PASCAL AND DISBELIEF

PASCAL AND DISBELIEF

Catechesis and Conversion in the *Pensées*

DAVID WETSEL

The Catholic University of America Press
Washington, D. C.

Printed in the United States of America
First paperback reprint 2002

The paper used in this publication meets the minimum requirements of American National Standards for Information Science—Permanence of Paper for Printed Library materials, ANSI Z39.48–1984.

∞

LIBRARY OF CONGRESS CATALOGING-IN-PUBLICATION DATA

Wetsel, David, 1949–
Pascal and disbelief : catechesis and conversion in the Pensées / by David Wetsel.
p. cm.
Includes bibliographical references and indexes.
ISBN 0-8132-0808-4 (hbk.; alk. paper)
ISBN 0-8132-1328-2 (pbk.)
1. Pascal, Blaise, 1623–1662. Pensées 2. Apologetics—17th century. 3. Libertines (French philosophers) 4. Faith. I. Title.
B1901.P43W48 1994
230'.2—dc20
93-51090

Contents

Illustrations

Acknowledgments

I owe a particular debt of gratitude to Professor Philippe Sellier (University of Paris IV—Sorbonne), who read and commented upon the text of this study at almost every stage in its writing and who invited me twice to present sections from the unfinished manuscript in his seminar on Classical French literature at the Sorbonne. In January of 1990, I presented a paper based on my research on Isaac de La Peyrère to his seminar "The Bible in the *Grand Siècle*." In November of 1991, I was again privileged to rehearse my research on "Pascal, *le libertinage* and Deism" in his seminar on the *Pensées*. I was especially honored to give these presentations in the presence of the doyen of Pascal studies in France, Professor Jean Mesnard, who had encouraged my emerging interest in Pascal in 1976 by inviting me to attend his seminar on Port-Royal, and without whose lifelong and inestimable contributions Pascal studies would be a much impoverished discipline.

It would hardly have been possible to complete this book had I not been hosted each summer for the past six years by my friend Christopher Chantrey, in whose guest room in the rue Papillon in Paris the greater part of this study was conceived, collated, and written. Financial assistance in the form of Faculty Grants was provided, for two of these summer sojourns, by the Office of Research and by the College of Liberal Arts and Sciences at Arizona State University.

The idea and initial research for this book grew out of a year I spent at the Divinity School of the University of Chicago in 1987–88. I would like to express my gratitude to three professors who directed my studies in religion at that illustrious institution: Wendy Doniger, David Tracy, and Anthony Yu.

During the writing of this study, I organized two seminars on Pascal which contributed much to my reflections on Pascal's apologetic enterprise. The first, underwritten by the Rose E. Tucker Foundation at Portland State University (Oregon) in 1989, permitted a significant exchange of ideas among four distinguished experts in Pascal studies: Pierre Force (Columbia University), Sara E. Melzer (University of California at Los Angeles), Charles Natoli (St. John Fisher College), and Philippe Sellier (University Paris IV—Sorbonne). The second, organized as a "special session" under the auspices of the Modern Language Association in 1991, featured important new papers given by John A. Gallucci (Colgate University), Erec Koch (Tulane University), François Lagarde (University of Texas at Austin), and Frank Mariner (Iowa State University). To these colleagues, and to Professor Wolfgang Leiner—who facilitated the publication of the papers from these two seminars in *Biblio 17* and *Papers on French Seventeenth Century Literature*—I would like to express my deep gratitude.

Other colleagues and friends (in truth too numerous to mention them all) who provided much appreciated advice and ideas include Professor Hugh Davidson (University of Virginia), Professor Guy Tessier (University of Tours), Professor Pierre Zobermann (University of Paris XIII), Mr. Bradley Berke, Professor Anthony Pugh (University of New Brunswick), M. Christian Belaygue (particularly for our extensive night-long conversation about Pascal's "wager"), the Reverend John M. Livingstone, Professor René Schérer (especially for our conversations on Leibniz, Gnosticism, and Manichaeism), Mme. Bernadette Perrin, and M. Olivier Leclair.

I owe special thanks to my friend Ceri Sherlock, Judith E. Wilson Visiting Fellow at Churchill College, Cambridge, in 1993, who invited me there in the late spring of that year for a period of reflection during which I undertook a major revision of my manuscript. I also am very much indebted to my colleagues Jeff Spires and Hélène Julien for their assistance in the rereading of the final draft of the manuscript and to Peter Lafford of the Arizona State University Humanities Computing Center for his infinite patience and invaluable help.

Avant-Propos

Dès 1981, le professeur David Wetsel s'était imposé dans l'ample mouvement des études pascaliennes avec une étude marquante, *L'Ecriture et le Reste: the "Pensées" of Pascal in the Exegetical Tradition of Port-Royal.* En faisant revivre l'ancienne vision biblique du monde, illustrée en particulier par l'auteur de la plus belle traduction française de la Bible, Sacy (1613–1684), l'ouvrage projetait une vive lumière sur le sens de nombreux fragments des *Pensées*, jusque là négligés. Il proposait en même temps une voie d'accès à une représentation de l'histoire qui, loin d'être propre à Port-Royal, a régné en Occident jusque dans la seconde moitié du XIXème siècle. C'est en effet seulement en 1872, lorsque fut présentée à Londres la XIème tablette de l'*Epopée de Gilgamesh*, que la Bible cessa officiellement d'être considérée, selon la formule de Pascal, comme "le plus ancien livre du monde."

Une pareille enquête révélait chez celui qui l'avait menée à bien le goût des recherches ambitieuses, la hardiesse intellectuelle. Elle laissait entrevoir un vif intérêt pour les sciences religieuses. Aussi n'est-il pas surprenant que M. Wetsel, déjà reconnu comme un excellent spécialiste de la littérature française, ait souhaité se doter aussi d'une solide formation en sciences des religions. De là l'acquisition d'un second domaine de compétence, grâce à un long séjour de recherches à la prestigieuse Ecole de Chicago.

De cette double culture est né *Pascal and Disbelief: Catechesis and Conversion in the "Pensées"*. Cette fois encore l'auteur innove. Certes divers travaux, en particulier un article décisif du grand spécialiste de la libre pensée, M. René Pintard, puis diverses publications de M. Jean Mesnard, s'étaient interrogés sur le type d'incroyant auquel s'adressait l'apologie pascalienne;

d'autres, par exemple sous la signature de M. Richard Popkin, s'étaient intéressés à cet étonnant "marginal" qu'est Isaac de La Peyrère, qui faisait rire son époque en assurant que les hommes avaient existé avant Adam. Mais la critique pascalienne, dans son ensemble, avait jusqu'ici prêté assez peu d'attention à la théorie des religions qui se dégage des *Pensées*: controverse avec l'Islam; discussion de la chronologie chinoise, qui menaçait ce qu'on tenait alors pour une chronologie révélée.

L'originalité de *Pascal and Disbelief* consiste à réunir sous un même regard critique les diverses cibles de l'apologiste: athées, déistes, tièdes (certains tenants de l'"honnêteté," soucieux avant tout d'exceller dans toutes les séductions de la vie), marginaux hétérodoxes (comme La Peyrère), musulmans, Chinois, païens de l'Antiquité. A lui seul le choix d'une telle perspective fait sortir de l'ombre toutes sortes de textes et crée des questions neuves. M. Wetsel, après avoir synthétisé l'apport de ses prédécesseurs, développe des analyses inédites. Très bien informé, il intègre les résultats les plus récents des études pascaliennes. Il donne vie à des mentions devenues imprécises, à trois siècles de distance: qu'était-ce qu'un "déiste" au temps de Pascal? Comment se représentait-on l'Islam à l'époque de la première traduction française du *Coran* (1647)? Que savait-on de la Chine?

L'intérêt de cette vaste exploration éclate, si l'on veut bien considérer qu'elle affronte deux interrogations capitales: Que nous dit le texte même des *Pensées* des interlocuteurs auxquels elles sont adressées? En quoi consiste la théorie pascalienne de la religion? Celle-ci devait occuper toute la fin de la première partie du projet d'apologie: "Connaissance de l'homme." On a beaucoup insisté sur l'étape philosophique de cette première partie, mais on a négligé le fait que Pascal prévoyait ensuite un examen des "fausses religions." Qui résoudra l'énigme de l'homme? "Sera-ce les philosophes . . .? Toutes les autres religions ne l'ont pu . . ." (fr. 149). Des fausses religions on devait passer, par contraste, à la véritable, en entrant dans la deuxième partie: "Connaissance de Dieu." *Pascal and Disbelief* attire donc vivement l'attention sur une pièce essentielle du dispositif envisagé.

Quant à la première interrogation, sur "l'inscription du lecteur" dans le texte pascalien, elle suscite deux riches chapitres: l'un sur l'Ouverture prévue pour l'apologie, avec la *Lettre pour porter à rechercher Dieu* et le *Discours de la machine* (le "pari"). En effet, ces deux développements inauguraux abondent en indications sur leurs destinataires; l'autre sur le chercheur de Dieu dans les *Pensées*.

On a pu parler récemment d'une "nouvelle vague" de la recherche pascalienne en Amérique du Nord. Bien évidemment M. Wetsel s'impose, avec ce nouvel ouvrage, comme une des personnalités les plus actives au sein de cette vitalité de la réflexion. *Pascal and Disbelief* éclaire, et provoque: il éclaire grâce à la diversité de ses apports; il provoque en ouvrant—comme *L'Ecriture et le Reste*—de nouveaux domaines où poursuivre les investigations.

PHILIPPE SELLIER
Université de Paris—Sorbonne

Already by 1981, Professor David Wetsel had made his presence felt in the world of Pascal studies with his ground-breaking book, *L'Ecriture et le Reste: The "Pensées" of Pascal in the Exegetical Tradition of Port-Royal.* By bringing back to life a Biblical worldview lost to the modern era—particularly well illustrated by that of Sacy (1613–1684), author of the most beautiful French translation of the Bible—Wetsel's book shed new light on the meaning of numerous previously neglected fragments of the *Pensées.* At the same time, Professor Wetsel offered a means of access to a representation of history which, far from being unique to Port-Royal, reigned in the West until the second half of the nineteeth century. Indeed, it was only in 1872, with the unveiling of the eleventh tablet of the *Epic of Gilgamesh*, that the Bible officially ceased being considered, to borrow Pascal's phrase, "the oldest book in the world."

A project of this scope revealed both an intellectual daring and a predilection for ambitious research in the scholar who so successfully carried it out. *L'Ecriture et le Reste* . . . also attested to a vivid interest in the field of the history of religions. Thus, one was hardly surprised that Professor Wetsel, already recognized as an excellent specialist on French literature, sought to acquire a solid foundation in the *sciences des religions.* Whence his mastery of a secondary field of scholarly expertise, acquired during a long period of research at the prestigious Divinity School of the University of Chicago.

Pascal and Disbelief: Catechesis and Conversion in the Pensées is the result of this dual scholarly apprenticeship. Once again, the author breaks new ground. Of course, a number of works—in particular a decisive article by the great specialist on *la libre pensée*, Professor René Pintard, and diverse works of Professor Jean Mesnard—had posed a critical question: to what kind of unbeliever would the Pascalian apology have been addressed?

Other studies, for example those of Professor Richard Popkin, had dealt with that astonishing eccentric Isaac de La Peyrère, whose contention that human beings had existed before Adam provoked ridicule among his contemporaries. However, as a whole, Pascalian criticism has until now paid but scant attention to the "theory of religions" implicit in the text of the *Pensées*: the controversy with Islam; the discussion of the Chinese chronologies, which called into question the divinely revealed status of Biblical chronology; and so on.

The originality of *Pascal and Disbelief* consists in its ability to draw together under a single critical scrutiny the diverse targets of the apologist: atheists, deists, the lukewarm (certain adherents of *l'honnêteté*, eager above all else to enjoy the charms of life on this earth), heterodox eccentrics (like La Peyrère), Muslims, Chinese, the pagans of classical antiquity. In and of itself, the choice of such a critical perspective illuminates all sorts of fragmentary texts found in the *Pensées* and brings to the fore a number of entirely new questions. Having synthesized the contributions of the commentators who preceded him, Professor Wetsel goes on to develop a series of completely innovative analyses. He is up to date on the most recent findings of Pascalian research, which he successfully integrates into his study. He gives new life to references which, from a distance of three centuries, have become vague or incomprehensible to the modern reader: What exactly was a "deist" in Pascal's day? How was Islam understood at the time of the first French translation of the Qur'an (1647)? What was really known about China?

This vast inquiry strikingly confronts two questions of capital importance: What do the texts of the *Pensées* themselves tell us about the interlocutors to whom they are addressed? What elements make up the Pascalian "theory of religion," which was to have constituted the conclusion of the first part of the apologetic project "Knowledge of man"? Much has been made of the philosophical aspects of this first section, but previous scholars have neglected the fact that Pascal then planned an examination of the "false religions." Who will resolve the enigma of the human condition? "Will it be the philosophers . . . ? All the other religions have failed to do so" (fragment 149). Pascal intended to make a transition from the "false religions" to the only true one ("la véritable"), upon entering the second part of the Apology: "Knowledge of God." *Pascal and Disbelief* therefore vividly draws our attention to an essential component of the schema envisaged by the apologist himself.

The first question confronted by Professor Wetsel's work, "the inscription of the reader" in the Pascalian text, gives birth to two rich chapters. The first is an analysis of the projected *Ouverture* to the Apology constituted by the *Letter urging men to seek God* and the *Discourse about the machine* (the "wager"), both of which abound in indications concerning their intended audience. A second and final chapter focuses on the "seeker of God" in the *Pensées*.

Recently it has become possible to speak of a veritable "new wave" of Pascalian research in North America. Without a doubt, this new work establishes Professor Wetsel as one of the most active participants at the center of this new and vigorous reflexion on Pascal's *Pensées*. *Pascal and Disbelief* both enlightens and provokes: it is illuminating because of the diversity of its scholarly contributions and challenging because—like *L'Ecriture et le Reste*—it opens new areas of scholarly investigation.

PASCAL AND DISBELIEF

Introduction

Rem viderunt, causam non viderunt.
—*Pensées*, fragment 206

In recent years, literary theorists have done well to remind us that the great texts of every culture ultimately begin to decay and to become subject to loss of meaning. It seems unfortunate, however, that many of the followers of these theorists have so often held up to derision the work of those still engaged in traditional historicocritical research. For who among professional interpreters of literature is better acquainted with the phenomenon of cultural slippage than the historical critic, whose very work consists in the painstaking attempt to restore texts to their original context?

Pascal's *Pensées* have proved particularly enticing to those commentators who have tried to apply contemporary critical theory to the "great" texts of the traditional canon. Misled by the fragmentary and seemingly highly unfinished state in which Pascal left his working notes, many of these commentators have reached what I believe to be the completely erroneous conclusion that Pascal never planned to rewrite the great majority of his more than eight hundred fragments into a finished Apology for the Christian religion. It is one thing to argue theoretically—and perhaps it is reasonable to do so—that it may be impossible to recover totally the *original* meaning of an unfinished text written over three hundred years ago. But, it is quite another to go on to argue that since such a recovery may prove ultimately impossible, the quest for a paleontological and thematic reconstruction of the Apology's final form should be abandoned as a vain, worn-out, and irrelevant endeavor.

Before taking up the thorny question of whether Pascal ever intended to produce a finished Apology for the Christian religion, an issue which has polarized Pascal studies in the United States (and to a lesser degree in France) in recent years, let us first return to the question of cultural slippage and the problem of the decay of literary texts. Let us take the example of that great galvanizing theme in the *Pensées*, the Christian doctrine of Original Sin, which, perhaps more than any other major Christian doctrine, has itself fallen victim to the phenomenon of cultural slippage over the past three hundred years. Here, in the concept of Original Sin, we encounter a theme central to the meaning of the *Pensées* that is likely to prove stubbornly inaccessible to a modern reader not intimately acquainted with the theological milieu that informs Pascal's text.

In Pascal's mind, only the Christian doctrine of the Fall, revealed to St. Paul (Romans 5:12–21) and elucidated by St. Augustine (*Quaestiones ad simplicianum*), can unravel the central enigma in human existence: the problem of evil and suffering. "Rem viderunt, causam non viderunt": "They saw the effect but not the cause" (fragment 206).[1] The greatest minds of antiquity, Augustine had observed, were able to reach the conclusion that the whole of the human condition is at its core deeply flawed. However, they were, Augustine had concluded, at a total loss to explain why. As Pascal understands it, the human mind—itself flawed in the Fall—will never be able to penetrate the enigma that stands at the heart of the human condition. Christianity alone, via a divinely revealed doctrine, can explain the truly cosmic cause of human suffering. As fragment 421 puts it, "Nulle religion que la nôtre n'a enseigné que l'homme naît en péché, nulle secte de philosophes ne l'a dit, nulle n'a donc dit vrai" ("No religion except ours has taught that man is born in sin, no philosophical sect has said it, so none has told the truth").

Few of Pascal's readers today, one suspects, will share Pascal's theological interpretation of the doctrine of the Fall. Fewer still will share his literal interpretation of the Genesis story.[2] The doctrine of Original Sin has, as an ideological, social, and theological construct, fallen victim to profound cultural slippage. An icon which, from Augustine at least to the Renaissance, constituted the principal theodicy of Western Christian cul-

1. See Philippe Sellier, ed., *Pensées, édition établie d'après la Copie de référence de Gilberte Pascal* (Paris: Bordas, 1991), p. 257, n.4.

2. For an analysis of Pascal's literal reading of Genesis, see Chapter IV ("Pascal's Biblicism: The Apologetic Consequences of a Literal View of the Fall") in my *L'Ecriture et Reste: the "Pensées" of Pascal in the Exegetical Tradition of Port-Royal* (Columbus: Ohio State University Press, 1981), pp. 99–123.

ture has, over the last three hundred years, been unable to withstand a fundamental shift in the whole Western religious sensibility. The myth of "man's first disobedience" simply no longer holds a real grip on the religious imagination.

A long tradition of humanistic and scientific ideas concerning the perfectibility of humanity and society has rendered the profound pessimism of the doctrine of the Fall less and less attractive to the modern Western mind. Geology and evolutionary biology have discredited what was, for over a thousand years, its grounding as historical fact. No orthodox theological tradition has rethought it in order to render it more accessible in a new allegorical form. Moreover, even official Christianity has tended to minimize its terrifying ideological implications, setting the vision of the Heavenly Jerusalem far closer to terra firma and stressing God's transcendence more than human corruption. The doctrine of Original Sin—at least as a psychologically believable defense of God's innocence—has decayed into a state of almost total incomprehensibility.

In all fairness to Pascal, we should not forget that he always qualifies the great doctrine of Original Sin as inherently "incompréhensible." But he goes on to make the case that in the absence of this revealed "mystère" the human condition must remain an enigma forever:

> Il est sans doute qu'il n'y a rien qui choque plus notre raison que de dire que le péché du premier homme ait rendu coupables ceux qui étant si éloignés de cette source semblent incapables d'y participer. Cet écoulement ne nous paraît pas seulement impossible. Il nous semble même très injuste car qu'y a(-t-)il de plus contraire aux règles de notre misérable justice que de damner éternellement un enfant incapable de volonté pour un péché où il paraît avoir si peu de part, qu'il est commis six mille ans avant qu'il fût en être. Certainement rien ne nous heurte plus rudement que cette doctrine. Et cependant sans ce mystère, le plus *incompréhensible* de tous, nous sommes incompréhensibles à nous-mêmes. Le noeud de notre condition prend ses replis et ses tours dans cet abîme. De sorte que l'homme est plus inconcevable sans ce mystère, que ce mystère n'est inconcevable à l'homme.

> Without a doubt, nothing more greatly shocks our reason than to say that the sin of the first human being has implicated in its guilt human beings so far from the original sin that they seem incapable of participating in it. This transmission of guilt seems to us not merely impossible. Indeed, it seems to us most unjust. For what could be more contrary to the rules of our miserable justice than the eternal damnation of a child, incapable of will, for an act in which he seems to have so little part, since it was committed six thousand years before he existed? Certainly nothing jolts us more rudely than this doctrine. And yet, without this mystery, the most *incomprehensible* of all, we remain incomprehensible to ourselves. The

knot of our condition is twisted and turned in that abyss. Thus, humanity is more inconceivable without this mystery than this mystery is inconceivable to the human mind. (131, italics mine)

Could any but the most strict Calvinist fundamentalist today agree with Pascal's thesis that only the divinely revealed "mystery" of the doctrine of Original Sin can clarify the enigma of the human condition? Will not the modern reader be taken aback by Pascal's contention that the Genesis story took place only six thousand years ago? Will he not be shocked by the notion that Adam's fall damns an unbaptized infant to eternal Hell? And make no mistake about it: these are Pascal's views. As Henri Gouhier insists:

> Aux yeux de Pascal et des théologiens qui lisent saint Augustin dans l'*Augustinus* de l'évêque Jansénius, le péché originel est une faute si radicale que la damnation de tous les fils d'Adam est pure justice et la rédemption de quelques uns, si petit que soit leur nombre, est pure miséricorde.[3]

> In the eyes of Pascal and those theologians who read Saint Augustine in the *Augustinus* of Bishop Jansen, Original Sin is so radical a crime that the damnation of all the sons of Adam is pure justice, and the redemption of a select group, however small their number, is pure mercy.

To what extent, I think we must ask, will the psychological inaccessibility of this major thesis in the *Pensées* hinder the modern reader's attempt to penetrate the meaning of this work?

One could always argue that a reader need not sympathize with Pascal's theological positions in order to appreciate his arguments intellectually. But is literary analysis—or indeed reading—ever a purely intellectual process? Or perhaps one could argue that one could take Pascal's exposition of Original Sin allegorically. Pascal's appeal for the modern reader could be said to reside in a dark and even "tragic"[4] view of the human condition which resembles our own.

In one of his most remarkable essays, "Survivals and Camouflages of Myths," the historian of religions Mircea Eliade argues that great mythological icons never simply decay to the point of disappearing. Rather, proteanlike, they transform themselves into new versions of the same "mythical thinking."[5] When the biologist Edward O. Wilson poses the question

3. Henri Gouhier, *Blaise Pascal: Conversion et apologétique* (Paris: Vrin, 1986), p. 22.

4. See Chapter IV, The Tragedy of Disbelief.

5. Mircea Eliade, "Survivals and Camouflages of Myths," in Diane Apostolos-Cappadona, ed., *Symbolism, the Sacred and the Arts* (New York: Crossroad, 1985), pp. 32–50.

"Is humanity suicidal?" he addresses the flawed nature of the human condition in a way which is a kind of "scientific" version of the theodicy of Original Sin. Will—neither human nor divine—plays no part in his thesis. But otherwise it is a vision which, if anything, is even more bleak than the one outlined in the first half of Pascal's projected Apology:[6]

> Darwin's dice have rolled badly for Earth. It was a misfortune for the living world in particular . . . that a carnivorous primate and not some more benign form of animal made the breakthrough. Our species retains hereditary traits that add greatly to our destructive impact. We are tribal and aggressively territorial, intent on private space beyond minimal requirements and oriented by selfish sexual and reproductive drives. Cooperation beyond the family and tribal levels comes hard. Worse, our liking for meat causes us to use the sun's energy at low efficiency.[7]

Anthropological and theological considerations aside, this is a vision of *concupiscientia* with which Saint-Cyran, Jansenius—and indeed Augustine—would have been in essential agreement. In their view as well, the fallen state of all Nature is to be laid at the feet of the progenitors of the human species.

When reading Pascal's *Pensées*, is it sufficient simply to make a psychological conversion of traditional Christian doctrine into more accessible modern modes? Or do we unconsciously distort the text by reflecting ourselves in doing so? After all, Pascal's version of Original Sin is not allegorical. It is intensely literal. Pascal believes that all of humanity is a *massa peccati*, damned to Eternal Hell though the fault of a historical Adam. Do we not essentially falsify and misread his text in our attempt to make him our philosophical contemporary?

Contemporary literary theory has duly warned us about the dangers which "projection" represents in literary interpretation. Sara Melzer makes a valid point when she argues that every reading of the *Pensées* is a "misreading."[8] However, should our fear of "misreading" a text mean that we abandon all attempts to elucidate what the text meant in the time in which it was written and for the writer by whom it was written? I think not. The study of Pascal's *Pensées* which follows is informed, I hope, at every level by my belief that the interpreter of a text stands under the

6. Cf. fragment 6: "Première partie: Que la nature est corrompue, par la nature même." ("First part: nature is corrupt: proved by nature itself").

7. Edward O. Wilson, "Is Humanity Suicidal?" *The New York Times Magazine,* May 30, 1993, p. 24.

8. Sara E. Melzer, *Discourses of the Fall: A Study of Pascal's Pensées* (Berkeley and Los Angeles: University of California Press, 1986), p. 137.

strictest of obligations at least to make the attempt to retrieve the meaning of a text in its own historical, sociopolitical, and intellectual context.

Philippe Sellier perhaps best expressed my own feelings on the matter during a discussion of this problem in the course of the "Journées de Portland" colloquium which I organized in 1989: "Je reconnais avec Sara Melzer le fait que toute lecture est une projection du lecteur. C'est la raison pour laquelle de chaque grand texte littéraire existe une multiplicité de lectures. Mais nous n'avons pas une liberté totale. Le texte n'est pas d'une plasticité illimitée. Nous sommes libres, mais *selon le texte*."[9] ("I recognize with Sara Melzer the fact that every reading is a projection on the part of the reader. This is why there exists a multiplicity of readings for each great literary text. But our liberty of interpretation is not absolute. A text is not of an unlimited plasticity. We are free, but *according to the text*.")

* * *

The study which follows takes as its primary objective an attempt to answer a question which has long dogged commentators on the *Pensées*: to whom does Pascal intend to address his itinerary for conversion to Christianity and his catechesis of Christian doctrine? The traditional view that Pascal intended to address his Apology to the professional *libertins* and the hardened atheists has been largely discredited. Some twenty years after the publication of his authoritative *Le Libertinage érudit dans la première moitié du XVIIe siècle* (1943), René Pintard reexamined the whole question and found few traces of that "adaptation constante aux curiosités des philosophes libertins"[10] ("constant adaptation to the objections of the libertine philosophers") which commentators had long claimed to see in the *Pensées*. In recent years, much of the discussion concerning Pascal's potential interlocutor(s) has revolved around Jean Mesnard's contention that the Apology was to have been principally addressed to those *honnêtes hommes* typified by Pascal's friends Mitton and Méré.[11]

In seeking to reexamine the whole question of Pascal's implicit audience for the Apology, it struck me that the most authentic version of Pascal's vision of disbelief might well be found within the text of the *Pensées* themselves. In fragment 427, which I believe to be a major section of a

9. "Panel Discussion: Order and Meaning in the Pensées." In D. Wetsel, ed., *Meaning, Structure and History in the "Pensées" of Pascal*. (Tübingen: Biblio 17, 1990), p. 99.

10. "Pascal et les libertins," in *Pascal Présent* (Clermont-Ferrand: G. de Bussac, 1962), p. 116.

11. See Chapter I, L'Honnête Homme.

draft of Pascal's general introduction to the Apology, Pascal gives a series of rather precise portraits of individuals afflicted with various degrees of religious disbelief. This highly polished *discours* has long been neglected by commentators because it stands outside the classified dossiers of 1658. In Chapters IV and V of the present study, I attempt to make the case that it contains the key to the whole question of Pascal's intended audience.

At the end of fragment 427, Pascal recapitulates a fundamental distinction he has made several times during the course of his draft of this "Lettre" (11). He insists upon a clear distinction between the hardened skeptics—whom he professes to have little hope of converting—and those seekers who will bring to the reading of his Apology "une sincérité parfaite et un véritable désir de rencontrer la vérité" ("an absolute sincerity and a real desire to find the truth") (427). Those guilty of only toying with *libertinage* are invited to recognize the truth of a single all-important theological principle: "Qu'ils reconnaissent enfin qu'il n'y a que deux sortes de personnes qu'on puisse appeler raisonnables: ou ceux qui servent Dieu de tout leur coeur parce qu'ils le connaissent, ou *ceux qui le cherchent de tout leur coeur parce qu'ils ne le connaissent pas*" ("Let them, in short, acknowledge that there are only two classes of persons who can be called reasonable: those who serve God with all their heart because they know him and *those who seek him with all their heart because they do not know him*") (427, italics mine).

If Pascal's Apology is to be addressed primarily to those unbelievers who are at least prepared to *seek* God, if the *libertins érudits* are essentially excluded from Pascal's projected audience, why has it been necessary to begin this study with a long chapter in which I attempt to trace the vast contours of scholarly disbelief in the forty years prior to the writing of the Apology? Given Pascal's striking portraits of hardened disbelief in his projected Preface, it seems a bit odd that these unbelievers are so rarely permitted to take the stage in the course of Pascal's notes for the main body of the Apology itself. Only in a handful of fragments are they ever again permitted to voice blatantly anti-Christian points of view. Why then go into the whole complicated history of *le libertinage érudit*?

The matter seems to me to boil down to an essential question. From which sources have the disbelievers (and particularly the seeking disbelievers) pictured in the *Pensées* derived their doubts concerning such essential Christian doctrines as the immortality of the soul, the intervention of God in human affairs, and the inevitability of divine judgment? Montaigne and the skeptics of classical antiquity of course remain prime potential sources, particularly for those fragments using the precise notations "pyrrhoniens(s)" and "pyrrhonisme." But is it entirely out of the question that Pascal's seeking unbelievers—whose portraits are surely based upon Pascal's encounters with them in the real world—have not been hindered in their search by having read or heard about the principal anti-Christian theses advanced by the *libertins érudits*?

The question is hardly one of direct sources. Nothing in the *Pensées* permits us even to conjecture concerning the extent to which Pascal himself was familiar with the anti-Christian ideas advanced by such writers as La Mothe le Vayer, Gabriel Naudé, or Cyrano de Bergerac. Indeed, it remains entirely possible that the living human beings upon whom Pascal modeled his portraits of the hardened disbelievers were far better acquainted with the precise tenets of active philosophical disbelief than was the apologist himself! The fact remains, however, that those aggressive unbelievers portrayed by Pascal in his projected Preface to the Apology and occasionally allowed to speak elsewhere in his texts have not pulled their objections to Christian doctrine out of thin air. When they deny the immortality of the soul, when they express their doubt that a God intervenes in human affairs, when they question the inevitability of judgment after death, when they refuse Christianity the status of a unique Revelation, and when they ridicule the credibility of Holy Scripture, these aggressive unbelievers seem to me to be doing more than simply drawing extreme conclusions from their readings in Montaigne or in the philosophers of classical antiquity. They seem to me to be speaking out of a living dialectic of disbelief, a tradition actively informed by such thinkers as La Mothe le Vayer and Gabriel Naudé.

In Chapter I, "Pascal and the *libertins*," I attempt to find in the works of a number of *philosophes libertins* a more complete exposition of the principal anti-Christian theses current in midseventeenth-century Paris than Pascal ever permits his aggressive disbelievers to voice. I do so in order that we may attempt to gauge the power and persuasive quality of these arguments and in some measure imagine how it might be that they have convinced the hardened atheists and hindered those who are still seeking. Making use of a far too neglected text, the *Quatrains du déiste*, I accord particular attention to the problem of Deism,[12] which Pascal addresses directly in fragment 449. I conclude that the disbelief advanced by those whom Pascal thinks still capable of being converted essentially represents

12. See Chapter I, Pascal and Deism.

a popularized version of deist ideas which have been combined with elements of neo-Pelagianism to form a kind of easy, skeptical religion described by one contemporary as "une religion à la mode."[13]

It would be a mistake to view Pascal's projected Apology as limited to the spiritual itinerary of drawing the seeking unbelievers back into the Church into which they have all presumably been baptized and confirmed. Nor would the Apology have been no more than a new kind of catechism, teaching them the fundamentals of the faith via an analysis of human corruption. It is both these things. But it is also a bulwark against unorthodoxy, an attempt to refocus the Christian religion according to the essential principles elucidated by St. Augustine and his interpreter Jansenius. Given the fundamental role of the doctrine of Original Sin in Pascal's arguments, we should not be surprised to find Pascal constantly attentive to the task of explaining and defending an orthodox, Augustinian version of the Fall and of the doctrine of Original Sin.[14]

In the dossiers "Contrariétés" (VII) and "A.P.R." (XI) and in the un-

13. See Chapter I, "La religion à la mode": The Popularization of Deist Ideas.

14. Saint Augustine, in his *Quaestiones ad simplicianum* (396), taught that Adam's guilt is transmitted to his descendants by concupiscence, thus making all of humanity a *massa damnata*. In the subsequent struggle against Pelagianism, the principles of Augustine's doctrine were confirmed by many Councils, especially the Second Council of Orange (A.D. 529).

Medieval theologians were much concerned with the nature and transmission of Original Sin. All of them hold that it is transmitted by the concupiscence accompanying the sexual act. Saint Thomas Aquinas brought in a new element, by distinguishing, in the state of Adam before the Fall, "pure nature," from the supernatural gifts which perfected it. Hence, for Aquinas, Original Sin consists primarily in the loss of these supernatural privileges. Aquinas' conception of Original Sin entails a more optimistic view of humanity than that of Saint Augustine: Original Sin is transmitted, not as the personal fault of Adam, but as a state of human nature.

The Thomist synthesis was not accepted everywhere. The old rigorous Augustinianism persisted among the Franciscans. In the later controversy with the Reformers, the teaching was made increasingly precise. To the exaggerated pessimism of Luther and Calvin, who equated it with concupiscence and argued that it persisted even after baptism, the Council of Trent opposed the teaching of the Schoolmen. In his condemnation of Jansenius' predecessor Baius (1567), Pius V condemned the identification of Original Sin with concupiscence and admitted the possibility of the right use of the will in the unbaptized.

In the seventeenth century, the Jesuits continued to develop the doctrine along the lines of the moderated optimism of the Schoolmen. In opposition to them, Port-Royal, and later Bossuet, reaffirmed the old Augustinian pessimism. From the eighteenth century onward, the influence of rationalism and natural science accelerated an attenuation of the doctrine of Original Sin. Liberal Protestantism abandoned it altogether.

See the article "Original Sin" in F. L. Cross, ed., *The Oxford Dictionary of the Christian Church* (Oxford: Oxford University Press, 1984), pp. 1010–12. The preceding summary has been taken from that article.

classed fragments which Philippe Sellier reads as a single "Discours de la Corruption"[15] (Lafuma fragments 436–450), Pascal presents the corruption of Adam and his posterity with a particular sense of urgency. The passion with which Pascal defends, in these dossiers and fragments, the orthodox, Augustinian version of the Fall and its fatal consequences for humanity has always struck me as suggesting that the apologist is consciously engaged in a mighty struggle with those who would dilute, weaken, or distort a doctrine which he views as at one with essential Christian truth.

In a sense, nearly all of Port-Royal's attacks upon those whom they viewed as deviating from or introducing innovations into received Christian truth involve a defense of the Augustinian version of Original Sin against the dangers of what they viewed as a new eruption of Pelagianism[16] within both the theological discourse and the traditional discipline of the Church. This is as true in all the quarrels about Grace evoked in the *Provinciales* as it is in the controversy over frequent communion, over the fate of the *anciens justes*,[17] or over the orthodoxy of the Jesuit mission to China.[18]

The book has yet to be written exploring the various unorthodox versions of the Genesis story that had been advanced in the Classical period in France prior to the writing of the *Pensées*. When it is, it will most certainly have to deal with Isaac de La Peyrère and his Pre-Adamite theory. There is but a single reference to La Peyrère's highly heterodox version of the Genesis story in the *Pensées* (fragment 576). However, the attention I accord this subject in Chapter II, I believe, is justified by the fact that La Peyrère's principal writings represent a veritable treasure house of unorthodox theories concerning the Fall, the antiquity of the human race, the

15. See Philippe Sellier, ed., *Pensées: édition établie d'après la Copie de référence de Gilberte Pascal,* Classiques Garnier (Paris: Bordas, 1991), p. 486, n. 1.

16. Pelagianism, a late fourth and early fifth century heresy, maintained that human beings may take, by their own efforts, the initial steps toward salvation. Though Pelagius, a British monk teaching in Rome, seems to have taken little interest in the problem of Original Sin, his followers (most notably, Rufinus and Celestius) denied the transmission of Adam's fault to his descendants. After the condemnation of Pelagius by the Council of Carthage in 411, St. Augustine attacked "Pelagian" doctrine in numerous works, particularly in his literary controversy with Julian of Eclanum. The controversy generated by the issues raised by Pelagianism continued to reappear during the Middle Ages and broke out with particular vehemence at the Reformation and during the Classical period in France. See the article "Pelagianism" in F. Cross, *Oxford Dictionary*, pp. 1058–59, from which this summary is taken.

17. See Chapter III, Le Vayer's *De la vertu des payens*.

18. See Chapter III, Pascal and the Jesuit Mission to China.

role of the Jews in the salvation of humanity, and the interpretation of Scripture.

From beginning to end, La Peyrère's writings are shot through with that very neo-Pelagianism which it was the principal mission of Port-Royal to oppose and against which the Apology was to have served as a bulwark of doctrinal orthodoxy. It would be pointless to attempt to argue that Pascal ever envisages a specific refutation of La Peyrère's theories. Fragment 575 aside, we simply have no information whatsoever regarding Pascal's knowledge of La Peyrère's writings. Rather, what La Peyrère brings to the present study is an invaluable glimpse into a whole world of heterodox thought which constitutes, in and of itself, a fundamental historical context for our examination of Pascal's defense of orthodox Christian doctrine.

In Chapter III, I propose to set Pascal's whole apologetic enterprise within another key historical context: the first stirrings, during the mid-seventeenth century in France, of the modern comparative study of religion. Throughout the *Pensées*, Pascal adheres strictly to the claim that Christianity represents God's sole and unique Revelation to the human race. Given this claim, in and of itself unremarkable for an orthodox Catholic churchman of the time, it seemed to me of inherent interest to ask precisely what Pascal knew about the non-Christian religions of the world.

In fact, if we are to judge by the *Pensées* themselves, it appears that Pascal had detailed knowledge of only two non-Christian living religious traditions: Islam and "[the religion] of China" (454). In the dossier "Fausseté des autres religions" ("Falseness of other religions"), Pascal's refutation of the religion revealed to the Prophet has a specific apologetic aim: to highlight the unique truth of the Christian Revelation by demonstrating the defective and deceptive character of a genuine "false" religion. Pascal never entertains the possibility that his seeking unbeliever might ever seriously consider a conversion to Islam. Rather, his purpose is to demonstrate, by examining the defective elements of this "false" religion, that outside the Christian Revelation there are to be found only pseudoreligions inspired and sustained by none other than the Old Deluder himself.

In my attempt to clarify Pascal's sources concerning Islam, I collate documentation of which Pascal in fact was probably not aware. This information, drawn from Du Ryer's Preface to the first vernacular translation of the Holy Qur'an (1647), from St. Thomas Aquinas' *Summa contra Gen-*

tiles, and from H. Grotius' *De veritate religionis christianae*, essentially serves to document how relatively little Pascal really knew about Islam. But it also serves to remind us of how little Pascal is really interested in the non-Christian traditions, which he de facto assumes not only to be false but to be demonically inspired.

If, in Pascal's view, the claims of Islam represent no challenge whatsoever to the authority of the Christian Revelation, such is not the case with what he calls the religion "of China" (454). Fragment 822, entitled "Histoire de la Chine" ("History of China"), would appear to echo Pascal's concern with refuting the claim that the chronologies of the Chinese could be shown to call into question the accuracy of those traditional Biblical chronologies upon which the apologist will rely in constructing his historical proofs of the credibility of Christianity. Once again, in attempting to elucidate Pascal's source—which has long been assumed to be Père Martini's *Sinicae Historiae* (1658) and which I have come to doubt that Pascal ever actually read—I suggest for the reader's perusal information which Pascal might never have consulted.

This new documentation, though of limited utility in interpreting fragment 822 ("Histoire de la Chine"), nonetheless serves to open a fascinating vista on Port-Royal's concerted attack on the Jesuit mission to China. Once again, the primary theological basis for the attack—as also in the case of Arnauld's and Pascal's assaults upon La Mothe le Vayer's *De la vertu des payens* (1642)—turns out to be the fear that the truth of Christian Revelation is being weakened and distorted via the introduction of theological and practical innovations which are essentially neo-Pelagian in their inspiration. This preoccupation with staying the tide of neo-Pelagian and liberal ideas, a preoccupation at the heart of Port-Royal's mission, will constitute an absolutely crucial theological context in the reading of the *Pensées* which is to follow.

One can hardly take up the question of Pascal's implicit audience in writing the Apology without first addressing the celebrated long fragment known as the "pari" ("wager") (418). Those seeking a detailed explication and analysis of this highly difficult text should consult Henri Gouhier's classic study of the fragment in chapter 5 of his *Blaise Pascal: Commentaires*[19] or chapter 7 in Laurent Thirouin's recent brilliant study, *Le Hasard et les règles: le modèle du jeu dans la pensée de Pascal.*[20] My aims in

19. Paris: Vrin, 1971, pp. 245–306 ("Le Pari de Pascal").
20 Paris: Vrin, 1991, pp. 130–89 ("Le Pari").

reviewing fragment 418 are far more modest. I focus upon only two questions: (1) what is the relationship between the "pari" and the Preface to the Apology partially sketched in fragment 427? and (2) to what extent does the portrait of that "libertin" whom commentators have always seen in this text correspond to the seeking unbeliever pictured in the Preface adumbrated by fragments 427–429?

After reviewing the opinions of various textual scholars as to the relationship between fragment 418 and fragments 427–429, I reach the conclusion that we would do well to trust Pascal's own note to himself on the matter. In fragment 11, he notes: "Ordre. Après la lettre qu'on doit chercher Dieu, faire la lettre d'ôter les obstacles, qui est le discours de la Machine, de préparer la Machine, de chercher par raison" ("Order. After the letter urging men to seek God, write the letter about removing obstacles, that is, the argument about the machine, how to prepare it and how to use reason for the search").

"La lettre qu'on doit chercher Dieu" ("the letter urging men to seek God"), which I take to be the same "lettre" referred to in fragment 5 as "une lettre à un ami pour le porter à chercher" ("a letter of exhortation to a friend to induce him to seek"), is obviously that major section of the general Preface to the Apology outlined in fragments 427–429. "La lettre d'ôter les obstacles" ("the letter about removing obstacles"), which fragment 11 indicates was to have been placed directly after "la letter qu'on doit chercher Dieu," is obviously fragment 418, "le pari." In other words, the Apology would have opened with the section of the Preface sketched in fragments 427–429. A text based upon the "wager" fragment would have then followed directly. I am emboldened in advancing this schema by the fact that Philippe Sellier, in his most recent revision of his edition of the *Pensées*, reaches precisely the same conclusion.[21]

My analysis of the "wager" fragment (418) deliberately sets aside other questions of great significance in this difficult text in order to focus upon one issue: the seven specific interventions ("i–vii" in my analysis)[22] which Pascal allows his interlocutor to make during the course of the fragment. So much has been written about Pascal's *libertin* in his "wager" text that we have almost come to think of Pascal's interlocutor as a fully drawn character with a life of his own. However, when we examine one by one

21. See Sellier, ed., *Pensées: édition établie,* p. 166, n. 7; p. 467, n. 2; p. 474, n. 1. See also Sellier's extremely convincing article, "L'ouverture de l'apologie pascalienne," *XVIIe siècle* 177 (1992); 437–49.

22. See Chapter IV, Pascal's Interlocutor in Fragment 418.

the seven brief responses he is allowed to make in the course of fragment 418, we realize that commentators have overdrawn and often exaggerated the portrait of the speaker who has come to be called Pascal's *libertin*. What we can make of him in fragment 418 certainly does not contradict—and in several instances reinforces—the portrait of the seeking unbeliever found in the Preface sketched in fragments 427–429. But he remains, at least in the text of fragment 418 itself, far from anything which one might be able to call a detailed portrait of a disbeliever.

If my exposition of fragment 418 is deliberately sketchy, I hope that my reading of fragments 427–429 will be perceived as far more detailed. For it is in these fragments—written as a major section of the general Preface to the entire Apology—that we find an essential distinction without which we can make hardly any sense at all of the rest of the collection of texts known as the *Pensées*. The distinction, between hardened and alterable disbelief, makes it eminently clear to whom the Apology will be addressed. Indeed, if we assume, as have so many commentators in the past, that the Apology was to be primarily addressed to hardened atheists, we are likely to misinterpret it not only in its larger meaning but in the meanings of its often terribly fragmented parts.

How different will be our reading of Pascal's unfinished Apology if we listen carefully to the final lines of fragment 427, lines which clearly indicate that the Apology which is to follow will *principally* be addressed to those unbelievers who are still seeking the truth. Having essentially despaired of saving the hardened skeptics, Pascal concludes:

> Mais pour ceux qui . . . apporteront [à cette lecture] une sincérité parfaite et un véritable désir de rencontrer la vérité, j'espère qu'ils auront satisfaction, et qu'ils seront convaincus des preuves d'une religion si divine, que j'ai ramassées ici, et dans lesquelles j'ai suivi à peu près cet ordre. . . .

> But as for those who approach [the work which is to follow] with absolute sincerity and a real desire to find the truth, I hope that they will be satisfied, and convinced by the proofs of so divine a religion which I have collected here, following more or less this order. . . . (427)

In Chapter V, I argue that Pascal's distinction between hardened and alterable disbelief—between the skeptics at the point of sinking into outright atheism (had they but the energy!) and the unbelievers who still "gémissent sincèrement" ("sincerely groan") in their doubts and who are still intent upon seeking the truth—is essentially grounded in the great

Augustinian doctrine of Predestination and Election. For Pascal, though he reminds himself toward the end of fragment 427 that no one can know for certain whom God will elect to save, the hardened skeptics are probably numbered among those for whom there is no hope. But what about these hardened skeptics? If they are not to be his audience, why has he gone to the trouble of painting them in such vivid detail in the part of the Preface to the Apology sketched in fragments 427–428? Indeed, the portrait of the seeking unbeliever drawn in fragment 429 pales in contrast with the terrifying and carefully drawn portraits of the hardened skeptics found in fragments 427–428.

The answer to this question, I believe, is to be found in Pascal's preparatory notes for the writing of the Preface. In "Série XXX" (fragment 821/432: [1]–[21]), the apologist essentially despairs of converting the hardened skeptics. He concludes that their disbelief cannot be modified by any human effort because it has supernatural origins. Any effort on his part will be futile. "Il n'y a rien à leur dire non par mépris, mais parce qu'ils n'ont pas le sens commun. Il faut que Dieu les touche" ("That shows that there is nothing to be said to them, not out of contempt, but because they have no common sense. God must touch them") (821/432–[4]).

God himself has blinded the hardened skeptics by taking away the most commonsense of desires: a desire for the life to come. Only He can open their eyes. However, these hardened skeptics will, paradoxically, play a central role in the conversion of the seeking disbelievers. "Même si nous ne pouvons les toucher, ils ne seront pas inutiles" ("But even if we cannot touch them, they will not be without their use") (821/432–[19]). "Ceux-là même qui semblent les plus opposés à la gloire de la religion n'y seront pas inutiles pour les autres" ("The very people who seem most opposed to the glory of religion will not be without their use for the others in this respect") (821/432–[19]).

Pascal's apologetic strategy could not be more explicit. The fatal indifference into which the hardened skeptics have sunk will be used to serve as a warning to those seeking unbelievers tempted by libertine ideas. Hardened skepticism will be shown to be tantamount to insanity. In the most essential of all matters, the question of a life beyond this one, the hardened unbelievers will be shown to act directly contrary to their most basic self-interest. Their very indifference will be shown to demonstrate the supernatural origin of their blindness and paradoxically will serve as a means by which those seekers tempted by *libertinage* will be saved from perdition:

Nous en ferons le premier argument qu'il y a quelque chose de surnaturel car un aveuglement de cette sorte n'est pas une chose naturelle. Et si leur folie les rend si contraires à leur propre bien, elle servira à en garantir les autres par l'horreur d'un exemple si déplorable. . . .

We will first base our argument on the fact that there is something supernatural about this, for such blindness is not a natural thing. And if their folly makes them run so counter to their own good, it will serve to protect the others from it by the horror of such a deplorable example. . . . (821/432–20)

The hardened skeptics, far from being granted the status of interlocutors in Pascal's unfinished *Apology for the Christian Religion*, will be made to serve the purposes of apologetic discourse by being reduced to the status of negative, indeed pitiable, examples of the tragedy to which toying with disbelief inevitably leads. They will figure in the Preface to the Apology—and, to the extent which they are allowed to speak at all, in the body of the Apology—not as philosophical adversaries, but as frightening examples of the folly to which an invasive and unbridled skepticism will always lead.

My study of disbelief, conversion, and catechesis in the *Pensées* is grounded in two assumptions which I believe are essential to an adequate understanding of that work. The first is that Pascal indubitably intended to reorganize his fragmented notes (already in the process of reorganization when he was forced to give up his enterprise) into a coherent, closely argued *Apology for the Christian Religion*. The fragmentary form so praised both by the contemporaries of La Rochefoucauld and by modern literary critics would not have constituted the final form of his text. My second assumption is that the long-ignored text constituted by fragments 427–429 represents a major section of the general Preface to the entire Apology. I intend to demonstrate that the composition of this section of the general Preface from two sets of fragmentary notes authorizes both these assumptions.

The idea advanced in recent years that we have no proof that Pascal ever intended to write an Apology for Christianity will, of course, appear patently absurd to those have followed the work of Louis Lafuma, Henri Gouhier, Jean Mesnard, and Philippe Sellier over the last forty years of Pascalian research. To be sure, the texts we read as the *Pensées* are not synonymous with Pascal's projected Apology. A certain amount of material found among Pascal's notes for the Apology clearly would not have been incorporated into the finished treatise. The dossier on miracles, abandoned early on by Pascal as a too-limited basis for a defense of Christian truth, would perhaps not have appeared in Pascal's final text at all. Nor would the various fragments continuing Pascal's campaign against the innovations of the Jesuits or the intensely personal writings such as the *Mémorial* and the *Mystère de Jésus*.

Philippe Sellier, while cautioning his readers that the title *Pensées* is, of course, not a synonym for the *Apology* itself, estimates that more than 80 percent of the texts we read as the *Pensées* bear directly upon Pascal's enterprise:

> Qu'est-ce que les *Pensées*? Environ huit cents fragments, qui furent trouvés chez Pascal à sa mort et conservés avec un soin, une vénération, dont aucune autre oeuvre de l'époque classique n'a bénéficié à ce point. Ils attestent la diversité des occupations du jeune savant, puisque s'y côtoient de nombreux textes en rapport avec la campagne des *Provinciales*, une note sur le vide, une attaque contre la théologie cartésienne de l'Eucharistie, plusieurs rédactions proches des *Ecrits sur la Grâce*, trois dossiers destinés sans doute à une *Lettre sur les miracles*, des vestiges de *Discours sur la condition des Grands*, des méditations ou des prières. . . . Néanmoins plus de 80% de ces fragments se rattachent à la préoccupation dominante du Pascal des dernières années, l'élaboration d'une *Apologie de la religion chrétienne*.[23]

> What exactly are the *Pensées*? Approximately 800 fragments which were found *chez* Pascal after his death and which were preserved with a care and a veneration to an extent accorded no other work of the Classical period. These fragments attest to the diversity of the interests of the young scientist. In the *Pensées*, one finds, side-by-side, numerous texts relating to the campaign of the *Provincial Letters*, a note on the problem of the vacuum, an attack on Cartesian Eucharistic theology, several compositions closely related to the *Writings on Grace*, three dossiers undoubtedly destined to form part of a *Letter on Miracles*, vestiges of the *Discourse on the Condition of the Great*, meditations or prayers. . . . Nonetheless, more than 80% of these fragments are directly related to the major preoccupation of the Pascal of those last years: the writing of an *Apology for the Christian Religion*.

The title *Apology* (or *Apologia*) is, of course, a modern denotation for Pascal's project. As Philippe Sellier is the first to point out, Pascal himself never used the word *apologie*. In the seventeenth century, the word had a far more restricted sense: "un livre ou discours fait pour justifier quelqu'un" ("a book or discourse written in defense of an individual") (*Dictionnaire de Furetière*, 1690). Sellier, however, finds the modern title an entirely appropriate one. It is entirely suitable, he thinks, to situate the greater part of the fragments making up the *Pensées* "à l'intérieur d'un

23. *Pensées* (1991), "Introduction," pp. 23–24.

genre littéraire et théologique qui remonte aux origines mêmes du christianisme, et . . . illustré dès le second siècle par une douzaine d'écrivains qu'on appelle précisément 'les apologistes' "[24] ("within a literary and theological genre going back to the very origins of Christianity and, . . . exemplified, as early as the second century, by a dozen or so writers whom we call, in fact, 'the [Christian] Apologists' ").

Sellier insists upon a clear distinction between Pascal and the great majority of Christian "apologists"—"souvent prétentieux et raisonneurs" ("often pretentious or argumentative")—who wrote from the seventeenth century onward. Pascal's enterprise, Sellier observes, is more like what we now call "la *théologie fondamentale*," that is, "l'activité d'une intelligence qui réfléchit avec profondeur sur le cheminement qui l'a conduite à croire en l'Absolu" ("the activity of a mind reflecting profoundly upon the itinerary which has led it to a belief in the Absolute"). The word *apologie,* Sellier concludes, is absolutely indispensable as a means of denoting, within that body of fragments known as the *Pensées*, "le massif des textes orientés vers la *Défense et illustration* de la vision catholique du monde"[25] ("that block of texts oriented toward a *Defense and Illustration* of the Catholic vision of the world").

In the light of the last forty years of Pascalian research, there remains not one inkling of doubt that Pascal intended to reorganize the great majority of his often-fragmented notes into a coherent defense and illustration of Christianity which would take the form of an invitation to conversion and a catechesis in Christian doctrine. The proof of this is everywhere: in Pascal's own notes to himself in the dossier "Ordre"; in the apologetic character of the great majority of the "fragments"; in the text (and particularly in the concluding lines) of the section of the Preface adumbrated in fragment 427; in the multiple contemporary accounts (Gilberte Périer, Etienne Périer, Filleau de la Chaise, and others) of those who had immediate access to Pascal's declarations of his intention to wage war on disbelief.

The evidence of Pascal's intention to reorganize his notes into a defense of Christianity in the form of an invitation to conversion is so overwhelming and so well documented that there is no need to rehearse it further here. Those unfamiliar with this evidence will find it nowhere more coherently presented than in Philippe Sellier's "Introduction" to his recent revi-

24. Ibid., p. 24.
25. Ibid., pp. 24–25.

sion of his edition of the *Pensées*.[26] Jean Mesnard's introduction to his long-awaited edition of the *Pensées* will undoubtedly only serve to reinforce our understanding of the essentially apologetic character of the *Pensées*.

One question remains: why the relatively recent vogue for denying that Pascal ever intended to write a defense of Christianity or for arguing that his finished text would have remained in fragmentary form? The "Edition de Port-Royal" of the *Pensées* does, from time to time, betray a taste for the fragmentary form which is unmistakably that of the contemporaries of La Rochefoucauld.[27] But the whole subsequent editorial history of the text has generally moved in the direction of synthesis, not fragmentation.

The modern view of the *Pensées* as an inherently fragmentary text ultimately finds its genesis, more than forty years ago, in Lucien Goldmann's *Le Dieu caché: étude sur la vision tragique dans les "Pensées" de Pascal et dans le théâtre de Racine*. Goldmann, arguing that the fragmentary state of Pascal's text reflects an existential dimension inherent in Pascal's thought, was the first critic to institute a radical break with the whole editorial tradition of synthesis:

> Chercher le "vrai" plan des *Pensées* nous paraît . . . une entreprise antipascalienne par excellence . . . Il n'y a, pour une oeuvre tragique, qu'une seule forme d'ordre valable, celui du fragment, qui est recherche d'ordre, mais recherche qui n'a pas réussi, . . . à l'approcher.[28]

> Searching for the "true" plan for the *Pensées* seems to us . . . the ultimate anti-Pascalian undertaking . . . For a tragic work, there is only one valid ordering principle, that of the fragment, which is a search for order but one which at the same time has not succeeded in reaching it.

With the advent of the new "science" of textual deconstruction, Louis Marin proposed an equally radical challenge to the traditional view of Pascal as Christian apologist. He proposed imagining the "author" cutting his pages into smaller and smaller bits in order to create a "possible du sens" ("possibility of meaning"), an infinite multiplicity of relationships among the fragments which constitute the *Pensées*.[29]

26. Ibid., pp. 5–83.

27. See Thérèse Goyet, "Le Visage de 1670 . . . Table de concordance entre l'édition des "Pensées" de 1670 et les éditions Lafuma (Luxembourg) et Brunschvicg" in *Les "Pensées" de Pascal ont trois cents ans* (Clermont-Ferrand: G. de Bussac, 1971), p. 77.

28. *Le Dieu caché* . . . (Paris: Gallimard, 1955), p. 220.

29. *La Critique du discours* (Paris: Minuit, 1975), pp. 133–34.

Most recently, Emmanuel Martineau has advanced the theory that Pascal actually wrote the *Pensées* in the form of a series of "discours," which he then cut up into myriad fragments. On the basis of this theory, he has produced an edition of the *Pensées*, entitled *Discours sur la religion et sur quelques autres sujets de Blaise Pascal, restitués et publiés par Emmanuel Martineau*,[30] in which he attempts to reconstitute the pages of Pascal's original text.

In contradistinction to Pol Ernst's *Géologie et stratigraphie des Pensées*, in which a reconstruction of the *feuilles* which Pascal later cut up and reclassed is based upon paleontological research involving the analysis of the material qualities of the pages themselves (watermarks, ink, handwriting, matching of cuts, and so on),[31] Martineau's reconstruction is based upon a thematic and philosophical reconstitution. Philippe Sellier observes that Martineau's thesis contradicts the whole tradition of Pascalian philological studies, which has always maintained that Pascal worked by first jotting down notes and fragments and then assembling these texts into larger unities.[32]

If the notion that Pascal meant to preserve the "fragmentary" form of his texts has remained in the margins of mainstream Pascalian research in France, such is not the case in the United States. During the past ten years, the notion of the essential fragmentary nature of the *Pensées* and the idea that there exists no proof that Pascal ever intended to write an Apology have been transformed into a kind of received dogma by an influential group of *pascalisants* working in American universities. Under their influence, more than one editor of scholarly journals dealing with French literature has refused to consider for publication any piece which dares refer to Pascal's "Apology" or argues that his work would not have remained in a fragmentary state.

In an attempt to initiate a dialogue between these two opposing camps in American Pascal studies, I organized two encounters between traditional and modernist *pascalisants*. The first, which took place under the aegis of Portland State University (Oregon) in 1989, served very much to clarify the distance which separates the two positions. Sara Melzer, whose *Discourses of the Fall* (1986) had been highly praised not only by those

30. Paris: Fayard/Armand Colin, 1992.

31. P. Ernst, *Géologie et stratigraphie des Pensées de Pascal* (Paris-Oxford: Universitas 1993).

32. See "Pascal: Pensées ou Discours?" in *Le Monde*, December 18 1992, p. 29. In this highly interesting "débat," Martineau discusses his theory with Philippe Sellier, Jean Mesnard, Pol Ernst, and Vincent Carraud.

much addicted to the theories of Jacques Derrida but by such traditional scholars as Anthony Pugh, finally articulated what a number of American critics had long thought but had never quite dared say. Arguing that the *aporia* constituted by the *Pensées* has significant implications for how we should read Pascal's text, Melzer observed:

> We are . . . cut off from Pascal, a *homo absconditus* who is hidden from his text since he has literally taken a scissors and cut it off from his originating intention. Given that Pascal is a *homo absconditus* whose true design is hidden from his text and from his reader, the traditional reading of the *Pensées* as an apology for the Christian religion must be seriously questioned.[33]

A second seminar, a "special session" held under the auspices of the Modern Language Association 1991 annual meeting, produced some excellent new papers on Pascal but failed, I think, to produce any real new dialogue. In his paper, "Le différement de Pascal," François Lagarde seemed to me to cut to the heart of the most puzzling question of all with regard to the recent critical challenge to the traditional reading of the *Pensées* as representing Pascal's preparatory notes for an *Apology for the Christian Religion*. "*Semiosis* a bel et bien chassé *Mimesis*," Lagarde observed, "mais pourquoi?"[34] ("*Semiosis* has indeed chased away *Mimesis*, but why?"). In other words, why have semioticians and deconstructionists struggled with such determination to obscure what, at least by the standards of orthodox seventeenth-century Catholicism, seems such an easily recognizable *Christian* system of thought?

Imagining that we may eventually be able to entice these new interpreters of the *Pensées* to come home to an exegesis of the *sensus litteralis* of Pascal's text may be a futile exercise. As Lagarde observed, "il serait vain de reprocher à cette critique de ne pas vouloir être mimétique, ne serait-ce que le temps d'une interprétation, puisqu'elle en éprouve l'impossibilité même" ("to object to this criticism's refusal to be mimetical, even if it were only an attempt, would be pointless, precisely since this kind of criticism

33. See "Panel Discussion: Order and Meaning in the *Pensees*" in D. Wetsel, ed., *Meaning, Structure and History in the "Pensées" of Pascal* (Tübingen: Biblio 17, 1990), p. 99.

34. "Le différement de Pascal," in *Papers on French Seventeenth Century Literature* 20:38 (1993), p. 186. The five English translations of the citations from his article were kindly furnished by François Lagarde.

The papers from the San Francisco special session "Pascal's *Pensées* and Recent Critical Theory: Illumination or Deformation of the Text," together with my introduction to them, were all published in the same volume of *Papers on French Seventeenth Century Literature*, pp. 117–97.

experiences the very impossibility of *Mimesis*"). One might, however, Lagarde concluded, take deconstructionist criticism to task for having been motivated by too strong a desire to demonstrate that Pascal's basic enterprise was a failure:

A trop vouloir que Pascal *ratât son coup*, on ne montre peut-être que le ratage du critique qui passe à côté de Pascal, ne le voit pas, ne veut pas le voir. La question est à la fin de savoir s'il y a ou s'il n'y a pas de pensée de Pascal! Et c'est là que la critique déconstructionniste est étonnante. Car en disant que Pascal n'est pas possible, elle croit tenir à distance un texte gorgé de ce qui fait peur et qui est, comme le texte le dit lui-même, la religion.[35]

When at all costs a critic wants Pascal *to fail*, he perhaps only demonstrates his own failure while avoiding Pascal and refusing to encounter his thought. For the ultimate question is to know if there is Pascalian thought or not, and this is where the deconstructionist is at his most astonishing. For by saying that Pascal is not constructible, he hopes to keep at arm's length a text overflowing with what scares him, and which is, as the text itself proclaims, religion.

Are Pascal's modern critical adversaries in the last analysis simply *néo-libertins*? Is not the whole debate ultimately one of ideology, one between traditional Christian truth and modernity, between the certainty and the impossibility of meaning? It is easy enough to imagine Pascal's own answer to these questions. For the apologist, all forms of disbelief are ultimately of supernatural origin. "On n'entend rien aux ouvrages de Dieu si on ne prend pour principe qu'il a voulu aveugler les uns et éclaircir les autres" ("We understand nothing of God's works unless we accept the principle that he wished to blind some and enlighten others") (232). "Les hommes ont mépris pour la religion. Ils en ont haine et *peur qu'elle soit vraie*" ("Human beings despise religion. They hate it and *are afraid it may be true*") (12, italics mine). "Les uns craignent de . . . perdre [Dieu], les autres *de le trouver*" ("Some fear . . . to lose [God], others *to find him*") (908, italics mine).

Is Pascal's own position adequate for, or even relevant to, the purposes of the present debate? In attempting to read the mind of the dead, Sara Melzer reminds us in her *Discourses of the Fall*, we risk falling into the trap of cultural projection. François Lagarde cautions that if recent critical theory has tended toward *libertinage*, traditional historical criticism has just as often veered in a hagiographic and overtly Christian direction.[36] Para-

35. "Le différement de Pascal," pp. 189–90.
36. Ibid., p. 191.

doxically, he argues, contemporary criticism has stumbled upon a Pascal "dans son attente linguistique de 'Dieu' " ("in his linguistic waiting for 'God' "):

> La critique contemporaine retrouve Pascal en le fuyant! . . . Elle rate le Pascal de la critique historique pour cependant aller droit au but. Car l'impossibilité du texte ou du sens qu'elle ressasse, l'indéfinitude tragique du langage qui la travaille, Pascal les a connues. En posant qu'au coeur des *Pensées* est un trou par où tout fuit, elle retrouve, et pourrait-on dire sans le savoir, le difficile et toujours incertain, l'infini passage de la connaissance au coeur, lieu a-textuel du Dieu sensible.[37]

> Contemporary criticism finally encounters Pascal by fleeing from him! . . . It misses the historical Pascal of scholars and nevertheless goes straight to his core. For the impossibility of meaning which today's critic feeds upon, the tragic indefinitude of language which torments the critic, Pascal has experienced all of that. By positing that at the core of the *Pensées* is a hole through which everything escapes, the critic recovers, but almost unknowingly, the painful and always uncertain, the interminable passage from the mind to the a-textual *locus* of a tender God which the heart is.

Without a doubt, semiological and deconstructive approaches to Pascal's text have served to dramatize the modern difficulty of reading the *Pensées* from what Sara Melzer calls the "perspective of faith." Is it possible, we must ask, for anyone—believer or skeptic—to suspend a whole array of post-Christian prejudices and *experience* Pascal's Apology from such a "perspective of faith"? All too often, I suspect, we really read the *Pensées* as if they were a kind of seventeenth-century version of that modern existentialist religious classic, Simone Weil's *L'Attente de Dieu*. In the final analysis, has recent critical theory, intent upon finding in the *Pensées* ideas and schemas which speak to the "postmodern" mind, really rendered the text more accessible to modern readers? Or has it unwittingly served to accelerate the process by which "classic" texts gradually but inexorably move in the direction of unintelligibility?

Only the work of historical criticism, in its attempt to restore meaning to its original context, I believe, has any chance of rescuing a philosophical and theological text like the *Pensées* from the very real phenomenon of cultural slippage. Posing new theories about the inherently fragmentary nature of Pascal's endeavor only serves, I think, to divert attention from the real issue at hand: restoring the text to its historical and intellectual

37. Ibid., p. 190.

context and from that position attempting to discern what Pascal meant to accomplish in his projected *Apology for the Christian Religion*.

The notion that Pascal's text would have remained in a fragmentary state can be easily dispatched. One need examine only one key text, fragment 427, and show how Pascal made use of two sets of fragmentary notes in writing this major *discours*. These two key sets of fragmentary notes are in the *Pensées* for our inspection. They are, in fact, Lafuma 821/432-[1]–[21], and the the dossier "Commencement" (XII).

In the book which follows, completed in 1991, I have perhaps used the term "Preface to the Apology" in too narrow a sense. I argue that the "Preface" would have essentially been constituted by the material found in fragments 427–429 and that the "wager" fragment (418) would have then directly followed in the form of an opening chapter. A new study by Philippe Sellier has convinced me that the "Preface" might well have included both of these major *discours* and perhaps several others. Sellier speaks of "une ample Ouverture de l'apologie" ("a well-developed Overture to the Apology") of which Pascal has left us two "*développements*": the "Lettre pour porter à rechercher Dieu" ("Letter urging men to seek God") (427–429) and the "Discours de la machine" ("Discourse about the machine") (418).[38]

As Sellier sees it, this "Ouverture de l'apologie," essentially growing out of dossiers XII ("Commencement") ("Beginning") and XIII ("Soumission et usage de la raison") ("Submission and Use of Reason"), might well have taken the ultimate form of four "Lettres" or "Discours": "une exhortation à rechercher Dieu, un appel à se dépouiller des passions païennes, une incitation au cheminement intellectuel, une *Critique* de la raison dans la recherche de l'infini"[39] ("an exhortation to seek God, a call to divest oneself of pagan passions, an incitement to take up an intellectual itinerary, a *Critique* of reason in the search for the infinite").

Sellier views the basic theme of the "Overture to the Apology" as that same great *leitmotif* of the *Pensées* themselves: "l'appel à mettre l'intelligence en mouvement, le rappel incessant de la nostalgie du vrai" ("the call to set the mind into motion, the incessant reminder of the yearning for what is true"). The unbeliever as Pascal pictures him both in the *liasse* "Commencement" (XII) and in fragments 427–428, Sellier observes, has become so accustomed to despairing of seeking the truth that he is almost

38. Philippe Sellier, "L'ouverture de l'apologie pascalienne," *XVIIe siècle* 177 (1992): 438.
39. Ibid., pp. 448–49.

unwilling to continue seeking.[40] The apologist's role is to awaken in him a desire to seek by convincing him that his dormant nostalgia for a never-found happiness is none other than an unrecognized yearning for a lost God. Fragment 427 will seek to set in motion this search by vividly picturing the trap of despair into which an intellectual torpor and an unbridled skepticism invariably lead. Fragment 418, will, on the other hand, seek to capture his immediate attention by proposing what Laurent Thirouin has so aptly labeled "un discours de commencement pour capter l'écoute"[41] ("an initial discourse aimed at catching his ear").

In 1976, I first noticed Philippe Sellier's notes to the effect that fragment 418, along with fragments 427–429, represent "une dilatation interne de la liasse 'Commencement' "[42] ("an internal expansion of the dossier 'Beginning' "). But, in the course of seventeen years, I never managed to grasp the profound significance of this observation. To date, Sellier has been the only editor of the *Pensées* to comprehend that *all* of the sixteen "pensées" in the *liasse* "Commencement" in fact constitute "des notes préparatoires aux deux premières 'Lettres' appelées à ouvrir l'apologie: la 'Lettre pour porter à rechercher Dieu' et la 'Lettre d'ôter les obstacles' "[43] ("preparatory notes for the first two 'Letters' called forth to open the Apology: the 'Letter urging men to seek God' and the 'Letter about removing obstacles' ").

It is crucial to remember that the sixteen fragments which constitute the *liasse* "Commencement" were not all written at the same time. Rather, they were written at different times and on different *feuilles* and then subsequently cut up and filed together, presumably during the course of the classification of 1658. The title assigned this dossier, "Commencement," is, of course, an entirely apposite one for a group of notes destined for a preface to an apology. Moreover, Sellier observes, this title appears to be the oldest of the titles which would be assigned to the classed dossiers:

> "Commencement" est le plus ancien des titres appelés à désigner un dossier. Il apparaît vraisemblablement dès l'automne 1656, dans le fragment [164], rédigé sur un papier filigrané "Cadran 1 // B coeur C":

40. Ibid., p. 446.

41. *Le Hasard et les règles: le modèle du jeu dans la pensée de Pascal* (Paris: Vrin, 1991), pp. 188–89.

42. *Blaise Pascal, Pensées* . . . (Paris: Mercure de France, 1976), p. 353, n. 2, and p. 360, n. 1.

43. "L'ouverture de l'apologie pascalienne," p. 444. Anthony Pugh, in his *The Composition of Pascal's Apologia* (Toronto: Toronto University Press, 1984), was perhaps the first

Commencement.
Cachot.

Je trouve bon qu'on n'approfondisse pas l'opinion de Copernic, mais ceci

---

Il importe à toute la vie de savoir si l'âme est mortelle ou immortelle.[44]

"Beginning" is the oldest of the titles invoked to designate a dossier. [This title] first appears in all probability in the autumn of 1656, in fragment [164], drafted on a sheet bearing the watermark "Cadran 1 // B coeur C":

Beginning.
Dungeon.

I agree that Copernicus' opinion need not be more closely examined, but this

---

It affects our whole life to know whether the soul is mortal or immortal. (164, italics mine)

Pol Ernst, Sellier tells us, has recently demonstrated that all the oldest fragments of the *Pensées*—that is, those on sheets bearing the watermarks "Cadran 1 // B coeur C" or "RCDV"—belong either to the future dossiers "Commencement" (XII) and "Soumission" (XIII) or to files concerning more traditional apologetic subjects (proofs of Christ, prophecies, controversies with the Jews, and so forth). Philippe Sellier draws two conclusions from Ernst's discovery, and these are fundamental to our understanding of the genesis of Pascal's apologetic enterprise. His first conclusion is that nothing suggests, at the time he set down fragment 164 and the title "Commencement," that Pascal had already conceived the notion of organizing his Apology into two parts and that consequently the idea of a vast "anthropological" study in the first part of the Apology is a late development. Sellier's second conclusion is that Pascal, as early as the autumn of 1656, was already thinking ahead to the way in which he would open his projected Apology.

Borrowing a phrase from M. Bakhtin, Sellier describes fragment 164 as a "dialogue sur le seuil"[45] ("dialogue on the threshold"), whose ultimate model is Plato's *Phaedon*:

Socrate dans sa prison et sur le point de mourir y médite sur la question de l'immortalité de l'âme. Or cette situation platonicienne au bord de la mort, c'est

---

commentator to postulate the extent of the relationship between "Commencement" and fragments 427 and 418. See pp. 149–63.

44. "L'ouverture de l'apologie pascalienne," p. 439.

45. M. Bakhtin, *La Poétique de Dostoïevski* (Paris: Seuil, 1970), p. 157.

la nôtre à tous (fr. 152). De là l'image du "cachot" (fr. 164 et 163) et le rappel obsédant de la proximité de la mort (fr. 151, 152, 154, 158, 163, 165, 166) qui occupent une ample partie du dossier "Commencement."

Pascal comptait donc faire retentir au seuil de l'apologie l'appel socratique à cesser de se perdre dans l'agitation au-dehors (comme font les "physiciens," Copernic), pour revenir à l'écoute de soi et scruter la seule réalité importante: notre destinée, "où il va de tout" (fr. 150).[46]

Socrates in his prison cell, death approaching, meditates on the question of the immortality of the soul. Now, this Platonic scenario at death's door is in fact the human condition (fr. 152). Thus Pascal's metaphor of the "dungeon" (frs. 164 and 163) and the obsessive reminders of the proximity of death (frs. 151, 152, 154, 158, 163, 165, 166) which make up a great part of the dossier "Beginning."

Pascal intended therefore to sound, at the threshold of the apology, the Socratic call to cease losing oneself (as do the "natural philosophers," Copernicus) in agitations external to one's own soul in order to turn inward and scrutinize the only truly important reality: our ultimate destiny, "where everything is at stake" (fr. 150).

This apologetic scenario, Sellier observes, represents but a transposition into a written form of the practical strategy which Gilberte Périer described as her brother's habitual way of instituting a dialogue with the unbelievers:

Quand il avait à conférer avec quelques athées, il ne *commençait* jamais par la dispute, ni par établir les principes qu'il avait à dire; mais il voulait connaître auparavant *s'ils cherchaient la vérité de tout leur coeur*; et il agissait suivant cela avec eux, ou pour les aider à trouver la lumière qu'ils n'avaient pas, *s'ils la cherchaient sincèrement*, ou pour *les disposer à la chercher* et en faire leur plus sérieuse occupation, *avant que de les instruire*, s'ils voulaient que son instruction leur fût utile.[47]

When he had to confer with several atheists, [Pascal] never *began* by initiating an argument nor setting forth the principles which he wanted to recount; rather, he first of all sought to learn *if they were seeking the truth with all their heart*; he subsequently used to act according to their response, either to help them find the light which they lacked, *if they were sincerely seeking it*, or to *motivate them to seek it* and to make this search their most serious enterprise. [He acted in this fashion] *before instructing them* [because he thought that this willingness to seek was essential] if they wanted his instruction to be truly useful to them.

46. "L'ouverture de l'apologie pascalienne," pp. 439–40.

47. Ibid., p. 440. The italics, serving to underscore the way in which these phrases are echoed in both the dossier "Commencement" and the "Lettre pour porter à rechercher Dieu," are Sellier's. The citation is from Gilberte Périer's *La Vie de Monsieur Pascal*. See Louis Lafuma, ed., *Pascal: Oeuvres complètes* (Paris: Seuil, 1963), p. 25.

How remarkably Mme. Périer's recollections echo that great theme of seeking God sincerely which so intimately links the dossier "Commencement" with the "Lettre pour porter à rechercher Dieu" set down in fragment 427! And how multiple are the other *leitmotifs* which link dossier XII with fragment 427. The notation "Cachot" in the very early fragment 164 is obviously developed into a full-blown metaphor for the human condition in fragment 163 of the same dossier. Now, the metaphor itself, that is, the first paragraph of fragment 163, does not appear in fragment 427. But its theological interpretation (paragraphs two and three of fragment 163) appears both in paragraph seventeen of fragment 427 and in another set of preparatory notes for the writing of this *discours*:

Fragment 163:

Un homme dans un cachot, ne sachant pas si son arrêt est donné, n'ayant plus qu'une heure pour l'apprendre, cette heure suffisant s'il sait qu'il est donné pour le faire révoquer. Il est contre nature qu'il emploie cette heure-là, non à s'informer si l'arrêt est donné, mais à jouer au piquet.

Ainsi il est surnaturel que l'homme, etc. C'est un appesantissement de la main de Dieu.

Ainsi non seulement le zèle de ceux qui le cherchent prouve Dieu, mais l'aveuglement de ceux qui ne le cherchent pas.

Fragment 821/432-[20]:

Nous en ferons le premier argument qu'il y a quelque chose de surnaturel car un aveuglement de cette sorte n'est pas une chose naturelle.

Fragment 427, par. 17:

C'est un enchantement incompréhensible, et un assoupissement surnaturel, qui marque une force toute-puissante qui le cause.

Fragment 163:

A man in a dungeon, not knowing whether sentence has been passed on him, with only an hour left to find out, and that hour enough, once he knows it has been passed, to have [the sentence] revoked. It would be unnatural for him to spend that hour, not finding out whether sentence has been passed, but playing piquet.

So it is beyond all nature that man, etc. It is the weighing down of the hand of God.

So it is not only the zeal of those who seek him that proves God's existence, but also the blindness of those who do not seek him.

Fragment 821/432-[20]:

We shall base our first argument on the fact that there is something supernatural about this, for such blindness is not natural.

Fragment 427, par. 17:

It is an incomprehensible spell, a supernatural torpor that points to an omnipotent power as its cause.

It is highly interesting that the editors of the "Edition de Port-Royal" of the *Pensées* inserted fragment 163 (cited previously)—along with two other fragments drawn from the dossier "Commencement," several parts of fragment 428, and two fragments drawn from Pascal's other set of preparatory notes for the writing of fragment 427 (821/432)—into their version of the discourse we read in fragment 427.[48] Fragment 163, inserted after paragraph seventeen of fragment 427, presents a metaphor for the human condition which in fact superbly illustrates, in its new context, the totally illogical element in the skeptics' failure to set about learning what happens after death. Even more interesting is the fact that these same editors set this new composite version of these texts (drawn from fragment 427, from the dossier "Commencement," and from fragment 821/432) at the very beginning of their edition of the *Pensées*. For them, it would appear, it seemed entirely obvious that these texts, which they entitled "Contre l'indifférence des athées," represented a logical reconstitution of Pascal's proposed introduction to his unfinished work.

An even more convincing argument that the "Lettre" partially adumbrated in fragment 427 would have been set at the very beginning of the Apology, Philippe Sellier observes, is contained in Pascal's own fragment 4 in the dossier "Ordre":

A peine constitués les vingt-six dossiers "Vanité" à "Conclusion," l'écrivain fait le point sur l'organisation de son ouvrage et ouvre un dossier "Ordre." Sur les dix "Pensées" qui y figurent deux fournissent des indications sur "la lettre qu'on doit chercher Dieu" (11), appelée aussi "Lettre pour porter à rechercher Dieu" (4). On reconnaît à ce seul titre le *leitmotiv* de "Commencement" et Pascal prend soin de préciser:

48. The "Edition de Port-Royal" inserts fragment 152 (from "Commencement") after the eighth paragraph of fragment 427. After the ninth paragraph, it inserts a passage beginning with the second sentence ("Que l'on juge donc . . . ") of the third paragraph of fragment 428 and running through the fourth paragraph of fragment 428. After the eleventh paragraph of fragment 427, it inserts fragment 821/432-(18) and then the final paragraph of fragment 428. Fragment 163 is inserted after paragraph seventeen, followed by fragment 166 (also from "Commencement"). Into paragraph eighteen, between the second and third sentences, it inserts fragment 821/432-(11). See A. Gazier, *Pensées de Pascal sur la religion et sur quelques autres sujets: Edition de Port-Royal* (Paris: Société Française d'Imprimerie, 1907), pp. 87–98. The paragraph numbers I give for fragments 427 and 428 are those of the text found in Lafuma's *Oeuvres complètes*.

> Lettre pour porter à rechercher Dieu.
> *Et puis* le faire chercher chez les philosophes, pyrrhoniens et dogmatistes, qui travailleront celui qui les recherche.

La "Lettre" se situe donc bien *avant* l'enquête anthropologique, donc tout au début du livre.[49] . . . Ainsi "Commencement" signifie clairement . . . "Commencement" de l'apologie, et non "Commencement" . . . de la deuxième partie, comme sont *contraints* de l'avancer ceux qui se tiennent au présupposé que [la table de dossiers][50] serait un Sommaire.[51]

The twenty-six dossiers ("Vanity" to "Conclusion") scarcely constituted, the writer takes his bearings with regard to the organization of his work and opens the dossier "Order." Out of the ten "Pensées" which figure in it, two furnish indications concerning "the Letter urging men to seek God" (11), also called the "Letter to induce men to seek God" (4). We will recognize in this very title the *leitmotiv* of "Beginning." Pascal takes care to specify:

> Letter to induce men to seek God.
> *And then* make them look for him among the philosophers, skeptics, and dogmatists, who will trouble the man who seeks.

This "Letter," therefore, is to be located well *before* the anthropological investigations, in other words, right at the beginning of the book. . . . Thus "Beginning" clearly signifies . . . "Beginning" of the apology, and not—as those who hold the presupposition that the ["liasse-table"] is a Table of Contents are *constrained* to have it—"Beginning" of the second part.

The "pensée" in the dossier "Commencement" which is most obviously linked to fragment 427 is fragment 160. In "Commencement" its formula-

49. "L'ouverture de l'apologie pascalienne," pp. 440–41, italics Sellier's.

50. Sellier prints the *liasse-table* as his fragment 1. See *Pensées* (1991), p. 153, n. 1. Lafuma, the first editor to make use of those *Copies* in which the "liasse-table" is included, did not consider it an arrangement of the titled dossiers which could be attributed to Pascal himself. No edition of the *Pensées* until that of Sellier ever included it as part of Pascal's text. Jean Mesnard, however, believes that it is a "copie figurée," i.e., a copyist's reproduction, of the exact arrangement on the page of yet another table, presumably in Pascal's own hand, which at some point became lost from the *Recueil original*.

Jean Mesnard concludes that "la table des matières est donc elle-même une *pensée,* la plus précise et la plus complète de toutes celles qui suggèrent un plan de l'*Apologie*" ("the table of contents is therefore itself a *pensée,* the most precise and most complete of all those which suggest a plan for the Apology"). See Mesnard's *Les Pensées de Pascal* (Paris: S.E.D.E.S., 1976), p. 28. Also, Mesnard's "Aux origines de l'édition: les deux copies," in *Les "Pensées" de Pascal ont trois cents ans* (Clermont-Ferrand: G. de Bussac, 1971), pp. 1–30. Whereas Mesnard insists that the "liasse-table" represents Pascal's more or less definitive ordering of his major chapters, Philippe Sellier sees it more as a provisional inventory of a preliminary classification. The order of titles given in the "liasse-table," therefore, for Sellier, by no means rules out seeing the chapter "Commencement" as containing Pascal's notes for the writing of the "Lettres" which would have constituted the Preface to the entire Apology.

51. "L'ouverture de l'apologie pascalienne," p. 441, n. 7, italics Sellier's.

tion covers all sorts and conditions of humanity and admits to no exception. In fragment 427 (paragraph nineteen), Pascal has transformed it to include only active believers and seekers:

Fragment 160:

Il n'y a que trois sortes de personnes: les uns qui servent Dieu, l'ayant trouvé, les autres qui s'emploient à le chercher ne l'ayant pas trouvé, les autres qui vivent sans le chercher ni l'avoir trouvé. Les premiers sont *raisonnables* et heureux, les derniers sont fous et malheureux, ceux du milieux sont malheureux et *raisonnables*.

Fragment 427, par. 19:

Qu'ils laissent donc ces impiétés donc à ceux qui sont assez mal nés pour en être véritablement capables; qu'ils soient au moins honnêtes gens s'ils ne peuvent être chrétiens, et qu'ils reconnaissent enfin qu'il n'y a que deux sortes de personnes qu'on puisse appeler *raisonnables*: ou ceux qui servent Dieu de tout leur coeur parce qu'ils le connaissent, ou ceux qui le cherchent de tout leur coeur parce qu'ils ne le connaissent pas.

Fragment 160:

There are only three sorts of people: those who have found God and serve him; those who are busy seeking him and have not found him; those who live without either seeking or finding him. The first are *reasonable* and happy, the last are foolish and unhappy, those in the middle are unhappy and *reasonable*.

Fragment 429, par. 19:

Let them leave such impiety to those ill-bred enough to be really capable of it; let them at least be decent people if they cannot be Christians; let them, in short, acknowledge that there are only two classes of persons who can be called *reasonable*: those who serve God with all their heart because they know him and those who seek him with all their heart because they do not know him.

What Philippe Sellier calls the "tripartition" of all humanity in fragment 160 of "Commencement" is the organizing force behind fragment 427:

Je fais une extrême différence de ceux qui travaillent de toutes leurs forces à s'en instruire [de l'éventuelle immortalité de l'âme], à ceux qui vivent sans s'en mettre en peine et sans y penser. (par. 4)

I make an absolute distinction between those who strive with all their might to instruct themselves [concerning the possibility of the immortality of the soul] and those who live without troubling themselves or thinking about it.

Je ne puis avoir que de la compassion pour ceux qui gémissent sincèrement dans ce doute, qui le regardent comme le dernier des malheurs, et qui n'épargnant rien pour en sortir font de cette *recherche* leurs principales et leurs plus sérieuses occupations. (par. 5)

I can feel nothing but compassion for those who sincerely lament their doubt, who regard it as the ultimate misfortune, and who, sparing no effort to escape from it, make their *search* their principal and most serious endeavor.

Mais pour ceux qui passent leur vie sans penser à cette dernière fin de la vie . . . cette négligence en une affaire où il s'agit d'eux-mêmes, de leur éternité, *de leur tout* . . . , c'est un monstre pour moi [. . .].[52] (pars. 6 and 7)

But as for those who spend their lives without a thought for this final end of life . . . this negligence in a matter in which they themselves, their eternity, *their all* are at stake . . . seems quite monstrous to me.

The great *leitmotif* of both fragment 427 and the dossier ("Commencement") from which it is constituted is that the search for God must be a prerequisite in any and every human life. Pascal begins his attack on the indifference of the skeptics in this all-important matter, Philippe Sellier notes, by denouncing the casual manner in which the skeptics claim to have already considered the case in favor of the Christian religion.

Il faudrait, pour la combattre, qu'ils criassent qu'ils ont fait tous leurs efforts pour *chercher* partout . . . Ils croient avoir fait de grands efforts pour s'instruire, lorsqu'ils ont employé quelques heures à la lecture de quelque livre de l'Ecriture. . . . (427, par. 2)

In order to really attack [the Christian religion] they would have to protest that they had made every effort to *seek* everywhere. . . . They think they have made great efforts to instruct themselves when they have spent a few hours reading some book of the Bible. . . .

Philippe Sellier sees in this second paragraph of fragment 427 a "reprise" of fragment 150 in the dossier "Commencement":

Les impies qui font profession de suivre la raison doivent être étrangement forts en raison.

Que disent-ils donc?

"Ne voyons-nous pas, disent-ils, mourir et vivre les bêtes comme les hommes, et les Turcs comme les chrétiens? Ils ont leur cérémonies, leurs prophètes, leurs docteurs, leurs saints, leurs religieux, comme nous," etc.

Cela est-il contraire à l'Ecriture, ne dit-elle pas tout cela?

Si vous ne vous souciez guère de savoir la vérité, en voilà assez pour vous laisser en repos. Mais si vous désirez de tout votre coeur de la connaître, ce n'est pas assez regardé au détail. C'en serait assez pour une question de philosophie, mais ici où il va de tout. . . .

Et cependant après une réflexion légère de cette sorte on s'amusera, etc. . . .

52. Ibid., p. 441, italics Sellier's.

> The ungodly who propose to follow reason must be singularly strong in reason.
> What do they say then?
> "Do we not see," they say, "animals live and die like men, Turks like Christians? They have their ceremonies, their prophets, their doctors, their saints, their religious, like us?" etc.
> "Is that contrary to Scripture? Does it not say all that?"
> If you hardly care about knowing the truth, that is enough to leave you in peace, but if you desire with all your heart to know it, you have not looked closely enough at the details. This would do for a philosophical question, but here where everything is at stake. . . . And yet, after superficial reflection of this kind, they go off to amuse themselves, etc. (150)

This important fragment, which we will treat in greater detail in Chapter III,[53] anticipates, in a very precise way, Pascal's critique of the indifference of the hardened skeptics in fragment 427. In particular, "ici où il va de tout" ("here where everything is at stake") anticipates the concluding lines of paragraph two: "Il ne s'agit pas ici de l'intérêt léger de quelque personne étrangère . . . il s'agit de nous mêmes, et de notre tout" ("It is not a question here of the trifling interest of some stranger . . . it is a question of ourselves and our all"). Moreover, Philippe Sellier demonstrates how fragment 150 can be used to identify precisely what book of the Bible ("quelque livre de l'Ecriture") the skeptics claim to have examined in the second paragraph of fragment 427.

In fragment 150, the first of the *libertins*' objections to Christianity—"Ne voyons-nous pas . . . mourir et vivre les bêtes comme les hommes?" ("Do we not see . . . animals live and die like men?")—is in fact a paraphrase of Ecclesiastes 3:19–21: "Indeed, the fate of man and beast is identical; one dies, the other too, and both have the selfsame breath; man has no advantage over the beast, for all is vanity. Both go to the same place; both originate from the dust and to the dust both return. Who knows if the spirit of man mounts upward or if the spirit of the beast goes down to the earth" (Jerusalem Bible). Sellier reminds us that the skeptics' predilection for Ecclesiastes was recognized by the more astute of the clergy in the Classical period. Fénelon, he points out, writing to the Bishop of Arras, cited the *libertins*' fondness for citing the more skeptical passages in Ecclesiastes as one reason for limiting direct access to the Bible to the less-educated faithful.[54]

Many other developments inspired by fragments in the dossier "Com-

53. See Chapter III, Fragment 822 and Neo-Augustinian Theology.

54. "L'ouverture de l'apologie pascalienne," p. 442, n. 10.

mencement" run right through the section of the Preface to the Apology found in fragment 427. Paragraphs three, four, and twenty-one of fragment 427 recapitulate the argument in fragment 164 that nothing in this life is more crucial than finding out whether the soul is mortal or immortal. Paragraph nine—"Faisons tant que nous voudrons les braves: voilà la fin qui attend la plus belle vie du monde" ("However brave a front we put on, [being annihilated or wretched throughout eternity] is the fate awaiting the world's most illustrious life")—echoes fragment 165: "Le dernier acte est sanglant quelque belle que soit la comédie en tout le reste. On jette enfin de la terre sur la tête et en voilà pour jamais" ("The last act is bloody, however fine the rest of the play. One ends up six feet under, and it is finished forever"). Fragment 156, "Plaindre les athées qui cherchent. . . . Invectiver contre ceux qui en font vanité" ("Pity the atheists who seek. . . . Inveigh against those who boast about it"), anticipates the whole apologetic strategy of fragment 427 that we shall examine in Chapters IV and V.

Philippe Sellier makes an extremely cogent case that the celebrated "wager" fragment (418), which he thinks would have also formed part of the Preface to the Apology, is directly anticipated in the dossier "Commencement" by at least three preparatory notes: fragments 154 ("Partis" ["Choices"]), 158 ("Pour les partis . . ." ["As far as the choices go . . ."]), and 159 ("Si on doit donner huit jours de la vie on doit donner cent ans" ["If we ought to give up one week of our life, we ought to give up a hundred years"]). The developments of the "wager" fragment (418) are also clearly anticipated, he demonstrates, by paragraph fourteen of fragment 427

> . . . je sais seulement qu'en sortant de ce monde je tombe pour jamais ou dans le néant, ou dans les mains d'un Dieu irrité. . . .

> . . . I know only that when I leave this world I shall fall forever either into nothingness or into the hands of an angry God. . . .

and the fourth paragraph of fragment 428

> La mort . . . les doit mettre infailliblement dans peu de temps dans l'horrible nécessité d'être éternellement ou anéantis ou malheureux. . . .[55]

55. Ibid., pp. 443–45.

Death . . . must inevitably and without much delay put them in the horrible alternative of being either eternally annihilated or eternally wretched. . . .

* * *

In addition to the fragments of "Commencement," there exists another entire group of fragments, filed in *série xxx* of the Lafuma edition, which are intimately related to the section of the Preface to the Apology represented by fragment 427. The relevant fragments in "Commencement" are essentially conceptional in nature and appear to have been set down well before the actual writing of fragment 427. To borrow Sellier's notion, Pascal uses them to "orchestrate" the "Letter urging men to seek God" (11). Fragments 821/432-[1]–[21] (see Plate X), along with their continuation in fragment 432 (*série iv*),[56] on the other hand, appear to be Pascal's actual working notes in preparation for writing fragment 427.

56. See Chapter IV, Fragments 418 and 427: The State of the Texts. These two sets of preparatory notes for the writing of fragment 427 represent something of a mystery. The *Recueil original,* as recorded by Z. Tourneur's "edition paléographique," places them immediately after the fragments joined to the "pari" (fragments 421, 426, 423, 422). See Z. Tourneur, *Pensées de Pascal. . . .* (Paris: Vrin, 1942), pp. 312–13. However, the *Recueil original* represents the arrangement of Pascal's texts, not in 1662, but in 1710, and does not necessarily demonstrate that they belong with other material destined for the Preface.

In the two *Copies,* a copyist's note indicates that fragment 432 should have been placed in the same dossier as fragment 427: "Ceci est dans le cahier commençant par ces mots: Qu'ils apprennent . . ." (i.e., 427). This notation (see Sellier, *Pensées* [1991], p. 484, n. 10) applies only to the seven fragments (432–[23]–[29]) which seem to be a continuation of the twenty-one or twenty-two fragments printed in Lafuma's edition as 821/432: [1]–[21]. How these twenty-one fragments came to be inserted in *série xxx* is a mystery.

Some of these notes are dictated. If one consults the *Recueil original,* it appears that these dictated notes (paragraphs two to four, six to nine, thirteen, fifteen, and sixteen) form the basic text. Pascal later added paragraphs one at the top, paragraphs eighteen to twenty at the bottom, paragraph five between paragraphs four and six, paragraph ten between nine and thirteen, paragraph seventeen between sixteen and eighteen, and paragraphs eleven, twelve, and fourteen in the left-hand margin, along with the second sentence of paragraph seven.

Anthony Pugh, whose explanation of the arrangement of these fragments in the *Recueil original* I follow, finds Lafuma's numbering "bizarre" and wonders why he did not give these fragments, which follow fragment 821 in *série xxx,* a number or numbers "appropriate to that position." Pugh explains: "The reason for the bizarre number 432 is that [série iv] records, after fragment 431, a series of seven jottings evidently closely related to the twenty-one short paragraphs [of 821/432]. Lafuma takes them to be the sequel and numbers them 23 to 29." See Pugh's *The Composition of Pascal's Apologia,* pp. 520–21, n. 16.

Sellier, while noting that the two sets of notes are obviously related as preparatory notes for the composition of fragment 427, prints them separately as his fragments 662 and 684 and refrains from numbering the paragraphs. See *Pensées* (1991), pp. 452–54 and 484–85.

Here is not the place for an exhaustive study of the relationships among these three sets of texts. However, a few examples will serve to show how Pascal moves from fragmentary notes to the composition of the long *discours* set forth in fragment 427. Many of the fragments found in 821/432 move directly into fragment 427, where they are then more fully elaborated:

Fragment 821/432-[2]:

Il faut bien être dans *la religion qu'ils méprisent pour ne les pas mépriser.*

One must belong to the religion they despise in order not to despise them.

Fragment 427, par. 20:

Mais pour ceux qui vivent sans le connaître et sans le chercher, ils se jugent eux-mêmes si peu dignes de leur soin, qu'ils ne sont pas dignes du soin des autres et qu'il faut avoir toute la charité de *la religion qu'ils méprisent pour ne pas les mépriser* jusqu'à les abandonner dans leur folie.

As for those who live without either knowing or seeking him, they consider it so little worthwhile to take trouble over themselves that they are not worth other people's trouble, and it takes all the charity of that religion they despise not to despise them to the point of abandoning them to their folly.

Fragment 821/432-[6]:

Vous me convertirez.

You will convert me.

Fragment 427, par. 19:

C'était ce que leur disait fort à propos une personne: "Si vous continuez à discourir de la sorte," leur disait-il, "en vérité *vous me convertirez.*"

As someone said to them very aptly one day: "If you go on arguing like that," he said, "you will convert me."

Fragment 821/432-[7]:

Je ne prends point cela par bigoterie, mais par la manière dont le coeur de l'homme est fait, non par *un zèle de dévotion* et de détachement, mais par *un principe* purement *humain*, mais par un mouvement d'*intérêt* et *d'amour-propre.*

I do not take that view out of bigotry, but because of the way man's heart is made; not out of zealous piety and detachment, but on purely human grounds and for motives of self-interest and self-love.

Fragment 427, par. 7:

Je ne dis pas ceci par *le zèle* pieux *d'une dévotion* spirituelle. J'entends au contraire qu'on doit avoir ce sentiment par un *principe* d'*intérêt humain* et par un *intérêt d'amour-propre*.

I do not say this prompted by the pious zeal of spiritual devotion. I mean on the contrary that we ought to have this feeling from principles of human interest and self-love.

Fragment 821/432-[9]:

C'est donc un malheur que de douter, mais c'est un *devoir indispensable de chercher dans* le *doute et ainsi celui qui doute et qui ne cherche pas est tout ensemble malheureux et injuste*; *que s'il est avec cela* gai et présomptueux, *je n'ai point de terme pour qualifier une si extravagante créature*.

Doubt is then an unhappy state, but there is an indispensable duty to seek in our doubt, and thus anyone who doubts and does not seek is at once unhappy and in the wrong. If, in addition, he is cheerful and presumptuous, I can find no words to describe so extravagant a creature.

Fragment 427, par. 10:

C'est donc un grand mal que d'être dans ce doute; mais c'est au moins *un devoir indispensable de chercher*, quand on est *dans ce doute*; *et ainsi celui qui doute et qui ne recherche pas est tout ensemble* et bien *malheureux* et bien *injuste*. *Que s'il est avec cela* tranquille et satisfait . . . *je n'ai point de termes pour qualifier une si extravagante créature*.

It is therefore quite certainly a great evil to have such doubts, but it is at least an indispensable obligation to seek when one does thus doubt; so the doubter who does not seek is at the same time very unhappy and very wrong. If in addition he feels a calm satisfaction . . . I can find no terms to describe so extravagant a creature.

Sometimes a fragment from 821/432 is absorbed into fragment 427 with a good deal of elaboration. The note serves to jog Pascal's memory on a particular point. Fragment 821/432-[12], "Est-ce une chose à dire avec joie? C'est une chose qu'on doit dire tristement" ("Is it a thing to be said with joy? It is a thing one should say with sadness"), serves to remind Pascal of a particular anecdote he wants to relate about the hardened skeptics:

Prétendent-ils nous avoir bien rejoui, de nous dire qu'ils tiennent que notre âme n'est qu'un peu de vent et de fumée, et encore de nous le dire d'un ton de voix fier et content? Est-ce une chose à dire gaiement? et n'est-ce pas une chose à dire tristement, au contraire, comme la chose du monde la plus triste?

Do they think they have given us pleasure by telling us that they hold our soul to be no more than wind or smoke, and saying it moreover in tones of pride and satisfaction? Is this then something to be said gaily? On the contrary, is it not something to be said sadly, as being the saddest thing in the world? (821/432-[12])

In the preceding passage, Pascal has greatly expanded a brief note and thus rendered it far more forceful. But sometimes the process works in reverse fashion. Fragment 821/432-[15] reads: "Est-ce courage à un homme mourant d'aller dans la faiblesse et dans l'agonie affronter un Dieu puissant et éternel?" ("Is it brave of a dying man to go in his weakness and agony to confront a powerful and eternal God?"). In paragraph twenty of fragment 427, the fragment is absorbed in a briefer, but far more striking form: "Rien n'est plus lâche que de faire le brave contre Dieu" ("Nothing is more cowardly than to attempt to stand up to God").

A number of the notes in *série xxx* are not absorbed directly. Rather, they are thematic and strategic. Fragment 821/432-[1], recalling fragments 156 and 162 in the dossier "Commencement," lays the groundwork for the distinction Pascal will make in fragment 427 (especially in paragraphs four to eleven) between his radically different attitudes toward the hardened skeptics and toward the seeking unbelievers:

On doit avoir pitié des uns et des autres, mais on doit avoir pour les uns une pitié qui naît de tendresse, et pour les autres une pitié qui naît de mépris.

We should pity both, but we should pity the former out of affection and the latter out of contempt.

Fragment 821/432-[5], which is never absorbed into fragment 427 at all, nevertheless provides a vital clue to the identity of the hardened skeptics in the Preface to the Apology. "Les gens de cette sorte sont académistes, écoliers, et c'est le plus méchant caractère d'homme que je connaisse" ("The people in this category are skeptics and scholars, and that is the meanest kind of man I have ever known"). Fragment 821/432-[21], on the other hand, gives rise to an important development orchestrated in paragraph seventeen of fragment 427. Whereas 821/432-[21] is but a fragmentary note containing a basic strategy

Est-ce qu'ils sont si fermes qu'ils soient insensibles à tout ce qui les touche? Eprouvons-les dans la perte des biens ou de l'honneur. Quoi? c'est un *enchantement*.

> Are they so closed as to be insensitive to everything that affects them? Put them to the test with the loss of their wealth or honor. What? It's an enchantment. (821/432-[21], italics mine)

paragraph seventeen of fragment 427 is a fully developed exposition of the enigma constituted by those who are indifferent to their ultimate fate:

> Rien n'est si important à l'homme que son état; rien ne lui est si redoutable que l'éternité. Et ainsi, qu'il se trouve des hommes indifférents à la perte de leur être et au péril d'une éternité de misères, cela n'est point naturel. Ils sont tout autres à l'égard de toutes les autres choses: ils craignent jusqu'aux plus légères, ils les prévoient, ils les sentent; et ce même homme qui passe tant de jours et de nuits dans la rage et dans le désespoir pour la perte d'une charge ou pour quelque offense imaginaire à son honneur, c'est celui-là même qui sait qu'il va tout perdre par la mort, sans inquiétude et sans émotions. C'est une chose monstrueuse de voir dans un même coeur et en même temps cette sensibilité pour les moindres choses et cette étrange insensibilité pour les plus grandes. C'est un *enchantement* incompréhensible, et un assoupissement surnaturel, qui marque une force toute-puissante qui le cause.

> Nothing is so important to man as his state of being: nothing more fearful than eternity. Thus the fact that there exist men who are indifferent to the loss of their existence and to the peril of an eternity of wretchedness is against nature. With everything else they are quite different; they fear the most trifling things, foresee and feel them; and the same man who spends so many days and nights in fury and despair at losing some office or at some imaginary affront to his honor is the very one who knows that he is going to lose everything through death but feels neither anxiety nor emotion. It is a monstrous thing to see one and the same heart at once so sensitive to minor things and so strangely insensitive to the greatest. It is an incomprehensible spell, a supernatural torpor that points to an omnipotent power as its cause.

We have by no means exhausted the highly complex issue of the relationship between this section of Pascal's Preface to the Apology set down in fragment 427 and those preparatory notes found in the dossier "Commencement" and in fragment 821/432. But, I have, I hope, demonstrated that Pascal never anticipated an Apology written in a fragmentary form. Indeed, the section of the Preface which we have seen him orchestrating with the help of these two collections of fragmentary notes probably represents the point in his work at which Pascal began to write the Apology itself in the form of a series of discourses and chapters.

Other more finished parts of the *Pensées*, put together from other sets of notes, indeed remain to be identified. The work of clarifying Pascal's methodology in this respect will without question be elevated to a more scientific plane once scholars have the chance to absorb the highly complicated revelations of Pol Ernst's recently published *Géologie et stratigraphie des Pensées*. Henceforth, scholars will know much more about the chronology of composition of the *Pensées*. Likewise, the introduction and notes to Jean Mesnard's long-awaited edition of the *Pensées* (in the sixth volume of his edition of the *Oeuvres complètes*) will certainly facilitate the opening of new vistas in research on the composition of the *Pensées*.

In a recent article Philippe Sellier has already identified another major *discours* which represents the orchestration of yet another set of Pascal's working notes. In "Une Préface 'retrouvée' de l'Apologie pascalienne," Sellier demonstrates that the dossier "Excellence" (XIV) constitutes the preparatory notes for the writing of the sketch of the Preface to the *second* part of the Apology set down in fragment 781 ("Préface de la seconde partie"). Moreover, he goes on to demonstrate that the *discours* erroneously broken up into fragments 438–450 by Lafuma[57] constituted an amplified and elaborated version of the "préface" sketched in fragment 781. At least twelve paragraphs of this newer version of the Preface to the second part of the Apology, Sellier goes on to show, are directly inspired by notes found in the dossier "Excellence."

Of even greater note, Sellier identifies a series of additional fragments which bear an intimate relationship to the two versions of the prefaces to the second half of the Apology adumbrated in fragments 781 and 438–450. The first of these, Lafuma 2–4, which Sellier gathers into a single fragment under the title "Ordre par dialogues" ("Order by dialogues"),[58] is pivotal to an understanding of how Pascal's proposed Apology would have differed from traditional apologies of a metaphysical orientation. In fragment 781, we find Pascal rejecting the metaphysical proofs of the existence of God, which have presumably been evoked by the unbelievers as unconvincing, found in all traditional apologetic works:

> J'admire avec quelle hardiesse ces personnes entreprennent de parler de Dieu.
>
> En addressant leurs discours aux *impies* leur premier chapitre est de prouver la divinité par les ouvrages de la nature. Je m'étonnerais pas de leur entreprise s'ils adressaient leurs discours aux fidèles . . . mais pour ceux en qui cette lumière est éteinte et dans lequels on a dessein de la faire revivre, ces personnes destituées de

57. Collated as fragment 690 in Sellier's edition.
58. Fragment 38 in Sellier's edition.

foi et de grâce, qui recherchant de toute leur lumiére tout ce qu'ils voient dans la nature qui les peut mener à cette connaissance ne trouvent qu'obscurité et ténèbres, dire à ceux-là qu'ils n'ont qu'à voir la moindre des choses qui les environnent et qu'ils y verront Dieu à découvert . . . c'est leur donner sujet de croire que les preuves de notre religion sont bien faibles et je vois par raison et *par expérience* que rien n'est plus propre à leur en faire naître le mépris. Ce n'est pas de cette sorte que l'Ecriture . . . en parle. Elle dit au contraire que Dieu est un Dieu caché et que depuis la corruption de la nature il les a laissés dans un aveuglement dont ils ne peuvent sortir que par J.-C., hors duquel toute communication avec Dieu est ôtée. . . .

I admire the boldness with which these people presume to speak of God. In addressing their arguments to *unbelievers*, their first chapter is the proof of the existence of God from the works of nature. Their enterprise would cause me no surprise if they were addressing their arguments to the faithful . . . but for those in whom this light has gone out and in whom we are trying to rekindle it, people deprived of faith and grace, examining with such light as they have everything they see in nature that might lead them to this knowledge, but finding only obscurity and darkness; to tell them that they only have to look at the least thing around them and they will see God plainly revealed . . . this is giving them cause to think that the proofs of our religion are very feeble, and reason and *experience* tell me that nothing is more likely to bring it into contempt in their eyes. This is not how Scripture . . . speaks. On the contrary, it says that God is a hidden God, and that since nature was corrupted he has left men to their blindness, from which they can escape only through Jesus Christ, without whom all communication with God is broken off. (781, italics mine)

In this crucial passage Pascal breaks with the entire apologetic tradition of beginning with the ontological proof of God's existence. Instead he invokes Augustine's *Deus absconditus*. This development, Sellier shows us, grows out of a much earlier—and far more fragmentary—notation in the dossier "Ordre":

ORDRE

PAR DIALOGUES

"Que dois-je faire? Je ne vois partout qu'obscurités. Croirai-je que je ne suis rien? Croirai-je que je suis dieu"

"Toutes choses changent et se succèdent."
"Vous vous trompez, il y a . . ."

"Et quoi ne dites-vous pas vous-même que le ciel et les oiseaux prouvent Dieu?" —— "Non." —— "Et votre religion ne le dit-elle pas?" —— "Non. Car encore que cela est vrai en un sens pour quelques âmes à qui Dieu donna cette lumière, néanmoins cela est faux à l'égard de la plupart."

ORDER
BY DIALOGUES

"What must I do? I see nothing but darkness on every side."
"Shall I believe I am nothing? Shall I believe I am God?"

"There is change and mutation in all things."
"You are wrong, there is . . ."

"Why, do you not say yourself that the sky and the birds prove God?"—"No."—"Does your religion not say so?"—No. For though it is true in a sense for some souls whom God has enlightened in this way, nevertheless it is untrue for the majority." (2–3)

Sellier finds five additional fragments which he views as flowing directly into the composition of the prefaces to the second part of the Apology sketched by fragment 781 and fragments 438–450. Fragment 417 anticipates the end of the fourth paragraph of fragment 781:

Non seulement nous ne connaissons Dieu que par Jésus-Christ. . . .

Not only do we only know God through Jesus-Christ. . . . (417)

Nemo novit patrem nisi filius et cui filius voluit revelare.

No one knows the Father except the Son and those to whom the Son chooses to reveal him. (Matthew 11:27) (781)

Fragment 394 announces a multiplicity of themes found in the *discours* constituted by fragments 438–450. Fragment 463 prefigures fragment 781 by recalling that no canonical author of Scripture ever made use of the ontological proof:

C'est une chose admirable que jamais auteur canonique ne s'est servi de la nature pour prouver Dieu.

It is a remarkable thing that no canonical author has ever called upon nature to prove God. (463)

Ce n'est pas de cette sorte que l'Ecriture . . . en parle. Elle dit au contraire . . .

This is not how Scripture . . . speaks. On the contrary it says . . . (781)

Fragment 460 directly anticipates paragraph ten of fragment 449, the penultimate section of the larger *discours* adumbrated by fragments 438–450:

Le Dieu des chrétiens est un Dieu qui fait sentir à l'âme qu'il est son unique bien; que tout son repos est en lui, qu'elle n'aura de joie qu'à l'aimer. . . .

The Christians' God is a God who makes the soul aware that he is its sole good; that in him alone can it find peace; that in loving him alone can it find joy. . . . (460)

Le Dieu des chrétiens . . . est un Dieu qui remplit l'âme et le coeur de ceux qu'il possède . . . qui les rend incapables d'autre fin que de lui-même.

The Christians' God . . . is a God who fills the soul and heart of those whom he possesses . . . who makes them incapable of having any other end but him. (449)

Fragment 464 either anticipates or amplifies the final paragraph of fragment 449 in a very direct fashion:

Je ne souffrirai point qu'il repose en l'un ni en l'autre afin qu'étant sans assiette et sans repos . . .

I will allow him no peace in the one or the other, so that with no place to settle or rest . . . (464)

Quelque parti qu'il prenne, je ne l'y laisserai point en repos . . .

Whatever course he adopts, I will not leave him in peace . . . (449)

Both these fragments, of course, refer to the strategy—outlined in the Preface to the first part of the Apology—of never letting the seeking unbeliever relapse into lethargy and finally into the fatal indifference of the hardened skeptics.

Philippe Sellier is extremely excited not only by the fact that it is becoming more and more possible to reconstitute major sections of the two Prefaces to the two great parts of the Apology, but by the very notion that we are now beginning to be able to identify which texts are in the process of taking their definitive forms:

Non seulement il devient possible d'accompagner "Pascal au travail," étape par étape, mais des thèmes capitaux se voient assigner la place privilégiée qui devait leur revenir dans le dispositif: ils en reçoivent un éclairage nouveau et un surcroît de sens. Enfin . . . nous disposerons pour la première fois d'une extraordinaire *succession* de textes décisifs. . . . Grâce au degré d'élaboration de la plupart de ces textes, déjà très travaillés, il deviendra concevable, enfin, de réfléchir sur ce que Pascal appelait *l'ordre du coeur* [298]. Pourquoi les études pascaliennes sont-elles restées si discrètes sur cette question si importante? C'est que pour découvrir *l'ordre du coeur*, il faut d'abord disposer d'un *ordre* authentiquement *pascalien*.[59]

Not only does it become possible to accompany "Pascal at work," stage by stage, but also we now find the major themes themselves assigned to the privileged status which was their due in Pascal's *dispositio*: as a result new light is shed upon them, yielding additional meaning.

Finally . . . we have at our disposal an extraordinary *succession* of definitive texts. . . . The degree to which the great majority of these already quite polished texts have been amplified means that it will finally become conceivable to reflect upon what Pascal called *the order of the heart* [298]. Why have Pascal studies had so little to say on such an important subject? It is because, in order to discover *the order of the heart*, one must first have at one's disposal an *order* which is authentically *Pascalian*.

* * *

Jésus sera en agonie jusqu'à la fin du monde.

(*Le Mystère de Jésus*, fragment 919)

Pascal's dark theodicy of the *Deus absconditus* must surely appear somewhat incomprehensible to a culture which has so sanitized death and suffering as has our own. We cannot hope, I think, to consider in all honesty Pascal's defense of God's essential goodness in the face of the reality of evil as proposed to us in the *Pensées* unless we are prepared to admit, in the first instance, that it strikes us as implying a kind of monster-God, capriciously damning and saving human beings on the basis of some unknown impulse. The notion, still so alive in the religion of the Prophet, of the inscrutability of God's will has simply withered away to the point of incomprehensibility during the three hundred years separating us from the author of the *Pensées*. Those "true believers" who would accept such a theodicy, I think we must admit, appear to us as barbarous as does the *bigot* ridiculed in the *Quatrains du déiste*:

Plein de trouble en son âme, il s'effraye de Dieu,
Ainsi que les enfans d'un monstre espouvantable,
Et tel l'imaginant, il le blasme en tout lieu
Sous ombre d'exalter sa justice ineffable.[60]

59. Philippe Sellier, "Une Préface 'retrouvée' de l'*Apologie* pascalienne," in *Travaux de littérature* (Paris: Klincksieck, 1993), p. 158.

60. See Chapter I, Pascal and Deism.

His soul full of turmoil, he is terrified of God / As children are of a horrible monster, / And imagining Him thus, he reproaches Him everywhere / Under cover of exalting his ineffable Justice.[61]

On the other hand, perhaps we should not be hasty in our rejection of Pascal's horrifyingly dark theodicy. Nor should we opt out of the dilemma which Pascal presents to us by simply labeling it "tragic."[62] After all, in the course of the last three hundred years, no Western theologian has successfully managed to rethink the problem of evil. Nor has any modern Christian theologian ever even begun to reconcile with any believability the traditional Christian reading of the Fall with the scientific revelations concerning the origins of humankind.

Pascal's critique of the indifference with which the great majority of human beings look upon the ultimate questions of existence (and the ultimate reality of death) is, of course, as valid as ever. At least in the West, the progress of modern public hygiene has shielded us from a direct contemplation of death and human suffering in a way which Pascal could have never imagined. Pascal, one supposes, could count upon the fact that very few of his projected readers would never have come upon corpses in the city streets nor ever have witnessed physical suffering of a kind from which our own culture routinely tries to shield us. Pascal's vision of suffering humanity, one suspects, is one which might meet with far more comprehension in the modern Third World.

How then should we attempt to read Pascal's *Pensées*? One can but hope that our contemporary Christian fundamentalists, be they Catholic[63] or Protestant, will never elevate Pascal as their standard-bearer. Their reading of his projected Apology could well prove to be more misguided (and far more dangerous) than that of the postmodernist critics. In the study which follows, I essentially propose reading the *Pensées* as Pascal's attempt—by parting company with traditional apologetics and attempting to "return to the origins"[64] of Christian doctrine—to stay the tide of an emerging liberalizing tendency in Catholic doctrine and practice.

61. Ibid.

62. See Chapter IV, The Tragedy of Disbelief.

63. Oddly enough, those Lefevrite Catholics who reject the reforms of the Second Vatican Council have automatically rejected Pascal (along with Port-Royal) as purveyors of the Jansenist "heresy."

64. This theme, M. Eliade points out, is hardly unique to the Reformation or the Counter-Reformation. A "return to the origins," he argues, is one of the most basic organizing principles of the myths of "archaic societies." See "Survivals and Camouflages of Myths," pp. 43–44.

However little we might sympathize with Pascal's doctrinal rigidity, we can, I think, come to share—at least temporarily—his nostalgia for a theodicy which genuinely speaks to the problem of evil and suffering. The doctrine of God's hidden nature expounded by Pascal in a more personal context, in the fourth letter to Charlotte de Roannez, has always struck me as more mystical (though hardly less rigorous) than the one he proposes in his attack on disbelief:

> Cet étrange secret dans lequel Dieu s'est retiré, impénétrable à la vue des hommes, est une grande leçon pour nous porter à la solitude loin de la vue des hommes. Il est demeuré caché sous le voile de la nature qui nous le couvre jusqu'à l'Incarnation; et quand il a fallu qu'il ait paru, il s'est encore plus caché en se couvrant de l'humanité. Il était bien plus reconnaissable quand il était invisible, que non pas quand il s'est rendu visible. Et enfin quand il a voulu accomplir la promesse qu'il fit à ses Apôtres de demeurer avec les hommes jusqu'à son dernier avènement, il a choisi d'y demeurer dans le plus étrange et le plus obscur secret de tous, qui sont les espèces de l'Eucharistie. C'est ce Sacrement que saint Jean appelle dans l'Apocalypse [II, 17] une manne cachée; et je crois qu'Isaïe le voyait en cet état, lorsqu'il dit en esprit de prophétie: *"Véritablement tu es un Dieu caché"* [Is., XLV, 15]. C'est là le dernier secret où il peut être.[65]

> This strange secret, into which God withdrew, impenetrable to the sight of men, is a great lesson which should urge us to seek solitude far from the sight of men. He remained hidden under the veil of nature which covers him until the Incarnation; and when he was obliged to appear, he hid himself even more profoundly by covering himself with humanity. He was far more recognizable when he was invisible than when he became visible. And finally, when he sought to accomplish the promise he made to his Apostles to remain with humanity until his last coming, he chose to remain with us in the most strange and the most obscure secret of all, in the species of the Eucharist. It is this Sacrament that St. John calls in his Apocalypse [2:17] a hidden manna; and I believe that Isaiah saw him in this state, when he said, animated by the spirit of prophecy: *"Truly thou art a hidden God"* [Is., 45:15]. The final secret where God can be is there.

In this more private statement of Pascal's theodicy, his theory of the "three orders," which Jean Mesnard has shown to be a major ideological organizing principle in the *Pensées*,[66] profoundly animates Pascal's schema of God's progressively hidden nature. Likewise, this same theory of the "three orders" is the fundamental organizing principle behind Pascal's conception of the progressive nature of Revelation itself:

65. Lafuma, *Pascal: Oeuvres complètes*, p. 267.

66. See Jean Mesnard's "Le thème des trois ordres dans l'organisation des *Pensées* in *Pascal: thématique des Pensées*, Lane M. Heller and Ian M. Richmond, eds. (Paris: Vrin, 1988), pp. 29–55.

Le voile de la nature qui couvre Dieu a été pénétré par plusieurs infidèles, qui, comme dit saint Paul, ont reconnu un Dieu invisible par la nature visible [Rom., I, 20]. Les Chrétiens hérétiques l'ont connu à travers son humanité et adorent Jésus-Christ Dieu et homme. Mais de le reconnaître sous des espèces de pain, c'est le propre des seuls Catholiques: il n'y que nous que Dieu éclaire jusque-là.[67]

The veil of nature concealing God was penetrated by a few among the pagans, who, as Saint Paul tells us, recognized an invisible God through visible nature [Rom., 1:20]. Heretical Christians have known him through his humanity and worship Jesus-Christ God and man. But to recognize him under the species of bread, that is the prerogative of Catholics alone: we alone have been enlightened by God to so great an extent.

* * *

I have chosen to cite the *Pensées* (by fragment number) in the body and notes of my study from the edition of Louis Lafuma (Collection l'Intégrale, Editions du Seuil, 1963) for one reason alone: it is the only modern edition of the *Pensées* based upon one of the *Copies* which can be found in English translations. For the same reason, I have accompanied all French citations, with the exception of a few notes which will interest only specialists, with an English translation. This constant process of translation has perhaps unduly cluttered the book which is to follow. But I long ago promised students and friends that the next book I wrote on Pascal would be accessible to those with a less than perfect reading knowledge of the French language.

For those who do read French, I can but recommend the edition of Philippe Sellier (Classiques Garnier, Bordas, 1991), in which I myself always choose to read Pascal's text and which I would have used as my edition of reference had I not been constrained by the promise made long ago. Sellier's edition, equipped with an admirable critical apparatus and whose notes and introduction are the best of any edition of the *Pensées*, not only corrects a number of misreadings in Lafuma's text, but also restores to Pascal's text many of the *discours* which Lafuma and other editors have unnecessarily fragmented.

67. Lafuma, *Pascal: Oeuvres complètes*, p. 267.

CHAPTER I

Pascal and the Unbelievers

In her *Vie de Monsieur Pascal*, Gilberte Périer gives the impression that her brother's unfinished *Apology for the Christian Religion* was originally undertaken out of a sense of outrage against the phenomenon of contemporary atheism. Mme Périer recounts that Pascal, while reflecting upon the light which miracles shed upon the truth of religion, "se sentit tellement animé contre les athées que, voyant dans les lumières que Dieu lui avait données, de quoi les convaincre et les confondre sans ressources, il s'appliqua à cet ouvrage . . ."[1] ("felt so outraged by the atheists that, seeing via the enlightenment that God had given him how to convince and utterly confound them, he undertook this great project . . .").

Other sources reinforce Mme. Périer's contention that Pascal's primary aim in writing the *Pensées* was to refute disbelief. In his "Préface" to the "Edition de Port-Royal" of the *Pensées*, Pascal's nephew, Etienne Périer, maintains that his uncle intended not only to refute "les raisonnements des athées" ("the arguments of the atheists") but to declare "la guerre . . . aux athées, aux infidèles et aux hérétiques"[2] ("war on the atheists, the unbelievers and the heretics"). Pascal's niece, Marguerite Périer, twice refers to her uncle's decision to "travailler contre les athées"[3] ("to work against the atheists"). Père Beurrier, who heard Pascal's last confession, recalls in

1. Louis Lafuma, ed., *Pascal: Oeuvres complètes* (Paris: Editions de Seuil, 1963), p. 24.

2. A. Gazier, ed., *Pensées de Pascal . . . Edition de Port-Royal* (Paris: Société Française d'Imprimerie, 1907), pp. 70–71.

3. "Mémoire sur Pascal et sa famille" in Jean Mesnard, *Blaise Pascal, Oeuvres complètes* (Paris: Desclée de Brouwer, Bibliothèque européenne, 1964), I, p. 1103.

his *Mémoires* that Pascal, after making a "retraite spirituelle,"[4] "avait pris résolution à combattre fortement les impies et les athées, qui étaient en grand nombre dans Paris"[5] ("resolved to mount a fierce fight against the unbelievers and atheists, who were very numerous in Paris").

Commentators on the *Pensées* have long struggled to reconcile the interlocutors whose presence we sometimes feel in the *Pensées* with these references to the practitioners of disbelief in midseventeenth-century Paris. Curiously enough, the one word which has come to characterize Pascal's interlocutor in the *Pensées* in much modern Pascalian scholarship never appears in that text. Not once does Pascal use the word *libertin* in the course of the *Pensées*.[6] The term *libertinage* figures only once in this vast text and then only in the relatively technical sense of "active disbelief" (179).

In his *Blaise Pascal: conversion et apologétique* (1986), Henri Gouhier cautions that the terms *libertins* and *libertinage* may well have been given a privileged status by modern historians of ideas in order to forge a convenient category comprehending the various forms and degrees of religious disbelief found in seventeenth-century France:

> La portée actuelle des mots "libertins" et "libertinage" appartient à la vision rétrospective où [les historiens des idées] introduisent quelque chose comme une catégorie de la pensée historique, qui va permettre d'opérer l'indispensable travail de classification et de dénomination. . . . Ni chez Pascal ni autour de lui, la notion de libertinage ne joue ce rôle de catégorie de la pensée historique. . . . Ainsi, dans la vision rétrospective à l'intérieur de laquelle nous étudions le XVIIe siècle, il est bien permis de montrer Pascal face aux libertins . . . mais il doit être entendu que, dans la vision contemporaine de Pascal, les incroyants à convertir peuvent apparaître sous d'autres noms.[7]

> The modern significance of the words *libertins* and *libertinage* belongs to a retrospective vision into which [historians of ideas] have attempted to introduce something like a category of historical thought. Their aim is to make possible the indispensable work of classification and designation. . . . Neither in Pascal's text nor in its intellectual setting does the notion of *libertinage* ever really constitute such a category of historical thought. . . . Thus, from within this retrospective

4. Perhaps a reference to Pascal's visit to Port-Royal-des-Champs in January 1655.

5. Mesnard, *Blaise Pascal, Oeuvres complètes,* 1, p. 868.

6. Henri Gouhier reminds us that Pascal had used the term *libertin* a single time in the fourth of the *Lettres Provinciales:* "ces *libertins* qui ne cherchent qu'à douter de la religion" ("those *libertines* who seek only to doubt religion") (italics mine). *Blaise Pascal: Conversion et apologétique* (Paris: Vrin, 1986), p. 117. Accordingly to Furetière's *Dictionnaire universel* (1690), *libertin* had a meaning much like that of *incrédule:* "Libertin, qui ne croit rien."

7. *Blaise Pascal: conversion et apologétique,* pp. 115–16.

vision we use to study the seventeenth century, it is perfectly permissible to present Pascal in confrontation with the *libertins* . . . but it must be understood that in Pascal's vision (and in that of his contemporaries), the unbelievers whom he seeks to convert may well appear under different names.

Pascal uses a variety of terms when alluding to disbelief: "les athées" ("atheists"), "les curieux" ("the curious"), "les incrédules" ("unbelievers"), "les impies" ("the impious").[8] However, even the most frequent of these references ("les impies") occurs only twelve times in the course of the text of the *Pensées*. Pascal's references to his more purely philosophical adversaries are more numerous. He refers to the "pyrrhoniens" ("skeptics") twenty-two times and invokes the doctrine of "pyrrhonisme" fourteen times.[9]

Given the length, scope, and complexity of the texts known as the *Pensées*, the sum total of Pascal's references to disbelief hardly constitutes an impressively consistent picture of those "athées" who, according to Mme. Périer, so aroused his indignation. Even less do these references give us anything like a detailed portrait of Pascal's potential interlocutors in his never-completed Apology.

Le Libertinage érudit

In its quest to understand the mentality to whom Pascal intended to address his Apology, modern scholarship has been unavoidably sidetracked by the difficult issue of scholarly disbelief. What is called *le libertinage érudit* is in fact an amalgam of several very different traditions of philosophical objections to the Bible, Christianity, and the existence of God. The matter is further complicated by the fact that the entire tradition undergoes considerable evolution in the course of the century which separates the Renaissance from the Enlightenment.

It is true that Italian neo-Averroism of the University of Padua, via its teaching that the operations of the natural world are regular and unvarying, furnished seventeenth-century *érudits* with three principal themes:

8. *Athées:* fragments 156, 161, 244, 449, 619, and 882; *Curieux:* fragments 60, 308, 933; *Incrédules:* fragments 162, 198, 224, 872; *Impies:* fragments 150, 208, 431, 441, 487, 618, 781, 840, 916, 923, and 903.

9. *Pyrrhonien(ne)(s):* fragments 131 (eleven references), 170, 170, 520, 886, 109, 694, 4, 33, 76, 619; *Pyrrhonisme:* fragments 33, 109, 131 (three references), 406, 521, 655, 658, 691, 896, 905.

the denial of miracles and divine providence, the negation of the Creation, and the refutation of the immortality of the soul. However, Pomponazzi's rethinking of Aristotle and the naturalism of Giordano Bruno are shot through with metaphysical implications which would become more and more alien to *le libertinage érudit* as it evolved toward the Enlightenment. As J. S. Spink notes in his discussion of this evolution, "the belief that an Intelligence is suffused throughout the universe and that the laws of nature are modes of that intelligence is probably the most attractive of all beliefs for the human mind." This whole belief, Spink explains, was radically undermined in the course of the Classical period by two major phenomena. On the one hand, the new mechanistic science stripped the Renaissance view of natural law of its metaphysical associations. It replaced them with what Spink calls "a simple and straightforward deism which separated God radically from his creation."[10] During the same period, the growing current of French skepticism began to eat away not only at Renaissance astrology and alchemy but at the very notion of a God implicated in every part of nature. This tendency was only further aggravated by the new Cartesian distinction between the mind and the extended world.

What came to be known as pantheism did not of course fade completely away from the history of ideas. As Spink observes, it crept into the purely rational systems of Leibniz and Spinoza and permitted Malebranche to Christianize Cartesianism.[11] It continues to influence Christian thought, from which it has never been entirely alien. However, the fact remains that this whole mode of thought is, with the possible exception of that of Cyrano de Bergerac, almost entirely absent from the irreligious systems of those seventeenth-century French skeptics whose ideas tempted or seduced those whom Pascal will attempt to reconvert to orthodox Christian belief. During the course of the Classical period in France, irreligious theory develops more and more in the direction of an increasingly mechanistic deism which always seems to be tottering on the brink of covert atheism. As we shall see, Pascal will come very close indeed to equating deism and atheism, calling them "deux choses que la religion chrétienne abhorre presque également" ("two things almost equally abhorrent to Christianity") (449).

The study of *le libertinage érudit* in the first half of the Classical period

10. J. S. Spink, *French Free-Thought from Gassendi to Voltaire* (London: Athlone Press, 1960), pp. 7–8.

11. Ibid., p. 8.

is complicated by a host of difficulties. First and foremost, our direct access to irreligious and anti-Christian writings is extremely limited. Like those scholars seeking to reconstruct second-century Christian Gnosticism from fragments cited by its orthodox antagonists, we are all too often reduced to studying the *libertins* via their detractors. Far too much of what we know about anti-Christian thought and theory in the period comes to us via such apologists as Père Garasse[12] and Père Mersenne.[13] Of the presumably many irreligious documents which circulated clandestinely in manuscript form, only a very few have been discovered by modern researchers. Key among these are the manuscript text of the *Quatrains du Déiste*[14] and the unexpurgated original text of Cyrano de Bergerac's *Etats et empires de la lune*. Another key text, which Georges Couton has shown to be particularly relevant to the *Pensées*, has never been found. The discovery of the famous *De Tribus Impostoribus*, which advanced the thesis that Moses, Christ, and Mohammed were all impostors of the same order, would represent a considerable contribution to the study of the problem of Pascal and scholarly disbelief.[15]

The relative paucity of books and manuscripts from the first half of the seventeenth century which espouse explicit anti-Christian theories is easily enough explained. J. S. Spink goes so far as to speak of a "'crisis' in French intellectual life" between the years 1619 and 1625 which was to have an extremely chilling effect on the open expression of libertine ideas right up until almost the end of the century.[16] In 1619, the openly freethinking Vanini was burnt at the stake by order of the Parlement of Toulouse. In 1625, the poet Théophile de Viau narrowly escaped the same fate.[17] During these years, violent attacks on free thought were published by the apologists Garasse and Mersenne and a series of repressive measures were instituted by the Parlements throughout France. In a moment of near-

12. *La Doctrine curieuse des beaux esprits de ce temps ou prétendus tels . . . combattue et renversée* (Paris, 1623).

13. *L'Impiété des déistes, athées et libertins de ce temps* (Paris, 1624).

14. Discovered by Frédéric Lachèvre in a Latin manuscript (B. N. f. lat 10329) and reproduced in Lachèvre's *Le Procès de Théophile* (Paris, 1909), 2 vols.

15. See Georges Couton, "Libertinage et apologétique: les *Pensées* de Pascal contre la thèse des Trois Imposteurs" in *XVIIe siècle* (April/June 1980, No. 127): 181–95.

16. *French Free-Thought*, pp. 5–6. See also, Joseph Beaude, *La Crise culturelle au début du XVIIe siècle (1600–1637) et le problème de Dieu*, thesis, University of Lille III, 1985.

17. On Théophile de Viau, see A. Adam, *Théophile de Viau et la libre pensée française* (Paris: Droz, 1936). Also, Théophile de Viau, *Oeuvres poétiques*, J. Strecher, ed. (Paris, 1951). The documents relevant to the trial of Théophile de Viau were published by Frédéric Lachèvre: *Le Procès de Théophile de Viau*, 2 vols. (Paris, 1909).

hysteria, Mersenne announced in his *Quaestiones in Genesim* (1623) that there were fifty thousand atheists in Paris alone.[18]

Père Garasse's attack on the open expression of *libertinage* in his *La Doctrine curieuse des beaux esprits de ce temps* was evidently provoked by a series of events which took place in 1622. A circle of young *seigneurs* attached to the Court had begun, in a rather daring and open fashion, to express their disdain for the rites and doctrines of Christianity. Around the same time, the *Parnasse des Poètes satyriques*, a volume of verse containing a number of quite obscene pieces, was published in Paris. On the first page of the collection there figured a signed sonnet by Théophile de Viau. Indignant, Père Garasse began an investigation and learned with horror that Théophile and his friends often gathered in drinking parties at which they pronounced "mille horribles blasphèmes."[19] Subsequently, he learned that Théophile had openly attacked the teachings of Christ in a blasphemous fashion and that his best friend, Jacques des Barreaux, had announced to one of his professors that he could no longer believe in the doctrine of the Incarnation:

> Il n'y a pas longtemps qu'un jeune esventé, qui est des principaux de la cabale mystérieuse, s'en vint . . . trouver un de nos Pères qui avoit esté jadis son maistre en Rhétorique . . . après quelques complimens, il luy va dire froidement, qu'il estoit là venu exprès, pour luy proposer une question, laquelle lui donnait bien de la peine: "C'est . . . que je ne puis me persuader que le Fils de Dieu se soit incarné depuis seize cens ans, comme on nous voudroit faire croire; car quelle apparence y peut-il avoir en cela, que Dieu se soit fait homme?"[20]

> Not so long ago, a young scatterbrain, one of the principal members of this mysterious cabal, came . . . to see one of our Fathers, who had formerly been his rhetoric master . . . after a polite exchange of greetings, he told him coldly that he had come there for the express purpose of putting a question to him which was giving him much trouble: "It's simply . . . that I cannot convince myself that the Son of God took on human flesh 1600 years ago as they would have us believe. What possible semblance of truth can there be in the idea that God became man in the Incarnation?"

Garasse's revelations provoked public scandal and action by the *procureur général*. Théophile managed to escape the death penalty (in this case being burned at the stake) sought by the religious party, but two

18. Cited by Louise Godard de Donville, *Le Libertin des origines à 1665: Un produit des apologètes* (Tübingen: Biblio 17, 1989), p. 331.
19. Antoine Adam, *Les Libertins au XVIIe siècle* (Paris: Buchet/Chastel, 1964), pp. 33–34.
20. Cited in ibid., p. 43.

years in prison ruined his health and he died in 1626.[21] Des Barreux, on the other hand, lived on until 1673 and continued to promulgate, though certainly more clandestinely, the radical libertinage of the early 1620s well beyond the time of Pascal. As late as 1666, Guy Patin would write: "Il a bien infecté de pauvres jeunes gens de son libertinage; sa conversation était bien dangereuse et fort pestilente au public"[22] ("He indeed infected many unfortunate young people with his *libertinage*; his conversations represented a deeply dangerous public pestilence").

In many ways, Des Barreaux's life spans the entire spectrum of Classical French free thought. As a young man, he had studied at the University of Padua. In spite of a terrible reputation as a *débauché*, he frequented the scientific circles of Gassendi, visited Descartes in Holland in 1641, and had been a friend of Pascal's friend the Chevalier de Méré.[23] Curiously enough, Des Barreaux is the sole *libertin* whose name figures in the text of the *Pensées*. In fragment 410, in which he contrasts the conflicting doctrines of the Stoics and the Epicureans, Pascal writes:

> La guerre intérieure de la raison contre les passions a fait que ceux qui ont voulu avoir la paix se sont partagés en deux sectes. Les uns ont voulu renoncer aux passions, et devenir Dieux. Les autres ont voulu renoncer à la raison et devenir bêtes brutes: Des Barreaux . . .
>
> The internal war of reason against the passions has made those who wanted peace split into two sects. Some wanted to renounce passions and become gods, others wanted to renounce reason and become brute beasts: Des Barreaux . . . (410)

Pascal's reference, perhaps gleaned from a conversation with Méré, is apparently to two lines of a now-lost song by Des Barreaux:

> Et par ma raison je butte
> A devenir bête brute.[24]

> And making use of my reason I aim / At becoming a beast without reason.

21 See Spink, *French Free-Thought*, pp. 42–45.

22. Cited by Adam, *Les Libertins au XVIIe siècle*, p. 193. On Des Barreaux, see Frédéric Lachèvre, *La Vie et les poésies libertines de Des Barreaux (1599–1673) et Saint-Pavin (1595–1670)* (Paris: Champion, 1911); *Le Prince des libertins du XVIIe siècle: Jacques Vallée des Barreaux, sa vie, ses poésies* (Paris: H. Leclerc, 1907).

23. Pintard, *Le Libertinage érudit dans la première moitié du XVIIe siècle* (Genèva-Paris: Slatkine, 1983), p. 204.

24. Cited by G. Couton, ed., *L'Edition de Port-Royal* (Saint-Etienne: Universités de la région Rhône-Alpes, 1971), Introduction, p. 18.

The editors of the Edition de Port-Royal of the *Pensées* (1670) suppressed both the adjective "brute" and the name "Des Barreaux." Though these editors suppressed the name of another living individual (Damien Mitton, in fragments 853, 597, and 642), their intention here would seem to be more than simply to suppress references to Pascal's contemporaries. Their suppression of the word "brute" and the name "Des Barreaux" would seem to be an attempt to remove any possible allusion to such a notorious evil-liver.

Commentators on the *Pensées* have repeatedly stressed that Pascal consciously avoids invoking the precise arguments by which the *libertins* sought to undermine Christianity. Pintard attaches major importance to the fact that Pascal's text bears so few traces of the doctrines of the *libertins savants*.[25] Jean Mesnard, invoking Pascal's repeated refusal to refute such arguments, argues that Pascal's intended audience could not possibly have been the *libertins érudits*.[26] However true it may be that the Apology will not represent an attempt to convert the hardened *libertins* by refuting their anti-Christian theses, it is nevertheless not quite true to say that they never appear in the *Pensées* at all. In fragment 427, Pascal's projected Preface to the Apology, he presents an unforgettable portrait of a hardened skeptic and impenitent Epicurean which is meant to horrify the skeptical potential convert and to shake him into examining the case for Christianity. Chapter IV will focus on an extended analysis of this portrait.[27] For the moment, let us not fail to take note of the significant affinities which link Pascal's portraits of the hardened *libertins* to Des Barreaux's sonnets on death.

In fragment 427, Pascal's principal theme will be the folly of those who consciously turn away from the contemplation of their own mortality:

> Rien n'est si important à l'homme que son état; rien ne lui est si redoutable que l'éternité. Et ainsi, qu'il se trouve des hommes indifférents à la perte de leur être et au péril d'une éternité de misères, cela n'est pas naturel. . . . C'est un enchantement incompréhensible, et un assoupissement surnaturel. . . .

> Nothing is so important to man as his state; nothing more fearful than eternity. Thus the fact that there exist men who are indifferent to the loss of their being and the peril of an eternity of wretchedness is against nature. . . . It is an incomprehensible spell, a supernatural torpor. . . . (427)

25. R. Pintard, "Pascal et les libertins" in *Pascal présent* (Clermond Ferrand: G. de Bussac, 1962), p. 125. See Chapter IV, The Unbelievers in Fragment 427 and The Tragedy of Disbelief.

26. Jean Mesnard, *Les Pensées de Pascal* (Paris: SEDES, 1976), p. 124.

27. See Chapter IV, The Unbelievers in Fragment 427 and The Tragedy of Disbelief.

Pascal can hardly bear to evoke the testimony of one so sunk in skepticism that he cannot be bothered to agonize over his eternal fate:

> "Comme je ne sais d'où je viens, aussi je ne sais où je vais; et je sais seulement qu'en sortant de ce monde je tombe pour jamais ou dans le néant ou dans les mains d'un Dieu irrité, sans savoir à laquelle de ces deux conditions je dois être éternellement en partage. Voilà mon état, plein de faiblesse et d'incertitude. Et, de tout cela, je conclus que je dois donc passer tous les jours de ma vie sans songer à chercher ce qui doit m'arriver. . . ."

> "Just as I do not know whence I come, so I do not know whither I am going. All I know is that when I leave this world I shall fall forever into nothingness or into the hands of a wrathful God, but I do not know which of these two states is to be my eternal lot. Such is my state, full of weakness and uncertainty. And my conclusion from all this is that I must pass my days without a thought of seeking what is to happen to me. . . ." (427)

Nor can Pascal bear the arrogant stoicism and passive resignation of an unbeliever who proposes confronting the greatest of all events by letting himself be carried limply away into the arms of death:

> "Je veux aller, sans prévoyance et sans crainte, tenter un si grand événement, et me laisser mollement conduire à la mort, dans l'incertitude de ma condition future."

> "I want to go without fear or foresight to face so momentous an event, and allow myself to be carried off limply to my death, uncertain of my future state for all eternity." (427)

In the sonnets of Des Barreaux, the terms are not precisely the same. For reasons which are obviously apologetic in nature, Pascal has introduced into his portrait an element, that is, the danger of falling into the hands of an angry God, which is entirely absent from the worldview of Des Barreaux. But otherwise the portraits have many potential affinities. For Des Barreaux, death is so surely an end to all things and to all consciousness that it would be folly to afflict this life with agonizing over the prospect of death. From Des Barreaux's perspective, Pascal's complacent skeptic articulates an eminently reasonable position with regard to life beyond the grave. A sonnet of Des Barreaux discovered by F. Lachèvre makes for fascinating reading in the context of Pascal's fragment 427:

> Mortel, qui que tu sois, n'aye plus à frémir
> De l'horreur de la mort et de la sépulture,
> Ce n'est qu'un doux repos où tombe la Nature,
> Dont l'insensible estat ne doit faire gémir.

Nos sens s'éteignent tous quand on vient à périr,
De l'âme avec le corps ne se fait pas rupture,
Ce n'est qu'extinction de chaleur toute pure.
Donc est-ce un si grand mal que d'avoir à mourir?

Peut-estre nostre mort sera-t-elle impréveue,
Peut-estre pourra-t-elle eschapper nostre veue
Par l'insensible effet d'un violent transport.

C'est pourquoy de tout point contentons nostre envie,
Du reste, chers amis, laissant faire le sort,
Des pensers de la mort, n'affligeons point la vie.[28]

O mortal, whoever you be, shudder no more / From the horror of death or the tomb; / It is but a sweet repose into which all Nature sinks, / A state whose total lack of sensation warrants no lamentation.

Our senses are all extinguished at the moment we expire; / There is no sensation of rupture between body and soul; / There is quite simply a complete and total extinguishing of a pure animating fire; / Thus is it such a great misfortune to have to die?

Perhaps unexpectedly our death will come; / It may even be that it will escape our notice / And that we will feel nothing when swept away by some violent delirium.

This is why we must satisfy our desires in all things. / For the rest, dear friends, let us let fate take charge / And afflict life no more with any thoughts of death.

To be sure, the two portraits are not precisely the same. Pascal's speaker is more skeptic than he is hard-core atheist. He cannot state with certainty that death will be followed by an annihilation of all consciousness. The speaker in another of Des Barreaux's sonnets shares no such ambivalence:

D'un sommeil éternel la mort sera suivie,
J'entre dans le néant quand je sors de la vie.[29]

By an eternal sleep will death be followed; / I will enter only into the annihilation when I exit this life.

Pascal's hardened skeptic has perhaps not yet imbibed the naturalist creed that death is but a natural part of the scheme of things. Not so for Des Barreaux's speaker:

28. Cited by A. Adam, *Les Libertins au XVIIe Siècle,* pp. 196–197, Sonnet 4. See F. Lachèvre, *Disciples et successeurs de Théophile de Viau* (Paris: H. Champion, 1908). Lachèvre found the sonnets reproduced by Adam in *Recueil de quelques pièces nouvelles et galantes* published in Cologne in 1667.

29. *Les Libertins au XVIIe siècle,* p. 195, Sonnet 1.

La Nature le veut, il faut que tout périsse
La plante, l'animal, la pierre, l'édifice.[30]

Nature wills it; all must perish; / Plants, animals, stones, the very world itself.

Nevertheless, both Pascal's hardened skeptic in fragment 427 and Des Barreaux's confirmed Epicurean both take refuge in Montaigne's school of ignorance as the only sure antidote to the inevitability of death:

"Voila mon état, plein de faiblesse et d'incertitude. . . . Et de tout cela, je conclus que je dois donc passer tous les jours de ma vie sans songer à chercher ce qui doit m'arriver."

"Such is my state, full of weakness and uncertainty. And my conclusion from all this is that I must pass my days without a thought of seeking what is to happen to me." (427)

Je me dégrade de raison,
Je veux devenir un oison,
Et me sauver dans l'ignorance

En buvant toujours du meilleur.
Celuy qui croist en connaissance
Ne fait qu'accroistre sa douleur.[31]

I climb down from lofty reason; / I want to become a simpleton / And save myself in ignorance by drinking always the best of the wine. / He who increases his knowledge / Only makes his pain grow full.

In Pascal's analysis of the human condition, "divertissement" functions in a way which is not unrelated to the true end of Epicureanism as described by the following lines of Des Barreaux:

Il faut estre bien fat, stupide ou malheureux
Pour n'avoir pas douleur de ton sort rigoreux
Qui t'oblige à la mort du jour de ta naissance.

Mais pour n'en point jetter d'inutiles soupirs
Et n'avoir pas toujours cet objet en présence,
Jette-toy comme moy dans le sein des plaisirs.[32]

You'd have to be a fool, stupid or an idiot / For the contemplation of your inevitable fate not to cause pain, / A fate which destines you to die on the day of your birth.

30. Ibid., p. 196, Sonnet 3.
31. Ibid., p. 195, Sonnet 2.
32. Ibid., p. 197, Sonnet 5.

So, to spare yourself useless laments / And to avoid the constant contemplation of death, / Throw yourself like me into the heart of pleasure.

I propose these fragments of Des Barreaux's sonnets less as precise historical models for Pascal's portraits of disbelief in fragment 427 than as a means of showing that the apologist is by no means unaware of that neopagan attitude toward death which had emerged in France since the Renaissance and particularly since the adoption of the *Essais* of Montaigne by the *libertins* as their private handbook in matters philosophical. Indeed, it would hardly be surprising to find that Montaigne is a source which inspires both Pascal's hardened skeptic in fragment 427 and the narrator in the sonnets of Des Barreaux. Montaigne, contrasting the intellectual's fear of death with the more healthy attitude of the peasant, had written:

> L'aigreur de cette imagination naît de notre curiosité. . . . Le commun n'a besoin ni de remède ny de consolation qu'au coup. . . . Est-ce pas ce que nous disons que la stupidité et faute d'appréhension du vulgaire lui donne cette patience aux maux présents et cette profonde nonchalance des sinistres accidents futurs? que leur âme pour être crasse et obtuse est moins pénétrable et agitable? Pour Dieu, s'il est ainsi, tenons dores en avant école de bêtise![33]

> The bitterness of this impression springs from our curiosity. . . . The common people need neither remedy nor consolation except when the blow falls. Isn't that what we say, that the stupidity and lack of apprehension of the vulgar give them this endurance of present troubles and this profound nonchalance about sinister accidents to come, that their souls, because they are thick and obtuse, are less penetrable and unstable. For Heaven's sake if that is so, let us henceforth hold a school of stupidity.[34]

Pascal, in fragment 680, would qualify Montaigne's "sentiments" concerning death as "tout païens" ("completely pagan").

In order to get an overview of the numerous libertine ideas to which Pascal's interlocutor may have been exposed, it may also prove useful to have a brief look at Père Garasse's inventory of the primary elements of that libertine thought which briefly emerged into the public arena in the early 1620s. Not that we shall expect to find an exact portrait of Pascal's unbeliever. Still less do we attempt to demonstrate Pascal's sources for that portrait. Rather, Garasse permits us access to major themes and or-

33. *Montaigne: Oeuvres complètes* (Paris: Editions du Seuil, 1967), *Essais,* 3:12, p. 423.

34. Donald M. Frame, ed., *The Complete Essays of Montaigne* (Stanford: Stanford University Press, 1965), 3:12, p. 805.

ganizing principles, which though they would be shortly driven underground, nonetheless continued to exert considerable influence both in the clandestine writings of the more radical atheists and in the more circumspect works of the new skeptics.

As will be Pascal's, Père Garasse's analysis of the major contours of libertine thought is often poorly focused and sometimes completely distorted. Therein, perhaps, lies its value. Like Pascal's, Garasses's picture of disbelief is a portrait viewed though the dual optics of orthodox Christian belief and Christian apologetics. A. Adam's summary of the credo of the first generation of *libertins*, pieced together from Père Garasse's prefaces to each of the eight books of the *Doctrine curieuse*, gives us an extremely useful picture of the major features of a *libre pensée* which was just on the point of being driven underground:

LES MAXIMES DES LIBERTINS:

I. Il y a fort peu de bons esprits au monde, et les sots, c'est-à-dire le commun des hommes, ne sont pas capables de nostre doctrine. Et partant il n'en faut pas parler librement, mais en secret, et parmy les esprits confidans et cabalistes.

II. Les beaux esprits ne croyent point en Dieu que par bien-séance et par maxime d'Estat.

III. Un bel esprit est libre en sa créance, et ne se laisse pas aisément captiver à la créance commune de tout plein de petits fatras qui se proposent à la simple populace.

IV. Toutes choses sont conduites et gouvernées par le Destin, lequel est irrévocable, infaillible, immuable, nécessaire, éternel et inévitable à tous les hommes, quoy qu'ils peussent faire.

V. Il est vray que le livre qu'on appelle la Bible, ou l'Escriture Saincte, est un gentil livre, et contient force bonnes choses. Mais qu'il faille obliger un bon esprit à croire sous peine de damnation tout ce qui est dedans, jusques à la queue du chien de Tobie, il n'y a pas d'apparence.[35]

35. "La Queue du chien de Tobie": Tobit, 6:1–2. Père Garasse cites eight common objections to Holy Writ advanced by the *libertins:* "1. Qu'il y a dans la Bible des choses de néant, indignes d'estre couchées par escrit, tant s'en faut qu'on doive attacher à ces bagatelles la damnation ou le salut d'un homme. 2. Des choses insupportables et quasi impossibles en leur execution. 3. Des choses qui se heurtent elles mesmes, et sont plenes de contradictions. 4. Des choses deshonnestes et meschantes qui doivent estres aneanties plustost que conservées dans les livres. 5. Des choses incroyables et qui surpassent l'apparence. 6. Des choses si obscures qu'il n'y a moyen de les concevoir. 7. Des sentences et periodes fautives, qui ont esté corrigées mille fois, et partant incapables d'affermir la creance soubs peine de damnation. 8. Les Chrestiens ne s'accordent pas avec les Juifs pour le nombre des livres canoniques, les Catholiques avec les Huguenots. . . ." ("1. That there are in the Bible things devoid of meaning, unworthy of being set down in writing, so much so that it is ridiculous that one should attach the salvation or damnation of a man to these trifles. 2. Intolerable things, nearly impossible to have been carried out. 3. Things which clash among themselves and are full of

VI. Il n'y a point d'autre divinité ny puissance souveraine au monde que la NATURE, laquelle il faut contenter en toutes choses sans rien refuser à nostre corps ou à nos sens de ce qu'ils désirent de nous en l'exercice de leurs puissances et facultez naturelles.

VII. Posé le cas qu'il y ait un Dieu, comme il est bien-séant de l'advoüer pour n'estre en continuelles prises avec les superstitieux, il ne s'ensuit pas qu'il y ait des créatures qui soient purement intellectuelles et séparées de la matière. Tout ce qui est en nature est composé. Et partant il n'y a ny Anges, ny Diables au monde, et n'est pas asseuré que l'âme soit de l'homme immortelle, etc.

VIII. Il est vray que pour vivre heureux il faut esteindre et noyer tous les scrupules. Mais si [pourtant] ne faut-il pas paroistre impie et abandonné, de peur de formaliser les simples, ou de se priver de l'abord des esprits superstitieux.[36]

I. There are indeed few truly enlightened minds in the world. The idiots, that's to say the great mass of humanity, are incapable of grasping our doctrine. Hence, we refrain from speaking openly. We converse only in secret and among the secret society of enlightened minds of whose confidence we are sure.

II. The truly enlightened have no belief in God at all except for the sake of propriety and the law of the land.

III. The enlightened man is a freethinker. He is not easily captivated by that kind of popular religious belief, full of bits of rubbish, which is proposed to the simple masses.

IV. All things are ruled and governed by Fate, which is irrevocable, infallible, immutable, necessary, eternal and inevitable for all men, whatever their efforts.

V. That book called the Bible, or the Holy Scriptures, is a truly excellent book containing a great many good things. But to oblige an intelligent person, under the pain of damnation, to believe everything in it (even including the tail of Tobias's dog) is completely ridiculous.

VI. There is no divinity nor power in the world but NATURE, which we have to satisfy in all things, refusing nothing to our body or senses which they desire from us in the exercise of their natural faculties and powers.

VII. Suppose we admit the possibility that God exists. This may be perfectly suitable so as not to be in constant conflict with the religious-minded ("superstitieux"). It does not necessarily follow that there are creatures which are purely spiritual and separate from matter. Everything in nature is made of something.

---

contradictions. 4. Indecent and vicious things which ought to be destroyed rather than preserved in books. 5. Incredible things which go beyond probability. 6. Things which are so obscure that there is no means of comprehending them. 7. Faulty phrases and sentences, which have been corrected a thousand times and which thus are incapable of being believed under pain of damnation. 8. Christians do not agree with Jews on the number of canonical books. Nor do Catholics with Protestants. . . .") *La Doctrine curieuse,* pp. 534–35. Cited by Louise Godard de Donville, *Le Libertin des origines à 1665,* pp. 225–26.

For an overview of libertine objections to the Bible, see Wetsel, *L'Ecriture et le Reste: The "Pensées" of Pascal in the Exegetical Tradition of Port-Royal* (Columbus: Ohio State University Press, 1981), pp. 56–67.

36. Cited by A. Adam, *Les libertins au XVIIe siècle,* pp. 41–42.

Hence, there are neither Angels nor Devils in the world. And it is by no means certain that the soul of man is immortal.

VIII. It is true that in order to live happily we must obliterate and drown every (religious) scruple. Yet one must not appear impious and given over to pleasures for fear of shocking the gullible masses or of losing the confidence of the superstitious.

Reading Père Garasse's account of the credo of the first generation of freethinkers leaves no doubt as to why the movement was driven underground so immediately and with such ferocity. Garasse's account, however out of focus and given to hyperbole, is one which must have terrified even the most open-minded civil and religious authorities of the time. Garasse penetrates right to the heart of things. He recognizes at once that the *beaux esprits* whose conversations he has investigated are neither deists nor unorthodox Christians. They are pure atheists and materialists. At the heart of reality, they enthrone only an infallible Fate, the only true author of both good and evil. Their only divinity is a Nature whose completely material expression leaves no place either for the moral regulations of Revelation or for spiritual beings. Their vision of reality is permeated by an Epicureanism whose limits are circumscribed only by the danger posed by the fact that the world is ruled by the "superstitieux." Hence the necessity not only of prudence but of secrecy among those all too few "esprits confidans et cabalistes."

Looking backward nearly four hundred years from the perspective of a post-Christian society, one is almost completely incapable of imagining the fury and horror which must have greeted the publication of Garasse's *La doctrine curieuse*. Unless we know something about those traditional religions which still today view things from a similar perspective, we can hardly imagine the free expression of disbelief, or indeed the questioning of Scripture or the immortality of the soul, as capital offenses. On the other hand, we should not be tempted to view the repression which was to follow solely as the product of the revelations of Père Garasse and the apologists who were to follow him. René Pintard reminds us that the silencing of the open expression of libertine ideas during the midseventeenth century in France was the result of the interplay of a far more complex set of religious and political factors:

Dans la France du XVIIe siècle, le renouveau spirituel, théologique, disciplinaire, ainsi que l'accroissement de l'autorité de l'Etat, s'ajoutent aux legs du passé pour contenir dans d'étroites limites les velléités de divergence des opinions hétérodoxes. Ecrits secrets maintenus, parfois pour des siècles, à l'abri des regards, livres publiés avec des précautions extrêmes, confidences démentant soudain un habituel conformisme, bien des indices prouvent la force des pressions qui s'exercent sur les esprits et la réserve que jugent indispensable ceux qui craignent d'être désapprouvés. Seules trois ou quatre oeuvres clandestines nous livrent les audaces anonymes d'auteurs inconnus. Partout ailleurs la discrétion d'un pseudonyme, les ambiguïtés propices de la fiction ou du dialogue, des critiques qui semblent pouvoir, au-delà de leur objet avoué, déboucher sur des zones interdites . . . suggèrent la vigilance d'autocensures s'exerçant à la fois sur la divulgation, l'expression, sans doute, même la conception des idées.[37]

In seventeenth-century France, the renewal of spirituality, theology and religious discipline, as well as the growing power of the authority of the State, combined with the legacy of the past in order to contain the divergent whims of heterodox opinions within extremely strict bounds. Secret writings, preserved, often for centuries, and sheltered from public inspection; books published with extreme precautions; disclosures suddenly contradicting habitual conformity. Multiple are the markers testifying to the strength of the pressures being exercised on the open expression of ideas. So too are those attesting that reserve which those who feared disapprobation judged indispensable. Only three or four clandestine works permit us access to the anonymous audacities of a few unknown authors. Everywhere else we find the prudence of a pseudonym, the ambiguities made possible by fiction or dialogues, criticisms which open onto forbidden subjects by overstepping their supposed subjects. . . . All these suggest the vigilance of the auto-censorship being exercised over the revelation, the expression—and indeed the very apprehension—of new ideas.

Within the public domain after 1625, open attacks on Christianity were more or less completely silenced. Into the void came such skeptics as François de la Mothe le Vayer and Gabriel Naudé. Here the problem for the modern student of *le libertinage érudit* is of an entirely different order. It is no longer a matter of seeking to discover long-lost clandestine manuscripts. The works of these thinkers exist in several printed editions. Rather, the problem becomes one of trying to read between the lines, of trying to penetrate the ambiguity of ideas presented in the form of fiction or dialogue. Most difficult of all is the attempt to gauge the import of explicit criticisms of libertine ideas which raise more questions than they answer and which provoke an unauthorized kind of speculation. For Pintard, writing nearly forty years after the publication of his magisterial *Le Libertinage érudit*. . . . , the last of these is among the most serious of all problems facing the modern student of *libertinage* in the Classical period:

37. René Pintard, "Les problèmes de l'histoire du libertinage, notes et réflexions," *XVIIe siècle* No. 127 (April/June 1980): 133.

Avons-nous affaire à des défenseurs de la religion ou à des "apologistes suspects"? Même les historiens les plus déterminés à maintenir leurs analyses au niveau de l'exprimé sont contraints de se poser des questions de cette sorte. . . . Si la lettre des textes ne nous révèle trop souvent qu'un compromis entre les convictions profondes et les nécessités de la prudence; si, à s'y tenir, on s'expose à laisser échapper le mouvement véritable de la pensée; si, pour éviter ce risque, le critique le plus objectif est entraîné à supputer la signification des lacunes, des ambiguïtés ou des contradictions, ne convient-il pas de tirer de ce constat ses pleines conséquences et de mettre en action tous les moyens d'éclairer les oeuvres par la connaissance de ceux qui les ont écrites, de leur formation, de leurs lectures, de leurs habitudes intellectuelles, des confidences qu'il leur est arrivé de livrer? Pourquoi refuserait-on à l'histoire des idées les approches psychologiques qui si souvent ont fecondé l'histoire littéraire?[38]

Are we dealing with defenders of religion or with "suspect apologists"? Even those historians who are the most set on maintaining their analysis on the level of what the text actually says are constrained to ask themselves such questions. . . . If the literal level of the text only too often reveals a compromise between deep convictions and the necessity of prudence; if one risks letting the real movement of ideas escape by taking the text too literally; if, to avoid this risk, the most objective critic must reckon the meaning of the lacunae, the ambiguities or the contradictions of the text, is it not admissible to clarify these works via a knowledge of those who wrote them, of their intellectual background, of what they read, of their habits of mind, of the confidences which they sometimes let slip? Why should we refuse to use in the history of ideas, psychological approaches which have so often enriched the study of literary history?

J. S. Spink makes the acute observation that this new tradition of critical skepticism inherited a key precept from the Italian naturalistic tradition of the previous century. While rejecting that tradition's preoccupation with metaphysics, astrology, and occultism, the new skeptics distilled from the writings of the Italian naturalists the notion of a basic distinction between the intellectual elite and the vulgar herd:

It was from the Italians that [the French skeptics] learned to distinguish between the virtue which the philosopher pursues for its own sake and the pragmatic rules which the mass of the people must be induced to observe if public order is to be preserved. They learned to look upon themselves as initiates (*déniaisés*), to distinguish between . . . rational knowledge and implicit faith, between philosophy and religion. The skeptics who are known to us were for the most part prudent and conservative scholars, safely ensconced in comfortable niches in the intellectual world. They showed no inclination to proselytize or parade their views before the public. They were academic in outlook and as exclusive as were the

38. Ibid., 133–34.

polite and literary salons surrounding the court. Their assumption of superiority led to the term "esprit fort" being used as a term of abuse, but they were not dogmatizers and their motto was that of Cremonini: *intus ut libet, foris ut moris est.*[39]

Two Cautious Skeptics: La Mothe le Vayer and Gabriel Naudé

Peter Gay makes the interesting observation that the libertine skeptics of the Classical period have all too often been viewed from the perspective of the Enlightenment *philosophes,* for whom "the line from Montaigne's to Bayle's skepticism was straight and unobstructed."[40] Gay insists upon an essential distinction between the "scrupulous scholarship" of Gassendi's revival of Epicureanism and those "libertins" who "misunderstood or deliberately misinterpreted it." According to Gay, it was the Enlightenment philosophes who, by greeting this "small but colorful group . . . with pleased recognition," "gave them an importance they do not deserve in their own right."[41] It is within this group of *libertins*, "not representative of their time" and "rarely even accurate transmitters of ancient doctrine," which Gay places François de La Mothe le Vayer (1588–1672).[42]

Professor Gay perhaps underestimates La Mothe le Vayer's importance within the context of the emerging crisis of religious skepticism among certain members of the Parisian intelligentsia in the 1640s and 1650s. That such a crisis existed, if nowhere else than in the minds of such orthodox Christians as Blaise Pascal, is testified to by the very existence of the Apology. True enough, we no longer read La Mothe le Vayer in the way in which we read Bayle, Montesquieu, or Diderot. There has been no new edition of any of his works since the late eighteenth century. Nevertheless, Le Vayer's extensive erudition commanded considerable respect well into the Enlightenment. And he was considered an important intellectual figure in his own time. An early member of the philosophical circle of the frères Dupuy and particularly attached to Gassendi, Diodati, and Naudé

39. Spink, *French Free-Thought*, p. 9.

40. Peter Gay, *The Enlightenment: The Rise of Modern Paganism* (New York: Norton, 1966), p. 290. The *philosophes,* Gay reminds us, always read Montaigne's own "opacity and evasiveness, not as signs of inner combat, nor as possible clues to a kind of wry fideism, but as tactical devices designed to spread a maximum of subversive information with a minimum of risk."

41. Ibid., p. 306.

42. Ibid., p. 307.

in a subcircle which called itself "la Tétrade," le Vayer wrote numerous political pamphlets in favor of Richelieu's policies and was eventually appointed tutor to the young Louis XIV in 1651.

Le Vayer's real position with regard to Christianity has always proved enigmatic and has been the subject of considerable controversy. Le Grand Arnauld, who had read all of his books, insisted that "il n'étoit pas chrétien"[43] ("he was no Christian"). J. S. Spink, looking at the same books from a modern perspective, judged La Mothe an "independent student of Christian thought" who was "not actually opposed to it."[44] Gérard Defaux goes so far as to call Le Vayer (and Naudé) "les héritiers directs—et fidèles—de la Sceptique chrétienne si intensément présente à la Renaissance"[45] ("direct and faithful inheritors of that Christian skepticism so intensely present during the Renaissance"). The view of Antoine Adam could be more different: "Nous savons par quelques témoignages concordants que La Mothe le Vayer . . . n'était pas simplement sceptique. Il était athée" ("We know via several corroborative accounts that La Mothe le Vayer was not simply a skeptic. He was an atheist"). Adam makes a crucial distinction between La Mothe and an earlier generation of *libertins*:

> Tandis que des hommes comme Théophile . . . comme les libertins attaqués par Garasse, opposent à une philosophie spiritualiste et chrétienne le naturalisme des Italiens, La Mothe le Vayer travaille à libérer l'esprit de toutes les métaphysiques, à ramener la science à l'observation exacte des faits. . . . Leçon d'une portée infinie. Bayle et Fontenelle ont, à la fin du siècle, développé les conséquences de cette leçon.[46]

> While men like Theophile . . . like the *libertins* attacked by Garasse, set the naturalism of the Italians up against a spiritual and Christian philosophy, La Mothe le Vayer worked to liberate the human mind from all metaphysical schemes, to return learning to a rigorous observation of fact. The lesson had an impact of infinite importance. Bayle and Fontenelle, at the end of the century, would develop the consequences of this lesson.

43. Pintard, *Le Libertinage érudit,* p. 145. On F. La Mothe le Vayer, see the following sources: F. L. Wickelgren *La Mothe Le Vayer, sa vie et son oeuvre* (Paris, 1934). R. Pintard, *Le libertinage érudit* . . . , pp. 131–47 and 505–38. J. Beaude, "Le Dialogue d'Orasius sur le sujet de la divinité," *Recherches sur le XVIIe siècle,* 1 (1976): 50–62. A. L. Sells, "Molière and La Mothe Le Vayer," *Modern Language Review* (1933). J. Eymard d'Angers, "Stoïcisme et libertinage dans l'oeuvre de François La Mothe Le Vayer" *Revue des sciences humaines* (1954).

44. *French Free-Thought,* pp. 18–19.

45. Gérard Defaux, "Un Evangélique au pays de la Contre-Réforme: Erasme en France au XVIIe siècle," in *Horizons européens de la littérature au XVIIe siècle* (Tübingen: G. Narr, 1988), p. 355.

46. *Les Libertins au XVIIe siècle,* pp. 122–23.

Basing my judgment entirely upon Le Vayer's *De la vertu des payens* (1641),[47] I once attempted to make the case that Le Vayer represented "the most radical wing of Christian humanist thought."[48] However, as René Pintard points out, *De la vertu des payens*, written at the request of Richelieu and published under the author's own name, is hardly the place to seek access to La Mothe's real attitude toward Christianity. As Pintard sees it, Le Vayer's real thought can only be assessed on the basis of his first *Dialogues*:

> Trois . . . volumes mûris pendant plus de quarante ans de vie privée, de voyages, de libre lecture et d'observation des hommes. Volumes entourés, à leur naissance, de bien des soins: faux nom d'auteurs, faux lieu et fausses dates d'impression, fausses marques de libraire, distribution à quelques amis sûrs d'un petit nombre d'exemplaires: ce luxe de précautions en dit assez long sur la crainte de l'auteur d'être trop bien compris. . . . Un secret aussi jalousement préservé ne saurait être celui d'un scepticisme chrétien ni celui d'un fidéisme sincère.[49]

> Three . . . volumes which matured during more than forty years of private life, travels, wide-ranging reading and observation of humankind. Volumes surrounded at their birth by the most careful protections: false names of authors, false place and dates of publication, false information regarding the publisher; the distribution of a small number of copies to a few trusted friends. This excessive precaution speaks volumes concerning the author's fear of being understood only too well. . . . Such a jealously guarded secret could hardly represent a Christian skepticism or a sincere fideism.

Pintard is careful to point out that a tradition of sincere fideism (largely inherited from Montaigne) did permit a number of "chrétiens embarrassés par des doutes mais désireux de les surmonter" ("Christians disturbed by their doubts but anxious to overcome them") to live at peace

47. For more on this text, see Chapter III, Le Vayer's *De la vertu des payens*.

48. D. Wetsel, "Biblicism and Historicity: The *Pensées* of Pascal and Christian Humanism," *South Central Review* 2, No. 4 (1985): 12.

49. "Les problèmes de l'histoire du libertinage," *XVIIe siècle*, 127, (April/June 1980): 154. In an article published in the same volume ("Libertinage et humanisme: une rencontre difficle"), Roger Zuber reaches a similar conclusion: "Dûment averti par la polémique de 1622–1624, [La Mothe le Vayer] n'ignorait pas qu'il utilisait contre la vérité chrétienne les subtilités éprouvées de la philosophie sceptique. Sauf documents nouveaux, il me semble difficile de ne pas lire Le Vayer avec les mêmes lunettes que Balzac et que Chapelain, qui s'inquiétaient de son athéisme, dans leurs échanges privés" ("Duly warned by the polemics of 1622–1624, [La Mothe le Vayer] was hardly unaware that he was making use of—against Christian truth—the well-tried subtlties of skeptic philosophy. In the absence of new documents, it seems to me difficult not to view Le Vayer in the same way that Balzac and Chapelain did. In their private exchanges these two were deeply disturbed by Le Vayer's atheism") (p. 172).

with themselves and with their more orthodox contemporaries.[50] Indeed, as Philippe Sellier has often pointed out to me, the entire tradition of Christian skepticism among the Parisian intelligentsia in the first half of the seventeenth century remains a largely uncharted territory. This is why La Mothe le Vayer, nowhere mentioned in the *Pensées* nor ever suggested as a direct target of the Apology, remains such an interesting and largely unexplored figure in connection with Pascal's apologetic enterprise. Pascal will make use of a skeptical fideism largely distilled from the *Essays* of Montaigne in order to attract the attention of those unbelievers who do harbor some secret desire to believe. But he never really hopes (see Chapter IV, The Uses and Dangers of Skepticism, and Chapter V, The Role of Argument in the *Pensées*: The Hardened Skeptics Reconsidered) to convert those hardened atheists who have been completely deprived of any inner light.

From a Pascalian perspective, La Mothe le Vayer stands as the great subverter of Montaigne's sincere fideism and Christian skepticism (see Plate I). Montaigne had elaborated an essentially profane philosophy, which Pascal would later condemn as leading to a pagan view of death (680), outside, rather than against, Christianity. La Mothe le Vayer, on the other hand, sought, at the very moment when the apologists were beginning to discover the potential dangers of Montaigne's ideas, to turn skepticism against the very notion of revealed religion. Hence the necessity of an ambiguous text directed to those few *déniaisés* who, as Pintard reminds us, knew how to read between the lines and how to interpret the meaning of what was left unsaid.[51]

La Mothe's expertise in what would much later come to be called the comparative study of religions far surpassed that of Montaigne. Not only had he read everything Montaigne had read on the subject of the non-Christian religions. He had read far more. Pintard's inventory of Le Vayer's readings is impressive. Almost every travelogue or mémoire coming out of the Age of Discovery was to his taste. So were the considerable number of new works being published toward 1630: *Voyage faict par terre depuis Paris jusques à la Chine*; *Relation du voyage de Perse*, *Relation de la Cochinchine*; *Grand voyage au pays des Hurons*.[52] But whereas Montaigne thought he could discern more resemblances than differences among the

50. "Les Problèmes de l'histoire de libertinage," p. 152.

51. *Le Libertinage érudit,* p. 147.

52. Ibid., p. 139.

PLATE 1. François de La Motte le Vayer (1583–1672). Gravé par Achille Ouvré. D'après le portrait de Nanteuil. The British Library.

different religions of the world, Le Vayer's preoccupation lay with documenting their total contradictions and lack of continuity.

Montaigne's penchant for setting up parallels between the various new religious doctrines and practices being discovered in various parts of the world by Christian explorers and missionaries left open two possibilities. Readers could have recourse to the traditional Christian explanation that the cults of the pagans were but *singeries* by which Satan had sought to ape Christianity and its predecessor Judaism.[53] Or they could conclude (as would the first generation of comparative religionists) that such parallels pointed either to the ultimate truth of Christianity or to the existence of some more primal religious truth. Le Vayer, on the other hand, sought to ruin the very notion of revealed truth by documenting the essential contradictions and incoherence of as many religious creeds as he could cite:

> Les uns veulent une religion cérémonieuse, y ayant des loix infinies prescrites sur ce sujet par la saincteté. . . . Les autres soutiennent qu'il ne faut adorer les Dieux qu'en pureté d'esprit. Nous nous lavons le front d'eau bénite à l'entrée des églises, comme les païens faisaient d'eau lustrale . . . les Indiens occidentaux de l'Ile Espagnole pensaient être purgés de tout crime quand ils s'étaient déchargés l'estomac par le vomissement au pied des autels. Les uns ont rougi les autels de sang humain, comme les Carthaginois et dernièrement ceux du Pérou, immolaient jusqu'à leurs propres enfants à leurs idoles. Les autres ont préféré les sacrifices qui se faisoient *farre pio et saliente mica*. . . .[54] Les uns veulent qu'on demande aux Dieux ce dont on croit avoir besoin. Pythagore le défend, n'y ayant personne, à son avis, qui sache au vrai ce qui lui est propre et utile. . . . Les Juifs ont leur jour du repos le samedi. . . . Les Turcs l'ont mis au vendredi. Les chrétiens sabbathisent le dimanche.[55]

> Some require a ceremonial religion and have an infinite series of legal prescriptions on the subject for the sake of holiness. Others maintain that the Gods must be worshiped in purity of spirit. We wash our foreheads with holy water upon entering our churches, as the pagans used to use purifying water. . . . The western Indians of the Spanish Island thought that they had purged themselves of all their crimes once they had discharged their stomachs and vomited at the foot of their altars. Some have made their altars run red with human blood. The people of Carthage, and more recently those of Peru, went so far as to sacrifice their own children. Others have preferred sacrifices made with "holy flour and shining crystals of salt." . . . Some want us to ask the Gods for what we think we need. Pythagoras forbids this, saying that no one, in his view, has true knowledge of what is proper and useful for him. . . . The Jews have their day of rest on Saturday. . . . The Turks have put it on Friday. . . . The Christians have turned Sunday into their Sabbath.

De la diversité des religions (*De la Divinité*), published anonymously and with false date and place of publication,[56] represents Le Vayer's most au-

53. See Chapter III, Le Vayer's *De la vertu des payens.*

54. Horace, *Odes,* III.23.20.

55. François de La Mothe le Vayer (Orasius Tubero), "Sur la Divinité" ("De la diversité des religions"), in *Deux Dialogues faits à l'imitation des anciens,* Ernest Tisserand, ed. (Paris: Editions Bossard, 1922), pp. 125–26.

56. "Orasius Tubero" is obviously a pseudonym. The date on the first edition of the *Dialogues*—1606—as well as the publisher and place of publication—"Francfort, par Jean Sarius"—have also been falsified to protect the author's identity.

dacious attack on the idea of revealed religion. To be sure, Le Vayer takes care to exclude Christianity itself from his analysis and to profess his adherence to Christian truth. However, his intention of casting indirect doubt on the Christian Revelation must have been perfectly clear to those who knew how to read between his lines. For instance, when discussing the problem of the existence of God, he does not fail to cite the traditional proofs in favor of the existence of Divinity. However, he goes on to elaborate the arguments which the atheists produce to the contrary. Drawing upon recent anthropological discoveries, he notes that there exist peoples possessing "aucune Loi ni vestige de religion" ("not a single law or vestige of religion"). The peoples of Mexico possess no word in their language for God. Those of New France "adoraient aucune divinité" ("worshiped no divinity"). The Mandarins who govern China believe in "point d'autre Dieu que la Nature"[57] ("no other God than Nature").

Le Vayer, again citing the "Athées," produces several arguments by which they explain the origin of the human belief in God or the Gods. Some, he explains, conjecture that primitive humans first conceived the notion of divinity by attempting to explain frightening natural phenomena: thunder, earthquakes, eclipses. Others, he notes, following Epicurus, explain the human experience of Divinity as having had its genesis in the dreams of primitive humans. In any event, Le Vayer explains, the earliest lawgivers in every culture made use of "l'opinion vulgaire" and the fear of the gods to control and manipulate "le sot peuple"[58] ("the gullible masses"). The greatest of the ancient philosophers, including Aristotle and his commentator "par excellence Averroès," says Le Vayer, recognized no other God than Nature itself, denied the creation of the world, affirmed the eternity of the universe, and rejected the notion of First Cause.[59]

Le Vayer is particularly subversive of revealed religion when he argues that even those who agree upon the existence of the Gods[60] cannot agree upon their nature. As will Pascal in fragment 449,[61] he makes an essential distinction between the Deist God and the God(s) who intervene(s) in

57. *Deux Dialogues,* pp. 91–95.
58. Ibid., pp. 94–95.
59. Ibid., pp. 98–99.
60. By using the plural, Le Vayer carefully avoids direct reference to the Christian God. However, the implications of his argument are clear.
61. See Chapter I, Pascal and Deism.

human affairs. Le Vayer's own prejudice in the matter is clear enough, as is his horror of the very notion of incarnation:

> Les uns . . . attribuent [aux Dieux] non seulement la direction générale de l'univers et le mouvement réglé de toutes ses machines et ses orbes, mais encore un soin particulier de tout ce qui se passe ici-bas, duquel s'ensuit la rémunération des actions vertueuses et la punition de celles qu'ils appellent vicieuses; les autres soutiennent qu'il vaudrait mieux nier les Dieux tout à fait que de les attacher à des soins si indignes, et les revêtir humainement de passions si honteuses, voire si incompatibles avec la Divinité.[62]

> Some . . . attribute [to the Gods] not only the general running of the universe and the regulation of the movement of its systems and celestial bodies, but a particular preoccupation with everything that happens here below. Thus follows the notion of the reward of virtuous actions and the punishment of those which they call vices. Others maintain that it would be better completely to deny the very existence of the Gods than to attach to them such unworthy preoccupations and to invest them with human passions which are shameful for, and indeed incompatible with, Divinity.

Le Vayer's principal motivation is to show that the various religions of the world possess not a single major doctrine in common. Whether among the ancients or the moderns, defenders of Divinity cannot even agree on whether the Gods require the worship of humankind. Some teach "qu'il faut révérer et servir religieusement les Dieux, qui connaissent toutes choses jusqu'aux mouvements de notre coeur, ayant en main la peine et la récompense" ("one must revere and religiously serve the Gods, who know everything, including our innermost thoughts, and who bear in their hands punishment and reward"). Others, like Epicurus, reject any kind of cult of worship or adoration.[63] Le Vayer evokes the particularly thorny issue of "la Providence." Whether in its Greek form as Fate or (by implication) in its Christian form as predestination, the problem of a world run by a wise and all-powerful God poses immense practical difficulties for the defenders of Divinity. Of what use are ceremonies, prayers, or even moral behavior if all is predestined by an omnipotent Divinity?

> Si toutes choses sont prédestinées inévitablement de toute éternité, ou dépendent absolument du sort ou de la Fortune . . . il s'ensuit d'une conséquence nécessaire que toutes nos dévotions, nos latries, nos prières et oraisons, sont choses

62. *Deux Dialogues* pp. 101–2.
63. Ibid., p. 102.

vaines et ridicules, inventées par ceux qui voulaient profiter de leur introduction, et confirmées ensuite par l'accoutumance aveugle et populaire, voire même par des clairvoyants, qui estimaient cette fiction fort utile à réprimer les plus vicieux.[64]

If all things have been unalterably predestined from the beginning of eternity, or depend absolutely on fate or fortune . . . it follows as a necessary consequence that all our devotions, praises, prayers and invocations are vain and ridiculous things, invented by those who wished to profit from their introduction. This is confirmed by the ease and blindness with which the masses adopted these things. Indeed, so too did even those more clear-sighted men who, though they saw through them, judged this fiction an extremely useful one for controlling those tending to criminal behavior.

When he argues that the various religions do not even agree on the crucial matter of the immortality of the soul, Le Vayer touches upon a matter to which Pascal is particularly sensitive. In a number of key fragments (164, 427, 612), Pascal tells the unbeliever that finding out whether the human soul is material or immortal is his most important task in deciding whether or not to embrace Christianity and to lead his life accordingly. "Il importe à toute la vie de savoir si l'âme est mortelle ou immortelle" ("It affects our whole life to know whether the soul is mortal or immortal") (164). Pascal takes it as a given that all humans—at least those whose hearts have not been predestined to disbelief—instinctively yearn for a life beyond this one. Indeed, he constitutes an entire dossier, "Le Souverain Bien" ("The Sovereign Good") (X), designed to prove that the eternal human search for happiness is in reality the search to be at one with a lost God.[65]

Le Vayer, while admitting that some religions teach the immortality of the soul and eternal reward or punishment, takes great pains to point out that these beliefs are not universal. Among the Jews, he observes, the Sadducees "croyaient l'âme mortelle et se mocquaient de cette prétendue résurrection, soutenant que dans tout le Pentateuque de Moïse, il n'y a rien sur quoi on puisse fonder l'immortalité de l'âme" ("believed the soul mortal and mocked this claim of resurrection, maintaining that in all of the Pentateuch of Moses there is nothing on which one might found a doctrine of the immortality of the soul"). Among the Chinese, he observes, there is a religious order which publicly preaches the mortality of the soul. And among the Anabaptists, there is a Sabbatarian sect which holds the

64. Ibid., pp. 113–14.

65. See Chapter V, The Role of Argument in the Apology: The Hardened Skeptics Reconsidered.

same doctrine. It was probably the early Greek philosophers, Le Vayer maintains, who first systematized the belief in the immortality of the soul.[66]

Ever advancing toward his thesis that all religious systems ultimately represent contradiction and incoherence, Le Vayer claims to be overwhelmed by the sheer number and diversity of human religions. Adroitly professing his own adherence to Christian truth, he claims to be horrified by the extent to which any given religion will go to perpetuate its claim to be the only true one:

> Au défaut d'avoir la foi pour aiguille aimantée qui tienne nostre esprit arrêté vers le pôle de la grâce divine, il est impossible d'éviter des erreurs et des tempêtes bien plus longues et plus périlleuses que celles d'Ulysse, puisqu'elles nous porteraient enfin à un spirituel naufrage. . . . Or, dans cette infinité de religions, il n'y a quasi personne qui ne croie posséder la vraie, et qui condamnant toutes les autres, ne combatte . . . jusqu'à la dernière goute de leur sang.[67]

> Lacking the compass of faith, which holds our minds fixed on the pole of divine grace, it is impossible to avoid longer and more perilous storms than those through which Ulysses passed, since they would ultimately carry us to spiritual shipwreck. . . . Indeed, among this infinity of religions there is hardly anyone who does not believe himself in possession of the one true religion, and who, condemning the adherents of all the others, would not fight until he had shed the last drop of their blood.

Curiously enough, this point in Le Vayer's dialogue parallels a crucial moment in Pascal's apologetic itinerary. In fragment 454, having guided his potential convert through "cette inconstante et bizarre variété de moeurs et de créances dans les divers temps" ("this shifting and odd variety of customs and beliefs in different ages"), Pascal begins to direct his interlocutor's attention to the peculiar circumstances surrounding God's Revelation of Himself to the Jews. At this point begin Pascal's series of historical proofs of Christianity.[68] Le Vayer's itinerary could not be more different. Horrified by the bloodshed which religious controversy has wrought upon the world, he directs his interlocutor's attention, not to the Judeo-Christian Revelation, but to those few moments in history in which certain rulers have authorized liberty of conscience. Invoking the example of the Emperor Valens, he lauds the Romans' building of their

66. *Deux Dialogues,* pp. 124–25.
67. Ibid., pp. 115–17.
68. See Chapter III, Pascal and Grotius.

Pantheon to all the Gods and Solomon's permitting his foreign wives to build temples to their own goddesses. Darius, he recalls, permitted the Jews to practice their own religion. He praises Manassas, King of Juda, for having installed idols and altars to a multiplicity of Gods in the Temple of Jerusalem. He goes so far as to commend the Hebrew kings Jehu and Joas for being been open-minded enough to sacrifice both to the God of their Fathers and to the "golden calves."[69]

No passage in Le Vayer's altogether heretical dialogue would have more enraged the neo–Augustinians of Port-Royal than this one. Arnauld constantly fulminated against the notion "qu'il faut avoir une religion, mais qu'elles sont toutes bonnes"[70] ("that one needs a religion but that they are all good") and was horrified by the very notion of religious toleration. Pascal, as Philippe Sellier has pointed out, was one of the rare thinkers in the Classical period to exclude the use of force in religious conversion (fragment 172).[71] But there is a vast difference between opposing coercion in religious matters and embracing the notion of religious tolerance. Le Vayer invokes contemporary examples of kingdoms permitting freedom of religious conscience. In India, he claims, "toutes religions sont indifférement admises" ("all religions are accepted indiscriminately"). He cites Père Trigault[72] to the effect that in China "on n'est jamais contraint ni travaillé sur le fait de la religion" ("there exists no coercion nor restraint in religious matters"). Other kingdoms, he notes, permit the coexistence of Judaism, Islam and Christianity.[73] Le Vayer's idea of complete freedom of religion remains almost unique in the seventeenth century in France. The idea would have to await the Enlightenment to be publicly propagated by the *philosophes*.

Toward the end of *De la diversité des religions*, Le Vayer ultimately qualifies all religions as "superstition." In an attempt to refute the accepted notion that atheism represents a danger to the political order, he translates word for word a key passage from the *Essays* of Bacon:

> Atheism leaves a man to sense, to philosophy, to natural piety, to laws, to reputation: all which may be guides to an outward moral. . . . Therefore atheism did never perturb states; for it makes men wary of themselves . . . we see the times

69. *Deux Dialogues*, pp. 119–20.

70. *Oeuvres de Messire Antoine Arnauld* (Paris: Gabriel de Bellegarde, 1775–83): 400–401.

71. "Seminar: Pascal's 'Trois Ordres,'" in *Meaning, Structure, and History in the "Pensées" of Pascal*, ed. D. Wetsel (Tübingen: Biblio 17, 1990), p. 83.

72. See Chapter III, "Histoire des la Chine": Pascal and the Challenge to Biblical Time.

73. *Deux Dialogues*, pp. 122–23.

inclined to atheism (as in the times of Augustus Caesar) were civil times; but superstitions hath been the confusion of many states and bringeth in a new *primum mobile*[74] that ravisheth all the spheres of government. The master of superstition is the people.[75]

* * *

Gabriel Naudé (1600–1653) takes as his major theme the idea that the masses are necessarily addicted to superstition and religion. Like La Mothe le Vayer, he thinks that the universal acceptance of an idea usually means that idea is false. Rejecting any kind of proof by universal consent, he goes on to develop a key theme in the libertine tradition of Classical France: the opposition of the ignorant masses to a necessarily tiny number of enlightened minds.The masses, by their very nature, are ready to take on any imposture which comes their way:

Cette populace est comparée à une mer sujète à toutes sortes de vents et de tempestes: au Caméléon qui peut recevoir toutes sortes de couleurs excepté la blanche, et à la sentine et cloaque dans laquelle coulent toutes les ordures de la maison. Ses plus belles parties sont d'estre inconstant et variable, appreuver et impreuver quelque chose en mesme temps, courir toujours d'un contraire à l'autre, croire de léger, se mutiner promptement, toujours gronder et murmurer. Bref, tout ce qu'elle pense n'est que vanité, tout ce qu'elle dit est faux et absurde, ce qu'elle improuve est bon, ce qu'elle approuve mauvais, ce qu'elle loue infame, et tout ce qu'elle fait et entreprend n'est qu'une pure folie.[76]

The English translation of 1711 renders this passage with particular vigor and color:

This populace is compared to a sea agitated with all sorts of Winds and Tempests, to the *Camelion*, which can appear in all sorts of colours, except the White: and to a Sink that all the Refuse of the House is thrown into. Its best Qualities are to be inconstant and variable, to approve and disapprove a thing at the same time, to run always from one contrariety to another, to believe groundlessly, Mutiny readily, Grumble, and Murmur incessantly: in short, whatever it thinks is

74. La Mothe le Vayer renders "bringeth in a new primum mobile" as "ayant porté à la nouveauté le premier mobile."

75. Cited by Adam, *Les Libertins au XVIIe siècle,* p. 139, n. 39.

76. Gabriel Naudé, *Considérations politiques sur les coups d'estat, par Gabriel Naudé, parisien* ("Sur la copie de Rome," 1679), pp. 248–49. For additional material on G. Naudé, see R. Pintard, *Le libertinage érudit . . .*, pp. 442–76. Sainte-Beuve, *Portraits littéraires* (Paris: Garnier frères, 1882), 2, pp. 467–512, 522–24. J. V. Rice, *Gabriel Naudé (1600–1653)* (Baltimore: Johns Hopkins University Press, 1939). D. E. Curtis, *Progress and Eternal Recurrence in the Works of Gabriel Naudé* (Hull, 1967). J. A. Clarke, *Gabriel Naudé 1600–1653* (Hamden, Conn.: Archon, 1970).

nothing but Vanity, all that it says is False and Absurd, what it dislikes is Good, what it practices is Evil, what it praises is Infamous, and all that it undertakes is pure Folly.[77]

How far we are indeed from Pascal's notation "Opinions du peuple saines" ("Opinions of the masses sound") (94). Whereas Pascal will commend to his unbeliever the example of those "personnes simples" who believe "sans raisonnement" ("without argument") (380) and even "sans avoir lu les Testaments" ("without having read the Testaments") (381),[78] Naudé delights in taking an inventory of the historic examples of the way in which religion has been used to dupe the masses. Delving into antiquity, he cites the instance of Romulus, who founded Rome by invoking his supposed connections with the god Mars.[79] After moving on to an account of how Mohammed duped an entire people into accepting his religion, Naudé invokes a series of more recent examples of the gullibility of the masses: Peter the Hermit, who preached a crusade using a relic made from a hair from his mule; Guillaume Postel, who convinced his followers that an old woman he met in Venice would complete the redemption of womankind since she was born of the same substance as Christ; the Anabaptists David George (who proclaimed himself the Son of God) and John of Leiden, who led his followers to the debacle at Münster in 1534.[80]

J. S. Spink qualifies Naudé as "one of the last humanists rather than one of the first philosophers" and describes him as a brilliant erudite who spent his life destroying myths and legends."[81] Doctor to Louis XIII and then librarian to Mazarin, Naudé never sought to propagate his ideas beyond his immediate circle of *déniasés*. Indeed, to have done so would have contradicted his central tenet that religion is a necessary evil, required to keep the masses under control and to oblige virtue. Spink notes with relish: "His very skepticism led him to prefer the old to the new in religious matters; all dogmatizers and provokers of disputes, Huguenots, Jansenists and promoters of new fashions of piety or belief were anathema to him."[82] In his *Considérations*, Naudé maintains that there exist only two

77. *Political Considerations upon Refined Politicks and the Master-Strokes of State as Practiced by the Ancients and Moderns Translated into English by Dr. King* (London: H. Clements, 1711), pp. 136–37.

78. See Chapter V, The Faith of the Simple.

79. *Considerations* (1679), p. 148.

80. Ibid., pp. 250–52.

81. *French Free-Thought*, pp. 20–21.

82. Ibid., p. 21.

means of keeping the masses under control: the fear of torture and the fear of the Gods. The latter, he insists, is by far the more effective method. Rulers, he observes, must convince their subjects that they are executing the will of the Gods, with whom they have a direct line of communication. They must make use of "miracles," "visions," and "prodiges" to inspire respect for the established religion.[83]

Naudé's attacks on astrology, occult science, magic, and cabalist speculation in his *Instruction à la France sur la vérité de l'histoire des frères de la Rose-Croix* (1623) and his *Apologie pour tous les grands personnages qui ont été faussement soupçonnés de magie* (1625) make for fascinating reading for the student of the history of religious thought. So too do those pages in the *Jugement de tout ce qui a été imprimé contre le cardinal Mazarin* (1649) in which he elucidates the political motivations behind the persecution of witches and relative to the famous cases of diabolical possession at Loudun and Louviers. However, at least from the perspective of Pascal's projected Apology, the most interesting passage in Naudé concerns his explanation of the origins of Islam.

In Chapter III (Pascal and Islam), we shall examine the way in which Pascal analyzes the Prophet and the origins of Islam in order to demonstrate the character of a genuinely false religion. By contrasting the founders and moral teachings of Islam and Christianity, Pascal will seek to demonstrate the true character of revealed religion. Seen in the context of his *Considérations* (1639), Naudé's aims are very different. He intends to demonstrate the extreme gullibility of humankind in general. Reading between the lines, it is perfectly possible to view his critique of the origins of Islam as capable of being read as an implicit critique of the origins of Christianity.

Naudé's text and the source on which he draws (probably Baudier's *Histoire générale de la religion des Turcs*, 1632) are too different from Pascal's discussion of Islam in the *liasse* "Fausseté des autres religions" (XVI) for Pascal to have used either as a source. However, it is conceivable that Naudé's source may have been known to Le Maistre de Sacy. In his critique of Islam in the Preface to his translation of Genesis,[84] Sacy makes use of a detail—attributing the Prophet's revelations to attacks of epilepsy—absent from the source (Grotius' *De Veritate religionis christianae*) which he generally follows in his attack on Islam.

83. *Considérations* (1679), pp. 260–64.

84. *La Genèse: traduite en français avec l'explication du sens littéral et du sens Spirituel* (Paris: Lambert Roulland, 1682), Préface, Première Partie, partic vii. Cf. *Pensées,* fragment 209.

Naudé's account of the origins of Islam is caricature at its most acerbic. Not only does the Prophet convince his friends that the "plus violents paroxismes de son épilepsie" ("most violent fits of his epilepsy") are a form of religious ecstasy. He dupes them into believing "qu'un pigeon blanc qui venoit manger des grains de bled dans son aureille esoit l'ange Gabriel qui lui venoit annoncer de la part . . . [de] Dieu ce qu'il avoit à faire"[85] ("that a white pigeon that he had taught to eat corn out of his Ear was the Angel Gabriel, who came from God to tell him what he was to do").[86] According to Naudé's account, the Prophet then used the help of a renegade monk, Sergius, in composing the Qur'an and falsely claimed that it was dictated to him "de la propre bouche de Dieu" ("from the mouth of God Himself"). He then made use of a famous astrologer to predict the coming of a great Prophet and a new Law. His "impostures" having been discovered by his secretary, he murdered him, set fire to his house, and presented the event as the wrath of heaven sent to punish the one who had tried to introduce the infamous "Satanic verses" into the text of the Qu'ran.[87]

Naudé's account of the origins of Islam is perfectly consonant with his general theory of how religions come to be foisted upon the gullible masses. A miracle is required to satisfy their inherent thirst for the supernatural. The one Naudé recounts could well be read (at least by initiates) as an attack on the authenticity of miracles in general:

> [Mahomet] persuada au plus fidèle de ses domestiques de descendre au fond d'un puits qui estoit proche d'un grand chemin, afin de crier lorsqu'il passeroit en compagnie d'une grande multitude de peuple qui le suivoit ordinairement, "Mahomet est le bien aymé de Dieu, Mahomet est le bien aymé de Dieu." Et cela estant arrivé de la façon qu'il avoit proposé, il remercia soudain la divine bonté d'un témoignage si remarquable, et pria tout le peuple qui le suivoit de combler à l'heure mesme ce puits et de bastir dessus une petite mosquée pour marque d'un tel miracle. Et par cette invention, ce pauvre domestique fut incontinent assommé et ensevely sous une gresle de cailloux, qui luy ostèrent bien le moyen de jamais descouvrir la fausseté de ce miracle.[88]

> [Mahomet] persuaded one of his most faithful domesticks to go down to the bottom of a Well that was near the highway and as he was passing by with a great Multitude following him, as there usually was, to cry out, "Mahomet is the beloved of God, Mahomet is the beloved of God." This being done in the manner

85. *Considérations* (1679), p. 152.
86. English translation (1711), p. 82.
87. *Considérations* (1679), pp. 152–53.
88. Ibid., pp. 153–54.

that was proposed, he immediately returned thanks to the divine Goodness for so signal a testimony, and desired all the People that attended him immediately to fill up this Well and to build a little Mosque upon it for the Memorial of such a Miracle. And by this Invention, the poor servant was soon knocked on the head and buried under a Heap of Stones, that hinder'd him from ever discovering this Miracle.[89]

The Survival of the Radical Tradition: Covert Atheism and Clandestine Manuscripts

The repression of libertine ideas in the 1620s and the relative discretion of La Mothe le Vayer and G. Naudé should serve to remind us of the danger occasioned by the open expression of atheism during the middle of the seventeenth century in France. How much more should we know had we access to any number of hypothetical private conversations transcribed by some daring listener! Indeed, there may be much more to be learned from a careful examination of the vast correspondence inventoried by Pintard in his monumental *Le Libertinage érudit*. . . . However, while awaiting further research into the incompletely understood phenomenon of the covert expression of atheistic ideas in the Classical period, we do have access to, and in one instance ample references to, a few clandestine manuscripts which circulated within libertine circles in the 1640s and 1650s. These include the *Quatrains du déiste*,[90] the *Theophrastus redivivus*,[91] numerous references to the never-discovered *De Tribus Impostoribus*, and Cyrano de Bergerac's *Etats et empires de la lune*.

We are probably unaccustomed to thinking of the last and most well known of these works as a "clandestine" manuscript. Nor have Cyrano's ideas often been invoked in connection with Pascal's freethinking interlocutor. However, the *Etats et empires de la lune* circulated only in manuscript form from the time it was written (1649) until it was published, two years after Cyrano's death, in 1657. And that edition, prepared by Cyrano's friend Lebret, prudently omitted a number of long passages containing Cyrano's most blatantly atheistic ideas. The authentic text of *Etats de la*

89. English translation (1711), pp. 83–84.

90. The complete text of *Les Quatrains du Déiste,* actually entitled the *Anti-Bigot ou le faux dévotieux,* can be found in F. Lachèvre's *La Procès de Théophile,* 2, pp. 105–126, and in his *Voltaire mourant* (Paris: H. Champion, 1908), pp. 110–36. A. Adam reconstructs a more accessible version of the text in *Les Libertins au XVIIe siècle,* pp. 90–109.

91. Bibliothéque Nationale, fonds latin 9324.

lune remained unpublished until early in this century.[92] Pascal may well have never heard of Cyrano's manuscript. But his mentor in matters exegetical, Le Maistre de Sacy, seems to have by the time he came to write the introduction to his translation of Genesis. Sacy blasts those who "se servent . . . de la personne de Moyse et de ce qu'il dit dans les premiers Chapitres de ce livre touchant la création du monde, le paradis terrestre, la chute d'Adam, et le péché originel, pour en prendre des sujets de leurs discours pleins d'insolence et de blasphème"[93] ("make use . . . of the person of Moses and of what he says in the first chapters of this book concerning the creation of the world, the Garden of Eden, the Fall of Adam and original sin in order to find subjects for their insolent and blasphemous discourses"). And what more blasphemous and notorious burlesque of Eden, the Patriarchs (Adam, Moses, Noah, Enoch), the Fall, and the Flood had ever been concocted than that of Cyrano in *Les Etats et empires de la lune*?

Scholars have only just begun to understand the full significance of Cyrano's place in the most radical stream of libertine thought. A pivotal figure, he links the Italian naturalistic tradition (via Campanella) with the open atheism of Père Meslier's "Testament"[94] at the end of the century. In the fictional guise of the *Etats et empires de la lune*, he effects what Olivier Bloch calls "la transformation d'un immanentisme métaphysique am-

92. The authentic text of *Les Estats et empires de la lune* is preserved in two manuscripts: ms. Munich 420 and ms. n. acq. fr. 4558, B.N. The Munich text was first published in 1910 by Leo Jordan in the *Gesellschaft für romanische Literatur,* v. 23. The Parisian text was published in 1922 by Frédéric Lachèvre in *Les Oeuvres libertines de Cyrano de Bergerac* (Paris: Champion, 1921).

On Cyrano de Bergerac, see the following: Spink, *French Free-Thought,* pp. 48–66. Olivier Bloch, "Cyrano de Bergerac et la philosophie," *XVIIe siècle* 149 (1985), 337–48. M. Alcover, *La Pensée philosophique et scientifique de Cyrano de Bergerac* (Geneva: Droz, 1970). J. J. Bridenne, "Cyrano de Bergerac," *Revue des sciences humaines* 75 (1954): 241–57. H. Weber, Introduction, Cyrano de Bergerac, *: L'Autre Monde* (Paris: Editions Sociales, 1960). G. Mongrédien, *Cyrano de Bergerac* (Paris: Berger-Levrault, 1964). E. W. Lanius, *Cyrano de Bergerac and the Universe of the Imagination* (Geneva: Droz, 1967). E. Harth, *Cyrano de Bergerac and the Polemics of Modernity* (New York: Columbia University Press, 1970).

93. *La Genèse: traduite en françois,* Première Partie, partie iii.

94. Jean Meslier (1664–1733), parish priest of Etrepigny in Champagne. On his death, there was found a large manuscript entitled *Mon testament,* in which Meslier repented for ever having taught and practiced Christianity. In 1763, Voltaire published extracts of the manuscript under the title *Testament de Jean Meslier*. This text includes two parts: (1) a scathing critique of all revealed religions, (2) a outright profession of atheism and materialism. See J. O. Wade, "The Manuscripts of J. Meslier's Testament," *Modern Philology* 30 (1932–33): 381–98.

bigu en un matérialisme pur et simple"[95] ("the transformation of an ambiguous metaphysical immanence into a pure and simple materialism"). The *Etats et empires de la lune* is in many ways a panegyric to the entire libertine tradition (see Plate II). Socrates' "daemon," whom Cyrano's traveler meets on the moon, has been an intimate, not only of Campanella, but of La Mothe le Vayer.[96]

At least two key passages from the *Etats et empires de la lune* bear noting with respect to Pascal's *Pensées*. As Antoine Adam observes, Pascal's famous "pari"[97] is anticipated by Cyrano in a libertine version suggesting the advantages of wagering that God does not exist.[98] Should God turn out not to exist, we lose nothing and gain the freedom to live a life free from the constraints of the Christian system. If God turns out to exist, we can hardly expect him to punish us, since he has furnished us with so little evidence of his existence. The God of Cyrano's wager is hardly Pascal's Christian God. At most, he is a kind of Deist God who never intervenes at all in human affairs. The argument, suppressed in all seventeenth-century editions of the *Etats et empires*, merits our close attention:

> Un homme, même tant soit peu sage, ne se picqueroit pas qu'un crocheteur l'eût injurié, si le crocheteur auroit pensé ne le pas faire, s'il l'avoit pris pour un autre ou si c'estoit le vin qui l'eut fait parler?
>
> Dieu, tout inébranlable, s'emportera-t-il contre nous pour ne l'avoir pas connu, puisque c'est Luy-même qui nous a refusé les moyens de le connoître. . . . Si la créance de Dieu nous étoit si nécessaire, enfin si elle nous importoit de l'éternité, Dieu lui-même ne nous en auroit-il pas infus à tous des lumières aussy claires que le Soleil, qui ne se cache à personne! Car de feindre qu'il ait voulu jouer entre les hommes à cligne-musette . . . c'est-à-dire tantôt se masquer, tantôt se démasquer, se déguiser à quelques-uns pour se manifester aux autres, c'est se forger un Dieu ou sot, ou malicieux. . . .[99]

> A man, even one with only a modicum of wisdom, would not get upset if a porter insulted him, if the porter did not realize what he was doing, mistook him for someone else, or if it were drink which had made him speak in such a fashion.
>
> Will God, who is completely unshakable, lose his temper with us for having failed to know him, since he himself has withheld from us the means of knowing him? If belief in God were truly necessary, indeed if it were a matter of our eternal

95. Bloch, "Cyrano de Bergerac et la philosophie," p. 347.

96. Frédéric Lachèvre, ed., Cyrano de Bergerac, *L'Autre Monde ou Les Etats et empires de la lune et soleil* (Paris: Garnier, 1938), p. 39.

97. See Chapter IV, Pascal's Interlocutor in Fragment 418.

98. *Les Libertins au XVIIe siècle,* p. 162.

99. *L'Autre Monde,* pp. 114–15.

PLATE 11. Cyrano de Bergerac, *Les Estats et empires de la lune* (1662). Service photographique, Bibliothèque Nationale.

reward or punishment, would not God himself have clarified the matter, giving us a light as bright as the sun, which hides itself from no one! To maintain the pretense that God has wanted to play hide-and-seek with humanity . . . that's to say, sometimes putting on a mask, sometimes taking it off, hiding himself from some in order to manifest himself to others: this is to invent a God who is either silly or malicious.

In fragment 232, Pascal writes: "On n'entend rien aux ouvrages de Dieu si on ne prend pour principe qu'il a voulu aveugler les uns et éclaircir les autres" ("We can understand nothing of God's works unless we accept the principle that he wished to blind some and enlighten others"). In rejecting the traditional Christian explanation for God's apparent absence in the world, Cyrano particularly blasts the Augustinian doctrine of predestination and election and Pascal's beloved theme of the *Deus absconditus*. Such a God, he insists, would be either a silly or a malicious Supreme Being. So too, he observes, would be a God who would damn humans when he had given them "un esprit incapable de le comprendre"[100] ("a mind incapable of understanding him"). The narrator of *Les Etats et empires de la lune* feigns horror upon hearing these propositions and concludes that the philosopher espousing such views must be the Anti-Christ himself. But make no mistake about it. These are the views of Cyrano. Just how dangerous he knows these views to be can be measured by the care he takes to have the speaker suddenly dragged down into hell by the devil himself.

A second passage, not suppressed in seventeenth-century editions of the *Etats et empires de la lune*, is particularly interesting in light of Pascal's apologetic itinerary. We have already noted Pascal's insistence that finding out whether the soul is mortal or immortal constitutes his inquirer's most important task (164, 427). Now, denying the immortality of the soul is almost a commonplace motif in the libertine tradition. Père Garasse cites his *libertins* as objecting that the existence of a God does not necessarily imply the immortality of the soul.[101] La Mothe le Vayer observes that not all religions agree on the subject.[102] A libertine lawyer tells the apologist Père Beurrier: "Nous croyons que quand nous mourons tout est mort pour nous"[103] ("We believe that when we die, everything dies with us"). A libertine poem cited by A. Adam makes the point with particular vigor:

100. Ibid., p. 115.
101. Adam, *Les Libertins au XVIIe siècle,* p. 42, "Maxime" VII.
102. *Deux Dialogues,* pp. 124–25.
103. Cited by A. Adam, *Les Libertins au XVIIe siècle,* p. 113.

Pourquoy prescher la mort aux hommes?
Ce sont des discours superflus.
Elle n'est pas tant que nous sommes,
Quand elle est, nous ne sommes plus.

Ah! qu'ils sont insensés, ces bougres,
    Avec leurs illusions
De croire ce qui est en poudre
    Sujet à résurrection!

Pourquoy tant de cloches, de messes?
Peut-on ressusciter les morts?
Nous devons croire avec sagesse
Que l'âme meurt avec le corps.

Les chiens, les oiseaux de rivière
Ne font pas tous un si grand bruit,
Qu'un prestre dans un cimetière,
En hurlant un *De Profundis*.[104]

Why preach to men about death? / It's all superfluous talk. / Death is not, as long as we are alive; / When it is, we are dead and gone.

Oh! they're insane, those poor buggers / With their delusions / Of believing what's been reduced to powder / Subject to resurrection!

Why so many bells, so many masses? / Can the dead be brought back to life? / Using our own common sense, we ought to believe / That the soul dies with the body.

Dogs and river birds / Make all together not so much noise, / As a priest in a cemetery / Howling a *De Profundis*.

In fragment 161, Pascal attempts to neutralize such objections to the immortality of the soul by injecting a clear note of skepticism into the whole affair. No one, he argues, has ever absolutely proved that the soul is material. "Les athées doivent dire des choses parfaitement claires. Or il n'est point parfaitement clair que l'âme soit matérielle" ("Atheists should say things that are perfectly clear. Now it is not perfectly clear that the soul is material"). One could only wish that Pascal had read Cyrano's argument on the subject. Not that it would have changed his mind. But the Pascalian counterargument would have made for intensely interesting reading. Cyrano's argument, probably already articulated in antiquity or by the Italian naturalists, nonetheless seems unique in the history of the seventeenth century in France. Not until Diderot and the Enlightenment

104. Ibid., p. 86.

would it be taken up again. Once again, Cyrano's argument is put in the mouth of a philosopher he meets on the moon:

> Si cette âme estoit spirituelle et par soy-même si raisonnable, comme ils disent, qu'elle fût aussy capable d'intelligence quand elle est séparée de notre masse qu'alors qu'elle en est revêtue, pourquoi les Aveugles-nés, avec tous les beaux avantages de cette Ame intellectuelle, ne sauroient-ils même s'imaginer ce que c'est que de voir? Pourquoi les Sourds n'entendent-ils point? Est-ce à cause qu'ils ne sont pas encore privés par le trépas de tous leurs sens? . . . Cependant, ils veulent que cette âme, qui ne peut pas agir qu'imparfaictement à cause de la perte d'un de ses outils dans le cours de la vie, puisse alors travailler avec perfection quand, après notre mort, elle les aura tous perdus.[105]

An English translation of 1687 renders the passage as follows:

> If that soul were Spiritual and of herself so rational, that being separated from our Mass, she understood as well as when clothed with a Body; why cannot blind men, born with all the fair advantages of that intellectual Soul, imagine what it is to see? Is it, because they are not as yet deprived of Sight, by the death of all their senses . . . they'll have this Soul, which can only act imperfectly, because of the loss of one of her Tools, in the course of life, to be able to work to Perfection, when after our death, she hast lost them all.[106]

It is of considerable interest that the preceding passage was not suppressed in seventeenth-century editions of the *Etats et empires*. Are we to conclude that speculation concerning the nature of the soul would have been considered less dangerous than Cyrano's attack upon the doctrine of the Hidden God of the Augustinian Christians? Interestingly enough, Pascal never actively censures speculation concerning the nature of the soul. In fact, in fragment 427 (see Chapter IV, The Unbelievers in Fragment 427), he encourages such speculation among those unbelievers who cannot be bothered to take up the question of the ultimate fate of their soul. Perhaps Cyrano's editors simply did not recognize the blatant atheism implicit in his critique of the doctrine of the immortality of the soul. But it is significant that they did recognize the completely anti-Christian character of his picture of a nonintervening and Deist God who could not be reasonably expected to punish the disbelief of those to whom he had

105. *L'Autre Monde*, p. 112.

106. *The Comical History of the States and Empires of the Worlds of the Moon and Sun, Written in French by Cyrano Bergerac and Newly Englished by A. Lovell, A.M.* (London: Henry Rhodes, 1687), pp. 134–35.

never actively revealed himself. In any event, we are once again reminded of the extent to which any kind of speculation concerning the Augustinian doctrines of predestination and election never failed to elicit extreme prudence during the course of the Classical period in France.

* * *

The anonymous *Theophrastus redivivus* (1659), though it could hardly have influenced Pascal's interlocutor, serves to remind us that it was possible for an atheism of the most radical sort to be rigorously elaborated right in the middle of the Classical period. As Gianni Paganini points out in his important study of this text, the *Theophrastus redivivus* represents the first complete rupture with the Italian naturalism of the previous century and anticipates the principal modalities of modern historical criticism.[107] J. S. Spink describes this immense Latin tome as a vast compendium of "all the thinkers in Antiquity and the Renaissance who were or could be considered as atheists, who denied the immortality of the soul, the existence of hell, demons, spirits and apparitions."[108] The first part (*De Diis*) of its two thousand folio pages uncompromisingly advances the thesis that the popular notion of God is but an expression of human fear. The God of the theologians is a pure abstraction with no independent existence. The second part of the *Theophrastus redivivus* is devoted to denying the creation and proving the eternity of the world. The third *Tractatus* (*de religione*) seeks to prove that all religions are an enormous deception practiced upon the masses in order to maintain order and effective government. Unlike Naudé, the author rejects the pretense of excepting Christianity from this general truth. He evokes the venerable libertine thesis of the Three Impostors: the proposition that Moses, Christ, and Mohammed seduced the human race in the pursuit of political power.

Georges Couton advances the idea that Pascal's historical proofs of the credibility of Christianity very much take into account the thesis of the Three Impostors. Pascal's careful attention to documenting the historicity of the Pentateuch and his attempt to characterize Islam as a demonstrably false religion make this entirely plausible. But why does Pascal never designate this famous libertine theory by name or describe it more clearly? Couton thinks that Pascal, aside from the fact that he would have considered the grouping of Moses and Christ with Mohammed a blasphemy in

107. Gianni Paganini, "L'Anthropologie naturaliste d'un esprit fort: thèmes et problèmes pomponaciens dans le *Theophrastus redivivus*," *XVIIe siècle* 149 (1985): 349–69.

108. *French Free-Thought*, p. 67. The summary which follows is taken from Spink's analysis.

and of itself, did not want to dignify it or accord it any importance even by mentioning it.[109]

That the thesis of the Three Impostors was part of the public domain and known to anyone of a libertine bent is certain. An atheist doctor questioned by the apologist Père Beurrier was particularly clear on the matter: "Il y a eu trois grands imposteurs au monde, à savoir Moïse, Jésus-Christ et Mahomet; mais Jésus-Christ est le plus grand; il a été le plus adroit et le plus subtil de tous"[110] ("There have been three great impostors in the history of the world, to wit, Moses, Jesus Christ and Mohammed; but Jesus Christ was the greatest of them, the most adroit, and the most subtle of them all"). An atheist priest, echoing a theme we have already seen in Naudé's *Considérations*,[111] explains to Père Beurrier the political implications of the thesis of the Three Impostors: "La police et la religion étaient des inventions des hommes qui voulaient se rendre maîtres des autres"[112] ("government and religion were inventions of men who wanted to rule over others").

Whether a real book or manuscript entitled *De Tribus Impostoribus* or *Traité des trois imposteurs* ever existed may never be known. Père Mersenne, whose scientific circle was frequented by Pascal and his father, believed in the existence of such a book, "très impie, très digne des flammes éternelles par lequel les Déistes et Athées essaient de persuader que Moïse et le Christ, à l'imitation de Mahomet, sont des imposteurs"[113] ("of great danger to religion and meriting hellfire, by which the Deists and atheists attempt to argue that Moses and Christ, after the fashion of Mohammed, were impostors"). Pintard recounts an amusing anecdote concerning Christina of Sweden's search for the mysterious manuscript:

> Les *Trois Imposteurs*, naturellement, sollicitent à leur tour sa gourmandise, ces *Trois Imposteurs* mentionnés partout, découverts nulle part, réfutés sans avoir été lus, recherchés de féroces autodafés ou pour les délectations d'une lecture secrète, et qui, parés d'un prestige unique par cent ans et plus de chuchotements et de légendes, ont tout pour enchanter d'avance son esprit romanesque. Elle a ouï dire qu'ils faisaient la parure cachée de la bibliothèque de Salvius, son plénipotentiaire à l'assemblée de Lubeck. . . . Or voici qu'il meurt vers la fin de 1652. Point de re-

109. Georges Couton, "Libertinage et apologétique: Les *Pensées* de Pascal contre la thèse des trois imposteurs," *XVIIe siècle* 127 (1980): 188.

110. Paul Beurrier, *Mémoires,* ms. 1885–1887, Bibliothèque Sainte Geneviève. Cited by Adam, *Les Libertins au XVIIe siècle,* p. 117.

111. See Chapter I, Two Cautious Skeptics: La Mothe le Vayer and Gabriel Naude.

112. Adam, *Les Libertins au XVIIe siècle,* p. 119.

113. Cited by Couton, "Libertinage et apologétique," p. 187.

tard: le corps du bonhomme est à peine froid que Bourdelot[114] est chez sa veuve, la priant, de la part de la Reine, de "satisfaire sa curiosité." On lui répond "que le malade, saisi de remors de conscience la veille de sa mort, avoit dans sa chambre fait jetter le livre au feu." Vérité ou mensonge? De toute façon, la Reine ne se consolera jamais de cette déconvenue: elle mettra en campagne "toutes sortes de furets de bibliothèque" pour dénicher, en quelque lieu d'Europe qu'il se dissimule, le dangereux et séduisant traité.[115]

These *Three Impostors*, naturally, in turn, whetted her appetite. Mentioned everywhere, discovered nowhere, refuted without ever having been read, sought in order to be consigned to a fierce *autodafé* or in order to be read in secret delection, adorned with a unique prestige by more than a hundred years of whispers and legends, [the *Three Impostors*] contained everything capable of enchanting [Queen Christina's] romantic mind. She heard it said that they formed the hidden embellishment of the library of Salvius, her plenipotentiary at the assembly of Lubek. . . . Then he died towards the end of 1652. She wasted no time. The gentleman's body was hardly cold before she dispatched Bourdelot to see his widow, to ask, on behalf of the Queen, "to satisfy her curiosity." [Bourdelot] was told that the dying man, seized with remorse the night before his death, had had the book thrown into the fire in his bedroom. Truth or fiction? At any rate, the Queen would never be consoled with regard to this disappointment. She dispatched into the breach "all sorts of librarian sleuths" to ferret out, wherever it might be hidden, in whatever country of Europe, the dangerous and seductive treatise.

Pascal and Deism

The exact nature of Pascal's acquaintance with the thesis of the *Trois Imposteurs* is far less problematic than the question of what Pascal means

114. Bourdelot (Pierre Michon), 1610–85. After graduating from the Medical Faculty in Paris, Bourdelot was called to Rome as the doctor to the French ambassador. After taking orders, he passed into the service of the Prince de Condé (1638), to whom he introduced Isaac de La Peyrère. On the recommendation of Claude Saumaise, he was called to serve Christina of Sweden, "dont il fut le professeur ès vices autant que le médecin" ("to whom he served as professor of vice as much as he did physician") (*Dictionaire des lettres françaises* [Paris: Fayard, 1954], p. 204). He returned to the service of Condé in 1653 and later treated Mme de Sévigny, the Princesses Palatine, and the Duchess of Longueville. A friend of La Mothe le Vayer and Gassendi, he is frequently mentioned in the annals of *la libre pensée*. Cf., Pintard, *Le Libertinage érudit*, pp. 219–20, 350–55, 356–62, 378–79. Also Gallois, *Conversations académiques tirées de l'Académie de M. Bourdelot* (Paris, 1684).

115. *Le Libertinage érudit*, pp. 394–95. The history of the search for the enigmatic manuscript is recounted in a letter attributed to La Monnoye (*Lettre à M. Bouhier sur le prétendu livre des trois imposteurs*, Paris, 16 juin 1712), which can be found in the *Menagiana*, 1715, 4, pp. 283–312. An additional account may be consulted in Prosper Marchand's *Dictionnaire historique* (1758).

when he uses the word *déisme* in fragment 449. Pintard insists that the "idée tout abstraite" ("completely abstract idea") that Pascal gives of Deism "convient beaucoup mieux au stoïcisme antique qu'à ce que les 'curieux' du siècle découvraient . . . dans les *Quatrains du Déiste* que Mersenne avait jugés dignes d'une longue réfutation"[116] ("fits Classical stoicism far better than it does what the *curieux du siècle* were discovering in the *Quatrains du Déiste*, which Mersenne had judged worthy of a long refutation"). Pintard's observation seems entirely reasonable with regard to fragment 142. In this fragment, entitled "(Contre les philosophes qui ont Dieu sans J.C.) Philosophes" ("[Against the philosophers who have God without Christ] Philosophers"), Pascal does seem to be thinking of the Stoics of antiquity. Indeed, the passage recalls his critique of Epictetus in the *Entretien avec M. De Sacy*:

> Ils croient que Dieu est seul digne d'être aimé et d'être admiré, et ont désiré d'être aimés et admirés des hommes, et ils ne connaissent pas leur corruption. S'ils se sentent pleins de sentiments pour l'aimer et l'adorer, et qu'ils y trouvent leur joie principale, qu'ils s'estiment bons à la bonne heure! Mais s'ils s'y trouvent répugnants s'(ils) n'(ont) aucune pente qu'à se vouloir établir dans l'estime des hommes, et que pour toute perfection, ils fassent seulement que, sans forcer les hommes, ils leur fassent trouver leur bonheur à les aimer, je dirai que cette perfection est horrible. Quoi, ils ont connu Dieu et n'ont pas désiré uniquement que les hommes l'aimassent, que les hommes s'arrêtassent à eux. Ils ont voulu être l'objet du bonheur volontaire des hommes.[117]

> They believe that God alone is worthy of love and admiration; they too wanted to be loved and admired by men and do not realize their own corruption. If their hearts are filled with the desire to love and worship him, and if this is their greatest joy, by all means let them think well of themselves. But if they find this repugnant,

116. R. Pintard, "Pascal et les libertins," in *Pascal présent* (Clermond Ferrand: G. de Bussac, 1962), p. 113.

117. In the *Entretien avec M. de Sacy,* Pascal lauds the way in which Epictetus teaches that man must regard God as "son principal objet," submitting his will to Divine Providence because he is persuaded that God cannot act otherwise than with justice. However, Pascal tells Sacy, Epictetus' view of things contains a serious flaw: "Il dit que Dieu a donné à l'homme les moyens de s'acquitter de toutes ses obligations; que ces moyens sont en notre puissance" ("He says that God has given man the means of fulfilling all his obligations; that these means are within our power"). When he maintains that man is able, through his own efforts, "connaître Dieu, l'aimer, lui obéir, lui plaire, se guérir de tous ses vices, acquérir toutes les vertus, se rendre saint ainsi et compagnon de Dieu" ("to know God, love him, obey him, please him, cure himself of all his vices, acquire all virtues, and thus render himself holy and the companion of God"), Epictetus loses himself "dans la présomption." Joseph Bédier, "Etablissement d'un texte critique de 'L'Entretien de Pascal avec M.de Saci," in *Etudes critiques* (Paris: A. Collin, 1903), pp. 55–56.

if their only inclination is to win men's esteem, if their only perfection lies in persuading men, without compelling them, that there is happiness in loving them, then I say such perfection is horrible. Why, they have known God and their sole desire has been, not that men should love him, but that they should stop short at them! They have desired to be the object of the happiness which men desire. (142)

It seems obvious that this passage is directed principally against the philosophers of pre-Christian antiquity. It is filed in the dossier ("Philosophes") (IX) dealing with Epictetus and the Stoics. Pascal's argument is essentially that those philosophers who were ignorant of the Incarnation were incapable of leading men to God because of the interference of their own ego, that human defect instituted by the Fall which cut off the direct line of communication with God. Only Christ, in his Incarnation, was able to restore this line of communication. This passage can hardly be seen as referring to contemporary non-Christian philosophers. Not once in the entire course of the *Pensées* does Pascal ever dignify his contemporary religious adversaries with the title "philosophers."

How startlingly different is fragment 449, directed squarely against the non-Christian thinkers of Pascal's own time and specifically naming the word *déisme*:

Ils prennent lieu de blasphémer la religion chrétienne, parce qu'ils la connaissent mal. Ils s'imaginent qu'elle consiste simplement en l'adoration d'un Dieu considéré comme grand et puissant; ce qui est proprement *le déisme*, *presque aussi éloigné de la religion chrétienne que l'athéisme*, qui y est tout à fait contraire. Et de là ils concluent que cette religion n'est pas véritable, puisque'ils ne voient pas que toutes choses concourent à l'etablissement de ce point, que Dieu ne se manifeste pas aux hommes avec toute l'evidence qu'il pourrait faire.

Mais qu'ils en concluent ce qu'ils voudront contre le *déisme*, ils n'en concluront rien contre la religion chrétienne.

They take occasion to blaspheme against the Christian religion, because they know so little about it. They imagine that it simply consists in worshiping a God considered to be great and mighty and eternal, which is properly speaking *deism*, *almost as remote from the Christian religion as atheism*, its complete opposite. And thence they conclude that this religion is not true, because they cannot see that all things combine to establish the point that God does not manifest himself to men as obviously as he might.

But let them conclude what they like against *deism*, their conclusions will not apply to Christianity. (449, italics mine)

Having explained why he will not undertake any kind of metaphysical proofs of Christianity, proofs which could hardly convince "des athées endurcis" ("hardened atheists"), Pascal then launches another broadside attack on those who seek to find God outside of Christ:

> Tous ceux qui cherchent Dieu hors de Jésus-Christ, et qui s'arrêtent dans la nature . . . arrivent à se former un moyen de connaître Dieu et de le servir sans médiateur, et par là ils tombent ou dans *l'athéisme ou dans le déisme*, *qui sont deux choses que la religion chrétienne abhorre presque également*.

> All those who seek God apart from Christ, and who go no further than nature . . . come to devise a means of knowing and serving God without a mediator, thus falling into either *atheism or deism*, *two things almost equally abhorrent to Christianity*. (449, italics mine)

Here, Pascal seems to be making a radical departure from Christian apologetics as practiced in the Western Church since the twelfth century. In this tradition, proofs of God's existence nearly always precede and make possible the elaboration of the doctrine of the Incarnation. Even the ancient Christian creeds establish "God the Father, Creator of all things" as the very first article of the Faith. From a modern religious perspective, Pascal's invective appears remarkably harsh. Deism is said to be "as far removed" from the Christian religion as "atheism." Deism and atheism are said to be "almost equally abhorrent to Christianity." One can hardly imagine even the most conservative modern Catholic calling his Unitarian neighbor an "atheist." On the other hand, Pascal seems curiously presentient. During the Enlightenment, Deism would indeed serve as a kind of halfway house for Diderot and many others before they later progressed to a completely materialistic atheism.

That Pascal refers to his contemporaries, and not to the ancient Stoics, seems completely clear. The Stoics had no knowledge of Christ. Those whom Pascal blasts know of Christ but deliberately seek God without reference to him. The only additional clue Pascal gives about these seekers (and they are seekers, not resigned atheists) is that they "s'arrêtent dans la nature" ("go no further than nature"). Who are they? And what can we find out about them? Our standard notion of what "Deism" represents has been so colored by the Enlightenment, and particularly by Voltaire's "Divine Watchmaker," that we perhaps need to delve further into what Deism represented a hundred or so years earlier.

During antiquity, several major philosophical traditions—among them the Platonic, the Stoic, and the Epicurean—rejected the anthropomorphic nature of the classical Gods and the notion of Incarnation. Scores of passages to this effect appear in Montaigne's *Essays*.[118] But at what point did premodern Europeans begin to apply these concepts to Christianity and to call themselves "Deists"? Pintard situates the origins of modern Deism in the fever of new ideas provoked by the Renaissance and the Reformation. He describes the first generation of Deists as men who, without wanting to deny the existence of God nor the utility of belief, stripped Christianity of its mysteries and constructed a religion more consonant with their philosophical ideas. The result was a pure "natural religion," accommodating and reasonable:

> Point de mysticisme, à part quelques exceptions, chez ceux-là: mais une longue et fervente pratique des oeuvres païennes; une foi réduite à celle de Cicéron et de Sénèque; une profonde répugnance pour les complications du dogme et même pour les élans de la piété, s'ils inspiraient du fanatisme; l'horreur des querelles religieuses; une préférence de principe pour le *credo* le plus court, celui qui pourrait diviser le moins. . . . Ces Déistes étaient très capables, à l'occasion, de penser: Jean Bodin l'avait suffisamment montré . . . par son *Heptaplomeres*. Ils recrutaient des partisans jusque dans le clergé. . . . Enfin ils répandaient leurs idées dans la foule elle-même: témoins, aux environs de 1620, ces *Quatrains du Déiste* qui fixaient pour tout le XVIIe siècle, leur physionomie intellectuelle et morale.[119]

> No mysticism at all, with a few exceptions, in the writings of these gentlemen. Rather a long and fervent study of the works of Classical antiquity; a faith reduced to that of Cicero and Seneca; a profound repugnance for the complications of dogma and even for pious impulses if inspired by fanaticism; a horror of religious disputes; in principal, a preference for the shortest and potentially least divisive creed. . . . These Deists were at times very capable of profound thought. Jean Bodin had sufficiently demonstrated this in his *Heptaplomeres*. They recruited their partisans even from within the ranks of the clergy. . . . Finally they began to spread their ideas into wider circles. The evidence for this? The appearance, around 1620,

118. For instance, *Essais,* 2:12: "Les choses les plus ignorées sont plus propres à être déifiées. Par quoi de faire de nous des dieux, comme l'ancienneté, cela surpasse l'extrême faiblesse de discours" ("The least-known things are the fittest to be deified; wherefore to make gods of ourselves, like antiquity, passes the utmost bounds of feeblemindedness") (*Oeuvres complètes,* p. 214); "L'ancienneté pensa, ce crois-je, faire quelque chose pour la grandeur divine, de l'apparier à l'homme, la vêtir de ses facultés et étrenner de ses belles humeurs et plus honteuses nécessités . . . " ("Antiquity thought, I believe, that it was doing something for divine greatness by likening it to man, investing it with his faculties, and presenting it with his fine humors and his most shameful needs. . . .") (*Oeuvres complètes,* p. 216); "Or rien du nôtre ne se peut assortir ou rapporter, en quelque façon que ce soit, à la nature divine qui ne la tache et marque d'autant d'imperfection" ("Now nothing of ours can be likened or compared in any way whatsoever to the divine nature without staining and marking it with just that much imperfection") (*Oeuvres complètes,* p. 217).

119. *Le Libertinage érudit* . . ., pp. 48–49.

of the *Quatrains du Déiste*, a work which would fix their intellectual and moral physiognomy for the whole seventeenth century.

The modern origins of Deism are particularly obscure. Douglas Bush advances the thesis that "deism of a kind may be said to have been alive since thought began."[120] However, the word *deism*, so far as we know, first appears only in the sixteenth century in the *Instruction chrétienne* (1564) of the Calvinist theologian Pierre Viret: "I have heard he is of that band who call themselves 'Deists,' a wholly new word which they would oppose to 'Atheist.'" Viret characterizes deists as "those who profess belief in God as creator of heaven and earth, but reject Jesus Christ and his doctrines."[121] The currency of the word's use during the Enlightenment was undoubtedly enhanced by the article on Viret in Bayle's *Dictionnaire historique et critique* (1697).

The Deism of the French Enlightenment has generally been thought to have been largely inspired by the long tradition of English Deism in the seventeenth century. References to Deism in seventeenth-century France are few and far between. Only a single extant text, the anonymous *Quatrains du Déiste*, survives. However, in England, Deism almost approached the status of a movement. Among its best-known representatives were Lord Herbert of Cherbury (1583–1648), author of the *De veritate* (1624); his disciple Charles Blount (1654–93); John Toland (1670–1722), author of *Christianity Not Mysterious* (1696); and Matthew Tindal (1657–1733), whose *Christianity as Old as the Creation* (1730) has often been described as "the Deist's Bible."[122]

The influence of English Deism on the French Enlightenment was undoubtedly of great importance. However, the origins of modern Deism may in fact be French rather than English. Scholars have often neglected to note that Lord Herbert of Cherbury, commonly christened the father of Deism, was English ambassador to Paris during the early 1620s, the very period during which he wrote his *De veritate*. This date coincides precisely with the appearance of the clandestine *Quatrains du Déiste*. Important differences exist, however, between the versions of Deism set forth in these two key texts. Lord Herbert's version of "natural religion," later expanded in *De Religione laici* (1645) and in the posthumous *De Reli-*

120. Douglas Bush, *English Literature in the Earlier Seventeenth Century 1600–1660* (Oxford: Clarendon Press, 1952), p. 322.

121. Allen W. Wood, "Deism," *Encyclopedia of Religions,* M. Eliade, ed. (New York: Macmillan, 1987), p. 262.

122. Ibid.

gione Gentilium (1663), contained five articles of faith: "that a supreme and providential Deity exists; that he ought to be worshiped; that virtue and piety are the essentials of worship; that men should repent of their sins; and that rewards and punishments are dispensed in a future life."[123]

The *Quatrains du Déiste*, on the other hand, belong to a much more extreme form of Deism, one which retains from Christianity only the notion that an intelligent and powerful God brought this world into being by imposing order on preexisting matter and by devising the natural laws according to which the universe functions. The God of the *Quatrains* does not intervene at all in the functioning of the universe. There can be no exception to natural law: hence the impossibility either of miracles or of incarnation. God is not concerned with the individual human being. There is no future life. Whatever happiness or sorrow a man experiences before his final annihilation in death has no relation to divine judgments. Virtue is its own reward.

Deistic ideas, much less detached from positive dogma, also took root during the Renaissance and Reformation among various minor Arian and anti-Trinitarian sects. They traveled to Holland, where they influenced a variety of mystical Anabaptist sects, and to Poland as Socinianism.[124] The Socinians denied the divinity of Christ and the propitiatory value of his sufferings. They viewed the Lord's Supper only as purely symbolic, denied predestination, and preached religious toleration. Their modern-day successors, via English Deism, are the Unitarians. It is not these organized Deist sects, however, with which we are primarily concerned in connection with Pascal's attacks on Deism. Rather, our attention is drawn to that

123. Bush, *English Literature in the Earlier Seventeenth Century,* p. 322.

124. Socinianism originated in Italy as an amalgam of Florentine Platonism, Paduan Aristotelianism, and Protestant Biblicism. In Poland, prior to its suppression, it was altered by Calvinist and Anabaptist ingredients. Characterized by a rationalist approach to Scripture (with a predilection for the New Testament), Socinianism accepted Jesus as a Revelation of God—but only as a human being. It rejected the doctrine of the resurrection of the body and taught the final resurrection of the soul and its investment with a "spiritual body."

Faustus Socinus (1539–1604) rejected Catholicism in 1563, arguing against the unconditional immortality of the soul. His treatise on Christology and soteriology—*De Jesu Christo servatore* (1578)—advanced the view that the ascended Christ, though not divine by nature, was divine "by office" and could thus be addressed in prayer. In Poland, Faustus Socinus' theology was fused with that of an antecedent anti-Trinitarian and partly Anabaptist Minor (Reformed) Church, suppressed in 1658. Socinus' ideas flourished in Holland, where the basic books of the movement were printed. In England, his ideas attracted such scientist-theologians as Sir Isaac Newton and influenced Cambridge Platonists. The first avowed English Socinian—John Biddle—is considered the father of English Unitarianism. See E. M. Wilbur, *A History of Unitarianism* (Cambridge, Mass.: 1945–52).

specifically French Deism which took the form of a philosophical movement, was never officially organized into a sect, and was spread from individual to individual via such manifestos as the *Quatrains du Déiste*.[125]

It seems unlikely that Pascal would not at least have heard the title of this work. Père Mersenne, whose scientific circle Pascal and his father frequented in the 1640s, had devoted some 1,340 pages to a point by point refutation of their 106 stanzas in *L'Impiété des Déistes, Athées et Libertins de ce temps, combattue et renversée de point en point par raisons tirées de la philosophie et de la théologie*.[126] Frédéric Lachèvre, who reproduces the entire text of the *Quatrains*, together with Mersenne's useful prose summaries of each stanza, in his *Voltaire mourant*, judges the work to contain "pas ombre de talent" ("not a shadow of talent"). However, he credits the work with immense influence in spreading ideas which he qualifies as ultimately pantheistic.[127]

The *Quatrains* reject all anthropomorphic conceptions of God, opposing "l'Estre éternel" ("the Eternal Being") to the God of the "superstitieux":

1
Puisque l'Estre éternel est éternellement
Très heureux, et parfait en toute suffisance,
. . .

2
Le superstitieux est-il pas insensé
De se le figurer constant et variable,
Embrazé de vengeance, et d'un rien offensé,
Ennemy des tyrans et plus qu'eux redoutable?

3
L'est-il pas derechef de se l'imaginer
De tout cet Univers la guide souveraine,
Et croire ensemblement qu'il se laisse mener
Selon les passions et la nature humaine.[128]

125. The *Anti-Bigot ou le faux dévotieux*, more often referred to as *Les Quatrains du Déiste*, has to have been composed before 1623. There is a specific reference to the work in Mersenne's *Quaestiones celeberrimae in Genesim*, published in that year. Mersenne attributes the composition of the poem to a philosophy master. See Spink, *French Free-Thought*, p. 45.

126. Paris: P. Bilaine, 1624, 2 vols. On Marin Mersenne, see Robert Lenoble, *Mersenne ou la naissance du mécanisme* (Paris: Vrin, 1971); D. De Ward, B. Rochot, and A. Beaulieu, eds., *Correspondence de Mersenne* (Paris: C.N.R.S., 1932–88), 18 vols; Joseph Beaude, "Le Déisme selon Mersenne," in Sergio Bertelli, ed., *Il Libertinismo in Europa* (Milan-Naples: R. Ricciardi, 1980), pp. 199–208.

127. Frédéric Lachèvre, *Voltaire mourant* (Paris: H. Champion, 1908), p. 109.

128. *Quatrains du Déiste*, stanzas 1–3. Cited by Adam, *Les Libertins au XVIIe siècle*, p. 90.

Since the Eternal Being eternally / Knows only great beatitude, perfect and all sufficient, . . . /
Is not the one sunk in superstition insane / To imagine Him both unchanging and changeable, / Inflamed with vengeance and offended by a thing of little consequence, / An enemy of tyrants, yet more redoubtable than they?
And is ["le superstitieux"] not yet again insane to imagine [God], / The Sovereign guide of the whole universe / And at the same time believe that He lets himself be swayed / According to the passions and human nature?

The *Quatrains* reject any belief in Heaven or Hell or in rewards or punishments. The doctrine of Original Sin is dismissed as incompatible with Divine justice and goodness. A wrathful God intent upon intervening in human affairs to reward or punish individuals or nations would be a mutable and less than perfect one:

5
Si ["le superstitieux"] ne voudroit pas engendrer des enfants
S'il pensoit que leur fin deust estre misérable,
Dieu de qui la bonté se voit à tous moments
Pourroit-il aux humains se monstrer dissemblable?

6
L'Eternel nous estant infiniment meilleur
Que n'est à ses enfans une soigneuse mère,
Nous peut-il imposer un infiny malheur
Pour le contentement d'une feinte colère?[129]

If the ["superstitieux"] would not want to engender children / If he thought they were destined to a miserable fate, / Then God, whose goodness is obvious at every moment, / Could He show himself to act in opposite fashion?
The Eternal, who being infinitely better / Than the most caring mother to her children, / Could He impose upon us an infinity of suffering / In order to satisfy some trumped-up anger?

For the author of the *Quatrains*, the fear of Hell is but "une fantasie et faiblesse d'esprit"[130] ("a fantasy and a weakness of mind"). Religion itself, in reality only a function of where a man happens to have been born,[131]

129. *Les Libertins au XVIIe Siècle,* p. 91.

130. Ibid., p. 98, stanza 49. Cf. stanza 72: "Qu'est-ce l'Enfer, qu'un masque et supposé tourment / Dont les religions maintiennent leur Empire?" ("What is Hell, but a pretense and a fictitious torment / With which religions maintain their ascendancy?") (Adam, p. 102).

131. *Les Libertins au XVIIe siècle,* p. 98, stanza 50: "Le Bigot suit la religion / Dont il est allaicté dès sa première enfance" ("The bigot follows that religion which he took in with his mother's milk").

ultimately represents the exercise of political power. Miracles and all the rest are an invention concocted to control the masses:

52

Utile invention pour brider les esprits
Des hommes insolents, qui pervers de nature
Mettent les magistrats et leurs loix à mespris
Pour vivre à l'abandon, sans reigle ny mesure,

53

A quoy semblent aussy viser finalement
Les merveilleux effects qu'on voit au monde naistre,
Dont les pipe-niais ombragent finement
Leurs contes fabuleux pour les simples repaistre.[132]

A useful invention to curb the minds / Of insolent men, who, perverse by nature, / Despise and ignore judges and their laws / And abandon themselves to a life with neither rule nor measure.

This too seems the ultimate aim / Of those miracles which we see spring up in the world, / With which those who con the masses subtly disguise their fabulous tales. / These they use to satiate the simple.

Père Mersenne was particularly infuriated by this line of reasoning, one which would be more fully elaborated in the *Considérations* of G. Naudé.[133] "Je crois que votre poète," he comments in his *L'Impiété des Déistes* . . . , "a ramassé toutes les impiétés de Lucien, de Machiavel, et de tous les libertins et athéistes qui furent jamais . . . [pour] persuader que c'était qu'une imposture que la loi divine"[134] ("I think that your poet has assembled all the impieties of Lucian, of Machiavelli and of all the libertines and atheists who ever existed . . . to argue that Divine Law is but an imposture").

In the view of Louise Godard de Donville, Père Mersenne views the whole doctrine of Deism as a plot ("complot") forged by the *libertins* in order to seduce the "naifs"—delighted to be liberated from the fear of Hell—into the first stages of atheism.[135] In Mersenne's *L'Impiété des Déistes*, the "Déiste," a melancholic character fleeing human society and anxious to find a God he can still believe in, is beginning to show the first

132. *Les Libertins au XVIIe siècle*, p. 99.

133. See Chapter I, Two Cautious Skeptics: La Mothe le Voyer and Gabriel Naudé.

134. Cited by G. Couton, "Introduction," *L'Edition de Port-Royal* (Saint-Etienne: Universités de la région Rhone-Alpes, 1971), p. 14.

135. *Le Libertin des origines à 1665*, p. 343.

signs of atheism. Eager to disassociate himself from the *libertins*, he thinks himself able to win them over to the cause of natural religion:

> "Estant armé de fortes raisons pour preuver que Dieu est, je retire beaucoup de libertins (avec lesquels je me trouve souvent) de leur impieté, et de leur aveuglement, qui est si grand qu'ils ne croyent à aucune divinité, quoy qu'on puisse dire."[136]
>
> "Being armed with strong arguments for proving that God exists, I win over a great many *libertins* (with whom I often find myself), from their impiety and blindness, which is so great that they believe in no divinity, whatever one says."

However, in Mersenne's view, it is the Deist who is caught in the net of those he is trying to convert. As in Pascal's fragment 449, Deism represents but the first step on the road to complete disbelief.

Joseph Beaude takes a very different view of Mersenne's relationship with his Deist adversary in *l'Impiété des Déistes*. . . . On the level of pure doctrine, he maintains, Mersenne's adversary is presented as not all that far removed from Mersenne's own position. According to Beaude, Mersenne himself shows signs of adhering to a kind of Deism which manifests a high idea of God as a Being incomprehensible to the workings of the human mind.[137] In those 521 pages which Mersenne devotes to a refutation of the *Quatrains*,[138] Beaude argues, Mersenne makes a transition from an "apologétique où il défend vigoureusement l'orthodoxie catholique à une sorte d'indifférence oecuménique" ("apologetic in which he vigorously defends Catholic orthodoxy to a kind of ecumenical indifference").[139]

Mersenne begins by declaring that the Deists are worse than atheists since "ils empruntent le nom et le titre de *Déistes* pour abuser les âmes les plus simples et crédules"[140] ("they borrow the name and title of *Deists* to lead astray the most simple and credulous souls") (cf. *Pensées*, 449). However, Beaude observes, Mersenne's critique of Deism—which rarely evokes Christ or Scripture—is purely philosophical. "Mersenne n'oppose . . . au déisme du Déiste, qu'un déisme du chrétien, à un déisme hétéro-

136. *L'impieté* . . ., 1, p. 71. Cited by L. Godard de Donville, *Le Libertin des origines* . . ., p. 342.

137. "Le Déiste selon Mersenne," in Sergio Bertelli, ed., *Il Libertinismo in Europa*, pp. 199–208.

138. *L'Impiété des Déistes* . . ., 1: 257–778.

139. "Le Déiste selon Mersenne," p. 200.

140. *L'Impiété* . . ., in the preface dedicated to Richelieu. Cited by Beaude, "Le Déiste selon Mersenne," pp. 200–201.

doxe, un déisme orthodoxe. . . . Au fond, le Déiste et Mersenne ont le même Dieu, ils ont . . . une théologie naturelle, une métaphysique de Dieu analogues"[141] ("Mersenne opposes . . . to the Deism of the Deist a Christian Deism, to heterodox Deism, an orthodox Deism. . . . In the last analysis, the Deist and Mersenne have the same God and a natural theology and metaphysics of God which are analogous").

According to Beaude, Mersenne taxes the Deism of the *Quatrains* with too little philosophical depth. "Je sçay bien," he scolds them, "qu'une legère cognoissance de la Philosophie peut porter l'inclination à l'irréligion, mais une plus forte teinture de la mesme science la peut aussi ramener . . . à la religion si on pénètre plus avant"[142] ("that a slight knowledge of philosophy can incline one to disbelief; however, a greater immersion in this same learning can also bring one back to religion if one penetrates deeply enough"). Mersenne opposes to Deist metaphysics, Beaude argues, a Christian metaphysics founded on "une meilleure idée de l'infini et de l'absolu divins" ("a better idea of the divine nature of the infinite and the absolute"). In the last analysis, concludes Beaude, the apologetics of *L'impiété. . .*, far from leading to Pascal's "Dieu d'Abraham, d'Isaac et de Jacob," proposes that God "des philosophes" whom Pascal specifically rejects.[143]

What so disturbs Mersenne about the God of the *Quatrains*, Beaude insists, is the way in which He is so far removed from the world of human actions. Without the presence of a just God reigning over human affairs, Mersenne fears, human society (and particularly that Church which holds it together) will totally collapse. Mersenne's ultimate apologetic aim, Beaude thinks, is far less doctrinal than it is social. Mersenne fears the Deism of the *Quatrains* far less for the damage it will do to Christian dogma than for the dangers of its implications for social order.[144]

From the perspective of the *Quatrains*, this is precisely the issue. Christianity, according to this text, is ultimately built upon social control. The Christian position lies open to charges of *l'amour propre*.The virtuous actions of the "bigots," insists the author of the *Quatrains*, are never disinterested but are always inspired by the hope of some reward (or the fear of some punishment) in the life to come:

141. "Le Déiste selon Mersenne," pp. 203–4.

142. *L'impiété des Déistes,* 1, 678. Cited by Beaude, "Le Déiste selon Mersenne," p. 205.

143. "Le Déiste selon Mersenne," p. 206. Cf. *Pensées,* fragment 449.

144. Ibid., p. 207.

98
Le Bigot ignorant ne fait rien sans espoir
De quelque récompense, et s'il fuit quelque vice
Ce n'est pas qu'à bien faire il ait un bon vouloir
Mais c'est pour éviter du meffait le supplice.[145]

The ignorant bigot does nothing without the hope / Of some reward, and if he flees any vice / It's not that he truly has the will and intent to do good, / But rather that he wants to avoid punishment for doing ill.

The Deist critique of the "bigot's" love of God as based only upon self-interest should perhaps serve to remind us that the whole question of "l'Amour pur" would emerge with particular acrimony in the debate over Quietism much later in the century. Bossuet would tax Fénelon not only with "déisme" but with "stoïcisme."[146] Writing to Madame Guyon, Bossuet would insist that prayers of petition and those motivated by desire are sanctioned and indeed prescribed both by Scripture and by Tradition.[147] "L'assimilation de la mystique au déisme et au stoïcisme," notes the author of the entry on "Quiétisme" in the *Dictionnaire de spiritualité*, "deviendra un lieu commun à l'époque du quiétisme."[148] Though Nicole would attempt to rehabilitate self-interest as an incentive for loving God in *De la charité et de l'amour propre*, Port-Royal in general always remained highly suspicious both of mystical spirituality and of the whole doctrine of "l'Amour pur."

For the author of the *Quatrains*, the religion of the "bigot"—Christianity by clear implication—is a religion based upon fear. The doctrine of Divine Justice turns God into a monster:

99
Plein de trouble en son âme, il s'effraye de Dieu,
Ainsi que les enfans d'un monstre espouvantable,
Et tel l'imaginant, il le blasme en tout lieu
Sous ombre d'exalter sa justice ineffable.[149]

His soul full of turmoil, he is terrified of God / As children are of a horrible monster, / And imagining Him thus, he reproaches Him everywhere / Under the cover of exalting his ineffable justice.

145. Adam, *Les Libertins au XVIIe siècle,* p. 106.

146. See Jacques Le Brun, *La Spiritualité de Bossuet* (Paris: Klincksieck, 1972), pp. 653–54.

147. Ibid., p. 553.

148. *Dictionnaire de spiritualité* (Paris: Beauchesne, 1986), 12, p. 2829.

149. *Les Libertins au XVIIe siècle,* p. 106.

The errors which have crept into natural religion via Christianity blind the poor *bigot* to his own inner light and hold his soul captive to fear:

100
Aussy est le Bigot entre les ignorans
Seul ennemy juré de sa propre lumière,
Pour ne voir les erreurs enfantez par les ans
Dans lesquels il détient son âme prisonniére.[150]

Thus the bigot remains among the ignorant, / The single sworn enemy of his own light, / Unable to recognize the errors engendered by the years, / In which he holds his own soul captive.

The Deist, on the other hand, "agit tant seulement / Pour amour du bien mesme" ("acts only for the love of virtue itself"). For him, virtue is never "servile et mercenaire."[151] The Deist creed is simple:

102
. . .
Nous devons adorer une Cause première
Aymant nostre prochain en elle seulement
Sans luy faire dommage en aucune manière.

103
Ennemy conjuré de l'irréligion,
Il vit paisiblement avecque tout le monde,
Et seul observateur de la religion
Il adore l'Auteur de la terre et de l'onde.

104
Mesme tout simplement il ayme l'Eternel,
Et en luy ce qui est, ce qui vit et respire,
Envers tous les humains se monstrant estre tel
Que mutuellement il souhaite et désire.[152]

. . . / We ought to worship a First Cause / Loving our neighbor only in It / Without doing him harm in any way.

The sworn enemy of impiety, / [The Deist] lives in peace with all men, / The only true observer of Religion, / He worships the Author of the earth and the sea.

With great simplicity, he loves the Eternal One, / And in Him everything that is, that lives and breathes. / Toward all humankind he acts as / In turn, he wishes and desires [to be treated].

150. Ibid., p. 107.
151. Ibid., stanza 101.
152. Ibid., p. 107.

The author of the *Quatrains* concludes his poem by situating the Deist in relation to both the atheist and the "bigot." Both of the latter, he insists, do violence to Divinity: the atheist by ungratefully denying "L'Eternel et sa saincte police" ("the Eternal and his sacred governing of the universe"); the "bigot" by attributing to God an erroneous scheme of justice. Only the Deist practices a religion which is pure, reasonable, and devoid of self-interest:

106
Ainsy l'Athée seul nie la Divinité.
Le Bigot, pirement, meilleur que Dieu s'estime;
Le Déiste entre tous l'adore en vérité,
Attendant qu'il parvienne où son but se termine.[153]

Thus the Atheist alone denies Divinity. / The Bigot, even worse, esteems himself better than God; / The Deist alone worships Him in truth, / While awaiting his arrival where his goal comes to an end.

A. Adam observes that the *Quatrains* contain not a trace of the naturalism of the Italian tradition.[154] And only in stanzas 52–53, we should note, is there a hint of that kind of historical critique of religion which would appear in Naudé and La Mothe le Vayer. The poem over and over again contrasts the God of the philosophers, the essence of Supreme Wisdom and Infinite Reason, with the anthropomorphic God of the Judeo-Christian tradition. Yet, interestingly enough, it contains but a single critique of the doctrines of the Incarnation and Redemption:

27
Si à l'Estre infiny rien ne peut estre osté
Ny soustrait du ressort de sa toute-puissance,
Comment a-t-il perdu et depuis racheté
Ce qui jamais ne fut qu'à sa divine essence?[155]

If nothing can be taken from the infinite Being, / Nor subtracted from the domain of his omnipotence, / How could he possibly have lost and then redeemed / That which was never anything but part of his divine essence?

Jesus the Sage is perhaps indirectly evoked by the fact that the Deist creed contains the Golden Rule: "Envers tous les humains se monstrant estre tel / Que mutuellement il souhaite et désire."[156] And the poet in-

153. Ibid., p. 108.
154. Ibid., p. 89.
155. Ibid., p. 94.
156. Ibid., p. 107, Stanza 104.

vokes, with apparent sincerity, God's command "d'aymer nos ennemis."[157] Yet nowhere in the poem is there anything like an elaboration of an anti-Christology or an explicit anti-Trinitarianism. Pintard sees the absence of any direct reference to Christ, to the Incarnation, or to the Redemption as intentional: "La religion simplifiée que définissaient les Déistes tendait à ruiner le christianisme en passant à côté du Christ lui-même."[158] ("The simplified religion that the Deists were defining . . . tended to ruin Christianity by completely bypassing Christ himself").

Curiously enough, Pascal and the author of the *Quatrains* are in significant agreement on a number of points. Both deny that the Deist position can in any way be viewed as a transitional stage on the way to revealed religion. Both reject the great libertine doctrine of the eternity of the world.[159] And whereas Pascal says that Deism is almost as far removed from Christianity as atheism, the author of the *Quatrains* insists that both atheism and Christianity are equally far removed from the purity of Deism. Indeed, for him, the "bigot" is quite clearly morally inferior ("pirement," v. 106) to the atheist since his beliefs and actions are motivated by *l'amour-propre*. Pascal says that those who fall into Deism because they seek God outside Christ "s'arrêtent dans la nature" ("go no further than nature") (449). The *Quatrains* do evoke "l'Auteur de la terre et de l'onde" ("the Author of the earth and the sea") but seem relatively impoverished as a great ode to Nature when compared to the writings of the great eighteenth-century French or English Deists. The God of the *Quatrains* is hardly experienced through a feeling of awe at the wonders of the universe. Rather, an immutable eternal essence in whom to know and to will are one and the same thing: He is experienced via the intellect, via reason. In short, He is the God of Stoic philosophy.

Perhaps the single most interesting thing about the *Quatrains du Déiste* is that the author of the poem spends the great majority of his time attacking those very ideas which Jansenius and Saint-Cyran were attempting to renew and which Pascal would later set at the heart of his Apology. The poet is horrified by any version of the traditional Christian

157. Ibid., p. 92, Stanza 11.

158. *Le Libertinage érudit* . . ., p. 49.

159. The *Quatrains* profess a belief in a Creator-Deity: Stanza 103: "*L'auteur* de la terre et de l'onde" ("the author of the earth and the sea"); Stanza 34: "Dieu estant un pur acte en son éternité / Qui *précède* en tout sens les choses temporelles" ("God being pure act in his eternity / Who precedes all temporal things in every sense"); Stanza 45: "Un mesme Dieu est *père* de nous tous" ("the same God is father of us all"); Stanza 102: "Nous devons adorer *une Cause première*" ("We ought to worship a First Cause") (italics mine).

theodicy. Better to deny Divinity completely, he thinks, than to imagine a God capable of punishing or torturing his creatures:

58
Pourroit-il de nos maux sa justice exalter
Et de nostre misère enrichir son essence?
Sçauroit-on faire pis que de luy adapter
L'office de bourreau pour vanger nos offenses?

59
Il n'est pas moins mauvais de nier simplement
Une Divinité, que de la croire telle
Qu'elle tire de l'heur et du contentement
A nous faire souffrir une peine immortelle.[160]

Could He use our misfortunes to exalt His justice / Or our wretchedness to enrich His essence? / How could we do worse than to assign Him / The role of hangman who avenges our crimes?

It would be less terrible simply to deny / A Divinity, than to believe Him capable / Of taking pleasure and finding happiness / In making us suffer unending punishment.

The author of the *Quatrains* views the Augustinian doctrine of predestination and election as particularly barbaric:

41
Si en soy l'Eternel voit tout présentement
Ce qui nous est futur, est-il imaginable
Qu'il nous ait défendu ce qu'infailliblement
Il sçait par son vouloir nous estre inévitable?

42
Nous peut-il commander de faire ce qu'il sçait
Que nous ne ferons point, ou par insuffisance
Retenir son vouloir sur le bien ou mal fait
Venant de nostre choix et pure contingence?

43
Bref, si le mesme Dieu sçait actuellement
Toute chose en soy-mesme, avec quelle ignorance
Le croirons-nous autheur d'une loy qui dément
Les effects descoulans de sa préconnoissance.[161]

160. *Quatrains du Déiste,* Stanzas 58–59. Cited by Adam, *Les Libertins,* p. 100.
161. Adam, *Les Libertins au XVIIe siècle,* p. 97.

If the Eternal One, in Himself, already now sees all / Which for us is the future, is it conceivable / That He would have forbidden us that which infallibly / He knows we will inevitably do at His command?

Can He command us to do that which He knows / That we will not do, or by what insufficiency / Does He withhold His will concerning the good or ill / Stemming from our choice or from sheer chance?

In short, if the same God knows at this very moment / Everything in His omniscience, are we not ignorant / To believe Him to be the author of a law which contradicts / The effects flowing from His foreknowledge?

In fragment 427, Pascal will qualify those who lack the desire for a life beyond this one as profoundly defective human beings. He will ultimately attribute this defect to the proposition that such persons must have been predestined to damnation:

Rien n'est si important à l'homme que son état, rien ne lui est si redoutable que l'éternité. Et ainsi, qu'il se trouvent des hommes indifférents à la perte de leur être et au péril d'une éternité de misères, cela n'est point naturel . . . C'est un enchantement incompréhensible, et un assoupissement surnaturel, qui marque une force toute-puissante qui le cause.

Nothing is so important to man as his state: nothing more fearful than eternity. Thus the fact there exist men who are indifferent to the loss of their being and to the peril of an eternity of wretchedness is against nature. . . . It is an incomprehensible spell, a supernatural torpor that points to an omnipotent power as its cause. (427)

The author of the *Quatrains* has a view on this matter which could not be more different from that of Pascal. For him, the whole notion of predestination and election is a smokescreen devised to cope with human fear of a monster-God. Whereas Pascal cannot conceive of anyone's not harboring a hope for a life beyond this one, the author of the *Quatrains* sees any such hope as unbelievably puerile. More than that, the doctrine of the immortality of the soul is a blasphemy. Who are we to criticize God for having failed to make us immortal according to some human standard? The ultimate theodicy of the *Quatrains* resides in the proposition that we have no right to claim immortality in the first place:

77

Et quand bien Dieu voudroit qu'à l'ancien chaos
Nous fussions tous réduits, n'est-ce pas un blasphème
De le vouloir taxer de nous mettre au repos
Où nous estions sans naistre en ce principe mesme?[162]

162. Ibid., p. 103.

> And when God wills that to the former chaos / We all be reduced, is it not a blasphemy / To proceed to tax Him for putting us in that state of rest / In which we were in the beginning before being born?

It would be interesting to know whether Pascal had any knowledge of the Deist critique of the Christian theodicy. But his rabid attack on "déisme" in fragment 449 is based upon a far simpler principle. The God of the philosophers is not the God incarnate in Jesus Christ. This principle, already enunciated in the personal revelation known as the *Mémorial*,

> Dieu d'Abraham, Dieu d'Isaac, Dieu de Jacob, non des philosophes et des savants

> God of Abraham, God of Isaac, God of Jacob, not of philosophers and scholars (913)

reemerges with particular force in fragment 449. Any knowledge, any proof of God's existence (or of the immortality of the soul) is devoid of value without knowledge of the doctrine of the Incarnation:

> Cette connaissance, sans Jésus-Christ, est inutile et stérile. Quand un homme serait persuadé que les proportions des nombres sont des vérités immatérielles, éternelles et dépendantes d'une première vérité en qui elles subsistent, *et qu'on appelle Dieu*, je ne le trouverais pas beaucoup avancé pour son salut.
>
> Le Dieu des chrétiens ne consiste pas en un Dieu simplement auteur des vérités géométriques et de l'ordre des éléments; c'est la part des païens et des épicuriens. . . .

> Such knowledge, without Christ, is useless and sterile. Even if someone were convinced that the proportions between numbers are immaterial, eternal truths, depending on a first truth in which they subsist, *called God*, I should not consider that he had made much progress toward his salvation.
>
> The Christian's God does not consist merely of a God who is the author of mathematical truths and the order of the elements. That is the portion of the pagans and the Epicureans. . . . (449, italics mine)

In this context, I think we must read "païens" ("pagans") as a reference to the pre-Christian philosophers of antiquity, of whom Pascal gives the Epicureans as an example. These philosophers could only posit the existence of an abstract mathematical "première vérité" ("first truth") because they were ignorant of God's Revelation of Himself: first to Moses ("le Dieu d'Abraham, le Dieu d'Isaac, le Dieu de Jacob"[163]) and then to the

163. In Exodus 3:6, where God first reveals Himself to Moses.

entire world in the Incarnate Person of Jesus Christ. Moreover, the pagan philosophers remained ignorant of another key Christian doctrine, that of Original Sin. The Christian God, fragment 449 goes on to stipulate, makes those who seek Him "sentir intérieurement leur misère" ("inwardly aware of their wretchedness"). The pre-Christian pagan philosophers, notes Pascal's mentor Le Maistre de Sacy, perceived the effects of the Fall within Nature. But they were at a loss to explain why this should have been so. Sacy cites St. Augustine: *"Rem viderunt, causam nescierunt."*[164]

The *déistes* described in the *Quatrains* are modern-day followers of the pagan philosophers of pre-Christian antiquity. Not only do they attempt to find God "hors de Jésus-Christ" ("apart from Christ"). They violently reject Original Sin and its terrible consequences for humanity. As Pascal sees it, their ignorance is far less excusable than that of their pagan masters. The latter could have had no knowledge either of the Incarnation or of the Fall. The modern *déistes,* on the other hand, reject a Revelation which is immediately available to them. It is this distinction, implicit in fragment 449, which can be taken to account for Pascal's extreme harshness on the subject of the modern-day Deists.

Interestingly enough, fragment 449 stands in direct conflict with the famous "wager" passage (418), which so many modern interpreters have taken as the heart of Pascal's apologetics. Moreover, fragment 449 is in some ways an indirect attack on Descartes' proofs of the existence of God. In a *propos* attributed to Pascal by Marguerite Périer (Lafuma 1001), Pascal comes very close to taxing Descartes with outright Deism:

> Je ne puis pardonner à Descartes: il voudrait bien, dans toute la philosophie, se pouvoir passer de Dieu; mais il n'a pu s'empêcher de lui donner une chiquenaude pour mettre le monde en mouvement; après cela, il n'a plus que faire de Dieu.
>
> I cannot forgive Descartes: in his whole philosophy he would like to do without God; but he could not help allowing him a flick of the fingers to set the world in motion; after that he had no more use for God. (1001)

From the perspective of fragment 449, neither the unbeliever at the end of the "wager" fragment nor the reader who accepts Descartes' proofs of the existence of God in the *Méditations* has made much progress toward his personal salvation. Nowhere in either of these texts is there mention either of the Incarnation or of the Fall. Ultimately, Pascal rejects any proof

164. *La Genèse,* Préface, Seconde Partie, partie ii. Cf. *Pensées,* fragment 206: "Rem viderunt, causam non viderunt" ("They saw the effect but not the cause").

of God which is based entirely upon defective human reason. It is of great significance that he appends two key fragments to the text of the "wager" passage. The first rejects human reason as a route to full knowledge of God: "C'est le coeur qui sent Dieu et non la raison" ("It is the heart which perceives God and not reason") (424). The second reminds the inquirer, who has read the pagan philosophers and perhaps flirted with the new Deist view of Divinity, that only Christianity has ever explained the reasons for human "misère" in the doctrine of Original Sin: "Nulle religion que la nôtre n'a enseigné que l'homme naît en péché, *nulle secte de philosophes* ne l'a dit, nulle n'a donc dit vrai" ("No religion except our own has taught that man is born sinful, *no philosophical sect* has said so, so none has told the truth") (421, italics mine).

The *Quatrains du Déiste* may not give us an exact portrait of those *déistes* whom Pascal assails in fragment 449. But that text, devoted as it is to a refutation of the Augustinian theodicy built around the doctrine of Original Sin, very much helps us to understand the violence with which Pascal attacks Deism in that fragment. Christianity, Pascal insists, finds Deism almost as abhorrent as it does atheism itself. From Pascal's perspective, this is so not just because the Deists reject the Incarnation. It is also because they attempt to subvert that other great doctrine, Original Sin, without which (at least in neo-Augustinian theology) the doctrine of the Incarnation is stripped of its true meaning. In Pascal's definition of Christianity, the doctrine of the Fall is always paired with that of the Incarnation. "La foi chrétienne ne va presque qu'à établir ces deux choses: la corruption de la nature et la Rédemption de Jésus-Christ" ("The Christian faith consists almost wholly in establishing these two things: the corruption of nature and the redemption of Christ") (427). "Toute la foi consiste en Jésus-Christ et en Adam" ("The whole of faith consists of Jesus Christ and Adam") (226).

"La Religion à la mode": The Popularization of Deist Ideas

The Deist doctrines set forth in the *Quatrains* seem to have remained the creed of an isolated elite in the 1620s. Within twenty or thirty years, however, these ideas seem to have considerably penetrated the sphere of worldly, but ostensibly still-practicing Christians. François de Grenaille, in his *La Mode ou charactère de la religion . . .* (1642), complains that all too many worldly Christians "veulent corriger les articles de nostre Foy, et en faire de nouveaux au lieu des anciens" ("want to correct the ancient articles of our Faith and make of them new ones"). Some reject the doctrine of the Trinity on grounds of "la bienséance." Some go even further, adopting a doctrine of universal salvation and a kind of neo-Pelagianism:

> D'autres s'imaginent encore que chacun se peut sauver dans sa Religion, pourvu qu'il adore un premier Estre, et que l'Auteur du monde ne nous ayant pas faicts pour nous perdre, nous ne sçaurions manquer à nous sauver infailliblement. Qu'au reste ce qu'on appelle commandements de Dieu n'est qu'un frein que les hommes ont voulu donner au peuple, et que rien de ce qui plaist à la nature ne sçauroit estre illicité.[165]

> Others imagine that each man can save himself in his own religion, provided that he worships a Supreme Being. They also imagine that the Author of the world, not having made us only to damn us, we could not possibly fail to save ourselves. As for the rest, they think that what are called the commandments of God are only a restraint which men have wished to put on the masses and that nothing which pleases Nature could possibly be illicit.

In this popularization of Deist ideas, the austere tenets of the *Quatrains*, which reject the whole notion of salvation and an afterlife, have gotten all mixed up with other libertine ideas: the idea that "natural" actions could hardly be immoral and the function of religious law as a "brake" on the masses. But many themes central to the *Quatrains* remain: anti-Trinitarianism, the notion that God's goodness is incompatible with the idea of divine punishment, an extreme critique of Augustinian ideas concerning Original Sin. This amalgam of Deism, libertine ideas, and neo-Pelagianism came to form a "religion à la mode" which may have been far more widespread than students of the Classical period have ever suspected. And it is this very accommodating kind of religion which will so horrify Pascal when he comes to write the *Apology*.

In his *Contre-Mode* (1642), Fitelieu laments that the "religion à la mode" is really a kind of Deistic Christianity. Its adherents "établissent véritablement une Divinité qu'ils adorent" ("truly establish a Divinity whom they worship") but choose to ignore the harder doctrines of the Redemption and Divine Justice. To this deistic theology, they append an indiffer-

165. François de Grenaille, *La Mode, ou Charactère de la religion. De la vie. De la conversation. De la solitude. Des complimens. Des habits et du style du temps* (Paris: N. Gassé, 1642), pp. 186–187. Cited by L. G. de Donville, *Le Libertin des origines à 1665*, pp. 394–95.

ence in religious matters which lets them "vivre à la mode," following the manners and opinions of those circles they happen to frequent:

> [Ils] prennent une liberté de vivre en s'acomodant au temps. Ils veulent qu'on les apele chrestiens sans en faire les actions, et pour passer la vie le plus doucement qu'il se peut ils se chargent autant de religions comme ils fréquentent des persones qu'ils pratiquent. Ils sont Athées avec ceux qui font une vie si miserable, Huguenots parmi les prétendus reformés, moines parmys les Religieux, Spirituels conversans avec ceux de qui la vie sert à l'esprit, et devots selon le temps et l'occasion qui leur en est.[166]

> They take the liberty of living in a way in which they tailor their ideas to suit the times. They want to be called Christians without acting like them. In order to spend life as pleasantly as possible, they take on as many religions as do those whom they frequent. They are atheists with those who lead such a wretched life, Protestants among the so-called "reformed," monks among religious, witty when they converse with those whose life is given over to wit, and even fervently devout when circumstances seem to warrant it.

These adaptable Christians, who have rejected every element of the traditional Christian doctrine of Judgment while retaining a vaguely Deist God, do not sound all that different from a group we shall meet in fragment 427 and call the "pseudo-*libertins*."[167] "Ce sont des gens qui ont ouï dire que les belles manières du monde consistent à faire l'emporté. C'est ce qu'ils appellent avoir secoué le joug et qu'ils essaient d'imiter" ("They are people who have heard it is good to display such extravagance. This is what they call shaking off the yoke, and what they are trying to imitate"). One of these will announce that he no longer believes "qu'il y ait un Dieu qui veille sur ses actions" ("that there is a God watching over his actions"). Others hold that the soul "n'est qu'un peu de vent et de fumée" ("is no more than a bit of wind or smoke").

This group, evoked by Pascal in fragment 427, have adopted a potpourri of libertine ideas from diverse sources. From Deist doctrine, they have culled the notion of a God who does not concern himself with particular human actions. From the materialists and their popularizers, they have adopted the idea of the mortality of the soul. These people consider themselves neither atheists nor *libertins*, but rather practitioners of a new, reasonable, and more believable version of Christianity. This is why they

166. Fitelieu, *La Contre-Mode* (Paris, 1642), p. 188. Cited by de Donville, *Le Libertin des origines à 1665*, pp. 393–94.

167. See Chapter IV, The Pseudo-*libertins*.

go on in such a light-hearted fashion. But Pascal is not amused. He sees through their innovations and is profoundly offended by this new version of Christianity which is so *à la mode*:

> Prétendent-ils nous avoir bien réjoui, de nous dire qu'ils tiennent que notre âme n'est qu'un peu de vent et de fumée, et encore de nous le dire d'un ton de voix fier et content? Est-ce donc une chose à dire gaiement? et n'est-ce pas une chose à dire tristement, au contraire, comme la chose du monde la plus triste?
>
> Do they think that they have given us great pleasure by telling us that they hold our soul to be no more than wind or smoke, and saying it moreover in tones of pride and satisfaction? Is this then something to be said gaily? Is it not on the contrary something to be said sadly, as being the saddest thing in the world? (427)

Pascal and the *Libertins érudits*: A Reassessment

In his landmark contribution to the volume *Pascal présent* (1962), René Pintard undertook a complete reassessment of Pascal's relationship to scholarly disbelief. He concluded that Pascal's portraits of the unbelievers bear few traces indeed of that whole challenge to Christian belief constituted by *le libertinage érudit* in the first half of the seventeenth century. Not once, he observes, does Pascal mention the name of a single of those Italian rationalists who so influenced the French *érudits*. Nor does he find any clear allusion to those "paradoxes nouveaux" which the scholarly *libertins* used to question Christian dogma. Pascal's versions of Epicureanism and skepticism, he insists, bear little resemblance to the renewal of those philosophies which was taking place just prior to the writing of the *Pensées*:

> Tout à côté de Pascal . . . Gassendi est en train de restaurer (en le purifiant) l'épicurisme . . . rien cependant n'indique, dans les *Pensées*, que Pascal ait cessé de voir seulement, dans l'épicurisme, l'attitude des débauchés vulgaires ou une secte antique définitivement déconsidérée. Tout près de Pascal, de même, le scepticisme se renouvelle. La Mothe le Vayer . . . prolonge, aggrave les analyses de Montaigne; il promène au coeur même du sanctuaire la lampe tremblotante du doute. . . . Point d'autre scepticisme, pour le Pascal de l'apologie, que celui des académiciens et des pyrrhoniens de l'antiquité ou que celui de leur disciple Montaigne. . . .
>
> Il me paraît donc difficile de découvrir dans les *Pensées*, ou cette adaptation constante aux curiosités des philosophes libertins que beaucoup de critiques y recon-

naissent, ou cette ampleur et cette minutie d'information que laissaient supposer le témoignage de Mme Périer et celui, plus sujet à caution, du Père Beurrier.[168]

Right next to Pascal . . . Gassendi was in the process of restoring a purified Epicureanism . . . nevertheless, nothing in the *Pensées* indicates that Pascal ever ceased to see in Epicureanism anything other than the attitude of the vulgar *débauchés* or an ancient and long-since discredited sect. Likewise, right within Pascal's intellectual world, skepticism was in a process of renewal. La Mothe le Vayer . . . was extending and rendering more seditious the analyses of Montaigne. He strolled right into the heart of the holy of holies, his flickering light of doubt in hand. . . . No other skepticism, for the Pascal of the Apology, than that of the Academicians and Pyrrhonists of antiquity or of their disciple Montaigne. . . .

It seems to me difficult to uncover in the *Pensées*, that constant adaptation to the innovations of the libertine philosophers which many critics think they recognize in that text, or the extent of detailed information implied by the accounts of Mme Périer or by that—more subject to caution—of Père Beurrier.

Pintard's conclusions may seem a bit disconcerting for those of us who would like to get a better feel for the religious and philosophical opinions of Pascal's potential interlocutors in the *Apology*! The *Pensées* are not utterly devoid of every trace of that disbelief which is characteristic of Pascal's own time. But precise references to specific persons or ideas are few indeed. In fact, I have only been able to discern four. We have already mentioned Pascal's allusion (in fragment 410) to the notorious *libertin* Jacques Des Barreaux.[169] Likewise, we have noted that fragment 161 ("il n'est point clair que l'âme soit matérielle") may evoke the libertine reanimation of a principle theme inherited from Italian neo-Epicureanism.[170] A third reference, in fragment 575, to the "pré-Adamites" and the theories of Isaac de La Peyrère seems to me to merit additional consideration. I will devote Chapter II, "Men Before Adam: Isaac de La Peyrère and the Discovery of Pre-Biblical Time," to a detailed examination of the way in which La Peyrère's theories potentially threaten Pascal's historical demonstrations of the truth of Christianity. A fourth reference, to the "impies" evoked in fragment 150, very well may contain an indirect reference to the theories of La Mothe le Vayer.[171] However, before considering this possibility, something more needs to be said about the larger subject of Pascal and *le libertinage érudit*.

168. René Pintard, "Pascal et les libertins" in *Pascal présent* (Clermond Ferrand: G. de Bussac, 1962), pp. 113–16.

169. See Chapter I, *Le Libertinage érudit*.

170. Ibid.

171. See Chapter III, Fragment 822 and Neo-Augustinian Theology.

René Pintard knows a good deal more about the scholarly libertine tradition in France prior to the writing of the *Pensées* than perhaps anyone else ever will. Does his conclusion that Pascal either does not know or deliberately ignores the whole tradition of *le libertinage érudit* mean that our brief survey of the subject in this chapter has been a waste of time? I think not. The question of Pascal's direct sources and specific allusions is an important one. So too are the identity and mind-set of Pascal's interlocutor in the Apology. However, if we are to appreciate the possible libertine prejudices to which Pascal's potential interlocutors may have been exposed, we simply must evoke the major objections to Christian dogma which were part of the public intellectual domain in the Paris of the 1640s and 1650s. Moreover, the modern reader of the *Pensées* will want to be able to imagine how the finished *Apology* might have struck those more aggressive freethinkers to whom Pascal will not necessarily direct his arguments.[172]

Some of the libertine attacks on Christian dogma which we have examined represent a greater challenge to Pascal's apologetic itinerary than others. The denial of the immortality of the soul, in and of itself, will not directly run counter to Pascal's major arguments in the *Pensées*. In fragment 449, he announces that his defense of Christianity will not be based upon metaphysical arguments designed to prove "par des raisons naturelles . . . l'immortalité de l'âme" ("by reasons from nature . . . the immortality of the soul"). But, on the other hand, the freethinker's indifference to the fate of his soul (see fragment 427) may well have been a product of hearing or reading the arguments of the scholarly libertines concerning the material nature of the soul.

The traditional libertine dichotomy between an elite—privy to philosophical truth—and the superstitious masses certainly contradicts Pascal's instinctive trust in the simple faith of "des personnes simples" (380, 94). But more dangerous still are those many libertine doctrines which call into question the Fall and Original Sin, those great Augustinian doctrines upon which Pascal will build his entire *Apology*. The Deist attack upon predestination and the enduring libertine doctrine, inherited from Italian naturalism (and ultimately from Aristotle's medieval commentators) of the eternity of the world, certainly do not predispose Pascal's potential readers to an easy acceptance of his exposition of the meaning and consequences of the Genesis story.

172. See Chapter V, The Role of Argument in the Apology: The Hardened Skeptics Reconsidered.

Pascal's ultimate defense of Christianity will consist of a demonstration of the historicity of sacred history as set forth in the two Testaments. How potentially dangerous, therefore, are the multiple libertine attacks on the truth and accuracy of the Bible.[173] And how very dangerous indeed is that emerging science of the comparative study of religions found in the works of La Mothe le Vayer. Fragment 150 may very well indicate that Pascal was perfectly aware of what the comparative religionists of his own time were up to. A distinguishing feature of the innovations of the *libres esprits* in seventeenth-century France was the way in which these thinkers had followed in Montaigne's footsteps, poring through the *mémoires* of missionaries to the Orient and the New World in order to document the thesis that little is unique to the rites and ceremonies of the Christian tradition. Those "impies" whom Pascal so severely censures in fragment 150 voice an objection to Christian Revelation which could come directly from the *Parallèles historiques* of La Mothe le Vayer:

> "Ne voyons-nous pas," disent-ils, "mourir et vivre les bêtes comme les hommes, et les Turcs comme les chrétiens: ils ont leurs cérémonies, leurs prophètes, leurs docteurs, leurs saints, leurs religieux comme nous, etc."[174]

> "Do we not see," they say, "animals live and die like men, Turks like Christians? They have their ceremonies, their prophets, their doctors, their saints, their religious like us, etc." (150)

In his *Parallèles historiques*, Le Vayer professes to subscribe to the traditional view that the pagan religions are but "singeries" by which Satan has sought to mock Christianity. The examples he produces, however, all point to the conclusion that very little indeed is peculiar to the rites of the Christian tradition. Circumcision, far from being unique to the Jews, is found "en usage dans beaucoup de provinces de l'Amérique" ("to be practiced in many provinces of America"). Nor is the monastic tradition found only in the Christian tradition. "Les Chinois à l'autre bout de la terre ont des personnes . . . consacrées au culte de leurs Pagodes, et l'on y voit des

173. See my discussion of the libertine attacks on the Bible in *L'Ecriture et le Reste: The "Pensées" of Pascal in the Exegetical Tradition of Port-Royal*, pp. 56–61.

174. The "impies," P. Sellier reminds me, could very well have found this argument in Montaigne. Cf., *Essais*, 2, 12: "La manière de naître, d'engendrer, nourrir, agir, mouvoir, *vivre et mourir des bêtes*, étant si voisine de la nôtre. . . ." However, the fact that Pascal specifically uses the word *impies*, a term far stronger than any he ever taxes Montaigne with, makes me think that he is referring specifically to a more contemporary scholarly *libertin* such as La Mothe le Vayer. Montaigne's observations, of course, may very well have oriented Le Vayer's research in this direction.

monastères . . . peu différents . . . de ceux du Christianisme" ("The Chinese at the other end of the earth have persons . . . ordained to the cult of their pagodas, and one sees there monasteries . . . very little different . . . from those of Christianity"). Pilgrimages, confession, and baptism are practiced in India, and the cult of relics has numerous parallels in Buddhism and Islam.[175]

Given his theological orientation, we should hardly expect Pascal to take such objections to the uniqueness of the Christian Revelation seriously. Pascal's unwillingness to admit the validity of evidence drawn from the pagan traditions reflects a constant theme in the writings of the theologians of Port-Royal. Evidence from outside the Christian Revelation is always subject to perversion and distortion by demonic forces. "Je vois dans l'Ecriture," Le Maistre de Sacy tells his secretary, Nicolas Fontaine, "que le feu qui ne venait point du sanctuaire était profane et étranger quoiqu'il pût être plus clair et plus beau que celui du sanctuaire"[176] ("I see in Scripture that the fire which did not come from the sanctuary was profane and alien even though it might have been brighter and more beautiful that the fire of the sanctuary").

Pascal's response to the objections to Christianity raised by the "impies" in fragment 150 is by no means a scholarly one. Rather, as Jean Mesnard points out, the apologist neutralizes such objections by mentioning them only in passing and by then dismissing them altogether: "L'objection est en général si sommairement esquissée que toute trace d'élaboration érudite en disparaît"[177] ("The objection is in general so summarily sketched that every trace of scholarly elaboration disappears from it"). Trying to refute such scholarly objections to the uniqueness of the Christian Revelation would run directly counter to Pascal's entire apologetic strategy, embroiling him in scholarly arguments and putting him on the defensive. It would also contradict his theological perspective. Scripture, according to Pascal, teaches that God allows error and contradiction to exist in the world in order to blind those who were not meant to see. "On n'entend rien aux ouvrages de Dieu si on ne prend pour principe qu'il a voulu aveugler les uns et éclairer les autres" ("We can understand nothing of God's works unless we accept the principle that he wished to blind some and enlighten others") (232).

175. *Oeuvres de la Mothe le Vayer* (Dresden: M. Groell, 1758), 7, pp. 287–97.

176. Nicolas Fontaine, *Mémoires pour servir à l'histoire de Port-Royal* (Utrecht, 1736), 2, pp. 510–11.

177. Mesnard, *Les Pensées de Pascal,* p. 122.

To those "impies" who argue that every religion has its ceremonies, prophets, and saints, Pascal can only reply: "Cela est-il contraire à l'Ecriture? ne dit-elle pas tout cela?" ("Is that contrary to Scripture? Does it not say all that?") (150).[178] Pascal always seems particularly inflexible in the face of those who intellectually question the Christian mysteries. The mere fact of taking such contradictions seriously strikes him as a potential sign of *aveuglement* and as yet another confirmation of the doctrine of *Deus absconditus*. At times, his impatience flares to the point of invective: "Que je hais ces sottises de ne pas croire l'Eucharistie, etc. Si l'Evangile est vrai, si J.-C. est Dieu, quelle difficulté y a(-t-)il là?" ("How I hate such foolishness as not believing in the Eucharist, etc. If the Gospel is true, if Jesus Christ is God, where is the difficulty?") (168).

Jean Mesnard reaches the conclusion that Pascal's intended audience for the *Apology* anticipated by the *Pensées* could not possibly have been those *libertins érudits* whose objections to Christianity he so summarily dismisses in fragment 150:

> La désinvolture relative avec laquelle l'auteur des *Pensées* traite les objections formulées par le "libertinage érudit" et le peu de cas qu'il fait des exigences critiques qui s'y rattachaient peuvent s'expliquer de plusieurs manières. Manque d'information? Peut-être, ou plutôt manque de rapports suivis avec les représentants de ce milieu. Raisons de méthode surtout. Réfuter une à une des objections de ce type serait tomber dans un véritable piège. Ce serait accorder à la raison une confiance qu'il suffit de lui refuser pour ébranler tout dogmatisme antichrétien. Ce serait adopter une attitude défensive, alors qu'il s'agit d'apporter des preuves positives. Ce serait faire de la vérité religieuse une somme de petites vérités, au lieu de les faire toutes dépendre d'une vérité fondamentale, inscrite dans l'Evangile et incarnée en Jésus-Christ.[179]

The relative offhandedness with which the author of the *Pensées* treats the objections formulated by *le libertinage érudit* and his almost complete disregard for the attendant critical claims might be explained in several ways. A lack of information? Perhaps. Or rather, a lack of sustained contacts with representatives of this milieu. The explanation relative to Pascal's methodology is particularly important. To refute objections of this type one by one would mean falling into a real trap. It would mean giving reason a priority which Pascal intends to refuse to give to it in order to unsettle every anti-Christian dogmatism. It would mean adopting a defensive posture, when his strategy is to produce positive proofs. It would make of religious truth a compendium of smaller truths, instead of making them all

178. For further discussion of this fragment, see Chapter III, Fragment 822 and Neo-Augustinian Theology, and Chapter V, Pascal's Categories of Disbelief.

179. *Les Pensées de Pascal*, p. 124.

dependent upon a fundamental truth, inscribed in the Gospel and incarnate in Jesus Christ.

L'Honnête Homme

Having dismissed the argument that the *Apology* was to be addressed primarily to scholarly disbelief, Jean Mesnard invokes another possibility. Perhaps, when formulating the apologetic strategy which governs the *Pensées*, Pascal had in mind a completely different category of unbeliever, "des champions de l'honnêteté."[180] Pascal knew two theorists of *l'honnêteté* via his friendship with the Duc de Roannez: the Chevalier de Méré (1604–84) and Damien Mitton (1618–90). Méré, characterized by Professor Mesnard as a "joueur, épicurien, libertin"[181] ("gambler, Epicurean, freethinker"), is never mentioned in the *Pensées* by name. Evidence suggests, however, that it was Méré who set Pascal to work on his theory of probability as a result of their conversations about gambling.[182] Mitton, on the other hand, is mentioned by name three times in the course of the *Pensées*.[183]

The first time, chronologically speaking, that Pascal evokes Mitton's name seems particularly significant. In an early dossier on miracles which predates the writing of most of the Apology, Pascal sets down the following note: "Reprocher à Miton [sic] de ne point se remuer quand Dieu le reprochera" ("Reproach Mitton for remaining unmoved at God's reproaches") (853). Anthony Pugh assigns the unit (série xxxii) in which this fragment figures to the winter of 1656–57.[184] This suggests that Pascal, well

180. Ibid.

181. Ibid., p. 125.

182. Lafuma, ed., *Pascal: Oeuvres complètes,* p. 658. For a detailed analysis of the precise problem put to Pascal by Méré, see Laurent Thirouin, *Le Hasard et les règles: Le modèle du jeu dans la pensée de Pascal* (Paris: Vrin, 1991), Chapter VI ("La Règle des partis"), pp. 107–29. The letter in which Pascal recounts his conversation with Méré to M. de Fermat (July 29, 1654) can be found in *Pascal, Oeuvres complètes,* éd. Jean Mesnard (Paris: Desclée de Brouwer, 1970), 2, p. 1137: "J'admire bien davantage la méthode des parties que celle des dés. J'avais vu plusieurs personnes trouver celle des dés, comme M. le Chevalier de Méré, qui est celui qui m'a proposé ces questions. . . ." See also Edmond Chamaillard, *Le Chevalier de Méré* (Paris: Niort, 1921), pp. 79–83, and Jean-Pierre Dens, "Le Chevalier de Méré et la critique mondaine," *XVIIe siècle* 101 (1973): 41–50.

183. Fragments 853, 597, and 642.

184. Anthony Pugh, *The Composition of Pascal's Apologia* (Toronto: University of Toronto Press, 1984), p. 319.

in advance of his formal organization of the dossiers of 1658, had in mind the kind of man to whom he would address his arguments. In the first of the ordered dossiers of 1658, Pascal speaks of "une lettre d'exhortation à un ami pour le porter à chercher" ("a letter of exhortation to a friend to induce him to seek") (5). Nothing necessarily links the "ami" mentioned in fragment 5 with Mitton. However, the arguments developed in fragment 427,[185] which Philippe Sellier identifies with the "Lettre" proposed in fragment 5,[186] certainly seem tailored to the Mitton pictured in fragments 853, 597, and 642.

Modern commentators have characterized Damien Mitton in rather different ways. For Brunschvicg, he was a disillusioned, enigmatic skeptic ("détaché des plaisirs, détaché de la vanité") whose "clairvoyance" was as "impitoyable" as were his "correction" and his "politesse."[187] Boudhors, the editor of Méré's *Oeuvres complètes*, on the other hand, came to view Mitton as little more than a rich, vulgar bourgeois who rather pathetically tried to pass himself off as a patron of letters.[188] In his biography of Mitton, H. A. Grubbs presents him as an "average if unenthusiastic" Catholic layman of the time who had "some pretentions to being a moralist." After considering the evidence that Mitton participated in an orgy of meat eating during Holy Week organized by Des Barreaux,[189] Grubbs concludes that "Mitton's *libertinage* was probably no more than the sowing of a few youthful wild oats." None of Mitton's extant writings, Grubbs observes, "contain indications of an impiety similar to that of a Des Barreaux."[190]

Nothing suggests that Mitton was anything approaching an aggressive unbeliever at the time Pascal came to know him. After all, any such active disbelief would have been at odds with Mitton's own definition of the dispassionate character of the *honnête homme*:

> L'honnête homme . . . n'est point intéressé . . . sa conduite est toujours réglée, et jamais il ne vit dans le désordre. . . .

185. See Chapter IV, The Unbelievers in Fragment 427, and, The Tragedy of Disbelief.

186. Philippe Sellier, ed., *Pensées, édition établie d'après la Copie de référence de Gilberte Pascal* (Paris: Bordas, 1991), p. 474, n. 1.

187. Léon Brunschvicg, *Oeuvres de Blaise Pascal* (Paris: Hachette, Les Grands Ecrivains de la France, 1908–14), 1, lxxxi–lxxxii.

188. Charles Boudhors, *Oeuvres complètes du Chevalier de Méré* (Paris: Editions Roche, 1930), 1, lx–lxv.

189. On Des Barreaux, see Chapter I, *Le Libertinage érudit*. and n. 22.

190. H. A. Grubbs, *Damien Mitton (1618–1690), bourgeois honnête homme* (Paris: P.U.F., 1932), p. 24.

L'honnête homme fait grand cas de l'esprit, mais il fait encore plus de cas de la raison . . . il veut tout savoir et ne se pique de rien savoir; il prend garde à tout; il n'estime les choses que selon leur véritable valeur. . . .

L'honnête homme enfin ne dit et ne fait jamais rien qui ne soit agréable et raisonnable, et qui ne tende à faire que tous les hommes soient heureux.[191]

The *honnête homme* . . . is not motivated by self-interest . . . his conduct is always moderate, and he never lives a dissolute life. . . .

The *honnête homme* attaches great importance to the intellect, but he attaches even more importance to reason . . . he wants to know all things but does not get upset at knowing nothing; he is attentive to everything; he esteems things only according to their true worth. . . .

In the last analysis, the *honnête homme* says and does nothing which is not agreeable and reasonable, and which does not tend to the greater happiness of all men.

"Reprocher à Miton [*sic*] de ne point se remuer" ("Reproach Mitton for remaining unmoved") (853). Pascal reproaches Mitton for that very indifference and dispassionate character which the *honnête homme* is supposed to cultivate. Pascal's notation in fragment 853 recalls a similar criticism of Montaigne in the *Entretien avec M. de Sacy*. Characterizing Montaigne as a "pur pyrrhonien" ("pure skeptic"), Pascal condemns his conception of virtue as "naïve, familière, plaisante, enjouée, et pour ainsi dire folâtre . . . couchée mollement dans le sein de l'oisiveté tranquille"[192] ("naive, familiar, agreable, jovial, that's to say, playful . . . comfortably lying on the breast of tranquil indolence"). In fragment 680, entitled "Montaigne," Pascal faults Montaigne for inspiring "une nonchalance du salut, sans crainte et sans repentir" ("indifference regarding salvation, without fear or repentance"):

Son livre n'étant pas fait pour porter à la piété il n'y était pas obligé, mais on est toujours obligé de n'en point détourner. On peut excuser ses sentiments un peu libres et voluptueux en quelques rencontres de la vie . . . mais on ne peut excuser ses sentiments tout païens sur la mort. Car il faut renoncer à toute piété si on ne veut au moins mourir chrétiennement. Or il ne pense qu'à mourir lâchement et mollement par tout son livre.[193]

191. *Description de l'honnête homme* in *Oeuvres mêlées de Saint Evremond* (Paris: C. Barbin, 1680), 6, 1–12. Cited by Grubbs, pp. 56–57. Grubbs gives an interesting account of how Mitton's writings came to be published among the *Oeuvres mêlées* of Saint-Evremond, pp. 53–54.

192. *Entretien avec M. de Sacy* in Lafuma, ed., *Oeuvres complètes*, p. 296.

193. Anthony Pugh points out that the word *mollement*, which links the passage cited from the *Entretien avec M. de Sacy* to fragments 680 and 427, is borrowed by Pascal directly from the *Essais* (3:9). See *The Composition of Pascal's Apologia*, p. 520, n. 15.

As his book was not written to encourage piety, he was under no obligation to do so, but we are always under an obligation not to discourage it. One may excuse his somewhat free and licentious views on certain situations in life . . . but his completely pagan views on death are inexcusable; for all hope of piety must be abandoned if we are not at least willing to die as Christians. Now, throughout his book he thinks only of dying a death of cowardly ease. (680)

In fragment 427, Pascal will reproach the *honnête homme* for the same kind of indifference and nonchalance concerning death and salvation.[194]

In fragment 597, Pascal addresses Mitton directly. He dismisses the entire concept of *honnêteté* as an impotent remedy for the misfortunes of the human condition:

Le moi est haïssable. Vous, Miton [*sic*], le couvrez, vous ne l'ôtez point pour cela: vous êtes donc toujours haïssable.

The self is hateful. You cover it up, Mitton, but that does not mean that you take it away. So you are still hateful. (597)

Mitton replies:

Point. Car en agissant, comme nous faisons, obligeamment pour tout le monde, on n'a plus sujet de nous haïr.

Not so, because by being obliging to everyone as we are, we give them no more cause to hate us. (597)

In other words, Mitton argues, one can opt out of the discord implicit in human relationships by means of a social code which abolishes the reasons for such discord. This code of behavior is based less on the notion of Christian charity than on the idea of limiting one's ego in the defense of one's own self-interest. As Mitton writes in his *Pensées sur l'honnêteté*, *l'honnêteté* ultimately consists in the successful regulation of one's own *amour propre*:

Pour se rendre heureux avec moins de peine, pour l'être avec sûreté, sans craindre d'être troublé dans son bonheur, il faut faire en sorte que les autres le soient avec nous: car si l'on prétend songer seulement à soi, on trouve des oppositions continuelles, et quand nous ne voulons être heureux qu'à condition que les autres le soient en même temps, tous obstacles sont levés, et tout le monde nous prête la main. C'est ce ménagement de bonheur pour nous et pour les autres que l'on doit appeler l'honnêteté, qui n'est, à le bien prendre, que l'amour propre bien réglé.[195]

194. See Chapter IV, The Tragedy of Disbelief.

195. *Pensées sur l'honnêteté* in *Oeuvres mêlées de Saint-Evremond*, 6, pp. 3–4.

To make oneself happy with less trouble and to be so with surety, with no fear of being troubled in one's happiness, we must act so that others are as happy as we are: because if one attempts to think only of oneself, he faces constant opposition. But when we want to be happy only on the condition that everyone else is as well, all obstacles are lifted, and everyone gives us his hand. It is the management of happiness—for us and for others—that is correctly called *honnêteté*. In the last analysis, it amounts to a well-regulated self-interest.

Such a social code might work, Pascal replies, only if there were nothing more inherently wrong with the ego than the pain and displeasure it causes others. But such is not the case. The ego is unjust and corrupt in and of itself:

Cela est vrai, si on ne haïssait dans le moi que le déplaisir qui nous en revient.
Mais si je le hais parce qu'il est injuste qu'il se fasse centre de tout, je le haïrai toujours.

True enough if the only hateful thing about the self were the unpleasantness it caused us.
But if I hate it because it is unjust that it should make itself center of everything, I shall go on hating it. (597)

The editors of the "Edition de Port-Royal" of the *Pensées* felt obliged to add an explanatory note to this passage to the effect that the word *moi* "ne signifie que l'amour propre" ("signifies only self-love").[196] Pascal's subsequent dissection of the characteristics of the *moi*, however, suggests that he means to go beyond a simple analysis of *amour propre*:

En un mot le moi a deux qualités: il est injuste en soi, en ce qu'il se fait centre de tout; il est incommode aux autres, en ce qu'il les veut asservir, car chaque moi est l'ennemi et voudrait être le tyran de tous les autres. Vous en ôtez l'incommodité, mais non pas l'injustice.
Et ainsi vous ne le rendez pas aimable à ceux qui en haissent l'injustice. Vous ne le rendez aimable qu'aux injustes, qui n'y trouvent plus leur ennemi. Et ainsi vous demeurez injuste, et ne pouvez plaire qu'aux injustes.

In a word the self has two characteristics. It is unjust in itself for making itself center of everything: it is a nuisance to others in that it tries to subjugate them, for each self is the enemy of all the others and would like to tyrannize them. You take away the nuisance, but not the injustice.
And thus, you do not make it pleasing to those who hate it for being injust; you only make it pleasing to unjust people who no longer see it as their enemy. Thus you remain unjust and can only please unjust people. (597)

196. A. Gazier, ed., *Pensées de Pascal . . . Edition de Port-Royal,* p. 437.

In the neo–Augustinian theology of Port-Royal, the *injustes* are those whom God has not justified, that is, redeemed. The ego, the *moi*, is not simply an otherwise natural and good human faculty corrupted by Original Sin. It is inherently *injuste* because it is itself that "mauvais levain" (cf. fragment 278) which the Fall *added* to original human nature. In fragment 421,[197] Pascal develops even more fully the notion that human beings are born into the world as *injustes* because of the consequences of the Fall. The *moi* is the ultimate source of all disorder. No system of law, no social code, no philosophy of purely human origin is able to neutralize its pernicious effects:

> Il est faux que nous soyons dignes que les autres nous aiment. Il est injuste que nous le voulions. Si nous naissions raisonnables et indifférents, et connaissant nous et les autres nous ne donnerions point cette inclination à notre volonté. Nous naissons pourtant avec elle, nous naissons donc injustes.
>
> Car tout tend à soi: cela est contre tout ordre.
>
> Il faut tendre au général, et la pente vers soi est le commencement de tout désordre, en guerre, en police, en économie, dans le corps particulier de l'homme.
>
> La volonté est donc dépravée. Si les membres des communautés naturelles et civiles tendent au bien du corps, les communautés elle-mêmes doivent tendre à un autre corps plus général dont elles sont membres. L'on doit donc tendre au général. Nous naissons donc injustes et dépravés.

> It is untrue that we are worthy to be loved by others. It is unfair that we should want such a thing. If we were born reasonable and impartial, with a knowledge of ourselves and others, we should not give our wills this bias. However, we are born with it, and so we are born unfair.
>
> For everything tends toward itself: this is contrary to all order.
>
> The tendency should be toward the general, and the bias toward self is the beginning of all disorder, in war, politics, economics, in man's individual body.
>
> The will is therefore depraved. If the members of natural and civil communities tend to the good of the whole body, the communities themselves should tend toward another more general body of which they are members. We should therefore tend toward the general. Thus we are born unfair and depraved. (421)

In a fragment appended to fragment 421, Pascal argues that only the Christian religion teaches that human beings are born in sin. Indeed, this is the principal sign of Christianity's claim to be the one true Revelation. "Nulle religion que la nôtre n'a enseigné que l'homme naît en péché, nulle secte de philosophes ne l'a dit, nulle n'a donc dit vrai" ("No religion ex-

197. In Lafuma's edition, two fragments are assigned the number 421. The first of these is the next fragment cited.

cept our own has taught that man is born sinful, no philosophical sect has said so, so none has told the truth") (421). However, in dossier XX, "Rabbinage," we find Pascal seeking to document a "tradition ample du péché originel selon les Juifs" ("ample tradition of original sin according to the Jews"). In fragment 278, he cites two rabbinical authorities from the Talmud:

> R. Moyse Haddarschan. Ce mauvais levain est mis dans l'homme dès l'heure où il est formé.
>
> *Massechet Succa.* Ce mauvais levain a sept noms: dans l'Ecriture il est appelé mal, prépuce, immonde, ennemi, scandale, coeur de pierre, aquilon, tout cela signifie la malignité qui est cachée et empreinte dans le coeur de l'homme.
>
> R. Moses Hadarshan. This evil leaven is put into man from the moment of his creation.
>
> *Massechet Sukkah*: This evil leaven has seven names; in the Scriptures it is called evil, foreskin, unclean, enemy, scandal, heart of stone, icy blast, which all represent the wickedness hidden and imprinted in the heart of man. (278)

In the same fragment, Pascal cites the *Bereshith Rabbah* to the effect that there is no greater tyrant than the evil leaven. *Tyran* ("tyrant") is the same word which Pascal uses in fragment 597 to describe the *moi*. Any doubt that Pascal means to identify the *moi* in the fragment addressed to Mitton with the "mauvais levain" ("evil leaven") of fragment 278 vanishes when we read fragment 211:

> On a fondé et tiré de la concupiscence des règles admirables de police, de morale et de justice.
>
> Mais dans le fond, ce vilain fond de l'homme, ce *figmentum malum* n'est que couvert. Il n'est pas ôté.
>
> We have established and developed out of concupiscence admirable rules of polity, ethics and justice, but at root, the evil root of man, this evil stuff of which we are made is only concealed; it is not pulled up. (211)

Figmentum malum ("*Figmentum* enim humani cordis *malum* est" [italics mine]) refers to Genesis 8:21, which Pascal had noted and translated in the course of his research in rabbinical texts: "Sur le mot de la Genèse 8, la composition du coeur est mauvaise dès son enfance" ("On the text of Genesis 8: 'the imagination of man's heart is evil from his youth'").

The terminology of fragment 211 is precisely that of Pascal's response to Mitton in fragment 597. "Vous," Pascal tells Mitton when speaking of the *moi,* "le couvrez, vous ne l'ôtez point" ("You cover it up, Mitton, but that does not mean that you take it away") (597). Fragment 211 makes it clear that Pascal means to identify the *moi* with that "vilain fond de l'homme" ("evil root of man") which the rabbinical authorities had called the "mauvais levain" ("evil leaven"). "Ce *figmentum malum* n'est que *couvert*. Il n'est pas *ôté*" ("This evil leaven is only *covered up*. It has not been *uprooted*") (211, italics mine). In both fragments, what Pascal means is clear. The ego, that evil leaven added to original human nature at the time of the Fall, can never be extirpated by any purely human remedy such as law or social codes. Rules of conduct only succeed in temporarily concealing it. "Vous en ôtez l'incommodité" ("You only take away the nuisance"), Pascal tells Mitton, "mais pas l'injustice" ("but not the injustice") (597). Human law, morality, and justice are ultimately impotent in the face of "ce vilain fond de l'homme" ("this evil root of man"). How then can Mitton expect his ridiculous code of *honnêteté* to succeed where morality and law have always failed?

In a third fragment concerning Mitton, Pascal notes that his friend lacks the theological background necessary to understand why human beings cannot help themselves:

> Miton [*sic*] voit bien que la nature est corrompue et que les hommes sont contraires à l'honnêteté. Mais il ne sait pas pourquoi ils ne peuvent voler plus haut.

> Mitton sees quite well that nature is corrupt and that men are opposed to integrity. But he does not know why they can fly no higher. (642)

This note perhaps suggests that Mitton's position has evolved, at least in Pascal's imagination. Mitton appears to have been disabused of the idea that *l'honnêteté* can ever be a viable remedy for the frailty of the human condition. He now understands that "les hommes sont contraires à l'honnêteté" ("men are opposed to integrity"). However, because Mitton's is still a purely human scheme of things, he fails to understand that the *moi* was irremediably corrupted in the Fall of Adam. Mitton acknowledges that human nature is "corrompue," but he understands the word *corrupted* only in a static and passive sense. He will never be able "voler plus haut" ("to fly higher") until he acknowledges his need for divine illumination. Until he understands the doctrine of Adam's Fall from Grace as recounted by Holy Scripture and elucidated by Saint Paul and Saint Augustine, he will never understand the truly cosmic dimension inherent in the human enigma.

Philippe Sellier reminds us that Pascal's analysis of Mitton has a distinct precedent in Saint Augustine's critique of Cicero:

Mitton ressemble . . . à Cicéron: Augustin souligne que dans le livre III du *De Républica* ce dernier présente l'homme comme un être produit par une nature-marâtre, nu, fragile, sans force . . . et pourtant habité d'une parcelle du feu divin. Le grand orateur accuse la nature. C'est donc qu'il a bien vu la réalité, mais en a ignoré la cause. . . . Parce qu'il n'était pas instruit de l'Ecriture, il ignorait les causes exactes de l'état présent.[198]

Mitton is not unlike . . . Cicero: Augustine underlines the fact that in the third book of his *De Républica*, Cicero presents man as a being produced by a Nature which is like a cruel stepmother: naked, fragile, without strength . . . yet inhabited by a bit of divine fire. The great orator accuses Nature. Thus he has perceived the reality of the human condition, but without understanding its cause. . . . Because he lacked the instruction of Holy Scripture, he remained ignorant of the precise causes of man's current state.

In the long fragment in which he sketches the Preface to his projected Apology, Pascal notes the example of those agnostics who think they have given Christianity a fair hearing when they have done no more than devote "quelques heures à la lecture de quelque livre de l'Ecriture" ("a few hours to reading some book of the Bible") (427). The apologetic itinerary anticipated in the *Pensées* envisages a far more detailed inquiry into Scripture, sacred history, and exegesis. Nothing suggests that Damien Mitton ever undertook any such investigation under Pascal's tutelage. Nor is there any reason to think that Mitton ever experienced the kind of profound religious conversion envisaged by the final chapters of the dossiers of 1658.

Grubbs speculates that it was Pascal's influence which caused Mitton to abandon his earlier "égarements" and to marry and settle down to a respectable life.[199] However, we have no evidence that Mitton went on to become particularly religious by the standards of his day in spite of a rather tragic final twenty years of his life in which he was beset by paralysis, financial troubles, and estrangement from his son. Toward the end of his life, we find him exhorting Protestant friends to convert to Catholicism at the time of the revocation of the Edict of Nantes. Yet his counsel that they take "la plus désintéressée de toutes les actions" ("the most unselfish of all possible actions") somehow still seems to come more from an *honnête homme* than it does from the kind of convinced convert anticipated by the *Pensées*.

Most scholars have refrained from drawing the conclusion that Pascal's

198. Philippe Sellier, *Pascal et Saint Augustin* (Paris: A. Colin, 1970), pp. 239–40.
199. *Damien Mitton,* p. 25.

interlocutor in the *Pensées* is necessarily any single historical figure. Domna Stanton, for instance, sees the Apology as addressed to "an anonymous individual, who may have been Mitton, Méré or some hypothetical imaginary prototype of *honnêteté*."[200] J.-J. Demorest describes Pascal's "homme sans religion" ("man without religion") as perhaps "un représentant de l'Honnêteté qu'il anime d'individualité"[201] ("a representative of *Honnêteté* whom he animates with individuality"). Henri Gouhier makes the illuminating point that the three fragments concerning Mitton may tell us as much about Pascal the apologist as they do about his potential interlocutor:

> Ce que n'auraient pu faire ni M. de Sacy, ni M. Singlin, ni même le docteur Arnauld, Blaise Pascal sait parler à Mitton. Sans doute, dans son dialogue avec Mitton, Pascal fait les demandes et les réponses; du moins celles-ci nous montrent-elles ce qu'il attend de son apologétique. Elle oblige "l'honnête homme" à constater que les hommes sont contraires à l'"honnêteté," ce qui est reconnaître une contradiction dans l'expression "honnête homme." Et voici que Mitton lui-même doit voir dans cette contradiction ou mieux: cette "contrariété" "une corruption de la nature." Rien de plus, bien sûr. Mais une apologétique qui conduirait Mitton jusque là ne serait pas vaine.[202]

> Neither M. de Sacy nor M. Singlin nor even Doctor Arnauld would have known what needs to be said to Mitton. But Blaise Pascal knows how to speak to him. No doubt, in his dialogue with Mitton, it is Pascal himself who invents the questions and the answers; but these questions and answers, at least, show us what results Pascal expects from his apologetic strategy. This strategy obliges the *honnête homme* to recognize that men are contrary to *honnêteté*, which means recognizing a contradiction in the term *honnête homme* itself. Thus we find Mitton himself obliged to recognize in this contradiction—or better still, in this contrariety—"a corruption of nature." Nothing more than this of course. But an apologetic strategy which would lead Mitton to this point would not have been undertaken in vain.

Mitton's small role in the *Pensées* is instructive in another way. It serves to remind us that Pascal's potential convert in the *Apology* must be carefully distinguished from that larger background of religious disbelief sketched in Pascal's text. In the course of the *Pensées*, Pascal only hints at

200. Domna Stanton, *The Aristocrat as Art: A Study of the Honnête Homme and the Dandy in Seventeenth- and Nineteenth-Century French Literature* (New York: Columbia University Press, 1980), p. 242, n. 59.

201. J.-J. Demorest, "L'Honnête Homme et le croyant selon Pascal," *Modern Philology* 53, no. 4 (May 1956): 217–20.

202. Henri Gouhier, *Blaise Pascal: Conversion et apologétique*, p. 111.

the rather vast contours of religious disbelief as he knows it. He includes not only two categories of atheists, the hardened and the *chercheurs*,[203] but also the *impies*,[204] the Deists,[205] and the skeptics.[206] To these we must add two other categories not usually thought of as disbelievers but constantly pilloried by Pascal in the course of his apologetic itinerary: the Christian humanists and the theologically suspect.

For purposes of contrast with Pascal's literal and neo-Augustinian reading of the Bible, the example of Isaac de La Peyrère particularly warrants our detailed examination. The following chapter, offered as an instructive excursion into the world of profound theological unorthodoxy during a period usually thought of as the high-water mark of Christian orthodoxy, seeks to bring into relief Pascal's intention of writing an Apology which defends the Apostolic Faith delivered once and for all time to the world by Saint Augustine.

203. See Chapter V, Pascal's *chercheur*.
204. Cf. fragment 150.
205. See Chapter I, Pascal and Deism.
206. See Chapter IV, The Unbelievers in Fragment 427.

CHAPTER II

Isaac de La Peyrère and the Discovery of Pre-Biblical Time

In fragment 575, Pascal evokes the "extravagances des Apocalyptiques et préadamites, millénaristes, etc." ("extravagances of the Apocalyptics, Pre-Adamites, Millenarists, etc.") (see Plate III). The fragment is an obvious reference to Isaac de La Peyrère (1596–1676) and his two most controversial books: *Du Rappel des Juifs* (1643) and *Systema theologicum ex prae Adamitarum hypothesi* (1655). Both Pascal and La Peyrère appear, at least by the standards of the apologists of their day, uncommonly obsessed with the election of the Jews as God's chosen people. But their perspectives could not be more different. For Pascal, the Jews survive only as a living testimony to the authenticity of a specific Revelation:

> Si les Juifs eussent été tous convertis par J.-C. nous n'aurions plus que des témoins suspects. Et s'ils avaient été exterminés, nous n'en aurions point du tout.
>
> If the Jews had been converted by Christ we should only have suspect witnesses left. And if they had been wiped out we should have none at all.[1] (592)

For La Peyrère, on the other hand, the Jews retain their original and universal vocation. Their recall to France, and thence to Jerusalem, will usher in the final Kingdom of God on earth.

La Peyrère's speculations concerning the "pré-Adamites," and his the-

1. Cf. fragment 492: "Sincères contre leur honneur et mourant pour cela. Cela n'a point d'exemple dans le monde ni sa racine dans la nature" ("Sincere against their honor and dying for it. This has no parallel in the world nor its roots in nature").

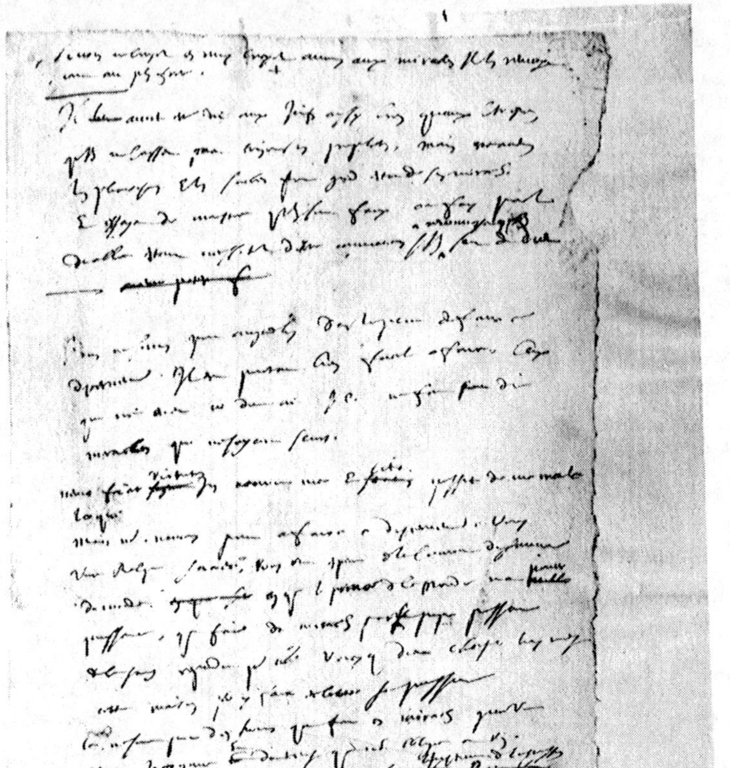

PLATE III. Fragment 575 (Lafuma): "Extravagances des Apocalyptiques et préadamites . . ." in the *Recueil original* (Bibliothèque Nationale, MS français 9202). Service photographique, Bibliothèque Nationale. Fragment begins in the fourth quarter of the manuscript page under "+."

ory that Adam was not the father of the human race, threaten Pascal's defense of Christianity far more than do any of the anti-Christian ideas propagated by the *libertins érudits*. For Pascal will build his entire *Apology* around a literal interpretation of the great Augustinian doctrine of Original Sin. His entire case will rest upon the literal truth of the Genesis story and upon the doctrine of all humanity's biological link to Adam. Over and over again, Pascal recapitulates the classical Pauline linking of Christ and Adam. "La foi chrétienne ne va presque qu'à établir ces deux choses: la corruption de la nature et la Rédemption de Jésus-Christ" ("The Christian faith consists almost wholly in establishing these two things: the corruption of nature and the redemption of Christ") (427). "Toute la foi consiste en Jésus-Christ et en Adam" ("The whole of faith consists in Jesus Christ and Adam") (226).

Paolo Rossi, in his *The Dark Abyss of Time*, puts Isaac de La Peyrère, along with Hobbes and Spinoza, in what he says subsequent Christian apologists would come to view as a "triumvirate of demons."[2] In many ways, La Peyrère's thesis that the Bible does not contain universal human history constituted as great a challenge to traditional Christian Revelation as did the new Copernican universe. La Peyrère did not hesitate to compare himself to Galileo.[3] Yet, this martyr of premodernism has remained long unknown to those interested in tracing the origins of the modern understanding of human history.

La Peyrère's *Systema theologicum ex prae Adamitarum hypothesi* (1655) has been called "the most refuted book of the seventeenth century."[4] Yet, La Peyrère's speculations failed to engender any serious subsequent inquiry into the notion that human history was of far greater antiquity than anyone in the Christian tradition had ever believed. His theories were thought to represent a serious threat to revealed religion, but hardly any of his contemporaries ever entertained the possibility that he might have stumbled upon the truth concerning the real historical status of the Bible. La Peyrère was dismissed as a madman and a visionary. Even when he ran afoul of the Inquisition, his censors seem to have regarded him more as

2. Paolo Rossi, *The Dark Abyss of Time: The History of the Earth and the History of Nations from Hooke to Vico* (Chicago: University of Chicago Press, 1984), p. 200.

3. See Jean-Paul Oddos, *Recherches sur la vie et l'oeuvre d'Isaac Lapeyère (1596?–1676)*, unpublished "thèse de 3ème cycle," 1971–74, Université des Sciences Sociales, Grenoble II, p. 178.

4. Ira Robinson, "Isaac de la Peyrère and the Recall of the Jews," *Jewish Social Studies*, 40 (1978): 128, n. 25.

a curiosity than as a serious intellectual threat to sacred doctrine. Pope Alexander VII, who received the official retraction of his theory, greeted him with humorous irony: "Embrassons cet homme qui est avant Adam"[5] ("Let us embrace this gentleman who is older than Adam").

The notion that human history might be older than Genesis appeared patently absurd to the seventeenth-century mentality. The mental universe of even the most cultivated individuals living between 1650 and 1700, Phillipe Sellier reminds us, remains strangely inaccessible:

> Ne faut-il pas se faire quelque peu ethnologue pour dialoguer avec des écrivains ou des penseurs qui datent la Création du monde de l'an 4004, croient connaître le jour où Abel fut tué par Caïn? Si les contemporains de Louis XIV s'ouvrent à l'idée d'un espace infini, combien fini demeure le temps de leur histoire! Combien erronée, ou lacunaire, leur connaissance des peuples! Impossible donc de comprendre pleinement un Pascal ou un Bossuet sans s'être familiarisé avec leur vision du monde, une vision à laquelle la Bible sert non seulement de centre, mais aussi de cadre.[6]

> Must not one almost play ethnologist in order to engage in a dialogue with writers or thinkers who place the Creation of the world in the year 4004, who believe they can pinpoint the very day on which Abel was killed by Cain? However open the contemporaries of Louis XIV appear to the notion of infinite space, how finite seem the limits of their history! How erroneous, or lacunary, their knowledge of the peoples of the world! It is impossible, therefore, to fully understand a Pascal or a Bossuet without familiarizing ourselves with their vision of the world. Not only does the Bible stand at the heart of this vision. It forms its outer limits.

La Peyrère's pre-Adamite theory seems oddly out of place in the age of French Classicism. To those for whom Genesis meant the beginning of time, the idea seemed not just incomprehensible but insane. Yet, at the same time, is it not strange that no one had advanced such a theory before the 1640s? Information concerning the histories and religions of America and the Orient had been flooding Europe for 150 years. Had it really occurred to no one that fitting all this new documentation into the framework provided by Genesis might prove problematic? The Enlightenment would begin to draw the contours of a more pluralistic vision of the origins of human history. Yet even Voltaire, we might remember, thought Newton's *Chronology of the Ancient Kingdoms Amended* (1728) to represent

5. Richard Simon, *Lettres choisies de M. Simon* (Rotterdam: R. Leers, 1702), 2, p. 28.

6. Philippe Sellier, "Avant-Propos," in David Wetsel, *L'Ecriture et le Reste: The Pensées of Pascal in the Exegetical Tradition of Port-Royal* (Columbus: Ohio State University Press, 1981), p. x.

an eminently reasonable shortening of the pretensions of the Chaldeans, Greeks, and Egyptians to great antiquity.[7]

La Peyrère's sense of the immense antiquity of human history would not really surface again until the advent of Darwin. The *Systema theologicum*, however, by no means anticipates modern evolutionary theory. La Peyrère theorizes that there were in fact two Creations: that of Adam, from whence sprang the Jews; and a much earlier one, lost in eternity, from which had emerged the rest of humankind. La Peyrère is not uninfluenced by the realization of how difficult it would be to absorb the rush of peoples discovered in the past 150 years into the framework of Genesis. Yet the writing of universal history is not his primary interest. His theory of the pre-Adamites is but the linchpin in a much greater scheme: the Election of the Jews. He seeks to reduce Genesis to the status of recounting but a single thread of human history in order to document his thesis that the history of the Jews stands totally apart from the universal history of the rest of humankind.

Du Rappel des Juifs

We know very little of La Peyrère's life prior to 1640, when he appears in Paris as a secretary to the Prince of Condé and surfaces in the circle of intellectuals attached to Père Mersenne.[8] Born in Bordeaux in 1596, La Peyrère was the oldest son of an affluent French Reformed family. Whether that family were Marranos of Portuguese origin has been a much-discussed question among the small circle of La Peyrère scholars in recent years. Richard H. Popkin devotes the first book ever written on La Peyrère (1987) to documenting the thesis that La Peyrère's theories can best be understood in the Marrano context.[9] In an unpublished French dissertation

7. Rossi, *The Dark Abyss of Time*, pp. 92, 163.

8. René Pintard, *Le Libertinage érudit dans la première moitié du XVIIe siècle* (Paris: Slatkine, 1983), p. 358. See also Oddos, *Recherches,* Chapter 3. Père Mersenne's circle of writers, scientists, and philosophers included Gassendi, La Mothe le Vayer, Naudé, Guy Patin, Grotius, Pascal, and Hobbes.

9. Richard H. Popkin, *Isaac La Peyrère (1596–1676): His Life, Works and Influence* (New York: E. J. Brill, 1987). See especially, pp. 21–25. Popkin concedes that the evidence concerning La Peyrère's Jewish origins is not conclusive: "My view is that the most likely explanation of La Peyrère's outlook was that he was of Jewish origins. The evidence is . . . not overwhelming. He said at one point he was a Jew, but a Jew like St. Paul. One obvious interpretation of that remark is that he was a convert. There were Marrano families with names like La Peyrère, and there were many Marranos who were Calvinists at the time. The epitaph

(1974), Jean-Pierre Oddos argues that it is unlikely that La Peyrère had Jewish origins. Oddos views La Peyrère's early preoccupation with the Jews and Jewish Messianic thought as growing out of the English Dissent, which maintained close contacts with Protestant circles in Bordeaux.[10]

When he arrived in Paris, La Peyrère seems already to have been long

---

written for him calls him 'that good Israelite.' This, I admit, is not decisive. One would like either some good archival evidence that traced his ancestors back to Spain or Portugal, or some document by La Peyrère or a close friend describing the family background. Since we have neither, we can only see what interpretation seems most probable. And it seems to me that the one that says he was a Marrano best fits the data. Whether or not he was a Marrano, his theory, I believe, is best explained as a vision of the world for the Marranos." *Isaac La Peyrère*, pp. 22–23.

10. Oddos, *Recherches*, pp. 185–204. "De quelle manière précise s'est exercée cette influence de la pensée juive sur Lapeyrère, si nous rejetons l'hypothèse de son origine marrane? Est-ce par une confrontation personnelle avec la petite communauté 'portugaise' de Bordeaux? A mon avis, le cheminement a pu être plus complexe encore. Car, si en France Lapeyrère représente une figure extrêmement originale, un cas presque unique, il n'en est pas de même dans l'Angleterre des années 1610–1620. Là, un fort courant philo-sémitique existe lié au développement de plusieurs sectes extrémistes. . . . Certains, poussant à son terme leur enthousiasme biblique, se proclament ouvertement 'juifs,' pratiquant la circoncision et observant le repos du Sabbath. . . . Or il existe d'étroites relations entre Bordeaux et l'Angleterre. . . . C'est peut-être sous l'influence de ces courants judaïsants que [La Peyrère] cherche ensuite à entrer en relation avec les marranes bordelais: car son philosémitisme, tel qu'il apparaîtra dans le *Rappel des Juifs,* se construit davantage sur un plan intellectuel que social, humain ou physique. Ainsi quand il confronte son propre acquis culturel avec la pensée juive, c'est à travers une sorte de prisme déformant une attitude intellectuelle déjà répandue chez ses sectaires anglais pour qui: 'the acceptance of the Jews into this society was not for the sake of its survival, but in order to lead [to] the realization of their eschatological hope, to the abolition of the existing order' " (*Recherches,* pp. 194–95).

"If we reject the hypothesis of his Marrano origins, how can we explain this influence of Jewish thought on La Peyrère? Did he have personal contacts with the tiny 'Portuguese' community of Bordeaux? In my opinion, the process was even more complicated. If La Peyrère represents an extremely original, indeed almost unique figure in France, such is not the case in the England of 1610–1620. In that country there existed a strong philo-Semitic current linked to the development of certain extremist sects. . . . Certain of these, pushing their biblical enthusiasm to the extreme, openly proclaimed themselves 'Jews,' practicing circumcision and observing the Sabbath. . . . As a matter of fact, there existed close contacts between Bordeaux and England. Perhaps it was under the influence of these Judaizing currents that [La Peyrère] sought to make contact with the Marrano community in Bordeaux. In the last analysis, [La Peyrère's] philo-Semiticism, such as it appears in the *Recall of the Jews,* is more intellectual than social, human or physical. Thus, when he confronts Jewish thought via his own cultural formation, it is through the deforming prism of an intellectual attitude already widespread among those English sectarians for whom: 'the acceptance . . . existing order.' " Oddos notes that La Peyrère's approach to Judaism is at many removes from the mystical speculations of the neo-Kabbalists: "Ce qu'il retient, c'est que cet évènement décisif—la venue du Messie—met en jeu non seulement le peuple élu, mais encore toute l'étendue de la création" ("What he retains [from the Jewish tradition] is that this decisive event—the coming of the Messiah—concerns not just the Chosen People but the whole Creation") at work on a magnum opus in which he intended to trace the Election, Rejection, and Recall of the Jews. He dedicated the work to Cardinal Richelieu, who banned its publication as soon as he saw La Peyrère's manuscript.[11] The work which was published in 1643, *Du Rappel des Juifs*, apparently represented the third volume in La Peyrère's grand theological project.[12] The pre-Adamite theory, which would be considerably refurbished in the years before its publication in Amsterdam in 1655, apparently constituted the first section of this now-lost manuscript. This first version of the *Systema theologicum ex prae Adamitarum hypothesi* appears to have circulated in manuscript form for nearly fifteen years. Hugo Grotius must have had a copy early on. He refutes La Peyrère's pre-Adamite thesis in 1643 in his *Dissertatio altera de origine Gentium Americanarum*.[13] The *libertins* whom La Peyrère met via Père Mersenne, observes René Pintard, immediately realized how potentially useful La Peyrère's speculations might be in the service of disbelief:

> Pour ceux-là, le système des Préadamites n'est pas une puérile ou inquiétante rêverie . . . c'est un gibier de choix. Aussi les voilà vite en chasse, les fins limiers! A peine Richelieu a-t-il proscrit le traité que ces rusés le transcrivent; et le bruit qu'ils font autour de l'étonnante production se répand jusqu'à Rome.[14]

(ibid., p. 196). Popkin observes that when Richard Simon suggested that La Peyrère could apply his theory to the Jewish Messianic movement of Sabbatai Zevi, La Peyrère showed no interest at all. Popkin, *Isaac La Peyrère,* p. 9.

11. Pintard, *Le Libertinage érudit,* p. 360.

12. *Du Rappel des Juifs* was published anonymously in Paris in 1643. See Popkin's article, "The Marrano Theology of Isaac La Peyrère," *Studi Internazionali di Filosofia,* 5 (1973): 99.

13. Hugo Grotius, *Dissertatio altera de origine Gentium Americanarum adversus obtrectatorem* (Paris: S. Cramoisy, 1643), pp. 13–14. In the *Systema theologicum* (Amsterdam, 1655), La Peyrère quotes Grotius as saying that the idea "that there were men before Adam, as one in France lately dreamed" represents "a great danger to Religion." La Peyrère objects that "Grotius had a little before read a little discourse of the Pre-Adamites undigested and about to be revised, which he under color of friendship had required of me, which I friendly did communicate to him: not that he should abuse me." *Systema theologicum* (1656 English edition), pp. 275–78.

Subsequent references to La Peyrère's *Prae Adamitae* and his *Systema theologicum ex prae Adamitarum hypothesi* will be to the English edition, in which both are translated and bound together: *Men before Adam, or a discourse upon the twelfth, thirteenth and fourteenth verses of the Epistle of the Apostle Paul to the Romans by which are proved that the first Men were created before Adam* (London: n.p., 1656); *A Theological Systeme upon that Presupposition that Men were before Adam* (London: n.p., 1655). La Peyrère was so offended by Grotius' refutation of his theory that he later threatened to entitle his work *Somnium Nobilis Aquitani de Prae-Adamitae.* Popkin discovered this amusing anecdote in Claude Sarrau's *Epistolae* (Orange: 1654). See his *Isaac La Peyrère,* pp. 10 and 179, n. 32.

14. Pintard, *Le Libertinage érudit,* p. 361.

For [the *libertins*], the pre-Adamite theory was not a puerile or disturbing reverie . . . it was a really choice quarry . . . like bloodhounds, they immediately went after it! No sooner had Richelieu proscribed the treatise than these crafty gentleman began to have it transcribed; the clamor they made conerning this astonishing piece of work spread all the way to Rome.

The *Du Rappel des Juifs* revolves around a central thesis which was clearly heretical by any orthodox Christian standards. The saving work of Christ, La Peyrère maintains, remains imperfect and incomplete so long as the Jews remain outside the drama of salvation. In all its phases, this drama is inexorably linked to the Election, Rejection, and Recall of God's original chosen people. The promise made to the nation of Israel in the Old Testament was imperfectly ("imparfaitement") accomplished in the New Testament.[15] The saving work of Christ grafted the Gentiles onto the Old Covenant, making them Jews in the mind of God ("Juifs . . . selon Dieu").[16] But the rejection of the Jews themselves by God, because they failed to recognize His Son, means that the larger cycle of salvation remains incomplete. Christians, La Peyrère maintains, will not receive their final and perfected salvation until they have brought about the conversion of the Jews. "Le Rappel des Juifs sera la plénitude des Gentils"[17] ("The Recall of the Jews will be the plenitude of the Gentiles").

According to La Peyrère, the Christian failure to perceive this larger cycle of salvation—and hence the delay in the coming of the Kingdom—springs from the malice which Christians mistakenly bear toward the Jews for having put to death their Savior. Christians manifest toward the Jews that very crime of ingratitude committed by the Jews when they rejected Jesus.[18] They fail to perceive that the specifically Christian cycle within the larger drama of salvation would have been impossible had the Jews not rejected and crucified Jesus. The Jews have every right to reply to the charge of Deicide by pointing out to the Christians that an act which has cost them so dearly was a necessary one from their perspective:

Si nos Pères n'avaient pas crucifié Jésus-Christ, Jésus-Christ ne serait pas mort pour toi. Et si Jésus-Christ n'était pas mort pour toi, tu serais mort en tes péchés,

15. *Du Rappel des Juifs* (Paris: n.p., 1643), p. 34.
16. Ibid., p. 27.
17. Ibid., p. 40.
18. Ibid., p. 155: "Nous Chrétiens, qui sommes ces Gentils qui avons reçu, et qui devons espérer tous ces biens des Juifs; . . . nous sommes . . . bien ingrats de traiter les Juifs comme nous les traitons" ("We Christians, who are those Gentiles who received and who must hope for these blessings from the Jews; . . . we are . . . truly ingrates to treat the Jews as we treat them").

et serais mort d'une mort éternelle. . . . Tu nous veux mourir pour ce que nos Pères ont péché. Tu ne peux le vouloir sans ingratitude: parce que tu nous poursuis pour un crime qui t'a été profitable.[19]

If our Fathers had not crucified Jesus Christ, Jesus Christ would not have died for you. And if Jesus Christ had not died for you, you would have died in your sins and that death would have been an eternal one. . . . You want us to die because our Fathers sinned. . . . This is not something you can desire without being ingrates: because you pursue us for a crime from which you have profited.

La Peyrère absolves the Jews of Deicide, not by blaming the Romans, but by arguing that their action was part of God's larger plan. God, he argues, has already sufficiently punished the Jews for their action. He does not need the help of Christians.[20] Both Jews and Christians must beg God's forgiveness:

Les Juifs pour le péché qu'ils ont commis contre Jésus-Christ. Les Gentils, pour le péché qu'ils commettent contre les Juifs. L'un et l'autre péché commis par mégarde et sans y penser, par une impétuosité de zèle qui nous porte bien souvent au mal une apparence de bien.[21]

The Jews for the sin which they committed against Jesus Christ. The Gentiles for the sin which they now commit against the Jews. Both sins committed inadvertently and without giving thought to the matter, in an excess of that zeal which deceives us by giving our evil actions the appearance of good.

La Peyrère buttresses his proposal for the cessation of the persecution of the Jews with two other arguments. First, he maintains, there remain hidden within the mass of unbelieving Jews a secret elect of seven thousand known only to God. Persecution of the Jews in general risks doing harm to this group of Elect. Next, La Peyrère takes a different tack. He argues that those Jews who continue to fulfill the Old Covenant in good faith and who believe in the Messiah to come have unconscious and implicit knowledge of Christ. Like the Patriarchs and Prophets of the Old Testament, they are Christians without knowing it.[22]

Pascal certainly evokes those Old Testament saints "qui attendaient en patience le Christ promis dès le commencement du monde" ("who patiently awaited the Christ promised since the world began") (281). However, like his mentor Le Maistre de Sacy, Pascal believes that only a few

19. Ibid., p. 162.
20. Ibid., pp. 156–60.
21. Ibid., p. 167.
22. Ibid., pp. 178–79, 193–94.

of the Jews of the Old Testament were able to penetrate the figurative veil under which the Law and the Prophets were hidden. Moses, Sacy writes, "a cru très certainement que Jésus-Christ naîtroit et mourroit pour les hommes" ("certainly believed that Jesus Christ would be born and die for humanity"). Joshua, David, and Samuel were likewise "Chrétiens effectivement par une anticipation de grâce" ("effectively Christians by an anticipation of Grace"). Sacy warns, however, that one should not imagine that this Grace was given to very many in the Old Covenant. Only a few of the Jews of old recognized that the manifold sacrifices and legal observations of the Law were but the "figure des choses qui devoient s'accomplir en la personne de Jésus-Christ"[23] ("figure of things which would be accomplished in the person of Jesus Christ"). There is no doubt whatsoever that both Pascal and Sacy would have rejected La Peyrère's thesis that the Jews of the post-Biblical world might be considered implicit Christians. And they would have deemed completely heretical his notion that the Jews had to be recalled to Jerusalem in order for the Second Coming of Christ to take place.

La Peyrère sets forth specific proposals which he says will serve to bring about the Recall of the Jews. First, the Jews will be officially readmitted to a France purged of all traces of anti-Semitism.[24] The Jews will be given the personal protection of the French monarch, who will reconquer Palestine for them, settle them there, and thus issue in the Kingdom and the reign of the Messiah.[25] When Jesus returns to rule from Jerusalem, the Jews will realize the wisdom of their conversion: they will find that their long-awaited Messiah and Jesus Christ are one and the same.[26]

23. *L'Exode et Le Lévitique: Traduits en françois* . . . (Lyon: Leonard Plaignard, 1683), Préface, pp. xxxiv–xxxvi. The Orthodox Church has long practiced the invocation of the Old Testament "saints" and the dedication of churches in their honor. Only since the Second Vatican Council has the practice been revived in modern Roman Catholicism. One now occasionally sees a Roman Catholic church dedicated, for example, to "St. Daniel the Prophet."

24. In her illuminating article, "La Religion de La Peyrère et 'Le Rappel des Juifs,' " in the *Revue d'histoire et de philosophie religieuse,* 51 (1971): 256, Miriam Yardeni points out that La Peyrère's program for readmitting the Jews to a country from which they had been banished during the Middle Ages had little in common with the Dutch and English proposals to readmit Jews to those countries. Whereas the Dutch and English patrons of the Jews argued on economic grounds and proposed accepting the Jews as Jews, La Peyrère's program was essentially theological: the Jews were to be admitted to France and sheltered from persecution as a prelude to their conversion to Christianity.

25. *Du Rappel des Juifs,* pp. 91–116.

26. Ibid., pp. 366–75.

The conversion of the Jews, which will take place in France, will in no way resemble the forced conversions of the medieval Church and the Inquisition. It will be more like an inquirer's class conducted under the patient and charitable aegis of the King of France. The Catholic Church, for its part, will set up and finance special temples, free of any images which might offend Jewish sensibilities. In these temples, special liturgies and catechisms which stress Old Testament texts and ceremonies will be used. "On fera entendre le christianisme par le judaïsme même"[27] ("Christianity will be made comprehensible via Judaism itself").

The Jews will gradually learn the Christian faith while continuing to practice their own. They will be taught a simple apostolic faith not unlike Erasmus' "philosophy of Christ." Only two sacraments will be retained for them: Baptism, which will eventually come to replace circumcision, and the Eucharist.[28] They will be exempted from having to confess any doctrines or creeds which have accrued to Christianity since the apostolic period, lest they complain to Christians, "Vos canons . . . et vos articles de Foi sont plus difficiles à comprendre que les règles et les cérémonies de Moïse ne sont difficiles à observer"[29] ("Your canons . . . and your articles of faith are more difficult to understand than the rules and ceremonies of Moses are to practice").

In La Peyrère's vision, the assimilation of the Jews into Christianity will be accomplished by a miraculous transformation of their physical characteristics. The dark coloring and repulsive physical traits which the Jews have borne since their expulsion from the Holy Land will disappear:

> Les Juifs de ce temps là n'auront plus cette couleur noire et basanée qu'ils ont contractée en leur Exil, et de l'injure du temps, et de l'injure des hommes. Ils changeront de visage dans ce Rappel, et la blancheur de leur teint aura le même éclat, dit le Psaume, qu'ont les ailes et la gorge d'un pigeon extrêmement blanc. Les Juifs ne sentiront plus le moisi ni le relent. Ce ne sera que douceur de leur haleine. Ce ne sera que musc et ambre qui sortira de leurs habits et de leurs transpirations.[30]

> The Jews of that latter time will no longer have that dark and swarthy color which they have contracted during their Exile, and from the injury of time and the injury of men. Their faces will change during their Recall, and the whiteness of their coloring will have the same lustre, says the Psalm, as the wings and the

27. Ibid., p. 356.
28. Ibid., pp. 330–56.
29. Ibid., p. 331.
30. Ibid., p. 81.

throat of an extremely white pigeon. The Jews will no longer smell musty or mouldy. Their breath will reek but of sweetness. Their clothes and sweat will give off only the odor of musk and amber.

The modern Israeli commentator on La Peyrère's Messianic vision Myriam Yardeni observes that unlike Richard Simon (whom he would know in the 1670s), La Peyrère had no significant appreciation of Jewish history and civilization in post-Biblical times. "En ce qui concerne les Juifs ses contemporains," she notes, "ses vues sont imprégnées de traditions et préjugés médiévaux, y compris une véritable répulsion physique"[31] ("With regard to those Jews who are his contemporaries . . . his views are impregnated with medieval traditions and prejudices, including a veritable physical repulsion"). Indeed, La Peyrère's only real interest in the Jews is their role in ushering in the final rule of God on earth. The King of France, prefigured in the Old Testament,[32] is a central figure in La Peyrère's scenario. He alone has the political power to force the nations of the Gentiles to accept the Jews as brothers in Christ.[33] He alone possesses the spiritual power to cure the Jews of their physical ills.[34] Alongside the Messiah and the recalled Jews, he will rule the world from Jerusalem, presiding over an everlasting era of unity and peace.[35]

La Peyrère's whole eschatological scenario may seem vaguely familiar to late-night television viewers who may have chanced to stumble upon the more extreme of the contemporary tele-evangelists. The same basic elements are present in both scenarios: the recall of the Jews (i.e., the establishment of the state of Israel), the Christian role in promoting and

31. Yardeni, "La Religion de La Peyrère," p. 248.

32. The royal symbol, the "fleur de lys" La Peyrère explains, corresponds to the Hebrew word *Susan,* the name of the city where the Jews were liberated: "La ville Royale de Susan qui est donc même chose que la ville Royale du lys: et même chose que la ville Royale de France." *Du Rappel des Juifs,* p. 138.

33. *Du Rappel des Juifs,* pp. 108–18.

34. The French King was thought to possess the divine gift of being able to cure scrofula, one of the maladies which, according to La Peyrère, had afflicted the Jews since their Rejection. See M. Block, *Les Rois thaumaturges* (Paris: A. Colin, 1961), pp. 120–40. Yardeni makes the interesting observation that during the Middle Ages, the Jews were less affected by the plague than the Christians because of their ritual hygienic practices. The Christians, however, attributed this phenomenon to the protection of Satan. "La Religion de La Peyrère," p. 255.

35. *Du Rappel des Juifs,* pp. 82–151. On the long and complicated history of the role of the King of France in Messianic literature, see Popkin, *Isaac La Peyrère,* pp. 62–68. Popkin traces the development of a tradition, extending from Joachim de Fiore to Guillaume Postel to Tommaso Campanella, in which the French Monarch played a crucial role in Messianism and Millenarianism.

protecting the secular New Jerusalem as a prelude to Christ's Second Coming (i.e., Evangelical Christian support for the new Jewish state), a the major role for the leader of the Christian world (i.e., the President of the United States). These parallels are not coincidental. Our latter-day preachers, inflamed by the advent of the third millennium, are at least in part the intellectual heirs—via a plethora of nineteenth- and early-twentieth-century sects (the various forms of Pentecostalism, the Seventh-Day Adventists, the Watchtower Society)—of that same left-wing Protestant Dissent which swept England and Holland in the seventeenth century.

This whole Millenarian tradition, of course, is far older than the various forms of Dissent unleashed by the Reformation. One only need mention the name of Joachim de Fiore in order to evoke its medieval manifestations. Yet, the fact remains that, at least from the perspective of post-Tridentine Catholic theology, all of its various manifestations are profoundly heretical. In the first place, the idea of the establishment of a temporal Kingdom of God on earth has never been a part of recent orthodox Catholic belief. Pascal, for instance, in those relatively rare instances in which he indulges in eschatological discourse, always invokes, not an earthly Kingdom of God, but the Heavenly and Celestial Jerusalem:

> Tout ce qui est au monde est concupiscence de la chair ou concupiscence des yeux ou orgueil de la vie. *Libido sentiendi, libido sciendi, libido dominandi.*[36] Malheureuse la terre de malédiction que ces trois fleuves de feu embrasent plutôt qu'ils n'arrosent. Heureux ceux qui . . . tendent la main à celui qui les doit élever pour les faire tenir debout et fermes dans les porches de la sainte Jérusalem . . . et qui cependant pleurent, non pas de voir écouler toutes les choses périssables, que ces torrents entraînent, mais dans le souvenir de leur chère patrie de la Jérusalem céleste, dont ils se souviennent sans cesse dans la longueur de leur exil.[37]

> "All that is in the world is lust of the flesh, lust of the eyes or pride of life." *Libido sentiendi, libido sciendi, libido dominandi.* Wretched is the cursed land consumed rather than watered by these three rivers of fire. Happy are those who . . . stretch out their hands to him who shall raise them to stand upright and steady in the porches of Jerusalem the blessed . . . and yet who weep, not at the sight of all the perishable things swept away by those torrents, but at the memory of their beloved home, the heavenly Jerusalem, which they constantly remember through the long years of their exile. (545)

36. 1 John 2:16.

37. See Philippe Sellier's lovely meditation on this fragment, "Sur les fleuves de Babylone: The Fluidity of the World and the Search for Permanence in the *Pensées*," in D. Wetsel, ed., *Meaning, Structure and History in the "Pensées" of Pascal* (Tübingen: Biblio 17, 1990), pp. 33–44.

The Catholicism of the Classical period, perhaps more influenced by a revival of Augustinian pessimism than is generally acknowledged, nearly always tended to stress the fate of the individual soul more than the New Testament emphasis on the coming of the Kingdom of God. This tendency is everywhere reflected in Pascal's *Apology*. Only rarely, as in the beautiful passage just cited, does Pascal give himself over to an eschatological kind of discourse. As an orthodox Catholic, Pascal obviously subscribes to traditional Christian belief about the Last Judgment. But there is very little mention of it in the *Pensées*, a work directed at the salvation of individual souls. Moreover, Pascal considers any kind of speculation on matters eschatological extremely dangerous and suspect. Thus his condemnation of the "extravagances des Apocalyptiques et préadamites, millénaristes":

> Qui voudra fonder des opinions extravagantes sur l'Ecriture en fondera par exemple sur cela.
>
> Il est dit que cette génération ne passera point jusqu'à ce que tout cela se fasse. Sur cela je dirai qu'après cette génération il viendra une autre génération et toujours successivement.

> Anyone wanting to base extravagant opinions on Scripture will, for example, base them on the following: "this generation shall not pass till all these things shall be fulfilled."[38] To that I reply that after this generation there shall come another and always another in succession. (575)

La Peyrère and the Problem of the Peoples of the New World

Du Rappel des Juifs, though full of heretical propositions, seems not to have brought La Peyrère to grief at the hands of ecclesiastical authorities. But, on the other hand, neither did it provoke any sign of a movement to recall the Jews to France and Christianity.[39] La Peyrère's major theses

38. Matthew 24:34.

39. Popkin has unearthed considerable data suggesting that *Du Rappel des Juifs* exercised a profound influence on the Jewish Messianic writer Rabbi Menasseh ben Israel. See *Isaac La Peyrère,* pp. 97–105. Noting that La Peyrère is sometimes mentioned as an early advocate of Zionism, Popkin concludes that "he seems to have had no further influence on the Jewish world" after Menasseh ben Israel. *Isaac La Peyrère,* p. 105. See also, Popkin's articles on this subject: "Menasseh ben Israel and Isaac La Peyrère," *Studia Rosenthaliana* 8 (1974): 59–63,

concerning the Election and Recall of the Jews would appear in the *Systema theologicum* (1655). In the intervening years, while his original manuscript continued to circulate, La Peyrère continued to refurbish and document his pre-Adamite theory. We find particular evidence of his continuing scholarly research during a voyage to Scandinavia he undertook in 1644–47.

In 1644, La Peyrère traveled to Denmark with the French ambassador as part of a diplomatic mission sent by France to mediate a conflict between Denmark and Sweden. In Stockholm, he met the young Queen Christina, who would later play a significant role in the publication of the *Systema theologicum*. In Copenhagen, he established a lasting friendship with the Danish scholar and scientist Ole Worm. Worm, who rescued Saxo Chronicles from oblivion in his *Danish Monuments* (1643), supervised La Peyrère's research into the history of Greenland and Iceland.[40] La Peyrère would later publish his findings in *Relation du Groenland* (1647) and *Relation de l'Islande* (1663) and would remain the leading scholarly authority on these two territories until well into the nineteenth century.[41] This research would also come to figure in the revised version of the *Systema theologicum* as further documentation of La Peyrère's thesis that Genesis does not contain the history of the newly discovered peoples of America.

For nearly 150 years, scholars had debated the origin of the American Indians, suggesting points of origin as diverse as China, Palestine (The Lost Tribes), Atlantis, and Norway. Early on, in the face of the possibility of Spanish and Portuguese extermination of the Indians of South and Central America, the Church had found itself forced to rule affirmatively on the question of whether or not these newly discovered peoples indeed were human and possessed souls. In 1607, G. Garcia, in his *Origen de los Indios*, warned that any attempt to assign these peoples a separate origin from that of the peoples of Europe and Asia would contradict the Chris-

and "Menasseh ben Israel and La Peyrère II," *Studia Rosenthaliana* 18 (1984): 12–20. Popkin has also discovered evidence that *Du Rappel des Juifs* influenced the Abbé Grégoire's theories on Jewish emancipation at the time of the French Revolution and contributed to Napoleon's attempt to reconstitute the Jewish Sanhedrin. See *Isaac La Peyrère*, pp. 107–14. Also, "La Peyrère, the Abbé Grégoire, and the Jewish Question in Eighteenth Century Culture," *Studies in Eighteenth Century Culture* 4 (1975): 209–22.

40. See Oddos, *Recherches*, pp. 56–60. Oddos gives a French translation of the extensive Latin correspondence between Worm and La Peyrère. *Recherches*, pp. 210–76.

41. Popkin, *Isaac La Peyrère*, p. 11.

tian teaching that all humanity shares an organic unity with a common father, Adam.[42]

Throughout the *Pensées*, Pascal continually reaffirms the biological unity of all humankind with its common father, Adam. Faced with the problem of explaining why the Fall and its consequences have never been obvious to human reason and were never perceived by the great philosophers of antiquity, Pascal has recourse to an idea borrowed from Jansenius: the notion of man's "deux états" ("two states").[43] Because human beings are not in the state of their Creation, they fail to perceive an event which resulted in the corruption of their reason:

> Nous ne concevons ni l'état glorieux d'Adam, ni la nature de son péché, ni la transmission qui s'en est faite en nous. Ce sont choses qui se sont passées dans l'état d'une nature toute différente de la nôtre et qui passent l'état de notre capacité présente.

> We cannot conceive of Adam's state of glory, or the nature of his sin, or the way it has been transmitted to us. These are things which took place in a state of nature quite different from our own and which pass our present understanding. (431)

In fragment 131, Pascal stresses that God has deliberately hidden the source of "la difficulté de notre être" ("the difficulties of our existence"), that is, Original Sin, from human reason. "Le mystère le plus éloigné de notre connaissance . . . est celui de la transmission du péché" ("The mystery furthest from our ken . . . is that of the transmission of [original] sin"). Indeed nothing shocks unilluminated human reason more than the true explanation of human blindness and weakness:

> Il n'y a rien qui choque plus notre raison que de dire que le péché du premier homme ait rendu coupables ceux qui étant si éloignés de cette source semblent incapables d'y participer. Cet écoulement ne nous paraît pas seulement impossible. Il nous semble même très injuste car qu'y a(-t-)il de plus contraire aux règles de notre misérable justice que de damner éternellement un enfant incapable de volonté pour un péché où il paraît avoir si peu de part, qu'il est commis six mille ans avant qu'il fût en être. Certainement rien ne nous heurte plus rudement que cette doctrine. Et cependant sans ce mystère, le plus incompréhensible de tous nous

42. Ibid., p. 50. Popkin notes that a second edition of Garcia's work would include a refutation of La Peyrère's pre-Adamite theory. See Gregoria Garcia, *Origen de los índios de el Nuevo Mundo e Indias Occidentales,* Seguanda Impresion (Madrid, 1729), Libro Quarto, Chapter 29, p. 248.

43. See Philippe Sellier, *Pascal et Saint Augustin* (Paris: A. Colin, 1970), pp. 236–37.

sommes incompréhensibles à nous-mêmes. Le noeud de notre condition prend ses replis et ses tours dans cet abîme.

Nothing is more shocking to our reason than to say that the sin of the first man has implicated in its guilt men so far from the original sin that they seem incapable of sharing it. This flow of guilt does not seem merely impossible to us, but indeed most unjust. What could be more contrary to the rules of our miserable justice than the eternal damnation of a child, incapable of will, for an act in which he seems to have so little part that it was actually committed 6,000 years before he existed? Certainly nothing jolts us more rudely than this doctrine, and yet, but for this mystery, the most incomprehensible of all, we remain incomprehensible to ourselves. The knot of our condition was twisted and turned in that abyss. (131)

La Peyrère's position on the transmission of Original Sin and the relationship of the great majority of humanity to Adam runs directly counter to that of Pascal. During the course of his research in Denmark, La Peyrère came to understand that the Eskimos represented the same problem as that of the new peoples of the Americas. Grotius, in the work in which he refuted La Peyrère's as yet unpublished pre-Adamite theory, had argued that the Eskimos—and hence all the new peoples of America—were descendants of Leif Erikson's Norwegian expeditions.[44] La Peyrère, examining the materials he received from Worm, discovered that the early Viking explorers had found the Eskimos already living in Greenland. Hence, La Peyrère concludes, the Eskimos are of Indian origin and came from America. In the *Systema theologicum*, the Scandinavian materials will be used to buttress the case that Genesis cannot account for the origin of the various peoples found in the New World.[45]

La Peyrère's exposition of his pre-Adamite theory will take place within the context of the intersection of two major traditions inherited from the Renaissance. The geographical Age of Discovery was also the period in which scholars began to unearth the ancient chronologies of classical pre-Christian antiquity. On his return from Scandinavia, La Peyrère stopped in Holland to present his theory to the Protestant scholar Claude Saumaise. Studying the history of astrology, Saumaise had reached the startling conclusion that the chronologies of the Chaldeans and the Egyptians predated Genesis by some thirty thousand years. Saumaise's conclusions,

44. Grotius, *Dissertatio altera de Origine Gentium Americanarum*, pp. 13–14. Cited by Popkin, "The Pre-Adamite Theory in the Renaissance," *Philosophy and Humanism: Renaissance Essays in Honor of Paul Oskar Kristeller* (Leiden: Brill, 1976), pp. 66, n. 51.

45. La Peyrère, *Relation du Groenland* (Paris, 1647), pp. 273–76; *A Theological Systeme*, Book 4, Chapter XIV.

in his *De annis climacteris* (1648), soon found their way into La Peyrère's evolving manuscript. La Peyrère would later declare that Saumaise had served as the "midwife" to his pre-Adamites.[46] Pascal, we should perhaps note in passing, denounces the "histoires" of the Egyptians, along with those of the Chinese and the Greeks, in fragments 436 and 454.[47]

La Peyrère's Arrest and Conversion

During the next nine years, La Peyrère continued to serve the House of Condé, moving with the new Prince to Belgium after the Fronde and from there undertaking a series of diplomatic missions to Spain and England.[48] Back in Antwerp, La Peyrère renewed his acquaintance with Queen Christina, who had just abdicated the throne of Sweden and who was preparing her conversion to Catholicism. Most sources agree that it was Christina who urged La Peyrère finally to publish his book and who financed its publication.[49] The work was published in Amsterdam in 1655 in three forms. There were four editions of the *Praeadamite*, three of the *Systema theologicum ex prae Adamitarum hypothesi* (an expanded version of the former), and one edition which included both. The following year, there appeared an English edition which incorporated the two works into one bound volume.[50] It is to this edition to which we will henceforth refer.

46. Oddos, *Recherches,* pp. 70–74, 166–167. Oddos reproduces La Peyrère's letter to Philibert de la Mare in which he says that when he received a copy of the *De annis climacteris,* he wrote to thank Saumaise "au nom de mes Préadamites" ("on behalf of my pre-Adamites") (ibid., p. 284). In a second letter to Philibert de la Mare, la Peyrère is more explicit: "Je puis dire qu'ils [les préadamites] doivent [leur existence] à Monsieur Saumaise qui a été comme leur sage-femme" ("I can say that they [the pre-Adamites] owe [their existence] to Monsieur Saumaise, who was like their midwife") (ibid., pp. 287–291). On La Peyrère's relations with Saumaise, see also Pintard, *Le Libertinage érudit,* p. 358, and Popkin, *Isaac La Peyrère,* pp. 11–12, 48.

47. See Chapter III, Pascal and the Non-Christian Religions.

48. Pintard, *Le Libertinage érudit,* p. 379. Oddos, *Recherches,* pp. 80–87. Popkin, *Isaac La Peyrère,* p. 12.

49. Pintard, *Le Libertinage érudit,* p. 399. Popkin, "Menasseh ben Israel and La Peyrère II," p. 13; *Isaac La Peyrère,* pp. 13, and 180, n. 50. Oddos, *Recherches,* pp. 90–91. See also, Sven Stolpe, *Christina of Sweden* (New York: Macmillan, 1966), p. 130.

50. La Peyrère, *Men before Adam; A Theological Systeme* (London: n.p., 1656) See n. 13 of the present chapter. Popkin has been unable to locate any evidence that La Peyrère made provisions for the translation and publication of his work in England during his visit to London three years before. *Isaac La Peyrère,* p. 12.

Though La Peyrère's book was published anonymously, his authorship was immediately recognized. Both Catholic and Protestant denunciations of the work began to appear at once.[51] In February of 1656, La Peyrère was arrested by the Inquisition and charged with heresy. The Prince of Condé's attempt to get him released proved futile, but a compromise was worked out by Condé's confessor, the Jesuit Pierre Lenet. The charges of heresy would be dropped in return for La Peyrère's conversion to the Roman Church and his formal retraction of his heretical propositions.[52] Although obstinately devoted to his pre-Adamites, La Peyrère did not long delay in accepting the proposition. As Pintard so aptly observes: "L'odeur du feu n'est pas passée très loin de ses narines"[53] ("He barely escaped the smell of smoke in his nostrils"). La Peyrère was escorted to Rome, where his formal retraction was published in 1657. He was presented to Alexander VII by the Superior General of the Jesuits, who hastened to assure him that the Holy Father had read his book and found his theories most amusing.[54]

In his formal retraction, written with the assistance of Cardinal Barberini, La Peyrère contends that he was led astray by the Calvinist notion that Scripture must be interpreted according to the lights of individual conscience. He abjures his book as "contraire aux sentiments des Saints Pères et aux Sacrées constitutions de l'Eglise Catholique" ("contrary to the teaching of the Holy Fathers and the Sacred Constitutions of the Catholic Church"), but explicitly refrains from retracting his conviction that the pre-Adamite theory contradicts neither Scripture nor reason.[55] The sincerity of La Peyrère's retraction is open to question.[56] His continu-

51. One of the first to condemn the book was the Bishop of Namur, who censured La Peyrère "comme Calviniste et comme Juif" ("as a Calvinist and as a Jew") (*Lettre de La Peyrère à Philotime* [Paris: A. Courbe, 1658], pp. 123–24). See Popkin, *Isaac La Peyrère,* pp. 14 and 181, nn. 55–59; "Marrano Theology," p. 122, nn. 71–72. Also, David Rice McKee, "Isaac La Peyrère, a precursor of the Eighteenth-Century Critical Deists," in *PMLA* 59 (1944): 458. McKee cites sources to the effect that in Paris the book was burned by the public hangman.

52. Pintard, *Le Libertinage érudit,* pp. 421–22. Also, Ira Robinson, "Isaac de la Peyrère and the Recall of the Jews," p. 119, who cites the *Lettres* of Richard Simon, pp. 24–25.

53. Pintard, *Le Libertinage érudit,* p. 424.

54. Louis Lafuma, *Pascal: Oeuvres complètes* (Paris: Seuil, 1963), p. 657.

55. See La Peyrère, *Lettre à Philotime, dans laquelle il expose les raisons qui l'ont obligé à abjurer la Secte de Calvin qu'il professait, et le Livre des Préadamites qu'il avait mis au jour. Traduit en Français du Latin imprimé à Rome, par l'auteur même* (Paris: Courbé, 1658), p. 168.

56. See Oddos, *Recherches,* pp. 107–9. Popkin thinks that the recantation described in the *Lettre à Philotime* "reeks with hypocrisy." *Isaac La Peyrère,* p. 15. Yardeni, on the other hand, noting that in *Rappel des Juifs,* La Peyrère proposes that the Catholic Church underwrite the construction of special temples for the returned Jews, senses that La Peyrère is attracted by

ing obsession with his grand scheme for the recall of the Jews is not. Indeed, in La Peyrère's letter to the Pope, it is Alexander VII (seven being the sign of the Sabbath and hence of the Jews) who replaces the French Monarch as the universal figure who will recall the Jews and settle them in Palestine.[57]

Though urged by the Pope to accept a benefice and remain in Rome, La Peyrère chose to return to his patron in Flanders. In 1659, he returned with Condé to Paris and accepted a post as his official librarian. In 1663, he wrote an *Apology* in which he attempted to justify his conversion. In the *Apologie de la Peyrère*, he claims that his theory, like that of Galileo, is a hypothesis which has yet to be disproved.[58] In 1665, La Peyrère retired as a lay brother to the Oratorian seminary at Aubervilliers, where he lived until his death in 1676. According to Richard Simon, who knew him throughout this last period, La Peyrère continued to work on a revised version of *Du Rappel des Juifs*. This last work, written in an odd phonetic French of La Peyrère's own devising, remained unpublished.[59]

The Oratorian Fathers apparently thought La Peyrère a bit mad and teasingly threatened to burn his papers after his death.[60] Richard Simon recounts that, on his deathbed, La Peyrère refused to abjure his pre-Adamite theory, invoking the Epistle of St. Jude: "*Hi quaecumque ignorant blasphemant*."[61] Pintard cites an anecdote from the *Mémoires* of Philibert de la Mare which casts some light on La Peyrère's lifelong unorthodoxy. As the priest who gave him extreme unction pronounced the words "*Pro-*

---

the universality of the Church of Rome: "Malgré ses multiples réserves à l'égard de la doctrine catholique, La Peyrère est finalement attiré par cette force massive, cette unité et cette autorité. Peut-être même que les pages farouchement anti-protestantes de sa . . . rétraction où il exaltera l'autorité qui émane de l'Englise Catholique, ne sont pas pure hypocrisie" ("In spite of his multiple reservations with regard to Catholic doctrine, La Peyrère is, in the last analysis, attracted by this massive force, unity and authority. Perhaps it may even be that those ferocious anti-Protestant pages of his . . . retraction, in which he exalts the authority which emanates from the Catholic Church, are not pure hypocrisy") ("La Religion de La Peyrère," pp. 250–51).

57. See Oddos, *Recherches,* pp. 107–11. La Peyrère's lettre, *A Notre Très Saint Père le Pape Alexandre VII,* constitutes the second half of the *Lettre à Philotime*. For an account of the Pope's role in La Peyrère's revised messianic scheme, see *Lettre à Philotime,* pp. 157–67.

58. *Apologie de la Peyrère* (Paris: L. Billaine, 1663), pp. 21–22.

59. See Richard Simon's letter, "Quelques particularités touchant l'Auteur et l'Ouvrage des Préadamites," in *Lettres choisies de M. Simon* (Rotterdam: R. Leers, 1702), 2, pp. 23–28. La Peyrère's last version of his magnum opus, *Des Juifs, Elus, Rejetés, et Rapelés,* reposes in the Cabinet des Manuscrits of the Musée Condé in Chantilly (ms. 191 [698]).

60. Pintard, *Le Libertinage érudit,* p. 430.

61. Simon, *Lettres choisies* (Amsterdam: P. Mortier, 1730), 2, pp. 28–30, 41–51.

ficiscere, anima Christiana, ex hoc mundi," the semiconscious father of the pre-Adamites could be heard to mutter: "Où voulez-vous qu'elle aille?"[62] ("Where the devil do you want it to go?"). An epitaph circulated after his death and collected by Bayle in the *Dictionnaire historique et critique* (1697) perhaps best sums up the spirit in which La Peyrère was remembered by his contemporaries:

> La Peyrère ici gît, ce bon Israélite
> Huguenot, Catholique, enfin Préadamite.
> Quatre Religions lui plurent à la fois;
> Et son indifférence était si peu commune,
> Qu'après quatre-vingts ans qu'il eut à faire choix;
> Le bon homme partit, et n'en choisit pas une.[63]

Here lies La Peyrère, that good Israelite / Huguenot, Catholic, and then pre-Adamite. / Altogether, he was attracted by four religions; / And his indifference was of such a rare quality, / That after the eighty years he had to make a choice; / The old fellow set off, and did not choose any of them.

The *Systema theologicum ex prae Adamitarum hypothesi*

When La Peyrère finally published the *Systema theologicum* in 1655, *Du Rappel des Juifs* had been in circulation for thirteen years. One can only wonder precisely what it was in the *Systema* that struck censors as more dangerous than the numerous heresies enunciated in the *Rappel*. Why was it that La Peyrère was only arrested for heresy in 1656? Oddos offers the hypothesis that the ecclesiastical authorities had been watching La Peyrère for a long time and had been carefully engineering his arrest and "conversion" in order to score a point against the Calvinists. Why, wonders Oddos, had La Peyrère's friend Bourdelot,[64] a freethinking doctor who had first introduced him to the Prince of Condé, sent a copy of the *Rappel* to Cardinal Barberini in Rome?[65] Around the time of La Peyrère's mission to Scandinavia, the Carthusian Christophe Dupuy had written to La Peyrère's friend Ismaël Boulliau in an attempt to find out more about the author of *Du Rappel des Juifs*:

62. Pintard, *Le Libertinage érudit,* p. 430. See n. 90 of the present chapter.
63. Pierre Bayle, *Dictionnaire historique et critique* (Rotterdam: R. Leers, 1697), 2, p. 767.
64. See n. 140 of present chapter.
65. Oddos, *Recherches,* p. 165. Also, Pintard, *Le Libertinage érudit,* pp. 421–22.

> Cet homme montre savoir quelque chose en ces matières de Rabbinisme, mais en beaucoup de lieux il donne des extravagances, nommément quand il parle des Rois de France. Cet homme est fils, à mon avis, de quelque espagnol, et son nom me le fait ainsi croire. J'ai su qu'il avait fait un livre intitulé *Des Préadamites*, qui doit être un dangereux ouvrage.[66]

> This man shows some evidence of knowledge in matters of Rabbinism, but in many areas he sets forth insanities, notably when he speaks of the Kings of France. In my opinion, this man is the son of some Spaniard. His name makes me think so all the more so. I learned that he had written a book entitled *Men Before Adam*, which must be a dangerous work.

Early on, we should perhaps note, La Peyrère's orthodox readers reached the conclusion that he must have been of Marrano extraction in order to take such an interest in the recall of the Jews.

Given how seriously quarrels over Grace and Original Sin were shaking the religious and political scene in seventeenth-century France, the most explosive element in La Peyrère's pre-Adamite theory must have seemed his claim that Adam was the biological father only of the Jews. From Augustine onward, orthodox doctrine had held that the stain of Original Sin was biologically transmitted to all of Adam's descendants and hence to all of the human race. The relative impunity with which La Peyrère enunciated his theory that only the Jews descended from Adam appears all the more striking when one bears in mind how savagely the Jansenists were persecuted for their interpretations of far more minor points concerning the doctrine of Original Sin. Claude Saumaise, to whom La Peyrère showed his manuscript in Holland on his way back to Paris from Denmark, immediately recognized that La Peyrère's straying from orthodox doctrine would bring him to grief. He advised La Peyrère to rethink the entire matter. Oddos speculates that it was Saumaise's warning which caused La Peyrère to devote almost the entire *Exercitio* attached to the *Systema theologicum* to an attempt to resolve this problem.[67]

Analyzing Romans 5:12–14, where St. Paul says that sin began with Adam, La Peyrère reaches the conclusion that a world of "natural" sin must have existed before "legal sin" was instituted by Adam's disobedience. In this state of nature, which is not unlike the one described by Hobbes, "warrs, Plagues and Fevers," together with all the other ills which afflicted the pre-Adamites, were the "consequences of natural sin."

66. Pintard, *Le Libertinage érudit,* pp. 361–62.
67. Oddos, *Recherches,* p. 166.

Adam put an end to the state of nature, but Christ put an end to the rule of law. Therefore true Original Sin extended only from Adam to Jesus. La Peyrère attempts to reconcile his theory with orthodox doctrine by arguing that Adam's sin, a sin which was spiritual and not material, may be "imputed backward" to embrace all men who lived before Adam.[68] La Peyrère's entire theory, Oddos observes, is shot through and through with the Pelagian heresy.[69]

The *Systema theologicum ex prae Adamitarum hypothesi* represents the first volume in La Peyrère's projected work concerning the Election, Rejection, and Recall of the Jews. Significantly, the *Praeadamitae* is dedicated "To all the Synagogues of the Jews dispersed over the face of the Earth."[70] La Peyrère intends to demonstrate the Election of the Jews by showing that their origin is completely separate from that of the rest of humankind. In his Preface, La Peyrère argues that his hypothesis strengthens rather than weakens the case for the truth of Christianity by putting belief on a more rational basis. He declares his fear of falling into heresy and states that he will willingly retract his hypothesis should anyone be able to demonstrate its error.[71]

In his letter to Pope Alexander VII, La Peyrère maintains that his pre-Adamite theory could be of great service to the Church "pour l'intelligence de l'Ecriture Sainte et pour l'éclaircissement des mystères de la foi" ("in the understanding of the Holy Scriptures and in the elucidation of the mysteries of the faith"). His hypothesis, he claims, dissolves the conflict between the Bible and "les histoires les plus anciennes des nations païennes" ("the most ancient histories of the pagan nations"). And even more importantly, La Peyrère argues, the pre-Adamite theory permits Christianity to absorb that rush of previously unknown peoples emerging from the Age of Discovery. "Par cette hypothèse se décid[ent] toutes les disputes qu'on fait aujourd'hui touchant l'origine des peuples que nos pères ont découverts aux deux derniers siècles"[72] ("This hypothesis resolves all the disputes taking place today concerning the origin of those peoples which our fathers have discovered in the last two centuries").

The *Systema theologicum* is divided into five major books. Book I describes the brutal and lawless "state of nature" of humankind before

68. *A Theological Systeme,* pp. 7–10. See Oddos, *Recherches,* pp. 142–51.
69. Oddos, *Recherches,* p. 151.
70. *Men Before Adam,* Preface.
71. Ibid., "Proeme."
72. *Lettre à Philotime,* pp. 111–12.

Adam. Human beings were profoundly attached to the matter from which they had been created. Nothing was a crime, since law had not yet been established. Both death and sin were "natural," inherent tendencies of that "matter" which man shares with the beasts.[73] It was only much later, with the creation of Adam, that sin and death took on any real meaning. Adam was the first human to be truly capable of sin, since he alone had been created in law. Likewise, he was the first human being for whom there existed the possibility of immortality.[74] Popkin wonders whether this "state of nature" theory was not borrowed from Hobbes, who wrote the *Leviathan* during his stay in Paris (1650–1655) and frequented the same circles as did La Peyrère.[75] J. S. Spink goes on to ask how much Pascal himself might have borrowed from Hobbes, neglecting the main framework of Hobbes' political philosophy and choosing "only those points which were useful for his own bitter arraignment of human nature."[76]

Book II treats the Election of the Jews in Adam. God, La Peyrère explains, confirmed this election by the Covenant with Abraham, in which he set the Jews apart from all nations and gave them an elected homeland.[77] La Peyrère underscores the abyss which separates the Jews from the Gentiles, who, though far more ancient than the Jews, make a tardy entrance into Providential History. To a one, the Gentiles were "Atheists and without a God."[78] The two Creation accounts found in Genesis, La Peyrère insists, speak to the separate creations of the Jews and the Gentiles. The Gentiles, as attested by Genesis 1:26–27, were made by "the Word of God." The Jews, on the other hand, were formed from "clay" (Genesis 2:7). The second chapter of Genesis, notes La Peyrère, is the only one of the two accounts which mentions Adam. La Peyrère thus concludes that the Jews in effect constitute a separate species of humankind.[79]

Book V recapitulates the arguments of Books I and II in reverse order, reading sacred history backward from Christ to Adam and explaining

73. *A Theological Systeme,* pp. 23–27. In his final work, *Des Juifs, Elus, Rejetés, et Rapelés,* La Peyrère derives *péché* from the Latin "*pecus*" (fol. 50). Cited by Oddos, *Recherches,* p. 151.

74. *A Theological Systeme,* pp. 49–54.

75. Popkin, *Isaac La Peyrère,* p. 45.

76. *French Free-Thought,* p. 73.

77. *A Theological Systeme,* Book 2, Chapters II–IV. Popkin observes that La Peyrère's conception of Eretz Israel might astonish even the most expansionist Israelis: the ancient Jewish concession included all the territory between the Nile and the Euphrates! Popkin, *Isaac La Peyrère,* p. 46.

78. Ibid., p. 92.

79. Ibid., pp. 113–14, 154–55. See Oddos, *Recherches,* p. 143.

how the Gentiles came to be grafted onto the Elect. Books III and IV, in which La Peyrère attempts to document the pre-Adamite hypothesis more scientifically, disappear completely from the final manuscript version of La Peyrère's magnum opus written after his conversion. The lacuna created by their removal, Oddos observes, deprives La Peyrère's whole system of the historical, philological, and exegetical bases on which it is founded.[80] It is in Books III and IV of the *Systema theologicum* in which La Peyrère stumbles into a vision of human history which is truly radical for his time.

La Peyrère's Critique of Genesis

La Peyrère begins by seeking to prove the existence of the pre-Adamites "out of Genesis itself."[81] In 1663, when writing his *Apology*, La Peyrère would explain that he had long sensed that the Old Testament we possess is incomplete. The Jews, interested only in their own history, had removed from the original text of the Old Testament much material related to the peoples who had come before them:

> Partout où je lisais l'Ecriture Sainte, je n'y trouvais ni suite, ni ordre, ni liaison solide d'un verset à l'autre. Ce que je rapportais à [ce] que, par le témoignage même de l'Ecriture Sainte, quantité de Livres originaux ont été perdus. Et que nous n'avons que des extraits des originaux qui ne sont plus.[82]

> Wherever I read in Holy Scripture, I found in it neither consistency nor order nor a firm linking from one verse to the next. I attributed this to the fact that, according even to the testimony of Scripture itself, a great many of the original Books have been lost. And we possess only extracts of original texts which no longer exist.

Genesis itself, La Peyrère maintains in Book III of the *Systema theologicum*, contains numerous textual relics which suggest the existence of the non-Adamic peoples. He points to Genesis 6:4 which speaks of "Giants upon the earth" and tells of the "sons of God" having married "the daughters of men." La Peyrère explains this verse as alluding to the intermarriage of the sons of Adam with the daughters of the Gentiles.[83] He devotes

80. Oddos, *Recherches,* p. 173.
81. *A Theological Systeme,* p. 129.
82. *Apologie de la Peyrère,* p. 81.
83. *A Theological Systeme,* p. 152, cf. pp. 216–17.

particular care to an analysis of the story of Cain and Abel. Abel, according to Genesis 4, was a shepherd. Why, asks La Peyrère, would Abel have kept sheep were there no other men to buy them? Cain was a "husbandman," a profession which required tools. Thus, there must have been "articifers in those days." Otherwise, Cain would have been "a very busybody," digging mines, constructing furnaces, and making the forge necessary for the fabrication of his plowshares. Indeed, does not the fact that Adam and Eve covered themselves with "garments" once they realized their nakedness suggest that "Curriers, Shoemakers and Skinners" were already exercising their trades "in those dayes"?[84]

La Peyrère identifies another element in the Cain and Abel story which suggests the existence of the pre-Adamic peoples. Having slain his brother, Cain becomes afraid and says to God, "Whosoever finds me shall slay me" (Genesis 4:14). Of whom, asks La Peyrère, was Cain afraid? Surely not of Adam and Eve, who were supposedly the only other people on the face of the earth? If there were no other people in the world, why did God set a mark on Cain in order to protect him? Cain's flight "east of Eden," where he took a wife and founded a city (Genesis 4:16–17), suggests to La Peyrère that Cain must have encountered the pre-Adamites. If he did not, where did he find a wife? "And with what workmen and carpenters, did Cain build this City?"[85]

In the course of Book III of the *Systema theologicum*, La Peyrère quickly moves toward the conclusion that Genesis cannot be read literally. All that is set down in the second chapter of Genesis, he objects, could not possibly have taken place in the second half of the sixth day. The naming of all the creatures of the earth by Adam would have required months if not years. The time required to bring the slow and lumbering elephants from India and Africa would have infinitely exceeded the half a day described by Genesis. And what of those innumerable species of animals which had to "swim so much sea, and pass over so much land to come from America to Mesopotamia"?[86]

84. Ibid., pp. 147–48.

85. Ibid., pp. 149–152. La Peyrère notes that these questions concerning the Cain and Abel story were put to him by Michel Marolles, the Abbot of Villeloin. *A Theological Systeme,* p. 149. After his conversion, La Peyrère collaborated with Marolles on the notes for Marolles' French translation of the Bible, suppressed by the Archbishop of Paris in 1671 before it reached the end of Leviticus. In his notes on Genesis, La Peyrère, while noting that it had been censured by the Church, presents evidence for his pre-Adamite theory. See Popkin, *Isaac La Peyrère,* pp. 19, 182–83, n. 92.

86. *A Theological Systeme,* pp. 138–39.

Behind La Peyrère's critique of Genesis as universal history obviously stands his realization of the complexity and immensity of the world as revealed by the Age of Discovery. In the Preface to his *Relation d'Islande* (1663), La Peyrère would later write:

> Nous ne connaissons pas la moitié du monde . . . les géographes inondent ce qu'ils ne connaissent pas et noyent dans leurs cartes quantité de peuples qui se portent bien dans les terres qu'ils habitent. . . . Je ne doute pas que tant de peuple inconnus soient quelque jour connus.[87]

> We know not half of the world . . . geographers flood [territories] which they do not know and drown on their maps a great number of peoples who are doing very well indeed in the lands where they live. . . . I have no doubt that ever so many unknown peoples will be known one day.

La Peyrère understands that Genesis made sense as universal history only so long as European geographical and ethnological knowledge remained extremely limited. The Fathers of the Church, though they had a sublime knowledge of "les choses du ciel" ("heavenly things"), were sadly ignorant concerning "celles de la Terre"[88] ("those of the earth"). "I would St. Augustine and Lactantius were now alive, who scoffed at the Antipodes," exclaims La Peyrère: "Truly they would pity themselves, if they should hear or see those things which are discovered in the East and West Indies in this clear-sighted age, as also a great many other countries full of men; to which it is certain that none of Adam's posterity ever arrived."[89]

Biblical History Versus the Deep Abyss of Time

In many ways, La Peyrère's grander scheme of things, founded upon the notion of two Creations and serving to buttress his Messianic vision, is more medieval than modern. Yet, another current running throughout his works signals the onset of the premodernism of the Enlightenment. La Peyrère, it may be argued, is one of the first figures in the intellectual history of Europe to set forth the thesis that the Bible does not represent the summa of all empirical knowledge. Once Scripture has been deprived of this status, profane history—always judged by the Christian tradition as fabulous—suddenly appeared less unreasonable and less defective. In

87. *Relation de l'Islande,* Préface.
88. Ibid.
89. *A Theological Systeme,* p. 276.

the course of the *Systema theologicum* there emerges an entirely new conception of time, a conception which had long lagged behind those other new dimensions of the world clarified by the Age of Discovery and by Copernicus' elaboration of a new cosmos.

A very major portion of the *Systema theologicum* is devoted to proving the immeasurable antiquity of human history. La Peyrère, we should note, hardly anticipates the New Geology. He shares with his predecessors of the Renaissance, who in turn inherited it via Averroes from the ancients, the conviction that the world is eternal and has always existed.[90] "They are very much deceived," La Peyrère boldly states, "who affirm that the world was made with Adam. They have streightened the beginning and the ending in such narrow bounds that it cannot by any means fit to so small room, which is read of the world created from eternity and which shall endure to eternity."[91] In seeking to demonstrate the extreme antiquity of human history, La Peyrère draws his proofs from two sources. First, he pores through the *mémoires* of those who have visited the new worlds found in the Age of Discovery to find evidence of the antiquity of peoples previously unknown to the Christian tradition. Then, he turns to the works of scholars, like his friend Claude Saumaise, who are in the process of documenting the ancients' claims of possessing chronologies far predating those of the Bible.

In the French translations of Gomara's *Histoire générale des Indes Occidentales et Terres Neuves* (1568) and G. de la Vega's *Histoire des Incas, rois du Pérou* (1633), La Peyrère finds evidence that the Mexicans and Peruvians possess chronologies beside which the six thousand years of Christian sacred history pale in comparison.[92] From Scaliger's *De Emendatione temporum* (1583), he mines the observation that the chronologies of the Chinese go back "eight hundred eightscore thousand and seventy-three years."[93] Turning to Classical pre-Christian antiquity, La Peyrère declares

90. Italian neo-Averroism of the Renaissance, we noted in Chapter I, *Le Libertinage érudit*, furnished seventeenth-century French *libertins érudits* with three principal themes: the denial of the immortality of the soul, the refutation of miracles, and the negation of the Creation. La Peyrère certainly subscribed to the latter of these two theses. If we can believe the anecdote cited by Pintard (see n. 62 of the present chapter), La Peyrère also endorsed the first.

91. *A Theological Systeme*, p. 258.

92. Ibid., p. 159.

93. Ibid., p. 177. On Joseph Scaliger (1540–1609), who created the first major new chronological system in the West after Bede's, see Donald J. Wilcox, *The Measure of Times Past: Pre-Newtonian Chronologies and the Rhetoric of Relative Time* (Chicago: The University of Chicago Press, 1987), pp. 196–203.

his intention to make use of "the most ancient and best-esteemed Philosophers and Historians": Herodotus, Diodorus Siculus, Strabo, and Cicero.[94] Were these philosophers such "blockheads," asks La Peyrère, "that they would not have found themselves grossly gull'd and abus'd in Histories of so many thousand years ago, if they had but smelled, or had the least hint that the world was so lately made, and only from the time of Adam?"[95]

La Peyrère then proceeds to reinforce the testimony of the ancients with facts gleaned from Scaliger's *De Emendatione temporum* and Saumaise's *De annis climacteris*. Scaliger had reconstructed Eusebius' *Chronicle*, according to which there had already been some sixteen Egyptian dynasties by the time of Abraham's birth. However, La Peyrère observes, the Christian chronologists have only allowed for some three hundred years "from the Flood of Noah to the birth of Abraham." How, he protests, can three hundred years have sufficed for sixteen Egyptian dynasties?[96] From Saumaise's treatise on the history of astrology, and magic, La Peyrère draws another set of parallel arguments. Abraham, he explains, learned the sciences of astronomy, astrology, and magic from the Chaldeans and taught them to the Egyptians, thus paving the way for the wisdom of Moses. How, he wonders, could the Chaldeans have perfected their knowledge of these sciences, which required "long observation and experiment," in the mere nineteen hundred years which Genesis assigns to the time between Adam and Abraham?[97]

La Peyrère's blending of modern and ancient sources in order to establish the prebiblical antiquity of human history should perhaps be taken to represent a growing awareness of some *érudits* that human history had to be older and more complicated than Christian chronologists had ever imagined. Christian apologists in midseventeenth-century France had already seen the necessity of countering such speculation. Just as La Peyrère was publishing his *Systema theologicum*, Pascal was setting to work on his *Apology for the Christian Religion*, in which he would defend the traditional chronology of the Bible. As part of his proof that the Jews constitute the world's oldest people, Pascal launches a broadside attack on the chronologies of the Chinese:

94. *A Theological Systeme*, pp. 155–77.
95. Ibid., p. 176.
96. Ibid., pp. 253–54.
97. Ibid., pp. 177–99.

Je ne crois que les histoires dont les témoins se feraient égorger.

Lequel est la plus croyable des deux, Moïse ou la Chine?

Il n'est pas question de voir cela en gros: je vous dis qu'il y a de quoi aveugler et de quoi éclairer.[98]

I only believe histories whose witnesses are ready to be put to death.

Which is the more credible of the two, Moses or China?

There is no question of the broad view. I tell you that there is enough here to blind and to enlighten. (822)

In Chapter III (Fragment 822 and Neo-Augustinian Theology), we will encounter Pascal arguing that the Chinese pretensions to extreme antiquity are but another instance of the way in which God has blinded the wise to the truth of Scripture. His tactic involves a neo–Augustinian variation on the traditional argument that the myths of the pagans have been concocted by Satan in order to cast doubt on the authority of Revelation. In fragments 481 and 436, we shall find him also rejecting the "histoires" of the Greeks, the Egyptians, and the Aztecs.[99] Pascalian scholarship has tended to assign Pascal's knowledge of the Aztec chronologies rejected in fragment 481 to his reading of Montaigne (*Essays*, 3, 6).[100] However, it remains a possibility, given the notoriety of La Peyrère's book and Pascal's reference to it in fragment 575, that Pascal was not unaware of the way in which La Peyrère and others were attempting to rehabilitate the historical status of non-Christian chronologies.

Pascal's reaction to such attempts to call into question the authority of Genesis could not be more uncompromising. In fragment 296, he proposes the astonishing thesis that only five generations of Patriarchs stood between Moses and Adam. "Sem qui a vu Lamech qui a vu Adam a vu aussi Jacob, qui a vu ceux qui ont vu Moïse: donc le déluge et la création son vrais" ("Shem, who saw Lamech, who saw Adam, also saw Jacob, who saw those who saw Moses: therefore the Flood and Creation are true") (296).[101] Pascal's hard-line stance in this matter should serve to remind us that La Peyrère, in attempting to argue that human history did not begin with Adam, confronted a unanimous Judeo-Christian tradition to the contrary.

The earliest Church Fathers had debated the issue with pagan philoso-

98. For a complete discussion of this fragment, see Chapter III, "Histoire de Chine": Pascal and the Challenge to Biblical Time.

99. See Chapter III, Pascal and the Non-Christian Religions.

100. See Philippe Sellier, ed., *Pensées* (1991), p. 506, n. 12.

101. See my discussion of this fragment in Wetsel, *L'Ecriture et le Reste,* pp. 63, 186–87.

phers. Theophilus of Antioch (170 A.D.) attempted to refute the claim of Apollonius the Egyptian that the world was some 153,075 years old.[102] However, Augustine had essentially closed that entire discussion in the tenth chapter of the twelfth book of *The City of God*, "Of the falseness of the history which allots many thousand years to the world's past":

> They are deceived [who believe] those highly mendacious documents which profess to give the history of many thousand years. . . . Reckoning [by our documents, which are truly sacred], we find that not 6000 years have yet passed. . . . How . . . can we believe these documents which, though full of fabulous and fictitious antiquities, [the pagans] would fain oppose to the authority of our well-known and divine books, which predicted that the whole world would believe them, and which the whole world accordingly has believed?[103]

One would be hard-pressed to demonstrate that the Christian tradition on the whole matter of the inadmissibility of non-Christian sources budged an inch between the fifth and the seventeenth century. Popkin finds occasional instances of heretics executed during the medieval period for denying the historicity of Genesis. He presents evidence that during the Renaissance, Paracelsus, Giordano Bruno, and the circle around Sir Walter Raleigh anticipated La Peyrère's pre-Adamite theory.[104] However, one may safely conclude that orthodox opinion among seventeenth-century theologians coincided perfectly with that of Augustine. Le Maistre de Sacy, Pascal's mentor in matters exegetical, reflects a long and unbroken Christian tradition when he maintains that pagan documents and myths are but *singeries* concocted by Satan in order to cast doubt on Revelation. For instance, in his commentary on Genesis, Sacy argues that the Greek poets forged the myth of Saturn (whose symbol recalls the Ark) from the Biblical story of Noah and the Flood.[105]

It is difficult to determine how relevant the Jewish rabbinical position on the matter of the historical accuracy of Genesis is to La Peyrère's hypothesis. La Peyrère does not appear to have been all that familiar with post-Biblical Jewish writings.[106] A number of thinkers in the rabbinical

102. See R. Popkin, "The Pre-Adamite Theory in the Renaissance," p. 51.

103. Saint Augustine *The City of God*, Marcus Dods, tr. (New York: Modern Library, 1950), pp. 390–91.

104. Popkin, "The Pre-Adamite Theory in the Renaissance," pp. 54–55, 58–61.

105. Louis-Isaac le Maistre de Sacy, *La Genèse: traduite en français avec l'explication du sens littéral et du sens spirituel* (Paris: Lambert Roulland, 1682), Chapter IX, pp. 350–51.

106. Myriam Yardeni, "La Religion de La Peyrère," p. 248. For another opinion, see Popkin's "The Marrano Theology of Isaac La Peyrère."

tradition, including Maimonides, had entertained the possibility that the world had always existed.[107] However, mainstream rabbinical opinion seems always to have viewed the historical sources of the pagans as but myth and fable. Popkin cites a fascinating episode from Judah Halevy's *Book of the Khazars*, written in twelfth-century Spain. The King of the Khazars has summoned to his court representatives of Aristotelian philosophy, Christianity, Islam, and Judaism. He asks the rabbi presenting the case for Judaism, "Does it not weaken thy belief if thou art told that the Indians have antiquities and buildings which they consider to be millions of years old?" The rabbi's answer reveals a position with regard to profane history which is not all that unlike the position held by Augustine, Pascal, and Le Maistre de Sacy:

> It would indeed weaken my belief had they a fixed form of religion, or a book concerning which a multitude of people held the same opinion, and in which no historical discrepancy could be found. Such a book, however, does not exist. Apart from this, they are a dissolute, unreliable people, and arouse the indignation of the followers of religions through their talk, whilst they anger them with their idols, talismans, and witchcraft.[108]

La Peyrère and *La Libre Pensée*

Book IV of the *Systema theologicum* is in many ways the most problematic of all the writings of Isaac La Peyrère. His aim in this section is to document further his thesis that the Old Testament recounts only the history of the Jews. However, in his attacks upon miracles, in his questioning of the literal inspiration of the sacred texts, and in his hypothesis that Moses did not write the Pentateuch, La Peyrère begins to undermine his own central thesis. Consciously or unconsciously, he stumbles into conclusions which recall those reached by the *libertins érudits*. After his conversion, La Peyrère repeatedly argued that his sole purpose was to defend religion by making it more believable. In his introduction to the final version of his magnum opus, written three years before his death, he insists that the pre-Adamite hypothesis was never anything more than a corollary to his grander thesis concerning the Jews:

107. See Robert M. Seltzer, *Jewish People, Jewish Thought* (New York: Macmillan, 1980), p. 399.

108. Judah Halevi, *The Kuzari* (New York: Schocken Books, 1964), Part I, p. 52. Cited by Popkin, "The Pre-Adamite Theory in the Renaissance," p. 52.

Quand je mis au jour les Préadamites, mon principal dessein n'était pas les Préadamites, mais celui que je traite en ce lieu, des juifs élus, rejetés et qui doivent être rapelés.[109]

When I brought to light the pre-Adamites, my principal intention was not the pre-Adamites but rather the one I deal with in this work: the Jews, elected, rejected and who must be recalled.

René Pintard judges La Peyrère's pre-Adamite theory as really more "heretical" than "libertine."[110] La Peyrère, he argues, was but a plaything in the hands of the real *libertins*. La Peyrère's "conversion," on the other hand, says Pintard, represented a considerable loss for *le libertinage érudit*: "Sa conversion, si peu de chose qu'elle soit en elle-même, aura eu des conséquences: elle aura été une perte pour le libertinage; elle l'aura privé d'un de ses plus originaux, d'un de ses plus plaisants hochets"[111] ("His conversion, of however little importance it was in and of itself, had consequences: it represented a loss for *le libertinage*; it deprived it of one of its most original and agreeable playthings"). As we examine Book IV of the *Systema theologicum*, we may do well to bear in mind that the fine line separating *libertinage* from belief often remained blurred in an age in which heresy still represented a crime against the state.

La Peyrère's approach to the problem of miracles would appear to be twofold. By reducing Biblical miracles to local dimensions, he hopes to underline the separateness of Jewish history and election. By preventing such miracles from intruding upon universal history, he aims to make the Old Testament text more believable as a whole. In general, La Peyrère either attempts to explain a given miracle in terms of natural causes or else reduces it to local status in which the laws of nature are perturbed only to a minor degree.

The first class of miracles, those which can be explained by natural phenomena, includes the various miracles assisting the Children of Israel during their wanderings in the wilderness. The clothes and shoes which last forty years (Deuteronomy 8:4, 29:5) are but symbolic of the fact that the Israelites were able to sustain themselves by a proper management of their herds.[112] Joshua's stopping of the sun (Joshua 10:13–14) can likewise be

109. *Des Juifs, Elus, Rejetés, et Rapelés,* Préface.

110. Pintard, *Le Libertinage érudit,* p. 361.

111. Ibid., p. 424.

112. *A Theological Systeme,* pp. 235–38. A *libertin* cited by Desmarests de Saint-Sorlin in his *Délices de l'Esprit* (Paris: A. Courbé, 1658), p. 23, argues that the passage of the Red Sea

explained as a natural phenomenon, the reflection of the sun's rays by the nearby mountain of Gibeon. He himself, La Peyrère insists, once witnessed a similar phenomenon which took place in the region near Montauban.[113] The star of Bethlehem, La Peyrère conjectures, must have really been a light or fire. How could a star have marked so small a place as a house? Besides, had such a star appeared in the heavens, "all famous historians would have spoken of it."[114]

Miracles which La Peyrère reduces to local status (and thus removes from universal history) include the column of fire guiding the Hebrews through the desert, the fiery army sent to Elijah (2 Kings 1:10–14), and the darkness which was supposed to have descended upon the earth at the death of Jesus.[115] Likewise, in the miracle wrought by Isaiah (2 Kings 20:8–12), God did not cause the sun to leave its orbit: he simply manipulated the shadow on the sundial built by Ahaz. Why, asks La Peyrère, would God have reversed the whole order of the universe for the benefit of one sick King?[116] In making sense of such miracles, La Peyrère insists, he is doing no more than rendering Scripture believable:

> I ingenuously confesse, I do not give in my name amongst those enormous upholders of miracles, who put all reason out of square. I am reasonable, and any thing that is belonging to reason I pretend an interest in. I believe those miracles of Josua and Isaiah, and do very magnify God in them, but think them no greater than they were, nor as is agreeable to reason, therefore I have contained them within their own limits.[117]

It is in the same spirit of reducing miracles to local and reasonable dimensions that La Peyrère approaches the thorny problem of Noah's Flood. More than any other, this problem bears directly on his pre-Adamite hypothesis. For if the Flood was indeed universal, wiping out all humans with the exception of Noah and his family, the pre-Adamites cannot have been the ancestors of the Gentiles. However, if La Peyrère can reduce the Flood to the status of a local miracle, Genesis is no longer incompatible with the new peoples and histories unveiled by the Age of Discovery.

---

can be explained in a similarly rational manner: Moses merely observed the tides and chose a favorable moment for his people to cross.

113. *A Theological Systeme*, pp. 229–31.

114. Ibid., pp. 220–22.

115. Ibid., pp. 219, 220, 224.

116. Ibid., pp. 222–28.

117. Ibid., p. 234.

Noah's Flood, La Peyrère reasons, must have been limited to "Palestine and the Land of the Jews." God's anger, directed at the Jews because they had violated the terms of their Election by intermarrying with pre-Adamites, can hardly be reckoned to have been justly visited upon "the Nations that dwelt in China, America, the South, or Greenland."[118] Examining the text of Genesis 8, La Peyrère notes that the olive branch brought back to the Ark by the dove sent out by Noah was not covered with mud. Therefore, some parts of the earth must have escaped inundation. Noah's flood could have extended no farther than the dove was able to fly in half a day. The "cataracts in the heavens" of which Genesis speaks are but hyperbole, resulting from a "high style" meant to express "the abundance of rain with which the land of the Jews was overflowed.[119]

La Peyrère's interpretation of the Flood of Noah serves to prevent Scripture from contradicting universal history. If the Flood had destroyed all the peoples of the earth, how could it have been possible for the sons of Noah to repopulate the entire world—including China, America, South America, and Greenland—within the space of five generations?[120] In 1627, the Jesuit Père Petau had calculated that Noah's male descendants could have numbered 623, 612, 358, 728 within 280 years.[121] How much more reasonable it is, urges La Peyrère, simply to conclude that the division of the "earth" recounted in Genesis 10 was really no more than the division of the Holy Land among the various Jewish tribes issued from Noah.[122]

In the final version of his projected work (written after his conversion), La Peyrère attempts to present a more orthodox interpretation of Genesis. However, since he has dropped the pre-Adamite theory contained in Books III and IV of the *Systema theologicum*, he can produce no satisfactory explanation for the origin of the Gentiles:

> Toute l'espèce de l'homme étant composée dans la seule famille de Noé . . . on ne saurait déterminer le temps ou le point auquel la ligne des gentils a commencé dans les descendants de Noé, car l'Ecriture ne le marque en façon quelconque.[123]

> The whole of human kind being composed only of the family of Noah . . . it would seem impossible to determine the time or the point at which the family line

118. Ibid., pp. 239–43.
119. Ibid., pp. 242–48.
120. Ibid., pp. 250–51.
121. *De Doctrina Temporum* (Paris, 1627), 2, p. 35. Cited by Oddos, *Recherches,* p. 183, n. 36.
122. *A Theological Systeme,* Book IV, Chapter 9.
123. *Des Juifs, Elus, Rejetés, et Rapelés,* folio 25. Cited by Oddos, *Recherches,* p. 184, n. 43.

of the Gentiles began within the descendents of Noah, since Scripture has nothing whatsoever to say on this matter.

La Peyrère and the Origins of Modern Biblical Criticism

In the *Systema theologicum*, La Peyrère reaches the remarkable conclusion that the entire Christian exegetical tradition has failed to understand the essentially figurative nature of Scripture. "How uncertain a Faith they do build," he laments "upon such weak conjectures, especially upon Hebrew speech, which is . . . so strange that it speaks almost nothing but Figures."[124] La Peyrère's Biblical criticism revolves around two fundamental propositions. The Bible, he thinks, is an entirely Judeocentric document which contains very little of universal history. Moreover, he argues, the text we possess of the Old Testament is a defective document, a truncated version of a lost original.

La Peyrère contends that the Old Testament contains far too much disorder and confusion; far too many inversions; repetitions and omissions; far too many obviously mutilated or truncated passages to represent Scripture's original text. Certain passages in Joshua, Chronicles, and Kings, he observes, are obviously taken from works which have long been lost. For instance, the miracle of Joshua's stopping the course of the sun and the moon (Joshua 12:10–14) is "manifestly copied out." Does not the passage conclude, "It is written in the books of the just?"[125] Other Old Testament passages are obviously mutilated, such as the speech of Lamech (Genesis 4:23–24)[126] and the episode of the circumcision of Moses' son (Exodus 4:24–26).[127]

La Peyrère, we should recall, knew neither Greek nor Hebrew and worked exclusively with the Vulgate text.[128] Nonetheless, almost after the fashion of a modern literary critic, he is able to see that certain passages of the Old Testament have been transposed. For instance, he remarks, the

124. *A Theological Systeme,* p. 252.

125. Ibid., p. 204.

126. "Those things which we had concerning Lamech, Gen. 4 are defective, 'Because I have slain a man to my hurt, and a young man to my grief.' For there is no mention made of that young man whom Lamech slew." *A Theological Systeme,* p. 208.

127. "That History . . . concerning the circumcision of the son of Moses is deficient, and conjectured to be deficient, because we clearly see what it should be." *A Theological Systeme,* p. 208.

128. Popkin, *Isaac La Peyrère,* p. 87.

episode of Abraham's sojourn with Abimelech at Gerar (Genesis 20) is obviously misplaced in the narrative: "For it is not likely that the King would lust after Sarah, who was an old woman who was not capable of pleasure."[129] Likewise, the tenth chapter of Deuteronomy, describing the separation of the tribe of the Levites as taking place at the time of the death of Aaron, must also have been transposed from its original position. The Levites, La Peyrère objects, had been chosen to be the guardians of the Ark long before Aaron's death.[130] La Peyrère devotes particular attention to the contradiction which exists between the fourth and eighteenth chapters of Exodus. Exodus 4:20 recounts that Moses took his wife and sons with him when he returned to Egypt to confront Pharaoh. Chapter 18, on the other hand, pictures Moses' father-in-law, Jethro, as bringing his wife and children to him after the going out from Egypt.[131] Here, as in several other instances, La Peyrère has inadvertently stumbled upon differences which exist between the "Yahwistic" and "Elohistic" texts of the Pentateuch.

La Peyrère was by no means the first Biblical commentator to notice such textual contradictions in the Old Testament. However, previous exegetes—with the glaring exception of the *libertins*—had almost all approached the problem from an apologetic perspective. Indeed, the Church Fathers and the Talmudic rabbis had perfected the art of Scriptural harmonization. In 1555, about the time of the first attacks upon the authenticity of the Bible by *la libre pensée*, Cumiranus had published his *Conciliatio omnium fere locorum totius sacrae scripturae, quae inter se pugnare videntur*. In 1648, the Protestant Thaddaeus sought to reconcile 1,050 apparent contradictions in both the Old and New Testaments. To those commentators, we may add the names Grotius, Lippomanus, Jansenius, and Le Maistre de Sacy without even beginning to exhaust the potential list.[132] In 1651, the rabbi Menasseh ben Israel, who would be much influenced by La Peyrère's *Du Rappel des Juifs*,[133] completed the publication of his *Conciliador*, in which he demonstrated how conflicting Scriptural passages could be reconciled without calling into question the inerrancy of the Bible.[134]

129. *A Theological Systeme,* pp. 208–9.

130. Ibid., p. 209.

131. Ibid., pp. 209–10.

132. See Geneviève Delassault, *Le Maistre de Sacy et son temps* (Paris: Nizet, 1957), pp. 205–10.

133. See n. 39 of the present chapter.

134. Popkin, *Isaac La Peyrère,* p. 50.

La Peyrère's analysis of the contradictions contained in Scripture, designed to demonstrate that the Old Testament is a defective text, has little in common with the earlier apologetic tradition. Rather, it recalls the attack upon the Bible by *la libre pensée*. The *libertins* cited by J. Boucher in *Les Triomphes de la religion chrestienne* (1638) find the Old Testament irrational and incoherent. "Mais pourquoi," they want to know, "y a-[t]-il tant de confusions dans les livres de la Bible, où l'on voit plusieurs discours sans aucun ordre, si peu arrangés et réglés, que dans un même chapitre on trouvera une si grande diversité de sentences et si éloignées les unes aux autres, qu'il est impossible d'y rien concevoir?"[135] ("But why are there so many confusions in the books of the Bible, in which one sees a number of discourses without any order, so little arranged and ordered, that in a single chapter one finds so great a diversity of contradictory maxims, that it is impossible to understand anything in it?").

The *beaux esprits* cited by Père Garasse in his apologetic work *La Doctrine curieuse* (1624) have trouble believing almost anything written in Genesis. They reject the first and second chapters (and particularly the story of the Fall) as "choses si étranges et de si dure créance qu'il faudrait avoir perdu le sens pour les recevoir sans contradiction"[136] ("things so strange and so hard to believe that one would have to have lost his mind to receive them without opposition"). Like La Peyrère, the skeptics cited by Boucher in *Les Triomphes* . . . are unable to accept any Biblical miracles which conflict with science. They find Scripture as a whole to be fraught with "grands manquements et défauts très-notables, touchant les propriétés naturelles des choses dont elle fait mention"[137] ("great omissions and extremely notable faults concerning the natural properties of the things which it mentions"). They dismiss such miracles as Joshua's stopping of the sun as pure invention.[138] Noah's flood particularly provokes their incredulity. "Comment est-il possible que la nature ait pu fournir

135. J. Boucher, *Les Triomphes de la religion chrestienne contenans les résolutions de trois cens soixante et six questions* (Paris: L. Sonnius, 1638), p. 174.

136. P. Garasse, *La Doctrine curieuse des beaux esprits de ce temps ou prétendus tels* (Paris: Chappelet, 1624), pp. 649–52. The *libertins* criticized by Père Garasse share with La Peyrère the conviction that the world has always existed. However, rejecting entirely the notion of Divine Creation of humanity, they go on to speculate that man "était né de pourriture comme les rats" ("was born from rotten matter as rats are"). Garasse identifies this theory as borrowed from "le maudit Lucilio Vanini." *La Doctrine curieuse,* p. 651. On Vanini, see Pintard, *Le Libertinage érudit,* pp. 20–21.

137. *Les Triomphes,* p. 177.

138. Ibid., p. 255.

d'une si grande quantité d'eaux pour noyer tout le monde?"[139] ("How is it possible that nature could have furnished enough water to drown the entire world?").

La Peyrère had undoubtedly encountered such objections to Holy Writ by the *libertins* whom he had known in the circle associated with Père Mersenne.[140] He obviously borrows many of their objections to the Bible. But to what end? Is he a covert *libertin* himself, taking cover behind his great Messianic vision? Or, as he insists in his letter to Pope Alexander VII,[141] is he attempting to answer the skeptics' objections to Christianity by rendering the Bible more rational and more believable? We will return to this important question. But first we should consider one final issue: La Peyrère's rejection of the Mosaic authorship of the Pentateuch, a theory which greatly alarmed the Inquisition and which he was specifically required to retract at the time of his conversion.[142]

La Peyrère's Rejection of the Mosaic Authorship of the Pentateuch

During the course of Book IV of the *Systema theologicum*, La Peyrère moves rather quickly from his hypothesis that the Old Testament has been corrupted by fallible human transcribers and copiers to the conclusion that the Pentateuch cannot have had a single author. Tradition, he notes, ascribes the entire first five books of the Bible to Moses. Yet, Scripture never once states this fact. Indeed, Holy Writ tends to imply the contrary, for Moses could certainly not have written the account of his own death! Nor could he have narrated those events which followed his death. How, asks La Peyrère, could Moses have written the words "These are the

139. Ibid., p. 205.

140. Among La Peyrère's closest friends we should probably count La Mothe le Vayer, Gassendi, Naudé, and Patin. Nor should we forget that it was Bourdelot, later physician to Christina after her abdication, who first brought La Peyrère to Paris and introduced him to the Prince of Condé and Père Mersenne's circle. See Oddos, *Recherches,* Chapter 3. For details on these particular individuals, see the extensive listings in the index of Pintard's *Le Libertinage erudit*. . . .

141. See Chapter II, *The Systema theologicum ex prae Adamitarum.*

142. Among the other specific heresies which La Peyrère was required to abjure: his pre-Adamite hypothesis and theory of Original Sin; his belief in the eternity of the world; his doubts concerning the universality of the Flood; his contention that only Palestine was darkened at the death of Christ. See Pintard, *Le Libertinage érudit,* p. 422.

words which Moses spake beyond the Jordan" (Deuteronomy 1:1) when he died before crossing the Jordan?

La Peyrère notes other texts in the Pentateuch which suggest a post-Mosaic authorship. Deuteronomy 3:14 recounts that a territory conquered by Jair is called by his name "even unto this day." Moses, observes La Peyrère, would hardly have added the phrase "even unto this day." La Peyrère, noting a reference in Numbers 21:14 to the "book of warrs of the Lord," concludes that there must have existed an earlier text of the Pentateuch than the one we possess.[143] Both the Jewish and Christian traditions had always explained Moses' knowledge of events which took place after his death as the result of the gift of prophecy. However, the medieval Jewish commentator Aben Ezra (1093–1167) had attributed the composition of the Pentateuch to Esdras. Just how popular this attribution had become by the middle of the seventeenth century may perhaps be judged by the care Pascal takes to refute the idea in fragments 970–972.[144]

In Chapter 33 of his *Leviathan*, Hobbes had posed similar questions concerning the Mosiac authorship of the Pentateuch. Popkin speculates that there may have been an exchange of ides between Hobbes and La Peyrère on the matter.[145] Hobbes published the *Leviathan* in 1651. La Peyrère had written the first version of the *Praeadamitae* in the early 1640s, but we have no way of knowing whether his theory concerning the Mosaic authorship of the Pentateuch figured in this manuscript, which has been lost for over three hundred years.

The controversy provoked by Hobbes and La Peyrère—and subsequently by Richard Simon in his *Histoire critique du Vieux Testament* (1678)—over the Mosiac authorship of the Pentateuch may seem almost unreal to those of us accustomed to a modern reading of the Bible. But for an apologist like Le Maistre de Sacy, the chief Biblical authority at Port-Royal, to question Moses' authority is to undermine the very foundations of Christian Truth. He directs his *Préface à la Genèse* specifically against those who "se servent de la personne de Moïse et de ce qu'il dit . . . touchant la création du monde . . . pour en prendre des sujets de leurs discours plein d'insolence et de blasphème" ("make use of the person of Moses and of what he says . . . concerning the creation of the world . . .

143. *A Theological Systeme,* pp. 204–6.

144. On the Esdras fragments (970–72), see my discussion in *L'Ecriture et le Reste,* p. 187. For a synthesis of the Jewish tradition on the Mosaic authorship of the Pentateuch, see Popkin, *Isaac La Peyrère,* pp. 49–50.

145. See *Isaac La Peyrère,* pp. 45, 49.

to find subjects for their writings full of insolence and blasphemy"). Sacy's position concerning the literal inspiration of Scripture could not be more clear: "Il n'importe que ce soit Moïse . . . qui en ait été le secrétaire. C'est Dieu certainement qui en est l'Auteur. *Ce sont ses pensées et ses paroles*"[146] ("It is of little importance that it was Moses . . . who was the scribe who wrote it down. It was God himself who was its author. *These are his thoughts and his words*).

By the standards of a Sacy or a Pascal, La Peyrère's conclusions concerning the Pentateuch and the Bible in general are very heretical indeed:

> I need not trouble the Reader much further to prove a thing in itself sufficiently evident, that the first five books of the Bible were not written by Moses, as is thought. Nor need any one wonder after this, when he reads many things confused, and out of order, obscure, deficient, many things omitted and misplaced, when they shall consider with themselves that they are a heap of Copie confusedly taken.[147]

What a tremendous abyss stands between Sacy's notion that the Bible constitutes God's very thoughts and words and La Peyrère's description of Scripture as "a heap of Copie confusedly taken"! How very accurate is Popkin's analysis of the relevance to modern thought of what La Peyrère stumbled onto as he sought to document his great Messianic vision:

> Whether La Peyrère realized it or not, when he developed his critique of Scripture in order to buttress his case for the pre-Adamite theory, he also began a chain of analyses that would end up transforming the evaluation of Scripture from a holy to a profane work. The Bible, for many, would no longer be looked upon as Revelation from God, but as tales and beliefs of the primitive Hebrews, to be compared with the tales and beliefs of other Near Eastern groups. This rather drastic consequence grew out of La Peyrère's need, for the sake of his theory, to be able to rewrite, eliminate, or ignore, passages in Scripture.[148]

The Legacy of La Peyrère

La Peyrère's influence during the Enlightenment, documented by Popkin, Rossi, and McKee,[149] cannot detain us here. We must let a single cita-

146. Le Maistre de Sacy, *La Genèse,* Préface, Première Partie, partie iii. Italics mine.

147. *A Theological Systeme,* p. 208.

148. Popkin, *Isaac La Peyrère,* p. 73.

149. Ibid., Chapter 9, "The Pre-Adamite Theory in the Enlightenment." Rossi, *Dark Abyss of Time,* pp. 159–61, 174–75, 186, 213, 251, 268–69. McKee, "Isaac de La Peyrère, a Precursor of Eighteenth-Century Critical Deists," pp. 473–85.

tion suffice. Surveying the damage done to the Mosaic authorship of the Pentateuch during the previous 150 years, Thomas Paine would note with satisfaction in *The Age of Reason* (1795): "Take away from Genesis that Moses was the author, on which only the strange belief that it is the word of God has stood, and there remains nothing of Genesis but an anonymous book of stories, fables and traditionary or invented absurdities or downright lies."[150]

Only in 1948 would the Pontifical Biblical Commission authorize Catholic scholars to make use of the Documentary Theory,[151] the fundamentals of which had been set down by Richard Simon in his *Histoire critique du Vieux Testament* (1678). The extent of Simon's debt to La Peyrère remains unclear. Simon had befriended the aged father of the pre-Adamites during his retirement at the Oratorian seminary at Aubervilliers. But he specifically rejected La Peyrère's pre-Adamite thesis. To argue that there were men before Adam, he told La Peyrère, would be to "combattre toute la tradition"[152] ("to wage war against the entire [Christian] tradition"). Nor could Simon give any credence at all to the ancient chronologies which La Peyrère had cited to prove the extreme antiquity of human history. "Il n'y en a point qui aient menti plus imprudemment," he writes to La Peyrère, "que les astrologues chaldéens" ("There have never been more imprudent liars than the Chaldean astrologers"). As for the Egyptians: "Leurs prêtres étaient des trompeurs de profession"[153] ("their priests were deceivers by profession").

Later, criticizing Spinoza's *Tractatus*, Simon would attribute Spinoza's irreligious conclusions to his reading of "le Système mal digéré de la Peyrère auteur des Préadamites"[154] ("the ill-digested system of La Peyrère, author of the pre-Adamites"). Ironically, Bossuet would later have both the *Tractatus* and the *Histoire critique du Vieux Testament* placed on the Roman Index.[155] At about the same time, Bossuet, at the invitation of

150. Thomas Paine, *The Age of Reason, Part the Second, Being an Investigation of True and Fabulous Theology* (London, 1795), p. 4. Cited by Popkin, *Isaac La Peyrère,* p. 73.

151. *The Jerusalem Bible* (New York: Doubleday, 1966) "Introduction to the Pentateuch," p. 7.

152. Richard Simon, *Lettres choisies,* 2, p. 1.

153. Ibid., p. 11.

154. Richard Simon, *De l'inspiration des Livres sacrés* (Rotterdam, 1687), p. 48. Cited by Popkin, *Isaac La Peyrère,* p. 88. On Richard Simon, see Jean Steinmann, *Richard Simon et les origines de l'exégèse biblique* (Paris: Desclée de Brouwer, 1959).

155. See Jean Orcibal, "Les Jansénistes face à Spinoza," *Revue de littérature comparée* (October 1949): 441–68.

Arnauld, undertook a defense of the Mosaic authorship of the Pentateuch in the second part of his *Discours sur l'histoire universelle*.[156]

Simon's expression "mal digéré" ("ill-digested") is perhaps not an altogether inappropriate description of La Peyrère's Biblical criticism, in which everything is ultimately subsumed into his Messianic vision and speculations concerning the Jews. For instance, though he many times advances the notion that the Pentateuch has been transcribed from multiple previous documents, La Peyrère fails to apply this hypothesis to the first two chapters of Genesis. Preoccupied with documenting the separate origins of the Jews and the Gentiles, he stops short of breaking through to Wellhausen's discovery that the two Creation accounts represent two different narrative traditions. Since Wellhausen, Genesis 2:4ff has been assigned to the "Yahwistic" ("J") source and Genesis 1 to the "Priestly" ("P") tradition.

In all fairness to La Peyrère, probably he could never have made this breakthrough, since he knew neither Greek nor Hebrew. But he comes remarkably close to it in his analysis of the two accounts of Creation found in Genesis:

> It is worth our taking notice that the men of the first creation (who, according to my supposition, are Gentiles), as also the whole world, were created *by the word*. The first chapter of Genesis hath this expressly, which is the chapter of the creation. *And God said, let us make man according to our own Image*. He said, *Let us make*. And by his word he made him. But not by his word, but of wrought clay, the Lord made Adam, Genesis 2.[157]

* * *

In and of itself, La Peyrère's whole Messianic scheme was, to say the least, wildly out of touch with reality. One can hardly imagine Louis XIV, who would subsequently expel the Protestants from France with the revocation of the Edict of Nantes (1685), even considering serving as the patron of the Jews' return to France. Nor, for that matter, can one quite conceive of the French Counter-Reformation Church's consenting to undertake the building of special temples for the Jews during their recall and conversion. Judged by the theological standards of his day, Oddos reminds us, there is hardly a single line in the *Systema* which is not "profon-

156. J.-B. Bossuet, *Discours sur l'histoire universelle* (Paris: Garnier-Flammarion, 1966), Chapter XXVIII, pp. 323ff.

157. *A Theological Systeme*, p. 113.

dément hérétique."[158] Yet, ironically, and perhaps because of his close association with the *libertins érudits*, La Peyrère comes to adopt an apologetic stance which in many ways prefigures the modern theological attempt to render Christianity more credible.

In the final chapters of the *Systema*, La Peyrère raises questions which are not irrelevant to Christianity's later struggle with modernity. Why does Scripture seem so contrary to reason? Why did God choose to reject his Chosen People? Why has Providence permitted so much schism, hatred, and division among Christians? In the *Apology*, Pascal will confront these questions. But he will answer them all from the perspective of the great Augustinian doctrines of Original Sin and *Deus absconditus*.[159] From the perspective of modern theology, La Peyrère, though in many ways an atavistic throwback to the Renaissance, seems curiously modern indeed.

At the very end of the *Systema*, La Peyrère enunciates a final, clearly heretical doctrine: the Universal Salvation of humankind. Citing the precedent of La Mothe le Vayer's *De la vertu des payens*, in which his friend had sought to prove that the great sages of pre-Christian antiquity had been saved,[160] La Peyrère extends the benefits of Christ's saving work to "those Gentiles in the first age, from the creation of the world, till the framing of Adam."[161] Citing Romans 8:14, La Peyrère asserts his belief that all "those Gentiles begotten before and after Adam" qualified as potential "bondsmen and servants of Christ":

> I think they had the spirit of Christ because I think they were . . . inspired by the spirit of Christ, which by secret operations and thoughts, wrought in them salvation to life eternal. The spirit of Christ was in the Gentiles, as the soul is in Infants . . . as reason is in Children. . . . The spirit of Christ was in them, as in a grain of Corn there is a vegetative power. . . . The spirit of Christ was given to the Gentiles not knowing, being supine and asleep. . . . The spirit of Christ was in them, but it was hidden and unknown, nor revealed itself unto them. They felt and worshiped that spirit; they felt that which they knew not, they worshiped that which they were ignorant of.[162]

La Peyrère's belief in the final salvation of all humankind could not be more profoundly in conflict with those great Augustinian doctrines which

158. Oddos, *Recherches*, p. 173.

159. See Chapter IV, The Uses and Dangers of Skepticism, and Chapter V, The Role of Argument in the *Apology:* The Hardened Skeptics Reconsidered.

160. On La Mothe le Vayer's *De la vertu des payens,* see Chapter III, Le Vayer's *De la vertu des payens*.

161. *A Theological Systeme,* p. 348.

162. Ibid., pp. 349–50.

so inform the *Pensées* of Pascal. However, assessing La Peyrère's system of Biblical interpretation from the perspective of that modern Catholic liberalism confirmed by the Second Vatican Council, Père Jean Steinmann found much to admire:

> Il est bien probable que depuis les Pères de l'Eglise, et André de Saint-Victor, on ne s'était jamais exprimé à ce sujet avec autant de science et de justesse. Les difficultés de l'Ecriture sont bien vues, et le sens des vraies solutions. Isaac La Peyrère avait du génie, mais il venait trop tôt. . . . Il pressentait la grandeur du monde et la vieillesse de l'homme. On lui opposait la tradition. Il était d'accord. Mais il pensait que l'Ecriture n'était pas opposée à sa thèse et il avait bien raison. Il ne fut compris par personne, excepté Spinoza. Richard Simon eut tort de le moquer car il devra lui-même beaucoup au *Systema*.[163]

> It is very likely indeed that since the Fathers of the Church and André de Saint-Victor, no one had ever expressed himself on this subject with so much learning and accuracy. The difficulties of Scripture are truly discerned. And La Peyrère had an innate sense of what would be the real solutions to them. Isaac La Peyrère had genius, but he came on the scene too early. . . . He had a presentiment of the immensity of the world and of the antiquity of humanity. He was told that he was in conflict with Holy Tradition. He agreed. But he thought that Scripture was not in conflict with his thesis and he was indeed right. No one understood him, with the exception of Spinoza. Richard Simon was quite wrong to make fun of him, because he himself would owe a very great deal to the *Systema*.

La Peyrère remains an eminently enigmatic figure. Seeking to synthesize the three great religious traditions of his time, he never fully identifies with any one of them. He is a Pelagian Calvinist, a philo-semite who knows little of rabbinical Judaism, and a Catholic whose only use for the Church is as an agent of universal reconciliation. He is a curious amalgam of historical perspectives. While his Messianic vision seems almost to belong to the world of Joachim of Fiore, his attempt to rationalize miracles is at one with the goals of the Enlightenment. He is profoundly a throwback to the Renaissance. At ease with Christian skepticism and pre-Christian antiquity, he is at the same time a student of the new pluralistic vision of culture and the world. His theory of two creations was wrong-headed, but it spoke to a growing intuition that human history had to be older and more complicated than anyone had ever imagined.

In the context of modernity, La Peyrère's thought is not without contradiction and ambiguity. He indeed anticipates the modern pluralistic vision of the world when he restores to Scripture a whole set of particular

163. Steinmann, *Richard Simon*, p. 57.

meanings which tradition had transformed into universal history. His most radical discovery was the dimension of Deep Time in human history. Another two centuries would pass before his intuitions would take the form of scientific theory. And yet, as Popkin so ably demonstrates, La Peyrère would leave a darker legacy to modernity. In the nineteenth century, his polygenetic origins theory, meant to separate Gentile from Jew, would reemerge as racist political doctrine.[164]

164. See Popkin, *Isaac La Peyrère,* Chapter 10, "Pre-Adamism and Racism."

CHAPTER III

Pascal and the Non-Christian Religions

The student of the comparative study of religions may well be disappointed by Pascal's scant knowledge of the non-Christian religions. Other than Islam, Pascal appears to be aware of the existence of only two religions: "celle de la Chine" (436, 454, 481, 822) and the religion recounted by "les historiens de Mexico" (481). To these, we might add Pascal's rather sketchy references to the no longer extant religions of the Greeks, the Romans, and the Egyptians (454, 451, 436).

Pascal makes short work of those ancient religions which are no longer extant. They are shown to have nothing to offer the *chercheur* because they have no verifiable history. When they are set up against the Old Testament, it becomes immediately evident that these antique religions were founded upon nothing but myth and fable. Unlike Moses, a quasi eyewitness to the Creation and the Flood (296, 290, 292), those who chronicled the ancient pagan religions were not contemporaries of the events they purported to recount:

> Qu'il y a de différence d'un livre à un autre! Je ne m'étonne pas de ce que les Grecs ont fait l'*Iliade*, ni les Egyptiens et les Chinois leurs histoires. Il ne faut que voir comment cela est né. Ces historiens fabuleux ne sont pas contemporains des choses dont ils écrivent. Homère fait un roman, qu'il donne pour tel et qui est reçu pour tel; car personne ne doutait que Troie et Agamemnon n'avaient non plus été que la pomme d'or. Il ne pensait pas aussi à en faire une histoire, mais seulement un divertissement; il est le seul qui écrit de son temps. . . . Quatre cents ans après, les témoins des choses ne sont plus vivants; personne ne sait plus par sa connaissance si c'est une fable ou une histoire. . . .
>
> Toute histoire qui n'est pas contemporaine est suspecte; ainsi les livres des sib-

ylles et de Trismégiste,[1] et tant d'autres qui ont eu crédit au monde, sont faux et se trouvent faux à la suite des temps. Il n'en est pas ainsi des auteurs contemporains.

What a difference there is between one book and another! I am not surprised that the Greeks composed the *Iliad*, nor the Egyptians and Chinese their histories. You have only to see how that came about. These historians of fable were not contemporary with the things they wrote about. Homer composed a tale, offered and accepted as such: for no one ever doubted that Troy and Agamemnon had never really existed any more than the golden apple. He never meant to write history about it, but only a diversion; he is the only writer of his times. . . . Four hundred years later the witnesses of these things are no longer alive; no one knows any longer from his own knowledge whether the work is fable or history. . . .

Any history that is not contemporary is suspect: thus the Sibylline books and those of Trismegistus, and many others which have enjoyed credit in the world, are false and have been found to be false in the course of time. This is not the case with contemporary authors. (436)

In fragment 343, Pascal dismisses the whole of the pagan religious traditions of antiquity with the following notation: "Prophéties. Le grand Pan est mort" ("Prophecies. The great Pan is dead"). The ruin of paganism, Pascal observes, was predicted even in the writings of the pagans themselves. Plutarch, in his *De defectu oraculorum*, recounts that during the reign of Tiberius a voice was heard proclaiming the death of the God Pan. Pascal, like many apologists in a tradition dating all the way back to Eusebius, takes Pan to represent polytheism and the oracle reported by Plutarch to be a prophecy of the ruin of the entire pagan tradition. The idea is a leitmotif of Christian apologetics in the Classical period. Guez de Balzac explicates the oracle as follows: "Le grand Pan est mort par la naissance du Fils de Dieu, ou plutôt par celle de sa doctrine; il ne faut pas le ressusciter. Au levé de cette lumière, tous les phantasmes du paganisme s'en sont enfuis; il ne les faut pas faire revenir"[2] ("The great Pan died with the birth

1. The Sibylline books, which Christian exegetes had attributed to the seventh century B.C., were supposed to have contained a prophecy of the rise of the Roman Empire. The God Hermes Trimegistus ("threefold great") was thought to be the author of forty-two Egyptian books treating all of knowledge. The Christian Middle Ages represented him as a pagan prophet who was a contemporary of Moses. Michel Le Guern notes: "On ne sait trop si Pascal nomme ces livres tout simplement parce qu'il s'agit d'oracles païens, ou s'il connaît l'utilisation abusive qu'avaient faite des apologistes chrétiens des IVe et Ve siècles d'interpolations que de pieux faussaires y avaient introduites" (*Pascal: Pensees II* [Paris: Gallimard, 1977], p. 281). Pascal's source concerning these books would seem to be St. Augustine's *The City of God* VIII.23–24, and XVIII.23.

2. *Oeuvres* (Paris: L. Billaine, 1665), 2, 533. Cited by Pintard, *Le Libertinage érudit dans la première moitié du XVIIe siècle,* rev. ed. p. 64.

of the Son of God, or rather with that of his doctrine; he must not be resurrected. At the rising of this light, all the phantasms of paganism fled; they should not be brought back"). In *Les Trois vérités*, Pierre Charron observes: "A la belle arrivée de Jésus-Christ, les oracles sont demeurés muets. . . . Plutarque en a fait un traité exprès, où il se morfond pour en trouver la cause" ("The oracles fell silent at the great arrival of Jesus Christ. . . . Plutarch dealt with the matter in a special treatise, in which he struggles unsuccessfully to determine the cause of this phenomenon").[3]

In the dossier "Prophéties" (XXIV), Pascal argues that the Old Testament itself contains texts predicting the cessation of the pagan religions and the conversion of the Gentiles to the religion of the God of Israel. From the time of God's revelation of himself to Moses until the coming of Christ, Pascal observes in fragment 338, "aucun païen n'avait adoré le Dieu des Juifs" ("no pagan had worshipped the God of the Jews"). Yet from the time of Christ onward, "la foule des païens adore cet unique Dieu, les temples sont détruits, les rois mêmes se soumettent à la croix" ("the mass of the heathen worshiped this one and only God, the [pagan] temples are destroyed, even kings make their submission to the Cross"). That monotheism to which Plato was able to convert only a few chosen and highly educated men remained the unique possession of the Jews for nearly two thousand years. Then suddenly, a secret force made hundreds of thousands of ignorant men believe by the power of a few words. The history of the Apostolic Church illustrates the dramatic nature of this conversion. "Les filles consacrent à Dieu leur virginité et leur vie, les hommes renoncent à tous plaisirs" ("Maidens consecrate their virginity and their life to God, and men renounce all pleasures"). "Les riches quittent leurs biens, les enfants quittent la maison délicate de leurs pères pour aller dans l'austérité" ("Rich men abandon their wealth, children abandon the luxury of their parents' home for the austerity of the desert").[4]

3. *Les Trois Vérités,* 2, 8. Cited by P. Sellier in *Pensées,* p. 190, n. 21.

4. Pascal seeks to document his assertion that this dramatic conversion was predicted throughout the Old Testament by collecting a whole series of key texts. Fragment 324, summarizing Ezekiel 30:13 and Malachi 1:11, documents the prophets' prediction of the ruin of the pagan religions: "Qu'alors l'idolâtrie serait renversée, que ce Messie abattrait toutes les idoles et ferait entrer les hommes dans le culte du vrai Dieu" ("That idolatry would then be overthrown, that the Messiah would cast down all idols, and would bring men to worship the true God"). "Que les temples des idoles seraient abattus et que parmi toutes les nations et en tous les lieux du monde lui serait offerte une hostie pure, non point des animaux" ("That the temples of the idols would be cast down, and that amongst all the nations and in

Throughout the whole course of Pascal's projected *Apology*, Judaism is expressly excluded from the category of non-Christian religions. Pascal intends to demonstrate that the religion of the Old Testament constitutes the same religion as Christianity. In fragment 453, he assembles a long series of Biblical citations aimed at demonstrating "que les vrais juifs et les vrais chrétiens n'ont qu'une même religion" ("that true Jews and true Christians have only one religion"). In his Preface to the Edition de Port-Royal of the *Pensées*, Etienne Périer describes the *chercheur*'s discovery of the people of the Old Testament as the key which eventually unlocks the entire enigma of the human condition for him:

> Enfin [M. Pascal] lui fait jeter les yeux sur le peuple juif, et il lui en fait observer des circonstances si extraordinaires qu'il attire facilement son attention. Après lui avoir représenté tout ce que ce peuple a de singulier, il s'arrête particulièrement à lui faire remarquer un livre unique par lequel il se gouverne, et qui comprend tout ensemble son histoire, sa loi et sa religion. A peine a-t-il ouvert ce livre qu'il y apprend que le monde est l'ouvrage d'un Dieu qui a créé l'homme à son image . . . dès qu'il poursuit la lecture de ce même livre, il y trouve qu'après que l'homme eût été créé de Dieu dans l'état d'innocence . . . la première action qu'il fit fut de se révolter contre son créateur. . . . M. Pascal lui fait alors comprendre que ce crime ayant été le plus grand de tous les crimes . . . il avait été puni non seulement dans ce premier homme . . . mais encore dans tous ses descendants, à qui ce même homme a communiqué et communiquera encore sa corruption dans toute la suite des temps.[5]

> Finally [Monsieur Pascal] causes him to cast his eyes on the Jewish people and makes him observe circumstances so extraordinary that he easily gains his attention. After having represented to him all which is so singular about this people, he directs his particular attention to a unique book by which this people governs itself, a book which includes the whole of their history, law and religion. No sooner does he open this book than he learns that the world is the work of a God and that it was this same God who created man in his own image. . . . As soon as he continues reading this same book, he finds in it that after man had been created by God in a state of innocence . . . the first action he took was to revolt against his

---

every place throughout the world a pure sacrifice would be offered up to him, and not that of animals").

Fragment 323 contains several citations destined to document the "vocation des gentils": "All the kindreds of the Gentiles shall adore in his sight" (Psalm 21:28); "Behold I have given thee to be a light of the Gentiles" (Isaiah 49, 6); "And all the kings of the earth shall adore him" (Psalm 71:11). In *série* XVII, Pascal copies out and translates several long passages from the book of Isaiah which he interprets as anticipating the conversion of the Gentiles (fragment 489). In fragment 498, he gathers an additional series of references under the rubric "vocation des gentils": Joel 2:28, Hosea 2:24, Deuteronomy 32:21, Malachi 1:11.

5. Lafuma, ed., *Pascal: Oeuvres complètes* pp. 495–96.

Creator. . . . Monsieur Pascal then causes him to understand that this crime having been the greatest of all possible crimes . . . it was punished not only in the person of this first man . . . but as well in all his descendants, to whom this same man communicated and will continue to communicate his corruption until the end of time.

It is in the Scriptures of the Jews that the seeker will find the key to the enigma ("grandeur"/"misère") with which he has been confronted in the first ten chapters of the Apology adumbrated by the dossiers of 1658. However, proving the credibility of the Fall means first demonstrating the authority and authenticity of the Old Testament. To this end, Pascal will open those dossiers which constitute the greater part of the second half of the Apology sketched by the *liasses* of 1658: "Rendre la religion aimable" ("Make religion attractive") (XVII), "Fondements" ("Foundations") (XVIII), "Loi figurative" ("Figurative law") (XIX), "Rabbinage" ("Rabbinism") (XX), "Perpétuité" ("Perpetuity") (XXI), "Preuves de Moïse" ("Proofs of Moses") (XXII), "Prophéties" ("Prophecies") (XXIV), and "Figures particulières" ("Particular figures") (XXV). Among the unclassified *liasses*, we find three rather finished fragments which recapitulate and reinforce Pascal's conclusions concerning the *témoignage* of the Jewish people: fragment 436, "Antiquité des Juifs" ("Antiquity of the Jews"); fragment 451, "Avantages du peuple juif" ("Advantages of the Jewish people"); and fragment 452, "Sincérité des Juifs" ("Sincerity of the Jews").

Five transitional chapters separate Pascal's exposition of the central paradox of the human condition ("misère"/"grandeur") in dossiers I–X from his demonstration of the authority of the Old Testament (and hence of the Fall) in dossiers XVI–XXV. Significantly enough, the fifth of these transitional chapters is entitled "Fausseté des autres religions" ("Falseness of other religions") (XVI). At the core of this chapter stands Pascal's analysis of the false religion constituted by Islam. It seems important to note that only one non-Christian religion warrants Pascal's detailed refutation in the course of the *Apology*. As far as Pascal is concerned, the demise of the pagan religions of antiquity speaks for itself. Those pagan religions which still exist in the New World, in India, and in Africa are not even worth a second glance. They are obviously the work of superstition and ignorance and have nothing in them which might interest "les gens habiles" ("clever men") (219). Islam, on the other hand, requires Pascal's refutation.

Pascal and Islam

In its "Declaration on the Relationship of the Church to Non-Christians," the Second Vatican Council extended a rather remarkable gesture of conciliation to the religion of the Prophet:

> Upon the Moslems . . . the Church looks with esteem. They adore one God, living and enduring, merciful and all-powerful, maker of heaven and earth and Speaker to men. They strive to submit wholeheartedly even to his inscrutable decrees, just as did Abraham, with whom the Islamic faith is pleased to associate itself. Though they do not acknowledge Jesus as God, they revere him as a prophet. They also honor Mary, his virgin Mother; at times they call on her, too, with devotion. In addition, they await the day of judgement. . . . Consequently, they prize the moral life, and give worship to God especially through prayer, almsgiving and fasting.[6]

Pascal's attitude toward Islam could hardly be more different. In the diagram sketched in fragment 565[7] (see Plate IV). Islam is distinguished from paganism (which for Pascal presumably includes all the other non-Christian religions) because it claims to be a revealed religion:

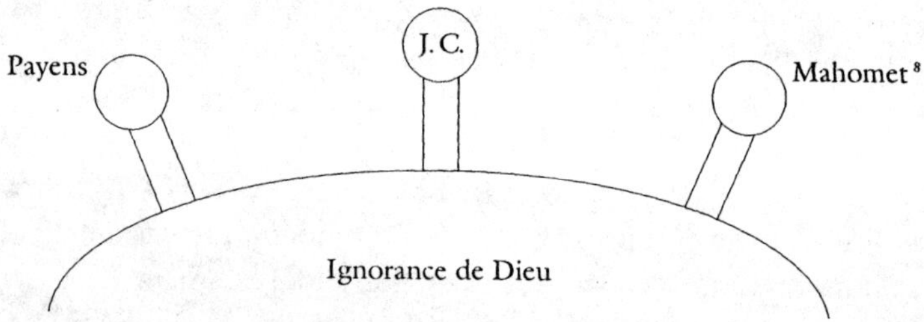

As a path to knowledge of God, Pascal asserts, Islam turns out to be as much a dead end as does paganism. The religion founded by Mohammed can be shown to be devoid of divine authority. "Tout homme peut faire

6. *The Documents of Vatican II,* Walter Abbott, S. J., ed. (New York: America Press, 1966), p. 663.

7. Lafuma's rendering of this diagram in the *Oeuvres complètes* seems to be defective. For a diagram based upon the autograph text, see Zacharie Tourneur, *Pensées de Blaise Pascal: Édition paléographique des manuscrits originaux conservés à la Bibliothèque Nationale* (Paris: Vrin, 1942), p. 78. See plate 4.

8. In his *Summa contra Gentiles,* Aquinas groups together the "pagans and Mohammedans who do not agree with us as to the authority of any Scripture." *The Summa contra Gentiles of Saint Thomas Aquinas* (London: Oates and Washborne, 1924), I: ii, p. 4.

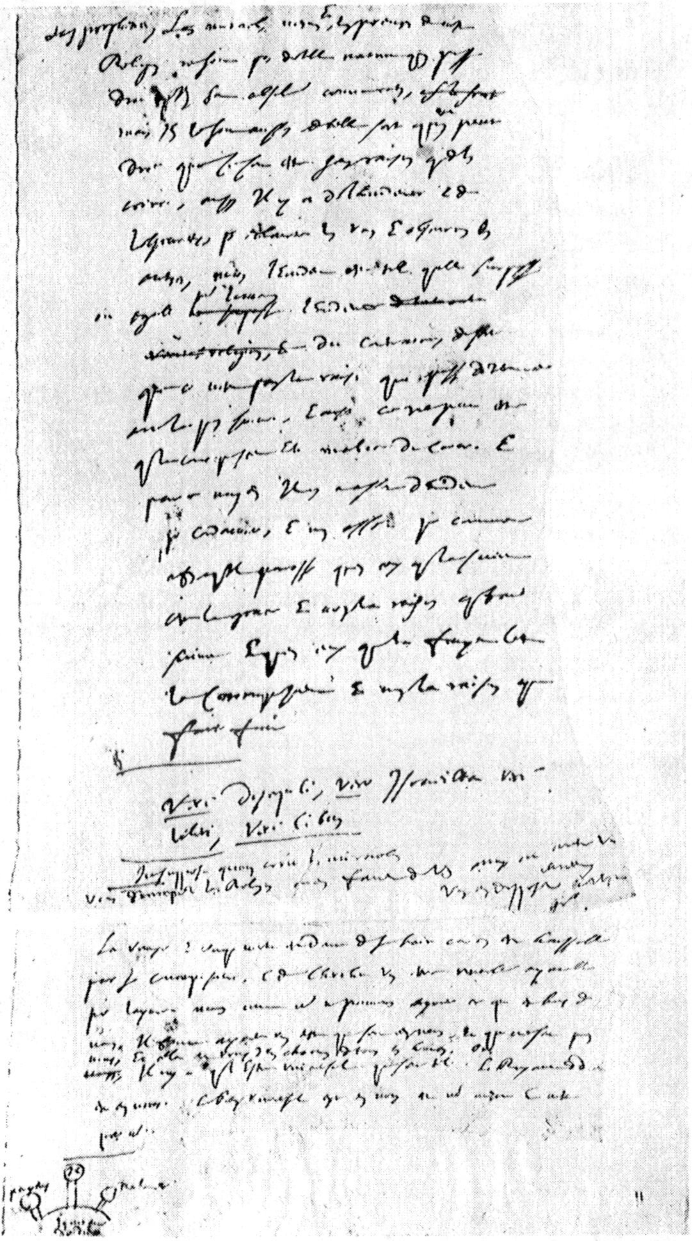

PLATE IV. Fragment 565 (Lafuma) in the *Recueil original* (Bibliothèque Nationale, MS français 9202). Service photographique, Bibliothèque Nationale. The tiny diagram contrasting "Mahomet" and the Christian Revelation is in the extreme lower-left-hand corner of the manuscript page.

ce qu'a fait Mahomet. Car il n'a point fait de miracles, il n'a point été prédit" ("Any man can do what Mahomet did. For he performed no miracles and was not foretold") (321). "Qui rend témoignage de Mahomet? lui-même" (Who bears witness to Mahomet? Himself") (1). Whereas Jesus was anticipated by the entire prophetic tradition elaborated in the *liasse* "Prophéties" (XXIV), Mohammed's coming was not predicted in earlier Scriptures. Moreover, he neither performed miracles nor revealed any new mysteries:

> La religion mahométane a pour fondement l'Alcoran, et Mahomet. Mais ce prophète qui devait être la dernière attente du monde a(-t-)il été prédit? Et quelle marque a(-t-)il que n'ait aussi tout homme qui se voudra prophète? Quels miracles dit-il lui-même avoir faits? Quel mystère a(-t-)il enseigné selon sa tradition même? Quelle morale et quelle félicité![9]

> The Moslem religion has the Koran and Mahomet for foundation. But was this prophet, supposedly the world's last hope, foretold? And what signs does he show that are not shown by anyone else who wants to call himself a prophet? What miracles does he himself claim to have performed? What mystery did he teach according to his own tradition? What notions of morality and of bliss! (243)

9. In composing this fragment (and perhaps fragments 207, 209, and 218), Pascal may well have taken his cue from the following passage in Thomas Aquinas' *Summa contra Gentiles* (Liber I, cap. 6, c–g) in which the Angelic Doctor discusses Mohammed: "Those who introduced the errors of the sects proceeded in contrary fashion, as instanced by Mohammed, who enticed peoples with the promise of carnal pleasures, to the desire of which the concupiscence of the flesh instigates. He also delivered commandments in keeping with his promises, by giving reins to carnal pleasure, wherein it is easy for carnal man to obey: and the lessons of truth which he inculcated were only such as can be easily known to any man of average wisdom by his natural powers: yea, rather the truths which he taught were mingled by him with many fables and most false doctrines.

Nor did he add any signs of supernatural agency, which alone are a fitting witness to divine inspiration, since a visible work that can be from God alone, proves the teacher of truth to be visibly inspired: but he asserted that he was sent in the power of arms, a sign that is not lacking even to robbers and tyrants. Again, those who believed in him from the outset were not wise men practiced in things divine and human, but beastlike men who dwelt in the wilds, utterly ignorant of all divine teaching; and it was by a multitude of such men and the force of arms that he compelled others to submit to his law.

Lastly, no divine oracles or prophets in a previous age bore witness to him; rather did he corrupt almost all the teaching of the Old and New Testaments by a narrative replete with fables, as one may see a perusal of his law. Hence by a cunning device, he did not commit the reading of the Old and New Testament Books to his followers, lest he should therefore be convicted of falsehood. Thus it is evident that those who believe his words believe lightly" (ibid., I.vi, p. 13).

Aquinas himself follows the Cluniac anti-Islamic tradition, basing his arguments upon passages in Peter the Venerable's *Summula quaedam brevis contra haereses et sectam diabolicae fraudis Saracenorum sive Ismaelitarum*.

Pascal's refutation of Islam never reaches the stage of a coherently organized chapter. Before attempting to make sense of the nine isolated fragments in which Pascal treats or mentions Islam,[10] it seems important to establish how much was known about Islam in France in the 1650s. According to the noted Islamicist Norman Daniel, the "Western 'canon' of what constitutes Islam" was firmly established in Europe by the middle of the fourteenth century. This "canon," formed during the twelfth and thirteenth centuries "by the absorption of Oriental, Byzantine and Mozarab traditions," would not be substantially altered until the advent of linguistic Orientalism in the eighteenth century.[11] It would prove strong enough to survive "the break-up of European ideological unity, both the division into Catholic and Protestant, and the growth of agnosticism and atheism."[12]

At the heart of this medieval Christian view of Islam stands a highly complicated series of texts, translations, and commentaries which Norman Daniel calls the "Cluniac corpus." These polemical writings, via which information about Islam first reached Western Europe from Muslim Spain, include the first Latin translation of the Qur'an commissioned by Peter the Venerable.[13] Out of this corpus of writings grew the major themes of subsequent Christian anti-Islamic polemic. Chief among these was the apologetic notion that the Qur'an represented an "involuntary witness" to the truth of Christianity and that Islam itself constituted the most heinous of all Christian heresies.[14] Other enduring motifs in this synthesis of the Christian critique of Islam included "the 'fraudulent' . . . character of Mohammed's claim to prophecy," attacks upon the moral character of the Prophet, "the ridicule and contempt of the Qur'anic Paradise," the censure of the use of force in establishing this religion, and attacks on the deficiencies in Islamic Christology.[15]

All these motifs recur in Pascal's sources, who themselves derive most of their theories and information from the "Cluniac corpus." Norman Daniel points to an organizing principle behind all these traditional Christian objections to the Qur'anic Revelation, "the medieval objection to the

10. Fragments 1, 203, 207, 209, 218, 243, 321, 794, and 454.

11. Norman Daniel, *Islam and the West: The Making of an Image* (Edinburgh: Edinburgh University Press, 1966), p. 275.

12. Ibid., p. 271.

13. Ibid., p. 18.

14. Ibid., pp. 272–73.

15. Ibid., pp. 274–76.

Islamic teaching that revelation might come down to solve problems of a transient nature":

> When the implications of this objection are considered, it will be seen that the objection . . . implies, in fact, all the detailed objections that were made to the character of Mohammed, and to his history, and that were thought definitively to preclude his claim to prophethood. . . . His prophethood was seen as alien to all known prophethood; non-prophetic, untruthful in utterance, evil of life, unverified by miracles. This absence of miracles was considered one of the most damning weaknesses in the Muslim case. . . . This attack on Muhammad's prophethood was worked out in great detail. . . . Heretical Jewish and Christian influences explained the content of his teaching; the manner of revelation alleged to him, and his solution of his immediate, temporary and often personal problems were all thought so suspicious as to amount in themselves to a disproof of the prophetic claim. . . . The salient elements in Muhammad's life, or in the Christian legend of his life, were reflected in the concept of Islam as a practical religion. Like its Prophet, it was said to be violent by nature.[16]

Du Ryer's *L'Alcoran*

The first French translation of the Qur'an appeared in Paris in 1647: *L'Alcoran de Mahomet translaté d'arabe en françois par le sieur du Ryer* (see Plate V). Norman Daniel qualifies this translation, the first in any modern vernacular, as "popular rather than academic."[17] Though its publication had been approved by the official censors, the religious party got wind of its imminent distribution and obtained an order blocking its sale. "Neantmoins," wrote one observer, [le libraire] s'en vend soubs la cappe et cela ne sert qu'à l'encherir"[18] ("Nevertheless, the publisher is selling it under the counter and this has only served to make it more expensive and sought after"). The introduction to Du Ryer's translation furnishes us with an extremely useful summary of what was known about Islam in the France of the Classical period. A short section entitled "Au lecteur" focuses upon the Qur'an itself. In it, we learn that the sacred book of Islam is essentially a human invention:

> Ce livre est une longue conférence de Dieu, des Anges, et de Mahomet, que ce faux prophète a inventée assez grossièrement. Tantôt il introduit Dieu qui lui parle et lui enseigne sa loi, après un ange, puis les prophètes, et souvent il fait parler

16. Ibid., pp. 273–74.
17. Ibid., p. 284.
18. Pintard, *Le Libertinage érudit,* p. 86.

SUITE
DE
L'ALCORAN
DE
MAHOMET.

Le Chapitre de la Beatitude *& de l'Enfer, contenant cent trente-cinq verſets, écrit à la Meque.*

Les Mahometans ont intitulé ce Chapitre طه Thé. *Ce ſont deux lettres de l'Alphabeth Arabe, ſavoir* ط Tt *&* ه Hé *ou* ط *En ce lieu* ط Tt *ſignifie* طوبا Thouba, *c'eſt-à dire* Beatitude *&* ه *ſignifie* هاوية Hahoihé, *c'eſt-à-dire* l'Enfer. *Voyez la gloſe & l'interpretation de Geladdin & du Bedaoi. Ils ont intitulé ce Chapitre* DE LA BEATITUDE ET DE L'ENFER.

AU nom de Dieu clement & miſericordieux. Nous ne t'avons pas donné l'Alcoran pour te tourmenter, mais pour l'enſeigner aux gens de bien. Il t'a été envoyé par celui qui a creé la Terre & les Cieux,

Tom. II. A le

PLATE V. Du Ryer's *L'Alcoran de Mahomet* (1647). Opening page, volume ii. Service photographique, Bibliothèque Nationale.

Dieu en pluriel par un style qui n'est pas ordinaire. Il déclame contre ceux qui adorent les idoles, particulièrement contre les habitants de la ville de Mecque. . . . Il a intitulé ce livre ALCORAN, comme qui dirait le Recueil des Préceptes. . . . Il l'a divisé en plusieurs chapitres, auxquels il donne telle inscription que bon lui semble. . . . Il divise [les chapîtres] en plusieurs lignes ou versets qui contiennent ses ordonnances ou fables, sans observation ni de suite ni liaison de discours, ce qui est cause que tu trouveras en ce livre un grand nombre de pièces détachées, et diverses répétitions de mêmes choses. Il a été expliqué par plusieurs docteurs mahométans. Leur explication est aussi ridicule que le texte. Ils assurent que l'original de l'Alcoran est écrit sur une table qui est gardée au ciel, que l'ange Gabriel a apporté cette copie à Mahomet qui ne savait ni lire ni écrire, et l'appellent le

Prophète. . . . Tu seras étonné que ces absurdités aient infecté la meilleure partie du monde, et avoueras que la connaissance de ce qui est contenu en ce livre rendra cette loi méprisable.[19]

This book is a long colloquium between God, the angels and Mohammed which this false prophet rather rudely invented. Right away, he introduces God, who speaks to him and teaches him his law; then [he introduces] an angel, then the prophets. Often he makes God speak in an out of the ordinary plural style. He inveighs against those who worship idols, particularly against the inhabitants of the city of Mecca. . . . He entitled this book the ALCORAN, that is to say the Collection of Precepts. . . . He divided it into several chapters, to which he gives whatever title comes into his head. . . . He divides [the chapters] into several lines or verses which contain his decrees and fables without observing any continuity or linking of discourse. As a result, you will find in this book a great number of disjointed writings and many repetitions of the same things. It has been explained by many Muslim doctors of the faith. Their explanation is as ridiculous as the text itself. They maintain that the original of the Alcoran is written on a tablet which is kept in heaven and that the angel Gabriel brought this copy to Mohammed, who knew neither how to read nor write. They call him the Prophet. . . . You will be astonished to learn that these absurdities have infected the better part of the world. You will be forced to admit that a knowledge of what is contained in this book will render this law worthy of scorn.

In a very useful "Sommaire de la Religion des Turcs," Du Ryer gives a series of details concerning the theology and religious practices of Islam. First of all, he emphasizes monotheism as the central tenet of the Islamic faith:

Les Turcs croient en un seul Dieu en une seule Personne, Créateur du ciel et de la terre, Rémunérateur des bons, et punisseur des méchants, qui a créé le paradis pour récompenser les gens de bien et l'enfer pour la dernière punition des crimes. Ils croient que Mahomet est un très grand prophète, que Dieu l'a envoyé au monde pour enseigner aux hommes le chemin de salut, et se nomment Musulmans, c'est-à-dire, les résignés en Dieu ou les sauvés.[20]

The Turks believe in only one God in a single Person, Creator of heaven and of earth, Rewarder of the good and Punisher of the evil, who created paradise to reward people who have lived virtuously and hell for the final punishment of crimes. They believe that Mohammed is a very great prophet, sent by God to the world to teach men the way of salvation. They call themselves Muslims, that is to say, those resigned to [the will of] God, or the elect.

19. *L'Alcoran de Mahomet translaté d'arabe en françois par le sieur du Ryer, sieur de la grade Malezaire* (Paris: chez Antoine de Sommaville, 1647), "Au lecteur."
20. Ibid., "Sommaire de la Religion des Turcs."

Du Ryer goes into some detail concerning the traditional Five Pillars of Islam. The Islamic faithful, he observes, are obliged to pray five times a day. Their prayers are preceded by ritual ablutions. "Ils croient qu'après s'être bien lavés le corps, disant quelque oraison appropriée à cette cérémonie, ils ont aussi l'âme nette . . . de péché" ("They believe that after a thorough cleansing of the body, while saying the appropriate prayers, the soul is also cleansed of sin"). Du Ryer compares the fast of the month of Ramadan, which he describes in some detail, to the Christian Lent and the breaking of the month-long fast to the Christian Easter. He notes that the Islamic faithful are "grands fondateurs de temples et hopîtaux" ("great benefactors of temples and hospitals") and that they are required to pay a 10 percent alms tax on their yearly earnings for the support of the indigent. He takes note of the pilgrimage to Mecca and cites the Islamic Profession of Faith: "Il n'y a qu'un seul Dieu; Mahomet est son Prophète et son Apôtre"[21] ("There is but one God; Mohammed is his Prophet and Apostle").

Interestingly enough, Du Ryer's account of the religious practices of Islam bears hardly any trace of that severity with which he censures that religion's holy book. He observes that wine and pork are forbidden under all circumstances and that circumcision, though not commanded by the Qur'an, constitutes Islam's only "sacrement." He compares the Moslem Friday to the Christian Sunday. He remarks that the Islamic faithful are obliged to observe the Decalogue of Moses. He notes without comment that the faithful are permitted four wives and as many female slaves as they can maintain. Indeed, his description of the liberal Islamic divorce laws seems almost positive in tone. One is very much reminded of the way in which Montesquieu's *Lettres persanes*, seventy-five years later, will attempt to make the Catholic position on divorce appear backward:

> Ils peuvent quitter leurs femmes quand bon leur semble, en leur payant ce qu'ils leur ont promis par leur contrat de mariage, et se remarier à leur volonté; mais les femmes sont obligées d'attendre jusqu'à ce qu'on soit assuré qu'elles ne soient pas grosses avant de se remarier, et les maris sont obligés de garder les enfants et d'en avoir du soin. Les enfants qu'ils ont de leurs esclaves sont traités indifféremment comme ceux qu'ils ont de leurs femmes et sont tous tenus pour légitimes.[22]

21. Ibid. Du Ryer's translation of the opening of the Qur'an, often called the Lord's Prayer of Islam, gives some notion of the tone and style of his translation: "Au nom de Dieu clément et miséricordieux, louange soit à Dieu clément et miséricordieux, Roy du jour du Jugement, c'est toy que nous adorons, c'est à toy que nous demandons secours; conduis nous au droict chemin, au chemin de ceux que tu as gratifiez, contre lesquels tu n'as pas esté courroucé, et nous ne serons pas dévoyés."

22. Ibid., "Sommaire."

They may leave their wives whenever they wish by paying them whatever they promised them in their marriage contract. [The men] may remarry at any time, but the women are required to wait until it has been established that they are not with child before remarrying. The husbands are required to keep the children and to care for them. The children of their slaves are treated no differently from those of their wives and are all held to be legitimate.

Du Ryer has a solid grasp on the theological differences which separate Islam and Christianity. He observes that though the Islamic faithful "invoquent leurs saints desquels ils ont une grande légende" ("invoke their saints, concerning whom they have a great many legends"), the doctrine of Purgatory is unknown. "Plusieurs d'entre eux estiment que les âmes et les corps demeurent ensemble dans le tombeau jusqu'au jour du Jugement" ("Many among them believe that the soul and the body remain together in the tomb until the day of Judgment"). He notes that Islamic doctrine maintains that the Jews and the Christians have altered their Holy Scriptures. The major difference between the two religions, he observes, concerns the matter of Christology. Islamic doctrine, while accepting the Virgin Birth of Jesus, denies both his divinity and his crucifixion:

Ils ne croient pas que Jésus-Christ soit Dieu, ni Fils de Dieu, ni croient pas en la Sainte Trinité. Ils disent que Jésus-Christ est un grand prophète, né de la Vierge Marie, Vierge devant et après l'enfantement, qu'il a été conçu par inspiration divine ou par un souffle divin sans père, comme Adam a été créé sans mère, et qu'il reviendra en terre avant la fin du monde pour confirmer la Loi de Mahomet. Ils assurent aussi que les Juifs croyant crucifier Jésus-Christ crucifièrent un homme d'entr'eux qui lui ressemblait.[23]

They do not believe that Jesus Christ is either God or the Son of God. Nor do they believe in the Holy Trinity. They say that Jesus Christ is a great prophet, born of the Virgin Mary, a virgin before and after childbearing. [They believe] that he was conceived without a father by divine inspiration or by a divine breath, just as Adam was created without a mother, and that he will return to the earth before the end of the world in order to confirm the Law of Mohammed. They also

23. Du Ryer's translation of a principal anti-Trinitarian passage in Book IV (v. 171) of the Qur'an bears noting: "O vous qui sçavez la loy escrite, obeîssez aux commandemens de Dieu, et ne parlez pas de sa divine Majesté qu'avec vérité. Le Messie Jésus, Fils de Marie, est Prophète et Apostre de Dieu, son Verbe et son Esprit qu'il a envoyé à Marie. Croyez donc en Dieu et en ses Prophètes, et ne dites pas qu'il y a trois Dieux. Mettez fin à ces discours. Vous ferez bien, car il n'y a qu'un seul Dieu, loué soit Dieu. Il n'a point enfant. Tout ce qui est au Ciel et en la Terre luy obéit. C'est assez qu'il en soit tesmoin. Le Messie ne tient pas à deshonneur d'estre serviteur de Dieu, ny les Anges, ny les Cherubins."

maintain that the Jews, while believing that they crucified Jesus Christ, actually crucified one of their own men who resembled him.

Du Ryer's extensive knowledge of Islamic religious practice reflects the fact that he spent a great part of his life in Islamic countries.[24] His detailed knowledge concerning Sufi brotherhoods and wandering ascetics represents information hardly known at all in seventeenth-century Europe:

> Ils ont des couvents de religieux qui vivent exemplairement. Ils obéissent à leurs supérieurs sans contradiction; et dansent au son des flûtes et d'autres instruments lors qu'ils font leurs oraisons. Ils ont encore une autre sorte de Religieux vagabonds par le monde, vêtus comme des fous de ce pays. Ils vont souvent nus, et découpent leur peau en plusieurs endroits. Ils sont tenus pour saints personnages et vivent d'aumône, qui ne leur est jamais refusée. L'une et l'autre sorte de religieux se nomment Dreuis. On les connaît à leur vêtements, et ils se peuvent retirer et marier quand bon leur semble.[25]

> They have convents of religious who live in an exemplary fashion. They obey their superiors without contradiction. They dance to the sound of flutes and other instruments while saying their prayers. Here and there one finds another kind of vagabond religious, who dress as do the insane of this country. Often they go about naked and cut their skin in several places. They are held to be holy men and live by begging alms, which are never refused to them. Both these kinds of religious men are called Druzes. One can recognize them by the way they dress. They may leave the religious state and marry whenever they decide to.

Georges Couton thinks that Du Ryer's Preface to his translation of the Qur'an served as one of Pascal's sources of information concerning Islam. Taking note of the censures of Mohammed and the Qur'an contained in the section "Au lecteur,"[26] Couton points to Pascal's use of the term "faux prophète" in fragment 207 and the words "il est ridicule" in fragment 218.[27]

Pascal's references appear to me to be too vague to warrant concluding with any certainty that Pascal made use of Du Ryer's Preface. Moreover,

24. Du Ryer (1580–1660) served as French consul in Egypt until 1630, when he went to Constantinople to undertake a mission to the French Court for the Sultan Marat IV. A knight of the Order of the Holy Sepulchre, he traveled extensively in the Islamic world on behalf of his order. Fluent in both Arabic and Turkish, he translated extracts from the *Empire des roses* (Paris: 1634) and prepared a never-published Latin-Turkish dictionary. The Bibliothèque Nationale possesses two copies of the manuscript of the latter work.

25. *L'Alcoran de Mahomet,* "Sommaire."

26. "que ce faux prophète a inventée assez grossièrement"; "l'explication [des docteurs mahométans] est aussi ridicule que le texte"; "ce faux prophète"; "Tu seras étonné que ces absurdités aient infecté la meilleure partie du monde . . . cette loi méprisable."

27. Introduction, *L'Edition de Port-Royal des Pensées* (Saint-Etienne: Universités de la région Rhône-Alpes, 1971), p. 15, n. 2.

had Pascal used the section "Au lecteur," would he not have read on to learn more about the religion he would attempt to refute? Pascal's nine fragments on Islam seem to me to betray little trace of Du Ryer's erudition. Nor do they contain any reference to the anti-Trinitarian doctrines so carefully explained by Du Ryer. Had he read Du Ryer's Preface, surely Pascal would have thought it necessary to refute the Islamic doctrine that Jesus did not die on the Cross. Pascal seems to have no inkling of this doctrine. In the *liasse* "Commencement," fragment 150 does make reference to the "cérémonies . . . prophètes . . . docteurs . . . religieux" of the "Turcs." However, this information is attributed to the "impies," who draw parallels between Christianity and Islam in order to call into question Christianity's claim to constitute a unique Revelation.[28]

Pascal occasionally betrays a more detailed knowledge of the doctrines of Islam. For instance, in fragment 243, he seems to refer to Mohammed's claim to be "the seal of the prophets." "Ce prophète qui devait être *la dernière attente* du monde a(-t-)il été prédit?" (italics mine) ("But was this prophet, supposedly the world's last hope, foretold?"). In fragment 218, he refers with irony to the paradise ("par son paradis") promised to the Muslim faithful. The second of these two references can probably be traced to Pascal's reading of Montaigne. In Book XII of the *Essais*, Montaigne observes: "Mahomet promet aux siens un paradis tapissé, paré d'or et de pierreries, peuplé de garces d'excellente beauté, de vins et de vivres singuliers"[29] ("Mohammed promises his followers a paradise tapestried,

28. See Chapter III, Fragment 822 and Neo-Augustinian Theology.

29. *Oeuvres complètes, Essais,* 2, 12, p. 215. Michel Le Guern (*Pensées* [Paris: Folio, 1977], 1, p. 305) refers us to Grotius' *De veritate religionis christiane,* VI.11: "Ils [les Mahométans] disent . . . que, dans la vie à venir, ce qu'on mangera se dissipera par les sueurs; qu'à chaque homme seront assignées des troupes de femmes pour assouvir ses passions" ("They [the Mohammedans] say that in the life to come what one eats will be dissipated via one's perspiration; that each man will be assigned a harem of women to gratify his passions"). Pascal may well have taken his cue for this censure of the Qu'ranic paradise from Thomas Aquinas' *Summa contra Gentiles,* Liber I, cap. 6, a–b: "Ut paret in Mahumeto qui carnalium voluptatum promissis, ad quorum desiderium carnalis concupiscentia instigat, populus illexit. Praecepta etiam tradidit promissis conformia, voluptati carnali habenas relaxans, in quibus in promptu est a carnalibus hominibus obediri." See n. 9 in the present chapter. Or, it may be that Aquinas is Grotius' source.

Both Aquinas and Grotius follow Peter the Venerable's *Summula quaedam brevis contra haereses et sectam diabolicae fraudis Saracenorum sive Ismaelitarum:* "Paradisum non societatis angelicae . . . sed vere talem, qualem caro et sanguis imo faex carnis et sanguinis concupiscebat, qualemque sibi parai optabat. Ibi carnium et omnigenorum fructuum esum, ibi lactis et mellis rivulos et aquarum splendentium, ibi pulcherrimarum virginum et mulierum amplexus et luxus, in quibus tota eius paradisus finitur, sectatoribus suis promisit."

adorned with gold and precious stones, peopled with wenches of surpassing beauty, with rare wines and foods").

Pascal and Grotius

Another possible candidate for Pascal's chief source of information about Islam is a second text suggested by Georges Couton: Grotius' *De veritate religionis christianae*.[30] According to Norman Daniel, Grotius "depended heavily upon the Cluniac corpus" and cites the Qur'an from the Latin translation commissioned from Robert of Ketton by Peter the Venerable.[31] Grotius' treatment of Islam in Chapters 1 and 2 of Book VI of *De veritate religionis christianae* is unabashedly written from the perspective of Christian apologetics. In Grotius' view, the rise of Islam constituted "a punishment of God." From the time of Constantine onward, he argues, sincere and simple Christian piety began "to wax cold" because of the "contentions" of the Christian bishops and the constant warfare among Christian princes. Christians began to prefer the "Tree of Knowledge" to the "Tree of Life." Religion was turned into an "Art" and began "everywhere to be placed not in purity of mind, but, as if Judaism was brought back into the world, in Rites and Ceremonies." By the time of the seventh century, there were "many Christians in name but few in deed."[32]

According to Grotius, the direction in which Christianity was evolving provoked God's ire. As a punishment, he decimated the existing Christian world with a new Flood in the form of a series of invasions. Christian Europe was ravaged by the pagan barbarians. Syria, Palestine, Persia, Egypt, Africa, and Spain—all Christian lands—were lost to the armies of Mohammed:

30. G. Couton, ed., *L'Edition de Port-Royal,* p. 15, n. 1. In her *Pascal's Unfinished Apology* (New Haven: Yale University Press, 1952), Sister Marie Louise Hubert, O.P., makes the best case for Grotius as Pascal's source; pp. 76–81. Also see Hubert's Appendix (p. 149), which gives a useful table of "Concordance Between Grotius' *De veritate religionis* and the *Pensées.*" On Grotius, see W. Knight, *The Life and Works of Hugo Grotius* (London: Sweet and Maxwell, 1925). Published in Latin in 1627, Grotius' *De veritate religionis christianae* was translated into French at least twice prior to 1660. Couton notes a translation by Mezeray and another by the Sieur de Beauvoir. In the following pages, I cite an English translation dating from 1689.

31. *Islam and the West,* p. 384.

32. Hugo Grotius, *The Truth of Christian Religion . . . translated into English . . . by Symon Patrick, Dean of Peterburg and Chaplain in Ordinary to Their Majesties* (London: Luke Meredith, 1689), 6, pp. 169–70.

God did not wink at these Vices of his people, but, out of the innermost parts of Scythia and Germany, poured forth like a Deluge, immense swarms of Barbarous Peoples into the Christian World. And when the vast slaughters which they made proved not sufficient to correct and amend the lives of those that survived, *Mahomet*, by God's just permission, sawed a new Religion in Arabia: and that directly opposite to the Christian Religion.[33]

Grotius' first critique of Islam focuses upon twin themes of ignorance and religious coercion. Islam, Grotius asserts, is a "religion altogether contrived for the shedding of blood."[34] "It is a religion which follows where Arms go before: of which it is an accessory and nothing of itself."[35] "[Islam] would be believed without all liberty of enquiry thereunto. Whence the vulgar are prohibited to read their books that are accounted holy." In Grotius' view, such coercion violates the very meaning of true religion:

Since that God hath implanted in the mind of man the power and faculty of judging, there is no part of truth that better deserves the employment thereof than that of which we cannot be ignorant, without the danger of losing eternal salvation.[36]

There is no true worship of God but which proceeds from a willing mind. And the will is to be wrought upon by good instruction and gentle persuasion but not by threats or violence.[37]

Pascal seems to be in complete agreement with Grotius on the question of religious coercion. Indeed, as Philippe Sellier, invoking fragment 172, points out, "au 17e siècle, Pascal est un des rares penseurs qui ait soutenu cette idée"[38] ("in the seventeenth century, Pascal is one of the rare thinkers who upheld this idea"):

La conduite de Dieu, qui dispose toutes choses avec douceur, est de mettre la religion dans l'esprit par les raisons et dans le coeur par la grâce, mais de la vouloir mettre dans l'esprit et dans le coeur par la force et par les menaces, ce n'est pas y mettre la religion mais la terreur. *Terrorem potius quam religionem.*

33. Ibid., pp. 170–71.
34. Ibid., p. 171.
35. Ibid., p. 177.
36. Ibid., p. 172.
37. Ibid., pp. 177–78.
38. "Seminar: Pascal's 'Trois Ordres' " in *Meaning, Structure and History in the "Pensées" of Pascal* (Tübingen: Biblio 17, 1990), p. 83.

The way of God, who disposes all things with gentleness, is to instill religion into our minds with reasoned arguments and into our hearts with grace, but attempting to instill it into hearts and minds with force and threats is to instill not religion but terror. *Terror rather than religion.* (172)

In fragment 209, which could well be a gloss on the first section of Book VI of Grotius' *De veritate religionis christianae*, Pascal underlines the contrast between Christianity and Islam concerning the reading of their Holy Scriptures. "Mahomet en défendant de lire, les apôtres en ordonnant de lire" ("Mahomet forbade reading, the Apostles commanded it") (209). In fragment 243, Pascal contrasts the commandments of Moses and Mohammed: "Au lieu que Mahomet pour faire subsister [son livre] a défendu de le lire, Moïse pour faire subsister le sien a ordonné à tout le monde de le lire" ("Whereas Mahomet tried to preserve his book by forbidding anyone to read it, Moses tried to preserve his by ordering everyone to read it") (243).

Both Grotius and Pascal would appear to have mistaken the traditional Islamic prohibition on translating the Holy Qur'an from the original Arabic into the vernacular[39] as a prohibition against the private reading of the sacred text. In fact, the public recitation of the Qur'an and its study in special classes have always formed an integral part of Islamic tradition (see Plate VI). In his essay "Des prières," Montaigne seems to have understood the matter more clearly. Commenting unfavorably upon the Protestants' reading of the Bible in the vernacular, he observes:

> Je crois aussi que la liberté à chacun de dissiper une parole si religieuse et importante à tant de sortes d'idiomes a beaucoup plus de danger que d'utilité. Les Juifs, les Mahométans et quasi tous autres ont épousé et révèrent le langage auquel originellement leurs mystères avaient été conçus; et en est défendu l'altération et changement.[40]

This freedom for everyone to disperse a word so sacred and important into so many kinds of idioms has in it much more danger than utility. The Jews, the Mohammedans, and almost all others have espoused, and revere, the language in

39. Even today Islamic scholars maintain that a translation of the Qur'an is not the Qur'an. An English convert to Islam, Mohammed Marmaduke Pickthall, maintains in his preface to his translation, *The Meaning of the Glorious Koran* (New York: Mentor, 1963): "The Koran cannot be translated . . . the Book is here rendered almost literally and every effort has been made to choose befitting language. But the result is not the Glorious Koran, that inimitable symphony, the very sounds of which move men to tears and ecstasy."

40. *Oeuvres complètes, Essais,* 1, 56, p. 139.

which their mysteries were originally conceived; and any alteration or change in them is forbidden, not without reason."[41]

As a Protestant, Grotius would have been especially sensitive to the faithful's not having access to vernacular versions of their sacred texts. Pascal's circle at Port-Royal took a similar position and undertook translations of the Bible and the liturgy.[42] Nonetheless, it seems as if Pascal, in fragments 209 and 243, mistakenly thinks that Mohammed had issued a direct prohibition against the reading of his Revelation by the ordinary Muslim faithful. Pascal's (and Grotius') source in this matter has proved completely elusive. It may by that Pascal (or Grotius) has misconstrued a passage in Thomas Aquinas' *Summa contra Gentiles*. The issue in Aquinas' text is not the reading of the Qu'ran, but of the Jewish and Christian Testaments by the Islamic faithful. Aquinas argues that the Prophet "by a cunning device did not commit the reading of the Old and New Testaments to his followers, lest he should therefore be convicted of falsehood."[43]

In fragment 209, Pascal notes another key difference between Jesus and Mohammed. "Mahomet en tuant, J.-C. en faisant tuer les siens" ("Mahomet slew, Jesus caused his followers to be slain"). This idea, of course, is one of the principal themes in the whole tradition of Christian anti-Islamic polemics. Le Maistre de Sacy, Pascal's mentor in matters exegetical, describes Islam as "une religion brutale très-propre à gagner des hommes brutaux" ("a brutal religion designed to attract brutal men"). It was propagated, asserts Sacy, "avec le fer et le feu"[44] ("by means of fire and the sword"). Grotius contrasts the first generation of those who embraced Islam ("thieves and robbers, men estranged from all humanity and piety") with the first Christians ("men of a plain and innocent life"). Islam was spread by the sword. Christianity was "enlarged and amplified" by the miracles of Christ and the Apostles and by the example of "the very patient enduring of the torments and punishments that the Christians suffered."[45]

As Grotius sees it, the first followers of Christianity and Islam reflected

41. Donald Frame, trans., *The Complete Essays of Montaigne* (Stanford: Stanford University Press, 1985), p. 232.

42. See my account of this matter in *L'Ecriture et le Reste: The "Pensées" of Pascal in the Exegetical Tradition of Port-Royal* (Columbus: Ohio State University Press, 1981), pp. 47–52.

43. *The Summa contra Gentiles of Saint Thomas Aquinas*, I:vi, p. 13. Philippe Sellier points to a key sentence in the *De veritate* (VI:2) as evidence of Pascal's use of Grotius: "La lecture de ses livres, prétendus saints, est interdite au peuple." See *Pensées de Pascal* (1991), p. 259, n. 7.

44. *La Genèse,* Préface, Première Partie, partie vii.

45. *The Truth of Christian Religion*, p. 176.

PLATE VI. The Public Recitation of the Holy Qur'an. Ravius [Christian Raue], *Prima tredecim partium Alcorani arabico-latin* (1646). Côte Bibliothèque Nationale 40 02g 122. Service photographique, Bibliothèque Nationale.

the character of the founders of their religions. Jesus led an "unblamable" life; Mohammed had been a "robber" before turning to prophecy. As does Pascal in fragment 321, Grotius contrasts Jesus and Mohammed on the question of miracles. Jesus gave sight to the blind, restored health to the sick, and made the lame walk. "Mahomet saith of himself that he was sent not with miracles but with arms." And those miracles which Mohammed's followers ascribed to him ("the dove which flew into his ear; the camel which had conference with him by night; the great part of the moon [which] fell into his lap") are nothing but "absurdities."[46] Unlike the Apostles, the "doctors of Mahometanism" "wrought no miracles at all." "Neither did they suffer any grievous persecutions or cruel kinds of death for their profession."[47]

In fragment 243, Pascal emphasizes the defective nature of Mohammed's moral teaching. "Quel mystère a(-t-)il enseigné selon sa tradition même? Quelle morale et quelle félicité!" ("What mystery did he teach according to his own tradition? What a [ridiculous] morality and heavenly reward!"). Going into greater detail, Grotius compares the "precepts of the two religions": Christianity teaches "loving one's enemies"; Islam, on the other hand, authorizes "revenge." Christianity teaches "the sanctity of marriage"; Islam tolerates polygamy and divorce. Christianity is a religion "rooted in the heart and soul"; Islam is a religion of the flesh which enjoins the obsolete ritual of circumcision. Christianity allows the "moderate use" of wine, "a great gift of God, beneficial both for body and mind if it be soberly taken." Islam absurdly forbids the eating of pork and the drinking of wine.[48]

Pascal sums up the differences between Jesus and Mohammed in lines which remind us of the extent to which the theory of the "three orders" pervades his thought in the course of the *Apology*.[49] Taking his cues from Grotius, he recasts the idea in a form which is uniquely Pascalian:

> Enfin cela est si contraire que si Mahomet a pris la voie de réussir humainement, J.-C. a pris celle de périr humainement et qu'au lieu de conclure que puisque Mahomet a réussi, J.-C. a bien pu réussir, il faut dire que puisque Mahomet a réussi, J.-C. devait périr.

46. Ibid., p. 175.
47. Ibid., p. 176.
48. Ibid., p. 178.
49. On this subject, see Jean Mesnard's landmark article, "Le Thème des trois ordres dans l'organisation des *Pensées*" in *Pascal: thématique des Pensées,* Lane M. Heller and Ian M. Richmond, eds. (Paris: Vrin, 1988), pp. 29–55.

In a word, the difference is so great that, if Mahomet followed the path of success, humanly speaking, Jesus followed that of death, humanly speaking, and, instead of concluding that where Mahomet succeeded Jesus could have done so too, we must say that, since Mahomet succeeded, Jesus had to die. (209)

In fragment 308, in which Pascal elaborates his theory of the "three orders," he makes a distinction between the separate orders of "chair" ("body"), "esprit" ("mind") and "charité" ("charity"):

La distance infinie des corps aux esprits figure la distance infiniment plus infinie des esprits à la charité, car elle est surnaturelle. . . .

La grandeur des gens d'esprit est invisible aux rois, aux riches, aux capitaines, à tous ces grands de chair.

La grandeur de la sagesse, qui est nulle sinon de Dieu, est invisible aux charnels et aux gens d'esprit. Ce sont trois ordres différents, de genre.

The infinite distance between body and mind symbolizes the infinitely more infinite distance between mind and charity, for charity is supernatural. . . .

The greatness of intellectual people is not visible to kings, rich men, captains, who are all great in a carnal sense.

The greatness of wisdom, which is nothing if it does not come from God, is not visible to carnal or intellectual people. They are three orders differing in kind. (308)

In Pascal's eyes, Mohammed is no more than a captain or a king. His success is entirely human, entirely of this world. Christ's success, on the other hand, is in the realm of the truly spiritual, in the order of charity. Similar dynamics operate in each of the three orders. But their consequences are very different. Mohammed succeeds according to the standards of this world; Christ's success is in the realm of holiness and sanctity. However, in the realm of the holy, success means the ultimate sacrifice of death. From the Christian perspective, it would be nonsense to think that Jesus could have succeeded in the way that Mohammed did. Rather, since Mohammed (who represents the dynamics of the carnal order) succeeded, it was inevitable that Jesus should die. "Puisque Mahomet a réussi, J.-C. devait périr" ("Since Mahomet succeeded, Jesus had to die"). Yet, in dying, Christ transcends that death which permeates the carnal and intellectual orders and breaks through to the order of charity and holiness:

J.-C. sans biens, et sans aucune production au dehors de science, est dans son ordre de sainteté. Il n'a point donné d'inventions. Il n'a point régné, mais il a été humble, patient, saint, saint, saint à Dieu, terrible aux démons, sans aucun péché. O qu'il est venu en grande pompe et en une prodigieuse magnificence aux yeux du coeur et qui voient la sagesse.

Jesus without wealth or any outward show of knowledge has his own order of holiness. He made no discoveries; he did not reign, but he was humble, patient, thrice holy to God, terrible to demons, and without sin. With what great pomp and marvelously magnificent array he came in the eyes of the heart, which perceive wisdom! (308)

In Chapter VI of the *De veritate religionis christianae*, Grotius devotes considerable effort to refuting what he views as the faulty Christology and anti-Trinitarian prejudices of the Qur'an. Grotius first notes that the Qur'an represents both Moses and Jesus as "holy men" sent by God. The Qur'an, however, "records many things contrary to the Old and New Testaments." The Gospels testify that Jesus was crucified and rose on the third day. "Mahomet teaches quite contrary, namely that Jesus was privily conveyed into Heaven and not himself but something in his likeness was nailed to the Cross; and consequently he did not die; but the sight of the Jews was deluded and deceived."[50]

Mohammed, observes Grotius, admits that Jesus was the Messiah and that he had no human father. However, the Qur'an refuses both the doctrine of the Incarnation and that of the Trinity. In order to refute these teachings, Grotius formulates the following "Answer to the Mahumetans' Objection Concerning the Son of God":

The Mahometans tell us they are not a little displeased with us for saying that God hath a Son, seeing he useth not a wife: As though the word *Son* could not have a more divine signification in God. But Mahomet himself attributes many things as dishonourable and ill-be-seeming God as if he should be said to have a wife. Thus he saith, that God had *a cold hand* . . . that God was carried in a chair and the like. . . .

When we say that Jesus is the Son of God we do but signify the same thing that he means when he calls him the *word* of God: for the *word* is often a sort begotten of the mind. And further, that he was born of a Virgin, only by the operation of God, supplying the *vertue* or efficacy of a father: that by the power of God, he was carried into Heaven: all which being confessed by Mahomet himself, do shew that Jesus by a singular prerogative and peculiar right, may and ought to be called the Son of God.[51]

Given the whole tradition of Christian hostility to Islamic theology, it is rather surprising to find Grotius taking such a conciliatory position. He argues that Christians actually mean the same thing by the term "Son of

50. *The Truth of Christian Religion,* p. 172. Scholars have noted that this version of Christ's death corresponds to versions current in the Gnostic and Docetist heresies.

51. Ibid., p. 179.

God" which the Qur'an means when it speaks of Jesus as having been created by the "word" of God. Grotius' attempt to explain Christian terminology as symbolic recalls Pascal's attempt to refute the Deist critique of the God of the Old Testament. Boucher, in *Les Triomphes de la religion chrestienne*, presents a group of *libertins* who claim to be horrified by the Old Testament's attribution of human features and gestures to God:

> Comment est-ce que cette Ecriture peut être inspirée de Dieu, puisqu'elle propose plusieurs choses injurieuses et indignes de sa Divine Majesté, lui attribuant des parties corporelles, des yeux, des oreilles, une bouche, des épaules, un ventre . . . et ce qui est plus injurieux, lui attribuant des passions d'esprit, disant qu'il travaille et se repose, qu'il sommeille . . . qu'il change ses oeuvres et se repent de quelques actions qu'il a faites, choses toutes indignes de la grandeur de sa Majesté infinie.[52]

> How can this Scripture be inspired by God, since it proposes many things injurious to and unworthy of his Divine Majesty, attributing to him corporeal parts, eyes, ears, a mouth, shoulders, a belly . . . and what is worse, attributing to him intellectual passions, saying that he works and rests, that he sleeps . . . that he changes his works and repents of actions which he has taken, things all unworthy of the greatness of his infinite Majesty.

Pascal, in the dossier "Loi figurative" (XIX), argues, like Grotius, that what is literally false can be spiritually true. The anthropomorphism of Scripture is a function of the limited nature of human language:

> Quand la parole de Dieu qui est véritable est fausse littéralement elle est vraie spirituellement. *Sede a dextris meis*[53]: cela est faux littéralement, donc cela est vrai spirituellement.
>
> En ces expressions il est parlé de Dieu à la manière des hommes. . . . C'est donc une marque de l'intention de Dieu, non de sa manière de l'exécuter.
>
> Ainsi quand il dit: Dieu a reçu l'odeur de vos parfums et vous donnera en récompense une terre grasse. . . . Ainsi *iratus est*,[54] Dieu jaloux, etc. Car les choses de Dieu étant inexprimables elles ne peuvent être dites autrement et l'Eglise d'aujourd'hui en use encore.

> When the word of God, which is true, is false in the letter it is true in the spirit. *Sit thou at my right hand* is false literally, so it is true spiritually.
>
> In such expressions God is spoken of in human terms. . . . Thus it indicates God's intention, not the way he will carry it out.

52. J. Boucher, *Les Triomphes de la religion chrestienne contenans les résolutions de trois cens soixante et six question* (Paris: L. Sonnius, 1628), p. 182.

53. Psalm 109:1.

54. Isaiah 5:25.

> Thus when it is written: "The Lord smelled a sweet savour"[55] and will reward you with a rich land. . . . Thus *the anger of the Lord is kindled*, "jealous God," etc. For as the things of God are inexpressible, they cannot be said in any other way and the Church still uses them today. (272)

Pascal admits that the Bible appears to contain much which is obscure and incomprehensible. But, he argues, the Bible also contains "des clartés admirables" ("things of striking clarity") and "des prophéties manifestes et accomplies" ("prophecies manifestly fulfilled") (218). One can therefore justify the Christian tradition of assigning a sacred or mysterious meaning to the "obscurités" found in the Old and New Testaments. However, the "clartés" found in the Qur'an—such as the paradise promised to the faithful—are patently absurd. Therefore, there can be no justification for attaching mysterious meanings to what is obscure in the Qur'an:

> Ce n'est pas par ce qu'il y a d'obscur dans Mahomet et qu'on peut faire passer pour un sens mystérieux que je veux qu'on en juge, mais par ce qu'il y a de clair, par son paradis et par le reste. C'est en cela qu'il est ridicule. Et c'est pourquoi il n'est pas juste de prendre ses obscurités pour des mystères, vu que ses clartés sont ridicules. Il n'en est pas de même de l'Ecriture. Je veux qu'il y ait des obscurités qui soient aussi bizarres que celles de Mahomet, mais il y a des clartés admirables et des prophéties manifestes et accomplies. La partie n'est donc pas égale. Il ne faut pas confondre et égaler les choses qui ne se ressemblent que par l'obscurité et non pas par la clarté qui mérite qu'on révère les obscurités.

> It is not by what is obscure in Mahomet, and might be claimed to have a mystical sense, that I want him to be judged, but by what is clear, by his paradise and all the rest. That is what is ridiculous about him, and that is why it is not right to take his obscurities for mysteries, seeing that what is clear in him is ridiculous. It is not the same with Scripture. I admit that there are obscurities as odd as those of Mahomet, but some things are admirably clear, with prophecies manifestly fulfilled. So it is not an even contest. We must not confuse and treat as equal things which are only alike in their obscurities, and not in the clarity which earns respect for the obscurities. (218)

Whereas Pascal mentions only the Qur'anic version of Paradise, Grotius goes into further detail concerning that which he finds "ridiculous" and "contrary to the truth of history" in the Qur'an:

> Such is that fable of a fair and beautiful woman that learned a solemn charm or song of some angels that were drunk, whereby she was wont to ascend in the sky and likewise descend again; and ascending once a great height into heaven, she was caught of God and there fixed and made that star which is called Venus.

55. Genesis 8:21.

> Like to this is that of a mouse in Noah's ark, that was bred of an elephant's dung; and an ant of the breath of a lion.
>
> More specially that most notorious fiction concerning Death to be changed into a ram, that must remain in the middle space between heaven and hell. And the fable of sweating out their good chear in the other life. When likewise (they imagine) there shall be whole troops of women assigned to every man for pleasures of carnal copulation.[56]

Grotius goes on to compare the Qur'an and the Christian Scriptures from several other perspectives. In the first place, he argues, the Christian Revelation was closed with the death of the last Apostle. Christ himself "foretold that after his time there should arise false Christs and false Prophets, which should lie and say they were sent of God." And even should an Angel descend from heaven, Grotius observes, "yet we may not receive or entertain any other doctrine than that which Christ hath left us." Moreover, whereas the Qur'an was written and dispersed in a single language, the Bible was preserved in many versions and even by "many sects" which differed greatly concerning its interpretation.[57] The Muslims, Grotius observes, claim that both the Torah and the Gospel represent corrupt texts. In particular, they are persuaded that in the fourteenth chapter of the Gospel of St. John (where the sending of a "Comforter" is mentioned), "there hath been something registered concerning Mahomet which the Christians have rayeded out."[58]

Replying to the notion that the Christian Gospels have been corrupted, Grotius argues (as does Pascal in fragment 207) that even the Jews and the pagans, writing five hundred years before the advent of Islam, never doubted the authenticity of these documents:

> Neither did ever the pagans or Jews raise any controversy about this, as if these were not the works of those men whose they were said to be: but Julian[59] himself plainly confesseth that those were the writings of Peter and Paul, Matthew, Mark and Luke . . . for as no man in his wits can doubt that those writings, which go under the names of Homer and Virgil are truly theirs . . . in like manner it were more absurd to bring the authors of those books in question.[60]

In fragment 207 (see Plate VII), Pascal restates what appears to be the same argument:

56. *The Truth of Christian Religion,* pp. 180–81.
57. Ibid., p. 183.
58. Ibid., p. 173.
59. The Emperor Julian ("the Apostate").
60. *The Truth of Christian Religion,* p. 183.

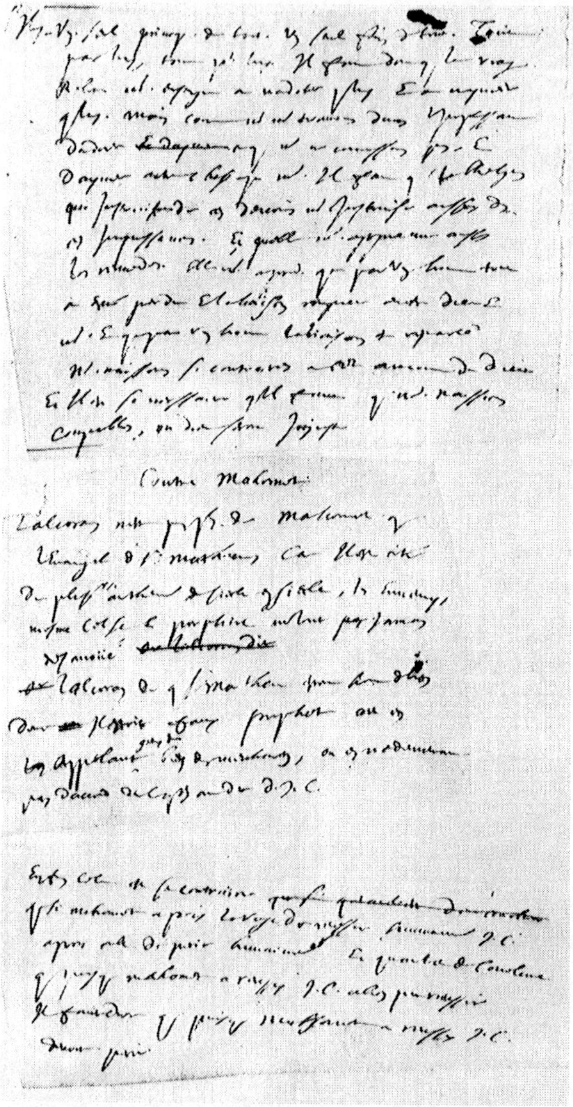

PLATE VII. Fragment 207 (Lafuma), "Contre Mahomet," in the *Recueil original* (Bibliothèque Nationale, MS français 9202). Service photographique, Bibliothèque Nationale. Fragment 207 is the middle section of the manuscript page.

Contre Mahomet.

L'Alcoran n'est pas plus de Mahomet que l'Evangile de saint Matthieu. Car il est cité de plusieurs auteurs de siècle en siècle. Les ennemis mêmes, Celse et Porphyre,[61] ne l'ont jamais désavoué.

L'Alcoran dit que saint Matthieu était homme de bien, donc il était faux prophète ou en appelant gens de bien méchants, ou en ne demeurant pas d'accord de ce qu'ils ont dit de J.-C.

Against Mahomet. The Koran is no more Mahomet's than St. Matthew's Gospel. For it is quoted by many authors from one century to another. Even its enemies, Celsus and Porphyry, never denied it.

The Koran says that St. Matthew was a good man, so he was a false prophet either in calling good men evil or in disagreeing with what they said about Christ. (207)

Fragment 207 has proved difficult to interpret. The argument of its concluding paragraph seems clear enough. The Qur'an is not consistent. Mohammed's sympathetic reference to St. Matthew contradicts his rejection of the divinity of Jesus. Mohammed demonstrated that he was a false prophet either by calling the Apostle "a good man" or by rejecting the Incarnation.[62] The first line of fragment 207, however, seems very obscure. "L'Alcoran n'est plus de Mahomet que l'Evangile de saint Matthieu" ("The Koran is no more Mahomet's than St. Matthew's Gospel"). Does Pascal mean to cast doubt on the origins of the Qur'an by arguing that Mohammed no more wrote the Qur'an than he did St. Matthew's Gospel? Or does he mean something quite different: that there is no more proof that Mohammed wrote the Qur'an than there is that St. Matthew really wrote the Gospel attributed to him? The second of these two readings seems to me the more likely. In the following lines, Pascal goes on to produce arguments which serve to buttress the case for the historical credibility of St. Matthew's Gospel. Unlike the Qur'an, it is cited by "plusieurs auteurs de siècle en siècle"[63] ("quoted by many authors from one

61. Celsus and Porphyry: pagan antagonists of early Christianity.

62. Something in Pascal's text seems odd. Who, in Pascal's hypothesis, are the "gens de bien" whom might have been called "des méchants"? Has Pascal not accidentally transposed the two categories? Should not his argument run as follows? Mohammed's status as a false prophet is proved by his inconsistency. He calls the authors of the Gospel "hommes de bien" yet rejects what they teach about Jesus. Tourneur's rendering of the original manuscript at this point seems to bear out such a reading. The words "*—gens de—bien des mechants*" seems to be some kind of correction. See Z. Tourneur, *Pensées de Blaise Pascal: édition paléographique* . . . , p. 246.

63. Pascal here seems to be drawing upon Grotius' argument in Book III of the *De veritate religionis christianae:* "Nous disons ensuite que les Livres dont on n'a jamais douté entre

century to another"). Even its enemies (the pagan antagonists to Christianity Celsus and Porphyry) never denied its authenticity.

Michel Le Guern demonstrates that Pascal has synthesized two different sources in formulating this argument. The first concerns Grotius' argument that even Julian the Apostate accepted the fact that the Gospels were written by those Apostles whose names they bear. The second source, which does not mention St. Matthew but contains the names of Celsus and Porphyry, is to be found in Charron's *Les Trois Vérités*:

> L'empereur Julien, Porphyre, Hiéroclès platoniciens, Celse épicurien, philosophes ennemis jurés du christianisme, ont avoué les miracles de Jésus-Christ.[64]

> The Emperor Julian, the Platonists Hierocles and Porphyry, the Epicurean Celsus, all philosophers who were sworn enemies of Christianity, accepted the miracles of Jesus Christ.

Francis Kaplan thinks that fragment 207 is less the result of a conscious synthesis than of Pascal's having confused two different texts: Grotius' and Charron's.[65] This seems possible. The two texts, which in fact deal with rather different subjects, are linked by a common reference to the Emperor Julian. Perhaps it was this common reference which caused Pascal to confuse the two when setting down the text of fragment 207.

Michel and Marie-Rose Le Guern remind us that Pascal's aims in the fragments dealing with Islam are not exactly the same as those of Grotius in the sixth chapter of the *De veritate religionis christianae*:

> L'intention de Pascal n'est sans doute pas celle de Grotius. Il ne destine pas son livre à des musulmans et il n'a donc aucune raison particulière de combattre le mahométisme. Il s'en sert surtout pour faire ressortir par contraste les qualités du christianisme. On sent bien que Pascal ne choisit le mahométisme que comme un

---

les Chrétiens, et qui sont attribués à un Auteur certain sont assurément de ceux dont ils portent le nom, parce que les plus anciens des écrivains Catholiques, comme un Justin, un Irenée, Clément d'Alexandrie et les autres qui les ont suivis, les ont allegués sous ces mêmes noms, parce que Tertullien rapporte que leurs originaux étaient encore de son temps, que les Eglises les ont reçus dans tout le monde . . . que les Juifs et les payens n'ont jamais mis en dispute s'ils étaient de ceux à qui on les donne et que Julien même a confessé ouvertement que les écrits que les chrétiens lisaient sous les noms de saint Matthieu, de saint Marc et de saint Luc, étaient véritablement d'eux." French translation cited from *De la vérité de la religion chréstienne par Hugue Grotius, traduit du latin par le sieur de Beauvoir* (Paris: chez Pierre le Petit, 1659), pp. 157–58.

64. Cited by Le Guern, *Blaise Pascal: Pensées* (Paris: Gallimard, 1977), I, p. 303, n. 2. Le Guern notes that in fact no such references exist in the works of Celsus or Porphyry.

65. *Les Pensées de Pascal* (Paris: Cerf. 1982), p. 410.

cas particulier en raison du caractère démonstratif des oppositions qu'il lui permet d'établir.[66]

Pascal's aim is obviously not that of Grotius. His book is not being written for Muslims, and he has no particular reason to combat Islam. He uses it to bring out, by way of contrast, the strong points of Christianity. One senses that Pascal has chosen the particular case of Islam only because of the oppositions which it permits him to establish.

Pascal's aims in demonstrating the character of a genuine "false religion" are obviously limited. He can hardly be said to undertake a full-scale refutation of the religion of the Prophet. Nonetheless, it still seems interesting that Pascal failed to take note of one central theme in anti-Christian Islamic polemic. Grotius reports with some insistence the Muslims' claim that the Christians have suppressed a reference to Mohammed in the fourteenth chapter of St. John and have corrupted the text of the Gospels.[67] Nowhere in the *Pensées* does Pascal ever refer to this challenge to the authority of Scripture. Did he find it simply too ridiculous? Did he know so little about Islam that the reference not make sense to him? Or perhaps he never read the relevant section of *De veritate religionis christianae*? In any event, the omission (assuming Grotius is really Pascal's principal source on Islam) is a bit curious. Throughout the *Pensées*, Pascal takes great pains to refute any challenge to the authenticity of the Christian Scriptures. Sometimes, he even manages to imagine objections which his libertine adversaries had not yet raised. In fragments 970–972, for instance, he goes to great length to refute the noncanonical Fourth Book of Esdras.[68]

Pascal's notes reveal a somewhat surprising lack of interest in Islam as a religious phenomenon. Even where Grotius provides key information, Pascal fails to take note of it. One almost wishes that he had found the subject more interesting. Given the kinds of arguments Pascal makes about Judaism, it would be fascinating to see what Pascal made of the Qur'an's claim to be part of the same Revelation (that "Mother of all Books") manifested in the Torah and the Gospels. What might he have

66. *Les Pensées de Pascal: De l'anthropologie à la théologie* (Paris: Larousse, 1977), p. 170.

67. *The Truth of Christian Religion,* p. 173.

68. The noncanonical Fourth Book of Esdras recounts that the original texts of the Pentateuch were burned during the Babylonian Exile and reconstituted by Esdras. In a dossier written prior to the classification of 1658, Pascal assembles a series of arguments aimed at proving that this account is but a "fable." These fragments, numbers 970–72 in Lafuma, were recorded only by the Second Copy.

thought of the Qur'an's rejection of the exclusivist claims of the Jewish Revelation? How might he have reacted to the Qur'an's censure of the central Christian doctrines of the Trinity and the Incarnation? How might he have refuted the Qur'anic teaching concerning Jesus?[69]

In the last analysis, Pascal's treatment of Islam is far from innovative. In many ways, it almost seems less derived from a direct reading of Grotius than of some intermediate source. Had it been published twenty years earlier, an excellent candidate for that source would be Le Maistre de Sacy's critique of Islam in the seventh section of Part I of his *Préface à la Genèse*. Sacy's analysis of Islam, which seems to be drawn directly from Grotius' *De veritate religionis christianae*, has much in common with the fragments of the *Pensées* we have just examined.[70] Its tone is generally more strident than is Grotius'. Sacy seeks to show those *libertins* who maintain that Christianity is an imposture what a genuine religious fraud looks like.

As does Pascal, Sacy contrasts the Qur'an and the Christian Scriptures. Whereas Christianity represents fifteen hundred years of continuous Revelation beginning with Moses and culminating in Christ, Sacy asserts, Islam is founded only on a single revelation purportedly received by Mohammed. The Old Testament is the testimony of an entire people. The Qur'an is but the testimony of a single unbalanced individual. Mohammed convinced his wife, "et par elle . . . beaucoup d'autres" ("and via her . . . many others"), that his attacks of epilepsy were "des communications . . . qu'il avait avec l'Ange Gabriel" ("revelations . . . which he had from the Angel Gabriel"). Christ was predicted by Moses and a great number of prophets. "Mahomet n'est prédit de personne"[71] ("Mohammed is predicted by no one").

Sacy invites his reader to compare the teachings of Jesus and Mohammed. The Gospels constitute "une morale divine et parfaitement sainte dans tous ses points" ("a teaching which is divine and perfectly holy in

69. Unlike Grotius, Pascal seems completely unaware that the Qur'an accepts the Virgin Birth of Jesus the Messenger and the Immaculate Conception of Mary while denying the doctrines of the Crucifixion and the Resurrection.

70. It is not completely out of the question that Pascal had access to Sacy's notes on Grotius' discussion of Islam. Philippe Sellier reminds us of the extent to which "les écrivains-théologiens de Port-Royal forment véritablement un 'groupe,' où circulent et s'échangent les textes-clés . . . et où se révèlent communs bien des principes de base" ("Avant-Propos," D. Wetsel, *L'Ecriture et le Reste,* p. xii).

71. *La Genèse: traduite en français avec l'explication du sens littéral et du sens spirituel* (Paris: Lambert Roulland, 1682), Préface, Première Partie, partie vii. Cf. *Pensées,* fragment 209.

every detail"). By contrast, the Qur'an is both morally defective and unoriginal. It amounts to no more than a plagiarism of the "vérités" which the great teachers had taught prior to Mohammed and which the Prophet and his followers "ont . . . souillées dans leur bouche par le mélange de l'impiété et de l'erreur" ("soiled in their mouths with a mixture of impiety and error"). Mohammed, with the help of an apostate Christian monk and a renegade Jew, simply invented a new religion under the cover of personal revelation. The Qur'an teaches "une religion brutale très propre à gagner des hommes brutaux" ("a brutal religion designed to win over brutal men"). Whereas Christianity was spread by martyrdom and by "une infinité de miracles," Islam was propagated "avec le fer et le feu"[72] ("the sword and the flame").

As a modern anti-Pelagian, Sacy can only regard with horror the Islamic tradition that those who die fighting for the defense of the faith will be reserved a place in Paradise. Nothing reveals more about a religion, he observes, than that "récompense à laquelle doivent tendre toutes les actions de ceux qui la suivent" ("reward toward which is directed the behavior of those who follow it"). That beatitude which he says Mahommed promises "ceux qui seront assez fous pour le croire" ("those who are insane enough to believe him") shocks Sacy's most fundamental opinions concerning the inscrutability of Grace. "Le Dieu de Mahomet qui promet aux siens une telle béatitude est digne, non de l'adoration, mais de l'exécration de tout le monde" ("The God of Mohammed, who promises his followers such happiness, merits, not the worship, but the execration of everyone"). As Sacy views it, Islam is a completely false religion. It is neither Christianity, from which it plagiarized its moral teachings, nor Judaism, from which it borrowed the obsolete rite of circumcision. Rather, it is "une secte monstrueuse" composed of "diverses erreurs qui s'entrecombattent"[73] ("many conflicting errors").

For Pascal as well, Islam stands as the perfect example of a false religion. It is a complete fabrication invented by its founder. It is as devoid of Revelation as any of the other pagan religions:

> Je vois donc des faiseurs de religions en plusieurs endroits du monde et dans tous les temps, mais ils n'ont ni la morale qui peut me plaire, ni les preuves qui peuvent m'arrêter . . . ainsi j'aurais refusé également, et *la religion de Mahomet* et celle de la Chine et celle des anciens Romains et celles des Egyptiens par cette seule

72. *La Genèse,* Préface, Première Partie, partie vii. Cf. Pensées, fragments 209 and 243.
73. *La Genèse,* Préface, Première Partie, partie vii.

raison que l'une n'ayant point plus (de) marques de vérité que l'autre, ni rien qui me déterminât nécessairement. La raison ne peut pencher plutôt vers l'une que vers l'autre.

I see then makers of religions in many parts of the world and throughout the ages, but their morality fails to satisfy me and their proofs fail to give me pause. Thus I should have refused alike *the religion of Mohammed*, that of China, of the ancient Romans, and of the Egyptians solely because, none of them bearing the stamp of truth more than another, nor anything which forces me to choose it, reason cannot incline toward one rather than another. (454, italics mine)

It would be a serious error to suppose that the speaker in the preceeding passage is Pascal himself in the role of the student of comparative religion. Pascal is hardly an inquirer into the conflicting truths of the world's great religions. He has hardly evoked the non-Christian religions because he seriously thinks they might contain some truth. Rather, he has used Islam and the ancient pagan religions as part of his apologetic strategy. These religions' lack of any "marque de vérité" ("stamp of truth") has served to sensitize Pascal's interlocutor to what is about to happen. The "je" of the passage represents Pascal's imagining himself in the role of the seeker. That seeker, according to the strategy sketched in fragment 454, is just on the verge of making his most crucial discovery so far in the course of the *Apology*. In the very next line, he will discover the Jews and their religion. That religion will be made to stand in complete contrast with all the other religions which have been examined to this point:

En considérant aussi cette inconstante et bizarre variété de moeurs et de créances dans les divers temps, je trouve en un coin du monde, un peuple particulier séparé de tous les autres peuples de la terre et dont les histoires précèdent de plusieurs siècles les plus anciennes que nous ayons.

Je trouve donc ce peuple grand et nombreux sorti d'un seul homme, qui adore un seul Dieu, et qui se conduit par une loi qu'ils disent tenir de sa main [et] ils soutiennent qu'ils sont les seuls du monde auxquels Dieu a révélé ses mystères. . . .

La rencontre de ce peuple m'étonne, et me semble digne de l'attention. . . .

As I consider this shifting and odd variety of customs and beliefs in different ages, I find in one corner of the world a peculiar people, separated from all the other peoples of the earth, who are the most ancient of all and whose history is earlier by several centuries than the earliest histories we have.

I find then this great and numerous people, descended from one man, worshipping one God, and living according to a law which they claim to have received from his hand. They maintain that they are the only people in the world to whom God has revealed his mysteries. . . .

My encounter with this people amazes me and seems worthy of attention. . . . (454)

Once again, the "je" in this passage is hardly Pascal, who is just now discovering the Jews and their monotheism. Rather, Pascal again imagines the reaction of his seeker. He gives him a voice and imagines his monologue. "La rencontre de ce peuple m'étonne et me semble digne de l'attention" ("My encounter with this people amazes me and seems worthy of attention"). Out of the seeker's encounter with the religion of the Old Testament will grow Pascal's entire historical demonstration of the truth of the Christian religion.

"Histoire de la Chine": Pascal and the Challenge to Biblical Time

If Pascal's information concerning Islam is sketchy, his knowledge of "la religion . . . de la Chine" (454) is practically nonexistent. However, the latter comes to threaten Pascal's version of the Christian Revelation in a way in which the former never did. This threat is not doctrinal. Rather, it takes the form of a challenge to the historical accuracy of Christian chronology. In fragment 454, Pascal appears to take it for granted that the Jews are the most ancient people on the earth ("le plus ancien de tous") and that they possess "histoires" which are several centuries older than any other human documents ("dont les histoires précèdent de plusieurs siècles les plus anciennes que nous ayons"). However, at some later point in the writing of the Apology, Pascal came across information which must have seemed to him to undermine traditional Biblical chronology.

Christian chronologists, calculating backward through the Old Testament, had fixed the date of the Creation of the world at the year 4404 B.C.[74] Documents discovered in the course of the Jesuit mission to China, however, placed the first Chinese emperor on the throne in the year 2952 B.C.—660 years before the Christian date for the Flood.[75] Pascal's reaction

74. In 1632, J. d'Auzoles had published *La Sainte Chronologie* (Paris: G. Alliot, 1632), in which he presented some seventy-nine different opinions, arrived at by 122 different chronologists, concerning the date of the Creation. The earliest date suggested by any of these chronologists was 6984 B.C.

75. *Histoire de la Chine, traduite du Latin du Père Martin Martini de la Compagnie de Jésus par l'abbé Le Peletier* (Paris: chez C. Barbin, 1692), 1, pp. 6–7.

to this discovery is vividly recorded in fragment 822 (see plate VIII) under the rubric "Histoire de la Chine":

> Je ne crois que les histoires dont les témoins se feraient égorger.
> (Lequel est le plus croyable des deux, Moïse ou la Chine?)
> Il n'est pas question de voir cela en gros: je vous dis qu'il y a de quoi aveugler et de quoi éclaircir.
> Par ce mot seul je ruine tous vos raisonnements; mais la Chine obscurcit, dites-vous. Et je réponds: la Chine obscurcit, mais il y a clarté à trouver. Cherchez-la.
> Ainsi tout ce que vous dites fait à un des desseins et rien contre l'autre. Ainsi cela sert et ne nuit pas.
> Il faut donc voir cela en détail. Il faut mettre papiers sur table.
>
> I only believe histories whose witnesses are ready to be put to death.
> (Which is the more credible of the two, Moses or China?)
> There is no question of the broad view. I tell you that there is enough here to blind and to enlighten.
> With this one word I destroy all your arguments.
> —"But China obscures the issue," you say.
> And I reply: "China obscures the issue but there is light to be found. Look for it."
> Thus all you say serves one of these purposes without telling against the other. So it helps and does not harm.
> We must look at this in detail then. We must put the evidence on the table. (822)

This brief exchange between Pascal and some imaginary interlocutor has no discernible context within the dossier (*série* XXX) in which it is filed. Most modern commentary on this enigmatic text has taken it to represent Pascal's reaction to a work published in Munich in 1658 by the Jesuit missionary Martin Martini: *Sinicae Historiae decas prima, Res a gentis origine ad Christum natum in extrema Asia*. According to Henri Gouhier, Père Martini's account of Chinese chronology disturbed Pascal because it seemed to cast doubt on the accuracy of Biblical history:

> D'après les Chinois, le monde est beaucoup plus ancien que ne le permet la chronologie établie par les spécialistes de l'Ecriture sainte qui mettent la création du monde en l'an 4404 avant Jésus-Christ. Le savant jésuite était prêt aux accommodements en interprétant les textes, ici et là, de façon à raccourcir la chronologie des Chinois et à allonger celle de la Bible. Pascal ôte au compromis toute raison d'être: nous n'avons pas même à prendre en considération la tradition des païens . . . Comme celles des Grecs et des Egyptiens, les "histoires" des Chinois ne sont pas de l'histoire puisqu'elles ne sont pas fondées sur des témoignages contemporains: elles sont du "roman."[76]

76. Henri Gouhier, *Blaise Pascal: Commentaires* (Paris: Vrin, 1971), pp. 228–29.

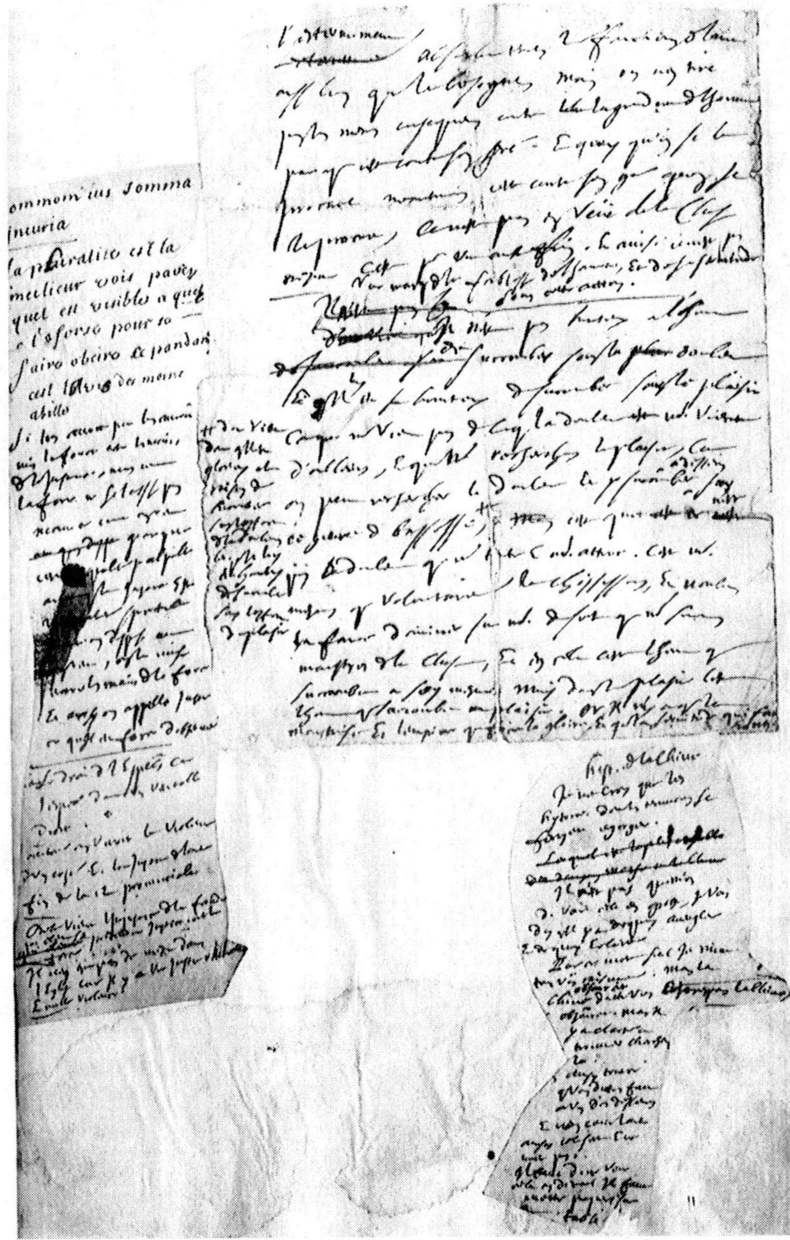

PLATE VIII. Fragment 822 (Lafuma), "Histoire de la Chine" in the *Recueil original* (Bibliothèque Nationale, MS français 9202). Service photographique, Bibliothèque Nationale. Fragment 822 is located in the lower-right-hand corner of the manuscript page.

According to the Chinese, the world is far older than the chronology established by the specialists of Holy Scripture, who put the Creation of the world in the year 4404 B.C., would allow. The scholarly Jesuit was prepared to compromise by interpreting the texts, here and there, so as to shorten the chronologies of the Chinese and lengthen those of the Bible. Pascal removes any reason for compromise: we need not even consider the traditions of the pagans. . . . Like those of the Greeks and the Egyptians, the "histories" of the Chinese are not historical since they are not founded upon the testimony of contemporary witnesses. They are completely fictitious.

Commentators on the *Pensées* have generally been less interested in the polemical implications of fragment 822 than in the way in which this text assists in the dating of those classified *liasses* which are so central to Pascal's apologetic strategy. Philippe Sellier notes that the fragment should logically figure in Chapter XVI, "Fausseté des autres religions" ("Falseness of other religions.")[77] Its absence from that chapter leads Jean Mesnard to conclude that Pascal's classification of the twenty-seven ordered *liasses* must have taken place before Pascal ever read Martini's *Sinicae Historiae* late in 1658.[78]

The usefulness of fragment 822 in dating significant parts of Pascal's projected Apology rests on the assumption that the fragment title, "Histoire de la Chine," is really a reference to Père Martini's *Sinicae Historiae*. Reevaluating the whole question, Anthony Pugh concludes that Père Martini's book is probably "the most likely candidate" for the reference contained in fragment 822. However, Pugh cautions that nothing necessarily links this fragment, or indeed Pascal's other references to China in fragments 436, 481, and 454, to the *Sinicae Historiae*. If we wish to maintain an earlier date for any of these fragments, Pugh reminds us, "we must look for another source."[79]

In an earlier discussion of fragment 822, I erroneously supposed that Pascal first learned of the Chinese pretensions to great historical antiquity when he came upon Martini's book.[80] In fact, what Pascal read in the *Sinicae Historiae*—if indeed he ever read it—should have come as no great surprise. Pascal had known about the conflict between the Bible and Chinese sources since his encounter with Jacques Forton, le sieur de Saint-Ange, in Rouen in 1647. Saint-Ange, a defrocked Capuchin, was ex-

77. Philippe Sellier, ed., *Pascal: Pensées* (Paris: Mercure de France, 1976), p. 341, n. 4.

78. Jean Mesnard, *Les Pensées de Pascal* (Paris: SEDES, 1976), p. 44.

79. Anthony R. Pugh, *The Composition of Pascal's Apologia* (Toronto: University of Toronto Press, 1984), p. 418.

80. David Wetsel, *L'Ecriture et le Reste*, p. 188.

pounding a number of less-than-orthodox propositions to the *curieux* of Rouen salon society. Among his teachings was the proposition that the end of the world could not come about until the entire physical mass of the earth had been exhausted in the furnishing of bodies for human souls. To this curious notion, Saint-Ange added a second heterodox principle: "Que Jésus-Christ est venu au milieu des siècles aussi bien qu'au milieu de la terre"[81] ("That Jesus Christ came in the middle of the Ages as well as in the middle of the earth").

Saint-Ange appears to have derived the notion that the earth must be spent in the production of physical bodies from the alchemical teaching concerning the necessity of the spiritualization of matter.[82] The idea that Christ came *"au milieu de la terre"* (italics mine) occupies an ancient place in Christian theological and philosophical speculation. As Mircea Eliade observes:

> The rock upon which the Temple of Jerusalem was built was considered as being the *umbilicus terrae*. The Irish pilgrim, Nicholas of Thvera, who had visited Jerusalem in the twelfth century, wrote of the Holy Sepulchre: "There is the Center of the World: there, on the day of the summer solstice, the sunlight fell perpendicular from the sky." A cosmological idea of indubitable archaism, and which survived into the late middle ages: on medieval maps, Jerusalem was always situated in the Center of the World. . . . Adam having been buried at the very place where he had been created, that is to say in Jerusalem, was redeemed by the Savior's blood on Golgotha.[83]

Pascal and a mathematician friend, Adrien Auzoult, took it upon themselves to inquire into Saint-Ange's teachings in order to denounce him to the local archbishop. They were immediately struck by the heretical character of Saint-Ange's version of sacred time and history. In order to prove the absurdity of his theory to Saint-Ange, they decided to calculate how long it would take to exhaust the physical mass of the earth in the production of human bodies. They told Saint-Ange that they would be generous with their numbers and assume that there are and have always been a greater number of people of the earth than there are or ever have

81. Léon Brunschvicg, ed., *Oeuvres de Blaise Pascal* (Paris: Hachette, 1908), "Récit de deux conférences," 1, 380–81, 399–400. For a detailed analysis of Pascal's encounters with Forton, see Henri Gouhier's *Pascal et les humanistes chrétiens: L'affaire Saint-Ange* (Paris: Vrin, 1974).

82. On this subject, see Mircea Eliade, *Forgerons et alchimistes* (Paris: Flammarion, 1977), pp. 126–29.

83. Mircea Eliade, *Symbolism, the Sacred, and the Arts* (New York: Crossroad, 1985), p. 109.

been. They would allow "trente pieds de terre" ("thirty feet of earth") for the composition of each human body and would assume that the recycling of souls into matter required a lifetime of fifteen years. Computing the volume of the earth in cubic feet from the earth's known circumference, they concluded it would take four billion years for the earth to be consumed by the production of human bodies. Thus, Christ would have been born into the world when it was already two billion years old. Pascal told Saint-Ange that the number was completely absurd. The most extreme figure any chronologist had ever advanced for the age of the world was "sept ou huit mille ans" ("seven or eight thousand years"). Saint-Ange replied that the Bible was obscure on this point but that the Chinese had "des mémoires de trente-six mille ans"[84] ("records of thirty-six thousand years").

Henri Gouhier was the first commentator to connect fragment 822 with the "affaire Saint-Ange." However, Gouhier admits that it is impossible to say whether Pascal remembered Saint-Ange's claim about the "mémoires" of the Chinese eleven years later. Nor have we any way of knowing whether Saint-Ange is Pascal's imagined interlocutor in fragment 822. Nonetheless, Gouhier insists, in light of that fragment, Saint-Ange's claim is striking:

> Ce dernier exemple est sérieux. Il le sera bien davantage après la publication de l'*Histoire de la Chine* par le P. Martini en 1658. Pascal en tiendra compte dans son *Apologie*. Se souvient-il alors de cet entretien avec Saint-Ange où, peut-être pour la première fois, on invoquait devant lui la chronologie chinoise pour justifier la réserve de l'historien devant les obscurités de la Bible? "La Chine obscurcit, dites-vous. . . ." Souvenir? Réminiscence? Idée neuve sans référence à un épisode complètement oublié? Qui le dirait?[85]

> This last example is serious. It will be even more so after the publication of the *History of China* by Père Martini in 1658. Pascal will take the matter into account in his *Apology*. Does he remember this conversation with Saint-Ange, in which he first perhaps heard the Chinese chronologies used to justify the historian's reserve in the face of the obscurities of the Bible? "China obscures the issue, you say. . . ." A memory? A reminiscence? A completely new idea with no reference to a completely forgotten episode? Who can say?

Given the fact that Pascal had known about the challenge to Christian chronology constituted by the Chinese "mémoires" long before 1658, only

84. Brunschvicg, ed., *Oeuvres de Blaise Pascal*, 1, 400–401.
85. *Pascal et les humanistes chrétiens: L'affaire Saint-Ange*, p. 5.

two solid arguments continue to suggest that Martini's *Sinicae Historiae* was the stimulus for the writing of fragment 822. First is the fact that Pascal does not mention China in the course of the twenty-seven classed *liasses* written before 1658.[86] Second is the similarity of the titles in fragments 822 and 481 (i.e., "Histoire de la Chine") to the Latin title *Sinicae Historiae*. However, neither of these arguments is conclusive. The title "Histoire de la Chine" might well refer to any one of a number of books written by Jesuit missionaries in the course of the previous fifty years. For instance, in Alvarez Semedo's *Histoire universelle . . . de la Chine*, translated from Italian into French in 1645, Pascal could have read that the Chinese language, one of the original seventy-two languages of the Tower of Babel, is written in characters that are over three thousand years old.[87] Pascal might also have consulted Gonzalès de Mendoça's *Histoire du grand Royaume de la Chine* (1589), Nicolas Trigault's *Histoire de l'expédition chrétienne au royaume de la Chine* (1618), or J.-J. Bellefleur's *Nouvelle Histoire de la Chine* (1622).

Pascal mentions China in three other fragments. In fragment 436, "Antiquité des Juifs," he lumps the chronologies of the Chinese with those of other civilizations of pagan antiquity. "Je ne m'étonne pas de ce que les Grecs ont fait l'*Iliade*, ni les Egyptiens et les Chinois leurs histoires" ("I am not surprised that the Greeks composed the *Iliad*, nor the Egyptians and Chinese their histories"). In fragment 454, he qualifies the religion of China, along with Islam and the religions of the Romans and Egyptians, as the product of "des faiseurs de religion" ("inventors of religions"). "J'aurais refusé également et la religion de Mahomet, et celle de la Chine, et celle des anciens Romains, et celle des Egyptiens" ("I should have refused alike the religion of Mahomet, that of China, of the ancient Romans, and that of the Egyptians"). In fragment 481, Pascal evokes the specific title *Histoire de la Chine*. "Contre l'*Histoire de la Chine*. Les histoires de Mexico, des cinq soleils, dont le dernier est il n'y a que huit cents ans" ("Against the *History of China*. The historians of Mexico, of the five suns, of which the last was only eight hundred years ago").

In the third of these three fragments, Pascal appears to argue that the chronologies of the Aztecs contradict those of the Chinese. According to Montaigne (*Essais*, III, 6), the Aztecs divided the history of the world into

86. See J. Mesnard, *Les Pensées de Pascal*, pp. 40–45. Also Philippe Sellier, ed., *Les Pensées de Pascal* (1976), pp. 16–18.

87. Alvarez Semedo, S. J., *Histoire universelle du grand royaume de la Chine, traduite en notre langue par Louis Coulon* (Paris: S. Cramoisy, 1645), pp. 46–48.

five ages, the first of which ended in a universal flood and the last of which began only eight hundred years before Montaigne's time.[88] Pascal, familiar with St. Augustine's theory of the six ages of the world (cf. fragment 283), appears to see a parallel in the "histoires de Mexico." Both the Aztecs and St. Augustine place the Flood at the end of the first age of the world. Apparently, Pascal thinks that the Aztecs provide a serious confirmation of Biblical chronology and contradict Chinese claims of extreme antiquity.[89]

In his *Histoire universelle . . . de la Chine*, Père Semedo faults the Chinese for failing to compute accurately the time between the Creation and the Patriarch Noah. As a result, the Chinese chronicles place the Emperor Yao, himself the successor of a long line of "anciens Patriarches," on the throne twelve years before the Christian date for the Flood. This is clearly impossible, observes Semedo, since all of humanity—with the exception of Noah and his family—perished in the Flood.[90]

Martini's *Sinicae Historiae*

In his *Sinicae Historiae*, translated into French by the Abbé Le Peletier in 1692, Père Martini devotes many pages to the problem of reconciling the universal Flood recounted by Genesis with the Great Flood described in the Chinese chronologies. The Chinese, Père Martini observes, have the most ancient calendar in the world. Consulting this calendar, which dates back to 2513 B.C., Martini draws a parallel between the astral conjunction observed by Chinese astronomers during the reign of the Emperor Yaus and a similar phenomenon "que les chronologistes de l'Europe assurent être arrivé du temps de Noé"[91] ("which European chronologists agree took place during the time of Noah"). Martini then argues that the legendary Emperor Yaus was probably none other than Noah. "On peut croire sans scrupule que *Yaus* est le même que *Janus*, tant à cause de la ressemblance des noms que de la proximité des temps, et que plusieurs ont cru que *Janus* et *Noé* était le même homme"[92] ("One may reasonably

88. See Donald Frame, ed., *The Complete Essays of Montaigne* (Stanford, Calif.: Stanford University Press, 1965), p. 698.

89. On this subject, see P. Sellier's useful note in *Pensées* (1991), p. 506, n. 12.

90. Semedo, *Histoire universelle . . . de la Chine,* p. 150.

91. Martini, *Histoire de la Chine,* p. 51.

92. Ibid., p. 65.

believe that *Yaus* is the same as *Janus*, as much because of the resemblance in the names as because of the proximity of their dates, and several have believed that *Janus* and *Noah* were the same man").

Père Martini's recourse to comparative mythology is not all that surprising. By the middle of the seventeenth century, comparatism had come to play an important role in Christian apologetics. In his *De veritate religionis christianae*, Grotius had attached great importance to the fact that traces of the Genesis story could be found in the mythologies of the Indians, the Egyptians, the Greeks, and the Romans.[93] Bogan (1658) composed an entire book of recollections of Genesis in the *Iliad* and the *Odyssey*.[94] An English apologist, E. Stillingfleet, sought to elucidate "what footsteps there are of the truth of Scripture history amid all the corruptions of heathen mythology."[95] Vossius, in his *De theologia Gentili*, ventured an even more daring interpretation. Pagan myth, he conjectured, was a kind of partial revelation by which the Gentiles were prepared to understand the Christian mysteries. Noah, for instance, is anticipated by three pagan deities: Bacchus, Janus (cf. Père Martini's speculation), and Saturn. The Dionysian mysteries recall Noah's discovery of intoxication (Genesis 9:21). Janus, represented in Roman mythology with two faces, recalls Noah's having seen two worlds. Saturn, whose symbol is the ship, divided the world among his three sons. Noah's sons fell heir to the postdiluvian world.[96]

Within Pascal's circle at Port-Royal, there was sharp disagreement concerning the utility of comparatism in Christian apologetics. Somewhat surprisingly, Le Maistre de Sacy found comparatism useful in establishing the antiquity of sacred history. In his commentary on Genesis, he theorizes that the Greek poets had forged the myth of Saturn—whose symbol recalls the Ark—from the Biblical account of Noah and the Flood.[97] Unlike Vossius, Sacy always insists that pagan myths are but parodies of Biblical events. They have been counterfeited by Satan in order to distort and cast doubt on Scripture. In his commentary on Leviticus 6:9, Sacy argues that the sacred fire tended by the vestal virgins in Roman mythology is

93. H. Grotius, *De veritate religionis christianae*, 1, p. 18ff.

94. Z. Bogan, *Homerus sive comparatio Homeri cum scriptoribus sacris quoad norman loquendi* (Oxford: n.p., 1658).

95. E. Stillingfleet, *Origines Sacrae or rational account of the grounds of Christian Faith as to the truth and divine authority of the Scriptures* (London: n.p., 1666), p. 599.

96. G.-J. Vossius, *De theologia Gentili et physiologia christiana sive de origine de progressu idolatriae* (Amsterdam: C. Blaen, 1642), 1, Chapter 19, pp. 75–77.

97. Le Maistre de Sacy, *Le Genèse*, pp. 350–51.

just such a parody. It is Satan's attempt to mock the perpetual fire which burned in the temple of the Jews. Sacy documents his argument with a citation from 1 Maccabees 3:48: "Ils ouvrirent les livres de la Loi, où les Gentils cherchaient à trouver quelque chose qui eût du rapport avec leurs idoles" ("They opened the books of the Law, in which the Gentiles sought to find something which might concern their idols") (Sacy's translation). "Les payens," Sacy explains, "cherchaient dans les livres saints quelque chose qu'ils pûssent imiter pour le culte de leurs idoles"[98] ("The pagans . . . sought to discover in the holy scriptures something which they might ape in the cult of their idols").

At Port-Royal, Sacy's colleague Antoine Arnauld feared that the comparative method might lead some to the conclusion that other religions or pagan myths might contain elements of divine truth. "Ce sont d'horribles choses et capables d'inspirer à de jeunes libertins: qu'il faut avoir une religion, mais qu'elles sont toutes bonnes, et que le paganisme même peut entrer en parallèle avec le christianisme"[99] ("These are horrible things, likely to inspire young libertines: that one needs to have a religion, but that they are all good, and that even paganism could be seen to run parallel to Christianity"). As we shall see, the Jesuit missionaries to China had come close to reaching such a conclusion. *Esprits forts* like La Mothe le Vayer had already reached it.[100]

In his *Sinicae Historiae*, Père Martini is extremely cautious when he draws parallels between the Bible and the "histoires" of the Chinese. Having ventured the hypothesis that perhaps the Flood spared Oriental Asia,[101] he then reconsiders the matter and evokes two other possibilities. Either prediluvian Chinese history is completely "fabuleuse" or else what the Chinese wrote concerning their history before the Flood was communicated to them by a survivor of Noah's Ark.[102] Martini had reason to be cautious about denying the universality of the Flood. As we saw in Chapter II, such a thesis had brought Isaac de La Peyrère to grief at the hands

98. *L'Exode et Le Lévitique: Traduits en français avec l'explication du sens littéral et du sens spirituel* (Lyon: L. Plaignard, 1683), p. 602. Sacy's argument is constructed on the basis of a faulty text. The correct reading of this text, in the translation of the Jerusalem Bible, is as follows: "For the guidance that the heathen would have sought from the images of their false gods, [Israel] opened the Book of the Law."

99. Antoine Arnauld, *Oeuvres* (Paris: Gabriel de Bellegarde, 1775–83), 3, 400–401.

100. See Chapter I, Two Cautious Skeptics: La Mothe le Voyer and Gabriel Naudé.

101. *Histoire de la Chine*, p. 6.

102. Ibid., pp. 63–65.

of the ecclesiastical authorities after the publication of his *Systema theologicum ex prae Adamitarum hypothesi* in 1655.[103]

Père Martini is by no means as rash as had been Isaac de La Peyrère. Early on in his treatise, he enunciates a cautious disclaimer concerning the strict veracity of the Chinese chronologies:

> Leurs annales sont remplies de grandes absurdités, tant à l'égard du long âge des hommes que de la durée des règnes de leurs souverains. Si l'on ajoutait foi à leurs historiens, il faudrait nécessairement croire que la naissance du monde a précédé le Déluge de plusieurs milliers d'années.[104]

> Their annals are full of great absurdities, both with regard to the extreme longevity of men and to the lengths of the reigns of their sovereigns. If one believed their historians, one would have to conclude that the Creation of the world preceded the Flood by many thousand years.

However, in the course of his exposition of the Chinese chronologies, Martini often seems more a mythographer than a Christian apologist. He is particularly fascinated by myths of origin. The Chinese, he observes, imagine that the first human emerged from a giant egg. "La coque fut enlevée dans le ciel; le blanc se répandit en l'air . . . le jaune demeura sur la terre" ("The shell was lifted up into the sky; the white spread out into the air . . . the yellow remained on the earth"). This same myth, Martini remarks, is also recounted by the Phoenicians.[105]

Martini explains that the Chinese are divided into two philosophical schools with regard to the origin of the world. One school holds that everything was produced by chance. A second teaches the eternity of the world. The second of these errors, Martini asserts, came to the Chinese—along with the practice of idolatry—from India in about A.D. 65.[106] Martini seems to think that the original religion of the Chinese was a kind of primal monotheism. He expresses his surprise that the Chinese language contains no particular word which might be translated as "God." However, Martini notes, the Chinese do have an expression, *Xang-ti* ("Seigneur et Conducteur du Ciel"), which indicates their belief in a Supreme Being who governs all things.

Knowledge of this Sovereign Being, Martini conjectures, was probably communicated to the Chinese by the descendants of Noah in the period

103. La Peyrère, English ed., pp. 239, 243.

104. *Histoire de la Chine,* p. 23.

105. Ibid., pp. 8–9.

106. Ibid., pp. 3–4.

immediately following the Flood.[107] Many of the Jesuit missionaries, Martini tells us, have come to believe that the Chinese chronicles contain numerous veiled references to the same sacred history recounted by the Old Testament. However, none of them has yet had the temerity to point this out to the Chinese themselves, "qui regardent leurs Histoires comme des Oracles et qui s'arrêtent avec opiniâtreté à leurs premiers sentiments"[108] ("who regard their histories as oracles and who obstinately cling to their traditional views").

Père Martini recounts that the Chinese *Traité de la Nature* divides the history of the world into twelve hours, each of which lasted eighteen hundred years. The Heavens were created at midnight; the earth at 1:00 A.M. Man appeared on the earth at 2:00 A.M. The Emperor Yaus (whom Martini identifies as Noah[109]) was born at noon the following day. In other words, some eighteen thousand years separated the beginning of the world from the Flood. If Pascal really read the *Sinicae Historiae*, he cannot have failed to note the discrepancy between the Chinese claim and the dates suggested by his own models. Pascal follows a radically conservative model borrowed from Le Maistre de Sacy. Only five generations of Patriarchs separate Moses, the author of the Pentateuch, from Adam and the Creation:

> Sem qui a vu Lamech qui a vu Adam a vu aussi Jacob qui a vu ceux qui ont vu Moïse: donc le déluge et la création sont vrais. Cela conclut entre de certaines gens qui l'entendent bien.

> Shem, who saw Lamech, who saw Adam, also saw Jacob, who saw those who saw Moses: therefore the Flood and the Creation are true. This evidence is conclusive among certain people who really understand the matter. (296)[110]

Père Martini admits to being startled by the implications of the chronological model proposed by the Chinese *Traité de la Nature*. "Si cette supputation était vraie . . . ces peuples seraient beaucoup plus anciens que ceux d'Egypte et de Chaldée qui se piquent d'une antique et fabuleuse origine" ("If these calculations were correct . . . these people would be

107. Ibid., pp. 4–5.

108. Ibid., p. 65.

109. Ibid.

110. Concerning Pascal's debt to Sacy, see D. Wetsel, *L'Ecriture et le Reste*, p. 63. Geneviève Delassault, in *Le Maistre de Sacy et son temps* (Paris: Nizet, 1957), observes that no historian before Sacy had ever advanced such a daring interpretation of early sacred history (p. 217).

far older than the Egyptians and the Chaldeans, who boast extravagantly concerning their ancient origins"). Moreover, the claim that the world is twenty-two thousand years old pales in the face of another Chinese claim. Confucius, according to another Chinese source, was born in the 667,000th year of the Creation![111] Père Martini's real attitude concerning the veracity of the Chinese pretentions to great antiquity is difficult to assess. In spite of his disclaimers, he often observes that *were* the Chinese figures correct, it would be necessary to revise radically the European version of history.

Père Martini's exposition of the Chinese chronologies would appear to have provoked considerable controversy. His French translator, the Abbé Le Peletier, seems to have felt obliged to append an additional disclaimer to his translation of the *Sinicae Historiae*:

> [Le père Martini] se moque de la vanité des Chinois sur leur opinion de l'ancienneté du monde, et ne l'a pas jugée plus préjudiciable à la chronologie chrétienne que le sentiment des Indiens, qui prétendaient être beaucoup plus anciens que la lune. Après avoir approfondi toutes les Annales de leur empire pour remonter à ce prodigieux nombre de siècles imaginaires, il n'a trouvé de véritable supputation de temps, que depuis l'invention d'un cycle . . . postérieur à la création du monde telle que le Saint Esprit l'a enseigné à Moïse.[112]

> [Père Martini] ridicules the vanity of the Chinese with regard to their opinion concerning the antiquity of the world, judging it no more prejudicial to the Christian chronology than that of the Indians, who claimed to be older than the moon. After having carefully studied all the Annals of their empire in order to trace backward this prodigious number of imaginary centuries, he concluded that the Chinese only began accurately calculating time with the invention of a cycle which postdates the Creation of the world as taught to Moses by the Holy Spirit.

It seems obvious that Pascal never examined Martini's *Sinicae Historiae* in any great detail. Had he done so, he would have found much that warranted his study and refutation. The general, if not vague, character of Pascal's four references to the Chinese question stands in considerable contrast to the detail with which he refutes the challenge to Biblical historicity posed by the apocryphal Fourth Book of Esdras.[113] It would probably be safe to conclude that Pascal only heard of Martini's book secondhand. This would be sufficient to explain the precise reference to the title *Histoire de la Chine* in fragments 822 and 481.

111. *Histoire de la Chine,* p. 10.
112. Ibid., in the introductory section, "Avertissement."
113. See n. 68 of present chapter.

Pascal may well have discussed the problem of the Chinese chronologies with Arnauld, who would later publish an extensive attack on the Jesuits' mission to China.[114] Another interesting text has often been overlooked. Père Beurrier, who heard Pascal's last confession, would later publish a work in which he would argue that the primitive religion of the Chinese contained all the fundamental doctrines of Christianity: the Fall, the Flood, the Trinity.[115] Beurrier maintains that the Chinese Emperor Fou-hi was the Patriarch Shem, who preached the cult of the true God in the Orient five hundred years after the Flood. According to Père Beurrier, Confucius taught moral doctrines anticipating those of Christ and predicted the birth of a Savior "in the West."[116]

Pascal and the Jesuit Mission to China

The sketchiness of Pascal's references to China in his draft of the *Apology* should not lead us to conclude that Pascal knew nothing about the Jesuit mission to China. A key reference in the Fifth *Provinciale* reveals the horror with which the future apologist had learned of the Jesuits' attempt to accommodate the religious tradition of the Chinese:

> Quand ils se trouvent en des pays où un Dieu crucifié passe pour folie, ils suppriment le scandale de la croix, et ne prêchent que Jésus-Christ glorieux, et non pas Jésus-Christ souffrant: comme ils ont fait dans les Indes et dans la Chine, où ils ont permis aux chrétiens l'idolâtrie même, par cette subtile invention, de leur faire cacher sous leurs habits une image de Jésus-Christ, à laquelle ils leur enseignent de rapporter mentalement les adorations publiques qu'ils rendent à l'idole Chacim-Choan et à leur Keum-fucum.[117]

114. Antoine Arnauld, *Morale pratique des Jésuites: Histoire des differens entre les missionaires Jésuites d'une part et ceux des ordres de St. Dominique et de St. François de l'autre, touchant les cultes que les Chinois rendent à leur Maître Confucius, à leurs Ancestres, et à l'idole Chin-Hoan* (Cologne: G. Quentel [Amsterdam; Elzevir] 1682).

115. Beurrier, *Speculum christianae religioniis in triplici, lege, naturali, mosaica et evangelica* (Paris: J. Langlois, 1662), p. 259.

116. Ibid., p. 271. Père Beurrier perhaps formulated these theories as a result of his discussions with the *libertins,* to whom he felt he had a special mission. See Beurrier's *Mémoires* in E. Jovy's *Pascal inédit* (Vitry-le-François: "l'auteur," 1910), Vol. 3. In his edition of Pascal's *Oeuvres complètes* (Paris: Desclée de Brouwer, 1964), Jean Mesnard reproduces the sections of Beurrier's *Mémoires* which are related to Pascal.

117. Lafuma, ed., *Oeuvres complètes,* p. 388. *Keum-fucum* is apparently a reference to Confucius. Pascal cites as his source Thomas Hurtado's *Martyre de la foi,* a text to which he was probably referred by Arnauld, who would later cite the same source in his attack on the China policy of the Jesuits.

When they are in countries where a crucified God is regarded as folly, they suppress the scandal of the Cross, and preach only a glorious and not a suffering Jesus Christ. This plan they allowed in the Indies and in China, where they have even allowed Christians to practice idolatry itself, with the aid of the following ingenious contrivance: they let their converts conceal under their clothes an image of Jesus Christ, to which they teach them to transfer mentally those adorations which they render publicly to the idol Chacim-Choan and to their Keum-fucum.

The quarrel of the *rites chinois* had pitted the Jesuits against the Franciscans and the Dominicans for decades. Pascal is the first writer to bring the dispute into the public domain. As Virgile Pinot observes, "[La Querelle des Cérémonies chinoises] devient ainsi un des moyens de combat que les jansénistes vont mettre en oeuvre pour abattre les Jésuites: elle sera désormais mêlée à toutes les luttes que vont se livrer ces ennemis irréconciliables"[118] ("[The quarrel over the Chinese rites] thus becomes one of the weapons which the Jansenists will use to attack the Jesuits: it will henceforth be a part of all the struggles in which are engaged these irreconcilable enemies"). In a passage which recalls the one just cited from the *Provinciales*, Du Cambout de Pontchâteau charges the Jesuits with having attempted to accommodate the Gospel "à l'humeur et aux coutumes des Chinois" ("to the temperament and customs of the Chinese"):

> [Les Jésuites] n'ont pas annoncé à la Chine J.-C. pauvre et crucifié . . . parce que, disent-ils, les Chinois l'ont en horreur. . . . Ils font passer les idolâtries des Chinois, comme des sacrifices à Kun-fu-zu et ceux qu'ils offrent à leur ancêtres pour des cérémonies politiques, et ils permettent aux mandarins de faire des offrandes à l'idole Chin-hoan, en dirigeant leurs intentions à une croix cachée sous les fleurs de l'autel de l'idole.[119]

> [The Jesuits] in China have failed to proclaim Jesus Christ poor and crucified . . . because, they say, the Chinese are horrified by such a figure. They attempt to pass off the idolatries of the Chinese, such as the sacrifices to Kun-fu-zu and those offered to the ancestors, as purely civil ceremonies. They permit the mandarins to make offerings to the idol Chin-hoan, while directing their intentions to a cross hidden under the flowers on the altar of the idol.

In the *Morale pratique des Jésuites*, Du Cambout de Pontchâteau devotes a particularly harsh chapter (see Plate IX) to "Martinius, Jésuite." An en-

118. Virgile Pinot, *La Chine et la formation de l'esprit philosophique en France (1640–1740)* (Paris: Librairie Orientaliste, 1932), p. 81.

119. Antoine Arnauld, *Morale pratique des Jésuites,* 2, "Table de matières." Long attributed to Arnauld, the first and second volumes of the *Morale pratique des Jésuites* were in fact the work of the abbé du Cambout de Pontchâteau. See Du Cambout de Pontchâteau (l'abbé

ATE IX. *Marche du P. M. Martinius, Mandarin du Premier Ordre*. Du Cambout de Pontchâteau, *La Morale Pratique de Jésuites* (1669). Côte Bibliothèque Nationale 80 Ld 39. 208. Service photographique, Bibliothèque Nationale.

graving attached to the chapter shows the author of the *Sinicae Historiae*, vested in silk mandarin robes bearing the image of a dragon, being borne on a portable throne. Père Martini casts a haughty gaze on a cowering, humble Franciscan, clad in the simple poverty of his order.

The Jesuit Fathers who undertook the first modern mission to China in 1563 discovered after much difficulty that this older civilization looked askance at the dogmatic pretensions of Christianity. The founder of the mission, Matteo Ricci, adopted the tactic of winning over the imperial intelligentsia by taking the robes of the Mandarins and studying everything from traditional Chinese philosophy to Chinese painting and calligraphy. The teachings of Confucius, he concluded, represented more of an ethical than a religious code. The cult of the ancestors, he reasoned, could be purified of superstition and reinterpreted in Christian terms.[120] Ricci's strategy showed some signs of working. By the middle of the seventeenth century, the Jesuits had established Christianity as an officially recognized religion in China and had made some 150,000 converts. At first, the Jesuits viewed the kinds of dispensations which so horrified Pascal as representing but a provisional stage in the conversion of China. The longer they stayed in China, however, the more they came to think that the Chinese philosophical and religious traditions contained a partial vision of the Christian Revelation.

Virgile Pinot cautions against interpreting the Jesuits' polemical writings on China as impartial studies which prefigure the modern science of the comparative study of religions. What Pinot says about the eighteenth century rings even more true when applied to the France of the Classical period:

> Le XVIIIe siècle, encore tout embarrassé dans les querelles théologiques, n'en demandait pas tant. Ce qu'il cherchait avant tout, s'il jetait un regard sur les exemples que lui fournissaient les peuples étrangers, c'était ou des raisons de croire ou des raisons de ne pas croire. . . . Or, les Jésuites, en donnant il est vrai quelques

Sébastien-Joseph), *La Morale pratique des Jésuites,* 1–2 (Cologne: C. Quentel, 1669). See Plate 9.

120. On Ricci's analysis of Chinese religion, see Jonathan Spence's *The Memory Palace of Matteo Ricci* (New York: Viking, 1984). On the controversy surrounding the *rites chinois,* see F. A. Rouleau's article ("Chinese Rites Controversy") in the *New Catholic Encyclopedia,* 3: 611–17 and the relevant chapters in Virgile Pinot's *La Chine et la formation de l'esprit philosophique en France (1640–1740)*. Also see Jacques Gernet, *Chine et christianisme* (Paris: Gallimard, 1982) (English translation, *China and the Christian Impact: A Conflict of Cultures* [Cambridge: Cambridge University Press, 1985]); and David E. Mungello, *Curious Land: Jesuit Accommodation and the Origins of Sinology* (Stuttgart: Steiner, 1985).

coups de pouce aux textes qui montraient le spiritualisme de la secte dominante des Lettrés de la Chine, pouvaient présenter la religion des anciens Chinois comme une religion spiritualiste qui ne répugnait pas à l'esprit chrétien, à condition de ne pas croire comme Arnauld à la nécessité de la foi explicite.[121]

The eighteenth century, still completely embroiled in theological disputes, hardly required as much from them. What it primarily sought, if it cast its gaze upon the examples furnished by foreign peoples, was reasons to believe or not to believe. . . . Now, the Jesuits, while, we must admit, presenting the texts which showed the spirituality of the dominant sect of the *lettrés* of Chine in their best light, managed to present the religion of the ancient Chinese as a spiritual religion which did not offend the Christian view of things, provided one did not believe, as did Arnauld, in the necessity of explicit faith.

Le Vayer's *De la vertu des payens*

It was not without reason that Arnauld (see Chapter III, Martini's *Sinicae Historiae*, n. 99) feared the consequences of those parallels which would inevitably be drawn between Christianity and the non-Christian religions. While Pascal was writing his celebrated defense of Christianity, La Mothe le Vayer pored through the *mémoires* of Jesuit missionaries to the Orient and the New World in order to document his thesis that Christianity could claim little that was unique.[122] On the question of the validity of non-Christian sources, Pascal and Arnauld had no greater adversary than La Mothe le Vayer. In his *Parallèles historiques*, Le Vayer ridicules those who fear that parallels drawn between Christian and Oriental texts will lead to a loss of faith. Why should Christianity, he asks, a religion which has already absorbed so many cultures, fear contamination from the Orient?

Si nous employons librement à l'embellissement des autels chrétiens quelques étoffes du Japon ou de la Chine que nous savons avoir été tissues et travaillées par des mains idolâtres, pourquoi ferions-nous difficulté de nous servir des dictions ou des pensées de ceux qu'une différente religion a séparés de nous et rendus mêmes ennemis de nos vérités Evangéliques?[123]

If we freely make use of fabrics for the decoration of Christian altars which we know have been woven and worked by idolatrous hands, why should we raise any

121. Pinot, *La Chine et la formation de l'esprit philosophique,* p. 184.

122. See Chapter I, Two Cautious Skeptics: La Mothe le Vayer and Gabniel Naudé.

123. La Mothe le Vayer, *Parallèles historiques,* in *Oeuvres de La Mothe le Vayer* (Dresden: M. Groell, 1758), 7, 287–97, "lettre cxvi."

difficulty concerning the use of thoughts or ideas of those whom a different religion has separated from us and even rendered enemies of the truth of the Gospel?

The quarrel over the *rites chinois*, which would engage Catholic polemicists until their final condemnation by Benedict XIV in 1742, needs to be considered in the context of a broader theological struggle. This conflict was provoked in the sixteenth century by the discovery of a multiplicity of peoples and religious traditions that were only with great difficulty integrated into a Christian worldview inherited from a thousand years before. Behind all the quarrels over Grace that shook the political and religious life of seventeenth-century France stood one larger question: How inclusive or exclusive, how implicit or explicit, was the redeeming work of Christ? How many, or indeed how few, would be saved?

The controversy over the fate of the *anciens justes*, which surfaces in fragment 960 of the *Pensées*, raises essentially the same question as that posed by the *rites chinois*. To whom does the saving work of Christ apply? Certain early Fathers had maintained that the virtuous lives of Socrates, Aristotle, and the other *anciens justes* suggested an implicit faith which might have saved them from eternal damnation. While Dante had created for them a not altogether unpleasant corner of Hell, Erasmus had gone so far as to invoke the name of Saint Socrates. The Augustinian tradition, however, renewed in France by the writings of Jansenius, held that only those having an explicit faith in Christ might be numbered among the elect.

In 1640, Jansenius' *Augustinus* was about to be published at Louvain. Cardinal Richelieu asked La Mothe le Vayer to produce a work aimed at countering Jansenius' attack on Christian humanism. In *De la vertu des payens* (1642), Le Vayer chose to defend the thesis that the virtuous among the ancient sages had indeed been saved:

> Dieu ne refuse jamais sa grâce à ceux qui font tout ce qu'ils peuvent pour s'en rendre dignes. Or les Payens qui ont vécu vertueusement suivant les lumières du droit de Nature et soumettant leur libre arbitre à la raison ont fait tout ce qui était de leur pouvoir, puisqu'ils ne connaissaient point d'autre loi que la naturelle. On doit donc croire que Dieu ne leur a pas dénié sa grâce, ni son assistance et par conséquent qu'ils peuvent être du nombre des Bien-heureux.[124]

> God never refuses his grace to those who do everything in their power to render themselves worthy of it. Thus the pagans who lived virtuously, following the lights of Nature's law and submitting their free-will to reason, did everything that

124. La Mothe le Vayer, *De la vertu des payens* (Paris: F. Targa, 1642), pp. 35–36.

was within their power since they knew no other law than the natural one. One must therefore believe that God did not deny them his grace nor his help and that consequently they can be numbered among the Blessed.

To an extensive list of Classical philosophers whom he deems worthy of salvation, La Mothe le Vayer adds the name of Confucius. The Sage's admonition "de ne faire jamais à autrui ce que nous ne voudrions pas qui nous fût fait" ("to never do unto others what we would not want to be done unto us") strikes La Mothe le Vayer as entirely consistent with "la morale chrétienne." Like Socrates, observes Le Vayer, Confucius believed in "un Dieu unique, créateur de toutes choses" ("a single God, creator of all things"). God therefore conferred on him that Grace which he never refuses to those who do everything in their power to obtain it.[125] La Mothe le Vayer argues that the primitive religion of the Chinese was always more pure than that of the Greeks and the Romans. "Les Chinois n'ont reconnu de temps immémorial qu'un seul Dieu qu'ils nomment le Roi du Ciel"[126] ("From time immemorial, the Chinese have recognized but a single God whom they call the King of Heaven").

Le Vayer also considers the fate of those multitudes who, though born after the Incarnation, have never received the Gospel. Have they not the right to complain, asks Le Vayer, as did the Japanese to Saint Francis Xavier, that God has treated them "avec tant de désavantage" ("with such great disadvantage")? To condemn them all to Hell, "sans réserve et sans miséricorde" ("without reserve and without mercy"), Le Vayer concludes, would be both inhumane and illogical.[127]

Port-Royal's response to Le Vayer's theses concerning the *anciens justes* and the unbaptized multitudes was swift. In his *De la nécessité de la foi en Jésus-Christ*, Arnauld mounts a broadside attack on *De la vertu des payens*. Le Vayer's attempt to rescue the *anciens justes* or those who never received the Gospel from the pains of Hell, Arnauld asserts, is tantamount to reviving the Pelegian heresy:

C'est se jouer de la religion . . . que de soutenir que dans les pays où l'Evangile n'a point été prêché, il y a des hommes qui meurent après avoir fait des actes de contrition. . . . C'est une rêverie pleine d'impiété de s'imaginer que des païens destitués de la lumière de l'Evangile, et vivant dans les ténèbres du paganisme puissent . . . faire des actes d'une sainte repentance par la seule lumière de la raison. L'ori-

125. Ibid., p. 291.
126. Ibid., p. 280.
127. Ibid., p. 59.

gine . . . de l'accès vers Dieu, c'est la foi en Jésus-Christ comme nous l'enseignent les Pères.[128]

It is to make a mockery of religion . . . to argue that in those countries where the Gospel has never been preached there exist men who are able to make sufficient acts of contrition before their deaths. . . . It is an impious dream to imagine that pagans deprived of the light of the Gospel and living in the darkness of heathen practices might succeed in achieving holy repentance by the light of reason alone. As the Fathers teach us, the [unique] source of access to God is faith in Jesus Christ.

In *De la vertu des payens*, Le Vayer had appealed for mercy on behalf of a young pagan who, pious according to the lights of nature, raises his thoughts to the Eternal Presence and prays: "Mon Dieu, qui connaissez le plus secret de mon âme, j'implore votre miséricorde, et je vous supplie de me conduire à la fin pour laquelle vous m'avez créé"[129] ("O God, you who know the innermost parts of my soul, I implore your mercy, and I beg you to lead me to the purpose for which you created me"). Arnauld does not hesitate for a moment before condemning Le Vayer's pious young pagan to that eternal punishment that has been reserved for him since the beginning of time. Nor does Arnauld see any reason to exempt "ces prétendus vertueux du paganisme" ("those supposed just pagans") from the common fate of the unredeemed.[130]

In fragment 960 of the *Pensées*, Pascal adopts precisely the same position with regard to the *anciens justes*. "Un bâtiment également beau par dehors, mais sur un mauvais fondement, les païens sages le bâtissaient, et le diable trompe les hommes par cette ressemblance apparente fondée sur le fondement le plus différent." "The heathen sages erected a structure equally fine outside, but upon an unsound foundation; and the devil deceives men by this apparent resemblance based upon the most different foundations."

In the dossier "Fausseté des autres religions" ("Falseness of other religions") (XVI), Pascal works out a detailed explanation of why the *anciens justes* cannot be thought to have worked out their own salvation. His argument hinges upon the paradox "misère"/"grandeur" as defined in the first ten *liasses* of the dossiers of 1658. Fragment 206 pluralizes an observation of St. Augustine in the *Contra Julianum* IV.12: "*Rem viderunt, causam*

128. Antoine Arnauld, *De la nécessité de la foi en Jésus-Christ* in *Oeuvres de Messire Antoine Arnauld* (Paris: chez d'Arnay, 1777), 10, 287–88.

129. La Mothe le Vayer, *De la vertu des payens,* p. 54.

130. Arnauld, *De la nécessité de la foi en Jésus-Christ,* p. 298.

non viderunt" ("They saw the effect but not the cause"). Augustine, in a reference to Cicero's description of human misery in the third book of his *De republica*, had written: "*Rem vidit*, causam nescivit" ("He saw the effect but knew not the cause"). Pascal generalizes Augustine's observation to include all of the *anciens justes*. These great philosophers managed to perceive the heart of the human paradox as contained in the formula "misère"/"grandeur." Yet, because they lacked the instruction of Scripture with regard to Original Sin, they were unable to make any sense of the fallen condition of humanity. Nor were they able to achieve that explicit virtue which alone ensures salvation:

> Sans ces divines connaissances qu'ont pu faire les hommes sinon ou s'élever dans le sentiment intérieur qui leur reste de leur grandeur passée, ou s'abattre dans la vue de leur faiblesse présente. Car ne voyant pas la vérité entière ils n'ont pu arriver à une parfaite vertu, les uns considérant la nature comme incorrompue, les autres comme irréparable, ils n'ont pu fuir ou l'orgueil ou la paresse qui sont les deux sources de tous les vices, puisqu'il ne peut sinon ou s'y abandonner par lâcheté, ou en sortir par l'orgueil. Car s'ils connaissaient l'excellence de l'homme, ils en ignorent la corruption de sorte qu'ils évitaient la paresse, mais ils se perdaient dans la superbe et s'ils reconnaissent l'infirmité de la nature ils en ignorent la dignité, de sorte qu'ils pouvaient bien éviter la vanité mais c'était en se précipitant dans le désespoir.
>
> De là viennent les diverses sectes des stoïques et des épicuriens, des dogmatistes et des académiciens, etc.[131]

Without this divine knowledge, how could men help feeling either exalted at the persistent inward sense of their past greatness or dejected at the sight of their present weakness? For unable to see the whole truth, they could not attain perfect virtue. With some regarding nature as incorrupt, others as irremediable, they have been unable to avoid either pride or sloth, the twin sources of all vice, since the only alternative is to give in through cowardice or escape through pride. For if they realized man's excellence they did not know his corruption, with the result that they certainly avoided sloth but sank into pride, and if they recognized the infirmity of nature, they did not know its dignity, with the result that they were certainly able to avoid vanity, only to fall headlong into despair.

131. In his commentary on *La Gènese*, Le Maistre de Sacy undertakes a similar critique of the *anciens justes*. In describing the pagan philosophers' perception of the effects of the Fall in nature, Sacy also cites the lines Pascal cites from Saint Augustine. Those "grands esprits" such as Aristotle and Cicero, he explains, realized that God could not be other than "souverainement bon et juste." Yet when they took stock of the human condition, they found it to be "visiblement un état de condamnation et de supplice." Since they had no knowledge of the Fall—"qui aurait autorisé cette misère de l'homme sans faire injure à la justice de Dieu"—these philosophers were forced to invent "une cause vraisemblable et très ingénieuse" to explain the contradiction between divine justice and human misery (pp. 250–52).

Hence the various sects of Stoics and Epicureans, Dogmatists and Academicians, etc. (208)

Recapitulating the arguments of the chapter "Philosophes" ("Philosophers") (IX), Pascal makes short work not only of Le Vayer's thesis concerning the salvation of the *anciens justes* but also of classical philosophy as an alternative to Christianity. In the last analysis, Pascal's critique of philosophy is far more central to the major aims of the Apology than is his refutation either of Islam or of the "religion de la Chine." In seventeenth-century France, conversion to a non-Christian religion was hardly a viable option for anyone unable to accept Christianity. However, as we saw in Chapter I (*Le Libertinage érudit*), the search for the truth in the various schools of classical philosophy had been the principal alternative to Christian belief for at least the previous 150 years. Why a few intellectuals began to become dissatisfied with the Christian vision of the world and of history is a highly complex question. The more widespread study and availability of pre-Christian schemes of meaning and reality certainly played a key role. So too did a shift in cosmological paradigms. But perhaps more than any other single factor was the way in which the Age of Discovery broadened the horizons of the known world.

Behind the quarrel over the *anciens justes* lies the same essential question behind the debate over the *rites chinois*. Is the received vision of Christian Revelation broad enough and flexible enough to comprehend that rush of new ideas, peoples, and cultures that emerged from the Age of Discovery? Those Christian humanists who invoke the notion of *foi implicite* in order to extend Revelation backward in time to the *anciens justes* are motivated by the same great historical and cultural impulse that led the Jesuits to attempt to graft Christianity onto an older non-Christian tradition. Both the Jesuits and the Christian humanists found fierce adversaries in the neo–Augustinians of Port-Royal. Arnauld, long the chief spokesman of the Jansenist movement, saw any compromise with such a new worldview as an imminent danger to received Revelation. In *De la nécessité de la foi en Jésus-Christ*, Arnauld savagely condemns the humanist notion that "Dieu a d'autres voies pour nous sauver que celles qui nous sont connues" ("God has other ways to save us in addition to those which are known to us"). He totally rejects the possibility that God has exercised mercy toward "une infinité de païens." He excoriates the proposition that "Dieu est trop bon pour être si rigoureux qu'on se persuade" ("God is too good to be as rigorous as has been thought"). He is infuriated by the notion that it is inhumane "à damner si facilement les hommes"[132] ("to damn men so easily").

The hundred years which separate Arnauld's treatise from the publication of the *Confessions* of Rousseau seem almost like light years in terms of the religious evolution of the French intelligentsia. The most original and influential thinkers will no longer find themselves on the side of traditional orthodox Christianity. The seeds planted by La Mothe le Vayer will bear remarkable fruit in the more modern religious sensibility of a Jean-Jacques Rousseau:

> En général, les croyants font Dieu comme ils sont eux-mêmes, les bons le font bon, les méchants le font méchant; les dévots haineux et bilieux ne voient que l'enfer, parce qu'ils voudraient damner tout le monde; les âmes aimantes et douces n'y croient guère . . .[133]

> In general, believers paint God in their own image; the good make him good; the bad make him bad; hate-filled and bilious fanatics see only hell because they would like to damn everyone; loving and gentle souls hardly believe [in hell] at all. . . .

In his subsequent attacks on the China policy of the Jesuits, Arnauld will attack the *rites chinois* for the very reason he censures the notion of the salvation of the *anciens justes*. Both, in his view, encourage *libertinage* by making Christian doctrine appear to be more flexible than it really is. Both violate the specific, explicit, and exclusive character of that closed Revelation received from the Fathers and the Apostolic Church. It is within this broader context of the struggle between Christian humanists and neo–Augustinians that Pascal's fragment 822, "Histoire de la Chine," takes on its true significance. Pascal's reaction to the claim that Chinese civilization predates Biblical history is telling. He does not pause for a moment to wonder whether the Chinese chronologies might constitute genuine empirical evidence. Rather, in order to explain their very existence, he invokes the doctrine of *Deus absconditus*: "Il y a de quoi aveugler" ("There is enough here to blind"). In other words, the apparent antiquity of Chinese chronology is but another example of the way in which God has hidden Revelation from the wise who were never meant to see. "La Chine obscurcit" (822).

132. Arnauld, *De la nécessité de la foi en Jésus-Christ*, pp. 304–5.
133. J.-J. Rousseau, *Les Confessions* (Paris: Pauvert, 1961), p. 351.

Fragment 822 and Neo-Augustinian Theology

Seen from the perspective of neo-Augustinian theology, fragment 822 can more easily be integrated into Pascal's larger apologetic strategy. His interlocutor in this brief exchange is hardly a hardened *libertin*. Rather, he figures among those *chercheurs* who will bring to a reading of Pascal's Apology "une sincérité parfaite et un véritable désir de rencontrer la vérité" ("absolute sincerity and a real desire to find the truth") (427). Pascal begins by invoking a traditional theme in Christian apologetics. The blood of the martyrs guarantees the authenticity of the Christian Scriptures. By implication, the "histoires" of the Chinese, like those promulgated by Islam, bear no such seal of authority.

Pascal seems unaware that the *libertins* had already attempted to refute this argument by pointing out that every religious tradition has its martyrs. At the beginning of the century, Vanini had constructed a flippant dialogue making light of the idea of martyrdom as a guarantor of truth:

> When I argued with the atheist from Amsterdam that Christians are not feeble-minded, as many glorious martyrdoms attest, this blasphemer attributed such martyrdoms to an exalted imagination, or the thirst for glory, or even a hypochondriacal humour. He added that all religions, even the most absurd, had their martyrs, that the Turks, the Indians and, in our own day, the heretics had produced believers whom no torture could daunt. How many English Protestants during the reign of Mary had suffered death for their beliefs?[134]

After having invoked the blood of the Christian martyrs as a seal of the credibility of Christian sources, Pascal then poses a question. "Lequel est le plus croyable des deux, Moïse ou la Chine?" ("Which is the more credible of the two, Moses or China?") Here Pascal's contrast of Christian and non-Christian sources reflects the arguments of Chapter XXII ("Preuves de Moïse") and XVI ("Fausseté des autres religions"). Non-Christian sources are completely suspect. The authenticity of the Pentateuch can be proved. However, Pascal strikes the line he has just written.[135] In this instance he wants to steer the *chercheur* away from a discussion of Biblical history and Chinese chronology. This tactic is typical of the way in which Pascal responds to the objections of the *libertins* throughout the course of

134. J. C. Vanini, *De admirandis naturae Reginae Deaeque mortalium Arcanis libri IV* (Lutetiae: Perier 1616). Translated and cited by J. S. Spink, *French Free-Thought from Gassendi to Voltaire* (London: The Athlone Press, 1960), p. 41.

135. In most modern editions of the *Pensées,* lines and passages struck by Pascal in the *Recueil original* are printed in italics.

the *Apology*. He avoids the trap of having to adopt a defensive attitude by placing the burden of proof squarely on the shoulders of his interlocutor.

In fragment 822, Pascal transforms the entire issue of the Chinese chronologies from a historical into a theological problem. "Il n'est pas question de voir cela en gros: je vous dis qu'il y a de quoi aveugler et de quoi éclairer" ("There is no question of the broad view. I tell you that there is enough here to blind and to enlighten"). Pascal brushes aside purely historical matters as unimportant. The important question is of a theological order. Why is there evidence in the world which seems to cast doubt on Christian Revelation? Having removed the question to the realm of higher theological truth, Pascal cannot resist teasing his interlocutor. "Par ce mot seul je ruine tous vos raisonnements" ("With this one word I destroy all your arguments") (822).

At this point, Pascal's interlocutor is permitted his single intervention during the entire exchange. He protests: "Mais la Chine obscurcit" ("But China obscures the issue"). Pascal cuts him off before he ever has the chance to invoke the historical difficulties posed by Chinese claims to pre-Biblical antiquity. Once again, the apologist directs his interlocutor to the theological realm of things. "La Chine obscurcit, mais il y a clarté à trouver. Cherchez-la" ("China obscures the issue but there is light to be found. Look for it") (822). "Cherchez-la" recalls a similar bit of dialogue set down in fragment 158:

> Vous devez vous mettre en peine de rechercher la vérité, car si vous mourez sans adorer le vrai principe vous êtes perdu. Mais—dites-vous, s'il avait voulu que je l'adorasse il m'aurait laissé des signes de sa volonté. Aussi a(-t-)il fait, mais vous les négligez. Cherchez-les donc; cela le vaut bien.

> You must take the trouble to seek the truth, for if you die without worshipping the true principle you are lost. "But," you say, "if he had wanted me to worship him, he would have left me some signs of his will." So he did, but you pay no heed. Look for them then; it is well worth it. (158)

According to neo-Augustinian theology, God has hidden Revelation in sacred history in such a way that its truth may only be perceived by the elect. "On n'entend rien aux ouvrages de Dieu si on ne prend pour principe qu'il a voulu aveugler les uns et éclaircir les autres" ("One understands nothing of God's works unless one accepts the principle that he wished to blind some and to enlighten others") (232). The seemingly misleading evidence of the Chinese chronologies is but another demonstration of the workings of divine predestination. Any argument Pascal's interlocutor attempts to invoke will only manifest his blindness without casting the slightest doubt on Christian truth. "Tout ce que vous dites fait à un des desseins et rien contre l'autre" ("All you say serves one of these purposes [i.e., to blind or to enlighten] without telling against the other"). Thus, the whole problem of China must ultimately reduce Pascal's interlocutor to silence. "Ainsi cela sert et ne nuit pas"[136] "So it helps and does not harm" (822).

Given Pascal's transformation of the issue of the Chinese chronologies from a historical to a theological problem, the two concluding sentences of fragment 822 seem unclear. "Il faut voir cela en détail. Il faut mettre papiers sur table" ("We must look at this in detail. We must put the evidence on the table"). Is this another admonition to Pascal's interlocutor? Or is it a note to himself to do some further research into the China question? "Il faut donc voir cela en détail" recalls Pascal's injunction to his interlocutor earlier in the fragment, "Il n'est pas question de voir cela en gros" ("There is no question of the broad view"). The words "en détail" also recall fragment 150, a text highly relevant to the question being dealt with in fragment 822. In this fragment, the *impies* attempt to discredit Christianity by pointing out that its rites and ceremonies have parallels in the non-Christian religions:

> Les impies qui font profession de suivre la raison doivent être étrangement forts en raison.
>
> Que disent-ils donc?
>
> Ne voyons-nous pas, disent-ils, mourir et vivre les bêtes comme les hommes, et les Turcs comme les chrétiens; ils ont leurs cérémonies, leurs prophètes, leurs docteurs, leurs saints, leur religieux comme nous, etc.
>
> Cela est-il contraire à l'Ecriture? ne dit-elle pas tout cela?
>
> Si vous ne vous souciez guère de savoir la vérité, en voilà assez pour vous laisser en repos. Mais si vous désirez de tout votre coeur de la connaître ce n'est pas assez regardé *au détail*. C'en serait assez pour une question de philosophie, mais ici où il va de tout. . . . Et cependant après une réflexion légère de cette sorte on s'amusera, etc.
>
> Qu'on s'informe de cette religion, même si elle ne rend pas raison de cette obscurité, peut-être qu'elle nous l'apprendra.

The ungodly who propose to follow reason must be singularly strong in reason.
What do they say then?

136. "Ainsi cela sert et ne nuit pas" recalls fragment 162: "Commencer par plaindre les incrédules, ils sont assez malheureux par leur condition. Il ne faudrait pas injurier qu'au cas que cela *servît*, mais cela leur *nuit*" (italics mine).

> "Do we not see," they say, "animals live and die like men, Turks like Christians? They have their ceremonies, their prophets, their doctors, their saints, their religious like us, etc."
>
> Is that contrary to Scripture? Does it not say all that?
>
> If you hardly care about knowing the truth, that is enough to leave you in peace, but if you desire with all your heart to know it, you have not looked closely enough *at the details*. This would do for a philosophical question, but here where everything is at stake. . . . And yet, after superficial reflection of this kind, we go off to amuse ourselves. . . .
>
> Let us inquire of this religion; even if it does not explain the obscurity away, perhaps it will teach us about it. (150, italics mine)

Pascal replies to the *impies* that they have failed to examine this question "au détail." Drawing such superficial parallels between Christianity and Islam might be sufficient were the subject at hand merely "une question de philosophie" ("some philosophical question"). However, in the present matter, everything is at stake: "Il va de tout. . . ." The question of whether or not to accept Christianity is hardly some purely academic matter. On it hinges the way in which one will wager the fate of one's immortal soul: "Il s'agit de nous-mêmes, et de notre tout" ("It is a question of ourselves and our all") (427). As Pascal warns his interlocutor in fragment 158, if one dies without worshiping "le vrai principe" ("the true principle") one is lost.

The *impies* of fragment 150 very much reflect the portrait of disbelief, set forth in Pascal's draft of his Preface to the Apology (fragments 427–428), which we will examine in Chapters IV and V. These unbelievers know little about the religion they are attempting to debunk. They have no idea that the paradoxes they point out are entirely consonant with what Scripture teaches about the hidden God of Christianity. "Cela est-il contraire à l'Ecriture? ne dit-elle pas tout cela?" (Is that contrary to Scripture? Does it not say all that?"). They can manage no better than "une réflexion légère" ("a superficial reflection") on the absolutely essential question of the fate of their souls.

The *impies* have missed the whole point of that "obscurité" which is so central to Christianity. Accustomed to dealing with "philosophical" matters, they think they have scored a point by asking a leading question. Rather than staying to learn the meaning of this "obscurité," they go off to amuse themselves. In fragment 822, Pascal's interlocutor at least recognizes the existence of something beyond his comprehension. He at least has the sense to complain, "Mais la Chine obscurcit." ("But China obscures the issue"). In fragment 150, "au détail" refers, not so much to the question of the parallels between Christianity and Islam, as to the far broader problem of the hidden quality of Revelation. So too, in fragment 822, "en détail" serves to direct Pascal's interlocutor away from the superficial dilemma posed by the Chinese chronologies to the hidden mystery of the *Deus absconditus*.

In the final line of fragment 822, Pascal seems to revert to the notion that Christianity can document its claim to possess final truth. In the Classical period, "papiers" had the primary meaning of *documents* or *pièces justificatives*. "Il faut mettre papiers sur table," whether an admonition to Pascal's interlocutor or a reminder to himself, seems to recall fragment 204: "Fausseté des autres religions. Ils n'ont pas de témoins" ("Falseness of other religions. They have no witnesses"). In Pascal's view, the Old Testament stands in obvious contrast to the "histoires" of the non-Christian religions:

> Il y a bien de la différence entre un livre que fait un particulier, et qu'il jette dans le peuple, et un livre que fait lui-même un peuple. On ne peut douter que le livre ne soit aussi ancien que le peuple.

> There is a great difference between a book composed by an individual, which he hands over to the people, and a book that a people composes itself. It is beyond doubt that the book is as old as the people. (436)

Unlike the other long-since-vanished peoples of antiquity, Pascal concludes, that people by whom the Old Testament was written mysteriously subsists in the world. The Jews survive as a people some seventeen hundred years after the foundation of Christianity. They serve as hostile, and therefore trustworthy, witnesses to the authenticity of the Old Testament. "Sincères contre leur honneur et mourant pour cela. Cela n'a point d'exemple dans le monde ni sa racine dans la nature" ("Sincere against their honor and dying for it. This has no parallel in the world nor its roots in nature") (492). Pascal's vision of the vocation of the Jews as hostile witnesses to the historical roots of Christianity finds an interesting parallel in Le Maistre de Sacy's Preface to his translation of Genesis. Sacy explains that God chose the Jews to be the guardians of his Scriptures at the beginning of the world. However, the Jews' ignorance of what was really written in their Scriptures was a necessary part of the economy of Salvation. Christ's Incarnation had to be announced by those who could later serve as nonsuspect witnesses. Had the Jews understood the hidden meaning of the Law, they would have received Christ as the Messiah. Had this happened, they could never have served as hostile, and therefore credible, witnesses concerning the authenticity of the Old Testament and its prophecies of the coming of Christ.[137]

Pascal's rejection of the antiquity of the Chinese chronologies proceeds from the same principle that leads him to reject the possibility of the salvation of the *anciens justes* and to condemn the *rites chinois*. As Pascal sees it, the received Christian vision of the world can be neither altered nor expanded without doing injury to that Revelation inherited from Scripture, the Primitive Church, and the Fathers. In taking such a position, Pascal resists that entire historical change in worldview that dominates the Classical period. As Sara Melzer points out, the seventeenth century experienced a radical transition from one worldview to another, from a mental universe reflecting the finite world to one grounded in the idea of an infinite universe:

> The *Pensées'* narrator is situated at a very specific moment in history . . . at the crossroads between what Michel Foucault calls the Renaissance and the classical *episteme*. According to the Renaissance *episteme*, nature spoke to humans through signs that situated them in a finite, ordered world. . . . With the discovery of the infinite, however, comes the realization that the former paradigm was illusory. In the classical *episteme*, the signs of nature are believed to lead to error.[138]

The way in which Melzer situates Pascal within a historical shift in cosmological paradigms provides a valuable perspective on the theological phenomenon of neo-Augustinianism. Pascal's obsession with the doctrine of the Fall, like that of Arnauld and Jansenius, represents more than simply a conservative reaction to the new Christian humanism originating in the Renaissance. It mirrors, though probably unconsciously, the collapse of a whole worldview that had endured for a thousand years. For Pascal, the failure of the traditional Christian cosmology serves only as further confirmation of the fallen state of nature. Any theological attempt to come to terms with the new cosmology would be, Pascal thinks, pointless. Even the infinite dimensions of the new Copernican model of the universe pale into insignificance when set up against the question of the ultimate fate of the human soul:

> Je trouve bon qu'on n'approfondisse pas l'opinion de Copernic. Mais ceci:
> Il importe à toute la vie de savoir si l'âme est mortelle ou immortelle.

137. Le Maistre de Sacy, *La Genèse,* Première Partie, partie v.

138. Sara E. Melzer, *Discourses of the Fall: A Study of Pascal's Pensées* (Berkeley and Los Angeles: University of California Press, 1986), p. 95.

I think it best that Copernicus' opinion not be more closely examined. But this: It affects our whole life to know whether the soul is mortal or immortal. (164)

Pascal instinctively realizes that the model of an infinite universe can no longer furnish a grid within which nature provides an immediate sense of ultimate meaning. He therefore attempts to reconstitute the essence of the old Christian worldview on the plane of theological truth and in the realm of sacred history. At several critical points during the drafting of his projected *Apology*, Pascal stages a retreat from an apologetic based on natural proofs of God. In fragments 190 and 449, he even goes so far as to argue that the argument from design was never consistent with true Christian doctrine. However, at some point Pascal must erect a final line of defense. He does so by projecting ultimate reality into sacred history. God, he argues, has lodged Revelation in sacred history in such a way as to blind those who were predestined not to see the truth. From such a perspective, even so-called secular history is imbued with meaning for those given the Grace to perceive it:

Qu'il est beau de voir par les yeux de la foi Darius et Cyrus, Alexandre, les Romains, Pompée et Hérode, agir sans le savoir pour la gloire de l'Evangile.

How fine it is to see with the eyes of faith, Darius and Cyrus, Alexander, the Romans, Pompey and Herod working, without knowing it, for the glory of the Gospel! (317)[139]

Throughout the course of his projected Apology, Pascal brilliantly struggles to resist any historical model which might subvert the strict accuracy of Biblical history. But his defense of the historicity of Biblical time would hardly survive him. A decade later, Bossuet would still be attempting to defend the strict historicity of the Flood. But the first stirrings of modern Biblical criticism would have already begun. During the course of the Classical period, a whole range of subjects once seen as outside the scope of human reason began to take their place within rational discourse. Astronomy and the natural sciences found their logical place alongside geometry and mathematics. Even Holy Scripture began to lose its exemp-

139. This fragment refers to Pascal's exegesis of the prophetic character of the eighth and ninth chapters of the book of Daniel in fragment 339. Darius, Cyrus, Alexander, and the Romans represent the four monarchies referred to by the Angel Gabriel in his explication of Daniel's dream (Daniel 8:20–25). Pompey, the conqueror of Jerusalem, and Herod act without knowing it to accomplish the prophecy concerning the removal of the "sceptre" from Judah.

tion from rational and textual analysis. It is no accident that Richard Simon, who first proposed the multiple-source theory for the Pentateuch, stood at the apogee of French Classical thought.

The total collapse of the authority of Biblical time would not take place until the nineteenth century. Even then, Darwin and modern geology would not convince everyone of the antiquity of human origins. However, the authority of the Biblical model had been seriously eroded before the end of the Enlightenment. In the 1650s, Isaac de La Peyrère was accused of heresy for publishing his theory of the "pré-Adamites." A century later, Voltaire, invoking the chronologies of the Chinese, denied the historicity of the Flood with relative impunity.[140] In the long run, the discovery of Deep Time came to alter Western consciousness as profoundly as had the advent of the Copernican cosmology.

140. See Virgile Pinot, *La Chine et la formation de l'esprit philosophique en France,* p. 279.

CHAPTER IV

The Preface to the Apology

Fragments 418 and 427: The State of the Texts

On occasion, Pascal lets his more aggressive adversaries voice their objections. The *athées* of fragment 244 ("Objections des athées"), for instance, protest, "Mais nous n'avons nulle lumière" ("But we have no light").[1] However, it is in his animation of the *honnête homme* in fragments 418 and 427 that Pascal gives us the most complete picture of his interlocutor and potential convert.

Both these long passages are difficult from a textual perspective. Neither stands within the classification of 1658. Neither has been assigned a date of composition on which most commentators can agree. Philippe Sellier views fragments 418 and 427 as linked by common themes and as representing internal developments of the dossier "Commencement." He assigns both fragments to the period 1659–62, that is, to a period posterior

1. See also fragments 156, 378, 748, and 760: "Mais—dites-vous, s'il avait voulu que je l'adorasse, il m'aurait laissé des signes de sa volonté" ("But—you say, if he had wanted me to worship him, he would have left me signs of his will") (156); "Si j'avais vu un miracle, disent-ils, je me convertirais" ("If I had seen a miracle, they say, I would be converted") (378); ("Obj. Ceux qui espèrent leur salut sont heureux en cela, mais ils ont pour contrepoids la crainte de l'enfer" ("Objection. Those who hope to be saved are happy in that; however, their hope is balanced out by the fear of hell") (748); "Ob. Visiblement l'Ecriture pleine de choses non dictées du Saint Esprit" ("Objection. Scripture is manifestly full of things not dictated by the Holy Spirit") (760).

to the classification of 1658.[2] A. Krailsheimer also thinks the two fragments are "probably contemporaneous."[3]

Jean Mesnard, on the other hand, dates fragment 418 from a period anterior to the classification of 1658. He assigns unit ii (in which fragment 418 figures) to a stage representing a "travail de préparation de l'*Apologie*."[4] Anthony Pugh also suggests a date prior to 1658 and argues that the "infini-rien" manuscript was composed "in the wake of the writings of 1655."[5] While reminding us that we are far from certain where fragment 418 would have been used in the finished Apology, Pugh sees no trouble accommodating it "as an appendix to section 12."[6]

Michel and Marie-Rose Le Guern argue that fragment 418 needs to be viewed as a project independent of the composition of the Apology: "La démonstration construite par Pascal sous ce titre *Infini-Rien* forme un tout qui n'appelle pas de développements extérieurs. Tout porte à penser que les quatre pages qui conservent ce fragment constituent à elles seules une apologie complète et indépendante qui se distingue de la grande apologie par le fait qu'elle est destinée à un public limitée et nettement caractérisé"[7] ("The demonstration constructed by Pascal under the title *Infini-Rien* forms a self-contained unit which does not call forth any external developments. Everything leads us to believe that the four pages which preserve this fragment constitute within themselves alone a complete and independent apology which needs to be distinguished from the grand apology because of the fact that they envisage a limited and clearly distinguished readership"). In fact, argue Michel and Marie-Rose Le Guern, the text of fragment 418 cannot have been set down in view of being included in some larger apologetic scheme. It must have been written, they think, rather as "un aide-mémoire destiné exclusivement à l'auteur lui-même"[8] ("a memorandum reserved for the author himself").

While also assigning fragment 418 to a period prior to 1658, Pol Ernst argues that fragment 427 is posterior to that classification.[9] On the basis

2. *Pensées: Nouvelle édition établie pour la première fois d'après la copie de référence de Gilberte Pascal par Philippe Sellier* (Paris: Mercure de France, 1976), p. 353, n. 2, and p. 360, n. 1.

3. *Pascal* (Oxford: Oxford University Press, 1980), p. 63.

4. *Les Pensées de Pascal,* p. 36.

5. *The Composition of Pascal's Apologia,* pp. 313–14 and 317.

6. Ibid., pp. 150–51.

7. Michel Le Guern and Marie-Rose Le Guern, *Les Pensées de Pascal: De l'anthropologie à la théologie* (Paris: Larousse, 1972), p. 35.

8. Ibid.

9. Review of Anthony R. Pugh, "*The Composition of Pascal's Apologia,*" *XVIIe siècle* 151 (April–June 1986): 184.

of what he calls "internal evidence," Pugh assigns fragment 427 to the year 1658.[10] Lafuma, on the other hand, thinks the fragment dates from a very late period (1661–1662).[11] Like Sellier, Pugh would like to read fragment 427 in the context of the dossier "Commencement."[12] Lafuma and H. Gouhier, on the other hand, view it as constituting a preface or introduction to the entire Apology.[13]

Fragment 418, the famous "infini/rien" passage, has been subject to so many variant readings precisely because we possess the original autograph of the text.[14] Fragment 427, on the other hand, is missing from the text of the *Recueil original*. In their respective editions, neither Lafuma nor Sellier notes that the original text of fragment 427 has been lost. In his edition, J. Chevalier notes that the fragment is recorded only by the two *Copies*.[15] The *Recueil original* (Folio 215) does record what are obviously the preparatory notes on which fragment 427 is based (see Plate X). These are reproduced according to the *Recueil original* on pages 313–15 of Z. Tourneur's "édition paléographique" of the *Pensées*.[16] Lafuma prints these fragments ("432 bis et ter") as part of his fragment 821. Sellier, following the Second Copy, includes them in his unit xl as his fragment 662. Chevalier inserts them as footnotes in the text of his fragment 335 (Lafuma 427). These preparatory notes, which seem to belong to unit iv, were filed by Pascal in unit xxx. Unit xxx contains what may be a reference to a book

10. *The Composition of Pascal's Apologia,* p. 414.

11. *Controverses pascaliennes* (Paris: Editions de Luxembourg, 1952), p. 86.

12. *The Composition of Pascal's Apologia,* p. 149.

13. See Chapter IV, The Unbelievers in Fragment 427.

14. Pugh describes the autograph of fragment 418 as being made up of several "different archeological layers which have been fused to make up the version we read in our editions" (*The Composition of Pascal's Apology,* p. 159). The bibliography of this fragment is vast. The most important commentaries include the following works: J. Lachelier, "Notes sur le pari de Pascal," *Revue philosophique de la France et de l'étranger* 51 (1901): 625–39; A. Valensin, "Note sur le pari de Pascal," *Revue pratique d'apologétique* (October 1919); Roger E. Lacombe, "Le pari de Pascal," *Revue philosophique* 137 (1997): 156–93; Jean Orcibal, "Le Fragment Infini-Rien et ses sources," *Blaise Pascal, l'homme et l'oeuvre* (Paris: Editions de Minuit, 1956), pp. 159–95; Georges Brunet, *Le Pari de Pascal* (Paris: Desclée de Brouwer, 1956); Henri Gouhier, "Le Pari de Pascal" in *Blaise Pascal: Commentaires* (Paris: Vrin, 1966); Michel Le Guern and Marie-Rose Le Guern, "Le Fragment Infini-Rien," in *Les Pensées de Pascal: De l'anthropologie à la théologie* (Paris: Larousse. 1972), pp. 34–55; P. Lønning, *Cet effrayant Pari* (Paris: Vrin, 1980); L. Thirouin, *Le Hasard et les règles: Le modèle du jeu dans la pensée de Pascal* (Paris: Vrin, 1991). Pugh's appendix E, "The Strata of Fragment 418," provides a particularly good overview of the textual difficulties of the fragment (pp. 467–68).

15. J. Chevalier, *Pascal: Oeuvres complètes* (Paris: Gallimard, 1954), p. 1172, n. 1.

16. Zacharie Tourneur, *Pensées de Blaise Pascal: Édition paléographique des manuscrits originaux conservés à la Bibliothèque Nationale* (Paris: Vrin, 1942).

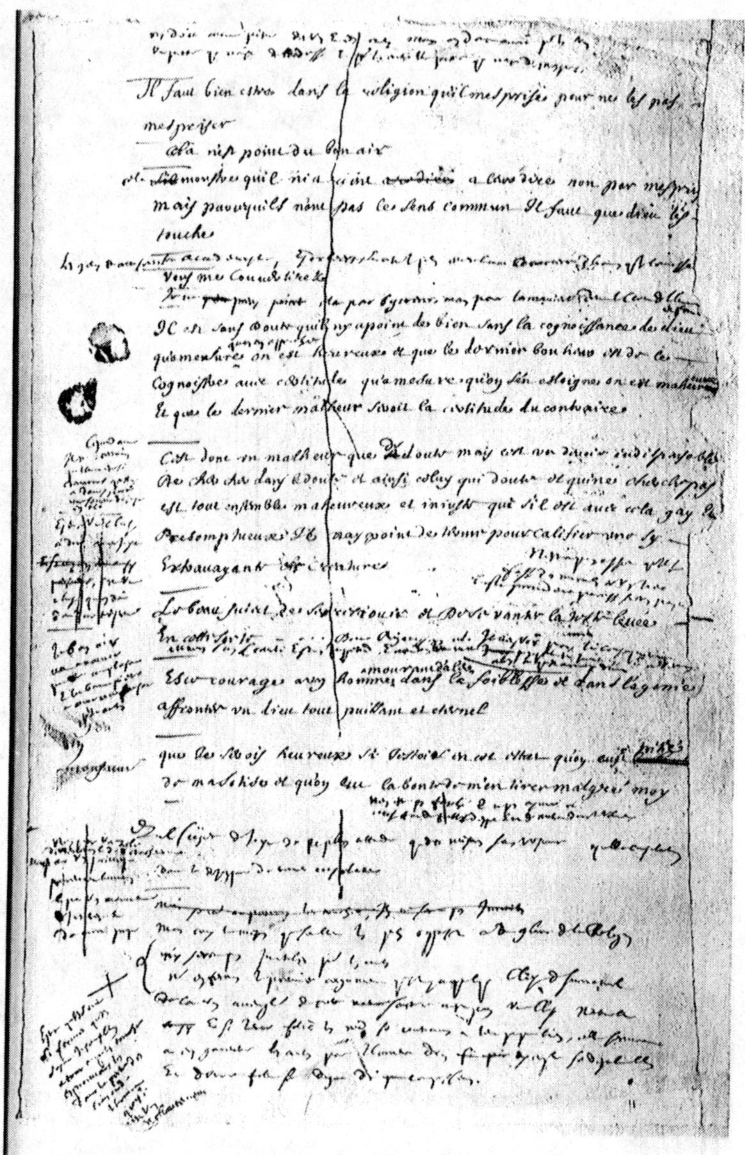

Il faut bien estre dans la religion qu'il mesprises pour ne les pas mespriser

cela n'est point du bon air

... monstre qu'il n'a ... a leur dire non par mespris mais parce qu'ils n'ont pas le sens commun Il faut que dieu les touche

Il est sans doute qu'il n'y a point de bien sans la cognoissance de dieu qu'a mesure qu'on en est heureux et que le dernier bonheur est de le cognoistre avec certitude qu'a mesure qu'on s'en esloigne on est malheureux Et que le dernier malheur seroit la certitude du contraire

C'est donc un malheur que d'estre dans le doute mais c'est un devoir indispensable de chercher dans le doute et ainsi celuy qui doute et qui ne cherche pas est tout ensemble malheureux et injuste que s'il est avec cela gay et presomptueux je n'ay point de termes pour qualifier une si extravagante creature

Est ce courage a un homme mourant d'aller dans la foiblesse et dans l'agonie affronter un dieu tout puissant et eternel

que je serois heureux si j'estois en cet estat qu'on eust pitié de ma sottise et qu'on eust la bonté de m'en tirer malgré moy

PLATE X. Pascal's Preliminary Notes for the Composition of the Preface to the Apology (Lafuma fragment 427) in the *Recueil original* (Bibliothèque Nationale, MS français 9202). Service photographique, Bibliothèque Nationale.

(Père Martini's *Sinicae Historiae*) published only in December of 1658. Mesnard therefore concludes that unit xxx (and by implication fragment 427) was written after the classification of 1658.[17]

The fact that we no longer possess the original text of fragment 427 means that we are unable to assess the process by which Pascal set down this important dialogue with disbelief. We lack the clues which might have been afforded by Pascal's usual hesitations, emendations, and marginal notes. In the absence of a manuscript version of fragment 427, we must rely upon the way in which the *Copies* organize the dialogue between Pascal and his antagonists. The example of fragment 418 serves to remind us of the extent to which modern editors have had to furnish quotation marks in order to clarify who is speaking in that fragment. One example will suffice. Compare Sellier's rendering of a key section from fragment 418 with the manuscript version as reproduced in Tourneur's "édition paléographique":

Sellier's edition:

Cela est démonstratif, et si
les hommes sont capables de
quelque vérité, celle-là
l'est.
"Je le confesse, je l'avoue,
mais encore. . . . N'y a-t-il
point moyen de voir le dessous
du jeu?"
—Oui, l'Ecriture et le
reste, etc.
—"Oui, mais j'ai les
mains liées et la bouche
muette. On me force à parier,
et je ne suis pas en liberté,
on ne me relâche pas. Et je
suis fait d'une telle sorte
que je ne puis croire. Que
voulez-vous donc que je
fasse?"
—Il est vrai. Mais
apprenez au moins. . . .[18]

Recueil original:

—Cela est demonstratif Et si
hommes sont Capables de
quelque Verité. Celle la l
est.
—[mais c] Je le confesse Je
l auoue, mais encore n y a Il
point moyen de Voir le dessous
du Jeu, ouy l Escriture Et le
reste &c. Ouy mais J ay les
mains liees Et la bouche [fer]
muette, on me force à parier,
ét Je ne suis pas en liberté,
on ne me relasche pas. [Il est
vray mais [—mais aprenez—]
—pas. —Et Je suis fait d
Une telle sorte que Je ne puis
croire que Voulez Vous donc
que Je face—
— Il est Vray [—Vous ne
pouuez croire—] mais
aprenez au moins . . . .[19]

17. *Les Pensées de Pascal,* p. 44.
18. *Pensées* (1976), p. 357.
19. Z. Tourneur, *Pensées: Édition paléographique,* p. 310.

Pascal's Interlocutor in Fragment 418

No other single passage in the *Pensées* has generated more commentary than the "infini/rien" fragment, popularly known as "the wager." On one memorable occasion, three eminent Pascal scholars proposed strikingly different portraits of Pascal's interlocutor in response to Lucien Goldmann's address, "Le pari est-il écrit 'pour le libertin'?"[20] ("Was the wager written 'for the *libertin*'?"). Henri Gouhier, arguing that the celebrated fragment hardly suits the mentality of the *libertin*, pointed to a key text found in the dossier "Commencement":

> Il n'y a que trois sortes de personnes: les uns qui servent Dieu l'ayant trouvé, les autres qui s'emploient à le chercher ne l'ayant pas trouvé, les autres qui vivent sans le chercher ni l'avoir trouvé. Les premiers sont raisonnables et heureux, les derniers sont fous et malheureux. Ceux du milieu sont malheureux et raisonnables.

> There are only three sorts of people: those who have found God and serve him; those who are busy seeking him and have not found him; those who live without either seeking or finding him. The first are reasonable and happy, the last are foolish and unhappy, those in the middle are unhappy and reasonable. (160)

Fragment 418, Gouhier insisted, represents a dialogue, not with a *libertin*, but rather with "celui qui commence à chercher Dieu ou du moins qui est malheureux"[21] ("one who is starting to seek God or who at least is unhappy"). Paul Bénichou could not have disagreed more strongly: "Je ne vois pas ici un libertin malheureux. . . . Je vois un sceptique, purement et simplement"[22] ("I do not see an unhappy *libertin* in this text. . . . I see a pure and simple skeptic"). Jean Mesnard reminded his colleagues that Pascal's unbeliever evolves considerably during the course of the dossiers of 1658 and is presented as practically converted by the time the Apology reaches the chapter "Morale chrétienne."[23]

At the risk of adding to the considerable weight of commentary generated by fragment 418, it seems worth pointing out the fact that the role of Pascal's interlocutor in this celebrated dialogue is quite minimal. Once we isolate the seven brief interventions (i–vii later) which Pascal permits him

20. Goldmann's paper and the observations of Professors Gouhier, Bénichou, and Mesnard are reproduced in *Blaise Pascal: L'Homme et l'oeuvre* (Paris: Editions de Minuit, 1956), pp. 139–56.

21. Ibid., pp. 139–40.

22. Ibid., p. 150.

23. Ibid., pp. 155–56.

in the course of the fragment, it becomes clear that the portrait of Pascal's unbeliever in this passage has perhaps been overdrawn by commentators and critics.

The first intervention of the unbeliever comes after a long preface in which Pascal demonstrates the finite in the face of the infinite:

Infini rien.

Notre âme est jetée dans le corps, où elle trouve nombre, temps, dimensions; elle raisonne là-dessus et appelle cela nature, nécessité, et ne peut croire autre chose.

L'unité jointe à l'infini ne l'augmente de rien, non plus que un pied à une mesure infini; le fini s'anéantit en présence de l'infini et devient un pur néant. . . .

Nous connaissons qu'il y a un infini, et ignorons sa nature, comme nous savons qu'il est faux que les nombres soient finis. Donc il est vrai qu'il y a un infini en nombre, mais nous ne savons pas ce qu'il est. Il est faux qu'il soit pair, il est faux qu'il soit impair; car en ajoutant l'unité il ne change point de nature. Cependant c'est un nombre, et tout nombre est pair ou impair. Il est vrai que cela s'entend de tout nombre fini. . . .

Nous connaissons donc l'existence et la nature du fini parce que nous sommes finis et étendus comme lui.

Nous connaissons l'existence de l'infini et ignorons sa nature, parce qu'il a étendue comme nous, mais non pas des bornes comme nous.

Mais nous ne connaissons ni l'existence ni la nature de Dieu, parce qu'il n'a ni étendue ni bornes.

Mais par la foi nous connaissons son existence, par la gloire nous connaîtrons sa nature.

Or j'ai déjà montré qu'on peut bien connaître l'existence d'une chose sans connaître sa nature.

Infinity—nothing. Our soul is cast into the body where it finds number, time, dimensions; it reasons about these things and calls them natural, or necessary, and can believe nothing else.

Unity added to infinity does not increase it at all, any more than a foot added to an infinite measurement: the finite is annihilated in the presence of the infinite and becomes pure nothingness. . . .

We know that the infinite exists without knowing its nature, just as we know that it is untrue that numbers are finite. Thus it is true that there is an infinite number, but we do not know what it is. It is untrue that it is even, untrue that it is odd, for by adding a unit it does not change its nature. Yet it is a number and every number is even or odd. (It is true that this applies to every finite number.)

Thus we know the existence and the nature of the finite because we too are finite and extended in space.

We know the existence of the infinite without knowing its nature, because it too has extension but unlike us no limits.

But we do not know either the existence or the nature of God, because he has neither extension nor limits.

But by faith we know his existence, through glory we shall know his nature.

Now I have already proved that it is quite possible to know that something exists without knowing its nature.[24]

Shifting to the perspective of "les lumières naturelles," Pascal goes on to establish the incomprehensibility of God:

S'il y a un Dieu, il est infiniment incompréhensible, puisque, n'ayant ni parties ni bornes, il n'a nul rapport à nous. Nous sommes donc incapables de connaître ni ce qu'il est, ni s'il est. Cela étant, qui osera entreprendre de résoudre cette question? Ce n'est pas nous, qui n'avons aucun rapport à lui.

If there is a God, he is infinitely beyond our comprehension, since, being indivisible and without limits, he bears no relation to us. We are therefore incapable of knowing either what he is or whether he is. That being so, who would dare to attempt an answer to the question? Certainly not we, who bear no relation to him.[25] (418)

Just prior to the unbeliever's first intervention, Pascal somewhat abruptly turns to the question of Christianity. Christians, he argues, cannot be blamed for not being able to justify their belief in God since finite human reason inevitably fails when it attempts to conceive of an infinite God:

Qui blâmera donc les chrétiens de ne pouvoir rendre raison de leur créance, eux qui professent une religion dont ils ne peuvent rendre raison? Ils déclarent en l'exposant au monde que c'est une sottise, *stultitiam*,[26] et puis vous vous plaignez de ce qu'ils ne la prouvent pas! S'ils la prouvaient, ils ne tiendraient pas parole. C'est en manquant de preuve qu'ils ne manquent pas de sens.

Who then will condemn Christians for being unable to give rational grounds for their belief, professing as they do a religion for which they can not give rational

24. Professor Jean Orcibal has demonstrated that a good deal of this preface to the dialogue was inspired by Pierre Charron's *Trois Vérités*. See "Le Fragment Infini-Rien et ses sources" in *Blaise Pascal: L'Homme et l'oeuvre* (Paris: Editions de Minuit, 1956), pp. 159–86.

25. In the larger context of the Apology, the doctrine of the Incarnation will furnish the answer to this key question. For the moment, Pascal seeks to engage the interest of the unbeliever by taking a position with which he can sympathize.

26. 1 Corinthians 1:21–25: "If it was God's wisdom that human wisdom should not know God, it was because God wanted to save those who have faith through the *foolishness* of the message that we preach." (Jerusalem Bible translation, italics mine).

grounds? They declare that it is a folly, *stultitiam*, in expounding it to the world, and then you complain that they do not prove it. If they did prove it they would not be keeping their word. It is by being without proof that they show they are not without sense. (418)

At this point in the text, Pascal's nameless interlocutor suddenly appears from nowhere. He assents to everything that Pascal has said so far but then protests that such a view does not excuse those who are examining the question from a rational point of view:

[i] "Oui, mais encore que cela excuse ceux qui l'offrent telle, et que cela les ôte du blâme de la produire sans raison, cela n'excuse pas ceux qui la reçoive."

"Yes, but although that excuses those who offer their religion as such, and absolves them from the criticism of producing it without rational grounds, it does not absolve those who accept it."

It is difficult to know what the first word uttered by the unbeliever really signifies. Does his "oui" mean that he assents to everything Pascal has said so far? Is he in agreement with Pascal's demonstration of the nothingness of the finite in the face of the infinite? Does he approve Pascal's statement concerning the incomprehensibility of God? Or does his "oui" only mark his assent to Pascal's contention that Christians would be contradicting themselves should they attempt to give a rational proof of the grounds of their faith? In any event, the unbeliever attempts to counter everything Pascal has said so far by drawing a fundamental distinction between those who believe by faith and those who would be converted by rational argument. Pascal's argument concerning the extrarational character of the Christian mysteries, he contends, excuses those believers who cannot produce rational grounds for their beliefs. However, he argues, it does not excuse those unbelievers being asked to consider such an argument from judging it from a rational perspective.

At this point, Pascal proceeds directly to his first exposition of the wager argument. Picking up his interlocutor's objection ("Examinons donc ce point . . ."), the apologist begins to lay the groundwork for his argument that belief, if not rational, is at least reasonable:

—Examinons donc ce point, et disons: Dieu est ou il n'est pas; mais de quel côté pencherons-nous? La raison n'y peut rien déterminer. Il y a un chaos infini qui nous sépare. Il se joue un jeu à l'extrémité de cette distance infinie, où il arrivera croix ou pile. Que gagerez-vous? Par raison, vous ne pouvez faire ni l'un ni l'autre; par raison, vous ne pouvez défendre nul des deux.

> Let us the examine this point, and let us say: "Either God is or he is not." But to which view shall we be inclined? Reason cannot decide this question. Infinite chaos separates us. At the far end of this infinite distance a coin is being spun which will come down heads or tails. How will you wager? Reason cannot make you choose either, reason cannot prove either wrong. (418)

Antony McKenna qualifies this point of departure in Pascal's argument as "une prise de position résolument anticartésienne" ("the taking of a resolutely anti-Cartesian position"). Pascal's emphasis on the absolute uncertainty of reason in this matter, observes McKenna, is a position characteristic of skeptical philosophy.[27] Yet while appealing to his interlocutor's skeptical bias, Pascal at the same moment admonishes him not to tax the believers for the choice they have made. The uncertainty of reason in the matter means that the unbeliever has no way of knowing whether believers in general have made a wise or a foolish choice. "Ne blâmez pas de fausseté ceux qui ont pris un choix, car vous n'en savez rien" ("Do not then condemn as wrong those who have made a choice, for you know nothing about it") (418).

In what is only his second intervention so far in the dialogue, Pascal's interlocutor displays the dispassionate character of the *honnête homme* at his most detached. He responds to the apologist that the best option is not to get involved at all in the question:

> [ii] "Non, mais je les blâmerai d'avoir fait, non ce choix, mais un choix. Car encore que celui qui prend croix et l'autre soient en pareille faute, ils sont tous les deux en faute. Le juste est de ne point parier."
>
> "No, but I will condemn them not for having made this particular choice, but any choice, for, although the one who calls heads and the other one are equally at fault, the fact is that they are both at fault: the right thing is not to wager at all." (418)

At this point, Pascal invokes an argument which Jean Mesnard qualifies as particularly adapted to the mentality of such *honnête hommes* as Mitton and Méré.[28] "Il faut parier. Cela n'est pas volontaire, vous êtes embarqué . . ." (see Plate XI) ("You must wager. There is no choice, you are already committed"). The rules of the game constrain one to wager one way or the other. Moreover, built into the proposition is an argument which the

27. "L'Argument 'Infini-Rien' " in *Méthodes Chez Pascal: Actes du Colloque tenu à Clermont-Ferrand 10–13 juin 1976* (Paris: Presses Universitaires de France, 1979), p. 498.

28. *Les Pensées de Pascal,* p. 126.

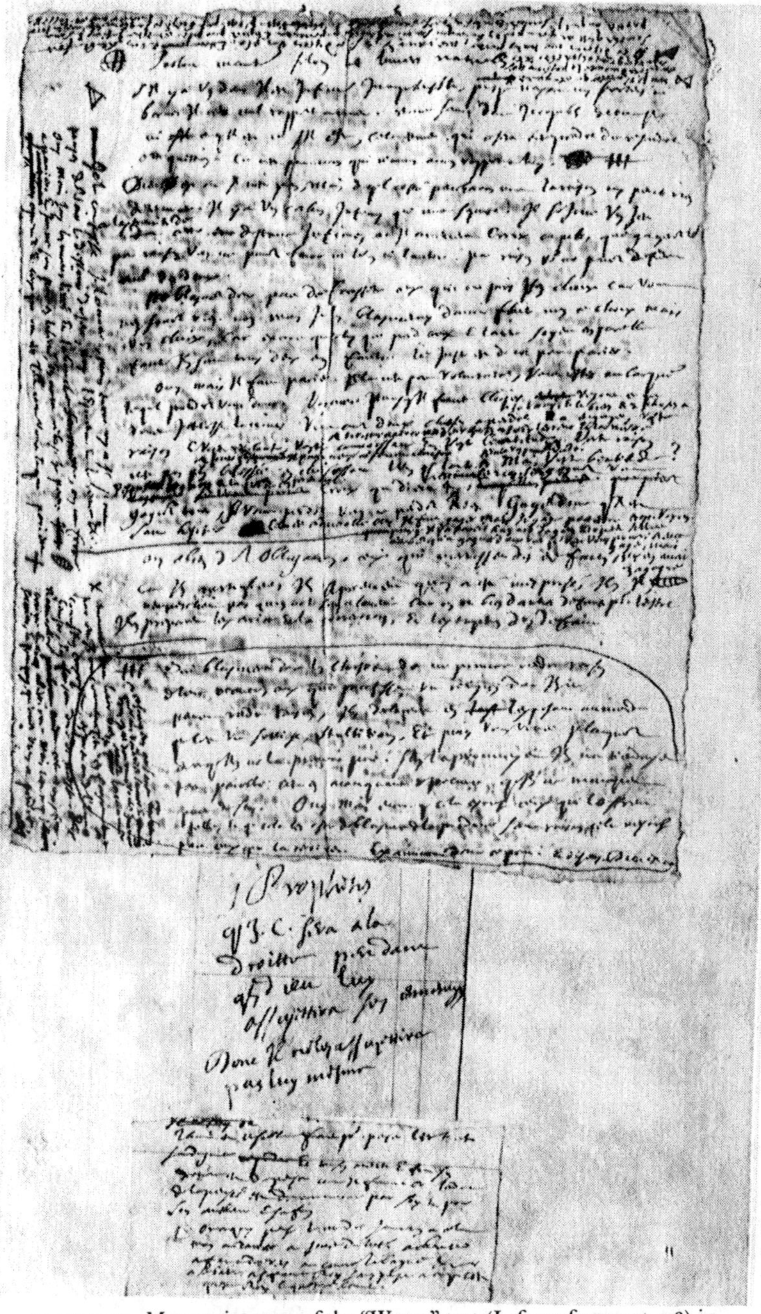

PLATE XI. Manuscript page of the "Wager" text (Lafuma fragment 418) in the *Recueil original* (Bibliothèque Nationale, MS français 9202):

—"Le juste est de ne point parier."
—"Oui, mais il faut parier. . . ."

Lines 13 and 14 at top of manuscript page, following "⊕." Service photographique, Bibliothèque Nationale.

honnête homme, whose rule is to seek the greatest possible happiness and avoid the greatest possible pain, cannot logically resist:

> Lequel prendrez-vous donc? Voyons, puisqu'il faut choisir, voyons ce qui vous intéresse le moins. Vous avez deux choses à perdre, le vrai et le bien, et deux choses à engager, votre raison et votre volonté, votre connaissance et votre béatitude, et votre nature deux choses à fuir, l'erreur et la misère. Votre raison n'est pas plus blessée, puisqu'il faut nécessairement choisir, en choisissant l'un que l'autre. Voilà un point vidé. Mais votre béatitude? Pesons le gain et la perte en prenant croix que Dieu est. Estimons ces deux cas: si vous gagnez, vous gagnez tout, et si vous perdez, vous ne perdez rien: gagnez donc qu'il est sans hésiter.[29]

> Which will you choose then? Let us see: since a choice must be made, let us see which offers you the least interest. You have two things to lose: the true and the good; and two things to stake: your reason and your will, your knowledge and your happiness; and your nature has two things to avoid: error and wretchedness. Since you must necessarily choose, your reason is no more affronted by choosing one rather than the other. That is one point cleared up. But your happiness? Let us weigh up the gain and the loss involved in calling heads that God exists. Let us assess the two cases: if you win you win everything, if you lose you lose nothing. Do not hesitate then; wager that he does exist. (418)

Pascal's formulation of the wager obviously implies a Christian view of things. The immortality of the soul hinges upon the existence of a God who will decide its fate. Pascal does not admit the possibility that the soul might be immortal in the absence of an omnipotent God. Nor does he allow the unbeliever to voice an objection noted in fragment 748: "Ceux qui espèrent leur salut sont heureux en cela, mais ils ont pour contrepoids la crainte de l'enfer" ("Those who hope for salvation are happy in that respect, but this is counterbalanced by their fear of Hell"). Indeed, throughout the entire "infini/rien" fragment, the possibility of Hell and eternal damnation is never explicitly mentioned. Wagering that God exists seems to entail only two possible consequences: (1) being wrong but never knowing that one has wagered incorrectly because consciousness is simply annihilated by death or (2) being correct and enjoying a subsequent "éternité de vie et de bonheur" ("eternity of life and happiness"). Nowhere does Pascal mention the possibility that one might wager for God's existence and still be condemned to an eternity of punishment. Nor does he invoke another possibility: being wrong in wagering that God does not exist and subsequently being condemned to Hell.

29. The primitive version of the wager stops at this point in the manuscript.

Pascal's interlocutor seems oblivious to the theological implications of the proposition he is being asked to accept. He reacts to Pascal's proposition, agrees to abide by the rules of the game, and focuses only upon his potential loss of terrestrial pleasures:

[iii] "Cela est admirable.[30] Oui, il faut gager. Mais je gage peut-être trop."

"That is wonderful. Yes, I must wager, but perhaps I am wagering too much." (418)

The unbeliever's third intervention seems to me quite problematic. Is it entirely contrived by Pascal to advance the course of his argument? Or does it contain the echo of a real conversation with an *honnête homme*? Pascal's interlocutor explains neither why he finds the apologist's proposition "admirable" nor why he has so suddenly abandoned his detachment and has agreed to become drawn into the wager. The only clue to his motives is contained in his reservation: "Mais je gage peut-être trop" ("But perhaps I am wagering too much"). In this statement at least, the unbeliever is in character with the victim of *divertissement* so convincingly painted in Chapter VIII of the *liasses* of 1658. Obsessed with the danger of failing to make the most of this life, he has been oblivious to the larger question of eternal life or annihilation. When the possible consequences of his position are put to him so bluntly and in such reasonable terms, is he simply so astonished that he utters the words "Cela est admirable"?

At this point in the dialogue, Pascal embarks on a long and difficult argument (the second version of the wager) designed to strengthen the case for wagering in favor of God's existence. He restates the wager in mathematical terms which recall his formulation of the rules for calculating probability in his letters to Fermat in 1654. Henri Gouhier gives a particularly cogent summary of Pascal's strategy at this point: "Au *rationnel* ce pari a substitué le *raisonnable*: on va maintenant montrer dans *raisonnable* une nouvelle espèce de *rationnel*, celle que découvrent les mathématiques les plus récentes . . . ce calcul qui rationalise la probabilité"[31] ("For

30. In his edition of the *Pensées* (Paris: Gallimard, 1977), Le Guern attributes the words "Cela est admirable" to Pascal and begins the unbeliever's third intervention with "Oui, il faut gager . . ." (p. 11). Lafuma does not make it clear to whom these words belong. Tourneur's rendering of the text of the *Recueil original,* however, suggests that "Cela est admirable" should be attributed to Pascal's interlocutor. Tourneur's edition reproduces a horizontal line before the word *Cela,* indicating that Pascal intended to open a new citation at this point (*Pensées: Édition paléographique,* p. 309).

31. *Blaise Pascal: Commentaires,* p. 259.

the *rational*, this wager has substituted the *reasonable*: a new kind of *rational* will now be shown to reside within the *reasonable*, the one being discovered by the newest mathematics . . . this calculation which rationalizes probability"). Michel Le Guern observes that whereas Pascal's first version of the wager can be analyzed from a psychological perspective, this second version can be explained only by "une exégèse mathématique qui laisse délibérément de côté tout aspect psychologique"[32] ("a mathematical exegesis which deliberately leaves aside all psychological aspects").

In order to introduce the concept of probability, Pascal first makes use of an example cast in the form of finite numbers:

> Voyons, puisqu'il y a pareil hasard de gain et de perte, si vous n'aviez qu'à gagner deux vies pour une, vous pourriez encore gager, mais s'il y en avait trois à gagner, il faudrait jouer (puisque vous êtes dans le nécessité de jouer) et vous seriez imprudent, lorsque vous êtes forcé à jouer, de ne pas hasarder votre vie pour en gagner trois à un jeu où il y a pareil hasard de perte et de gain.

> Let us see: since there is an equal chance of gain and loss, if you stood to win only two lives for one you could still wager, but supposing you stood to win three? You would have to play (since you must necessarily play) and it would be unwise of you, once you are obliged to play, not to risk your life in order to win three lives at a game in which there is an equal chance of losing and winning. (418)

As Pascal explains it, the perspective changes once what could be won outweighs what might be lost. Given a one in two chance of winning three times what one has wagered, it might normally be reasonable to hesitate to gamble the life one has and risks losing. However, one is obliged to wager. It would therefore be unreasonable not to wager on the side of the greater possible gain. Pascal next applies the same formula to a hypothesis which makes use of infinite numbers. The greater possible gain jumps suddenly from 3/2 lives to "une éternité de vie et de bonheur" ("an eternity of life and of happiness"):

> Mais il y a une éternité de vie et de bonheur. Et cela étant, quand il y aurait une infinité de hasards dont un seul serait pour vous, vous auriez encore raison de gagner un pour avoir deux, et vous agirez de mauvais sens, en étant obligé de jouer, de refuser de jouer une vie contre trois à un jeu où d'une infinité de hasards, il y en a un pour vous, s'il y avait une infinité de vie infiniment heureuse à gagner.

> But there is an eternity of life and happiness. That being so, even though there were an infinite number of chances, of which only one were in your favor, you

32. *Les Pensées de Pascal: De l'anthropologie à la théologie,* p. 46.

would still be right to wager one in order to win two; and you would still be acting wrongly, being obliged to play, in refusing to stake one life against three in a game, where out of an infinite number of chances there is one in your favor, if there were an infinity of infinitely happy life to be won. (418)

J. Lachelier once qualified this passage as "à la fois incohérent et absurde"[33] ("both incoherent and absurd"). Le Guern explains its elliptical character by again reminding us that the entire text of fragment 418 is more of an "aide-mémoire" than a finished text.[34] In any case, we should once again note, nowhere in Pascal's formula does there appear the possibility of eternal damnation. Winning the wager automatically means winning "une infinité de vie infiniment heureuse" ("an infinity of infinitely happy life"): "Mais il y a ici une infinité de vie infiniment heureuse à gagner, un hasard de gain contre un nombre fini de hasards de perte, et ce que vous jouez est fini" ("But here there is an infinity of infinitely happy life to be won, one chance of winning against a finite number of chances of losing, and what you are staking is finite") (418).

At this point, Pascal draws a practical conclusion on behalf of his silent interlocutor. Rational behavior demands wagering for God's existence. Deciding to keep one's life instead of wagering it would amount to renouncing the use of reason itself:

> Cela ôte tout parti partout où est l'infini et où il n'y a pas infinité de hasards de perte contre celui de gain. Il n'y a point à balancer, il faut tout donner, et ainsi quand on est forcé à jouer, il faut renoncer à la raison pour garder la vie plutôt que de la hasarder pour le gain infini aussi prêt à arriver que la perte du néant.

> That leaves no choice; wherever there is infinity, and where there are not infinite chances of losing against that of winning, there is no room for hesitation, you must give everything. And thus, since you are obliged to play, you must be renouncing reason if you hoard your life rather than risk it for an infinite gain, just as likely to occur as a loss amounting to nothing. (418)

In the lines which follow, Pascal seems to broaden his perspective and to consider using the wager demonstration for a larger audience. As Le Guern observes,[35] the objection he now presents and then refutes is hardly an objection that a professional gambler would make. Nor is it directly attributed to his interlocutor in the dialogue:

33. Cited by Gouhier, *Blaise Pascal: Commentaires,* p. 261.
34. *Les Pensées de Pascal: De l'anthropologie à la théologie,* p. 47.
35. Ibid., p. 49.

Car il ne sert de rien de dire qu'il est incertain si on gagnera, et qu'il est certain qu'on hasarde, et que l'infinie distance qui est entre la certitude de ce qu'on expose et l'incertitude de ce qu'on gagnera égale le bien fini qu'on expose certainement à l'infini qui est incertain. Cela n'est pas ainsi. Tout joueur hasarde avec certitude pour gagner avec incertitude, et néanmoins il hasarde certainement le fini pour gagner incertainement le fini, sans pécher contre la raison. Il n'y a pas infinité de distance entre cette certitude de ce qu'on s'expose et l'incertitude du gain; cela est faux. Il y a, à la vérité, infinité entre la certitude de gagner et la certitude de perdre, mais l'incertitude de gagner est proportionnée à la certitude de ce qu'on hasarde selon la proportion des hasards de gain et de perte. Et de là vient que s'il y a autant de hasards d'un côté que de l'autre, le parti est à jouer égal contre égal. Et alors la certitude de ce qu'on s'expose est égale à l'incertitude du gain, tant s'en faut qu'elle en soit infiniment distante. Et ainsi notre proposition est dans une force infinie, quand il y a le fini à hasarder, à un jeu où il y a pareils hasards de gain que de perte, et l'infini à gagner.

Cela est démonstratif et, si les hommes sont capables de quelque vérité, celle-là l'est.

For it is no good saying that it is uncertain whether you will win, that it is certain that you are taking a risk, and that the infinite distance between the certainty of what you are risking and the uncertainty of what you may gain makes the finite good you are certainly risking equal to the infinite good that you are not certain to gain. This is not the case. Every gambler takes a certain risk for an uncertain gain, and yet he is taking a certain finite risk for an uncertain finite gain without sinning against reason. Here there is no infinite distance between the certain risk and the uncertain gain: that is not true. There is, indeed, an infinite distance between the certainty of winning and the certainty of losing, but the proportion between the uncertainty of winning and the certainty of what is being risked is in proportion to the chances of winning or losing. And hence if there are as many chances on one side as on the other you are playing for even odds. And in that case the certainty of what you are risking is equal to the uncertainty of what you may win; it is by no means infinitely distant from it. Thus our argument carries infinite weight, when the stakes are finite in a game where there are even chances of winning and losing and an infinite prize to be won.

This is conclusive and if men are capable of any truth this is it. (418)

Here the dialogue begins again. However, the unbeliever's response (only his fourth intervention so far) to Pascal's long and complicated demonstration seems curiously inadequate. He makes no reference at all to the details, mathematical or otherwise, of Pascal's second exposition of the wager. Rather, he seems to accept the whole argument as irrefutable. He adds only a request for information as to how he can increase his odds of wagering correctly:

[iv] —Je le confesse, je l'avoue, mais encore n'y a-t-il point moyen de voir le dessous du jeu?

"I confess, I admit it, but is there really no way of seeing what the cards are?" (418)

If the unbeliever's protestations of agreement ("Je le confesse, je l'avoue") seem somewhat contrived, his appeal for additional empirical data does have a certain ring of authenticity. "Le dessous du jeu" is an analogy taken from a card game. The agnostic wants to know what aces are being reserved for the critical moment. This plea for help gives Pascal the opportunity to plant an idea in his interlocutor's mind which will later be of capital importance: "Oui, l'Ecriture et le reste, etc." ("Yes. Scripture and the rest, etc."). Scripture, the source of Revelation, contains hidden clues which will provide an edge over the purely mathematical chances of making the correct wager. Fragment 158, which contains an allusion to eternal punishment absent in the "infini/rien" fragment, makes it clear that God has left signs in Revelation so that those who search with all their heart may come to believe:

Pour les partis vous devez vous mettre en peine de rechercher la vérité, car si vous mourez sans adorer le vrai principe vous êtes perdu. Mais—dites-vous, s'il avait voulu que je l'adorasse il m'aurait laissé des signes de sa volonté. Aussi a(-t-)il fait, mais vous les négligez. Cherchez-les donc; cela le vaut bien.

As far as the choices go, you must take the trouble to seek the truth, for if you die without worshiping the true principle you are lost. "But," you say, "if he had wanted me to worship him, he would have left me some signs of his will." So he did, but you pay them no heed. Look for them then; it is well worth it. (158)

In the course of the Apology sketched by the dossiers of 1658, the "signes" alluded to in fragment 158 are shown to be hidden in "l'Ecriture et le reste." However, at this point in fragment 418, the unbeliever does not seem to grasp the implications of "Oui, l'Ecriture et le reste, etc." He never pursues Pascal's response to his question "N'y a-t-il point moyen de voir le dessous du jeu?" He dismisses Pascal's answer with a "Oui, mais . . ." and then goes on to formulate what is his most memorable intervention in the course of the entire dialogue:

(v) "Oui, mais j'ai les mains liées et la bouche muette. On me force à parier, et je ne suis pas en liberté, on ne me relâche pas. Et je suis fait d'une telle sorte que je ne puis croire. Que voulez-vous que je fasse?"

"Yes, but my hands are tied and my lips are sealed; I am being forced to wager and I am not free; I am being held fast and I am so made that I cannot believe. What do you want me to do then?" (418)

At this point, the unbeliever attempts to cry foul. He protests that his forced assent to the wager that God exists by no means makes him a believer. While agreeing to make a conscious, albeit obligatory, decision to believe, he lacks inner conviction. He attributes this lack of inner conviction to a deficiency in his constitution: "Je suis fait d'une telle sorte que je ne puis croire" (see Plate XII). ("I am so made that I cannot believe"). "Que voulez-vous donc que je fasse" ("What do you want me to do then?") represents not so much a cry of despair as a final attempt to be let off the hook. The entire wager is beside the point, he seems to be telling Pascal, in the absence of an inner faculty of belief.

Pascal immediately seizes upon this opening. He explains to the unbeliever that since reason compels him to believe, his inability to do so must be the product of his carnal nature:

Il est vrai, mais apprenez au moins que votre impuissance à croire vient de vos passions, puisque la raison vous y porte et que néanmoins vous ne le pouvez. Travaillez donc non pas à vous convaincre par l'augmentation des preuves de Dieu, mais par la diminution de vos passions.[36] Vous allez à la foi et vous n'en savez pas le chemin. Vous voulez vous guérir de l'infidélité et vous en demandez les remèdes, apprenez de ceux, etc., qui ont été liés comme vous et qui parient maintenant tout leur bien. Ce sont gens qui savent ce chemin que vous voudriez suivre et guérir d'un mal dont vous voulez guérir; suivez la manière par où ils ont commencé. C'est en faisant tout comme s'ils croyaient, en prenant de l'eau bénite, en faisant dire des messes, etc. Naturellement même cela vous fera croire et vous abêtira.

36. Le Guern (*Pensées,* 2, p. 13) inserts two fragments in the margin of the autograph (Lafuma fragments 424 and 423) at this point:

C'est le coeur qui sent Dieu et non la raison. Voilà ce que c'est que la foi. Dieu sensible au coeur, non à la raison (424).

Le coeur a ses raisons que la raison ne connaît pas; on le sait en mille choses.

Je dis que le coeur aime l'être universel naturellement et soi-même naturellement, selon qu'il s'y adonne, et il se durcit contre l'un ou l'autre à son choix. Vous avez rejeté l'un et conservé l'autre; est-ce par raison que vous vous aimez? (423).

(It is the heart which perceives God and not reason. That is what faith is: God perceived by the heart, not by reason (424).

The heart has its reasons of which reason knows nothing: we know this in countless ways.

I say that it is natural for the heart to love the universal being or itself, according to its allegiance, and it hardens itself against either as it chooses. You have rejected one and kept the other. Is it reason that makes you love yourself?) (423).

Folio 8

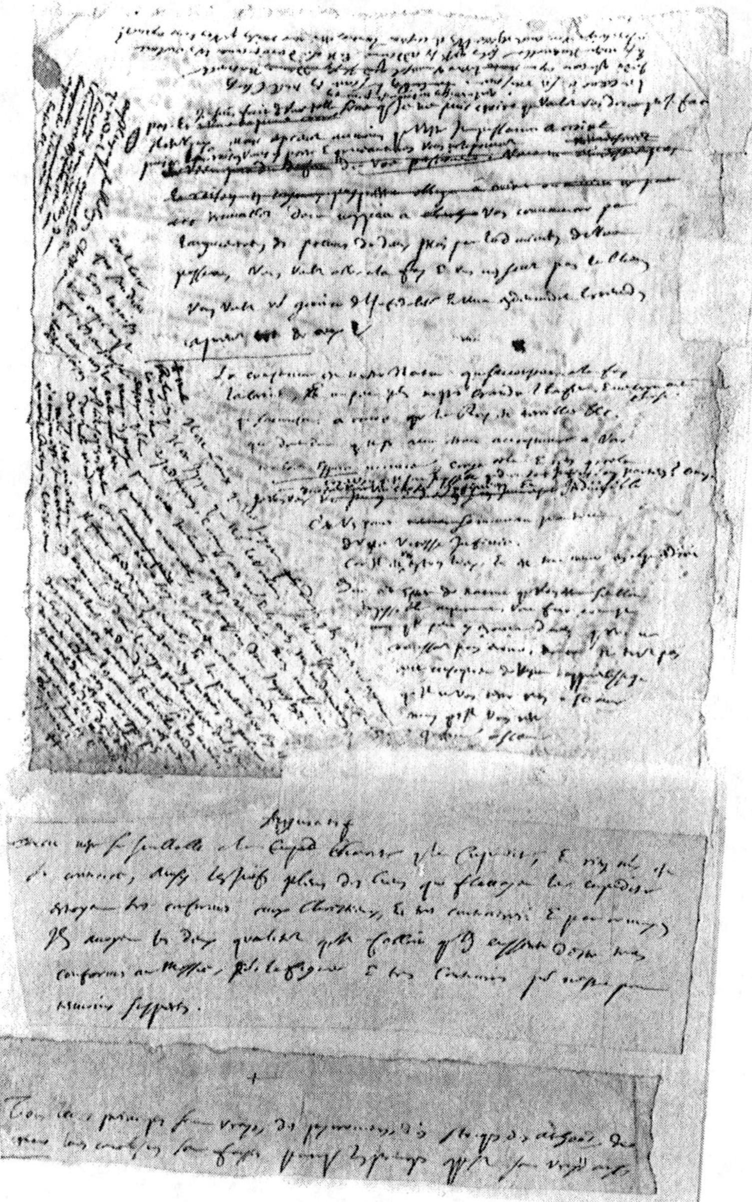

PLATE XII. Manuscript page of the "Wager" text (Lafuma fragment 418) in the *Recueil original* (Bibliothèque Nationale, MS français 9202):

"Je suis fait d'une telle sorte que je ne puis croire. Que voulez-vous donc que je fasse?"

The *libertin's* intervention (v) cited above begins in the middle of the sixth line from the top of the manuscript page. The first four lines (upside down) on the page are reproduced by Lafuma as fragment 423: "Le coeur a ses raisons. . . ." Lafuma fragment 426 is constituted by the lines in the upper-left-hand margin. Service photographique.

That is true, but at least get it into your head that, if you are unable to believe, it is because of your passions, since reason impels you to believe and yet you cannot do so. Concentrate then not on convincing yourself by multiplying proofs of God's existence but by diminishing your passions. You want to find faith and you do not know the road. You want to be cured of unbelief and you ask for the remedy: learn from those who were once bound like you and who now wager all they have. These are people who know the road you wish to follow, who have been cured of the affliction of which you wish to be cured: follow the way by which they began. They behaved just as if they did believe, taking holy water, having masses said, and so on. That will make you believe quite naturally, and will make you more docile. (418)

Pascal insists that the work which the unbeliever must now undertake is not of an intellectual order. Attempting to augment the number of traditional proofs of God's existence will not help him. Rather, he must work to counteract his carnal nature by following in the tried and true path of those who have found themselves in the same dilemma.[37] He must *act* as though he believed, blessing himself with holy water as he enters a church and requesting masses to be said for his inner conversion. In wagering that God exists, the unbeliever does not automatically receive God's Grace. However, in removing the obstacles to faith constituted by the passions, he opens himself to this possibility.

"Abêtira" invokes the Cartesian model of the "bête-machine." By training oneself to adopt reflexes of religious significance, one opens oneself to the possibility of the gift of Grace. As Pascal notes in fragment 944:

Il faut que l'extérieur soit joint à l'intérieur pour obtenir de Dieu, c'est-à-dire que l'on se mette à genoux, prie des lèvres, etc., afin que l'homme orgueilleux qui n'a voulu soumettre à Dieu soit maintenant soumis à la créature. Attendre de cet extérieur le secours est être superstitieux; ne vouloir pas le joindre à l'intérieur est être superbe.

We must combine outward and inward to obtain anything from God; in other words, we must go down on our knees, pray with our lips, etc., so that the proud man who would not submit to God must now submit to his creature. If we expect help from this outward part we are being superstitious, if we refuse to combine it with the inward we are being arrogant. (944)

"Cela vous fera croire et vous abêtira" ("That will make you believe and will make you more docile"). The prospect of such a program of spiritual

37. It is not clear to whom Pascal refers. Is the reference to particular penitents or particular methods of spiritual direction?

apprenticeship provokes from Pascal's interlocutor a reaction which has not always been properly understood:

(vi) "Mais c'est ce que je crains."

"But that is what I am afraid of."

Just what is it that the unbeliever fears? Is it the prospect of having to diminish his passions and the resulting loss of terrestrial pleasures? Or is it the prospect of having to exhibit the kind of external religious conformity which he has ridiculed in the past? In attempting to make sense of the unbeliever's response, we encounter a problem of tone. Is the agnostic acknowledging genuine fear? Or might not his comment simply be wry and ironic?

Perhaps the unbeliever is simply accusing Pascal of having ended up by telling him what believers always end up telling agnostics: "Act as though you believed, behave as though you believed and perhaps God will grant you the gift of his grace." Down through the ages, Christians have counseled doubters to pray the prayer of the father of the epileptic boy in Mark 9:24: "Lord I believe, help thou my unbelief." What if "Mais c'est ce que je crains" reveals less a sense of fear and trembling than the agnostic's wry realization that in the last analysis he is being told nothing new?

Pascal completely ignores the irony implicit in the statement "Mais c'est ce que je crains." Taking the statement at face value, he pretends to understand that the unbeliever really fears having to part company with his passions. He restates the idea that acting as if he were a believer will help the unbeliever mortify his passions and adds that he has nothing to lose in adopting such a course:

—Et pourquoi? Qu'avez-vous à perdre? Mais pour vous montrer que cela y mène, c'est que cela diminue les passions, qui sont vos grands obstacles, etc.

—But why? What have you to lose? But to show you that this is the way, the fact is that this diminishes the passions which are your great obstacles, etc. (418)

In the original autograph, the exact position of the final intervention by the unbeliever is unclear. Sellier, following the Second Copy, places the agnostic's final words

[vii] "O ce discours me transporte, me ravit," etc.

"How these words fill me with rapture and delight!" etc. (418)

immediately following the "etc." which concludes Pascal's restatement of the necessity of mortifying the passions. Lafuma, following the First Copy, inserts two paragraphs found in the margin under the rubric "Fin de ce discours" (see Plate XIII) ("End of this address") just before the unbeliever's final intervention:

> Or quel mal vous arrivera-t-il en prenant ce parti? Vous serez fidèle, honnête,[38] humble, reconnaissant, bienfaisant, ami, sincère, véritable. . . . A la vérité, vous ne serez point dans les plaisirs empestés, dans la gloire, dans les délices, mais n'en aurez-vous point d'autres?
>
> Je vous dis que vous y gagnerez en cette vie, et que, à chaque pas que vous ferez dans ce chemin, vous verrez tant de certitude de gain, et tant de néant de ce que vous hasardez, que vous connaîtrez à la fin que vous avez parié pour une chose certaine, infinie, pour laquelle vous n'avez rien donné.

> Now what harm will come to you from choosing this course? You will be faithful, honest, humble, grateful, full of good works, a sincere, true friend. . . . It is true you will not enjoy noxious pleasures, glory and good living, but will you not have others?
>
> I tell you that you will gain even in this life, and that at every step you take along this road you will see that your gain is so certain and your risk so negligible that in the end you will realize that you have wagered on something certain and infinite for which you have paid nothing. (418)

Lafuma's reading has the value of providing an antecedent for the word *discours* in the unbeliever's last response. However, neither reconstruction of the text sheds much light on the unbeliever's final position. Does Pascal mean for this final interjection to signal the agnostic's total capitulation? Or, is it meant to show him in a state of hesitation, unnerved by the argument of the wager and ready to inquire more carefully into the arguments in favor of Christianity? Pascal's response to the unbeliever's final words is instructive:

> Si ce discours vous plaît et vous semble fort, sachez qu'il est fait par un homme qui s'est mis à genoux auparavant et après, pour prier cet être infini et sans parties, auquel il soumet tout le sien, de se soumettre aussi le vôtre pour votre propre bien et pour sa gloire; et qu'ainsi la force s'accorde avec cette bassesse.

> If my words please you and seem cogent, you must know that they come from a man who went down upon his knees before and after to pray this infinite and

38. Cf., the penultimate paragraph of fragment 427: "qu'ils soient au moins *honnêtes* gens s'ils ne peuvent être chrétiens . . ." ("let them at least be decent people if they cannot be Christians.") (italics mine).

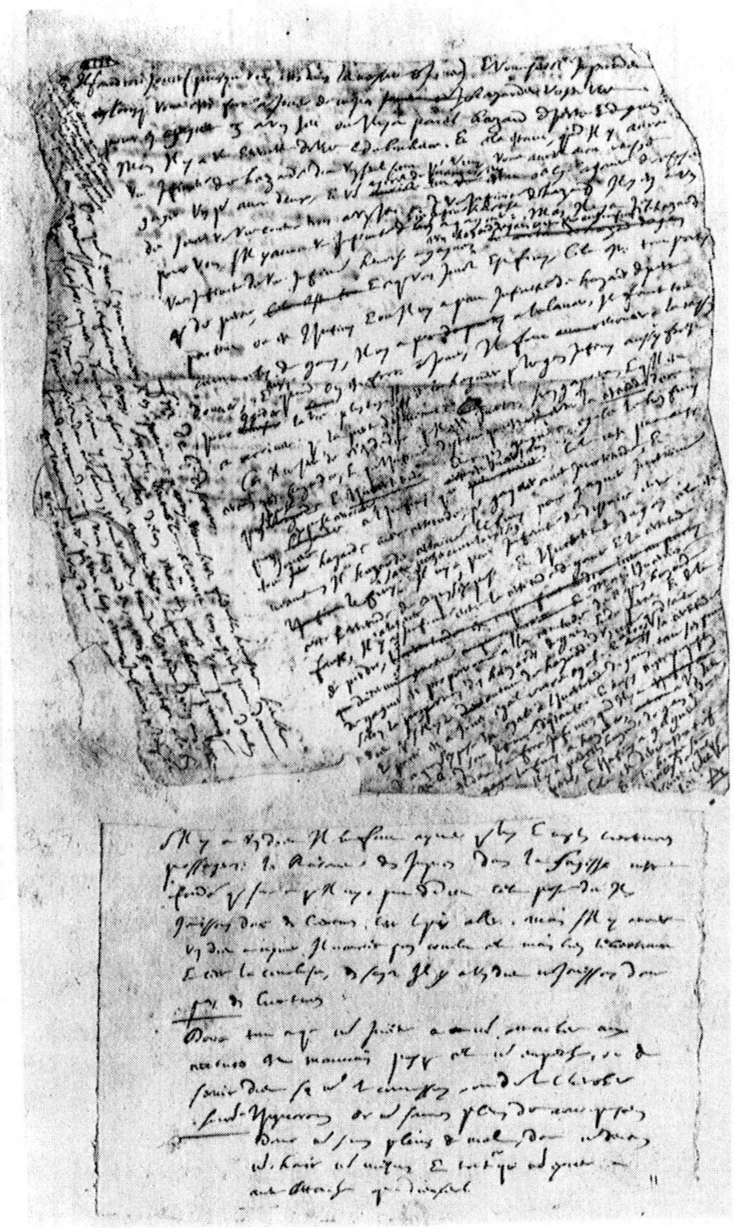

PLATE XIII. Manuscript page of the "Wager" text (Lafuma fragment 418) in the *Recueil original* (Bibliothèque Nationale, MS français 9202). The section entitled "Fin de ce discours" is set down in the left-hand margin. Service photographique, Bibliothèque Nationale.

indivisible being, to whom he submits his own, that he might bring your being also to submit to him for your own good and for his glory: and that strength might thus be reconciled with lowliness. (418)

Henri Gouhier suggests that the model for the dialogue found in the "infini/rien" fragment is that of spiritual direction:

> Ainsi se précise le visage de celui qui va tenir le rôle du directeur: c'est un homme qui a vécu l'expérience que l'interlocuteur est en train de vivre; il n'argumente pas: il raconte ce qu'il a fait. Pascal retrouve ici le thème de l'habitude indiqué dans la première des notes jetées à la suite de son exposé: il y a des conduites religieuses qui disposent l'âme à recevoir la foi qu'elles supposent. N'oublions pas que le conseil de "faire comme si" s'adresse non pas à n'importe quel incrédule mais à quelqu'un qui voudrait bien croire et qui, ne le pouvant pas au moment où sa raison l'y pousse, risque de se décourager. Pascal ne dit pas: "prenez de l'eau bénite" à l'athée ou au sceptique; ce serait absurde et même offensant; le dialogue n'irait pas au delà de: "pour qui me prenez-vous?"[39]

> Thus is revealed the face of the one who will take the role of spiritual director: a man who has lived through the experience which the interlocutor is undergoing. He does not construct an argument. Rather, he recounts what he has done in a similar situation. Pascal here takes up again the theme of habit, as indicated in the first of those notes set down directly following his exposition of the wager: there are kinds of religious behavior which dispose the soul to receive the grace which they imply. We must not forget that the advice to "act as if" is addressed, not to just any unbeliever but to someone who wants to believe and who, unable to believe even though motivated by his reason, is in danger of becoming discouraged. Pascal hardly says "take holy water" to an atheist or a skeptic. That would be absurd and even offensive. The dialogue would go no further than: "for whom do you take me?"

In many ways, Gouhier's interpretation of the model for Pascal's dialogue makes a good deal of sense. In his final response to the unbeliever, Pascal says that he, like a good confessor or spiritual director, prays before and after the encounter that his actions may advance the salvation of a soul and the glory of God. Moreover, the very brevity of the unbeliever's responses in the dialogue fits the model of spiritual direction. In such an exchange, the penitent's role is hardly to give a full defense of his own position. Yet, however useful this model is, we are still faced with the fact that the unbeliever's final position is far from clear.

At the risk of taking the unbeliever's seven interventions out of context, it seems worth asking what picture of disbelief they really add up to. In

39. *Blaise Pascal: Commentaires*, p. 272.

interventions i and ii, Pascal's interlocutor seems principally to display the dispassionate character of the *honnête homme*. At the same time, however, he is not portrayed as an aggressive opponent of Christianity. He readily assents to the way in which Pascal excuses believers from having to justify their belief rationally. In interventions iii, iv, and vii, Pascal's interlocutor seems almost a cardboard antagonist. The apologist seems to be placing his responses directly into his mouth. Only in interventions v and vi ("je suis fait d'une telle sorte"; "C'est ce que je crains") do his responses seem to have a ring of authenticity and originality. In the last analysis, his conversion is far from certain. He has assented to the fact that he must wager. But, in spite of his protestations of amazement ("Je le confesse, je l'avoue; O ce discours me transporte, me ravit"), it is not clear that he ever actually agrees to begin behaving as if he were a believer.

In all fairness to Pascal, we must remember how unfinished is the original text of the "infini/rien" fragment.[40] As Jean Mesnard observes: "Le texte se réduit à un brouillon si éloigné de son achèvement qu'il aurait certainement subi d'importantes retouches"[41] ("In the last analysis, the text is such a rough draft so far from completion that it would most certainly have undergone a significant touching up"). Nevertheless, like other commentators who have overdrawn the sketch of the unbeliever contained in fragment 418, I find it hard to resist speculating what psychological state Pascal means to indicate when he has his interlocutor speak

40. The last two sheets of the "infini/rien" fragment in the *Recueil original* contain eight additional fragments. Sellier incorporates them into the end of the "infini/rien" fragment itself. Lafuma gives them new numbers: 419–26.

Two of these fragments (419 and 420) follow a line separating them from the last manuscript page of the text. Four (421, 424, 426, and 423) are found in the margin of the same page. Two additional fragments (422 and 425) figure in the margin of the preceding page, next to the text contained under the rubric "Fin de ce discours."

Henri Gouhier qualifies these fragments as "des additions à un exposé futur du pari" and advises against including them in the text of fragment 418. "En les incorporant à l'exposé actuel," he writes in his *Blaise Pascal: Commentaires* (p. 274), "on risque de briser sa continuité et de troubler son intelligibilité." ("By incorporating [these additions] into the draft as it exists . . . one takes the risk of interrupting its continuity and obscuring its intelligibility").

Only one of these fragments (420) contains an exchange with the unbeliever: "—Croyez-vous qu'il soit impossible que Dieu soit infini, sans parties?—Oui.—Je vous veux donc faire voir une chose infinie et indivisible: C'est un point se mouvant partout d'une vitesse infinie" (—" 'Do you believe that it is impossible for God to be infinite and indivisible?' "—'Yes.'—'Very well, I will show you something infinite and indivisible: it is a point moving everywhere at an infinite speed' ").

This exchange obviously belongs to the beginning section of the dialogue. It would be a mistake to read it as coming after the unbeliever's last intervention.

41. *Les Pensées de Pascal,* p. 316.

the words "Je le confesse, je l'avoue" ("I confess, I admit it") and "O ce discours me ravit" ("How these words fill me with rapture and delight"). Does he imagine that unbeliever has suddenly been seized with fear and anxiety concerning the state of his soul and the prospect of his eventual damnation or salvation?

I hardly think so. Pascal's interlocutor could scarcely be more unlike the young Rousseau pictured in his *Confessions*. Obsessed with the prospect of death and with a "cruelle incertitude" concerning his salvation, the young Rousseau engages in a kind of wager:

> Je me dis: je m'en vais jeter cette pierre contre l'arbre qui est vis-à-vis de moi. Si je le touche, signe de salut; si je le manque, signe de damnation. Tout en disant ainsi, je jette ma pierre d'une main tremblante et avec un horrible battement de coeur, mais si heureusement qu'elle va frapper au beau milieu de l'arbre. . . . Depuis lors je n'ai plus douté de mon salut.[42]

> I said to myself: I'm going to throw this rock against the tree which is in front of me. If I hit it, this is a sign that I am saved; if I miss it, it means that I am damned. While saying this, I threw my rock, my hand trembling and my heart racing. Fortunately, it struck right in the middle of the tree. . . . Since that time, I have never doubted that I have been saved.

The modern reader will perhaps be tempted to attribute Rousseau's obsession with death and the possibility of eternal damnation to some deep neurosis. It will perhaps appear to him very unhealthy. Pascal's perspective on the matter could not be more different. As we shall see in our analysis of fragment 427, Pascal qualifies such an attitude as eminently reasonable. The truly insane are those skeptics who have consciously cultivated an attitude of indifference, complacency, or acceptance in the face of man's ultimate fate.

In the "infini/rien" fragment, the unbeliever seems to me to be relatively indifferent to the state of his soul or the prospect of his salvation or damnation. The words "O ce discours me transporte, me ravit" ("How these words fill me with rapture and delight!") hardly reveal the unbeliever in a state of fear and trembling. Rather, they are an expression of his fascination with the rational force of Pascal's mathematical argument. Like Le Maistre de Sacy in the *Entretien*,[43] Pascal adapts his apologetic strategy to the pri-

42. *Confessions,* (Paris: Pléiade, 1959), 4, p. 243.

43. "La conduite ordinaire de M. de Saci, en entretenant les gens, était de proportionner ses entretiens à ceux à qui il parlait. S'il voyait par exemple M. Champaigne, il parlait avec lui de la peinture. S'il voyait M. Hamon, il l'entretenait de la médecine. S'il voyait le chirur-

mary interest of his interlocutor. Mathematics is, in a sense, the religion of the unbeliever. It is that final truth to which all other truths can be reduced. A celebrated scene in Molière's *Dom Juan* reminds us of the extent to which this association was a commonplace in the Classical period:

> Dom Juan. —Je crois que deux et deux sont quatre, Sganarelle, et que quatre et quatre sont huit.
>
> Sganarelle. —La belle croyance et les beaux articles que voilà! Votre religion, à ce que je vois, est donc l'arithmétique?[44]

> Dom Juan. —I believe that two plus two make four, Sganarelle, and that four and four make eight.
>
> Sganarelle. —What a pretty statement of your faith and articles of belief! Your religion, from what I see, is thus arithmetic?

In the *Lettres philosophiques*, Voltaire claims to be shocked by the very premises underlying the wager argument. "Cet article," he observes, "paraît un peu indécent et puérile; cette idée du jeu, de perte et de gain ne convient point à la gravité du sujet"[45] ("This argument . . . seems a bit indecent and puerile; this metaphor of gambling, of winning and losing, hardly suits the gravity of the subject"). In point of fact, Pascal's interlocutor in fragment 418 never really seems very impressed by the gravity of the subject of eternal death or eternal life. Rather, he is transfixed by the mechanical brilliance of the argument. Only at one point in the dialogue does the unbeliever appear to me to be slightly unnerved. Whether ironic

---

gien du lieu, il le questionnait sur la chirurgie. . . . Tout lui servait pour passer aussitôt à Dieu, et pour y faire passer les autres" ("The ordinary conduct of M. de Saci, when conversing with people, was to tailor his conversation to those with whom he was speaking. If he were speaking with M. Champaigne, he spoke with him about painting. When he saw M. Hamon, he got him on to the subject of medicine. If he saw the local surgeon, he questioned him about surgery. . . . He used everything as a means of then going on to talk about God and as a means of getting others onto that subject") *Oeuvres complètes* (éd. Lafuma), p. 292.

44. *Dom Juan,* Act III, scene 1.

45. *Lettres philosophiques* (Oxford: Blackwell, 1965), p. 98. Voltaire goes on to criticize the wager argument from the perspective of Pascal's neo-Augustinian theology: "Commencez, pourrait-on dire à M. Pascal, par convaincre ma raison. J'ai intérêt, sans doute, qu'il y ait un Dieu. Mais si, dans votre système, Dieu n'est venu que pour si peu de personnes; si le petit nombre des élus est si effrayant; si je ne puis rien du tout par moi-même, dites-moi, je vous prie, quel intérêt j'ai à vous croire? N'ai-je pas pas un intérêt visible à être persuadé du contraire? De quel front osez-vous me montrer un bonheur infini, auquel, d'un million d'hommes, à peine un seul a droit d'aspirer? Si vous voulez me convaincre, prenez-vous-y d'une autre façon, et n'allez pas tantôt me parler du jeu, de hasard, de pari, de croix et de pile, et tantôt m'effrayer par les épines que vous semez sur le chemin que je veux et que je dois suivre. Votre raisonnement ne servirait qu'à faire des athées, si la voix de toute la nature ne nous criait qu'il y a un Dieu, avec autant de force que ces subtilités ont de faiblesse."

or not, the words "Mais c'est ce que je crains" ("But that is what I am afraid of")—following on the heels of Pascal's admonition "Cela vous fera croire et vous abêtira" ("That will make you believe quite naturally and will make you more docile")—seem to betray an extreme uneasiness about the prospect of giving up the pleasures of life in this world.

As we shall see in fragment 427, Pascal finds the attachment to life in this world so profoundly unreasonable that he credits its power over humans to the supernatural consequences of Original Sin. When he reads the *Essais*, Pascal is no less offended by his project of exploring his own personality ("le sot projet qu'il a de se peindre") (780) than by Montaigne's "pagan" attitude toward death ("sentiments tout païens sur la mort") (680). In the last analysis, the final chapter of the *Essais* ("De l'expérience") must have seemed as illogical and as incomprehensible to Pascal as the final scene of Camus' novel *L'Étranger* appeared to traditional Catholic readers fifty years ago.

At the end of Camus' novel, the dilemma of his protagonist Meursault is not unlike that of Pascal's "homme dans un cachot" ("man in a dungeon"). In fragment 163, Pascal creates an analogy meant to demonstrate the supernatural origin of that illogicality which underlies human complacency in the face of death:

> Un homme dans un cachot, ne sachant pas si son arrêt est donné, n'ayant plus qu'une heure pour l'apprendre, cette heure suffisant s'il sait qu'il est donné pour le faire révoquer. Il est contre nature qu'il emploie cette heure-là, non à s'informer si l'arrêt est donné, mais à jouer au piquet.
>
> Ainsi il est surnaturel que l'homme, etc. C'est un appesantissement de la main de Dieu.
>
> Ainsi non seulement le zèle de ceux qui le cherchent prouve Dieu, mais l'aveuglement de ceux qui ne le cherchent pas.

> A man in a dungeon, not knowing whether sentence has been passed on him, with only an hour left to find out, and that hour enough, once he knows it has been passed, to have it revoked. It would be unnatural for him to spend that hour not finding out whether sentence has been passed but playing piquet.
>
> So it is beyond all nature that man, etc. It is the heavy weight of the hand of God.
>
> Thus it is not only the zeal of those who seek him that proves God's existence, but also the blindness of those who do not seek him. (163)

While awaiting execution, Camus' Meursault is able to think only of two things. During the night, he is obsessed only with living to see the following dawn:

C'est à l'aube qu'ils venaient, je le savais. En somme, j'ai occupé mes nuits à attendre cette aube. Je n'ai jamais aimé être surpris. Quand il m'arrive quelque chose, je préfère être là. C'est pourquoi j'ai fini par ne plus dormir qu'un peu dans mes journées et, tout le long de mes nuits, j'ai attendu patiemment que la lumière naisse sur la vitre du ciel. Le plus difficile, c'était l'heure douteuse où je savais qu'ils opéraient d'habitude. Passé minuit, j'attendais et je guettais. Jamais mon oreille n'avait perçu tant de bruits. . . . Je peux dire, d'ailleurs, que d'une certaine façon j'ai eu de la chance, puisque je n'ai jamais entendu de pas. Maman disait souvent qu'on n'est jamais tout à fait malheureux. Je l'approuvais dans ma prison, quand le ciel se colorait et qu'un nouveau jour glissait dans ma cellule. Parce qu'aussi bien, j'aurais pu entendre des pas et mon coeur aurait pu éclater. Même si le moindre glissement me jetait à la porte, même si, l'oreille collée au bois, j'attendais éperdument jusqu'à ce que j'entende ma propre respiration, effrayé de la trouver rauque et si pareille au râle d'un chien, au bout du compte mon coeur n'éclatait pas et j'avais gagné vingt-quatre heures.[46]

They always came for one at dawn; that much I knew. So, really, all my nights were spent in waiting for that dawn. I have never liked being taken by surprise. When something happens to me I want to be ready for it. That's why I got into the habit of sleeping off and on in the daytime and watching through the night for the first hint of daybreak in the dark dome above. The worst period of the night was that vague hour when, I knew, they usually come; once it was midnight I waited, listening intently. Never before had my ears perceived so many noises. . . . Still I must say that I was lucky in one respect; never during any of those periods did I hear footsteps. Mother used to say that however miserable one is, there's always something to be thankful for. And each morning, when the sky brightened and light began to flood my cell, I agreed with her. Because I might just as well have heard footsteps, and felt my heart shattered into bits. Even though the faintest rustle sent me hurrying to the door and, pressing an ear to the rough, cold wood, I listened so intently that I could hear my breathing, quick and hoarse like a dog's panting—even so there was an end; my heart hadn't split, and I knew I had another twenty-four hours respite.

During the day, Meursault is absorbed by the thought of whether or not he will be pardoned. His reflections, of a kind commended in fragment 163, take the form of a kind of wager:

Je calculais mes effets et j'obtenais de mes réflexions le meilleur rendement. Je prenais toujours la plus mauvaise supposition: mon pourvoi était rejeté. "Et bien, je mourrai donc." Plus tôt que d'autres, c'était évident. Mais tout le monde sait que la vie ne vaut pas la peine d'être vécue. Dans le fond, j'ignorais pas que mourir à trente ans ou à soixante-dix ans importe peu puisque, naturellement, dans les deux cas, d'autres hommes et d'autres femmes vivront, et cela pendant des milliers

46. Albert Camus, *L'Etranger* (Englewood Cliffs, N.J.: Prentice-Hall, 1955), pp. 129–30. English translation adapted from the translation of Stuart Gilbert (New York: Vintage, 1954).

d'années. Rien n'était plus clair, en somme. C'était toujours moi qui mourrais, que ce soit maintenant ou dans vingt ans. A ce moment, ce qui me gênait un peu dans mon raisonnement, c'était ce bond terrible que je sentais en moi à la pensée de vingt ans de vie à venir. Mais je n'avais qu'à l'étouffer en imaginant ce que seraient mes pensées dans vingt ans quand il me faudrait quand même en venir là. Donc (et le difficile, c'était de ne pas perdre de vue tout ce que ce "donc" représentait de raisonnements), donc, je devais accepter le rejet de mon pourvoi.

A ce moment, à ce moment seulement, j'avais pour ainsi dire le droit, je me donnais en quelque sorte la permission d'aborder la deuxième hypothèse: j'étais gracié. L'ennuyeux, c'est qu'il fallait rendre moins fougueux cet élan du sang et du corps qui me piquait les yeux d'une joie insensée. Il fallait que je m'applique à réduire ce cri, à le raisonner. Il fallait que je sois naturel même dans cette hypothèse, pour rendre plus plausible ma résignation dans la première. Quand j'avais réussi, j'avais gagné une heure de calme. Cela, tout de même, était à considérer.[47]

I calculated the consequences of my situation and I obtained from my reflections the maximum of consolation. Thus, I always began by assuming the worst; my appeal was dismissed. That meant, of course, I was to die. Sooner than others, obviously. "But," I reminded myself, "it's common knowledge that life isn't worth living, anyhow." And, on a wide view, I could see that it makes little difference whether one dies at the age of thirty or seventy—since, in either case, other men and women will go on living as before. Also, whether I died now or forty years hence, this business of dying had to be got through, inevitably. Still, somehow this line of thought wasn't as consoling as it should have been; the idea of all those years of life in hand was a galling reminder! However, I could argue myself out of it, by picturing what would have been my feelings when my term was up, and death had cornered me. Once you're up against it, the precise manner of your death has obviously small importance. Therefore—but it was hard not to lose the thread of the argument leading up to that "therefore"—I should be prepared to face the dismissal of my appeal.

At this stage, but only at this stage, I had, so to speak, the *right*, and accordingly I gave myself leave, to consider the other alternative: that my appeal was successful. And then the trouble was to calm down that sudden rush of joy racing through my body and even bringing tears to my eyes. But it was up to me to bring my nerves to heel and steady my mind; for, even in considering this possibility, I had to keep some order in my thoughts, so as to make my consolations, as regards the first alternative, more plausible. When I'd succeeded, I had earned a good hour's peace of mind; and that, anyhow, was something.

Meursault's intense emotional involvement in the question of whether he will survive another twenty-four hours serves to remind us of the essentially dispassionate emotional state of Pascal's interlocutor in fragment

47. Ibid., pp. 130–31.

418. Nowhere in the fragment is there the slightest indication that he has been moved to wager because of either a fear of death or a desire to gain immortality. He wagers only because he has been constrained to wager. In the course of the *Apology*, Pascal will present a picture of the fragility of human life designed to propel the unbeliever toward the conclusion that reason dictates living as if the present hour were the last:

> Partis:
> Il faut vivre autrement dans le monde, selon ces diverses suppositions . . . s'il est sûr qu'on y sera toujours . . . s'il est sûr qu'on n'y sera pas longtemps, et incertain si on y sera une heure.
>
> Choices.
> Our life in the world must vary according to these different assumptions . . . if it is certain that we shall always be here . . . if it is certain that we shall not be here for long, and uncertain whether we shall be here even one hour. (154)

However, the unbeliever pictured in fragment 418 has not yet been pushed to make an emotional identification with the common fate of humankind. His wager, unlike Meursault's, is not being made from the perspective of possibly having to face death within a day or an hour. For him, the wager proposition remains entirely theoretical.

From the larger perspective of the *Apology*, the unbeliever sketched in fragment 418 seems to display an odd lack of curiosity concerning the very immortality for which he is being urged to wager. Is he simply naive concerning the Christian notion of immortality? Or, like Meursault, is he inherently prejudiced against it?

In the final pages of *L'Etranger*, Meursault encounters, in the person of the prison chaplain, a Christian perspective on death which is not unlike that of Pascal. The priest attempts to convince Meursault that his situation is a paradigm of the human situation since we are all condemned to death. Like Pascal, the chaplain is mystified by his interlocutor's attachment to the life of this world: "Aimez-vous donc cette terre à ce point?" ("Do you really love these earthly things so very much?"). He attempts to counter Meursault's lack of interest in the fate of his soul by forcing him to admit that he has at least entertained the fantasy of a life beyond this one:

> "Non, je ne peux pas vous croire. Je suis sûr qu'il vous est arrivé de souhaiter une autre vie." Je lui ai répondu que naturellement, mais cela n'avait pas plus d'importance que de souhaiter d'être riche, de nager très vite ou d'avoir une

bouche mieux faite. C'était du même ordre. Mais lui m'a arrêté et il voulait savoir comment je voyais cette autre vie. Alors, je lui ai crié: "Une vie où je pourrais me souvenir de celle-ci."[48]

"No! No! I refuse to believe it. I'm sure you've often wished there was an after-life." Of course I had, I told him. Everybody has that wish at times. But that had no more importance than wishing to be rich, or to swim very fast, or to have a better-shaped mouth. It was in the same order of things. I was going on in this same vein when he cut in with a question. How did I imagine that life after the grave? I fairly bawled out at him: "A life in which I could remember this one."

Meursault's reaction to the Christian perspective on death and immortality is not significantly different from that of the skeptics whom Pascal will present in fragment 427. In the first place, he dismisses the Christian promise of a life to come as but an illusion. It is a fantasy of the same order as wishing one were rich or more handsome. Pascal's skeptics will similarly dismiss the entire notion of life after death as belonging to "ces opinions que le peuple reçoit avec une facilité trop crédule" ("those opinions which are accepted by the masses with too ready credulity") (428). Meursault's second criticism of the Christian notion of immortality is even more far-reaching. Even if the Christian hypothesis were true, Meursault would not be interested in it. The only immortality which would have any meaning for him would be one which would be of a kind with life in this world. Such an attachment to this world, betrayed by the unbeliever's hesitancy to wager in fragment 418 and implicit in the portrait of the skeptics in fragment 427, is essentially incomprehensible to Pascal. With the entire Christian tradition, he takes it as a given that this life is but a vale of tears, an inherently flawed, miserable, and unhappy state. For Pascal, the attachment to this world and its passing joys is but a symptom of the human malady engendered by the Fall. Indeed, the entire first half of the *Apology* anticipated by fragment 6 ("Misère de l'homme sans Dieu") seeks to make the case for this position.

Much contemporary commentary on the *Pensées* seems to accept as a given that the celebrated wager fragment is the key to the meaning of the work as a whole. Much energy has been expended on trying to decide how and where the fragment was to be incorporated in the finished Apology. Professor Le Guern's contention that the fragment constitutes "une apo-

48. Ibid., p. 135.

logie complète et indépendante qui se distingue de la grande apologie"[49] ("a complete and independent apology which must be distinguished from the grand Apology") perhaps provides a needed corrective to this obsession with integrating the wager fragment into the movement and vision of the Apology as a whole. Not only is the unbeliever in the wager fragment an incomplete portrait of the mentality of disbelief envisaged by the Apology. The apologetic strategy of the wager fragment is fundamentally unlike that of the Apology as a whole. Nothing in that fragment gives us the impression that Pascal's interlocutor has yet realized that he shares in the human condition. Indeed, nowhere in the fragment is the tragedy of the human condition yet invoked.

As I see it, we should perhaps best think of the wager fragment as a kind of prelude to the Apology sketched by the dossiers of 1658. Perhaps it is a kind of lure, intended to draw a certain kind of unbeliever into the chapters which will follow. Reading it in isolation is, however, perhaps a mistake. For Pascal, in fragment 11, gives it a specific context. It will follow the introduction to the Apology which is constituted by fragment 427:

> Ordre. Après la lettre qu'on doit chercher Dieu, faire la lettre d'ôter les obstacles qui est le discours de la Machine, de préparer la Machine, de chercher par raison.

> Order. After the letter urging men to seek God, write the letter about removing obstacles, that is the argument about the Machine, how to prepare it and how to use reason for the search. (11)

Whether the wager fragment was written before or after the "lettre" constituted by fragment 427 remains a thorny problem. But one thing is certain. Reading that dialogue in the light of the portraits of disbelief sketched in fragment 427 gives us a far better perspective on Pascal's celebrated interlocutor.

The Unbelievers in Fragment 427

The picture of disbelief presented in the wager fragment seems sketchy indeed when set up against the portraits of the unbelievers found in fragments 427 and 428. If fragment 418 is essentially a rough draft, fragments 427 and 428 are two of the most finished of the major "pensées." Jean

49. *Les Penseés de Pascal: De l'anthropologie à la théologie*, p. 35.

Mesnard calls fragment 427 "un des plus travaillés" ("one of the most carefully polished") of the major fragments and qualifies it as "incontestablement des plus beaux"[50] ("incontestably one of the most beautiful"). Both Lafuma and Gouhier regard the text of this fragment as very late, dating from 1661–62. Both think the fragment was composed as an introduction to the Apology as a whole.[51] Indeed, at the end of fragment 427 we read: "Qu'ils donnent à cette lecture quelques-unes de ces heures qu'ils emploient si inutilement ailleurs" ("Let them spend on reading about it a few of the hours they waste on other things"). Gouhier notes, "C'est donc bien un auteur qui s'adresse à des lecteurs"[52] ("Obviously this is an author addressing himself to his readers").

Jean Mesnard calls fragment 427 a kind of psychodrama: "un jeu se joue par lequel le 'libertin' doit être arraché à son indifférence malsaine et entrer dans la catégorie de 'ceux qui cherchent en gémissant' (405)"[53] ("a scenario is played out in which the *'libertin'* wrested from his unhealthy indifference and made to enter the category of 'those who seek with groans' [405]"). It is in this fragment that we find Pascal's clearest portraits of those to whom he will address his Apology.

Before embarking on a demonstration of "les preuves de la religion chrétienne," Pascal tells his readers in fragment 428, he wants first to focus on the "injustice" of those who are indifferent to the ultimate fate of their souls. As it did in the brief exchange with Mitton in fragment 597,[54] "injustice" once again has critical theological overtones. The very indifference

50. *Les Pensées de Pascal,* p. 340. It is a considerable loss that the original of fragments 427–428 is missing from the *Recueil original.* We possess only the preparatory notes for the writing of fragment 427, constituted by fragments 432 and 821 (see Chapter IV, Fragments 418 and 427: The State of the Texts). The *Copies* seem to transcribe a fairly straightforward text. The versions recorded by the First and Second *Copies* are very similar.

51. Louis Lafuma, *Histoire des Pensées de Pascal* (Paris: Editions de Luxembourg, 1954), p. 22. Henri Gouhier, *Blaise Pascal: Conversion et apologétique,* p. 103: "[le fragment 427] appartient, semble-t-il, à un projet d'introduction au livre présentant la nouvelle Apologie de la religion chrétienne" ("[fragment 427] belongs, it seems, to [Pascal's] draft of the introduction to the book presenting his new Apology for the Christian Religion").

52. *Blaise Pascal: Conversion et apologétique,* p. 103. Fragment 428 likewise seems destined to figure in such a preface or introduction: "Avant que d'entrer dans les preuves de la religion chrétienne . . . ("Before going into the proofs of the Christian religion . . . "). Anthony Pugh thinks fragment 428 "reads more like a preface to part two than a general preface." *Composition of Pascal's Apologia,* p. 585, n. 77. J. Chevalier makes 428 precede 427 in his edition of the *Pensées.* Lafuma, in his Delmas edition of 1948, places 428 after 427. It might be argued that the word *preuves* in the first sentence of fragment 428 refers to the word *preuves* in the last sentence of fragment 427.

53. *Les Pensées de Pascal,* pp. 312–13.

54. See Chapter I, *L'Honnête Homme.*

of the agnostics would seem to number them among those who have not been justified, that is, predestined to redemption. They risk a terrible consequence: "ils sont dans le péril de l'éternité de misères" ("they risk an eternity of wretchedness") (428). Their failure to examine whether the beliefs of ordinary (and sometimes ignorant) Christians have any merit is an indictment of their blindness in and of itself. Like those condemned in Isaiah 43:8, they look without seeing and listen without hearing:

> Ils . . . ont [les preuves] devant les yeux; ils refusent d'y regarder, et, dans cette ignorance, ils prennent le parti de faire tout ce qu'il faut pour tomber dans ce malheur au cas qu'il soit, d'attendre à en faire l'épreuve à la mort, d'être cependant forts satisfaits en cet état, d'en faire profession et enfin d'en faire vanité.
>
> The proofs lie before their eyes, but they refuse to look, and in this state of ignorance they choose to do everything necessary to fall into this calamity, if it exists, to wait for death before testing the proofs, while yet remaining highly satisfied in that state, professing it openly, and indeed with pride. (428)

The unbelievers described in fragment 428 are essentially skeptics who have deliberately chosen to live "dans cette ignorance de ce qu'ils sont et sans rechercher d'éclaircissement" ("without knowing what they are and without seeking enlightenment"). Their rule of life, borrowed from Montaigne, is "Je ne sais." Pascal cannot even contemplate the way in which they turn aside from the most serious of all matters without being filled with horror:

> Peut-on penser sérieusement à l'importance de cette affaire sans avoir horreur d'une conduite si extravagante?
>
> Ce repos dans cette ignorance est une chose monstrueuse, et dont il faut sentir l'extravagance et la stupidité à ceux qui y passent leur vie, en la leur représentant à eux-mêmes, pour les confondre par la vue de leur folie.
>
> Can we seriously think how important this matter is without being horrified at such extravagant behavior?
>
> To settle down in such ignorance is a monstrous thing, and those who spend their lives thus must be made to feel how extravagant and stupid it is by having it pointed out to them so that they are confounded by the sight of their own folly. (428)

Nothing, Pascal argues, is more obvious to common sense nor more strongly urged by "les sentiments de la nature" than the fact that death, whatever its consequences, puts a definitive end to this life. As Pascal restates the idea in fragment 427, one need be neither particularly bright nor particularly religious in order to see something so obvious:

Il ne faut pas avoir l'âme fort élevée pour comprendre qu'il n'y a point ici de satisfaction véritable et solide, que tous nos plaisirs ne sont que vanité, que nos maux sont infinis, et qu'enfin la mort, qui nous menace à chaque instant, doit infailliblement nous mettre, dans peu d'années, dans l'horrible nécessité d'être éternellement ou anéantis ou malheureux.

One needs no great sublimity of soul to realize that in this life there is no true and solid satisfaction, that all our pleasures are mere vanity, that our afflictions are infinite, and finally that death which threatens us at every moment must in a few years infallibly face us with the inescapable and appalling alternative of being annihilated or wretched throughout eternity. (427)

In the course of the Apology, Pascal will demonstrate how the curse of Original Sin and the consequent folly of *divertissement* do in fact blind many if not most people to this all too obvious truth. Disbelief, attacked here merely as unreasonable, will turn out to have supernatural origins. However, in his projected Preface, Pascal means to attract the curiosity of his potential readers by presenting the whole matter as a great enigma. How is it possible for people to behave so unreasonably? Do they really believe that they can annihilate death and eternity by turning their thoughts to things terrestrial? Such a fantasy, Pascal observes, only serves to put them in grave danger. Reality is otherwise:

Cependant, cette éternité subsiste, et la mort, qui la doit ouvrir et qui les menace à toute heure, les doit mettre infailliblement dans peu de temps dans l'horrible nécessité d'être éternellement ou anéantis ou malheureux, sans qu'ils sachent laquelle de ces éternités leur est à jamais préparée.[55]

However, eternity exists, and death, which must begin it and which threatens at every moment, must infallibly face them with the inescapable and appalling alternative of being either eternally annihilated or wretched, without their knowing which of these two forms of eternity stands ready to meet them forever. (428)

Pascal seems to have a somewhat ambivalent attitude toward the unbelievers described in fragment 428. On the one hand, he seems to think that their behavior and attitude condemn them to the category of the *réprouvés*. On the other hand, he expresses some hope that they can be made to feel

55. Compare this passage to the passage just cited from fragment 427: Fragment 428: "et *la mort,* qui la doit ouvrir et *qui* les *menace* à toute heure, les *doit mettre infailliblement dans peu* de temps *dans l'horrible nécessité d'être éternellement ou anéantis ou malheureux,* sans qu'ils sachent . . ." (italics mine). Fragment 427: "et qu'enfin *la mort, qui* nous *menace* à chaque instant, *doit infailliblement* nous *mettre, dans peu* d'années, *dans l'horrible nécessité d'être éternellement ou anéantis ou malheureux*" (italics mine).

("sentir") the stupidity of their position by confronting them ("en la leur représentant à eux-mêmes") with "la vue de leur folie" ("the sight of their folly"). In attempting to shake these unbelievers out of their passive skepticism, Pascal intends to invoke both common sense and natural instincts ("les premières vues du sens commun et . . . les sentiments de la nature").

Fragment 427 reveals a far more complicated scenario. At first, Pascal seems to be addressing his arguments even to the most hardened skeptics and adversaries of Christianity. However, as the fragment progresses, it appears that the apologist harbors but slight hope for their conversion. Fragment 427 is not really a dialogue with disbelief on the order of the "infini/rien" fragment. Rather, it is a series of *tableaux* presented for the benefit of potential converts who themselves are not yet all that advanced in the ways of disbelief. The real purpose of Pascal's portraits of hardened disbelief in his projected Preface to the Apology is to serve as a negative example for those pseudoskeptics only superficially infected with disbelief.

Fragment 427 commences with a broadside attack on those who actively attack Christian belief. "Qu'ils apprennent au moins quelle est la religion qu'ils combattent avant que de la combattre" ("Let them at least learn what this religion is which they are attacking before attacking it"). Pascal sets out to neutralize the influence of the active opponents of Christianity by immediately turning the tables on them. They know nothing, he asserts, about true Christianity. They erroneously suppose that Christianity teaches that God has openly revealed Himself. When they find no evidence of God's intervention in the world or in human life, they conclude that the Christian God is a fable. Such a conclusion, Pascal asserts, shows that these opponents of Christianity are completely ignorant of what this religion really teaches about God. Far from asserting that it is possible to know God directly, Pascal insists, Christianity teaches that He has hidden Himself from human knowledge. "C'est même le nom qu'il se donne dans les Ecritures, *Deus absconditus*" ("This is the very name he gives himself in Scripture: *Deus absconditus*").[56]

Christianity does teach, Pascal explains, that God has established "des marques sensibles" ("visible signs") in Holy Revelation for the benefit of those who seek him. However, these signs have been veiled so that only those who seek God with all their hearts will find him:

> [Cette religion] travaille également à établir ces deux choses: que Dieu a établi des marques sensibles dans l'Eglise pour se faire reconnaître à ceux qui le cherche-

56. "The hidden God": Isaiah 45:15.

raient sincèrement; et qu'il les a couvertes néanmoins de telle sorte qu'il ne sera aperçu que de ceux qui le cherchent de tout leur coeur.

[This religion] strives equally to establish these two facts: that God has appointed visible signs in the Church so that he shall be recognized by those who genuinely seek him, and that he has nonetheless hidden them in such a way that he will only be perceived by those who seek him with all their heart. (427)

In the very first paragraph of his projected Preface, Pascal seeks to silence the aggressive enemies of Christianity by arguing that this religion teaches precisely what they themselves have deduced: God's apparent absence from the world. The darkness in which the skeptics and agnostics find themselves serves only to confirm the great Augustinian doctrine of *Deus absconditus*. Explicit in Pascal's opening broadside attack on disbelief is another great Augustinian doctrine, that of Predestination and Election. All human beings are not destined to find God. As fragment 232 will state the matter in the dossier "Fondements":

On n'entend rien aux ouvrages de Dieu si on ne prend pour principe qu'il a voulu aveugler les uns et éclaircir les autres.

We can understand nothing of God's works unless we accept the principle that he wished to blind some and enlighten others. (232)

Fragment 449 sheds a great deal of light on the theology implicit in the opening of Pascal's projected Preface and on the identity of Pascal's adversaries. Like fragments 427–31, this fragment is missing from the *Recueil original*. Commentators like Roger Lacombe[57] and Patricia Topliss[58] have thought that fragment 449 would have been joined to fragments 427–31 as part of Pascal's general Preface to the Apology. Anthony Pugh, on the other hand, sees fragment 449 as the key to the dossier "Excellence."[59] Philippe Sellier thinks that fragments 438–50 represent a single "Discours de la Corruption," which he prints as his fragments 688–90.[60]

Fragment 449 begins with a sentence which recalls the opening of fragment 427: "Ils blasphèment ce qu'ils ignorent"[61] ("They blaspheme

57. *L'Apologétique de Pascal: Etude critique* (Paris: PUF, 1958), p. 35.

58. *The Rhetoric of Pascal* (Leicester: Leicester University Press, 1966), p. 178.

59. *The Composition of Pascal's Apology*, p. 175.

60. *Pensées* [1991], p. 486, n. 1. The entire dossier (*série v*) constituted by these fragments is missing from the *Recueil original*.

61. Cf. fragment 427: "Qu'ils apprennent au moins quelle est la religion qu'ils combattent avant que de la combattre" ("Let them at least learn what this religion is which they are attacking before attacking it").

against that which they are ignorant of"). Just who are these enemies of Christianity and why, according to Pascal, are they ignorant of its true teachings? It is obvious that these aggressive detractors of Christianity constitute a special class of unbelievers. Pascal's relatively docile interlocutor in the "infini/rien" fragment hardly belongs to this category. Nor do "ceux qui cherchent en gémissant" ("those who seek with groans") (405). Rather, these aggressive unbelievers are the professional *libertins*, the "athées endurcis" ("hardened atheists") (449), whose objections to Christianity we examined in Chapter I.

In Pascal's definition of these unbelievers as "blasphemers," Henri Gouhier senses a reference to Jude 10:10: "These people abuse anything they do not understand; and the only things they do understand—just by nature like unreasoning animals—will turn out to be fatal to them.[62] In effect, Pascal explains that those who blaspheme Christianity attack this religion from the perspective of the false light of nature. Via natural reason, they conclude that if there is a true religion, it should teach God's manifest presence in the world.[63] They erroneously suppose that Christianity consists only of the worship of "un Dieu considéré comme grand et puissant et éternel" ("a God considered to be great and mighty and eternal"). However, they could not be more mistaken. Their natural reason has turned out to be fatal for them.

What these critics think is Christianity, Pascal insists, is only Deism, a system of belief "presque aussi éloigné de la religion chrétienne que l'athéisme" ("almost as remote from the Christian religion as atheism"). Refuting Deism, Pascal observes, is a completely separate matter from disproving Christianity:

> Ils concluent que cette religion n'est pas véritable, parce qu'ils ne voient pas que toutes choses concourent à l'établissement de ce point, que Dieu ne se manifeste pas aux hommes avec toute l'évidence qu'il pourrait faire.

62. *Blaise Pascal: Conversion et apologétique,* p. 127. Translation cited from *The Jerusalem Bible* (New York: Doubleday, 1966), pp. 422–423. See also Jude 10:18–19: "But remember, my dear friends, what the apostles of our Lord Jesus Christ told you to expect. 'At the end of time,' they told you 'there are going to be people who sneer at religion and follow nothing but their own desires for wickedness.' "

63. Compare the beginning of fragment 427: "Si cette religion se vantait d'avoir une vue claire de Dieu, et de le posséder à découvert et sans voile, ce serait la combattre que de dire qu'on ne voit rien dans le monde avec cette évidence" ("If this religion boasted that it had a clear sight of God and plain and manifest evidence of his existence, it would be an effective objection to say that there is nothing to be seen in the world which proves him so obviously").

Mais qu'ils en concluent ce qu'ils voudront contre le déisme, ils n'en concluront rien contre la religion chrétienne, qui consiste proprement au mystère du Rédempteur, qui unissant en lui les deux natures, humaine et divine, a retiré les hommes de la corruption du péché pour les réconcilier à Dieu en sa personne divine.

They conclude that this religion is not true, because they cannot see that all things combine to establish the point that God does not manifest himself to men as obviously as he might.

But let them conclude what they like against Deism, their conclusions will not apply to Christianity, which properly consists in the mystery of the Redeemer, who, uniting in himself the two natures, human and divine, saved men from the corruption of sin in order to reconcile them with God in his divine person. (449)

Deism, Pascal insists, is easy enough to refute. One only need demonstrate that God is not manifestly present in the world. But such a demonstration has no implications whatsoever for Christianity, which teaches the opposite doctrine. Moreover, if one examines "l'ordre du monde" ("the order of the world"), one finds neither "une exclusion totale" ("the total absence") nor "une présence manifeste" ("the manifest presence") of Divinity. Rather, an examination of what can be seen on earth reveals, for those who have the eyes to see it, the presence of a hidden God ("la présence d'un Dieu qui se cache"). In other words, whereas nature reveals no clear-cut evidence of God's existence, it does point to the reality of human corruption. This, in turn, points to the theological doctrine of the Fall.

It is via this route that the Apology will attempt to lead those who sincerely seek him to a knowledge of God. Pascal insists that he will not even attempt to invoke natural reason in proofs of God's existence, of the nature of the Trinity, or even of the immortality of the soul.[64] In the first

64. In the matter of proofs of the existence of God, one might have expected Pascal to follow the example of St. Augustine, who gathered the speculations of the Fathers into a powerful synthesis. In various works, Augustine gives a whole series of proofs for the existence of God: from the contingency of the created world in utter contrast with the necessary being of God, from the order and beauty of the world, from the eternal principle of human reason and the moral argument from conscience. In Augustine's works, however, these proofs were not yet elaborated with the systematic methods of the Middle Ages.

Under the influence of the newly discovered Aristotle, St. Thomas Aquinas rejected the a priori Ontological Argument first elaborated by St. Anselm and later defended by Descartes. The Ontological Argument is as follows: since by the very notion of God we mean "that than which nothing greater can be conceived," we would be involved in contradiction if we supposed that God did not exist since we could at once conceive of a greater entity than a nonexisting God, namely a God who existed.

In his famous fivefold proof for the existence of God (*Quinque viae*), Aquinas sought to prove the existence of God a posteriori, from those effects of His being which are known to us: (1) that motion implies a First Mover; (2) that a sequence of efficient causes, and their

place, Pascal explains, he is not "assez fort pour trouver dans la nature de quoi convaincre des athées endurcis" ("competent to find in nature arguments which would convince hardened atheists"). Moreover, such proofs, in the absence of faith, might prove even more fatal to hardened unbelievers:

> Cette connaissance, sans Jésus-Christ, est inutile et stérile. Quand un homme serait persuadé que les proportions des nombres sont des vérités immatérielles, éternelles et dépendantes d'une première vérité en qui elles subsistent, et qu'on appelle Dieu, je ne le trouverais pas beaucoup avancé pour son salut.
>
> Such knowledge, without Christ, is useless and sterile. Even if someone were convinced that the proportions between numbers were immaterial, eternal truths, depending on a first truth in which they subsist, called God, I should not consider that he had made much progress toward his salvation. (449)

These lines provide a key perspective on the celebrated "infini/rien" fragment. Pascal admits that geometrical reasoning has a strictly circumscribed value within the field of Christian apologetics. Indeed, from a strictly theological perspective, the unbeliever at the end of the wager fragment has not significantly advanced in the direction of his salvation. Is Pascal thinking of the wager text? The question is difficult to answer, since we have no way of dating fragment 449, which is missing from the *Recueil original*. In this fragment, Pascal is enunciating nothing less than what he views as the Christian doctrine of God. As he sees it, the Christian God is not simply the author of geometric truths and of the order of the elements. That would be the God of the pagans and the Epicureans. Nor is He only the God who exercises his Providence over human affairs and grants favors to those who worship him: "C'est la portion des Juifs" ("That is the portion of the Jews"). Only Christianity, and here the text of the *Memorial* breaks through into fragment 449, reveals God in all his truth:

---

effects, such as we find in the world, implies an uncaused First Cause; (3) that the existence of things which logically might not exist implies some necessary being (the Cosmological Argument); (4) that the comparisons we make imply a standard of comparison which is in itself perfect; (5) that the fulfillment by inanimate or unintelligent objects of an end to which they are evidently designed to work implies a purposive intelligence in their creation and direction (the Physico-Theological Argument).

Though Aquinas' rejection of the Ontological Argument was not followed by the theologians of the Franciscan schools (Bonaventure and Duns Scotus), his proofs of God's existence eventually became the officially accepted basis of the teaching of Tridentine Catholic theology. See F. L. Cross, ed., *The Oxford Dictionary of the Christian Church* (Oxford: Oxford University Press, 1984), art. "God," p. 576.

Mais le Dieu d'Abraham, le Dieu d'Isaac, le Dieu de Jacob, le Dieu des chrétiens, est un Dieu d'amour et de consolation; c'est un Dieu qui remplit l'âme et le coeur de ceux qu'il possède; c'est un Dieu qui leur fait sentir intérieurement leur misère, et sa miséricorde infini; qui s'unit au fond de leur âme; qui la remplit d'humilité, de joie, de confiance, d'amour; qui les rend incapables d'autre fin que de lui-même.

But the God of Abraham, the God of Isaac, the God of Jacob, the God of the Christians is a God of love and consolation: he is a God who fills the soul and heart of those whom he possesses: he is a God who makes them inwardly aware of their wretchedness and his infinite mercy: who unites himself with them in the depths of their soul: who fills it with humility, joy, confidence and love: who makes them incapable of having any other end but him. (449)

Pascal's Doctrine of God completely rules out the possibility of any kind of partial revelation. As we noted in Chapter III, Le Vayer's *De la vertu des payens*, and Pascal and the Jesuit mission to China, Pascal's hostility to the notion of the salvation of the *anciens justes* and to the Jesuit mission to China was a direct corollary of his Christocentric understanding of Revelation. Like the non-Christian religions, any search for God outside the person of Christ is a dead end, ultimately leading either to Deism or to atheism:

Tous ceux qui cherchent Dieu hors de Jésus-Christ, et qui s'arrêtent dans la nature, ou ils ne trouvent aucune lumière qui les satisfasse, ou ils arrivent à se former un moyen de connaître Dieu et de le servir sans médiateur, et par là ils tombent ou dans l'athéisme ou dans le déisme, qui sont deux choses que la religion chrétienne abhorre presque également.

All those who seek God apart from Christ, and who go no further than nature, either find no light to satisfy them or come to devise a means of knowing and serving God without a mediator, thus falling either into atheism or deism, two things almost equally abhorrent to Christianity. (449)

Taken by itself, Pascal's doctrine of the hidden God, knowable only by implication (i.e., via the evidence of human corruption), seems almost an unorthodox departure from classical Christian theology. As Henri Gouhier reminds us, Pascal dismisses not only the Thomist proofs which lead to God via physical phenomena but also Saint Augustine's demonstration which concludes the existence of the Eternal Word from preexisting truths in the human soul.[65] However, in fragment 449 Pascal balances the

65. *Blaise Pascal: Conversion et apologétique,* pp. 140 and 234, n. 39.

doctrine of *Deus absconditus* with a Christology which sets the Incarnation at the heart of meaning itself:

Jésus-Christ est l'objet de tout, et le centre où tout tend. Qui le connaît connaît la raison de toutes choses. . . .

Sans Jésus-Christ, le monde ne subsisterait pas; car il faudrait, ou qu'il fût détruit, ou qu'il fût comme un enfer.

Si le monde subsistait pour instruire l'homme de Dieu, sa divinité y reluirait de toutes parts d'une manière incontestable; mais comme il ne subsiste que par Jésus-Christ, et pour Jésus-Christ et pour instruire les hommes de leur corruption et de leur rédemption, tout y éclate des preuves de ces deux vérités.

Jesus-Christ is the object of all things, the center towards which all things tend. Whoever knows him knows the reason for everything. . . .

But for Christ the world would not go on existing, for it would either have to be destroyed or be a kind of hell.

If the world existed in order to teach man about God, his divinity would shine out on every hand in an incontestable manner: but as it only exists through Christ, for Christ, and to teach men about their corruption and redemption, everything in it blazes with proofs of these two truths. (449)

In the entire Catholic tradition, observes Philippe Sellier, "il y a peu de mystiques de Christ aussi étonnants que Pascal"[66] ("there are few Christocentric mystics as singular as Pascal"). When he sets Christ at the heart of meaning itself, calling him "le centre où tout tend" ("the center toward which all things tend"), Pascal invokes a vision which transcends both doctrine and apologetics. The world exists for and through Christ. Even the Fall, when viewed from this mystical Christocentric perspective, turns out to be the most fortunate of events. As the *felix culpa* verse from the liturgy of Holy Saturday puts it: "O bienheureuse faute qui a été réparée par un remède et par un Sauveur si grand et si divin" ("O blessed iniquity, for whose redemption such a price was paid by such a Savior").[67]

Fragment 449 begins with an attack on the unbelievers: "ils blasphèment ce qu'ils ignorent. . . ." But toward the end of the fragment, we see a modulation to the third person singular:

Il ne faut pas qu'*il* ne voie rien du tout; il ne faut pas aussi qu'*il* en voie assez pour croire qu'*il* le possède, mais qu'*il* en voie assez pour connaître qu'*il* l'a perdu;

66. *Meaning, Structure and History in the "Pensées" of Pascal* (Tübingen: Biblio 17, 1990), p. 104.

67. French translation by Le Maistre de Sacy, *Lettres chrestiennes et spirituelles* (Paris: Desprez, 1690), 2, p. 307.

car, pour connaître qu'on a perdu, il faut voir et ne voir pas; et c'est précisément l'état où est la nature.

Quelque parti qu'*il* prenne, je ne *l*'y laisserai point en repos. . . .

He must not see nothing at all, nor must *he* see enough to think that *he* possesses God, but *he* must see enough to know that *he* has lost him. For, to know that one has lost something one must see and not see: such precisely is the state of nature.

Whatever course *he* adopts I will not leave *him* in peace. . . . (449, italics mine)

The apologetic strategy sketched in these final lines of fragment 449 will be that of the Apology as a whole. Nature, and more precisely human nature, will be shown to proclaim everywhere a lost God. But just who is it who will be made to understand this? Of whom is Pascal speaking when he says, "Quelque parti qu'*il* prenne, je ne *l*'y laisserai point en repos" ("Whatever course *he* adopts I will not leave *him* in peace")? Obviously this potential convert to Christianity is not a hardened atheist. He must be disabused of certain ideas which he has picked up from the aggressive enemies of Christianity. He must learn that Christianity is nothing like Deism. But his heart has not yet been so hardened by active disbelief that he cannot be made to see that the whole world proclaims a lost God. Before returning to the picture of disbelief sketched by fragment 427, we might do well to recall the "Avis" attached to the "infini/rien" fragment by the editors of the Edition de Port-Royal. This description of Pascal's interlocutor is equally pertinent to the picture of the *chercheur* which emerges in the course of fragment 427:

Presque tout ce qui est contenu dans ce chapitre ne regarde que certaines sortes de personnes, qui n'étant pas convaincues des preuves de la Religion, et encore moins des raisons des athées, demeurent dans un état de suspension entre la foi et l'infidélité.[68]

Almost everything contained in this chapter pertains only to certain kinds of persons, who not being convinced by the proofs of religion and even less by the reasoning of the atheists, remain in a state of suspension between faith and disbelief.

In fragment 427, Pascal tries to present the most negative possible picture of those who are actively hostile to Christianity. Not only are they portrayed as ignorant of what Christianity really teaches about God. Pascal pictures them as imagining that they have made a great effort to find out whether Christianity is true when they have done nothing more than

68. *Pensées de Pascal . . . Edition de Port-Royal,* A. Gazier, ed., p. 137.

spend a few hours reading "quelque livre de l'Ecriture" ("some book of the Bible") or questioning "quelque ecclésiastique" ("some clergyman") concerning the Christian articles of faith. Their lack of genuine passion for the truth, conveyed by Pascal's repetition of the word *quelque,* appears to the apologist to be completely intolerable ("insupportable"). They seem to think that the whole question of man's ultimate fate is some purely academic or esoteric matter. They seem blind to the fact that finding out the truth concerning the nature of the soul is a matter of eternal life or eternal death. "Il s'agit de nous-mêmes, et de notre tout" ("It is a question of ourselves and our all"). Only upon resolving this most essential of all questions can one make a truly reasonable decision concerning how one should live this life:

> L'immortalité de l'âme est une chose qui nous importe si fort, nous touche si profondément, qu'il faut avoir perdu tout sentiment pour être dans l'indifférence de savoir ce qui en est. Toutes nos actions et nos pensées doivent prendre des routes si différentes, selon qu'il y aura des biens éternels à espérer ou non, qu'il est impossible de faire une démarche avec sens et jugement, qu'en les réglant par la vue de ce point, qui doit être notre dernier objet.
>
> Ainsi notre premier intérêt et notre premier devoir est de nous éclairer sur ce sujet, d'où dépend toute notre conduite.

> The immortality of the soul is something of such vital importance to us, affecting us so deeply, that one must have lost all feeling not to care about knowing the facts of the matter. All our actions and thoughts must follow such different paths, according to whether there is hope of eternal blessings or not, that the only possible way of acting with sense and judgment is to decide our course in the light of this point, which ought to be our ultimate objective.
>
> Thus our chief interest and chief duty are to seek enlightenment on this subject, on which all our conduct depends. (427)

At this point, Pascal professes to make a critical distinction ("une extrême différence") between two classes of unbelievers: (1) "ceux qui travaillent de toutes leurs forces à s'en instruire" ("those who strive with all their might to learn the truth [concerning the true nature of the soul]") and (2) "ceux qui vivent sans s'en mettre en peine et sans y penser" ("those who live without troubling themselves or thinking about it"). For those who seriously lament their doubt ("ceux qui gémissent sincèrement dans ce doute"), Pascal professes only compassion. However, the negligence and indifference of the second category of disbelievers irritate rather than touch him. His horror in the face of such indifference, Pascal insists, has nothing to do with his own religious perspective. What so shocks him, he claims, is the way in which such indifference contravenes the most essential principles of self-preservation and "amour-propre":

> Je ne puis avoir que de la compassion pour ceux qui gémissent sincèrement dans ce doute, qui le regardent comme le dernier des malheurs, et qui, n'épargnant rien pour en sortir, font de cette recherche leurs principales et leurs plus sérieuses occupations.
>
> Mais pour ceux qui passent leur vie sans penser à cette dernière fin de la vie, et qui, par cette seule raison qu'ils ne trouvent pas en eux-mêmes les lumières qui les en persuadent, négligent de les chercher ailleurs, et d'examiner à fond si cette opinion est de celles que le peuple reçoit par une simplicité crédule, ou de celles qui, quoique obscures d'elles-mêmes, ont néanmoins un fondement très solide et inébranlable, je les considère d'une manière toute différente.
>
> Cette négligence en une affaire où il s'agit d'eux-mêmes, de leur éternité, de leur tout, m'irrite plus qu'elle ne m'attendrit; elle m'étonne et m'épouvante: c'est un monstre pour moi. Je ne dis pas ceci par le zèle pieux d'une dévotion spirituelle. J'entends au contraire qu'on doit avoir ce sentiment par un principe d'intérêt humain et par un intérêt d'amour-propre: il ne faut pour cela que voir ce que voient les personnes les moins éclairées.
>
> I can feel nothing but compassion for those who sincerely lament their doubt, who regard it as the ultimate misfortune, and who, sparing no effort to escape from it, make their search their principal and most serious business.
>
> But as for those who spend their lives without a thought for this final end of life and who, solely because they do not find within themselves the light of conviction, neglect to look elsewhere, and to examine thoroughly whether this opinion is one of those which people accept out of credulous simplicity or one of those which, though obscure in themselves, nonetheless have a most solid and unshakable foundation; as for them, I view them differently.
>
> This negligence in a matter where they themselves, their eternity, their all are at stake, fills me more with irritation than pity; it astounds and appalls me; it seems quite monstrous to me. I do not say this prompted by the pious zeal of spiritual devotion. I mean on the contrary that we ought to have this feeling from principles of human interest and self-esteem. For that we need only see what the least enlightened see. (427)

Pascal's expression of compassion for "ceux qui gémissent sincèrement dans ce doute" ("those who sincerely lament their doubt") serves a key function in terms of the overall apologetic strategy of fragment 427. The *chercheurs*, who at least indirectly manifest their will to believe, provide a powerful foil for the folly of the second category of unbelievers. Indeed, most of fragment 427 is oriented toward documenting the insanity of those agnostics whose indifference puts them in such great peril. Pascal's potential interlocutor in the Apology which is to follow this projected Preface will over and over be invited to identify himself with those who at least desire to seek the truth. This identification will be negatively reinforced by Pascal's exposition of the dangers inherent in indifference and active disbelief.

Those unbelievers in the grip of indifference, Pascal observes, profess only one excuse to justify their position. They claim they can find no light within themselves which might persuade them that the soul is immortal. Therein, Pascal thinks, lies their capital error. Seduced by the philosophers into thinking that truth is only to be found within (cf. fragment 143),[69] they fail or refuse to look for light or guidance *outside* themselves. "[Ils] négligent de . . . chercher [les lumières] *ailleurs*" (427, italics mine). They reject the possibility of the immortality of the soul out of hand as the wishful thinking of the credulous masses. They never even entertain the possibility that there might be some truth to such a venerable and widespread belief. They never pause to wonder whether this idea might be one of those truths which are not immediately obvious.

Pascal qualifies the doctrine of the immortality of the soul as one of those *opinions* which though obscure are nevertheless grounded in "un fondement très solide et inébranlable" ("a most solid and unshakable truth").[70] Does Pascal mean to evoke the difference between ordinary perception and scientific truth? Does he mean to suggest that the immortality of the soul, like the existence of a vacuum in nature or the fact that the world is round, is empirically demonstrable even though not obvious to the senses? Or, like the doctrine of the Eucharist, is the doctrine of the immortality of the soul demonstrable only in terms of faith and belief? Is it one of those transcendent truths which stands in the definition of fragment 185, "above" the senses rather than in opposition to them?:

> La foi dit bien ce que les sens ne disent pas, mais non pas le contraire de ce qu'ils voient; elle est *au-dessus*, et non pas contre.

> Faith certainly tells us what reason does not, but not the contrary of what they see; it is *above*, not against them. (185, italics mine)

In what is perhaps a pitch to the mentality of the *honnête homme*, Pascal insists that his horror in the face of the indifference of the agnostics does not issue from "le zèle pieux d'une devotion spirituelle" ("the pious zeal

69. See Chapter V, Pascal's *Chercheur*.

70. "Si cette opinion . . . que le peuple reçoit" perhaps anticipates the arguments which would have been filed in the chapter envisaged by the *liasse-table* of 1658: "Opinions du peuple saines." This chapter was never created. The title itself is struck out in the *liasse-table*. "Un fondement très solide et inébranlable" perhaps anticipates the chapter "Fondements."

of spiritual devotion"). Rather, he claims to be shocked by their failure to display the normal reaction to danger dictated by the principles of self-interest and *amour-propre*. Even the least enlightened of human beings, Pascal maintains, ought to be able to see that the question of whether or not it is possible to survive physical death is the most critical question confronting anyone. This question, Pascal insists, bears directly on how one decides to organize his or her life in this world. If the soul is material and mortal, the path counseled by the Epicureans might make perfect sense. If the soul is immortal and the Christian vision of the last things is true, however, self-denial, disciplining the passions, and "une vie toute crucifiée"[71] make even more sense:

> Toutes nos actions et nos pensées doivent prendre des routes si différentes, selon qu'il y aura des biens éternels à espérer ou non, qu'il est impossible de faire une démarche avec sens et jugement, qu'en les réglant par la vue de ce point, qui doit être notre dernier objet.

> All our actions and thoughts must follow such different paths, according to whether there is hope of eternal blessings or not, that the only possible way of acting with sense and judgment is to decide our course in the light of this point, which ought to be our ultimate objective. (427)

The reader of the *Pensées* will easily detect in Pascal's projected Preface the apologist's constant hints that man's seeming indifference to his ultimate fate has supernatural origins. It is the result of the debasement of his reason in the Fall. However, a general preface to an apology for Christianity is hardly the place to enter immediately into such a theological argument. The *honnête homme* would probably close the Apology before ever reaching the first chapter. In chapters such as "Vanité" (II), "Misère" (III), "Ennui" (IV), and "Divertissement" (VIII), the apologist will amply document the human obsession with avoiding thinking about death. In the chapter "A.P.R." (XI), he will begin to reveal the Fall as the true reason for such apparently inexplicable behavior. However, in the Preface adumbrated by fragment 427, Pascal's principal aim is to pique his readers' curiosity by presenting the indifference of the agnostics as a complete enigma.

Pascal injects into this enigma what might be qualified as a profoundly "tragic" vision of life on this earth. One needs no great sublimity of soul,

71. "Comparaison des chrétiens des premiers temps avec ceux d'aujourd'hui," in Lafuma, *Oeuvres complètes*, p. 362.

he asserts, to reach the conclusion that "il n'y a point ici de satisfaction véritable et solide" ("in this life there is no true and solid satisfaction"). Our earthly pleasures are fleeting if not completely illusory. Our sufferings, both physical and mental, are innumerable. And death, whose jaws yawn open at every moment, will eventually and inexorably put an end to life as we know it now: "Il n'y a rien de plus réel que cela, ni de plus terrible" ("Nothing could be more real, or more dreadful, than that"). The misguided stoicism affected by the indifferent is totally impotent in the face of the reality of such a tragic vision:

> Faisons tant que nous voudrons les braves: voilà la fin qui attend la plus belle vie du monde. Qu'on fasse réflexion là-dessus, et qu'on dise ensuite s'il n'est pas indubitable qu'il n'y a de bien en cette vie qu'en l'espérance d'une autre vie, qu'on n'est heureux qu'à mesure qu'on s'en approche, et que, comme il n'y aura plus de malheurs pour ceux qui avaient une entière assurance de l'éternité, il n'y a point aussi de bonheur pour ceux qui n'en ont aucune lumière.

> Let us put on as bold a face as we like: that is the end awaiting the world's most illustrious life. Let us ponder these things, and then say whether it is not beyond doubt that the only good thing in this life is the hope of another life, that we become happy only as we come nearer to it, and that, just as no more unhappiness awaits those who have been quite certain of eternity, so there is no happiness for those who have no inkling of it. (427)

However successfully the "braves"[72] think they have mastered the Stoic ideal of indifference, they too must face the inevitable horror of the void. As Pascal sees it, human life necessarily takes on tragic dimensions when divorced from the Christian promise of a life to come. Death, the final common denominator, reduces "la plus belle vie du monde" ("the world's most illustrious life") to the value of the most miserable existence ever endured. In one of the earlier of the *Essais*, "Qu'il ne faut juger de notre heur qu'après la mort" ("That our happiness must not be judged until after our death"), Montaigne had argued that how one confronts death is the ultimate measure of the serenity which one has achieved in life:

> Ce même bonheur de notre vie, qui dépend de la tranquillité et contentement d'un esprit bien né, et de la résolution et assurance d'une âme réglée, ne se [doit] attribuer à l'homme, qu'on ne lui ait vu jouer le dernier acte de sa comédie, et sans

72. Cf., Montaigne, *Essais* in *Oeuvres complètes* (Paris: Seuil, 1967), 2, 18, p. 276: "Que peut-on imaginer plus vilain que d'être couard à l'endroit des hommes et *brave* à l'endroit de Dieu?" ("For what can you imagine uglier than being a coward toward men and *bold* toward God?") (italics mine).

doute le plus difficile. En tout le reste il y peut avoir du masque: ou ces beaux discours de la philosophie ne sont en nous que par contenance; ou les accidents ne nous essayant pas jusques au vif, nous donnent loisir de maintenir toujours notre visage rassis. Mais à ce dernier rôle de la mort et de nous, il n'y a plus que feindre, il faut parler français, il faut montrer ce qu'il y a de bon et de net dans le fond du pot . . . Voilà pourquoi se doivent à ce dernier trait toucher et éprouver toutes les autres actions de notre vie. C'est le maître jour, c'est le jour, dit un ancien, qui doit juger de toutes mes années passées. Je remets à la mort l'essai du fruit de mes études. Nous verrons là si mes discours me partent de la bouche, ou du coeur.[73]

This same happiness of our life, which depends on the tranquillity and contentment of a well-born spirit and the resolution and assurance of a well-ordered soul, should never be attributed to a man until he has been seen to play the last act of his comedy, and beyond doubt the hardest. In everything else there may be sham: the fine reasonings of philosophy may be a mere pose in us; or else our trials, by not testing us to the quick, give us a chance to keep our face always composed. But in the last scene, between death and ourselves, there is no more pretending; we must talk plain French, we must show what there is that is good and clean at the bottom of the pot. . . . That is why all the other actions of our life must be tried and tested by this last act. It is the master day, the day that is judge of all the others. "It is the day," says one of the ancients [Seneca], "that must judge all my past years." I leave it to death to test the fruit of my studies. We shall see then whether my reasonings come from my mouth of from my heart.[74]

In fragment 165, Pascal takes up Montaigne's metaphor but gives it a new twist:

Le dernier acte est sanglant, quelque belle que soit la comédie en tout le reste. On jette enfin de la terre sur la tête, et en voilà pour jamais.

The last act is bloody, however fine the rest of the play. They throw earth over your head and it is finished forever. (165)

In Pascal's version, the comedy of life always turns out to be tragedy. The last act is always bloody. Even those who face death serenely end up two feet under.

In fragment 427, Pascal does not yet attempt to argue that the Christian vision of the last things is true. Rather, he simply notes the observable phenomenon that "une entière assurance d'une autre vie" ("a sure confidence in the life to come") renders the sufferings of this life—including

73. *Montaigne: Oeuvres complètes,* 1:19, p. 47.

74. Donald M. Frame, tr., *The Complete Essays of Montaigne* (Stanford: Stanford University Press, 1965), p. 55.

the inevitable approach of death—more bearable for those who believe. Life and death are all that much more unbearable for those who have no inkling of any such assurance. It would not be unfair to say that most modern thinkers have come to agree with Pascal's adversaries that the hope of a life to come is but an opiate of the masses. The Swiss psychiatrist C. G. Jung, however, agrees with Pascal that such a hope is a salutary medicine for the suffering soul:

> Critical rationalism has apparently eliminated, along with so many other mythic conceptions, the idea of life after death. . . . Leaving aside the rational arguments in these matters, we must not forget that for most people it means a great deal to assume that their lives will have an indefinite continuity beyond their present existence. They live more sensibly, feel better, and are more at peace. . . . Such reasoning does not apply to everyone. There are people who feel no craving for immortality. . . . There are also quite a few who have been so buffeted by life . . . that they prefer absolute cessation. But in the majority of cases the question of immortality is so urgent, so immediate, and also so ineradicable that we must make an effort to form some sort of view about it. . . .
>
> A man should be able to say he has done his best to form a conception of life after death . . . even if he must confess his failure. Not to have done so is a vital loss. For the question that is posed to him is the age-old heritage of humanity: an archetype, rich in secret life, which seeks to add itself to our individual life in order to make it whole.[75]

The Pascalian equivalent, so to speak, of the Jungian archetype of immortality is that "marque et . . . trace toute vide" ("empty print and trace") (148) which the Fall has left in the human heart. According to Pascal, men long for immortality because somewhere in the depths of their hearts they retain "quelque instinct impuissant du bonheur de leur première nature" ("some feeble instinct from the happiness of their first nature") (149). Human experience, Pascal explains in fragment 117, demonstrates that men legitimately yearn only for what was once rightfully theirs:

> Qui se trouve malheureux de n'être pas roi sinon un roi dépossédé? Trouvait-on Paul Emile malheureux de n'être pas consul? au contraire tout le monde trouvait qu'il était heureux de l'avoir été, parce que sa condition n'était pas de l'être toujours. Mais on trouvait Persée si malheureux de n'être plus roi, parce que sa condition était de l'être toujours qu'on trouvait étrange de ce qu'il supportait la vie. Qui se trouve malheureux de n'avoir qu'une bouche et qui ne se trouverait

75. C. G. Jung, *Memories, Dreams, Reflections* (New York: Random House, 1965), pp. 300–302.

> malheureux de n'avoir qu'un oeil? On ne s'est peut-être jamais avisé de s'affliger de n'avoir pas trois yeux, mais on est inconsolable de n'en point avoir.

> Who indeed would think himself unhappy not to be king except one who had been dispossessed? Did anyone think Paulus Emilius was unhappy not to be consul? On the contrary, everyone thought he was happy to have been so once, because the office was not meant to be permanent. But people thought Perseus so unhappy at finding himself no longer king, because that was meant to be a permanent office, that they were surprised that he could bear to go on living. Who would think himself unhappy if he only had one mouth and who would not if he only had one eye? It has probably never occurred to anyone to be distressed at not having three eyes, but those who have none are inconsolable. (117)

Immortality is that "Souverain Bien" ("Sovereign Good") for which all men yearn whether they know it or not. Unlike Jung, who concedes that a few people exist who feel no craving for immortality, Pascal is unwilling to allow even a single exception to this principle. In the chapter "Le Souverain Bien," he attempts to make the case that this yearning—manifested as the desire for happiness—is universal and without exception:

> Tous les hommes recherchent d'être heureux. Cela est sans exception, quelques différents moyens qu'ils y emploient. Ils tendent tous à ce but. Ce qui fait que les uns vont à la guerre et que les autres n'y vont pas est ce même désir qui est dans tous les deux accompagné de différentes vues. La volonté fait jamais la moindre démarche que vers cet objet. C'est le motif de toutes les actions de tous les hommes, jusqu'à ceux qui vont se pendre.

> All men seek happiness. There are no exceptions. However different the means they may employ, they all strive toward this goal. The reason why some go to war and some do not is the same desire in both, but interpreted in two different ways. The will never takes the least step except to that end. This is the motive of every act of every man, including those who go and hang themselves. (148)

In the context of *liasses* VI–X, "le Souverain Bien" is of course happiness. But in the chapter "A.P.R." (XI), Pascal demonstrates that happiness is but a symptomatic and purely human construct. The human yearning for happiness, dictated by that "marque . . . toute vide" ("empty print") which the Fall left imprinted in the human heart, is really a longing for our immortal life with God before Adam's Fall. Indeed, as the Preface sketched by fragment 427 puts it: "Qu'on fasse réflexion là-dessus, et qu'on dise ensuite s'il n'est pas indubitable qu'il n'y a de bien en cette vie qu'en l'espérence d'une autre vie" ("Let us ponder these things [the vanity of human aspirations, the fragility of human life, and the inevitability of death], and then say whether it is not beyond doubt that the only good thing in this life is the hope of another life").

Indifference is the way in which the hardened disbelievers attempt to cope with an unbearably tragic vision of human life. "N'ayant pu guérir la mort, la misère, l'ignorance, ils se sont avisés, pour se rendre heureux, de n'y point penser" ("Being unable to cure death, wretchedness and ignorance, they have decided, in order to be happy, not to think about such things"). Those who have no hope of a life to come or even any inkling that the soul might be immortal must repress the thought of their own mortality in order to survive psychically. The dilemma of the unbeliever is in some sense simply an exaggerated version of the human condition as defined by Pascal in the chapter "Divertissement" ("Diversion") (VIII):

> Nonobstant ces misères il veut être heureux et ne veut être qu'heureux, et ne peut ne vouloir pas l'être.
>
> Mais comment s'y prendra(-t-)il? Il faudrait pour bien faire qu'il se rendît immortel, mais ne le pouvant il s'est avisé de s'empêcher d'y penser.

> Despite these afflictions man wants to be happy, only wants to be happy, and cannot help wanting to be happy.
>
> But how shall he go about it? The best thing would be to make himself immortal, but as he cannot do that, he has decided to stop himself thinking about it. (134)

The Tragedy of Disbelief

In the nearly forty years since the appearance of Lucien Goldmann's *Le Dieu caché*,[76] much has been written about Pascal's "tragic vision." If by "tragic" we mean something inherent in the human condition which can be ameliorated by neither human reason, will, nor progress, then Pascal's vision of the human condition from the perspective of "Misère de l'homme sans Dieu" ("Wretchedness of man without God") (6) merits being included among the most profound tragic visions produced by our culture. Modern family counseling has hardly modified the tragic vision of Sophocles' *Oedipus Rex*. Nor has better care for the aged altered that set forth in *King Lear*. Advances in modern medicine have sanitized death and have sometimes offered stays of execution, but they have not funda-

76. Lucien Goldmann, *Le Dieu caché: Étude sur la vision tragique dans les Pensées de Pascal et dans le théâtre de Racine* (Paris: Gallimard, 1955).

mentally altered the tragic vision of human life which Pascal expresses in fragments 434 and 151:

> Qu'on s'imagine un nombre d'hommes dans les chaînes, et tous condamnés à la mort, dont les uns étant chaque jour égorgés à la vue des autres, ceux qui restent voient leur propre condition dans celle de leurs semblables, et, se regardant les uns et les autres avec douleur et sans espérance, attendent à leur tour. C'est l'image de la condition des hommes.
>
> Imagine a number of men in chains, all under sentence of death, some of whom are each day butchered in the sight of the others; those remaining see their own condition in that of their fellows, and looking at each other with grief and despair await their turn. This is an image of the human condition. (434)
>
> Nous sommes plaisants de nous reposer dans la société de nos semblables, misérables comme nous, impuissants comme nous; ils ne nous aideront pas: on mourra seul.
>
> It is absurd of us to rely on the company of our fellows, as wretched and helpless as we are; they will not help us; we shall die alone. (151)

If Pascal's vision of the human condition in the first part of the Apology ("[1.] Partie. Misère de l'homme sans Dieu.") (6) can indeed be described as "tragic," this is not the case for the vision of the Apology as a whole. The second stage in Pascal's apologetic itinerary, anticipated by the note ("[2.] Partie. Félicité de l'homme avec Dieu" ["Second part: Happiness of man with God"] in fragment 6, envisages "un Réparateur" ("a Redeemer") who enables human beings to transcend the human condition. It is a mistake to read the entire Apology from the perspective of but one of its parts. As Jean Mesnard so aptly points out, Goldmann's Pascal, though perhaps tragic, is most assuredly "moliniste."[77] From the perspective of Pascal's larger apologetic scheme, it is hardly man who transcends the human condition by working out his own salvation. That, Pascal might say, would be Pelagianism or even Deism. Rather, as Pascal sees it, the tragedy of the human condition was remedied by the intervention of God into human history. The Incarnation and Christ's unique Sacrifice reverse the effects of the Fall and restore fallen man's communication with God.

From the Christian perspective, Pascal will argue in the second half of the Apology, the human condition is no longer irreparably "tragic." However, Pascal seems to suggest in fragment 427, the instance of the

77. *Les Pensées de Pascal,* p. 308.

hardened disbelievers does figure forth a classical tragic impasse. Those unbelievers who consciously cultivate doubt and indifference in order to insulate themselves from the fear of their own mortality somehow blind themselves to the benefits of the remedy to the human condition which God has provided to suffering humanity. Their indifference engenders despair. Their doubt generates what Pascal terms "la fausse crainte" ("false fear"):

> Crainte mauvaise. Crainte, non celle qui vient de ce qu'on croit Dieu, mais celle de ce qu'on doute s'il est ou non. La bonne crainte vient de la foi, la fausse crainte du doute; la bonne crainte jointe à l'espérance, parce qu'elle naît de la foi et qu'on espère au Dieu que l'on croit; la mauvaise jointe au désespoir parce qu'on craint le Dieu auquel on n'a point eu foi. Les uns craignent de le perdre, les autres de le trouver.

> Wrong fear. Fear: not that which comes from believing in God, but from doubting whether or not he exists. The right fear comes from faith, false fear from doubt; the right fear is linked with hope, because it is born of faith and one hopes in the God in whom one believes; the wrong fear is linked with despair, because one fears the God in whom one has not put one's faith. Some fear to lose him, others to find him. (908)

Unconsciously, Pascal believes, the unbelievers fear the very God in whom they do not believe. But their "mauvaise crainte" ("wrong fear") engenders only more doubt and despair, which they vainly attempt to neutralize by cultivating the Stoic virtue of passive indifference. In doing so, they tragically forfeit any real desire to find the Truth. In Pascal's view, the behavior of the hardened unbelievers violates every canon of common sense and the most elementary human instinct for self-preservation. Between our souls and heaven or hell stands only this fragile bit of life (cf. 152). Not to use it well, Pascal thinks, is both insane and "contre nature" ("beyond all nature") (163).

Pascal can only conclude that those who squander the opportunity to "buy terms divine" obviously demonstrate the truth of the doctrine of Predestination and Election. "Non seulement le zèle de ceux qui le cherchent prouve Dieu, mais l'aveuglement de ceux qui ne le cherchent pas" ("It is not only the zeal of those who seek him that proves God's existence, but also the blindness of those who do not seek him") (163). Such behavior, inconsonant with the norms of common sense, is obviously of supernatural origin. "C'est un appesantissement de la main de Dieu" ("It is a chastisement of the hand of God"). The indisputable fact that we must die alone would reasonably seem to impose the obligation to act as if we were alone in this world ("comme si on était seul") (151). Instead of storing up treasures on earth and building "des maisons superbes" ("superb houses"), we should unhesitatingly look for the truth ("on chercherait la vérité sans hésiter"). However, fallen man prefers "l'estime des hommes" ("men's esteem") to "la recherche de la vérité" ("the pursuit of the truth") (151).

From a theological perspective, the unbelievers bring into focus what is a universal human phenomenon. Pascal's "homme dans un cachot" (163) stands as a metaphor for all of fallen humanity. Yet, in this projected Preface to the Apology, Pascal hardly fits Voltaire's description of "ce misanthrope sublime."[78] His irritation is not generalized to humanity as a whole. Rather, his indignation is focused on the hardened unbelievers who have abandoned the search for the truth. As fragment 156 reminds us, Pascal constantly bears in mind a fundamental distinction between two kinds of unbelievers:

> Plaindre les athées qui cherchent, car ne sont-ils assez malheureux. Invectiver contre ceux qui en font vanité.

> Pity the atheists who seek, for are they not unhappy enough? Inveigh against those who boast about it. (156)

This dichotomy means two different attitudes toward these two very different kinds of unbelievers. The seekers merit the apologist's compassion. Those so hardened in disbelief as to brag about it merit only invective.

The vehemence of Pascal's invective against the hardened disbelievers is comprehensible only if we are able to see the "braves" pictured in fragment 427 from his perspective. For Pascal, the hardened unbeliever is a man laughing himself all the way to hell. He is a necessarily tragic figure who has doomed himself by rejecting that "devoir indispensable de chercher" ("indispensable duty to seek") imposed by doubt itself and by a healthy fear of death and eternal punishment. Midway through the draft of his projected Preface, Pascal can no longer contain his horror in the face of what he sees as self-satisfied arrogance:

> C'est donc assurément un grand mal que d'être dans ce doute; mais c'est au moins un devoir indispensable de chercher, quand on est dans ce doute; et ainsi celui qui doute et qui ne recherche pas est tout ensemble et bien malheureux et bien injuste. Que s'il est avec cela tranquille et satisfait, qu'il en fasse profession,

78. *Lettres philosophiques,* p. 94.

et enfin qu'il en fasse le sujet de sa vanité, je n'ai point de termes pour qualifier une si extravagante créature.

Où peut-on prendre ces sentiments? Quel sujet de joie trouve-t-on à n'attendre plus que des misères sans ressources? Quel sujet de vanité de se voir dans des obscurités impénétrables, et comment se peut-il faire que ce raisonnement se passe dans un homme raisonnable?

It is therefore quite certainly a great evil to have such doubts, but it is at least an indispensable obligation to seek when one does thus doubt; so the doubter who does not seek is at the same time very unhappy and very wrong. If in addition he feels a calm satisfaction, which he openly professes, and even regards as a reason for joy and vanity, I can find no terms to describe so extravagant a creature.

What can give rise to such feelings? What reason for joy can be found in the expectation of nothing but helpless wretchedness? What reason for vanity in being plunged into impenetrable darkness? And how can such an argument as this occur to a reasonable man? (427)

In the passage which follows the one just cited, Pascal gives us a detailed portrait of the hardened unbeliever. This portrait, cast in the first person, is not a dialogue between apologist and unbeliever. The speaker does not respond to Pascal's invective against indifference. Nor does the apologist intervene during the course of the unbeliever's testimony. In the portrait we are about to examine, Pascal holds up a mirror for the *honnête homme* to whom the Apology will be addressed. However, the reflection in the mirror is not the *honnête homme* as he is now. Rather, like the reflection proposed to the miser in Dickens' *A Christmas Carol* by the Ghost of Christmas Future, the image in Pascal's mirror reveals what the *honnête homme* may become if he progresses further in the ways of disbelief. This portrait, designed to startle and frighten Pascal's potential interlocutor in the Apology, presents the testimony of an agnostic whose heart and soul have been devoured by skepticism and disbelief.

In the first paragraph of his testimony, the unbeliever presents himself as a complete skeptic who professes "une ignorance terrible de toutes choses" ("a terrible ignorance of all things"). Skepticism has eaten away even his thinking faculty. He is unable even to reach Descartes' elementary conclusion, "Cogito, ergo sum":

"Je ne sais qui m'a mis au monde, ni ce que c'est que le monde, ni que moi-même; je suis dans une ignorance terrible de toutes choses; je ne sais ce que c'est que mon corps, que mes sens, que mon âme et cette partie même de moi qui pense ce que je dis, qui fait réflexion sur tout et sur elle-même, et ne se connaît non plus que le reste."

"I do not know who put me into the world, nor what the world is, nor what I am myself. I am terribly ignorant about everything. I do not know what my body is, or my senses, or my soul, or even that part of me which thinks what I am saying, which reflects about everything and about itself, and does not know itself any better than it knows anything else." (427)

Pascal's portrait of the complete skeptic has a satirical edge. Having professed his ignorance of the nature, meaning, or even existence of his own body, senses, and soul, the unbeliever extends his skepticism to the universe around him. He claims he has not the slightest hint as to his relationship to time, space, or infinity. To this profound skepticism concerning all things, he adds an Epicurean, materialistic atomism:

"Je vois ces effroyables espaces de l'univers qui m'enferment, et je me trouve attaché à un coin de cette vaste étendue, sans que je sache pourquoi je suis plutôt placé en ce lieu qu'en un autre, ni pourquoi ce peu de temps qui m'est donné à vivre m'est assigné à ce point plutôt qu'à un autre de toute l'éternité qui m'a précédé et de toute celle qui me suit. Je ne vois que des infinités de toutes parts, qui m'enferment comme un atome et comme une ombre qui ne dure qu'un instant sans retour. Tout ce que je connais est que je dois bientôt mourir, mais ce que j'ignore le plus est cette mort même que je ne saurais éviter."

"I see the terrifying spaces of the universe hemming me in, and I find myself attached to one corner of this vast expanse without knowing why I have been put in this place rather than that, or why the brief span of life allotted to me should be assigned to one moment rather than another of all the eternity which went before me and all that which will come after me. I see only infinity on every side, hemming me in like an atom or like the shadow of a fleeting instant. All I know is that I must soon die, but what I know least about is this very death which I cannot evade." (427)

This vision is most certainly tragic by any standards. But is it Pascal's ultimate vision of reality? Here perhaps we should recall the debate which once centered on a similar fragment filed in the *liasse* "Transition": "Le silence éternel de ces espaces infinis m'effraie" ("The eternal silence of these infinite spaces fills me with dread") (201). A Romantic tradition, which regarded the *Pensées* as Pascal's intimate spiritual journal, was fond of attributing this profession of fear and trembling to Pascal himself. Valéry, in his *Variation sur une pensée*, judged the fragment too studied to convey a sincere feeling of terror.[79] A. Béguin, in his *Pascal par lui-même*, argued that the fragment should be placed in the mouth of the *libertin*, a

79. In *Revue hebdomadaire* special issue (1932): 161–72.

conclusion seconded by Jean Mesnard.[80] Philippe Sellier, on the other hand, judges the sentiment expressed in fragment 201 to be exemplary of the believer's reaction to divine omnipotence in the tradition of Augustinian spirituality.[81]

In fragment 427, it is clear that Pascal places the lines "Je vois ces effroyable espaces . . ." in the mouth of the unbeliever. When the unbeliever raises his eyes to behold the terrifying spaces of the universe, he experiences neither the fear of God nor the desire to plumb the great secrets of existence. Like one of the early Soviet cosmonauts, he takes pleasure in announcing that he has failed to catch a glimpse of God in outer space. Instead, he sees only an infinite expanse of space and time which renders his tiny existence insignificant and meaningless. "Je ne vois que des infinités de toutes parts, qui m'enferment comme un atome et comme une ombre qui ne dure qu'un instant sans retour" ("I see only infinity on every side, hemming me in like an atom or like the shadow of a fleeting instant") (427). As Pascal sees it, the unbeliever has thus blinded himself to the God who stands behind his Creation.

At two critical junctures during the course of the Apology (449, 781), Pascal will reject the utility of proofs of God drawn from natural religion. These, Pascal will observe, contain nothing capable of opening the eyes of the hardened atheists ("des athées endurcis") (449). A believer beholds the heavens and immediately recognizes that everything which exists is the work of the God whom he worships . The unbeliever, however, scans the very same heavens and finds nothing but obscurity and darkness. Thus, traditional apologies for Christianity, which begin with a chapter proving the existence of God, have misjudged the fundamental nature of disbelief:

> Préface de la seconde partie.
> Parler de ceux qui ont traité de cette matière.
> J'admire avec quelle hardiesse ces personnes entreprennent de parler de Dieu.
> En adressant leurs discours aux impies leur premier chapitre est de prouver la divinité par les ouvrages de la nature. Je ne m'étonnerais pas de leur entreprise s'ils adressaient leurs discours aux fidèles, car il est certain que ceux qui ont la foi vive dedans le coeur voient incontinent que tout ce qui est n'est autre chose que l'ouvrage du Dieu qu'ils adorent, mais pour ceux en qui cette lumière est éteinte et

80. A. Béguin, *Pascal par lui-même* (Paris: Seuil, 1952), pp. 47–48. Jean Mesnard, *Les Pensées de Pascal,* pp. 312 and 340. Anthony Pugh gives an excellent account of the history of commentary on this fragment in his *The Composition of Pascal's Apologia,* pp. 523–24, n. 5.

81. *Pensées* (1991), p. 256, n. 19.

dans lesquels on a dessein de la faire revivre, ces personnes destituées de foi et de grâce, qui recherchant de toute leur lumière tout ce qu'ils voient dans la nature qui les peut mener à cette connaissance ne trouvent qu'obscurité et ténèbres, dire à ceux-là qu'ils n'ont qu'à voir la moindre des choses qui les environnent et qu'ils y verront Dieu à découvert et leur donner pour toute preuve de ce grand et important sujet le cours de la lune et de planètes et prétendre avoir achevé sa preuve avec un tel discours, c'est leur donner sujet de croire que les preuves de notre religion sont bien faibles et je vois par raison et par expérience que rien n'est plus propre à leur en faire naître le mépris.

Preface to the second part.

Discuss those who have dealt with this subject.

I marvel at the boldness with which these people presume to speak of God.

In addressing their arguments to unbelievers, their first chapter is the proof of the existence of God from the works of nature. Their enterprise would cause me no surprise if they were addressing their arguments to the faithful, for those with living faith in their hearts can certainly see at once that everything which exists is entirely the work of the God they worship. But for those in whom this light has gone out and in whom we are trying to rekindle it, people deprived of faith and grace, examining with such light as they have everything they see in nature that might lead them to this knowledge, but finding only obscurity and darkness; to tell them, I say, that they have only to look at the least thing around them and they will see in it God plainly revealed; to give them no other proof of this great and weighty matter than the course of the moon and the planets; to claim to have completed the proof with such an argument; this is giving them cause to think that the proofs of our religion are indeed feeble, and reason and experience tell me that nothing is more likely to bring it into contempt in their eyes. (781)

The reality of the Fall voids the very premises of natural religion. Pascal's neo–Augustinian perspective is greatly clarified by the Preface of the 1702 edition of the Sacy Bible. This Preface opens by describing the universe as "un grand volume dans lequel Dieu a imprimé tous les caractères de sa Divinité" ("an enormous book in which God has printed all the characters of his Divinity"). However, the Preface continues, the consequences of the Fall mean that "la lumière naturelle" ("man's natural light") is too weak to enable him to perceive God in Creation. The contemplation of the universe clouds the human mind more than it enlightens it ("dissipe beaucoup plus notre esprit qu'elle ne l'éclaire"):

> Le péché originel a tellement brouillé ces divins caractères . . . a répandu de si profondes ténèbres sur nos esprits . . . a corrompu nos coeurs jusqu'à un tel point, que l'ignorance et la faiblesse sont devenues notre partage. Si nous étendons nos vues sur tout ce monde visible, c'est bien moins pour nous élever jusqu'à son Au-

teur, que pour chercher . . . l'objet de nos désirs corrompus, de nos attaches criminelles, de nos passions déréglées.[82]

Original sin so blurred these divine characters . . . spread such shadows across our minds . . . corrupted our hearts to such a point, that ignorance and weakness have become our natural state. When we extend our view out over the visible world, this is less to raise ourselves up to its Author than to seek the object of our corrupt desires, our criminal bonds and our unbridled passions.

In some sense, the unbeliever's testimony in fragment 427 serves to validate the apologist's decision to use neither philosophy nor natural religion in proving the truth of Christianity. Philosophical arguments are unlikely to impress an unbeliever so sunk in skepticism that he denies the first principle of consciousness. Nor will proofs drawn from natural religion alter his vision of a universe crushing man into oblivion. The unbeliever of fragment 427 claims to know a great deal about human "misère." But he knows nothing of man's "grandeur." He lacks an innate sense that consciousness—of whose existence he is uncertain—gives man an advantage over the infinite universe. Attempting to evoke this latent sense of human "grandeur" will constitute a major strategy in the Apology:

L'homme n'est qu'un roseau, le plus faible de la nature, mais c'est un roseau pensant. Il ne faut pas que l'univers entier s'arme pour l'écraser, une vapeur, une goutte d'eau suffit pour le tuer. Mais quand l'univers l'écraserait, l'homme serait encore plus noble que ce qui le tue, puisqu'il sait qu'il meurt et l'avantage que l'univers a sur lui. L'univers n'en sait rien.

Man is only a reed, the weakest in nature, but he is a thinking reed. There is no need for the whole universe to take up arms to crush him: a vapour, a drop of water is enough to kill him. But even if the universe were to crush him, man would still be nobler than his slayer, because he knows that he is dying and the advantage the universe has over him. The universe knows none of this. (200)

Up until this point, the unbeliever portrayed in fragment 427 might perhaps be said to be not that different from the *libertin* sketched in the wager passage. However, a critical distinction soon emerges. In the wager, the unbeliever is taken aback when confronted with his own mortality and the choice between eternal life and complete annihilation. The unbeliever pictured in fragment 427 does not flinch for a moment in the face

82. *La Sainte Bible . . . traduite en françois . . . avec de courtes notes tirées des Saints Pères* (Liège: Chez Broncart, 1702), Préface, p. 1.

of the same prospect. He claims to have looked death squarely in the eyes. His own mortality, he maintains, is the only fact of which he can be certain. But, in turn, the consequences of his death are the subject of his most profound skepticism of all. "Tout ce que je connais est que je dois bientôt mourir, mais ce que j'ignore le plus est cette mort même que je ne saurais éviter" ("All I know is that I must soon die, but what I know least about is this very death which I cannot evade").

The unbeliever of fragment 427 freely admits that when he departs this life he must fall either into absolute nothingness or into the hands of an angry God. But, undaunted by such a prospect, he concludes that speculation is a waste of time since it is impossible to know what happens after death. The only sane course, he maintains, is to live this life without seeking to know what cannot be known. For Pascal's hardened skeptic, as for La Mothe le Vayer, skepticism constitutes "l'unique port de salut"[83]

> "Comme je ne sais d'où je viens, aussi je ne sais où je vais et je sais seulement qu'en sortant de ce monde je tombe pour jamais ou dans le néant, ou dans les mains d'un Dieu irrité, sans savoir à laquelle de ces deux conditions je dois être éternellement en partage. Voilà mon état, plein de faiblesse et d'incertitude. Et, de tout cela, je conclus que je dois donc passer tous les jours de ma vie sans songer à chercher ce qui doit m'arriver. Peut-être que je pourrais trouver quelque éclaircissement dans mes doutes; mais je n'en veux pas prendre la peine, ni faire un pas pour le chercher; et après, en traitant avec mépris ceux qui se travailleront de ce soin (quelque certitude qu'ils en eussent, c'est un sujet de désespoir, plutôt que de vanité) je veux aller, sans prévoyance et sans crainte, tenter un si grand événement, et me laisser mollement conduire à la mort, dans l'incertitude de l'éternité de ma condition future."

> "Just as I do not know whence I come, so I do not know whither I am going. All I know is that when I leave this world I shall fall for ever into nothingness or into the hands of a wrathful God, but I do not know which of these two states is to be my eternal lot. Such is my state, full of weakness and uncertainty. And my conclusion from all of this is that I must pass my days without a thought of seeking what is to happen to me. Perhaps I might find some enlightenment in my doubts, but I do not want to take the trouble, nor take a step to look for it: and afterwards, as I sneer at those who are striving to this end—(whatever certainty they have should arouse despair rather than vanity)—I will go without fear or foresight to face so momentous an event, and allow myself to be carried off limply to my death, uncertain of my future state for all eternity." (427)

The unbeliever pictured in this tableau is no passive agnostic ready to be convinced of the utility of seeking the truth. He aggressively sneers at

83. La Mothe le Vayer, *Petit traité sceptique* in *Oeuvres*, 10, p. 201.

those *chercheurs* who devote their lives to resolving the enigma of death, the soul, and the meaning of existence. He claims to be frightened neither by the prospect of total extinction nor by that of eternal damnation. He is reasonably confident that death puts an end to all consciousness. But should he be wrong, he—like Molière's Dom Juan—is prepared to storm the very portals of Hell. Casting himself in the heroic role, he intends to depart this life as captain of his fate, scorning those who fear the unknown: "Je veux aller, sans prévoyance et sans crainte, tenter un si grand événement, et me laisser mollement conduire à la mort, dans l'incertitude de l'éternité de ma condition future" ("I want to go and face without fear or foresight so momentous an event, and allow myself to be carried off limply to my death, uncertain of my future state for all eternity") (427).

Pascal's aggressive skeptic would seem to be a composite portrait drawn from yet unidentified sources. In the passage cited "mollement" and "sans crainte" recall Pascal's fragment 680 ("Montaigne"):

> Les défauts de Montaigne sont grands. . . . Il inspire une nonchalance du salut, *sans crainte* et sans repentir. Son livre n'étant pas fait pour porter à la piété il n'y était pas obligé, mais on est toujours obligé de n'en point détourner. On peut excuser ses sentiments un peu libres et voluptueux en quelques rencontres de la vie—730, 331—mais on ne peut excuser ses sentiments tout païens sur la mort. Car il faut renoncer à toute piété si on ne veut au moins mourir chrétiennement. Or il ne pense qu'à mourir lâchement et *mollement* par tout son livre.[84]

> Montaigne's faults are great. . . . He inspires indifference regarding salvation: "without fear or repentance." As his book was not written to encourage piety, he was under no obligation to do so, but we are always under an obligation not to discourage it. One may excuse his somewhat free and licentious views on certain situations in life (pp. 730, 331) but his completely pagan views on death are inexcusable; for all hope of piety must be abandoned if we are not at least willing to die as Christians. Now, throughout his book he thinks only of dying a death of cowardly ease. (680)

84. Italics mine. The pagination noted by Pascal refers to the 1652 edition of the *Essais* (Paris: A. Courbe), 1 vol.

For Pascal's references to the *Essais,* see the edition of M. V.-L. Saulnier (Paris: P.U.F., 1965): for "sans crainte et sans repentir", 2, 2, pp. 806 and 816; for "ses sentiments tout païens sur la mort," 3, 9, pp. 981–84, and 2, 12, p. 461; for "lâchement et mollement," 3, 9, p. 949.

"Mollement" also recalls Pascal's critique of Montaigne in the "Entretien avec M. de Sacy": "Il rejette donc bien loin cette vertu stoïque. . . . La sienne est naïve, familière, plaisante, enjouée, et pour ainsi dire folâtre: elle suit ce qui la charme, et badine négligemment des accidents bons ou mauvais, couchée *mollement* dans le sein de l'oisiveté tranquille, d'où elle montre aux hommes, qui cherchent la félicité avec tant de peine, que c'est là seulement où elle repose, et que l'ignorance et l'incuriosité sont deux doux oreillers pour une tête bien faite, comme il dit lui-même" (Lafuma, *Oeuvres complètes,* p. 296).

Since the 1640s, the *Essais* of Montaigne had come to have the reputation of what J. Lhermet calls "le livre cabalistique des sceptiques et des libertins."[85] Pascal's hardened atheist has obviously derived some of his skepticism from Montaigne. But, as René Pintard points out with regard to fragment 131 ("Les principales forces des pyrrhoniens . . ."), Pascal's portrait also owes a considerable debt to the "académiciens."[86] The unbeliever portrayed in fragment 427 is of course not a neo-Stoic. His complete atheism runs counter to the Deism or Monism which the neo-Stoics found in the *Manuel* and *Propos* of Epictetus.[87] He is far from aspiring to the "haut degré de sagesse" of the Stoics Pascal describes in fragment 144. But he does derive from the Stoic tradition the ideal of passive resignation in the face of death, an idea which Pascal thinks contradicts the dictates of both common sense and human nature.[88]

In drawing the *libertin* of fragment 427, Pascal throws in a good measure of arrogance, an element not entirely consonant with the skeptical tradition of Montaigne. Montaigne had counseled against the folly of attempting to play the "brave" with regard to God.[89] Pascal's *libertin* claims that he will let himself be carried away "mollement" by death. But he reveals his desire to play the hero, to play the "brave," when he describes his confrontation with death with the expression "tenter un si grand événement" ("brave so great an event"). The *libertin* of this tableau is certainly not a model *honnête homme*, aspiring to the ideal of "l'amour propre bien réglé."[90] He mocks not only the believers but those among his fellow agnostics who would seek "quelque éclaircissement" ("some enlightenment"). Pascal's purpose in painting him as so arrogant seems obvious. The apologist wants to alienate from him the *honnête homme* whose natural feelings have not yet been completely destroyed by hardened disbelief.

Pascal's portrait of the hardened *libertin* may not strike the modern

85. J. Lhermet, *Pascal et la Bible* (Paris: Vrin, 1930), p. 489.

86. See "Pascal et les libertins" in *Pascal présent,* p. 114.

87. See Julien-Eymard d'Angers, "Le Stoïcisme d'après l'*Humanitas theologica* de Pierre Lescalopier, S.J.," *Bulletin de littérature ecclésiastique* 56 (1955): 35.

88. A possible source for Pascal's portrait might be the stoicism of Montaigne's "That to philosophize is to learn to die": "Premeditation of death is premeditation of freedom. He who has learned how to die has unlearned how to be a slave. Knowing how to die frees us from all subjection and constraint. There is nothing evil in life for the man who has thoroughly grasped the fact that to be deprived of life is not an evil" (Frame, ed., *Complete Essays,* 1, 20, p. 60).

89. "Car que peut-on imaginer plus vilain, que d'être couard à l'endroit des hommes, et brave à l'endroit de Dieu" (*Essais* 2, 18).

90. See Chapter I, *L'Honnête homme*.

reader as entirely unsympathetic. We have come to admire not only Byronic and Faustian heroes but also the more contemporary ideal of the "good clean atheist." Often cited with admiration for sheer honesty are Simone de Beauvoir's words upon the death of Jean-Paul Sartre: "Sa mort nous sépare. Ma mort ne nous réunira pas"[91] ("His death separates us. Mine will not reunite us"). The post-Christian sensibility reserves a special admiration for those said to be able to create their own meaning in a meaningless universe. Pascal himself has sometimes been called a precursor of existentialism. However, the fact remains that the author of the *Pensées* never betrays the slightest sympathy for the heroic atheist, existential or otherwise. For Pascal, the person who has no desire for a life to come is profoundly defective as a human being. No one, Pascal argues, could possibly want such a man for a friend. This observation, following immediately upon the portrait of the hardened skeptic, is obviously meant to appeal to the *honnête homme*, for whom friendship has been elevated to the level of dogma:

> Qui souhaiterait d'avoir pour un ami un homme qui discourt de cette manière? Qui le choisirait entre les autres pour lui communiquer ses affaires? Qui aurait recours à lui dans ses afflictions? Et enfin, à quel usage de la vie le pourrait-on destiner?

> Who would wish to have as his friend a man who argued like that? Who would choose him from among others as a confidant in his affairs? To what use in life could he possibly be turned? (427)

Through fragment 427 is not a dialogue, Pascal at times acts as though it is. However, he addresses, not the *libertin* who has just been presented, but rather the silent *honnête homme*. At this point Pascal takes the offensive. The testimony of the *libertin*, he tells his silent interlocutor, serves only to glorify the Christian religion and to illustrate the truth of its doctrines:

> Il est glorieux à la religion d'avoir pour ennemis des hommes si déraisonnables; et leur opposition lui est si peu dangereuse, qu'elle sert au contraire à l'établissement de ces vérités.

> It is truly glorious for religion to have such unreasonable men as enemies: their opposition represents so small a danger that it serves on the contrary the truths of religion. (427)

91. Simone de Beauvoir, *La Cérémonie des adieux* (Paris: Gallimard, 1981), p. 159.

Pascal then reiterates the two essential doctrines of Christianity set forth at the beginning of fragment 427: "La foi chrétienne ne va presque qu'à établir ces deux choses: la corruption de la nature, et la redemption de Jésus-Christ" ("The Christian faith consists almost wholly in establishing these two things: the corruption of nature and the redemption of Christ"). The unreasonable and perverted ("dénaturés")[92] sentiments of the hardened unbelievers admirably demonstrate "la corruption de la nature." The unnatural heroics of the atheists in the face of death contradict ordinary human experience. Braving the peril of eternal punishment and risking the loss of one's soul are inconsistent with the way human beings act in far less consequential matters:

> Rien n'est si important à l'homme que son état; rien ne lui est si redoutable que l'éternité. Et ainsi, qu'il se trouve des hommes indifférents à la perte de leur être et au péril d'une éternité de misères, cela n'est point naturel. Ils sont tout autres à l'égard de toutes choses; ils craignent jusqu'aux plus légères, ils les prévoient, ils les sentent; et ce même homme qui passe tant de jours et de nuits dans la rage et dans le désespoir pour la perte d'une charge ou pour quelque offense imaginaire à son honneur, c'est celui-là même qui sait qu'il va tout perdre par la mort, sans inquiétude et sans émotion. C'est une chose monstrueuse de voir dans un même coeur et en même temps cette sensibilité pour les moindres choses et cette étrange insensibilité pour les grandes. C'est un enchantement incompréhensible, et un assoupissement surnaturel, qui marque une force toute-puissante qui le cause.

> Nothing is so important to man as his state: nothing more fearful than eternity. Thus the fact that there exist men who are indifferent to the loss of their being and the peril of an eternity of wretchedness is against nature. With everything else they are quite different; they fear the most trifling things, foresee and feel them; and the same man who spends so many days and nights in fury and despair at losing some office or at some imaginary affront to his honor is the very one who knows that he is going to lose everything through death but feels neither anxiety nor emotion. It is a monstrous thing to see one and the same heart at once so sensitive to minor things and so strangely insensitive to the greatest. It is an incomprehensible spell, a supernatural torpor that points to an omnipotent power as its cause. (427)

In commenting on the enigma just cited, Pascal postulates that human nature must have undergone some "étrange renversement" ("strange reversal") in order for a single person to be capable of boasting that he is

92. Cf., Montaigne, *Essais,* 2, 12: "L'athéisme étant une proposition *dénaturée* et monstrueuse. . . ."

unafraid of death. This "renversement" is of course the Fall. However, in this draft of the Preface to the Apology, Pascal refrains from elaborating the Christian doctrine of Original Sin in any great detail. It better serves his purpose—gaining his potential reader's attention—to let the source of this "enchantement incompréhensible" remain a mystery.

The Pseudo-*Libertins*

Pascal begins his treatment of an entirely new category of disbelievers by pointing out that he has personally encountered a great number of people who profess indifference toward death and the fate of their souls. Such an observation, Pascal explains, would be horrifying if we did not know that the great majority of these people are only faking this entirely unnatural attitude. Pascal at this point very subtly switches to the first person plural: "si *nous* ne savions pas que la plupart de ceux qui s'en mêlent se contrefont et ne sont pas tels en effet" ("if *we* did not know that most of those concerned in this are pretending and are not really what they seem"). By switching to the first person plural, Pascal automatically includes his silent interlocutor (or reader) in his point of view. In the observations which follow, Pascal continues—for the sake of rhetorical effect—to promote the impression that he assumes that his interlocutor (or reader) shares his perspective. He likewise intends to convey the impression that his interlocutor (or reader) does not, of course, figure among the category of people he is about to discuss.

The pseudo-*libertins*, probably provincials or *arrivistes*, think that "les belles manières du monde" ("fashionable manners") dictate affecting a certain agnosticism in matters religious. "C'est ce qu'ils appellent avoir secoué le joug,[93] et qu'ils essayent d'imiter" ("This is what they call having shaken off the yoke, and what they are trying to imitate"). They have adopted a conscious veneer of religious doubt because they think that it is intellectually avant-garde to do so. They think they are shocking stodgy matrons and pious old gentlemen when they whisper that "the soul is only a puff of wind or smoke" ("que notre âme n'est qu'un peu de vent et de fumée") or when they assert that "God is not watching over human affairs" ("qu'il[s] ne croi[ent] pas qu'il y ait un Dieu qui veille sur

93. Pascal attributes this expression to the *libertins* themselves: "C'est ce qu'*ils* appellent avoir secoué le joug." Cf. Matthew 11:30: "For my *yoke* is easy and my burden is light."

[leurs] actions").[94] They think they are making a place for themselves in intellectual society. But, says Pascal, they could not be more mistaken: "Ils s'abusent en cherchant par là l'estime" ("They are very mistaken to court esteem in this way"). Those "personnes du monde" whose opinions really count in society are neither amused nor shocked by such talk. They are saddened.

Pascal insists that anyone aspiring to the status of *honnête homme* must refrain from espousing such agnostic and libertine sentiments. Those who brag that they have cast off the yoke of religion only fall in the estime of the true *honnêtes hommes*. Instead of advancing their progress in society, these poor *arrivistes* create the worst sort of impression:

> Il ne serait pas difficile de leur faire entendre combien ils s'abusent en cherchant par là de l'estime. Ce n'est pas le moyen d'en acquérir, je dis même parmi les personnes du monde qui jugent sainement des choses et qui savent que la seule voie d'y réussir est de se faire paraître honnête, fidèle, judicieux et capable de servir utilement son ami, parce que les hommes n'aiment naturellement que ce qui peut leur être utile. Or, quel avantage y a-t-il pour nous à ouïr dire à un homme qu'il a donc secoué le joug, qu'il ne croit pas qu'il y ait un Dieu qui veille sur ses actions, qu'il se considère comme seul maître de ses actions, qu'il ne pense en rendre compte qu'à soi-même? Pense-t-il nous avoir porté par là à attendre des consolations, des conseils et de secours dans tous les besoins de la vie? Prétendent-ils nous avoir bien réjoui, de nous dire qu'ils tiennent que notre âme n'est qu'un peu de vent et de fumée, et encore de nous le dire d'un ton de voix fier et content? Est-ce donc une chose à dire gaiement? Et n'est-ce pas une chose à dire tristement, au contraire, comme la chose du monde la plus triste?

It would not be difficult to show them how mistaken they are to court esteem in this way. This is not how to acquire it, not even, I would say, among worldly people, who judge things sensibly and who know that the only way to succeed is to appear honest, faithful, judicious and capable of rendering service to one's friends, because by nature men only like what may be of use to them. Now what advantage is it to us to hear someone say that he has shaken off the yoke, that he does not believe that there is a God watching over his actions, that he considers himself sole master of his behavior, and that he proposes to account for it to no one but himself? Does he think that by so doing he has henceforth won our full confidence, and made us expect from him consolation, counsel and assistance in all life's needs? Do they think that they have given us great pleasure by telling us that they hold our soul to be no more than wind or smoke, and saying it moreover

94. "Que notre âme n'est qu'un peu de vent et de fumée" represents the materialist doctrine of the soul advanced by the neo-Epicureans. Not believing that there is a God who watches over human affairs represents the Deist doctrine of the watchmaker God. Or perhaps it represents total atheism.

in tones of pride and satisfaction? Is this then something to be said gaily? Is it not on the contrary something to be said sadly, as being the saddest thing in the world? (427)

Pascal's purpose in this part of fragment 427 is obviously to make the affectation of *libertinage* and agnosticism appear both contrary to the ideals of the *honnête homme* and socially unacceptable. "Athéisme," Pascal had noted in "Commencement" (XII), "marque de force d'esprit, mais jusqu'à un certain degré seulement" ("Atheism indicates strength of mind, but only up to a certain point") (157). In society, Pascal argues in fragment 427, affecting disbelief means incurring considerable social stigma. If those who affect this fashion thought about it seriously, he argues, they would see that their *bons mots* are very poorly received in respectable social discourse. *Libertinage*, they would realize, is both "opposé à l'honnêteté" ("opposed to *honnêteté*") and "éloigné en toutes manières de ce bon air qu'ils recherchent" ("remote in every way from the good form they seek") (427).

Pascal is a merciless satirist. He observes that those who attempt to impress *le beau monde* by affecting *libertinage* are not very good at it. They would be more likely to reform than to corrupt these who might feel inclined to follow them ("Ils seraient plutôt capables de redresser que de corrompre ceux qui auraient quelque inclination à les suivre"). They are perfectly incapable of logically explaining their objections to religion. Their arguments are so silly that those whom they can convince to hear them out usually conclude that the opposite of what they are saying must be true. Pascal urges, "Faites-leur rendre compte de leur sentiments et des raisons qu'ils ont de douter de la religion" ("Make them describe the feeling and reasons which inspire their doubts about religion"). Their reply, he claims, will be instructive: "Ils vous diront des choses si faibles et si basses, qu'ils vous persuaderont du contraire" ("What they say will be so feeble and cheap as to persuade you of the contrary").

"Des choses si faibles" would seem to indicate that those who are attempting to affect a facade of *libertinage* do not really understand the traditional antireligious arguments formulated by classical atheism and skepticism. Instead, they regurgitate an incoherent and poorly digested version of arguments which they have heard used by more adept unbelievers. "Si basses" perhaps refers to those blasphemous or sacrilegious *bons mots* with which the pseudo-*libertins* attempt to disguise their ignorance in matters religious and philosophic.

The parish clergy in midseventeenth-century Paris routinely inveighed against blasphemy as a symptom of growing disbelief. Pintard cites the interesting testimony of a certain Monseigneur Grillet, who laments that sacrilegious talk, "par une licence effrénée et sans bornes" ("with unlimited and unbridled license"), is to be found everywhere and "en la bouche de toutes sortes de personnes" ("in the mouths of all sorts and conditions of persons"). "Les personnes de haute condition" ("people of high social rank"), he declares, are particularly guilty of profaning the name of God. They profane the name of God and soil His most august sacraments in order to ornament their "detestable galanteries." Blasphemy, he protests, has come to be accepted in *le beau monde* not only as licit but even as "louable" ("praiseworthy"). Those who utter them do so "non par jeu, non par colère, non par aucune passion . . . mais de sang froid, à dessein, et par désir déliberé de paraître . . . ennemis de Dieu et de toute religion" ("neither in jest, nor in anger, nor in a state of any passion whatsoever . . . but coldbloodedly, with premeditation and with the deliberate design of appearing to be . . . enemies of God and of all religion"):

> Ces déstestables vomissent . . . des injures, des outrages, des salletez, des blasphemes . . . qu'ils prononcent avec délices . . . [ils] pratiquent des profanations publiques des choses les plus saintes, exercent ridiculement des idolatries payennes, mais mélées avec des mocqueries des plus augustes Mystères de notre foy . . . pour . . . introduire . . . l'athéisme dans un Royaume très-chrétien, et avec lui toutes sortes d'ordures, de crimes et de vices.
>
> Ce mal est un mal qu'on commet serieusement, froidement, à dessein et de propros déliberé; et mal, qui pis est . . . venant de personnes considérables et de condition, s'imprime . . . dans les coeurs de toute la Noblesse. . . . Ce n'est plus un simple ulcère . . . c'est une plaie gangrenée, qui augumente tous les jours . . . les vanités d'une fausse galanterie, poisons des jeunes esprits . . . pour appeler à son mortel appât des âmes que déjà l'oisiveté, l'orgueil et l'abondance rendent d'ailleurs très dereglées.[95]

> These detestable people vomit forth . . . abusive language, outrages, filth, blasphemies . . . which they pronounce with delectation . . . [they] practice public profanations of the most holy things [and] ridiculously practice pagan idolatries, mixing them up with mockeries of the most august Mysteries of our Faith . . . in order to . . . introduce . . . atheism into a most Christian Kingdom, and along with it, all sorts of filth, crimes and vices.
>
> This evil is one which they commit seriously, coldly, purposefully and with premeditated words; it is an evil, even worse to say . . . [which], coming from persons of rank and condition, takes root . . . in the hearts of all the Nobility. . . . This is not a simple sore . . . it is a gangrenous ulceration, which every day causes the

95. René Pintard, *Le Libertinage érudit*, pp. 35–36.

augmentation of . . . the vanities of a false gallantry, poisonous to young minds . . . in order to snare with its deadly bait souls which ease, pride and wealth have already rendered dissolute.

Pintard makes the important observation that the upper classes largely escaped prosecution for blasphemy or impiety. Severe punishments—the stake, hanging, amputation of the hand or tongue—were meted out to those *petites gens* found guilty of la "grossièreté des mœurs." For instance: "trois gais compères, déguisés en ermites, qui avaient distribué aux dames des chapelets munis de médailles obscènes" ("three jokers, disguised as hermits, who had distributed rosaries with obscene medals to unsuspecting ladies"). However, Pintard stresses, impious opinions remained largely unpunished. *Laquais* or drunkards who had carelessly uttered obscene oaths were subjected to torture and sometimes death. However, "les athées, les vrais, faisaient élégamment retenir leurs éperons sur les pavés de la Place Royale"[96] ("the atheists, the real ones, continued to sound their spurs on the pavingstones of the Place Royale").

Pascal refrains from telling us precisely what "choses . . . si basses" ("cheap things") the pseudo-*libertins* have gleaned from the *propos* of the *libertins de profession*. Their denial that God watches over human behavior suggests that they go so far as to deny the existence of the Christian God. But to what extent are they familiar with scholarly disbelief? Do they advance the thesis of "les trois imposteurs"?[97] Or do they simply make light of the fervor of the *dévots*? Whatever their comments, Pascal insists, they make a ridiculous impression. The real unbelievers are quite frankly embarrassed by the nonsense they spout. Pascal cites the instance of a confirmed atheist who, upon hearing their garbled version of *libertinage*, could only exclaim: "Si vous continuez à discourir de la sorte . . . vous me convertirez"[98] ("If you go on arguing like that . . . you really will convert

96. Ibid., pp. 24–26.

97. In his *Mémoires,* Père Beurrier tells of an atheist Parisian doctor who explains that his creed is based upon "trois articles": "le premier, que la plus grande de toutes le fables, c'est la religion chrestienne; le second, que le plus ancien de tous les romans, c'est la Bible; le troisième, que le plus grand de tous le fourbes et de tous les imposteurs, c'est Jésus-Christ." Cited by Antoine Adam, *Les Libertins au XVIIe siècle* (Paris: Buchet/Chastel, 1964), pp. 115–16. See Georges Couton's article, "Libertinage et Apologétique: Les *Pensées* de Pascal contre la thèse des Trois Imposteurs," *XVIIe siècle* (April–June 1980): 181–95.

98. The preparatory notes for fragment 427 contain the following notation: "Vous me convertirez" (821/432-[6]). This *bon mot,* dictated by Pascal to his secretary (see Tourneur, édition paléographique, p. 313), may well be derived from a real conversation heard by Pascal.

me"). Once again, we find Pascal drawing a critical distinction between the true unbelievers and the pseudo-*libertins*. In an ironic twist, Pascal goes so far as to express approval of the reaction of the real unbeliever. "Il avait raison, car qui n'aurait horreur de se voir dans des sentiments où l'on a pour compagnons des personnes si méprisables" ("He was right, for who would not shrink from finding himself sharing the feelings of such contemptible people?").

The section of fragment 427 concluded by this anecdote should perhaps be compared to a key passage in the "wager" fragment. Pascal has argued that *libertinage* is completely contrary to true *honnêteté*. The only way to succeed in gaining the estime of those who really count in society is "se faire paraître *honnête*, *fidèle*, judicieux et capable de servir utilement son ami" ("to appear honest, faithful, judicious and capable of rendering useful service to one's friends") (427). Does this not recall Pascal's statement toward the end of the "wager" fragment of those supererogatory benefits which accrue when one behaves as if one believes: "Vous serez *fidèle*, *honnête*, humble, reconnaissant, bienfaisant, ami sincère, véritable"? ("You will be faithful, honest, grateful, full of good works, a sincere, true friend") (418) (italics mine).

The Uses and Dangers of Skepticism

Pascal's recourse to irony when he satirizes the pseudo-*libertins* by no means means that he does not view the feigning of *libertinage* as a dangerous business. Rather, he sees it as potentially lethal to the immortal souls of those involved in it. Disbelief, like the unclean spirit described in Matthew 12:43–45, lies in wait to invade a mind emptied by skepticism and irreligious thoughts. A single expression of doubt, no matter how benignly intended, returns sevenfold into the vacuum which its utterance has created in the human heart.

In the *Entretien avec M. de Sacy*, the future apologist had scandalized the pious Sacy by suggesting that Montaigne's skepticism might be enlisted in the service of Christian apologetics. Montaigne's methods, Pascal had suggested, might provide the means of humbling "la raison dénuée de la foi" ("reason stripped of faith"). Sacy, thinking first of the risks of such an enterprise, had expressed serious reservations concerning any such method:

Qu'avait besoin Montaigne de s'égayer l'esprit en renouvelant une doctrine qui passe maintenant aux Chrétiens pour une folie? . . . Vous êtes heureux, Monsieur, de vous être élevé au-dessus de ces personnes qu'on appelle des docteurs plongés dans l'ivresse de la science, mais qui ont le coeur vide de vérité. Dieu a répandu dans votre coeur d'autres douceurs que ceux que vous trouviez dans Montaigne. . . . Ce sont des viandes dangereuses . . . que l'on sert dans de beaux plats . . . au lieu de nourrir le coeur, elles le vident.[99]

But why did Montaigne need to enliven the mind by reviving a doctrine which now appears to be foolishness to Christians? . . . You are fortunate, sir, in having raised yourself above these people who are called learned, immersed in the drunkenness of knowledge, but whose hearts are devoid of truth. God has diffused other attractions in your heart than those you used to find in Montaigne. . . . These are dangerous meats . . . served in lovely dishes . . . instead of nourishing the heart, they empty it.

In Pascal's Apology, skepticism (much of it borrowed from Montaigne) has a strictly purificatory function. It takes place only within the larger context of catechesis and conversion. Pascal never tires of repeating to the *chercheur* that the only knowledge which does not ultimately leave one empty is the knowledge of Christ's saving work: "Hors de J.-C. nous ne savons ce que c'est ni que notre vie, ni que notre mort, ni que Dieu, ni que nous-mêmes" ("Apart from Jesus Christ we cannot know the meaning of our life or our death, of God or of ourselves") (417). According to Pascal's apologetic scheme, true conversion can take place only when a skepticism which is peculiarly Christian has dethroned Reason and emptied the heart of such alien doctrines as Deism or nihilism.

At no point in the spiritual itinerary traced by the dossiers of 1658 is the *chercheur* more vulnerable to eternally crippling disbelief than the moment at which he emerges from the purificatory rite of skepticism. He has been stripped of his preconceptions, illusions, and false beliefs. But he has yet to receive that catechesis which will bring him to the point of conversion. In the chapter "Transition" (XV), the *chercheur* wakes into the brave new world described by fragment 198:

En voyant l'aveuglement et la misère de l'homme, en regardant tout l'univers muet, et l'homme sans lumière, abandonné à lui-même et comme égaré dans ce recoin de l'univers, sans savoir qui l'y a mis, ce qu'il est venu faire, ce qu'il deviendra en mourant, incapable de toute connaissance, j'entre en effroi, comme un homme qu'on aurait porté endormi dans une île déserte et effroyable et qui s'éveil-

99. Lafuma, *Oeuvres complètes,* p. 37.

lerait sans connaître où il est, et sans moyen d'en sortir. Et, sur cela, j'admire comment on n'entre point en désespoir d'un si misérable état. Je vois d'autres personnes auprès de moi, d'une semblable nature: je leur demande s'ils sont mieux instruits que moi; ils me disent que non; et sur cela, ces misérables égarés, ayant regardé autour d'eux, et ayant vu quelques objets plaisants, s'y sont donnés et s'y sont attachés. Pour moi, je n'ai pu y prendre d'attache et, considérant combien il y a plus d'apparence qu'il y a autre chose que ce que je vois, j'ai recherché si ce Dieu n'aurait point laissé quelques marques de soi.

When I see the blind and wretched state of man, when I survey the whole universe in its dumbness and man left to himself with no light, as though lost in this corner of the universe, without knowing who put him there, what he has come to do, what will become of him when he dies, incapable of knowing anything, I am moved to terror, like a man transported in his sleep to some terrifying desert island, who wakes up quite lost and with no means of escape. Then I marvel that so wretched a state does not drive people to despair. I see other people around me, made like myself. I ask them if they are any better informed than I, and they say they are not. Then these lost and wretched creatures look around and find some attractive objects to which they become addicted and attached. For my part I have never been able to form such attachments, and considering how very likely it is that there exists something besides what I can see, I have tried to find out whether God has left any traces of himself. (198)

What a contrast this portrait forms when set beside the portrait of the hardened skeptic in fragment 427. Both speakers find themselves in an unfathomable universe. However, here the resemblance ends. The unbeliever of fragment 198 has gained a crucial critical perspective. He sees the folly of *divertissement*. Unlike his fellow creatures, he is unable to attach himself to transitory objects. He intuitively feels that something lies behind the visible universe. He is determined to find out whether God has left any traces of himself. Here we have Pascal's portrait of the *chercheur*. In the definition of fragment 160, he is the man who seeks God because he has yet to find Him. He is unhappy but reasonable. From this point onward, the schema of conversion proposed by the *liasses* of 1658 will be fairly straightforward. After having been shown the vanity of the non-Christian religions, the seeker will work his way through the complexities of Scripture to that ultimate proof constituted by the prophecies (335).

But what of the pseudo-*libertins* satirized in fragment 427? Are they candidates for the status of *chercheur*? Or are they doomed to evolve into hardened disbelievers? How do they fit into Pascal's elaboration of a theory of inner conversion? Like the hardened skeptics, they are a negative example. They serve to turn the *honnête homme* away from active disbelief. Yet is Pascal's strategy not a bit duplicitous? Even if only used as bait for the *honnête homme*, is not the notion of feigning belief (or at least of repressing *libertinage*) in order to facilitate social advancement at odds with the notion of inner conversion?

René Pintard reminds us that the middle of the seventeenth century was a time in which overt disbelief was being driven underground. Active *libertinage* was giving way to hypocrisy. The role once played by Vanini and Théophile de Viau was being replaced by the more prudent model of La Mothe le Vayer:

> L'impiété se confinera dans le for intérieur, elle ne passera plus dans les actes, elle ne percera que rarement dans les paroles. On fera extérieurement profession du christianisme; on fréquentera les sacrements; on ira dans les paroisses, on s'abstiendra de jurer et, sans incliner le coeur, on pliera la machine. Sauver les dehors, quel 'honnête homme' le refuserait, fût-ce au prix de la duplicité?[100]

> Disbelief would confine itself to the inner mind; it would no longer manifest itself in actions and would only rarely pierce through the veil of words. Unbelievers would make an external profession of Christianity; they would frequent the sacraments and be seen in church; they would refrain from swearing, and, without inclining the heart, they would make the body conform. In order to save one's skin, what "honnête homme" would refuse? Even if at the price of duplicity.

Pascal knows that the frontiers between *honnêteté* and hypocrisy are not always sharply delineated in the minds of those who frequent *le beau monde*. Indeed, the Church itself knowingly harbors hypocrites whose piety is purely superficial:

> Dieu ne regarde que l'intérieur, l'Eglise ne juge que par l'extérieur. . . . Dieu fera une Eglise pure au-dedans, qui confonde par sa sainteté intérieure et toute spirituelle, l'impiété des superbes et des pharisiens. Et l'Eglise sera une assemblée d'hommes dont les moeurs extérieures soient si pures qu'elles confondent les moeurs des payens; s'il y en a d'hypocrites, non si bien déguisés qu'elle n'en reconnaisse point le venin, elle les souffre. Car encore qu'ils ne sont pas reçus de Dieu qu'ils ne peuvent tromper, ils le sont des hommes qu'ils trompent. Et ainsi elle n'est pas déshonorée par leur conduite, qui paraît sainte.[101]

100. *Le libertinage érudit,* p. 37.

101. The context of this fragment is that of "les confessions et absolutions sans marques de regret" ("confession and absolution without signs of repentance"). Pascal accuses the Jesuits of going too far when they allow active disbelievers to remain within the sacraments of the Church: "Vous retenez dans l'Eglise les plus débordés et ceux qui la déshonorent si fort que les synagogues des Juifs et sectes des philosophes les auraient exclus comme indignes et les auraient abhorrés comme impies" ("You keep within the Church the most dissolute and those who dishonor it to such an extent that the Jewish synagogues and philosophical sects would have kept them out as unworthy and would have loathed them as impious") (923).

> God only looks at what is inward, the Church judges only by what is outward. . . . God will create an inwardly pure Church, to confound by its inward and complete spiritual holiness the inward impiety of the proud and Pharisees. And the Church will be a gathering of men whose outward conduct is so pure as to confound pagan conduct; if some of them are hypocrites, not so well disguised that it fails to recognize their poison, she endures them. For although they are not accepted by God, whom they cannot deceive, they are accepted by men, whom they do deceive. And so the Church is not dishonored by their conduct, which looks saintly.

Though Pascal insists that the sanctity of the Church is not tainted by the presence of those whose belief is only superficial, external conformity is by no means an acceptable goal in the conversion process envisaged by the Apology. The model of the "bête-machine" is valid only in the specific case of the *chercheur*, who genuinely wants to believe. It is useless, if not fatal, for those who use it to veil their real lack of belief.

In fragment 427, Pascal adapts his schema of conversion to the perspective of the *honnête homme*. His strategy is twofold. First, he uses the testimony of the hardened *libertin* to alienate the *honnête homme* from the position of active disbelief. Then, he produces his caricature of the pseudo-*libertins*. This second portrait does more than simply brand feigned *libertinage* as socially dangerous. It provides an escape hatch for those unbelievers who genuinely feel that they have no light but wish they did. Pascal subtly maneuvers the *honnête homme* into an identification with those who "gémissent sincèrement" about their lack of light.

Pascal initially spoke of the pseudo-*libertins* in a way which let his potential interlocutor (or reader) distance himself from them. His interlocutor was invited to dissociate himself from their ridiculous example. Now, in a sudden about-face, the apologist begins to urge his interlocutor (or reader) to identify with them. Those only superficially infected with disbelief are now viewed from a more favorable perspective. Active disbelief has not yet completely eaten away their natural instincts ("leur naturel"); indeed, they have to constrain those instincts in order to feign that *libertinage* which they think will enhance their social advancement. In doing so, Pascal observes, they do themselves a great injustice. Not only do they give the false impression that they are "les plus impertinents des hommes" ("the most impertinent of men"). They lay themselves open to an invasion of more serious disbelief.

Pascal now invites those who have genuine doubts or scruples concerning Christianity to lay down their yoke. Those genuinely disturbed ("fâchés dans le fond de leur coeur")[102] because they find no light in the depths of their hearts should make a clean confession of their spiritual state. "Cette déclaration ne sera point honteuse" ("It would be no shame to admit it"). The very fact that one is disturbed by not having more inner light is a healthy sign. It means that one's natural instincts urging one to seek a lost God are still operative. "Il n'y a de honte qu'à n'en point avoir" ("There is no shame except in having none"). Feeling no shame or distress—or worse, feeling satisfaction —because of one's spiritual ignorance would be a very bad sign. It might very well mean that one had not been numbered among the elect:

> Rien n'accuse davantage une extrême faiblesse d'esprit que de pas connaître quel est le malheur d'un homme sans Dieu; rien ne marque davantage une mauvaise disposition du coeur que de ne pas souhaiter la vérité des promesses éternelles; rien n'est plus lâche que de faire le brave[103] contre Dieu.

> There is no surer sign of extreme weakness of mind than the failure to recognize the unhappy state of a man without God; there is no surer sign of an evil heart than failure to desire that the eternal promises be true; nothing is more cowardly than to brazen it out with God. (427)

Those from whom God's Grace has been withdrawn are defective both intellectually and spiritually. They are simply unable to recognize the basic premise—"Misère de l'homme sans Dieu" ("Wretchedness of man without God") (6)—which the apologist seeks to document in the first half of the Apology. Not only do these potential *réprouvés* have no hope of a life to come. They do not even harbor the wish that such a thing were true. "Rien ne marque davantage une mauvaise disposition du coeur" ("There is no surer sign of an evil heart"). A third sign marks out the hardened unbelievers as figuring among the *réprouvés*: their arrogance in the face of death and the possibility of divine judgment. The tenor of their attitude is abnormal by any human standard. They lack even the normal human fear of the unknown. In the preparatory notes for his draft of fragment 427,[104]

102. "Fâchés dans le fond de leur coeur" perhaps indicates that Pascal thinks that the pseudo-*libertins* have resorted to impious talk out of a sense of frustration at finding no light within themselves. Their response is one of anger. They have yet to learn that they must seek the truth outside themselves. Cf. fragment 143.

103. See n. 72.

104. See Chapter IV, Fragments 418 and 427: The State of the Texts. Pugh devotes an illuminating discussion to the difficulties of fragment 821–432-bis. See *The Composition of Pascal's Apologia*, p. 520, n. 16.

Pascal had written, "Est-ce courage à un homme mourant d'aller dans la faiblesse et dans l'agonie affronter un Dieu puissant et éternel?" ("Is it brave for a dying man to go in his weakness and agony to confront a powerful and eternal God?") (821/432-[15]). In fragment 427, Pascal turns to his own uses Montaigne's statement of the same idea: "Rien n'est plus lâche que de faire le brave contre Dieu" ("Nothing is more cowardly than to brazen it out with God").

At this point, Pascal attempts to effect a final separation of those *honnêtes hommes* to whom he will address the Apology from the company of the hardened disbelievers. Those guilty only of feigning indifference and disbelief are invited to see themselves as *chercheurs*:

> Qu'ils laissent donc ces impiétés à ceux qui sont assez mal nés pour en être véritablement capables; qu'ils soient au moins honnêtes gens s'ils ne peuvent être chrétiens, et qu'ils reconnaissent enfin qu'il n'y a que deux sortes de personnes qu'on puisse appeler raisonnables: ou ceux qui servent Dieu de tout leur coeur parce qu'ils le connaissent, ou ceux qui le cherchent de tout leur coeur parce qu'ils ne le connaissent pas.[105]
>
> Let them leave such impiety to those ill-bred enough to be really capable of it; let them at least be *honnête hommes* if they cannot be Christians; let them, in short, acknowledge that there are only two classes of persons who can be called reasonable: those who serve God with all their heart because they know him and those who seek him with all their heart because they do not know him. (427)

In what sense are those truly capable of impiety "mal nés"? Does Pascal mean to suggest that the *libertins* are simply "ill bred"? Or does "mal nés" have a theological implication? True unbelievers, Pascal seems to be suggesting, may indeed have been condemned to disbelief from the beginning of time. They may have been born into the world in order not to see. Aggressive disbelief may have supernatural origins. As Pascal notes in fragment 232: "On n'entend rien aux ouvrages de Dieu si on ne prend pour principe qu'il a voulu aveugler les uns et éclaircir les autres" ("We can understand nothing of God's works unless we accept the principle that he wished to blind some and enlighten others").

In order to capture the attention of the *honnête homme* to whom he will address the argument of his Apology, Pascal proposes *honnêteté* as a provisional stage on the way to true belief. "Qu'ils soient au moins *honnêtes gens* s'ils ne peuvent être chrétiens" ("Let them at least be decent people if they

105. See Chapter V, Pascal's Categories of Disbelief, for a discussion of the source of this key principle.

cannot be Christians") (427, italics mine). In the passages associated with Mitton (597, 642), Pascal demonstrates that *honnêteté* is an impotent remedy for the human condition because it fails to take into account the inherent corruption of the human ego. But in this draft of the Preface, Pascal is willing to allow his potential interlocutors to cling temporarily to the ideal of *honnêteté*. Those "honnêtes gens" who make a cult of reason, however, will be obliged to recognize that only two categories of human beings can be called truly reasonable: those who serve God because they know him and those who seek God because they do not know him.

In the *liasse* "Commencement," fragment 160 envisages three universal categories: "Les uns qui servent Dieu l'ayant trouvé, les autres qui s'emploient à le chercher ne l'ayant pas trouvé, les autres qui vivent sans le chercher ni l'avoir trouvé" ("those who have found God and serve him; those who are busy seeking him and have not found him; those who live without either seeking or finding him"). The true believers, who constitute the first category, are reasonable and happy ("raisonnables et heureux"). The hardened unbelievers, who make up the third category, are insane and unhappy ("fous et malheureux"). "Ceux du milieu" ("those in the middle"), who seek God for the very reason that they do not know him, are unhappy but reasonable ("malheureux et raisonnables"). In the context of fragment 427, the very fact that the *chercheurs* are unhappy signifies that they are not beyond hope and help. Their dissatisfaction with their lack of inner light probably means that their natural instinct urging them to seek a lost God is still intact. As the suffering Christ tells the seeker in the *Mystère de Jésus*: "Console-toi. Tu ne me chercherais pas si tu ne m'avais trouvé" ("Take comfort. You would not seek me if you had not found me") (919).

In the closing paragraph of fragment 427, Pascal appears to rethink the whole issue of the utility of dialogue with the hardened unbelievers from the perspective of the inscrutability of Grace. In a fragment figuring among those set down in preparation for the writing of fragment 427,[106] Pascal had concluded that the hardened unbelievers are completely immune to the effects of apologetic dialogue. "Cela montre qu'il n'y a rien à leur dire non par mépris, mais parce qu'ils n'ont pas le sens commun. Il faut que Dieu les touche" ("That shows that there is nothing to be said to them, not out of contempt, but because they have no common sense. God must touch them") (821/432–[4]). In fragment 427, Pascal moderates this

106. See Chapter IV, Fragments 418 and 427: The State of the Texts.

conclusion. Christianity, he realizes, admits no exception to the Golden Rule. It teaches the inscrutability of Grace and obliges us to treat even the most hardened and vicious enemies of the Christian faith as capable of being filled with Grace until the moment in which they draw their last breath. The recalcitrant blasphemer may well be granted repentance and salvation in the last instant of his life on earth. The believer of a lifetime may be plunged into perdition in the same split second.

Pascal calls upon the charity mandated by that very religion which the unbelievers despise in order to resist the temptation to abandon them to their folly. He insists that the apologist must do unto the unbelievers as he would wish them to do unto him were he in their blindness. He must call upon them to have pity upon themselves and to take at least a few hesitant steps in the direction of finding divine illumination:

> Pour ceux qui vivent sans le connaître et sans le chercher, ils se jugent eux-mêmes si peu dignes de leur soin, qu'ils ne sont pas dignes du soin des autres et qu'il faut avoir toute la charité de la religion qu'ils méprisent pour ne les pas mépriser jusqu'à les abandonner dans leur folie. Mais parce que cette religion nous oblige de les regarder toujours, tant qu'ils seront en cette vie, comme capables de la grâce qui peut les éclairer, et de croire qu'ils peuvent être dans peu de temps plus remplis de foi que nous ne sommes, et que nous pouvons au contraire tomber dans l'aveuglement où ils sont, il faut faire pour eux ce que nous voudrions qu'on fît pour nous si nous étions à leur place, et les appeler à avoir pitié d'eux-mêmes, et à faire au moins quelques pas pour tenter s'ils ne trouveront pas de lumières.

> As for those who live without either knowing or seeking him, they consider it so little worthwhile to take trouble over themselves that they are not worth other people's trouble, and it takes all the charity of that religion they despise not to despise them to the point of abandoning them to their folly. But as this religion obliges us always to regard them, as long as they live, as being capable of receiving grace which may enlighten them, and to believe that in a short time they may be filled with more faith than we are, while we on the contrary may be stricken by the same blindness which is theirs now, we must do for them what we would wish to be done for us in their place, and appeal to them to have pity on themselves, and to take at least a few steps in an attempt to find some light. (427)

Pascal does not have a great deal of hope that the hardened unbelievers can be rescued by apologetics. However, he may have known of the occasional spectacular conversions which the Parisian clergy claimed to have brought about. Père Beurrier, who heard Pascal's last confession, claimed to have converted a hardened atheist by the name of Basin. Pintard describes Basin as an archetypal Deist and scoffer at Christian belief:

Séduit par de mauvaises compagnies, corrompu par de longs voyages qui l'avaient mêlé à des protestants et à des juifs, à des musulmans et à des idolâtres, il avait abjuré toute croyance chrétienne, et auprès de sa bibliothèque remplie de livres "dangereux et hérétiques," il se complaisait à ruminer des sentences impies. Le christianisme? Une fable. La Bible? Un roman. Le Christ? Un imposteur. Basin acceptait . . . "un Dieu premier principe de toute choses"; mais il pensait "qu'il ne se mêlait point de nos affaires."

Seduced by low companions, corrupted by long voyages which put him into constant contact with Protestants, Jews, Muslims and idolaters, he had abjured all Christian belief. In his library, filled with "dangerous and heretical" books, he delighted in mulling over impious propositions. Christianity? A fable. The Bible. Myth. Christ? An impostor. Basin accepted "a God author of all things"; but he thought "that he did not concern himself with human affairs."[107]

Basin is not unlike the "impies" censured in fragment 150 or the Deists pilloried in fragment 449. However, the fact remains that the argument of the Apology is not primarily directed to those from whom God has apparently so withdrawn His Grace that they lack "le sens commun" (821/432–[4]). Pintard, who has studied the dossiers of the *libertins érudits* more carefully than practically anyone else, cannot imagine that many of them might have been susceptible to Pascal's apologetic strategy:

Plus qu'en des philosophes de profession présentant des objections bien classées, Pascal a trouvé ses interlocuteurs en ces esprits brillants et désinvoltes, en ces hommes avides de vivre, êtres de chair et de sang qui ont des convoitises, des joies, des déceptions, des vanités, des faiblesses et qui s'offrent par elles à ses prises. Il ne les lâchera plus; et c'est ainsi que leur image s'imprimera fortement dans ce texte même des *Pensées* qui garde si peu de traces des doctrines des savants libertins.[108]

More than from the ranks of professional philosophers, presenting carefully ordered objections [to Christianity], Pascal recruited his interlocutors from among those brilliant and impertinent intellects, from among those men filled with desire for life, beings of flesh and blood endowed with lusts, joys, disappointments, vanities and weaknesses, and who, because of these very qualities, fall into his grasp. He will not let them go. And thus it is that their image will be strikingly engraved in the very text of the *Pensées*, a text which retains so few traces of the doctrines of the *savants libertins*.

While drafting the conclusion of his Preface for the Apology, Pascal realizes that he must at least issue a summons to conversion to those

107. *Le libertinage érudit,* p. 81. Pintard cautions that Père Beurrier's portraits are often "types conventionnels . . . inventés, ou du moins déformés, dans une intention apologétique" (pp. 589–90, n. 2 for p. 81).

108. "Pascal et les libertins" in *Pascal présent,* p. 124.

"athées endurcis" ("hardened atheists") (cf. 449) for whom he has little hope. Not to do so would invalidate his entire belief in the mysterious workings of Grace:

> Qu'ils donnent à cette lecture [i.e., to the Apology which will follow] quelques-unes de ces heures qu'ils emploient si inutilement ailleurs; quelque aversion qu'ils y apportent, peut-être rencontreront-ils quelque chose, et pour le moins, ils n'y perdront pas beaucoup.

> Let them spend reading what follows a few of the hours they waste on other things: however reluctantly they may approach the task they will perhaps hit upon something, and at least they will not be losing much. (427)

But, Pascal makes clear, his efforts in the Apology will principally be addressed to those *chercheurs* who sincerely desire to seek the truth:

> Pour ceux qui y apporteront une sincérité parfaite et un véritable désir de rencontrer la vérité, j'espère qu'ils auront satisfaction, et qu'ils seront convaincus des preuves d'une religion si divine, que j'ai ramassées ici, et dans lesquelles j'ai suivi à peu près cet ordre. . . .

> But as for those who approach it with absolute sincerity and a real desire to find the truth, I hope that they will be satisfied, and convinced by the proofs of so divine a religion which I have collected here, following more or less this order. . . . (427)

The Preface outlined by fragment 427 breaks off at this point. Anthony Pugh suggests invoking two unclassified fragments to complete Pascal's unfinished sentence.[109] Fragment 482 outlines a series of twelve proofs which very much reflect the major themes, if not the order, of the Apology outlined by the *liasses* of 1658:

> PREUVES—1. la religion chrétienne, par son établissement, par elle-même établie si fortement, si doucement, étant si contraire à la nature.—2. La sainteté, la hauteur et l'humilité d'une âme chrétienne.—3. Les merveilles de l'Ecriture sainte.—4. Jésus-Christ en particulier.—5. Les apôtres en particulier.—6. Moïse et les prophètes en particulier.—7. Le peuple juif.—8. Les prophéties.—9. La perpétuité; nulle religion n'a la perpétuité.—10. La doctrine, qui rend raison de tout.—11. La sainteté de cette loi.—12. Par la conduite du monde.

> PROOFS—1. The Christian religion, by the fact of being established, by establishing itself so firmly and so gently, though so contrary to nature—2. The holiness, sublimity and humility of a Christian soul—3. The miracles of Holy Scrip-

109. *The Composition of Pascal's Apologia*, p. 158.

ture—4. Jesus Christ in particular—5. The apostles in particular—6. Moses and the prophets in particular —7. The Jewish people —8. Prophecies—9. Perpetuity: no religion enjoys perpetuity—10. Doctrine, accounting for everything—11. The holiness of this law—12. By the order of the world. (482)

Fragment 402, which Pugh judges later than fragment 482,[110] gives a more schematic version of the proofs which will govern the argument of the *Apology*: "Preuves de la religion. Morale. / Doctrine. / Miracles. / Prophéties. / Figures" ("Proofs of religion. Morality / Doctrine / Miracles / Prophecies / Figures"). Fragment 482 appears to have been written well before the Preface drafted in fragment 427.[111] However, its concluding lines nicely complete the line of reasoning outlined in the projected Preface:

Il est indubitable qu'après cela on ne doit pas refuser, en considérant ce que c'est que la vie, et que cette religion, de suivre l'inclination de la suivre, si elle nous vient dans le coeur; et il est certain qu'il n'y a nul lieu de se moquer de ceux qui la suivent.

Without any doubt after this, considering the nature of life and of this religion, we ought not to resist the inclination to follow it if our hearts are so inclined: and it is certain that there are no grounds for laughing at those who do follow it. (482)

110. Ibid., p. 585, n. 83.
111. See Jean Mesnard, *Les Pensées de Pascal,* p. 47.

CHAPTER V

Catechesis and Conversion in the *Pensées*

Pascal's *Chercheur*

At the end of the draft of his Preface to the Apology (fragment 427), Pascal undertakes a radical reassessment of the whole problem of disbelief. Making use of a principle borrowed from Saint Augustine's *De utilitate credendi*,[1] Pascal attempts to separate those to whom he will address his Apology from the company of the hardened disbelievers. Those guilty only of feigning skepticism or religious indifference in order to pass themselves off as worldly are invited to leave aggressive impiety to those ill bred enough to be really capable of it ("à ceux qui sont assez mal nés[2] pour en être véritablement capables") (427). If they cannot see their way to being Christians, Pascal's future interlocutors are invited at least to be "honnêtes gens" ("decent people") and to recognize the veracity of the following essential principle:

Qu'ils reconnaissent enfin qu'il n'y a que deux sortes de personnes qu'on puisse appeler raisonnables: ou ceux qui servent Dieu de tout leur coeur parce qu'ils le

1. See Philippe Sellier, *Pascal et Saint Augustin* (Paris: A. Colin, 1970), p. 520. Pascal derives this principle, enunciated at the end of fragment 427 and formulated in a different version in fragment 160, from chapter 11 of Saint Augustine's *De utilitate credendi:* "There are [only] two [classes of] persons in religion who are praiseworthy: the one consists of those who have already found out . . . the other of those who are seeking very studiously and in the correct way." Cited from *The Advantage of Believing,* trans. L. Meagher, in *Writings of Saint Augustine* (New York: Cima, 1947), 2, 423–424.

2. See Chapter IV, The Uses and Dangers of Skepticism.

connaissent, ou ceux qui le cherchent de tout leur coeur parce qu'ils ne le connaissent pas.

Let them, in short, acknowledge that there are only two classes of persons who can be called reasonable: those who serve God with all their heart because they know him and those who seek him with all their heart because they do not know him. (427)

In the course of fragment 427, Pascal has made what he considers a critical distinction ("une extrême différence") between two fundamentally different kinds of unbelievers. On the one hand are those unbelievers who, unnerved by their ignorance concerning the fate of the human soul after death, devote their every effort to finding the answer to this all-important question. On the other hand are the hardened unbelievers, who never trouble themselves with the question of their fate after this life. The indifference of this second class of unbelievers irritates Pascal to the point of horror: "C'est un monstre pour moi" ("It seems quite monstrous to me") (427). However, Pascal claims, the example of the first category of unbelievers provokes only his compassion:

Je ne puis avoir que de la compassion pour ceux qui gémissent dans ce doute, qui le regardent comme le dernier des malheurs, et qui, n'épargnant rien pour en sortir, font de cette recherche leurs principales et leurs plus sérieuses occupations.[3]

I can feel nothing but compassion for those who sincerely lament their doubt, who regard it as the ultimate misfortune, and who, sparing no effort to escape from it, make their search their principal and most serious business. (427)

Pascal's description of those disbelievers who do seek to learn the truth concerning ultimate human destiny constitutes a crucial and often neglected key to his entire apologetic discourse. It is to this specific class of unbelievers that the Apology sketched in the *Pensées* will be addressed. Commentators on the *Pensées* have perhaps misfocused a vital question when seeking to pinpoint the identity of Pascal's *libertin*. Perhaps the crucial question is less "Who is the *libertin*?" than "Who are the *chercheurs*?"

As we attempt to understand who it is precisely that Pascal means to include in the class of "ceux qui cherchent en gémissant" ("those who seek with groans") (405), we must beware of our own curiously modern perspective on the pursuit of religious truth. The passage under consideration might at first seem to imply that the essential criterion for inclusion

3. Cf. fragment 405: "Je ne puis approuver que ceux qui cherchent en gémissant" ("I can only approve of those who seek with groans").

among the category of the *chercheurs* is sincerity: "Je ne puis avoir que de la compassion pour ceux qui gémissent *sincèrement*" ("I can feel nothing but compassion for those who *sincerely* lament their doubt") (427, italics mine). However, it may be that the notion of "sincerity" evokes a very different constellation of beliefs and value systems for us than it did for Pascal. Whereas we tend in our culture to value sincerity as an end in itself, Pascal, convinced of the truth of only one system of belief (orthodox Christianity), views sincerity rather as a means to an end. For instance, what of those *libertins érudits* who have carefully examined the case for Christianity but who, in all good conscience, must reject it as unconvincing? We may consider them to be the model *chercheurs*. As we follow the argument of the *Pensées*, however, it becomes clear that Pascal does not. We might well sanction the quest of those who seek the answer to the nature of the soul in science or philosophy. We might be impressed by the alternative of exploring the Buddhist solution to the problem of the soul. Pascal, it must be said, includes none of the above when he speaks of "seeking sincerely."

It is, of course, impossible to read the mind of the dead. However, we can refrain from projecting our perspective into the mental universe of a neo-Augustinian thinker living in the midseventeenth century. We may be tempted to include in Pascal's category of *chercheurs* those in our own time who look to the modern science of physics, anthropology, and comparative religion in an attempt to resolve the enigma of the human condition. Moreover, more than one modern religious thinker has come to have a kind of grudging respect for what is sometimes called "good clean atheism." But could Blaise Pascal have ever even conceived of the "purificatory atheism" advocated by a Simone Weil? Indeed, might not Pascal have found it exceedingly odd that modern French Catholics often regard Simone Weil as a modern saint and compare her self-immolation to that of the author of the *Mémorial*?

Clarifying our own modern liberal perspective on the pursuit of religious truth can help to prevent us from misreading the mental universe of Pascal. It can serve to remind us that the *Pensées* have a particular historical context which has been all too often obscured by the attempt to read Pascal as a modern religious thinker. This specific historical context is that of the hardening of an entire doctrinal tradition horrified by the first stirrings of a more pluralistic view of human beings and of the world. In midseventeenth-century France, a central question was taking on increasing importance with each passing decade: Can religious truth exist outside the Christian Revelation? A major controversy pitted Christian humanists against a conservative tradition which held that any similarities to Christian truth appearing in ancient myth, pagan philosophy, or the non-Christian religions were but *singeries* by which Satan had sought to ape and thus undermine Christian belief. This controversy came to a head in two major quarrels: the first concerned the salvation of the *anciens justes*[4]; the second involved the Jesuit mission to China and the dispute over the *rites chinois*.[5] Port-Royal played a central role in both these confrontations. Both are invoked in the course of the *Pensées*.[6]

The same essential question underlies both the quarrel over the *anciens justes* and the debate over the *rites chinois*: Is the received vision of the Christian Revelation flexible enough to comprehend that rush of new peoples, ideas, and cultures which emerged from the Renaissance and the Age of Discovery? When La Mothe le Vayer invokes the notion of *foi implicite* (implicit faith) in order to extend Revelation backward in time to the *anciens justes*,[7] he is motivated by the same great historical and cultural impulses which led the Jesuits to attempt to graft Christianity onto an older non-Christian tradition in the case of the *rites chinois*.[8] Both La Mothe le Vayer and the Jesuits found fierce adversaries in the neo–Augustinians of Port-Royal. *Le grand* Arnauld, long the chief spokesman for the Jansenist movement, saw any compromise with such a new and more flexible view of the world and of history as an imminent danger to received Revelation.

In his *De la nécessité de la foi en Jésus-Christ*, Arnauld condemns four propositions which were, from the Enlightenment onward, more and more to find a place in modern Christian thought:

(1) "Que Dieu est trop bon pour être si rigoureux qu'on se persuade."

(2) "Qu'il y a de la témérité, aussi bien que l'inhumanité à damner si facilement les hommes."

(3) "Que Dieu a d'autres voies pour nous sauver que celles qui nous sont connues."

(4) "Que l'on peut croire raisonnable [que Dieu] a usé de miséricorde envers une infinité de payens."[9]

4. See Chapter III, Le Vayer's *De la vertu des payens*.

5. See Chapter III, Pascal and the Jesuit Mission to China.

6. Cf. fragments 960 and 822.

7. See Chapter III, Le Vayer's *De la vertu des payens*.

8. See Chapter III, Pascal and the Jesuit Mission to China.

9. *De la nécessité de la foi en Jésus-Christ* in *Oeuvres* (Paris: Chez d'Arnay, 1777), 10, pp. 304–5.

(1) "That God is too good to be as rigorous as has been thought."
(2) "That it is both overbold and inhumane to damn men so easily."
(3) "That God has means of saving us other than those which are known to us."
(4) "That we can reasonably believe that God has exercised mercy toward an infinite number of the pagans."

Arnauld's condemnation of these propositions can serve to remind us of the theological gulf which separates the modern liberal religious sensibility from the worldview of Port-Royal. We should not be surprised to find Pascal's position in the *Pensées* no less rigorous than that of Arnauld. Because Pascal's God is a *Deus absconditus*, hiding himself in Revelation, "natural religion" turns out to be a totally false construct built upon deception and false premises. It can lead only to Deism, which, Pascal insists, true Christianity abhors almost as much as atheism.[10] Outside the Church, which contains the unique deposit of Revelation, Pascal maintains, "il n'y a que malédiction" ("there is only damnation").[11] The virtues of the *anciens justes* are but deception of a diabolical origin:

> Un bâtiment également beau par dehors, mais sur un mauvais fondement, les payens sages le bâtissaient. Et le diable trompe les hommes par cette ressemblance apparante fondée sur le fondement le plus différent.

> A building of equal beauty outside, but on unsound foundations, built by heathen sages; the devil deceives men because of an apparent resemblance, based on quite different foundations. (960)

In the last analysis, Pascal has little use for the whole endeavor of philosophical inquiry. As he sees it, the inward search proposed by philosophy is even more misdirected than the more mundane folly of *divertissement*. For, in coveting created things, human beings at least follow the promptings of an inner instinct urging them to yearn for a lost God. All human beings, "jusqu'à ceux qui vont se pendre" ("including those who go and hang themselves"), search for God without knowing the object of their search (148). Philosophy, on the other hand, counsels an agenda based upon a total misunderstanding of the human condition:

10. Cf. fragment 449: "Tous ceux qui cherchent Dieu hors de Jésus-Christ, et qui s'arrêtent dans la nature . . . tombent ou dans l'athéisme ou dans le déisme, qui sont deux choses que la religion chrétienne abhorre presque également" ("All those who seek God apart from Christ, and who go no further than nature . . . fall into either atheism or deism, two things almost equally abhorrent to Christianity").

11. "Lettre à Mlle de Roannez" [III], in Lafuma, *Pascal: Œuvres complètes* (Paris: Seuil, 1963), p. 267.

Philosophes. Nous sommes pleins de choses qui nous jettent au-dehors. Notre instinct nous fait sentir qu'il faut chercher notre bonheur hors de nous. Nos passions nous poussent au-dehors, quand même les objets ne s'offriraient pas pour les exciter. Les objets du dehors nous tentent d'eux-mêmes et nous appellent, quand même nous n'y pensons pas. Et ainsi les philosophes ont beau dire: "Rentrez-vous en vous-mêmes, vous y trouverez votre bien." On ne les croit pas. Et ceux qui les croient sont les plus vides et les plus sots.

Philosophers. We are full of things that impel us outward. Our instinct makes us feel that our happiness must be sought outside ourselves. Our passions drive us outward, even without objects to excite them. External objects tempt us in themselves and entice us even when we do not think about them. Thus philosophers in vain tell us: "Withdraw into yourselves and there you will find your good." We do not believe them, and those who do believe them are the most empty and silly of all. (143)

Obviously, those sincere unbelievers commended by Pascal in fragment 427 are not those who look to philosophy to provide an answer concerning the ultimate fate of the human soul. Those seekers seduced by the philosophers are "les plus vides et les plus sots" ("the most empty and silly of all") (143). If not in philosophy then, in what domain do those who seek to resolve their doubts concerning the immortality of the soul legitimately pursue "cette recherche" ("this search")? We need not delve too deeply into Pascal's attitude toward the "New Science."[12] In his scientific writings, Pascal makes his position very clear. Science can no more be used to resolve metaphysical problems than can religious doctrine be used to settle scientific disputes. Religious and scientific truth belong to separate, though equally valid, orders.

In an attempt to deny the validity of Pascal's experiments on the possibility of a vacuum existing in nature, Père Noël had invoked the doctrine of the Real Presence of Christ in the Holy Eucharist. In his *Préface sur le Traité du Vide,* Pascal responds to Père Noël's attempt to confuse science and religion by formulating the notion that religious and scientific truth are not of the same order. Theology inhabits the closed realm of Revelation. Nothing can be added to the deposit of faith delivered by Christ to the Apostles. Geometry and physics, on the other hand, belong to that order of sciences which are "soumises à l'expérience et au raisonnement" ("subject to experient and reason"). These disciplines, unlike theology,

12. For an interesting interpretation of Pascal's reaction to the "New Science," see Sara Melzer's *Discourses of the Fall: A Study of Pascal's Pensées* (Berkeley and Los Angeles: University of California Press, 1986), pp. 95–105.

"doivent être augmentées pour devenir parfaites" ("must be augmented in order to become perfect").[13]

The implications of Pascal's theory for the seeking unbelievers are clear. Asking science to prove the immortality of the soul is as vain an endeavor as trying to refute the thesis that a vacuum can exist in nature by invoking Eucharistic doctrine. Religious and scientific truth inhabit separate orders. However, for Pascal it is manifestly clear in which of these two orders the "recherche" (427) of the sincere unbeliever should be conducted. As Pascal states the matter in fragment 164, the religious problem concerning the nature of the soul is vastly more crucial to the *chercheur* than even the most burning of contemporary scientific disputes:

> Je trouve bon qu'on n'approfondisse pas l'opinion de Copernic. Mais ceci:
>
> Il importe à toute la vie de savoir si l'âme est mortelle ou immortelle.
>
> I agree that Copernicus' opinion need not be more closely examined. But this:
>
> It affects our whole life to know whether the soul is mortal or immortal. (164)

If neither science nor philosophy constitutes, in Pascal's view, a legitimate domain of inquiry for those sincere unbelievers who are unhappy but reasonable, what then is the nature of "cette recherche"? Fragment 160 describes the unbelievers worthy of the apologist's attention as those "qui s'emploient à . . . chercher [Dieu], ne l'ayant pas trouvé" ("who spend their time seeking God, not having yet found him"). But exactly where are they supposed to seek God? Certainly not in the created universe. God's presence there is far from manifest: "La nature est corrompue."[14] Original Sin veils human discernment of God in Creation. At most, one can only conclude "la présence d'un Dieu qui se cache" ("the presence of a hidden God") (449). Short of reconsidering Christianity's claim to reveal God and the solution of the human condition, what options are left for those unbelievers who "gémissent sincèrement" (427)?

According to Etienne Périer, Pascal intended to invite the unbeliever

13. *Préface sur le Traité du Vide* in Lafuma, *Pascal: Oeuvres complètes,* p. 231. See also Pascal's exchange of letters with Père Noël, pp. 199–221 and 230–32.

14. This chapter title is envisaged by the *liasse-table* of 1658 but was never constituted by Pascal himself. Anthony Pugh proposes a useful reconstruction of the chapter. See, *The Composition of Pascal's Apologia* (Toronto: University of Toronto Press, 1984), pp. 180–82. Philippe Sellier refers us to dossier XLVII of the Second Copy (Lafuma 438–50). Sellier gives this section the title "Discours de la corruption" in his edition, *Pensées* (Paris: Bordas, 1991). See especially p. 154, n. 2, and p. 486, n. 1.

to examine the various solutions to the riddle of human existence proposed by the non-Christian religions:

> M. Pascal, l'ayant mis dans cette disposition de chercher à s'instruire sur un doute si important . . . lui fait ensuite parcourir tout l'univers et tous les âges, pour lui faire remarquer une infinité de religions qui s'y rencontrent; mais il lui fait voir en même temps, par des raisons si fortes et si convaincantes, que toutes ses religions ne sont remplies que de vanités, que de folies, que d'erreurs, que d'égarements et d'extravagances, qu'il n'y trouve rien encore qui le puisse satisfaire.[15]

> M. Pascal, having motivated him to seek to resolve such an important doubt . . . then makes him cast his eyes over the whole world and over all of history in order to encounter that infinity of religions which are found there; however, at the same time, using a reasoning which is strong and convincing, he makes him see that all these religions are filled with nothing but vanities, insanities, errors, aberrations and extravagances and that he will find nothing in them which might satisfy him.

As we saw in Chapter III, Pascal's treatment of the non-Christian religions remains in a rather embryonic form in the text of the *Pensées*. Indeed, the modern student of the comparative study of religions may be astonished by Pascal's scant knowledge of the religions of the world beyond Europe; aside from Islam, Pascal appears to be aware of the existence of only two others: "celle de la Chine" ("that of China") (454, 822, 436, 481) and the pagan religion described by "les historiens de Mexico" (481). To these, we might add Pascal's rather sketchy references to the no longer extant religions of the Greeks, the Romans, and the Egyptians (454, 451, 436). Pascal excludes, of course, Judaism from the category of the non-Christian religions. In the course of the Apology, he intends to demonstrate "que les vrais juifs et les vrais chrétiens n'ont qu'une même religion" ("that true Jews and true Christians have the same religion") (453).[16]

However sketchy Pascal's perspective on the non-Christian religions seems, it is nonetheless abundantly clear that the apologist does not intend for his *chercheur* to waste very much time exploring them. As Pascal sees it, seeking knowledge concerning the fate of the soul after death in the non-Christian religions is no more a legitimate concern for the seeking unbeliever than is the search for religious truth in the realms of science or philosophy. When he commends those unbelievers who seek the truth, Pascal hardly has in mind the pursuit of science, philosophy, or compara-

15. "Préface de l'Edition de Port-Royal" in Lafuma, *Pascal: Oeuvres complètes*, p. 495.

16. An entire dossier, *série viii*, contains a long list of Scriptural citations with which Pascal evidently intended to document this theme.

tive religion. "Sans Jésus-Christ," Pascal insists in fragment 449, any knowledge gained in such an endeavor would remain "inutile et stérile." In the last analysis, he thinks, the only logical alternative to being a convinced believer is being what the early Church called a "catechumen," that is, one who seeks instruction while awaiting the gift of Grace. Those unbelievers who really "cherchent en gémissant" ("seek with groans") must ultimately do so under the guidance of Holy Mother Church.

The Catechumenate as a Model for Conversion

After having fallen into disuse for many centuries, the catechumenate was restored in 1962 by the Second Vatican Council as a necessary prelude to all adult Baptisms. On entering the catechumenate, candidates are marked with the Sign of the Cross. During a lengthy "Time of Purification and Enlightenment," they are obliged to attend services of Scriptural reading and doctrinal instruction. Their election for sacramental initiation normally takes place on the first Sunday in Lent and is followed by "scrutinies" on the third, fourth, and fifth Sundays of Lent. On Holy Saturday, the final ceremonies take place: the public recitation of the Creed, the Ephphata,[17] and the anointing of the candidates with oil. Baptism, Confirmation, and Communion follow during the Easter Vigil Service.

Pascal learned of the central role of the catechumenate in the Primitive Church through consulting Saint Augustine's *De catechizandis rudibus*.[18] Philippe Sellier has demonstrated that Pascal borrows a cardinal principle of Scriptural exegesis from this text. Augustine had recommended that the inquirer into Christianity interpret spiritually and figuratively everything in Scripture which does not manifestly lead to the love of God. In fragment 270, Pascal renders this principal as follows:

> Tout ce qui ne va point à la charité est figure.
>
> L'unique objet de l'Ecriture est la charité.
>
> Tout ce qui ne va point à l'unique but en est la figure. Car puisqu'il n'y a qu'un but, tout ce qui n'y va point en mots propres est figure.

17. The ceremony in the Roman Baptismal Rite during which the celebrant, pronouncing the words "Ephphata, that is Be opened" (cf. Mark 7:34), touches the ears and mouth of the candidate and prays that he may hear and preach the Gospel. It is found from an early date in the Baptismal Rite for Easter Eve in the Roman Usage.

18. See Philippe Sellier, *Pascal et Saint Augustin*, p. 414.

> Everything which does not lead to charity is figurative.
>
> The sole object of Scripture is charity.
>
> Everything that does not lead to this sole good is figurative. For, since there is only one goal, everything that does not lead to it explicitly is figurative. (270)

The context in which Pascal enunciates this central exegetical principle bears directly upon his conception of the nature of true conversion. The Jews, he explains, had always interpreted God's promises literally, believing that He had favored them materially above all peoples and that He would send a Messiah to make them masters of the world. "Le monde ayant vieilli dans ces erreurs charnelles, J.-C. est venu dans le temps prédit, mais non pas dans l'état attendu, et ainsi ils n'ont pas pensé que ce fût lui" ("When the world had grown old in these carnal errors, Jesus Christ came at the time appointed, but not in the expected blaze of glory, and thus they did not think it was he") (270). Only after Christ's death did Saint Paul unlock the true meaning of the Scriptures by explaining that everything had come to pass figuratively:

> Que le royaume de Dieu ne consistait pas en la chair, mais en l'esprit, que les ennemis des hommes n'étaient pas les Babyloniens, mais leurs passions, que Dieu ne se plaisait pas aux temples faits de main, mais en un coeur pur et humilié, que la circoncision du corps était inutile, mais qu'il fallait celle du coeur, que Moïse ne leur avait pas donné le pain du ciel, etc.

> That the kingdom of God was not in the flesh but in the spirit, that the enemies of men were not the Babylonians but their passions, that God did not delight in temples made with hands but in a pure and humble heart, that the circumcision of the body was useless, but that there must be circumcision of the heart; that Moses had not given them the bread from heaven, etc. (270)

Pascal's *chercheur*, like the Jews of old, is obsessed with the literal, the carnal, and the material. He understands that nature is corrupt and that human beings are contrary to *honnêteté*. But he is unable "voler plus haut" ("to penetrate the matter further") (642). He has not yet broken through to the spiritual order of *charité*. This is why proofs of God's existence drawn from "les ouvrages de la nature" ("the works of nature") are useless in bringing about his conversion. Those believers who possess "la foi vive dedans le coeur" ("living faith in their hearts") are able to see God in His Creation. When they look at the universe they automatically understand that "tout ce qui est n'est autre chose que l'ouvrage du Dieu qu'ils adorent" ("everything which exists is entirely the work of the God they worship"). However, this is not the case at all for those who have yet to be touched by Grace:

> Pour ceux en qui cette lumière est éteinte et dans lesquels on a dessein de la faire revivre, ces personnes destituées de la grâce, qui recherchant de toute leur lumière tout ce qu'ils voient dans la nature qui les peut mener à cette connaissance ne trouvent qu'obscurité et ténèbres, dire à ceux-là qu'ils n'ont qu'à voir la moindre des choses qui les environnent et qu'ils y verront Dieu à découvert . . . c'est leur donner sujet de croire que les preuves de notre religion sont bien faibles.

> For those in whom this light has gone out and in whom we are trying to rekindle it, people deprived of faith and grace, examining with such light as they have everything they see in nature that might lead them to this knowledge, but finding only obscurity and darkness; to tell them, I say, that they have only to look at the least thing around them and they will see in it God plainly revealed . . . this is giving them cause to think that the proofs of our religion are indeed feeble. (781)

Perhaps nowhere in the *Pensées* does Pascal more perfectly define his apologetic mission. His role as apologist means attempting to rekindle the inner light which has been extinguished by disbelief in those "personnes destituées de foi et de grâce" ("people deprived of faith and grace"). Because they lack the inner light which Grace alone can rekindle, these unbelievers—even when their intentions are right and they are seeking the truth—simply cannot see what believers see when they look at the world around them. They are like those who seek the light at noonday or water in the sea. God has left them "dans un aveuglement dont ils ne peuvent sortir que par J.-C., hors duquel toute communication avec Dieu est ôtée" ("in a blindness from which they can escape only through Jesus Christ, without whom all communication with God is broken off"). "*Nemo novit patrem nisi filius et cui filius voluit revelare*" ("Neither knoweth any man the Father save the Son, and he to whomsoever the Son will reveal him")[19] (781).

A text which has often been overlooked by commentators on the *Pensées* affords us great insight into Pascal's understanding of the nature of Christian conversion. His *Comparaison des chrétiens des premiers temps avec ceux d'aujourd'hui* (*Comparison of the Early Christians with Those Today*) is essentially a panegyric on the ancient initiation rite of the Primitive Church:

> Dans le temps de l'Eglise naissante, on enseignait les catéchumènes, c'est-à-dire ceux qui prétendaient au baptême, avant que de le leur conférer, et on ne les y

19. Matthew 11:27.

admettait qu'après une pleine instruction des mystères de la religion, qu'après une pénitence de leur vie passée, qu'après une grande connaissance de la grandeur et de l'excellence de la profession de la foi et des maximes chrétiennes où ils désiraient entrer pour jamais, *qu'après des marques d'une conversion véritable du coeur*, et qu'après un extrême désir du baptême.[20]

In the days of the Primitive Church, the catechumens, i.e., those who aspired to Christian Baptism, were instructed before receiving it; they were admitted to Baptism only after having received a full instruction in the mysteries of our holy religion, only after having done penance for their past life, only after having understood the majesty and excellence of that profession of faith and of those articles of the Christian religion into which they desired to enter forever, only after having manifested *signs of a true conversion of the heart*, only after having shown an extreme desire to receive the sacrament of Baptism.

In Pascal's view, the loss of the Church's ancient initiation rite, the catechumenate, has resulted in a scandalous deterioration of Christian devotion and sacramental life. In the days of the Primitive Church, most Christians were extensively instructed in the mysteries of their religion. Christians today, says Pascal, "sont dans une ignorance qui fait horreur" ("are in a horrifying state of ignorance"). Because Baptism now precedes instruction, "on croit pouvoir demeurer chrétien sans se faire instruire" ("people think they can remain Christians without receiving instruction"). Early Christians, Pascal observes, abjured the world at their Baptism. Contemporary practice could hardly be more different. "On fréquente les sacrements et on jouit des plaisirs du monde" ("People frequent the sacraments while enjoying worldly pleasures"). Those who had experienced the ancient initiation rite rarely fell away from the Church and back into the ways of the secular world. The Christians of Pascal's time, he observes, abuse the sacraments in order to facilitate their "chutes et rechutes continuelles" ("constant lapses and relapses"):

L'Eglise des saints se trouve donc maintenant toute souillée par le mélange des méchants, et ses enfants qu'elle a conçus, portés et nourris dès l'enfance dans ses flancs, sont ceux-là mêmes qui portent dans son coeur, c'est-à-dire jusqu'à la participation de ses plus augustes mystères, le plus cruel de ses ennemis, c'est-à-dire l'esprit du monde, l'esprit d'ambition, l'esprit de vengeance, l'esprit d'impureté, l'esprit de concupiscence: et l'amour qu'elle a pour ses propres enfants, l'oblige d'admettre jusque dans ses entrailles le plus cruel de ses persécuteurs.[21]

20. *Comparaison des chrétiens des premiers temps avec ceux d'aujourd'hui* in Lafuma, *Pascal: Oeuvres complètes*, p. 360. Italics mine.

21. Ibid., p. 361.

The Church of the saints now finds her purity soiled by the contamination of the evildoers; her own children which she has conceived, carried and nourished from childhood in her entrails, are the very ones who now carry into her heart, that is to say, even into the participation in her most august mysteries, the most cruel of her enemies, which is to say, the spirit of the world, of vengeance, of impurity, of lust: the love which she bears her own children forces her to admit into her very womb the most cruel of her persecutors.

Despite his admiration for the catechumenate of the Primitive Church, Pascal is never tempted by the heresy of the Anabaptists. The long-standing and venerable practice of the Baptism of infants, he maintains, is warranted by serious theological considerations. In her great mercy, the Church does not condemn to everlasting Hell those many children who would die before receiving Baptism at the age of reason:

Ce n'est pas à l'Eglise que l'on doit imputer les malheurs qui ont suivi un changement de discipline si salutaire; car elle n'a pas changé d'esprit, quoiqu'elle ait changé de conduite. Ayant donc vu que la dilation du baptême laissait un grand nombre d'enfants dans la malédiction d'Adam, elle a voulu les délivrer de cette masse de perdition, en précipitant les secours qu'elle leur donne. Et cette bonne mère ne voit qu'avec regret extrême que ce qu'elle a procuré pour le salut de ses enfants, devienne l'occasion de la perte des adultes.[22]

The Church should not be blamed for the misfortunes which have followed upon such a salutary change of discipline; she has not changed her mind, even though she has changed her conduct. Having seen that the delay in Baptism left a great number of children in the grips of Adam's curse, she wanted to deliver them from this mass of perdition by coming to their aid more quickly. And this good Mother sees with extreme regret that the means by which she has procured the salvation of her children becomes the very means by which adults are lost.

Pascal leaves no doubt as to his literal view of the transmission of the stain of Original Sin. Unbaptized children, along with the *anciens justes* and those who have never heard the Gospel, will receive the eternal punishment which all humanity ("cette masse de perdition") merited in Adam's Fall. Those who have received the free gift of Baptism should beware of abusing it to their perdition. All baptized Christians, Pascal urges, must seek to imitate the example of the catechumens of the Primitive Church:

Il faut qu'ils se mettent devant les yeux l'exemple des catéchumènes, et qu'ils considèrent leur ardeur, leur dévotion, leur horreur du monde, et leur généreux renoncement à toute ses pompes. Car, si on ne jugeait pas ceux-là dignes de rece-

22. Ibid.

voir le baptême sans ces dispositions, n'est-il pas juste que ceux qui ne les trouvent pas en eux après l'avoir reçu, fassent tous leurs efforts pour former d'aussi généreux sentiments, se soumettant à une pénitence salutaire le reste de leurs jours, et qu'ils aient moins d'aversion pour une vie toute crucifiée qu'ils ne trouvent de charme dans l'usage des délices empoisonnées du péché.[23]

They must hold before their eyes the example of the catechumens. Let them reflect upon their ardor, their devotion, their horror of the world and their generous renunciation of all its pomp. Indeed, if the catechumens were not judged worthy to receive Holy Baptism without this frame of mind and these inclinations, is it not just that those who do not find them in themselves after having received it, make every effort to form such noble sentiments, submitting themselves to a salutary penitence for the rest of their days; let them at least have less aversion for the crucified life than they have attraction for the poisonous delights of sin.

Pascal's enthusiasm for the catechumenate of the early Church serves to remind us that he is not calling the seeking unbeliever to be a nominal or conventional Catholic Christian, no better or no worse than any other. Rather, the *chercheur* is being challenged to a true inner conversion which requires no less than the total annihilation of self. Those in whom the inner light has been extinguished, Pascal observes, flippantly imagine dramatic scenes of conversion. "'Si j'avais vu un miracle,' disent-ils, 'je me convertirais'" ("'If I had seen a miracle,' they say, 'I would be converted'") (378). Pascal can only answer that such unbelievers fail completely to understand what true conversion entails:

Comment assurent-ils qu'ils feraient ce qu'ils ignorent? Ils s'imaginent que cette conversion consiste en une adoration qui se fait de Dieu comme un commerce et une conversation telle qu'ils se la figurent. La conversion véritable consiste à s'anéantir devant cet être universel qu'on a irrité tant de fois et qui peut vous perdre légitimement à toute heure, à reconnaître qu'on ne peut rien sans lui et qu'on n'a rien mérité de lui que sa disgrâce. Elle consiste à connaître qu'il y a une opposition invincible entre Dieu et nous et que sans un médiateur il ne peut y avoir de commerce.

How can they be sure that they would do what they know nothing about? They imagine that such a conversion consists in a worship of God conducted, as they picture it, like some exchange or conversation. True conversion consists in self-annihilation before the universal being whom we have so often vexed and who is perfectly entitled to destroy us at any moment, in recognizing that we can do nothing without him and that we have deserved nothing but his disfavor. It consists in knowing that there is an irreconcilable opposition between God and us, and that without a mediator there can be no exchange. (378)

23. Ibid., p. 362.

For Pascal, true inner conversion means accepting the call to "une vie toute crucifée"[24] ("the completely crucified life"). In the liturgy renewed in 1962 by the ordo "De Initiatione Christiana Adultorum," the catechumen is first claimed for Christ by being marked with the Sign of the Cross. At the end of the "wager" fragment (418), the unbeliever who seeks to believe is told by Pascal to signify his will to believe by making the Sign of the Cross with holy water ("en prenant de l'eau bénite"). Significantly enough, he is not encouraged to strengthen his fledgling faith by receiving Holy Communion. The theologians of Port-Royal discouraged reception of the sacrament except when accompanied by thorough preparation and proper interior disposition. In his *De la fréquente communion* (1643), Arnauld had attacked the Jesuits' practice of advising penitents to receive communion frequently in order to attract an increase of interior Grace. Nowhere in the apologetic itinerary sketched by the *Pensées* does Pascal ever recommend that the *chercheur* return to the sacraments as a means of attracting the Grace necessary for true conversion.

According to the ordo "De Initiatione Christiana Adultorum," the catechumen must go through a lengthy period of "Purification and Enlightenment" before proceeding to his Profession of Faith. During this period, he learns the inner and spiritual meanings of the Scriptures and the Creeds. In the first half of the Apology anticipated by the *Pensées*, the *chercheur* also passes through a kind of purification. He is disabused of his illusions concerning the scope and power of human reason. He vicariously experiences the vanity of human wishes, the impotence of human desires, and the ultimate meaninglessness of man without God. Only after having descended to the depths of human *misère* in the school of *expérience* is he prepared to receive Divine Enlightenment. Like the catechumen, he will study the Scriptures and learn how to interpret their inner meaning. Chapters XVIII–XXV in the *liasses* of 1658 ("Fondements," "Loi figurative," "Rabbinage," "Perpétuité," "Preuves de Moïse," "Preuves de Jésus-Christ," "Prophéties" and "Figures particulières") will unfold the drama of Salvation as revealed in the Scriptures. Pascal's *chercheur* will learn that God has hidden many signs in Revelation so that those who search with all their hearts may believe.

The paradigm of conversion represented by the ancient catechumenate rite logically leads to a Profession of Faith and Holy Baptism. But what of Pascal's initiate? The catechumenate dates from a time when Christians

24. Ibid.

were a distinct minority. Pascal's inquirer, a nominal Catholic, lives in a Catholic society in which almost everyone has been baptized as an infant. Re-Baptism, of course, is out of the question. To advocate it would be to fall into the heresy of the Anabaptists or that of the Donatists. Pascal seeks to rekindle the inner light within the soul of the seeker. Indeed, if we can judge by the evidence of fragment 418, the apologist himself prays to God that the *chercheur* will be granted the gift of Grace and a true inner conversion:

> Si ce discours vous plaît et vous semble fort, sachez qu'il est fait par un homme qui s'est mis à genoux auparavant et après, pour prier cet être infini et sans parties, auquel il soumet tout le sien, de se soumettre aussi le vôtre pour votre propre bien et pour sa gloire.

> If these words please you and seem cogent, you must know that they come from a man who went down upon his knees before and after to pray this infinite and indivisible being, to whom he submits his own, that he might bring your being also to submit to him for your own good and for his glory. (418)

The apologist cannot, of course, mandate such a conversion. He can do no more than serve as a catechist, instructing the *chercheur* and preparing him to receive the gift which Grace alone can dispense. Pascal may well have seen himself as having been vouchsafed this kind of second Baptism of inner conversion. "FEU," the first word set down in the *Mémorial* (see Plates XIV and XV) after the date, has been the subject of much speculation by psychiatrists, commentators on the *Pensées*, and students of the mystical tradition.[25] Henri Gouhier suggests "une source littéraire précise": the episode in Exodus 3 which also inspires the second line of the *Mémorial*.[26] Both "FEU" and "Dieu d'Abraham, Dieu d'Isaac, Dieu de Jacob" (913) obviously invoke the God of Israel's revelation of Himself in the Burning Bush of Exodus 3:1–6. But might not "FEU" also recall the descent of the tongues of fire upon the Apostles on the Day of Pentecost (Acts 2:1–4) or the fire from Heaven which blinded Saint Paul on the road to Damascus (Acts 9:3–9)?

The neo-Augustinian theology formulated by the theologians of Port-Royal has of course been much oversimplified by the symbol of "le Christ aux bras étroits."[27] However, one must admit the existence of a certain

25. See Henri Gouhier, *Blaise Pascal: Commentaires* (Paris: Vrin, 1971), pp. 57–65.
26. Ibid., p. 65.
27. According to Philippe Sellier, there exists no trace of any such crucifix in the iconography of Port-Royal (conversation, 1990).

tendency toward a doctrine of soteriological elitism in the writings of Saint-Cyran, Arnauld, and others. Pascal himself plainly makes the point that true believers in his time are every bit as much in the minority as were Christians in the days of the Primitive Church:

> Il y a peu de vrais chrétiens. Je dis même pour la foi. Il y en a bien qui croient mais par superstition. Il y en a bien qui ne croient pas, mais par libertinage; peu sont entre-deux.
>
> Je ne comprends pas en cela ceux qui sont dans la véritable piété de moeurs et tous ceux qui croient par un sentiment du coeur.

> There are few true Christians. I mean even as regards faith. There are plenty who believe, but out of superstition. There are plenty who do not believe, but because they are libertine; there are few in between.
>
> I do not include those who lead a really devout life, nor all those who believe by intuition of the heart. (179)

The Faith of the Simple

In the *liasse* "Conclusion" (XXVII), Pascal goes to great lengths to justify the faith of those "personnes simples" who are able to believe "sans raisonnement" ("without reasoning"). The *chercheur*, whom Jean Mesnard qualifies as "considéré comme pratiquement converti"[28] ("considered as practically converted") by this point in the Apology, is warned by the apologist not to be surprised by this phenomenon. God accords to such believers, Pascal explains, the two essential interior dispositions necessary for belief. "Dieu leur donne l'amour de soi et la haine d'eux-mêmes" ("God makes them love him and hate themselves") (380). Christianity is the only religion which teaches a doctrine of God and a doctrine of man which is perfectly attuned to the paradox of the human condition:

> Le christianisme est étrange; il ordonne à l'homme de reconnaître qu'il est vil et même abominable, et lui ordonne de vouloir être semblable à Dieu. Sans un tel contrepoids cette élévation le rendrait horriblement vain, ou cet abaissement le rendrait horriblement abject.

> Christianity is strange. It bids man to recognize that he is vile, and even abominable, and bids him want to be like God. Without such a counterweight his exaltation would make him horribly vain or his abasement horribly abject. (351)

28. In *Blaise Pascal: L'Homme et l'oeuvre,* Cahiers de Royaumont (Paris: Editions de Minuit, 1956), pp. 155–56.

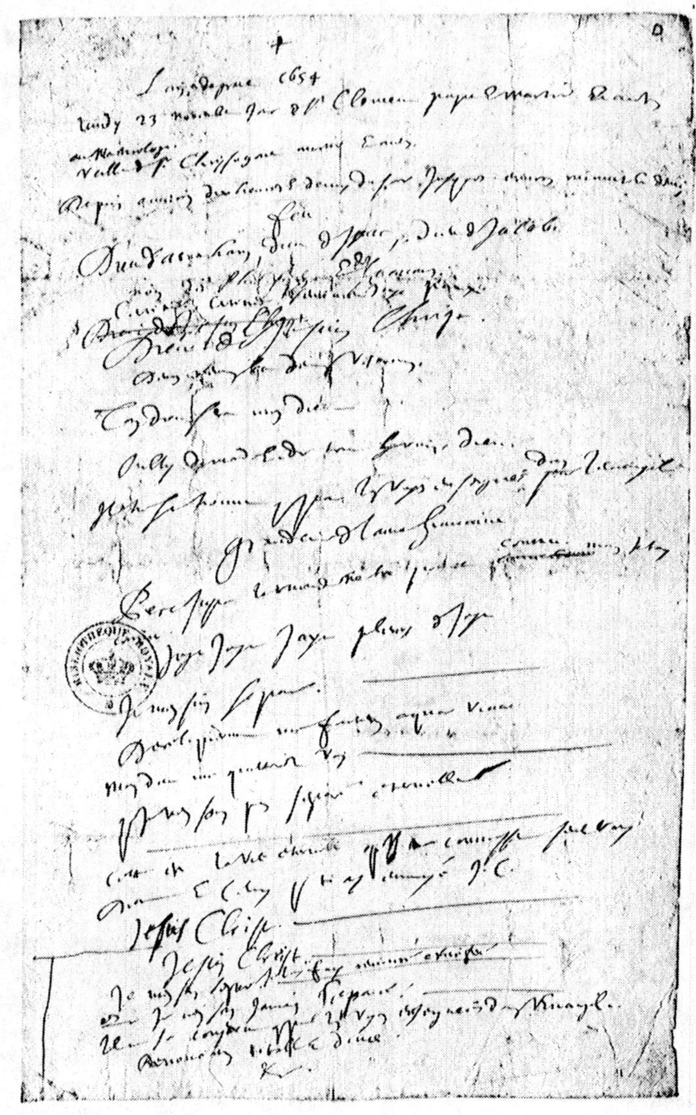

PLATE XIV. The autograph text of the *Mémorial* (Lafuma fragment 913) written by Pascal the night of November 23, 1654 and found sewn into the lining of his doublet at his death:

"FEU

Dieu d'Abraham, Dieu d'Isaac, Dieu de Jacob,
non des philosophes et des savants. . . ."

Citation begins on the sixth line of the manuscript page. Service photographique, Bibliothèque Nationale.

E.

L'an de grace 1654.
Lundy 23e Nov.bre jour de St. Clement
Pape et m. et autres au martirologe Romain
veille de St. Crysogone m. et autres &c.
Depuis environ dix heures et demi du soir
jusques environ minuit et demi

FEV.

Dieu d'Abraham. Dieu d'Isaac. Dieu de Jacob
non des philosophes et sçavans.
certitude joye certitude sentiment veue joye
Dieu de Jesus Christ.
Deum meum et Deum vestrum.
Jeh. 20. 17.
Ton Dieu sera mon Dieu. Ruth.
oubly du monde et de Tout hormis DIEV
Il ne se trouve que par les voyes enseignées
dans l'Evangile. Grandeur de l'ame humaine.
Pere juste, le monde ne t'a point
connu, mais je t'ay connu. Jeh. 17.
Joye Joye Joye et pleurs de joye
Je m'en suis separé
Dereliquerunt me fontem
mon Dieu me quitterez vous
que je n'en sois pas separé eternellement.

Cette est la vie eternelle qu'ils te connoissent
seul vray Dieu et celuy que tu as envoyé
Jesus Christ
Jesus Christ
je m'en suis separé, je l'ay fui renoncé crucifié
que je n'en sois jamais separé.
il ne se conserve que par les voyes enseignées
dans l'Evangile.
Renontiation Totale et douce
Soûmission totale a Jesus Christ et a mon directeur.
eternellemt. en joye pour un jour d'exercice sur la terre.
non obliviscar sermones tuos. amen.

C'est icy la copie figurée d'un parchemin trouvé apres la mort de Mr. Pascal mon oncle écrit de sa main, et cousu dans la doublure de son pourpoint.

PLATE XV. Facsimile copy of the *Mémorial* made by Louis Périer. The notation in the margin reads: "C'est icy la copie figurée d'un parchemin trouvé après la mort de M. Pascal mon oncle écrit de sa main, et cousu dans la doublure de son pourpoint." Service photographique, Bibliothèque Nationale.

The one true religion ("la vraie religion"), Pascal insists, must fulfill four criteria: (I) It must teach the love of God; (II) It must take into account the reality of fallen human nature; (III) It must teach hatred of self; (IV) It must teach the remedy necessary to redeem the corruption of humanity in the Fall. Christianity fulfills all four criteria:

(I) La vraie religion doit avoir pour marque d'obliger à aimer son Dieu. Cela est bien juste et cependant aucune ne l'a ordonné, la nôtre l'a fait.

The sign of the true religion must be that it obliges men to love God. That is quite right, yet while none enjoined it, ours has done so. (214)

(II) (Après avoir entendu toute la nature de l'homme) il faut pour faire qu'une religion soit vraie qu'elle ait connu notre nature. Elle doit avoir connu la grandeur et la petitesse et la raison de l'une et de l'autre. Qui l'a connu que la chrétienne?

(After hearing the whole nature of man.) For a religion to be true it must have known our nature; it must have known its greatness and smallness, and the reason for both. What other religion but Christianity has known this? (215)

(III) Nulle autre religion n'a proposé de se haïr, nulle autre religion ne peut donc plaire à ceux qui se haïssent et qui cherchent un être véritablement aimable. Et ceux-là s'ils n'avaient jamais ouï parler de la religion d'un Dieu humilié l'embrasseraient incontinent.

No other religion has proposed that we should hate ourselves. No other religion therefore can please those who hate themselves and who seek a being who is really worthy of love. And if they had never [before] heard of the religion of a humiliated God, they would at once embrace it. (220)

(IV) [La vraie religion] doit . . . avoir apporté des remèdes [à la concupiscence et à l'impuissance]. (214) L'Incarnation montre à l'homme la grandeur de sa misère par la grandeur du remède qu'il a fallu.

[The true religion] must have provided the remedies [for concupiscence and weakness]. (214) The Incarnation shows man the greatness of his wretchedness through the greatness of the remedy required. (352)

No other religion, Pascal argues in the *liasse* "Fausseté des autres religions" ("Falseness of other religions") (XVI), has ever proposed self-hatred. Yet only a religion which teaches self-hatred will make sense to those who have truly experienced the depths of human "misère." Christ's poor experience this "misère" every day in the very reality of their lives. The *chercheur* has had to be convinced of the reality of "misère" via an intellectual analysis of the human condition. Even those who had never heard of

Christianity ("la religion d'un Dieu humilié), but who were wise enough to hate themselves, would unhesitatingly embrace it ("l'embrasseraient incontinent") should they encounter this religion by chance (200). Such, presumably, is Pascal's answer to those who pity the plight of the *anciens justes* and that of those who never had a chance to hear the Gospel. As Pascal sees it, the religion of a suffering God ("un Dieu humilié") is the only theodicy which is left intact in the face of the problem of evil.

When God inclines the hearts of the simple toward belief, he does not simply give them love for Himself and for things eternal. Such a gift ("cette élévation") would only serve to make them "horriblement vain[s]" (351). God also accords the simple an instinctive self-hatred which leads to true belief:

> Ne vous étonnez pas de voir des personnes simples croire sans raisonnement. Dieu leur donne l'amour de soi et la haine d'eux-mêmes. Il incline leur coeur à croire. On ne croira jamais, d'une créance utile et de foi si Dieu n'incline le coeur et on croira dès qu'il l'inclinera.

> Do not be astonished to see simple people believing without argument. God makes them love him and hate themselves. He inclines their hearts to believe. We shall never believe, with an effective belief and faith, unless God inclines our hearts, and we shall believe as soon as he does so. (380)

In one of the very last fragments of the *Apology* sketched by the dossiers of 1658, Pascal again reminds the *chercheur* that the single indispensable ingredient in belief is an initiative by God himself. "On ne croira jamais, d'une créance utile et de foi si Dieu n'incline le coeur" ("We shall never believe, with an effective belief and faith, unless God inclines our hearts"). Once this happens, everything else—including both the search of the unbeliever and the efforts of the Christian apologist—pales into insignificance. "On croira dès qu'il l'inclinera" ("We shall believe as soon as he disposes [the heart] to believe") (380).

The simple do not need the "raisonnement" of philosophy in order to become conscious of human "misère." Nor do they need the itinerary traced in the first half of the *Apology* in order to be prompted to seek God. Via the gift of Grace, they instinctively grasp the implications of the human condition. Within themselves they instinctively perceive via the heart everything which Pascal means when he uses the shorthand expression "misère." Their self-hatred is instinctive. Their belief proceeds from the heart:

> Ceux qui croient sans avoir lu les Testaments c'est parce qu'ils ont une disposition intérieure toute sainte et que ce qu'ils entendent dire de notre religion y est

conforme. Ils sentent qu'un Dieu les a faits. Ils ne veulent aimer que Dieu, ils ne veulent haïr qu'eux-mêmes. Ils sentent qu'ils n'en ont pas la force d'eux-mêmes, qu'ils sont incapables d'aller à Dieu et que si Dieu ne vient à eux ils sont incapables d'aucune communication avec lui et ils entendent dire dans notre religion qu'il ne faut aimer que Dieu et ne haïr que soi-même, mais qu'étant tous corrompus et incapables de Dieu, Dieu s'est fait homme pour s'unir à nous. Il n'en faut pas davantage pour persuader des hommes qui ont cette disposition dans le coeur et qui ont cette connaissance de leur devoir et de leur incapacité.

Those who believe without having read the Testaments do so because their inward disposition is truly holy and what they hear about our religion matches it. They feel that a God made them, they only want to love God, they only want to hate themselves. They feel that they are not strong enough to do this by themselves, that they are incapable of going to God, and that if God does not come to them they are incapable of communicating with him at all. They hear it said in our religion that we must only love God and only hate ourselves, but that, since we are all corrupt and incapable of reaching God, God made himself man in order to unite himself with us. It takes no more than this to convince men whose hearts are thus disposed and who have such an understanding of their duty and incapacity. (381)

Pascal has an immediate apologetic reason for focusing upon those who believe "sans avoir lu les Testaments" ("without having read the Testaments") (381). The apologetic itinerary which has led the *chercheur* to the threshold of belief has climaxed with a study of those proofs of Christianity found in the Scriptures. Throughout the Apology, Pascal has labored to convince the seeking unbeliever that God has modified his unknowable nature ("tempéré sa connaissance") (149) in order to save those "qui le cherchent de tout leur coeur" ("who seek him with all their heart") (149). God has hidden in Revelation "des marques de soi visibles à ceux qui le cherchent" ("signs of Himself visible to those who seek Him") (149). Chief among these "marques . . . visibles" are the Old Testament prophecies and their accomplishment in the New Testament. "La plus grande des preuves de J.-C. sont les prophéties" (335).[29] That "miracle subsistant"

29. Pascal makes it clear that "la plus grande des preuves" originates with God himself: "C'est . . . à quoi Dieu a le plus pourvu" ("It is for them that God made most provision") (335). Le Maistre de Sacy, Pascal's mentor in matters exegetical, insists that it is the prophecies which distinguish "la véritable religion" from all other religions: "Dieu ayant résolu de sauver le monde quatre mille ans après sa création par la mort et par la résurrection de son Fils . . . a voulu fonder cette foi sur des preuves convaincantes qu'elles puissent distinguer la véritable religion de toutes les sociétés sacrilèges que le démon avait déjà inventés ou qu'il pourrait inventer dans la suite de tous les siècles" ("God, having resolved to save the world four thousand years after its creation by the death and resurrection of his Son . . . wanted to found this faith on convincing proofs capable of distinguishing this true religion from all

("continuing miracle") (180) constituted by "les prophéties accomplies" ("fulfilled prophecies") has played a critical role in bringing the *chercheur* to the threshold of conversion. But what will be his reaction when he goes out into the world and encounters "ceux que nous voyons chrétiens sans la connaissance des prophéties et des preuves" ("those whom we see to be Christians without knowledge of the prophecies and proofs") (382)? Will he not be taken aback by the fact that the vulgar masses already believe what he has come to believe via a painful rite of purification, initiation, and study?

Pascal obviously means to anticipate such a potentially harmful realization by the *chercheur*. He warns him to expect to encounter many Christians "qui croient sans avoir lu les Testaments" ("who believe without having read the Testaments") (381). Not only is the belief of these people valid; it is every bit as valid as the belief of those who have a knowledge of the prophecies and other proofs of Christianity. "Ils en jugent par le coeur comme les autres en jugent par l'esprit. C'est Dieu lui-même qui les incline à croire et ainsi ils sont très efficacement persuadés" ("They judge with their hearts as others judge with their minds. It is God himself who inclines them to believe and thus they are most effectively convinced") (382).

The *chercheur* might logically then ask why he has had to labor so hard to acquire "par esprit" ("with his mind") what the simple have been granted "par le coeur" ("by means of their hearts"). At this point, we might imagine Pascal admonishing his interlocutor that his conversion is by no means complete. "Qu'il y a loin de la connaissance de Dieu à l'aimer" ("What a long way it is between knowing God and loving him!") (377). The *chercheur*, though indeed practically converted, must understand that his ultimate fate is neither in his own hands nor in those of the apologist. He must still await the gift of Grace; indeed, true belief is completely impossible without it. "On ne croira jamais, d'une créance utile et de foi, si Dieu n'incline le coeur et on croira dès qu'il l'inclinera" ("We shall never believe, with an effective belief and faith, unless God inclines our hearts, and we shall believe as soon as he does so") (380). As Anthony Pugh so justly remarks:

---

those unholy sects which the devil had already invented or might yet invent in the course of the centuries to come"). Cited from *Les douzes petits prophètes: traduits en français . . . par Le Maistre de Sacy, Prêtre* (Brussels: Chez Fricx, 1700), Préface, p. iv. For a longer discussion of the role of the Old Testmanent prophecies in the *Apology*, see pp. 193–205 in my study, *L'Ecriture et le Reste: The "Pensées" of Pascal in the Exegetical Tradition of Port-Royal* (Columbus: Ohio State University Press, 1981).

Pascal does not want to give the impression that Christians are created by arguments, however sound. All we can do is to help others and ourselves to remove obstacles of our own creating, but if Christianity is right in its insistence on man's corruption and God's initiative in restoring the broken relationship, then the last step can only be taken with God's grace; the apologist retires before the last round, like a trainer who has to leave his charge to run the race on his own.[30]

In his final chapter of the Apology, Pascal seems to have another reason for drawing a distinction between the status of the *chercheur* and that of those simple Christians who believe without having read the Scriptures. Those Christians, though their belief is equally valid, would have great difficulty convincing an unbeliever of the truth of what they believe. Those, on the other hand, who possess the proofs of Christianity will be able to justify intellectually not only their belief but that of the simple Christians as well:

J'avoue bien qu'un de ces chrétiens qui croient sans preuves n'aura peut-être pas de quoi convaincre un infidèle, qui en dira autant de soi, mais ceux qui savent les preuves de la religion prouveront sans difficulté que ce fidèle est véritablement inspiré de Dieu, quoiqu'il ne peut le prouver lui-même.

I freely admit that one of these Christians who believe without proof will perhaps not have the means of convincing an unbeliever, who might say as much for himself, but those who do know the proofs of religion can easily prove that this believer is truly inspired by God, although he cannot prove it himself. (382)

Herein, perhaps, lies the divine raison d'être of Christian apologetics. The *chercheur* is being called to the Christian faith for more than one reason. His conversion will serve to justify the faith of the great majority of Christians who are simple believers. It will serve as an example of the power and divine inspiration of Christian catechesis. And, perhaps, he himself will be ultimately used as an instrument of Grace for the benefit of others who seek to believe.

The Limits of Apologetics

Pascal has no illusions about the limits of apologetic discourse. The ultimate end of Christian apologetics, he believes, is to vindicate the faith of those who already believe. In the instance of the *chercheur*, the apologist

30. *The Composition of Pascal's Apologia*, p. 265.

must not even think of attempting to force the hand of God or the mysterious work of his Divine Grace. In the *Mystère de Jésus*, a devotional meditation composed by Pascal during his retreat at Port-Royal-des-Champs in 1655, Christ himself admonishes the future apologist: "C'est mon affaire que ta conversion" ("Your conversion is my concern") (919). In fragment 588, Pascal reminds the *chercheur*: "La foi est un don de Dieu. Ne croyez pas que nous disions que c'est un don de raisonnement" ("Faith is a gift of God. Do not imagine that we describe it as a gift of reason"). Indeed, the doctrine of Grace is another one of those signs which distinguish Christianity from all other religions which have ever existed. "Les autres religions ne disent pas cela de leur foi. Elles ne donnaient que le raisonnement pour y arriver, et qui n'y mène pas néanmoins" ("Other religions do not say that about their faith. They offered nothing but reason as a way to faith, and yet it does not lead there") (588).

That Grace which effects true conversion flows from a unique source: Christ's redemptive work. Those Christian humanists who would seek to extend the benefits of Christ's unique sacrifice to the *anciens justes* or to adherents of those religions whose teachings seem to point toward the Gospel have failed to heed Saint Paul's warning: *Ne evacuetur crux Christi* (802).[31] Neither the Jews nor the *anciens justes* were able to bring about the conversion of the pagans:

> La conversion des païens n'était réservée qu'à la grâce du Messie. Les Juifs ont été si longtemps à les combattre sans succès: tout ce qu'en ont dit Salomon et les prophètes a été inutile. Les sages, comme Platon et Socrate, n'ont pu les persuader.
>
> The conversion of the heathen was solely reserved for the grace of the Messiah. The Jews had been attacking them for so long without success: everything that Solomon and the prophets said was useless. Wise men, like Plato and Socrates, failed to persuade them. (447)

In other words, disbelief—exemplified in its most extreme form by the pagans—was finally only confounded by the unique Grace dispensed in the Incarnation and sanctifying work of Jesus Christ.

The operation of Grace on the plane of history mirrors the conversion experience of the individual. In fragment 808, Pascal explains that there

31. Cf. 1 Corinthians 1:17–18: "For Christ did not send me to baptize but to preach the Gospel, and not with worldly wisdom, *lest the cross of Christ be emptied of its power*. For the word of the cross is folly to those who are perishing, but to us who are being saved it is the power of God" (Revised Standard translation, italics mine).

are "trois moyens de croire" ("three ways to believe"): (1) "la raison" ("reason"); (2) "la coutume" ("habit"); (3) "l'inspiration" ("inspiration"). Unlike all the other religions, Christianity does not acknowledge as its true children ("ses vrais enfants") those who believe "sans inspiration" ("without inspiration"). Christianity does not exclude reason and habit as a means to belief: "Au contraire." Yet reason and habit are useless without the operation of Grace:

> Il faut ouvrir son esprit aux preuves, s'y confirmer par la coutume, mais s'offrir par les humiliations aux inspirations, qui seules peuvent faire le vrai et salutaire effet, *ne evacuetur crux Christi.*
>
> We must open our mind to the proofs, confirm ourselves in it through habit, while offering ourselves through humiliations to inspiration, which alone can produce the real and salutary effect. *Lest the Cross of Christ be made of none effect.* (808)

This paradigm of conversion seems extremely pertinent to the progress of Pascal's *chercheur* in the course of the Apology. The first half of the Apology, which corresponds to the rite of purification in the ancient catechumenate liturgy, has served to open the mind of the *chercheur* to the proofs of Christianity by shocking him out of his illusions concerning the reliability of reason. The second half corresponding to the ancient initiation rite of Enlightenment, has consisted of the proofs of Christianity themselves. Habit has its role in this rite of Enlightenment. The more the *chercheur* studies and meditates upon the proofs of Christianity drawn from the Scriptures, the more sense they will begin to make to him. At the same time, he is presumably following Pascal's admonition to "s'offrir par les humiliations aux inspirations" ("to offer himself through humiliations to inspiration") (808). This element in the conversion schema proposed by fragment 808 corresponds, of course, to the regimen prescribed by Pascal at the end of the wager fragment. The external practice of gestures of religious significance will help (via habit) to prepare the way for true inner conversion.[32]

The actual conversion of the *chercheur*, of course, stands beyond the end of the text of the Apology itself. However, a fragment discovered by Jean Mesnard suggests that Pascal is already thinking ahead to the kind of spiritual care which the *chercheur* will need after his conversion. Once he returns to the active practice of the Christian faith, the new convert will have to be placed in the hands of a skilled spiritual director who will not

32. See Chapter IV, Pascal's Interlocutor in Fragment 427.

overburden him with works of piety and penitence during the crucial phase of inner renewal which follows upon his being touched by Grace:

> Il est bon de porter les personnes renouvelées intérieurement par la grâce à faire des oeuvres de piété et de pénitence proportionnées à leur portée. . . . Quand on contraint à des oeuvres extraordinaires de piété et de pénitence celui qui n'est pas encore renouvelé intérieurement, on gâte l'un et l'autre, l'homme par sa malice corrompant les oeuvres, et les oeuvres accablant la débilité de l'homme, qui n'est pas capable de les porter. C'est un mauvais signe de voir une personne produire au-dehors dès l'instant de sa conversion. L'ordre de la charité est de s'enraciner dans le coeur avant que de produire de bonnes oeuvres au-dehors.[33]

> It is a good thing to encourage those persons inwardly renewed by grace to undertake works of piety and penitence which are within their capacity. . . . When one requires the person who is not yet renewed inwardly to perform extraordinary works of piety and penitence, both are spoiled. Through his malice, the person corrupts the good works; at the same time, the good works overburden the weakness of the person, who is unable to bear their weight. It is a very bad sign to see a person begin to produce external good works from the moment of his conversion. The order of charity is to first take root in the heart before then producing external good works.

This fragment casts a good deal of light on Pascal's understanding of the nature of true conversion. Inner conversion, he insists, must always precede works of piety or penitence. Done in the absence of inner Grace, such works are both counterproductive and devoid of spiritual value. They may even be spiritually harmful if undertaken in an attempt to attract inner Grace. "C'est un mauvais signe de voir une personne produire au-dehors dès l'instant de sa conversion" ("It is a very bad sign to see a person begin to produce external good works from the moment of his conversion"). Not once during the course of the Apology sketched by the *Pensées* do we see Pascal urging the *chercheur* to attempt to attract inner Grace by returning to the sacraments.[34] But, in light of this fragment, what are we to make of Pascal's admonition to the *libertin* at the end of the wager fragment that he most undertake mortification of the passions as a means of removing obstacles to belief? Perhaps these works of self-mortification do not fall under the category of "extraordinary" works of penitence. After all, blessing oneself with holy water and having masses

33. This fragment, discovered by Professor Mesnard in a manuscript entitled *Pensées à imprimer* (ms. 2466, Bibliothèque Nationale), is reproduced by Philippe Sellier in his edition as fragment 772.

34. See Chapter V, the Catechumenate as a Model for Conversion.

said is not exactly the same thing as undertaking austere fasts and a strict regimen of prayer. Nonetheless, it seems somewhat difficult to reconcile Pascal's advice in fragment 418 with the idea that conversion must always *precede* its external manifestations. "L'ordre de la charité est de s'enraciner dans le coeur avant que de produire de bonnes oeuvres au-dehors" ("The way of charity is always to root itself in the heart before producing external good works").[35]

In the celebrated "wager" fragment (418), Pascal evokes the Cartesian model of the *bête-machine* as a means by which the unbeliever may work toward achieving belief. In Chapter IV, we analyzed this passage from the perspective of the apologetic argument constituted by fragment 418 itself.[36] Let us now look at it again within the context of Pascal's theory of conversion:

> Travaillez donc, non pas à vous convaincre par l'augmentation des preuves de Dieu, mais par la diminution de vos passions. Vous voulez allez à la foi, et vous n'en savez pas le chemin? Vous voulez vous guérir de l'infidélité, et vous en demander les remèdes? Apprenez de ceux qui ont été liés comme vous et qui parient maintenant tout leur bien: ce sont gens qui savent ce chemin que vous voudriez suivre et guéris d'un mal dont vous voulez guérir. Suivez la manière par où ils ont commencé: c'est en faisant tout comme s'ils croyaient, en prenant de l'eau bénite, en faisant dire des messes, etc. Naturellement même cela vous fera croire et vous abêtira.
>
> Concentrate then not on convincing yourself by multiplying proofs of God's existence but by diminishing your passions. You want to find faith and you do not know the road. You want to be cured of unbelief and you ask for the remedy: learn from those who were once bound like you and who now wager all they have. These are people who know the road you wish to follow, who have been cured of the affliction of which you wish to be cured: follow the way by which they began. They behaved just as if they did believe, taking holy water, having masses said, and so on. That will make you believe quite naturally, and will make you more docile. (418)

Jean Mesnard reminds us that in general Pascal rejects Descartes' entire philosophical system and that he describes *Les Principes de la philosophie* as "une rêverie" ("a fantasy") (1005) and as "le roman de la nature, semblable à peu près à l'histoire de Dom Quichot" ("the Romance of Nature, something like the story of Don Quixote") (1008). According to Mesnard, the theory of the *bête-machine* is the single element in the whole Cartesian

35. See Chapter IV, Pascal's Interlocutor in Fragment 418.
36. Ibid.

system which Pascal retains and adapts to the purposes of his apologetic strategy:

> L'analyse de la croyance et la pratique de la persuasion ne sauraient ignorer ce rôle de la coutume, cet automatisme du corps. A l'apologiste d'y songer. L'opinion du "libertin" s'est fait habitude et le poids de cette habitude l'empêche d'écouter les raisons de se convertir. D'où la nécessité, à une étape du cheminement apologétique, de susciter un changement d'habitudes, de réformer l'automate: ce sera "le discours de la machine."[37]

> An analysis of belief and the practice of persuasion can hardly fail to take into account this role of habit, this automatism of the body. The apologist ought to think about it. The opinions of the *libertin* have turned themselves into habit, and it is this habit which prevents him from being able to understand the logical reasons requiring his conversion. Hence, the necessity, at one stage of the apologetic itinerary, of instigating a change in habit, of reforming the automaton: this will be "the argument about the Machine."

Professor Mesnard makes a key observation concerning Pascal's conception of the nature of disbelief. Disbelief, which begins as a set of opinions, transforms itself by force of habit into a mechanism which, by extinguishing the inner light of belief, prevents the *libertin* from being able to recognize the truth when he hears it. Likewise, those "personnes destituées de foi et de grâce" ("people deprived of faith and grace"), even though they are seeking the truth "de toute leur lumière" ("with such light as they have"), fail to perceive God in his creation (781). The regimen of suppressing the passions and acting as if one believed, ordered by the apologist in fragment 418, is a kind of shock tactic. Disbelief is counteracted by the very mechanism—habit—by which it has installed itself in the mind of the *libertin*. However, as Mesnard points out, this tactic is appropriate to only one "étape" of the apologetic itinerary. The actions of the *libertin* which will result from Pascal's prescription cannot really be called works of piety or penitence. His conversion still stands far off and is far from certain. All this should serve to remind us that Pascal's portrait of the seeking unbeliever in the *Pensées* is far from static. It is in constant evolution. After all, the entire rite of Purification and Enlightenment stands between the *libertin* of fragment 418 and the practically converted *chercheur* of the final chapter of the *Apology*.

In "Ordre," the first of the *liasses* of 1658, Pascal twice mentions "le discours de la machine" ("the argument about the machine"). In fragment 7,

37. Jean Mesnard, *Les Pensées de Pascal,* pp. 79–80.

he proposes a "Lettre qui marque l'utilité des preuves. Par la Machine" ("Letter showing the usefulness of proofs, by the machine"). In fragment 11, he specifies that this "lettre"[38] will immediately follow "la lettre qu'on doit chercher Dieu" ("the letter urging men to seek God"). Following the judgment of Philippe Sellier,[39] I have identified "la lettre qu'on doit chercher Dieu" as the long draft of the Preface to the Apology constituted by fragments 427–29. Now, neither fragment 418 nor fragments 427–29 were ever placed by Pascal in the body of the Apology sketched by the *liasses* of 1658. However, the unclassified dossier *série xxx* joins two fragments which are extremely pertinent to both the "wager" fragment and the fragments which constitute the Preface. In the dossier *série xxx* we find both Pascal's preparatory notes for the writing of fragment 427 (821/432-[1]-[21]) and the main text of fragment 821 itself, in which he adapts the Cartesian model of the *bête-machine* to the uses of Christian apologetics.

In fragment 821, Pascal makes the case that intellectual and rational proofs, in order to have staying power, must be reinforced by those other proofs constituted by custom and habit:

> Il ne faut pas se méconnaître, nous sommes automate autant qu'esprit. Et de là vient que l'instrument par lequel la persuasion se fait n'est pas la seule démonstration. Combien y a(-t-)il peu de choses démontrées? Les preuves ne convainquent que l'esprit, la coutume fait nos preuves les plus fortes et les plus crues. Elle incline

38. "La lettre d'ôter les obstacles qui est le discours de la Machine, de préparer la Machine, de chercher par raison" ("the letter about removing obstacles, that is the argument about the machine, how to prepare it and how to use reason for the search").

39. *Pensées* (1991), pp. 39, 467, n. 2, and 474, n. 1. Fragment 11 again raises the difficult problem concerning the chronological relationship between fragments 418 and 427. In what is apparently a note to himself, Pascal specifies, "Ordre. *Après* la lettre qu'on doit chercher Dieu, *faire* la lettre d'ôter les obstacles qui est le discours de la machine. . . " (italics mine). I can only read this as meaning that Pascal intended to write the "wager" passage once he had already written the long passage constituted by fragment 427. If this is so, and if fragment 427—as Lafuma thought (see Chapter IV, n. 11)—dates from the late period 1661–62, then fragment 418 cannot have been written—as Jean Mesnard (see Chapter IV, n. 4) and Pol Ernst (see Chapter IV, n. 9) both think—prior to the classification of 1658. I have always had a weakness for Mesnard's description of fragment 418 as belonging to a stage representing a "travail de préparation de l'*Apologie*" (see Chapter IV, Fragments 418 and 427: The State of the Texts). However, if fragment 11 really means what it seems to, then Sellier's view that both fragments 418 and 427 belong to a period posterior to the classification of 1658 (see Chapter IV, n. 2) seems the more reasonable one. We should note that fragment 11, though it appears in the classification of 1658, could conceivably have been written several years earlier. Moreover, fragment 11 gives the impression that neither of the "lettres" has actually yet been written. Indeed, Pascal may not have followed the writing plan sketched in fragment 11. If this were the case, then fragment 418 could well have been written several years before fragment 427.

l'automate qui entraîne l'esprit sans qu'il y pense. Qui a démontré qu'il sera demain jour et que nous mourrons, et qu'y a(-t-)il de plus cru? C'est donc la coutume qui nous en persuade. C'est elle qui fait tant de chrétiens, c'est elle qui fait les Turcs, les païens, les métiers, les soldats, etc. Il y a la foi reçue dans le baptême de plus aux chrétiens qu'aux païens.

We must make no mistake about ourselves: we are as much automaton as mind. As a result, demonstration is not the only instrument for convincing us. How few things can be demonstrated! Proofs only convince the mind; habit provides the strongest proofs and those that are the most believed. It inclines the automaton, which leads the mind unconsciously along with it. Who ever proved that it will dawn tomorrow, and that we shall die? And what is more widely believed? It is, then, habit that convinces us and makes so many Christians. It is habit that makes Turks, heathens, trades, soldiers, etc. The faith received at baptism is the advantage Christians have over heathen. (821)

Commenting upon this passage, Charles Natoli makes the point that, for Pascal, custom is a kind of proof: "The repetition of past events is proof that these events or similar ones will recur. . . . For Pascal, proof can hardly be equivalent to demonstration. He is willing to call 'proofs' arguments that are neither deductive nor proceeding from indubitable premises. Moreover, a probative agent, custom, is not an argument at all. It bypasses reason and persuades the mind through the body."[40] Echoing Charron[41] and Montaigne,[42] Pascal evokes a human world whose mistress is custom. Her reign extends even into the domain of religion. "C'est elle qui fait tant de chrétiens, c'est elle qui fait les Turcs, les païens . . ." ("It is habit that makes so many Christians. It is habit that makes Turks, heathen . . .") (821). However, qualifying Montaigne's premise that religion is only a function of the country in which one happens to be born, Pascal adds that Christians receive a special dispensation of faith at their Baptism. "Il y a la foi reçue dans le baptême de plus aux chrétiens qu'aux païens" ("The faith received at Baptism is the advantage Christians have over heathen").

In the Apology outlined by the *liasses* of 1658, Pascal's ultimate emphasis

40. Charles M. Natoli, "Proof in Pascal's *Pensées:* Reason as Rhetoric" in *Meaning, Structure and History in the "Pensées" of Pascal* (Tübingen: Biblio 17, 1990), p. 24.

41. *De la sagesse,* L. 2, Chapter 5: "[Les religions] sont reçues par mains et moyens humains . . . l'on est de celle que le lieu où l'on est né et élevé tient: nous sommes circoncis, baptisé, Juifs, Mahométans, Chrétiens, avant que nous sachions que nous sommes hommes."

42. *Oeuvres complètes, Essais,* 2, 12, p. 184: "Nous sommes chrétiens à même titre que nous sommes ou périgourdins ou allemands."

is on a demonstration of the historical truth of Christianity. What role, we may well ask, does that "croyance plus facile, qui est celle de l'habitude" ("easier belief, which is that of habit") play in Pascal's larger apologetic scheme? Fragment 7 says that the "Lettre . . . par la Machine" ("Letter . . . by the Machine") will demonstrate "l'utilité des preuves" ("the usefulness of proofs"). Are custom and habit viewed as useful in preparing the way for the *chercheur*'s acceptance of the proofs of Christianity? Is the model that of fragment 418: mortification of the passions? Or do habit and custom only come into play once the *chercheur* has acknowledged the truth of Revelation? Fragment 821 provides a clear answer to this central question concerning Pascal's apologetic strategy. The role of habit is to fix in consciousness a truth which has been perceived via demonstration:

> Enfin il faut avoir recours à [la coutume] *quand une fois l'esprit a vu où est la vérité* afin de nous abreuver et nous teindre de cette créance, qui nous échappe à toute heure. Car d'en avoir toujours les preuves présentes, c'est trop d'affaire. Il faut acquérir une créance plus facile, qui est celle de l'habitude, qui sans violence, sans art, sans argument nous fait croire les choses et incline toutes nos puissances à cette croyance, en sorte que notre âme y tombe naturellement. Quand on ne croit que par la force de la conviction, et que l'automate est incliné à croire le contraire, ce n'est pas assez. Il faut donc faire croire nos deux pièces: l'esprit, par les raisons, qu'il suffit d'avoir vues une fois en sa vie; et l'automate, par la coutume, en ne lui permettant pas de s'incliner au contraire. *Inclina cor meum deus.*[43]

> In short, we must resort to habit *once the mind has seen where the truth lies*, in order to steep and stain ourselves in that belief which constantly eludes us, for it is too much trouble to have the proofs always present before us. We must acquire an easier belief, which is that of habit. With no violence, art or argument it makes us believe things, and so inclines all of our faculties to this belief that our soul falls naturally into it. When we believe only by the strength of our conviction and the automaton is inclined to believe the opposite, that is not enough. We must therefore make both parts of us believe: the mind by reasons, which need to be seen only once in a lifetime, and the automaton by habit, and not allowing it any inclination to the contrary. *Incline my heart.* (821, italics mine)

In this fragment, Pascal is adapting Montaigne's theory about custom and habit to the uses of Christian catechesis. No Christian could be expected to keep the proofs of his religion constantly present in his mind. Even the strongest of convictions is likely to be contravened by the carnal inclinations of the automaton or by the demonic forces of doubt. Hence

43. Psalm 119:36.

the necessity of habit. In Christian terms, this means not only ritual gestures such as crossing oneself, genuflecting, and repeating set prayers and pious ejaculations. The Creed and the yearly round of the liturgy recapitulate both Christian doctrine and the drama of Salvation contained in the Scriptures. Fragment 821 explains the mechanism by which habit and custom go about anchoring belief, perceived clearly and rationally only in a fleeting moment of demonstration, in the bedrock of *sentiment*:

> La raison agit avec lenteur et avec tant de vues sur tant de principes, lesquels il faut qu'ils soient toujours présents, qu'à toute heure elle s'assoupit ou s'égare manque d'avoir tous ses principes présents. Le sentiment n'agit pas ainsi; il agit en un instant, et toujours est prêt à agir. Il faut donc mettre notre foi dans le sentiment, autrement elle sera toujours vacillante.

> Reason works slowly, looking so often at so many principles, which must always be present, that it is constantly nodding or straying because all its principles are not present. Feeling does not work like that, but works instantly, and is always ready. We must then put our faith in feeling, or it will always be vacillating. (821)

In *The Idea of the Holy*, Rudolf Otto asserts that the experience of "the holy" is always achieved via the avenue of "creature-feeling." Otto invites his reader "to direct his mind to a moment of deeply-felt religious experience, as little as possible qualified by other forms of consciousness":

> Whoever cannot do this, whoever knows no such moments in his experience, is requested to read no further; for it is not easy to discuss questions of religious psychology with one who can recollect the emotions of his adolescence . . . but cannot recall any intrinsically religious feelings. We do not blame such a one, when he tries for himself to advance as far as he can with the help of such principles of explanation as he knows, interpreting "aesthetics" in terms of sensuous pleasure, and "religion" as a function of the gregarious instinct and social standards, or as something more primitive still. But the artist, who for his part has an intimate personal knowledge of the distinctive element in the aesthetic experience, will decline his theories with thanks, and the religious man will reject them even more uncompromisingly.[44]

In the course of the *Pensées*, Pascal does not fail to take into account the role of *sentiment* in religious belief. That religious feeling which crystallizes belief and gives it durability, at least in the case of Pascal himself, flows directly from his Christocentric spirituality. The mere evocation of

44. Rudolf Otto, *The Idea of the Holy: An Inquiry into the Nonrational Factor in the Idea of the Divine and Its Relation to the Rational* (Oxford: Oxford University Press, 1958), p. 8.

the name of Jesus—"saint, saint, saint à Dieu" (308)—and of his Eternal Presence in the Holy Eucharist works instantly to evoke the whole of Christian belief. "C'est le coeur qui sent Dieu et non la raison. Voilà ce que c'est que la foi. Dieu sensible au coeur, non à la raison" ("It is the heart which perceives God and not reason. That is what faith is: God perceived by the heart, not by reason") (424).

Pascal's adherence to the Augustinian concept of inner conversion effectively rules out the use of habit and custom to *attract* Grace. To put one's faith in such external realities would be "superstitious." However, to be unwilling to submit to the external symbols and manifestations of Christian belief would suggest a heart hardened against the very possibility of conversion and belief:

> Il faut que l'extérieur soit joint à l'intérieur pour obtenir de Dieu; c'est-à-dire que l'on se mette à genoux, prie des lèvres, etc., afin que l'homme orgueilleux qui n'a voulu se soumettre à Dieu soit maintenant soumis à la créature. Attendre de cet extérieur le secours est être superstitieux; ne vouloir pas le joindre à l'intérieur est être superbe.

> We must combine outward and inward to obtain anything from God; in other words we must go down on our knees, pray with our lips, etc., so that the proud man who would not submit to God must now submit to his creature. If we expect help from this outward part we are being superstitious; if we refuse to combine it with the inward we are being arrogant. (944)

In fragment 7, Pascal makes a crucial distinction between faith and proof. "La foi est différente de la preuve. L'une est humaine et l'autre est un don de Dieu. *Justus ex fide vivit*.[45] C'est de cette foi que Dieu lui-même met dans le coeur, dont la preuve est souvent l'instrument, *fides ex auditu*,[46] mais cette foi est dans le coeur et fait dire non *scio* mais *Credo*" ("Faith is different from proof. One is human and the other a gift of God. *The just shall live by faith*. This is the faith that God himself puts into our hearts, often using proof as the instrument. *Faith cometh by hearing*. But this faith is in our hearts, and makes us say not *I know* but *I believe*"). Proof, when taken from Revelation itself, can be an instrument of Grace. Though human in and of itself, proof taken from Scripture is one of the ways in which God reaches out to man. Custom and habit can prepare the way for illumination via proof by rooting out resistance to belief. Once

45. Romans 1:17: "The just man liveth by faith" (Douay-Rheims translation).

46. Romans 10:17: "Faith then cometh by hearing; and hearing by the word of Christ" (Douay-Rheims translation).

insight is achieved, custom and habit can serve to anchor belief in *sentiment*. But only God can give the gift of faith itself.

For Pascal, true conversion is the most radical of all possible acts. Once he has accepted the apologist's demonstration of the historical truth of Christianity, the *chercheur* must then manifest his conversion by the act of self-annihilation ("s'anéantir") (378). A purely intellectual submission to Christianity is absolutely insufficient. "Qu'il y a loin de la connaissance de Dieu à l'aimer" ("What a long way it is between knowing God and loving him!") (377). The modern, post-Christian reader may very well find Pascal's notion of self-annihilation tinged with a certain degree of fanaticism. However, as Rudolf Otto reminds us in *The Idea of the Holy*, "annihilation of self" and its complement ("the transcendent as the sole and entire reality") represent "the characteristic notes of mysticism in all its forms, however otherwise various in content."[47]

This radical element in the neo-Augustinian schema of conversion seemed to the Jesuits to have distinct overtones of soteriological narrowness. The Jesuits attributed to Jansenius himself the second of the notorious Five Propositions condemned by Innocent X in the bull "Cum occasione" (1653): "Dans l'état de la nature déchue, on ne résiste pas à la grâce intérieure"[48] ("In the state of fallen nature, one cannot resist interior Grace"). While preparing the eighteenth of his *Lettres provinciales*, Pascal found the passage in the *Augustinus* in which Jansenius affirms the teaching of the Council of Trent "qu'on a toujours le pouvoir de résister à la grâce"[49] ("that one always retains the power to resist Grace"). Free will plays an essential role in Pascal's understanding of the nature of conversion and belief. "La volonté est un des principaux organes de la créance, non qu'elle forme la créance, mais parce que les choses sont vraies ou fausses selon la face par où on les regarde" ("The will is one of the chief organs of belief, not because it creates belief, but because things are true or false according to the aspect by which we judge them") (539).

In the neo-Augustinian scheme of things, the will cannot mandate or create belief in the absence of Grace. Yet Grace cannot operate to effect conversion without the assent of the will. Those unbelievers who so flippantly maintain that they would undergo a conversion if they witnessed a miracle (378) have the matter completely backward: "Les miracles ne

47. *The Idea of the Holy*, p. 21.

48. See Tetsuya Shiokawa, *Pascal et les miracles* (Paris: Nizet, 1977), p. 174.

49. Lafuma, *Pascal: Oeuvres complétes,* p. 464. Pascal cites the precise reference in the *Augustinus:* "au t. 3, 1.8, c. 20."

servent pas à convertir mais à condamner"[50] ("Miracles do not serve to convert but to condemn") (379). "Ce sera une des confusions des damnés de voir qu'ils seront condamnés par leur propre raison par laquelle ils ont prétendu condamner la religion chrétienne" ("One of the ways in which the damned will be confounded is that they will see themselves condemned by their own reason, by which they claimed to condemn the Christian religion") (175). Those "unhappy but reasonable" unbelievers (160) who will be the intended readers of the *Apology* demonstrate—though perhaps unconsciously—their will to believe when they make finding out the nature of the soul ("cette recherche") (427) their principal business in life.

The Evolution of the *Chercheur*

Fragment 429 is sometimes read as if it were a redraft of Pascal's portrait of the hardened *libertin* in fragment 427. Such a reading hardly makes sense. The portrait sketched in fragment 427 is meant to alienate the *honnête homme* from the poisonous influence of aggressive disbelief. Fragment 429, on the other hand, pictures an unbeliever who is evolving into a *chercheur*. Though perhaps still an agnostic, he at least hopes that God exists. He no longer feigns playing "le brave contre Dieu." He has been stripped of his indifference. Grace has been awakened in his heart, which now strains to perceive "le vrai bien" ("the true good"). He even envies the certitude and inner peace of the believers, whom he no longer mocks. He is prepared to make any sacrifice, no matter how high the price, to win eternal life:

> Voilà ce que je vois et ce qui me trouble. Je regarde de toutes parts, et je ne vois partout qu'obscurité. La nature ne m'offre rien qui ne soit matière de doute et d'inquiétude. Si je n'y voyais rien qui marquât une Divinité, je me déterminerais à la négative; si je voyais partout les marques d'un Créateur, je reposerais en paix dans la foi. Mais, voyant trop pour nier et trop peu pour m'assurer, je suis dans un état à plaindre, et où j'ai souhaité cent fois que, si un Dieu la soutient, elle le

50. The reference "l.p.q. 113. a. 10. ad. 2.") appended to this fragment refers to Thomas Aquinas' *Summa theologica.* Sellier notes: "Pascal s'insurge contre un lieu commun de la 'piété': les vrais miracles seraient ceux qui s'opèrent dans les coeurs. Appuyé sur saint Thomas, qui dénie tout caractère miraculeux aux conversions (sauf 'Chemins de Damas'), Pascal conclut que les vrais miracles servent à condamner ceux qui y résistent" (*Pensées* [1991], p. 318, n . 1). Cf. fragments 574 and 846. See also Shiokawa, *Pascal et les miracles,* pp. 174–75.

marquât sans équivoque; et que, si les marques qu'elle en donne sont trompeuses, elle les supprimât tout à fait; qu'elle dît tout ou rien, afin que je visse quel parti je dois suivre. Au lieu qu'en l'état où je suis, ignorant ce que je suis et ce que je dois faire, je ne connais ni ma condition, ni mon devoir. Mon coeur tend tout entier à connaître où est le vrai bien, pour le suivre; rien ne me serait trop cher pour l'éternité.

Je porte envie à ceux que je vois dans la foi vivre avec tant de négligence, et qui usent si mal d'un don duquel il me semble que je ferais un usage si différent.

This is what I see and what troubles me. I look around in every direction and all I see is darkness. Nature has nothing to offer me that does not give rise to doubt and anxiety. If I saw no sign there of a Divinity I should decide on a negative solution: if I saw signs of a Creator everywhere I should peacefully settle down in the faith. But, seeing too much to deny and not enough to affirm, I am in a pitiful state, where I have wished a hundred times over that, if there is a God supporting nature, she should unequivocally proclaim him, and that, if the signs in nature are deceptive, they should be completely erased; that nature should say everything or nothing so that I could see what course I ought to follow. Instead of that, in the state in which I am, not knowing what I am nor what I ought to do, I know neither my condition nor my duty. My whole heart strains to know what the true good is in order to pursue it: no price would be too high to pay for eternity.

I envy those of the faithful whom I see living so unconcernedly, making so little use of a gift which, it seems to me, I should turn to such different account. (429)

The unbeliever pictured in fragment 429 has received neither divine illumination nor Christian instruction. Like the hardened skeptic of fragment 427, he perceives only "obscurité" when he beholds the created universe. Nature reveals nothing to him "qui ne soit matière de doute et d'inquiétude" ("that does not give rise to doubt and anxiety"). However, unlike the hardened unbeliever, he has not yet lost an innate sense that nature itself bears the imprint of something far more deeply interfused. To use the description which the editors of the "Edition de Port-Royal" applied to Pascal's interlocutor in fragment 418, the unbeliever in fragment 429 finds himself "dans un état de suspension entre la foi et l'infidélité"[51] ("in a state of suspension between faith and disbelief"). He cannot opt for total disbelief since he is not convinced that nothing in the created world might point to the hidden presence of "une Divinité." However, at the same time, Nature furnishes insufficient "marques d'un Créateur" ("signs of a Creator") to warrant his concluding that God really exists.

What the agnostic of fragment 429 sees when he scans the created universe—that is, "trop pour nier" ("too much to deny") yet "trop peu pour

51. *Pensées de Pascal . . . Edition de Port-Royal,* A. Gazier, ed., p. 137.

[s]'assurer" ("too little to affirm") —squares perfectly with Pascal's neo-Augustinian conception of God's hidden presence in the world. "Ce qui y paraît" ("what can be seen on earth"), Pascal insists in fragment 449, "marque ni une exclusion totale, ni une présence manifeste de divinité, mais la présence d'un Dieu qui se cache" ("indicates neither the total absence, nor the manifest presence of divinity, but the presence of a hidden God"). What the unhappy unbeliever concludes in fragment 429 matches perfectly the apologetic strategy proposed in fragment 449. The future *chercheur* is precisely where the apologist wants him to be:

> Il ne faut pas qu'il ne voie rien du tout; il ne faut pas qu'il en voie assez pour croire qu'il le possède, mais qu'il en voie assez pour connaître qu'il l'a perdu. Car pour connaître qu'on a perdu, il faut voir et ne voir pas: et c'est précisément l'état où est la nature. Quelque parti qu'il prenne, je ne l'y laisserai point en repos.
>
> He must not see nothing at all, nor must he see enough to think he possesses God, but he must see enough to know that he has lost him. For, to know that one has lost something one must see and not see: such precisely is the state of nature. Whatever course he adopts I will not leave him in peace. (449)

Unlike the hardened skeptic of fragment 427, the agnostic of fragment 429 is fully conscious of the precarious state in which he finds himself. Unlike the indifferent *libertin*, he burns with the desire to solve the riddle of existence:

> Voyant trop pour nier et trop peu pour m'assurer, je suis en un état à plaindre, et où j'ai souhaité cent fois que, si un Dieu la soutient [i.e., la nature],[52] elle le marquât sans équivoque; et que, si les marques qu'elle en donne sont trompeuses, elle les supprimât tout à fait; qu'elle dît tout ou rien, afin que je visse quel parti je dois suivre.
>
> Seeing too much to deny and not enough to affirm, I am in a pitiful state, where I have wished a hundred times over that, if there is a God supporting nature, she should unequivocally proclaim him, and that, if the signs in nature are deceptive, they should be completely erased; that nature should say all or nothing so that I could see what course I ought to follow. (429)

The hardened unbeliever of fragment 427 cultivates the ideal of *nonchalance* and total indifference to the riddle of existence. He has concluded that passive resignation is the only sane alternative to the horror of im-

52. The antecedent of "la" ("si un Dieu *la* soutient") and of "elle," in four subsequent instances is obviously "la nature," occurring two sentences earlier. "La foi," though it stands closer, makes no sense as an antecedent to "la" and "elle."

aging oneself crushed by the universe. The attitude of the potential *chercheur* in fragment 429 could hardly be more different. He finds being suspended between belief and disbelief intolerable. He burns to settle the matter once and for all. A hundred times, he protests, he has called upon Nature—if indeed a hidden God is her First Cause and sustainer[53]—to figure Him forth in no uncertain terms ("sans équivoque") so that he may believe. Or, if those signs in the design of Creation which seem to denote Divinity really have no significance, he pleads with Nature to suppress them completely so that he may resign himself to living in a meaningless universe.

Because he does not yet understand the doctrine of *Deus absconditus*, the potential *chercheur* of fragment 429 still clings intellectually to the notion that God's presence in the world ought to be evident and manifest. He calls upon Nature to reveal "tout ou rien" ("all or nothing"). Nature, however, refuses to oblige. The seeking unbeliever, therefore, is forced to reevaluate the usefulness of the argument from design as a proof of the existence of God. This reevaluation is crucial to Pascal's apologetic strategy. The potential *chercheur* can progress no further until he is disabused of the idea that it is man who must strain his intellect and imagination in order to perceive God in His Creation. Nature is incapable of figuring forth the architect of the universe to fallen, faulty reason. God has deliberately hidden Himself from rational scrutiny. The potential *chercheur* must learn that it is futile for human beings to attempt to reach out with their intellects and to catch a glimpse of God. God must reveal Himself to them.

By the time the Apology reaches the chapter "Transition" (XV), the *chercheur* will have understood the futility of straining the intellect in an effort to see God face to face. He will have learned that God can be found only in that deposit of Revelation in which he has revealed Himself to the human species. Instead of wasting his time scanning the horizons of the created universe, the *chercheur* will have begun to seek the signs which God has hidden in Revelation. If he stays on course, his search will lead him to the Prophecies, which set Christianity apart from the conflicting pretensions of all other religions which have ever existed:

53. "Si un Dieu la soutient": the agnostic appears to have borrowed this notion from Cartesian metaphysics. In fragment 449 Pascal observes that the person persuaded of "une première vérité . . . qu'on appelle Dieu" ("a first truth . . . called God") is not "beaucoup avancé pour son salut" ("very advanced in the direction of his salvation").

Considérant combien il y a plus d'apparence qu'il y a autre chose que ce que je vois, j'ai recherché si ce Dieu n'aurait point laissé quelque marque de soi.

Je vois plusieurs religions contraires et partant toutes fausses, excepté une. Chacune veut être crue par sa propre autorité et menace les incrédules. Je ne les crois donc pas là-dessus. Chacun peut dire cela. Chacun peut se dire prophète mais je vois la chrétienne et je trouve des prophéties, et c'est ce que chacun ne peut pas faire.

Considering how very likely it is that there exists something besides what I can see, I have tried to find out whether God has left any traces of himself.

I see a number of religions in conflict, and therefore all false, except one. Each of them wishes to be believed on its own authority and threatens unbelievers. I do not believe them on that account. Anyone can say that. Anyone can call himself a prophet, but I see Christianity, and find its prophecies, which are not something that anyone can do. (198)

The potential *chercheur* portrayed in fragment 429 still stands far off from the knowledge which brings salvation. He has a long way to travel before reaching the state of partial Enlightenment portrayed in fragment 198. He knows neither his "condition" ("state") nor his "devoir" ("duty"). Yet how different he is from the hardened skeptic portrayed in fragment 427! The very fact that his heart is set ("tend tout entier") on discovering "le vrai bien" ("the true good") points toward his eventual conversion. His innate instincts, which prompt him to seek a lost God, are still more or less intact. The hardened unbeliever in fragment 427 numbers himself among the perishing when he vaunts his success in having overcome the desire for a life beyond this one. The unhappy unbeliever of fragment 429, on the other hand, separates himself forever from the company of the *réprouvés* when he declares: "Rien ne me serait trop cher pour l'éternité" ("No price would be too high for me to pay for eternity") (429).

Pascal's Categories of Disbelief

Many sections of the *Pensées* must remain enigmatic until we are able to reconstruct more completely the mental universe of Pascal's potential convert. But, once again, who is he? The *Pensées* give us a number of quite dissimilar portraits of disbelief. Is Pascal's potential interlocutor the hardened skeptic of fragment 427? Or is he the troubled agnostic of fragment 429? The question is crucial to an understanding of the scope of Pascal's unfinished Apology. First, let us take the hypothesis that the Apology would have been addressed to the hardened atheist portrayed in fragment

427. If this is the case, we must explain how this hardened skeptic will be transformed into the unhappy agnostic sketched in fragment 429. We could, of course, try to argue that the first half of the Apology is designed to shock the hardened atheist into the uncertainty of agnosticism. However, to do so would mean having to ignore the important theological dimensions inherent in Pascal's apologetic strategy.

From a theological perspective, the distance between the unhappy unbeliever portrayed in fragment 429 and the *chercheur* of fragment 198 is not all that great. It can be bridged by the process of Christian catechesis. From the same perspective, however, the distance between the hardened disbelief of fragment 427 and the unhappy disbelief of fragment 429 is tantamount to a yawning abyss. Hardened disbelief, in Pascal's view, is more or less immune to the effects of apologetics or catechesis. No human remedy can reverse a blindness which is supernatural in origin. Only the workings of Grace might serve to convert those who are truly sunk in disbelief. "Il n'y a rien à leur dire non par mépris, mais parce qu'ils n'ont pas le sens commun. Il faut que Dieu les touche" ("That shows that there is nothing to be said to them, not out of contempt, but because they have no common sense. God must touch them") (821/432-4).

Much modern commentary on the *Pensées* seems to accept as a given that the itinerary traced by the first half of the Apology will so shake the hardened unbeliever that he will somehow be transformed into the *chercheur* who suddenly emerges in the *liasse* "Transition" (XV). However, given Pascal's neo-Augustinian theories of Grace and conversion, is such a transformation really possible? Let us one last time review the evidence as contained in Pascal's texts on the subject of disbelief.

In the *liasses* of 1658, Pascal draws a clear distinction between his more strident opponents (the hardened atheists, the *impies*, and the *libertins de profession*) and those whom apologetic discourse may possibly convert. The distinction is Pascal's own, reiterated three times in the *liasse* "Commencement" (XII):

> Plaindre les athées qui cherchent. Car ne sont -ils pas assez malheureux? Invectiver contre ceux qui en font vanité.

> Pity the atheists who seek, for are they not unhappy enough? Inveigh against those who boast about it. (156)

> Il n'y a que trois sortes de personnes: les uns qui servent Dieu l'ayant trouvé, les autres qui s'emploient à le chercher ne l'ayant pas trouvé, les autres qui vivent

sans le chercher ni l'avoir trouvé. Les premiers sont raisonnables et heureux, les derniers sont fous et malheureux, ceux du milieu sont malheureux et raisonnables.

There are only three sorts of people: those who have found God and serve him; those who are busy seeking him and have not found him; those who live without either seeking or finding him. The first are reasonable and happy, the last are foolish and unhappy, those in the middle are happy and reasonable. (160)

Commencer par plaindre les incrédules. Ils sont assez malheureux par leur condition. Il ne les faudrait injurier qu'au cas que cela servît. Mais cela leur nuit.

Begin by pitying the unbelievers; their condition makes them unhappy enough. They ought not to be abused unless it does them good, but in fact it does them harm. (162)

In these texts, Pascal's distinction between two categories of unbelievers very much reflects the conflicting portraits of disbelief presented in fragments 429 and 427. The potential *chercheur* pictured in fragment 429 clearly falls into the category of "les athées qui cherchent" ("the atheists who seek") (156). Like that class of people who seek God for the very reason that they have not yet found Him (160), the agnostic of fragment 429 is unhappy yet reasonable. He can be numbered among those "incrédules" ("unbelievers") who, "assez malheureux par leur condition" ("very unhappy because of their state"), should not be abused because it will only do them harm (162). The hardened skeptic of fragment 427, on the other hand, obviously figures among those who are blind to their true "condition." They are not just "malheureux" ("unhappy"); they are "fous" ("insane") (160). They have neither found God nor taken the trouble to seek Him. They merit, not compassion, but the most harsh criticism: "Invectiver contre ceux qui en font vanité" ("Inveigh against those who boast about it") (156).

Clarifying Pascal's fundamentally different attitudes toward what he sees as two distinct categories of disbelief helps to give us a new perspective on the entire Apology. Pascal's projected work had several objectives. In the first place, it was to be a defense of Christianity's claim to be the one revealed Truth. At the same time, it was written as a refutation of disbelief's claim to be based upon rational principles. Superimposed upon these two objectives—and at times not yet perfectly integrated into them—is a third process: a call to inner conversion issued to those among the unbelievers whose hearts have not yet been completely hardened against the Truth. It seems fairly clear that the finished Apology would not have contained a series of point by point refutations of the historical and philosophical objections to Christianity outlined by the *libertins érudits*. However, this is not to say that Pascal is not vitally concerned with refuting the premise that disbelief is an intellectually tenable position. Indeed, Pascal's critique of the hardened skeptic in fragment 427 is designed to demonstrate that disbelief is not only profoundly unreasonable but contrary to common sense and, in the final analysis, tantamount to insanity.

Pascal's ultimate objective in neutralizing disbelief is to shield his potential *chercheur* from what has been a poisonous influence. But it does not necessarily follow that those hardened atheists already sunk deep in unbelief will somehow be transformed into "ceux qui cherchent en gémissant" ("those who seek with groans") (405). For Pascal, hardened atheism and unhappy agnosticism are not simply greater and lesser degrees of some abstract construct called disbelief. Rather, they are mutually exclusive categories. The hardened skeptic who brags that he has transcended the desire for a life beyond this one is, for Pascal, fundamentally different from the unhappy agnostic who declares, "Rien ne me serait trop cher pour l'éternité" ("No price would be too high for me to pay for eternity") (429).

In order to understand disbelief as a fundamental context in the *Pensées* properly, we must reconstruct not one, but two, mentalities. But upon what texts shall we draw? The theoretical concept of two very different categories of disbelief is clearly enunciated in the *liasse* "Commencement." However, elsewhere in the dossiers of 1658 the unbelievers are rarely allowed to speak their minds. When they do, it is far from easy to decide to which category they belong. The unbelievers cited in the following fragments could well be hardened skeptics. But, on the other hand, might they not just as well be seekers legitimately struggling with their doubts? One can imagine the fragments which follow spoken either in a cynical tone by a hardened skeptic or in a sincere and disquieted manner by a *chercheur*:

> "Ne voyons-nous pas," disent-ils, "mourir et vivre les bêtes comme les hommes, et les Turcs comme les chrétiens; ils ont leurs cérémonies, leurs prophètes, leurs docteurs, leurs saints, leurs religieux comme nous, etc."

> "Do we not see," they say, "animals live and die like men, Turks like Christians? They have their ceremonies, their prophets, their doctors, their saints, their religious like us, etc." (150)

> "S'il avait voulu que je l'adorasse il m'aurait laissé des signes de sa volonté."

"If he had wanted me to worship him, he would have left me some signs of his will." (158)

"Si j'avais vu un miracle," disent-ils, "je me convertirais."

"If I had seen a miracle," they say, "I would be converted." (378)

Pascal identifies the unbelievers cited in the first of these three fragments as "les impies qui font profession de suivre la raison" ("the ungodly who propose to follow reason") (150). One might suppose that these "impies" are hardened disbelievers. Their argument, which could have been lifted almost verbatim from La Mothe le Vayer's *Parallèles historiques*,[54] sounds like one formulated by the more erudite *libertins*. However, Pascal appears unsure whether the "impies" are hardened skeptics or potential *chercheurs*. When he addresses them directly, he seems prepared to give them the benefit of the doubt:

> Si vous ne vous souciez guère de savoir la vérité, en voilà assez pour vous laisser en repos. Mais si vous désirez de tout votre coeur de la connaître ce n'est pas assez regardé au détail. C'en serait assez pour une question de philosophie, mais ici où il va de tout. . . . Et cependant après une réflexion légère de cette sorte on s'amusera, etc.
>
> If you hardly care about knowing the truth, that is enough to leave you in peace, but if you desire with all your heart to know it, you have not looked closely enough at the details. This would do for a philosophical question, but here where everything is at stake. . . . And yet, after superficial reflection of this kind we amuse ourselves, etc. (150)

As in fragment 427, Pascal makes a fundamental distinction between those whose skepticism has seduced them into a fatal "repos" ("state of rest") and those who are bent upon knowing the truth. Those who cannot be bothered to seek the truth will treat Christianity's claims to possess the one revealed truth as some mere philosophical matter. As a result, they will be blinded by the superficial resemblances between Christianity and other religions. Likewise, because their reason is illuminated only by the false lights of nature, they will erroneously conclude that the ultimate fate of human beings does not differ from that of the other animals. "Après une réflexion légère de cette sorte" ("after superficial reflection of this

54. See Chapter I, Two Cautious Skeptics: La Mothe le Vayer and Gabriel Naudé. The ultimate source of this argument is of course Montaigne. See *Oeuvres complètes, Essais,* 2, 12, pp. 238–39. Cf. fragment 149: "Ceux qui nous ont égalé aux bêtes et les mahométans qui nous ont donné les plaisirs de la terre, même dans l'éternité . . ."

kind"), they will turn back to *divertissement* in an attempt to divert their thoughts from the sorry spectacle of their own mortality.

Those whose hearts are fixed upon knowing the truth will instinctively realize that the question of the mortality or immortality of the soul is far more than a mere academic or philosophical question: "Ici . . . il va de tout"[55] ("Here . . . everything is at stake"). Those who truly seek will be persuaded to examine in detail ("au détail") the false premise that Christianity is like every other religion. They can be made to understand the warning of Scripture that Revelation has been hidden from those who are wise by the standards of this world. "Cela est-il contraire à l'Ecriture, ne dit-elle pas tout cela?" ("Is that contrary to Scripture? Does it not say all that?") (150). Indeed, Christianity teaches the existence of that very "obscurité" which has so deceived the philosophers and skeptics. "Qu'on s'informe de cette religion, même si elle ne rend pas raison de cette obscurité, peut-être qu'elle nous l'apprendra" ("Let us inquire of this religion; even if it does not explain the obscurity away, perhaps it will teach us about it" (150).

Those "impies" cited in fragment 150 may well turn out to number among the hardened skeptics whom Pascal analyzes in fragment 427, where he enters into a detailed analysis of their "négligence en une affaire où il s'agit d'eux-mêmes, de leur éternité, de leur tout" ("negligence in a matter where they themselves, their eternity, their all are at stake") (427). The unbeliever with whom Pascal imagines a brief exchange in fragment 158, on the other hand, more closely resembles the potential *chercheur* of fragment 429. Pascal warns the unbeliever who speaks in fragment 158, "Vous devez vous mettre en peine de rechercher la vérité, car si vous mourez sans adorer le vrai principe vous êtes perdu" ("You must take the trouble to seek the truth, for if you die without worshipping the true principle you are lost"). The unbeliever's reply is significant: "Mais . . . s'il avait voulu que je l'adorasse il m'aurait laissé des signes de sa volonté" ("But . . . if he had wanted me to worship him, he would have left me some signs of his will"). Pascal seems to think that this unbeliever is on the right track. Some innate instinct prompts him to postulate the possible existence of a God who reaches out to humankind. In this instance, encouragement, not invective, is in order. The unbeliever complains that

55. This line recalls fragment 427: "L'immortalité de l'âme est une chose qui nous importe si fort, qui nous touche si profondément, qu'il faut avoir perdu tout sentiment pour être dans l'indifférence de savoir ce qui en est" ("The immortality of the soul is something of such vital importance to us, affecting us so deeply, that one must have lost all feeling not to care about knowing the facts of the matter").

God has not shown him "des signes de sa volonté" ("signs of his will"). Pascal is then able to reply: "Aussi a(-t-)il fait, mais vous les négligez. *Cherchez-les*; cela le vaut bien" ("So he did, but you pay no heed. *Look for them* then; it is well worth it") (158, italics mine).

It is difficult to know which category of disbelief best suits the unbelievers cited in fragment 378. Once again, they protest that they have been denied divine illumination: "'Si j'avais vu un miracle,' disent-ils, 'je me convertirais'" ("'If I had seen a miracle,' they say, 'I should be converted'"). This time, however, their complaint merits, not the sympathy, but rather the invective of the apologist: "Comment assurent-ils qu'ils feraient ce qu'ils ignorent . . ." ("How can they be positive they would do what they know nothing about . . ."). (378) "Les miracles ne servent pas à convertir mais à condamner." ("Miracles do not serve to convert but to condemn.") (379)

We have already discussed how fragments 378 and 379 figure in Pascal's theory of conversion.[56] However, we have yet to account for why such an exchange occurs in the final chapter ("Conclusion") of the Apology envisaged by the *liasses* of 1658. Surely Jean Mesnard is correct when he asserts that Pascal's interlocutor is considered to be almost converted by the time the Apology reaches this final chapter.[57] Yet is it not odd that the unbelievers cited in this chapter are still speaking about conversion in such a hypothetical way? Indeed, they protest that it would take a miracle to convert them. The answer must be that the *chercheur* whose spiritual evolution we have tried to trace no longer figures among their number. After all, their protestation about requiring a miracle to convert them is precisely the kind of "réflexion légère" ("superficial reflection") which Pascal so severely censures in fragment 150.

Perhaps Pascal cites this flippant "réflexion légère" as a kind of warning to the *chercheur* who stands on the threshold of conversion. The *chercheur* must not be tempted to suppose that his intellectual assent to Christianity means that his conversion is complete. True conversion is inner conversion, conversion of the heart. "Qu'il y a loin de la connaissance de Dieu à l'aimer" ("What a long way it is between knowing God and loving him!") (377). "La conversion véritable consiste à s'anéantir devant cet être universel . . . à reconnaître qu'on ne peut rien sans lui et qu'on n'a rien mérité de lui que sa disgrâce" ("True conversion consists in self-annihilation be-

56. See Chapter V, The Catechumenate as a Model for Conversion.
57. *Blaise Pascal: L'Homme et l'oeuvre*, pp. 155–56.

fore the universal being . . . in recognizing that we can do nothing without him and that we have deserved nothing but his disfavor") (378).

The Role of Argument in the Apology: The Hardened Skeptics Reconsidered

While always keeping in mind that Pascal believes that only Grace can effect a conversion of the heart, we should not underestimate the role of intellectual assent to Christianity in Pascal's theory of conversion. Pascal views the *chercheur*'s very ability to recognize the truth of Revelation when it is presented to him in the course of the apologist's historical demonstrations as a sign that his conversion is possible. To be sure, the intellectual assent of the *chercheur* is no guarantee that he will come to be numbered among the elect. The ways of Grace are inscrutable. But it is as a result of his acceptance of the historical truth of Christianity that the *chercheur* will make the conscious decision to return to the practice of the Christian faith.

The emergence of the *Pensées* as a literary text has often served to obscure the centrality of Pascal's historical demonstrations both in his apologetic schema and in his theory of conversion. R. E. Lacombe speaks for most modern readers of the *Pensées* when he concludes, "Ce qui fait l'originalité de l'apologétique pascalienne, c'est d'abord la place qu'y occupe la peinture de la misère humaine"[58] ("The great originality of Pascal's apologetics is constituted first of all by the place he gives to the depiction of the human condition"). In Lacombe's estimation, nearly all the most celebrated fragments of the *Pensées*—"ceux qui font la gloire de Pascal et sont susceptibles de toucher l'incrédule" ("those for which Pascal is so celebrated and which may really come to influence the unbeliever")—belong to the first part of the Apology.[59]

Lacombe's assessment goes to the heart of the modern conception of what the *Pensées* are about. Those who have experienced the *Pensées* primarily as a literary text will not easily be persuaded that the most significant meaning of Pascal's projected Apology lies outside those fragments which Lacombe qualifies as most celebrated. When we think of disbelief, we almost automatically think of that modern disbelief inspired by the

58. R. E. Lacombe, *L'Apologétique de Pascal* (Paris: P.U.F., 1958), p. 306.
59. Ibid., p. 312.

revelations of science. We do not easily conceive of an agnostic's being convinced by Pascal's historical demonstrations. We are far more drawn to Pascal's attempt to unsettle disbelief than we are to his exposition of the historical truth of Christianity. Yet, if we really desire to avoid projecting our own preconceptions into the mental universe of the author of the *Pensées*, then we must make an honest attempt to grasp Pascal's own conception of the ultimate goal of his apologetic discourse.

Fragment 12 ("Ordre"), I believe, begins to make a good deal more sense in light of our attempt to elaborate Pascal's twin theories of conversion and catechesis:

> Les hommes ont mépris pour la religion. Ils en ont haine et peur qu'elle soit vraie. Pour guérir cela il faut commencer par montrer que la religion n'est point contraire à la raison. Vénérable, en donner respect.
>
> La rendre ensuite aimable, faire souhaiter aux bons qu'elle fût vraie et puis montrer qu'elle est vraie.
>
> Vénérable parce qu'elle a bien connu l'homme.
>
> Aimable parce qu'elle promet le vrai bien.

> Men despise religion. They hate it and are afraid it may be true. The cure for this is first to show that religion is not contrary to reason, but worthy of reverence and respect.
>
> Next make it attractive, make good men wish it were true, and then show that it is.
>
> Worthy of reverence because it really understands human nature.
>
> Attractive because it promises true good. (12)

In the Apology anticipated by the *liasses* of 1658, Pascal sets out to demonstrate that Christianity is "vénérable" if only because it is the only system of thought which has taken into account humankind's fallen condition ("misère"). Christianity cannot be shown to be contrary to reason ("contraire à la raison"), because reason itself can be shown to be an inadequate vehicle for the perception of truth. The unbelievers, who profess to make a cult of reason, hate Christianity. They do, not because they truly believe it to be false, but because they are unconsciously afraid that it is true. Pascal's ultimate mission is to separate those who can be made to wish that Christianity were true from the company of the hardened unbelievers. "Faire souhaiter *aux bons* qu'elle fût vraie" ("Make *good men* wish it were true") (12, italics mine). The demonstration which will follow ("montrer qu'elle est vraie" ["show that it is true"]) will be addressed, not to the mass of unbelievers, but only to those whose hearts can be made to burn to know the truth. "*Faire souhaiter* aux bons qu'elle fût vraie" ("*Make* good men *wish* it were true") (12, italics mine). Once again, we find Pascal making a basic distinction between two kinds of disbelief. Those whose disbelief is conditioned by the possibility of making them wish that Christianity were not just an illusion (i.e., the "bons") are fundamentally different from those whose hatred of Christianity proceeds from their unconscious fear that it is true.

In fragment 12, Pascal's fundamental distinction between hardened and alterable disbelief enters into one of his key statements of his plan for structuring the Apology. Other fragments (156, 160, 162) in the *liasses* of 1658 take this fundamental dichotomy into account. Yet, as we have observed, nowhere in those dossiers does Pascal ever anchor these hypothetical categories in fully human portraits. It is this paucity of concrete description in the *liasses* of 1658 which renders fragments 427–429 so valuable. Without the conflicting portraits of the hardened skeptic and the seeking agnostic in fragments 427 and 429, Pascal's theories of conversion and catechesis remain extremely theoretical. However, these fragments—so crucial to the larger meaning of the *Pensées*—themselves pose a critical problem related to the history of the composition of the Apology. Why is it that these crucial portraits of disbelief, if we can believe those who have studied these texts most carefully,[60] were composed so late in the course of the writing of the Apology? Has Pascal had these portraits in mind all along? Or does he only finally realize to whom the Apology will be expressly addressed once he is involved in the writing of the Preface?

It can be argued, I believe, that the Preface or *Lettre* (cf. fragment 11) constituted by fragments 427–29 represents Pascal's resolution of a problem which bears directly upon the shape and character of the Apology as a whole. In short, it is in these texts that Pascal finally decides to whom the Apology will be addressed. In fragment 427, we find Pascal deciding that the Apology cannot be primarily addressed to those hardened disbelievers whose hearts have been sealed in disbelief by God himself. This is not to say that the apologist is not obligated to invite the hardened skeptics to read the Apology. Not to do so would be to fail to take into account the inscrutability of Grace. "Quelque aversion qu'ils y apportent, peut-être rencontreront-ils quelque chose" ("However reluctantly they may approach the task they will perhaps hit upon something"). However, the real audience of the Apology will be those unhappy unbelievers who will bring to their reading of Pascal's arguments and proofs "une sincérité par-

60. See Chapter IV, nn. 2, 9, 11, and 51.

faite et un véritable désir de rencontrer la vérité" ("absolute sincerity and a real desire to find the truth"). They are those, exemplified by the potential *chercheur* of fragment 429, who seek God with all their hearts because they have yet to find Him.

Pascal seems to have long harbored the hope that even the hardened skeptics might be shaken from their indifference by turning skepticism itself to the uses of Christian apologetics. During the first half of the Apology anticipated by the *liasses* of 1658, his principal strategy seems to be to question the ultimate authority of human reason and thus to deprive "les impies qui font profession de suivre la raison" ("the ungodly who propose to follow reason") (150) of any logical basis for their disbelief. By the time he comes to write fragment 427, however, Pascal seems to have reached the conclusion that hardened disbelief cannot be modified because it has supernatural origins. Pascal's portrait of the hardened skeptic horrifies its creator: "C'est un monstre pour moi" ("It seems quite monstrous to me") (427). The inability of the *braves* even to act in their own self-interest with regard to the possibility of a life beyond this one convinces Pascal that any effort by him will be futile: "Il n'y a rien à leur dire . . . il faut que Dieu les touche" ("There is nothing to be said to them . . . God must touch them") (821/432-[4]). God Himself has blinded the hardened unbelievers. Only He can open their eyes.

Though they are themselves seemingly immune to seeing the truth, the hardened unbelievers paradoxically have a central role to play in the conversion of those who as yet are only feigning *libertinage*. "Même si nous ne pouvons les toucher, ils ne seront pas inutiles" ("But if we cannot touch them, they will not be without their use") (821/432-18). "Ceux-là même qui semblent les plus opposés à la gloire de la religion n'y seront pas inutiles pour les autres" ("The very people who seem most opposed to the glory of religion will not be without their use for others in this respect") (821/432-[19]). In his notes for the writing of fragment 427,[61] Pascal makes his strategy perfectly clear. The fate of the hardened disbelievers and the fatal indifference into which they have sunk will serve as a warning to those toying with libertine ideas. Hardened disbelief will be shown to be tantamount to insanity. In the most essential of all matters, that is, the question of a life beyond this one, the hardened skeptics can be shown to act directly contrary to their most basic self-interest. They thus demonstrate the supernatural origin of their blindness and paradoxically serve as

61. See Chapter IV, Fragments 418 and 427: The State of the Texts.

the means by which their potential disciples (the pseudo-*libertins*) are to be saved from perdition:

> Nous en ferons le premier argument qu'il y a quelque chose de surnaturel car un aveuglement de cette sorte n'est pas une chose naturelle. Et si leur folie les rend si contraires à leur propre bien, elle servira à en garantir les autres par l'horreur d'un exemple si déplorable, et d'une folie si digne de compassion.

> We shall base our first argument on the fact that there is something supernatural about this, for such blindness is not natural. And if their folly makes them run so counter to their own good, the horror of such a deplorable example and so pitiful a folly will help to keep others from it. (821/432-[20])

This important and long-ignored fragment, another of those found among Pascal's preliminary notes for fragment 427,[62] clearly demonstrates the use to which Pascal intended to put his portraits of the hardened skeptics. The evident insanity ("folie") of the hardened skeptics "*servira à en garantir* les autres par l'horreur d'un exemple si déplorable" ("*will serve to keep others from it* by the horror of such a deplorable example") (821/432-20, italics mine). In other words, the hardened skeptics, far from being granted the status of interlocutors in the Apology, will be made to serve the purposes of apologetic discourse by being reduced to a negative, indeed pitiable, example of the tragedy to which toying with disbelief inevitably leads.

Pascal's rethinking of the nature and apologetic uses of disbelief in fragments 427–29 in a sense reorients his entire apologetic project. Henceforth, his demonstration of the credibility of Christianity will be addressed only to those who possess the innate capacity to recognize the truth when it is presented to them. The hardened skeptics will figure in the Apology less as philosophical opponents than as negative examples of the dangers to which an unbridled and invasive skepticism can lead. Now, this is not to say that Pascal's potential *chercheurs* will appear, at the beginning of the Apology, superficially much different from those whose hearts have been eaten away by disbelief. Indeed, these potential future *chercheurs* may consider themselves thoroughly convinced that Christianity is the greatest of all fables. Their true status as *chercheurs* will emerge only as a result of their participation in Pascal's radical analysis of the vanity of human illusions.

This purificatory rite, which corresponds more or less to the first half

62. I.e., fragment 821/432 [1]–[21].

of the Apology anticipated by the *liasses* of 1658, will serve to separate the potential *chercheurs* from the ranks of those who are truly beyond human help. Having experienced Pascal's vision of the "misère de l'homme sans Dieu" ("wretchedness of man without God") (6), they will come at least to wish that the Christian version of reality were true. It is only at this point, or so thinks Pascal, that they can legitimately claim the status of *chercheurs*. The *réprouvés*, on the other hand, can never be made to see the truth. No matter how hard they are forced to look at human suffering, they are simply unable even to *wish* that Christianity were true. Their inherent inability to make this leap of volition stands, for Pascal, as the chief sign of their irremediable blindness. Far from being a virtue, the stoic indifference they cultivate is a mortal poison. "Est-ce qu'ils sont si fermes qu'ils soient insensibles à tout ce qui les touche? Eprouvons-les dans la perte des biens ou de l'honneur[63] Quoi? C'est un enchantement"[64] ("Are they so firm as to be insensitive to everything that affects them? Try them with the loss of their wealth or honor. What? It is a magic spell") (821/432-[21]).

If Pascal is pessimistic concerning the utility of apologetic discourse in the face of hardened disbelief, he is adamant with regard to the apologist's obligation to rescue those for whom there may be hope. The Second Vatican Council's "Statement on Religious Freedom" speaks of an inherent

63. Pascal seems to have expanded this sentence into the section of fragment 427 which reads as follows: "Et ce même homme qui passe tant de jours et de nuits dans la rage et dans le désespoir pour *la perte* d'une charge ou pour quelque offense imaginaire à son *honneur,* c'est celui même qui sait qu'il va tout perdre par la mort, sans inquiétude et sans émotion. C'est une chose monstreuse de voir dans un même coeur et en même temps cette sensibilité pour les moindres choses et cette étrange insensibilité pour les plus grandes" ("And the same man who spends so many days and nights in fury and despair at losing some office or at some imaginary affront to his honor is the very one who knows that he is going to lose everything through death but feels neither anxiety nor emotion. It is a monstrous thing to see one and the same heart at once so sensitive to minor things and so strangely insensitive to the greatest"). In fact, Pascal changes his original idea (the indifference of the stoical skeptics to the loss of goods or honor) when he rewrites the passage. In fragment 427, the unbelievers take on a more universal aspect. There are no longer stoics but rather emblems of a more universal human blindness.

64. These words seem to be the basis for the following section of fragment 427: "C'est un enchantement incompréhensible, et un assoupissement surnaturel, qui marque une force toute-puissante qui le cause. Il faut qu'il y ait un étrange renversement dans la nature de l'homme pour faire gloire d'être dans cet état, dans lequel il semble incroyable qu'une seule personne puisse être" ("It is an incomprehensible spell, a supernatural torpor that points to an omnipotent power as its cause. Man's nature must have undergone a strange reversal for him to glory in being in a state in which it seems incredible that any single person should be").

right to the freedom from "psychological" coercion in religious matters, "an immunity which continues to exist even in those who do not live up to their obligation of seeking the truth and adhering to it."[65] Philippe Sellier, invoking fragment 172, points out that Pascal is "un des rares penseurs" ("one of the very few thinkers") in the entire seventeenth century who completely excludes the use of force in religious conversion[66]:

> La conduite de Dieu, qui dispose toutes choses avec douceur, est de mettre la religion dans l'esprit par les raisons et dans le coeur par la grâce, mais de vouloir mettre dans l'esprit et dans le coeur par la force et par les menaces, ce n'est pas y mettre la religion mais la terreur. *Terrorem potius quam religionem.*

> The way of God, who disposes all things with gentleness, is to instill religion into our minds with reasoned arguments and into our hearts with grace, but attempting to instill it into hearts and minds with force and threats is to instill not religion but terror. *Terror rather than religion.* (172)

Though Pascal excludes "la force" and "les menaces" from any role in religious conversion, it could not be said that he shares the modern notion, enunciated in the Second Vatican Council's "Statement on Religious Freedom," that the inherent right to freedom from psychological coercion in religious matters "continues to exist even in those who do not live up to their obligation of seeking the truth."[67] Indeed, his entire apologetic strategy is predicated upon the notion that those capable of grasping the truth must be forced to seek it in every way possible. The kind of psychological coercion implicit in the first half of the Apology, he seems to think, is the only possible antidote to that indifference spawned by doubt. Were he himself in the position of losing his immortal soul, Pascal notes, he would be grateful to be made to see the truth. "Que je serais heureux si j'étais en cet état qu'on eût la bonté de m'en tirer *malgré moi*" ("How happy I should be if I were in such a state and someone took pity on my foolishness, and was kind enough to save me from it *in spite of myself*") (821/432-[16], italics mine).

The compassion which Pascal professes to feel for "ceux qui cherchent en gémissant" ("those who seek with groans") (405) ultimately proceeds from a somewhat different source than that pity which Christian charity compels him to feel for the hardened atheists unable even to act in their

65. *Documents of Vatican II,* p. 679.

66. Philippe Sellier, "Seminar: Pascal's 'Trois Ordres' " in *Meaning, Structure and History in the "Pensées" of Pascal,* ed. D. Wetsel (Tübingen: Biblio 17, 1990), p. 83.

67. *Documents of Vatican II,* p. 679.

own self-interest. "On doit avoir pitié des uns et des autres, mais on doit avoir pour les uns une pitié qui naît de tendresse, et pour les autres une pitié qui naît de mépris. Il faut être dans la religion qu'ils méprisent pour ne les pas mépriser" ("We should feel sorry for both, but we should feel sorry for the former out of affection and the latter out of contempt. One must belong to the religion they despise in order not to despise them"). In Pascal's view, the act of seeking the truth is laudable and profitable only insofar as it remains oriented toward the ultimate goal of discovering the Christian Revelation. The apologist stands under the strictest of obligations to hold the *chercheur* to this fixed and unalterable course.

During the first half of the Apology anticipated by the *liasses* of 1658, Pascal makes use of a skepticism essentially distilled from the *Essais* of Montaigne in order to dismantle the complex scaffolding of reason, custom, and illusion which underpins the mental universe of his interlocutor. However, once this purificatory rite is past, skepticism never again enters into Pascal's apologetic strategy. Pascal's purpose has been to create a void within the mind of the *chercheur* which only Revelation can fill. However, the creation of such an epistemological vacuum entails great risks. Custom, illusion, and doubt stand ready to gush into and fill the mind cleared of belief, certainty, or even indifference. Like the unclean spirit of Matthew 12:43–45, disbelief lies in wait to invade the newly swept mind of the agnostic who is at the point of turning *chercheur*. At no point in the course of the Apology is the apologist's role more critical. Fortunately for the future *chercheur*, Pascal is a skilled practitioner. In the words of Monsieur de Sacy, he is like "ces médecins habiles qui, par la manière adroite de préparer les plus grands poisons, en savent tirer les plus grands remèdes" ("those skillful physicians, who by the way in which they manipulate the most deadly poisons, turn them into the most powerful medicines").[68]

It would be unwise to push the preceding analogy, which draws upon Pascal's "Expériences . . . touchant le vide" ("Experiments . . . concerning the vacuum"), much further. After all, Pascal's theology does not really admit the possibility of creating a true tabula rasa in the mind of the unbeliever. That "mauvais levain" ("evil leaven") instituted by Original Sin is not content but structure. The true source of fallen and faulty reason cannot be extirpated by any human means. Even in the hands of a practitioner as skilled as Pascal, skepticism can do no more than disabuse the potential *chercheur* of his reliance on reason, custom, and illusion. Even were it pos-

68. "Entretien avec M. de Saci" in Lafuma, *Pascal: Oeuvres complètes,* p. 297.

sible to create a true tabula rasa in the human mind, the underlying mental apparatus would still be incapable of correctly processing reality. It would distort truth from the moment it sought to generate first principles. Hence the necessity of Revealed Truth.

Pascal knows he cannot impose revealed truth on the *chercheur* without impugning the doctrine of Free Will. The assertions of the Jesuits to the contrary, Pascal, following Jansenius and Saint-Cyran, affirms Augustine's teaching that one always retains the power to resist Grace.[69] However, leading the unbeliever to an epistemological impasse via the purificatory rite of skepticism is an altogether different matter. Once the unbeliever utters the wish that Christianity were true, Pascal can legitimately unfurl the mystical garment of Revelation without doing injury to the doctrine of Free Will. This is precisely what happens in that so often misunderstood *liasse* "A.P.R." (XI).

"A.P.R." (see Plate XVI) immediately precedes "Commencement," the *liasse* in which Pascal draws the crucial distinction between hardened and alterable disbelief. In "Commencement" (XII), Pascal begins the laborious process of erecting the new epistemological scaffolding which will eventually underpin his historical demonstration of the truth of Christian Revelation. He elaborates this new epistemology in three subsequent *liasses*: "Soumission et usage de la raison" ("Submission and Use of Reason") (XIII), "Excellence [de cette manière de prouver Dieu]" ("Excellence of This Means of Proving God") (XIV), and "Transition [de la connaissance de l'homme à Dieu]" ("Transition from Knowledge of Man to Knowledge of God") (XV). Only once he has constructed the epistemological basis for his subsequent historical arguments does Pascal begin to close the hermeneutic circle: the prophecies will demonstrate the truth of Scripture, which will in turn prove the validity of the doctrine of the Fall. In the last analysis, it is the doctrine of Original Sin which will account for the central enigma of the human condition.

At first glance, the *liasse* "A.P.R." seems to be out of place.[70] It proposes a theoretical exposition of the doctrines of the Fall and Redemption before Pascal has worked out either an epistemology of Revelation or the historical grounds for claiming the historicity of the Fall. Why, one wonders, has Pascal chosen to set such a chapter—which in a sense contains

69. See Chapter V, The Limits of Apologetics, n. 49.

70. Whether "A.P.R." signifies "A Port-Royal" is a related but different question. See Sellier, *Pensées* (1991), p. 227, n. 1; Pugh, *Composition of Pascal's Apologia*, pp. 379–80; Mesnard, *Les Pensées de Pascal*, pp. 206–7.

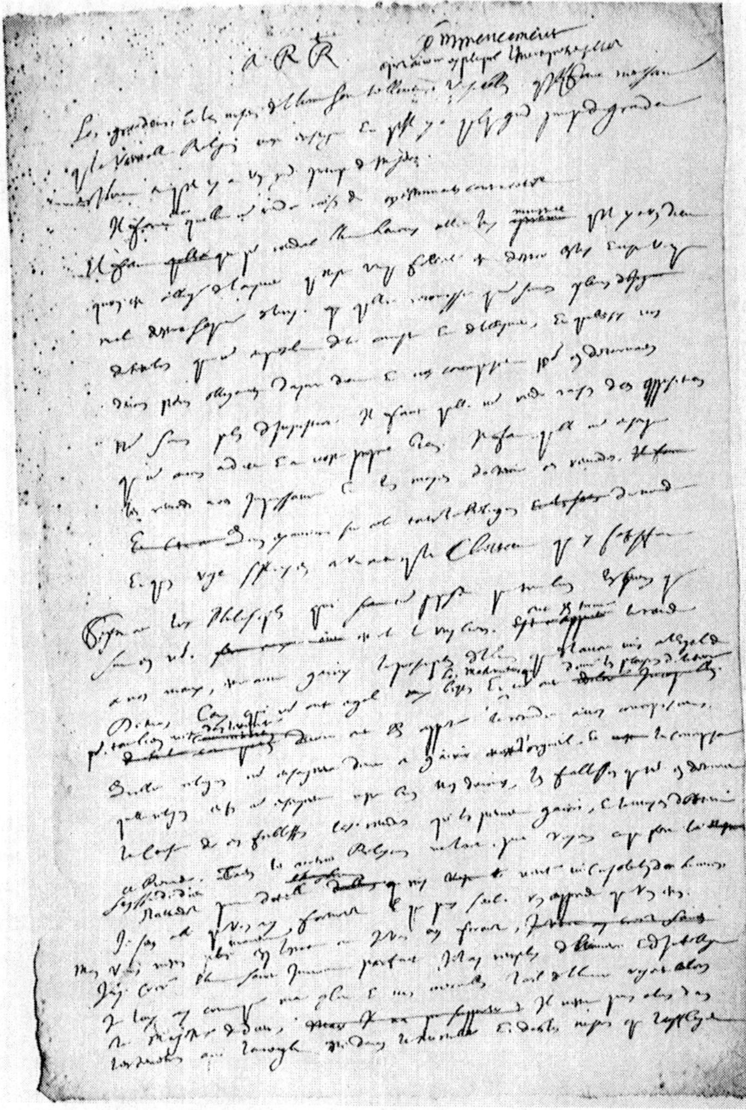

PLATE XVI. First page of the dossier "A.P.R." (Lafuma fragment 149) in the *Recueil original* (Bibliothèque Nationale, MS français 9202): "Le grandeurs et les misères de l'homme sont tellement visibles qu'il faut nécessairement que la véritable religion nous enseigne et qu'il a quelque grand principe de grandeur en l'homme et qu'il y a un grand principe de misère." Service photographique, Bibliothèque Nationale.

his entire theology—between the end of his anthropological reflections in *liasses* II–X and the beginning of his elaboration of a new epistemology in "Commencement" (XII)? The answer to this question once again lies in Pascal's apologetic strategy. "Faire souhaiter aux bons qu[e la religion] fût vraie et puis montrer qu'elle est vraie" ("Make good men wish that religion were true; then show that it is") (12). Before he can legitimately wish that Christianity were true, the *chercheur* needs a rudimentary working definition of a religion concerning which he has some very mistaken notions. "A.P.R." will give him this preliminary, global overview of what true Christianity means.

A significant epistemological break takes place at the end of the chapter "Philosophes" (IX). All that remains of human knowledge and custom has been reduced to a single principle set forth at the beginning of the *liasse* "Le Souverain Bien" ("The Sovereign Good") (X): "Tous les hommes recherchent d'être heureux" ("All men seek happiness") (148). This irreducible principle, the single common denominator of all human beings who have ever lived, immediately gives rise to the hypothesis of a lost God:

> Qu'est-ce donc que nous crie cette avidité et cette impuissance sinon qu'il y a eu autrefois dans l'homme un véritable bonheur, dont il ne lui reste maintenant que la marque et la trace toute vide, et qu'il essaie inutilement de remplir de tout ce qui l'environne, recherchant des choses absentes le secours qu'il n'obtient pas des présentes, mais qui en sont toutes incapables parce que ce gouffre infini ne peut être rempli que par un objet infini et immuable, c'est à dire par Dieu même.

> What else does this craving, and this helplessness, proclaim but that there was once in man a true happiness, of which all that now remains is the empty print and trace? This he tries in vain to fill with everything around him, seeking in things that are not there the help he cannot find in those that are, though none can help, since this infinite abyss can be filled only with an infinite and immutable object; in other words by God himself. (148)

The opening sentences of "A.P.R." (XI) recast this hypothesis in epistemological terms. "Les grandeurs et les misères de l'homme sont tellement visibles qu'il faut nécessairement que la véritable religion nous enseigne et qu'il y a quelque grand principe de grandeur en l'homme et qu'il y a un grand principe de misère. Il faut encore qu'elle nous rende raison de ces étonnantes contrariétés" ("Man's greatness and wretchedness are so evident that the true religion must necessarily teach us that there is in man some great principle of greatness and some great principle of wretchedness. It must also account for such amazing contradictions") (149).

It is precisely at this point that Revelation, in the person of Divine Wisdom, breaks through the epistemological impasse to which the unbeliever has been led via the purificatory rite of skepticism. "N'attendez pas, dit-elle, ô hommes, ni vérité ni consolation des hommes. Je suis celle qui vous ai formés et qui peux seule vous apprendre qui vous êtes" (" 'O men' says [Divine Wisdom], 'do not expect either truth or consolation from men. It is I who have made you and I alone can teach you what you are' ") (149).

What follows is not an historical exposition of the Fall. Rather, Revelation—in the guise of Divine Wisdom, a model borrowed from the Book of Proverbs—paints the great contours of the Christian vision of reality. The detailed brushwork, in which will be elaborated those "preuves convaincantes" ("convincing proofs") of which Divine Wisdom speaks, will come later. At this point in the projected Apology, Pascal is more concerned with tracing the parameters of a conceptual framework into which the *chercheur* will be able to fit all that is to follow. This provisional version of Revelation will temporarily serve to fill the epistemological void left in the mind of the *chercheur* by the rite of skepticism.

In her final discourse, Divine Wisdom directly addresses the *chercheur*. She assures him that he will retain both his powers of reason and his Free Will as he considers the case for Christian Revelation:

> "Je n'entends pas que vous soumettiez votre créance à moi sans raison, et ne prétends pas vous assujettir avec tyrannie. Je ne prétends pas aussi vous rendre raison de toutes choses. Et pour accorder ces contrariétés, j'entends vous faire voir clairement, par des preuves convaincantes, des marques divines en moi, qui vous convainquent de ce que je suis, et m'attirer autorité par des merveilles et des preuves que vous ne puissiez refuser; et qu'ensuite vous croyiez les choses que je vous enseigne, quand vous n'y trouverez autre sujet de les refuser, sinon que vous ne pouvez par vous-même connaître si elles sont ou non."

> "I do not mean you to believe me submissively and without reason; I do not claim to subdue you by tyranny. Nor do I claim to account to you for everything. To reconcile these contradictions I mean to show you clearly, by convincing proofs, marks of divinity within me which will convince you of what I am, and establish my authority by miracles and proofs that you cannot reject, so that you will then believe the things I teach, finding no reason to reject them but your own inability to tell whether they are true or not." (149)

Divine Wisdom then turns to the most difficult question of all: why Revelation has been given to some and withheld from others. Her exposition of the doctrine of *Deus absconditus* lays the theological groundwork for Pascal's subsequent distinction between hardened and alterable disbelief in the following *liasse*. The hardened unbelievers (the "endurcis") are explicitly contrasted with those who seek God with all their hearts:

"Dieu a voulu racheter les hommes, et ouvrir le salut *à ceux qui le cherchaient*. Mais les hommes s'en rendent si indignes *qu'il est juste que Dieu refuse à quelques-uns*, à cause de leur *endurcissement*, *ce qu'il accorde aux autres* par une miséricorde qui ne leur est pas due.

S'il eût voulu surmonter l'obstination des plus *endurcis*, il eût pu, en se découvrant si manifestement à eux qu'ils n'eussent pu douter de la vérité de son essence, comme il paraîtra au dernier jour. . . .

Ce n'est pas en cette sorte qu'il a voulu paraître dans son avènement de douceur; parce que, tant d'hommes se rendant indignes de sa clémence, il a voulu les laisser dans la privation du bien qu'ils ne veulent pas. Il n'était donc pas juste qu'il parût d'une manière manifestement divine, et absolument capable de convaincre tous les hommes; mais il n'était pas juste aussi qu'il vînt d'une manière si cachée, qu'il ne pût être reconnu de *ceux qui le chercheraient sincèrement*. Il a voulu se rendre parfaitement connaissable à ceux-là et ainsi, voulant paraître à découvert à *ceux qui le cherchent de tout leur coeur*, *et caché à ceux qui le fuient de tout leur coeur*, il a tempéré sa connaissance, en sorte qu'il a donné des marques de soi visibles à *ceux qui le cherchent*, et non à *ceux qui ne le cherchent pas*.

Il y a assez de lumière pour ceux qui ne désirent que de voir et assez d'obscurité pour ceux qui ont une disposition contraire."

"God's will has been to redeem men and open the way of salvation *to those who seek him*, but men have shown themselves so unworthy *that it is right for God to refuse to some* for their *hardness* of heart, what he grants to others by a mercy they have not earned. If he had wished to overcome the obstinacy of the most *hardened*, he could have done so by revealing himself to them so plainly that they could not doubt the truth of his essence, as he will appear on the last day. . . .

This is not the way he wished to appear when he came in mildness, because so many men had shown themselves unworthy of his clemency, that he wished to deprive them of the good they did not desire. It was therefore not right that he should appear in a manner manifestly divine and absolutely capable of convincing all men, but neither was it right that his coming should be so hidden that he could not be recognized by *those who sincerely sought him*. He wished to make himself perfectly recognizable to them. Thus wishing to appear openly to those *who seek him with all their heart* and *hidden from those who shun him with all their heart*, he has qualified our knowledge of him by giving signs which can be seen by *those who seek him* and not by *those who do not*.

There is enough light for those who desire only to see, and enough darkness for those of a contrary disposition." (149, italics mine)

In the last analysis, Pascal's distinction between hardened and alterable disbelief is but a corollary of the great Augustinian doctrine of Election and Predestination. In condemning some and saving others, God does not act arbitrarily or contrary to mercy and justice. Because they bear the imprint of Adam's Fall, all human beings who have ever lived merit eternal damnation. God simply abandons "ceux qui le fuient de tout leur coeur" ("those who shun him with all their heart") to a fate which by right all—including those who seek Him—justly deserve. God has hidden Himself in Revelation so as to separate the *élus* from the *réprouvés*:

> Il y a assez de clarté pour éclairer les élus et assez d'obscurité pour les humilier. Il y a assez d'obscurité pour aveugler les réprouvés et assez de clarté pour les condamner et les rendre inexcusables.

> There is enough light to enlighten the elect and enough obscurity to humiliate them. There is enough obscurity to blind the reprobate and enough light to condemn them and deprive them of excuse. (236)

In saving the elect, God transcends His own hidden nature. In the Incarnation, God has modified His unknowable nature in order to reveal Himself to those who seek Him with all their hearts. Revelation as recorded in Scripture is a kind of extraordinary dispensation of Grace:

> Voulant paraître à découvert à ceux qui le cherchent de tout leur coeur, *Dieu a tempéré sa connaissance* en sorte qu'il a donné des marques de soi visibles à ceux qui le cherchent et non à ceux qui ne le cherchent pas.

> Wishing to appear openly to those who seek him with all their heart and hidden from those who shun him with all their heart, *God has qualified our knowledge of him* by giving signs which can be seen by those who seek him and not by those who do not. (149, italics mine)[71]

Those whose hearts are fixed on earthly and temporal things will, like the hardened skeptics, fail to penetrate the figurative veil of Revelation in Scripture. In Pascal's scheme of things, however, those who seek God sincerely and with all their hearts must somehow have already been touched by Grace. Their hearts must have already been turned away from earthly and temporal treasures. Otherwise, they would not be searching. "Tu ne me chercherais pas" ("You would not be seeking me"), Christ tells the seeker in a fragment destined for the *Mystère de Jésus*, "si tu ne me possédais" ("if you did not possess me") (929).

71. Pascal transposes the final part of this passage (beginning with the word *tempéré* to the *liasse* "Fondements" (XVIII). See Sellier, *Pensées* (1991), p. 223, n. 7.

Bibliography

References to the *Pensées*, that is, to the fragment numbers cited in the text, are to the edition of Louis Lafuma's *Pascal: Œuvres complètes* (Paris: Seuil, 1963).

Abbott, Walter, S.J., ed. *The Documents of Vatican II*. New York: America Press, 1966.

Adam, Antoine. *Théophile de Viau et la libre pensée française*. Paris: Droz, 1936.

———. *Les Libertins au XVIIe siècle*. Paris: Buchet/Chastel, 1964.

Alcover, M. *La Pensée philosophique et scientifique de Cyrano de Bergerac*. Geneva: Droz, 1970.

Alquié, Ferdinand. "Pascal et la critique contemporaine." *Critique* 13 (1957): 126.

Aquinas, Saint Thomas. *The Summa contra Gentiles of Saint Thomas Aquinas*. London: Oates and Washborne, 1924.

Arnauld, Antoine. *Morale pratique des Jésuites VI: Histoire des differens entre les missionaires Jésuites d'une part et ceux des ordres de St. Dominique et de St. François de l'autre, touchant les cultes que les Chinois rendent à leur Maître Confucius, à leurs ancestres, et à l'idole Chin-hoan*. Cologne: G. Quentel [Amsterdam: Elzevir], 1692. *Morale pratique des Jésuites*. . . . 8 vol. 1669–95.

———. *Oeuvres de Messire Antoine Arnauld*. Paris: Gabriel de Bellegarde, 1775–83.

———. *De la nécessité de la foi en Jésus-Christ*. In *Oeuvres de Messire Antoine Arnauld*. Paris: chez d'Arnay, 1777.

Augustine, Saint. *The Advantage of Believing*. Translated by L. Meagher. In *Writings of Saint Augustine II*. New York: Cima, 1947.

———. *The City of God*. Translated by Marcus Dods. New York: Modern Library, 1950.

Balzac, Guez de. *Oeuvres*. Paris: L. Billaine, 1665.

Bayle, Pierre. *Dictionnaire historique et critique*. Rotterdam: R. Leers, 1697.

Beaude, Joseph. "Le Dialogue d'Orasius sur le sujet de la divinité." *Recherches sur le XVIIe siècle* 1 (1976): 50–62.

———. "Le Déisme selon Mersenne." In *Il Libertinismo in Europa*. Edited by Sergio Bertelli. Milan-Naples: R. Ricciardi, 1980. 199–208.

———. *La Crise culturelle au début du XVIIe siècle (1600–1637) et le problème de Dieu*. Thesis, University of Lille III, 1985.

Beauvoir, Simone de. *La Cérémonie des adieux*. Paris: Gallimard, 1981.

Bédier, Joseph. "Etablissement d'un texte critique de 'L'Entretien de Pascal avec M. de Saci.' " In *Etudes critiques*. Paris: A. Collin, 1903. 19–80.

Béguin, Albert. *Pascal par lui-même*. Paris: Seuil, 1952.

Beurrier, Père Paul. *Speculum christianae religioniis in triplici, lege, naturali, mosaica et evangelica*. Paris: J. Langlois, 1662.

———. *Mémoires*. Ms.1885–87, Bibliothèque Sainte Geneviève. Extracts related to Pascal reproduced in Jean Mesnard's edition of the *Oeuvres complètes*. Bibliothèque Européenne. Paris: Desclée de Brouwer, 1964. I, 866–75.

Bloch, Olivier. "Cyrano de Bergerac et la philosophie," *XVIIe siècle* No. 149 (1985): 337–48.

Block, Marc. *Les Rois thaumaturges*. Paris: A. Colin, 1961.

Bogan, Z. *Homerus sive comparatio Homeri cum scriptoribus sacris quoad norman loquendi*. Oxford: n.p., 1658.

Bossuet, J.-B. *Discours sur l'histoire universelle*. Paris: Garnier-Flammarion, 1966.

Boucher, J. *Les Triomphes de la religion chrestienne contenans les résolutions de trois cens soixante et six questions*. Paris: L. Sonnius, 1638.

Boudhors, Charles. *Oeuvres complètes du Chevalier de Méré*. Paris: Editions Roche, 1930.

Bridenne, J.J. "Cyrano de Bergerac." *Revue des sciences humaines* 75 (1954): 241–57.

Brunet, Georges. *Le Pari de Pascal*. Paris: Desclée de Brouwer, 1956.

Brunschvicg, Léon, ed. *Oeuvres de Blaise Pascal*. Paris: Hachette, Les Grands Ecrivains de la France, 1908–14.

Bush, Douglas. *English Literature in the Earlier Seventeenth Century 1600–1660*. Oxford: Clarendon Press, 1952.

Busson, Henri. *La Pensée religieuse de Charron à Pascal*. Paris: Vrin, 1933.

Camus, Albert. *L'Etranger*. Englewood Cliffs, N.J.: Prentice-Hall, 1955.

Cantillon, Alain. "Vérité des *Pensées*: Proposition pour une théorie de l'énonciation littéraire." *Poétique* 76 (1988): 395–413.

Carraud, Vincent. *Pascal et la philosophie*. Paris: P.U.F., coll. "Epiméthée," 1992.

Chamaillard, Edmond. *Le Chevalier de Méré*. Paris: Niort, 1921.

Charles-Daubert, Françoise. "Le Libertinage et la recherche contemporaine." *XVIIe siècle* 149 (1985): 409–32.

Chevalier, J. *Pascal: Oeuvres complètes*. Paris: Gallimard, 1954.

Clarke, J.A. *Gabriel Naudé 1600–1653*. Hamden, Conn.: Archon, 1970.

Couton, Georges. Introduction. In *L'Edition de Port-Royal des Pensées*. Saint-Etienne: Universités de la région Rhône-Alpes, 1971.

———. "Libertinage et apologétique: Les *Pensées* de Pascal contre la thèse des Trois Imposteurs." *XVIIe siècle* 127 (1980): 181–95.

Croquette, Bernard. *Pascal et Montaigne*. Genève: Droz, 1974.

Cross, F.L., ed. *The Oxford Dictionary of the Christian Church*. Oxford: Oxford University Press, 1984.

Curtis, D.E. *Progress and Eternal Recurrence in the Works of Gabriel Naudé*. Hull, 1967.

Cyrano de Bergerac. *The Comical History of the States and Empires of the Worlds of the Moon and Sun, written in French by Cyrano Bergerac and Newly Englished by A. Lovell, A.M.*. London: Henry Rhodes, 1687.

———. *L'Autre Monde ou Les Etats et empires de la lune et soleil*. Edited by F. Lachèvre. Paris: Garnier, 1938.

Daniel, Norman. *Islam and the West: The Making of an Image*. Edinburgh: Edinburgh University Press, 1966.

D'Auzoles, J. *La Sainte Chronologie*. Paris: G. Alliot, 1632.

Davidson, Hugh M. *The Origins of Certainty: Means and Meaning in Pascal's Pensées*. Chicago: Chicago University Press, 1979.

Davidson, Hugh M, and Dubé, P. *A Concordance to Pascal's Pensées*. Ithaca: Cornell University Press, 1975.

Defaux, Gérard. "Un Evangélique au pays de la Contre-Réforme: Erasme en France au XVIIe siècle." In *Horizons européens de la littérature au XVIIe siècle*. Tübingen: G. Narr, 1988.

Delassault, Geneviève. *Le Maistre de Sacy et son temps*. Paris: Nizet, 1957.

Demorest, J.-J. "L'Honnête Homme et le croyant selon Pascal." *Modern Philology* 53.4 (1956): 217–20.

Dens, Jean-Pierre. "Le Chevalier de Méré et la critique mondaine." *XVIIe siècle* 101 (1973): 41–50.

Dictionnaire des lettres françaises. Paris: Fayard, 1954.

Dictionnaire de spiritualité. Paris: Beauchesne, 1986.

Dorival, Bernard. *Album Pascal*. Paris: Gallimard, "Bibliothèque de la Pléiade," 1978.

Du Cambout de Pontchâteau, l'abbé Sébastien-Joseph. *La Morale pratique des Jésuites*. Cologne: C. Quentel, 1669. Côte. Bibliothèque Nationale: 80 Ld 39. 208.

Du Ryer, André. *L'Alcoran de Mahomet translaté d'arabe en françois par le sieur du Ryer, sieur de la grande Malezaire*. Paris: Chez Antoine de Sommaville, 1647.

Eliade, Mircea. *Forgerons et alchimistes*. Paris: Flammarion, 1977.

Eliade, Mircea. "Survivals and Camouflages of Myths." In *Symbolism, the Sacred and the Arts*. Edited by Diane Apostolos-Cappadona. New York: Crossroad, 1985. 32–52.

Ernst, Pol. *Approches pascaliennes*. Gembloux: Duculot, 1970.

———. Review of *The Composition of Pascal's Apologia*, by Anthony Pugh. *XVIIe siècle* (April-June 1986): 183–85.

———. *Géologie et stratigraphie des Pensées*. Paris-Oxford: Universitas, 1993.

Ferreyrolles, Gérard. "L'Imagination en procès." *XVIIe siècle* 177 (1992): 469–79.

Fitelieu (De), Sieur de Rodolphe et du Montour. *La Contre-Mode*. Paris: L. de Heuqueville, 1642.

Fontaine, Nicolas. *Mémoires pour servir à l'histoire de Port-Royal*. Utrecht: n.p., 1736.

Force, Pierre. *Le Problème herméneutique chez Pascal*. Paris: Vrin, 1989.

Gallucci, John. "Pascal poeta-theologus." *Papers on French Seventeenth Century Literature* 17.32 (1990): 151–70.

———. "Faith and Language: Allegories of Interpretation in Pascal." *French Forum* 16.2 (1991): 149–75.

———. "Pascal and Kenneth Burke: An Argument for a 'Logological' Reading of the *Pensées*." *Papers on French Seventeenth Century Literature* 20.38 (1993): 123–50.

Garasse, Père François. *La Doctrine curieuse des beaux esprits de ce temps ou prétendus tels . . . combattue et renversée*. Paris: S. Chappelet, 1624.

Gay, Peter. *The Enlightenment: The Rise of Modern Paganism*. New York: Norton, 1966.

Gazier, A., ed. *Pensées de Pascal . . . Edition de Port-Royal*. Paris: Société Française d'Imprimerie, 1907.

Gernet, Jacques. *Chine et christianisme*. Paris: Gallimard, 1982. English translation: *China and the Christian Impact: A Conflict of Cultures*. Cambridge: Cambridge University Press, 1985.

Godard de Donville, Louise. *Le Libertin des origines à 1665: Un produit des apologètes*. Tübingen: Biblio 17, 1989.
Goldmann, Lucien. *Le Dieu caché: Étude sur la vision tragique dans les Pensées de Pascal et dans le théâtre de Racine*. Paris: Gallimard, 1955.
———. "Le Pari est-il écrit 'pour le libertin'?" In *Blaise Pascal: L'Homme et l'oeuvre*. Edited by M.-A. Bera. Paris: Editions de Minuit, 1956. 139–56.
Gouhier, Henri. *Blaise Pascal: Commentaires*. Paris: Vrin, 1971.
———. *Pascal et les humanistes chrétiens: L'affaire Saint-Ange*. Paris: Vrin, 1974.
———. *Blaise Pascal: Conversion et apologétique*. Paris: Vrin, 1986.
———. *L'Anti-Humanisme au XVIIe siècle*. Paris: Vrin, 1987.
Goyet, Thérèse. "Table de concordance entre l'édition des "Pensées" de 1670 et les éditions Lafuma (Luxembourg) et Brunschvicg." In *Les "Pensées" de Pascal ont trois cents ans*. Clermont-Ferrand: G. de Bussac, 1971. 42–78.
Grenaille, François de. *La Mode, ou Charactère de la religion. De la vie. De la conversation. De la solitude. Des complimens. Des habits et du style du temps*. Paris: N. Gassé, 1642.
Grotius, Hugo. *Dissertatio altera de origine Gentium Americanarum adversus obtrectatorem*. Paris: S. Cramoisy, 1643.
———. *De la Vérité de la religion chrestienne par Hugue Grotius, traduit du latin par le sieur de Beauvoir*. Paris: chez Pierre le Petit, 1659.
———. *The Truth of Christian Religion . . . translated into English . . . by Symon Patrick, Dean of Peterburgh and Chaplain in Ordinary to Their Majesties*. London: Luke Meredith, 1689.
Grubbs, H. A. *Damien Mitton (1618–1690), bourgeois honnête homme*. Paris: P.U.F., 1932.
Halevi, Judah. *The Kuzari*. New York: Schocken Books, 1964.
Harrington, Thomas. *Pascal philosophe*. Paris: S.E.D.E.S., 1982.
Harth, Erica. *Cyrano de Bergerac and the Polemics of Modernity*. New York: Columbia University Press, 1970.
Hubert, Sister Marie Louise, O.P. *Pascal's Unfinished Apology*. New Haven, Conn.: Yale University Press, 1952.
Jerusalem Bible. New York: Doubleday, 1966.
Jovy, E. *Pascal inédit*. 3. Vitry-le-François: "l'auteur," 1910.
Julien-Eymard d'Angers. *Pascal et ses précurseurs*. Paris: Nouvelles Editions Latines, 1954.
———. "Stoïcisme et libertinage dans l'oeuvre de François La Mothe Le Vayer." *Revue de sciences humaines* 75 (1954): 259–84.
———. "Le Stoïcisme d'après l'*Humanitas theologica* de Pierre Lescalopier, S.J." *Bulletin de littérature ecclésiastique* 56 (1955): 23–36.
Jung, C. G. *Memories, Dreams, Reflections*. New York: Random House, 1965.
Kaplan, Francis. *Les Pensées de Pascal*. Paris: Cerf, 1982.
Kelly, Van. *Pascalian Fictions: Antagonism and Absent Agency in the Wager and Other "Pensées."* Birmingham, Ala.: Summa Publications, 1992.
Knight, W. *The Life and Works of Hugo Grotius*. London: Sweet and Maxwell, 1925.
Koch, Erec. "Rhetorical Aesthetics and Rhetorical Theory in Pascal." *Papers on French Seventeenth Century Literature* 20:38 (1993): 151–70.
Krailsheimer, A. J. *Pascal*. Oxford: Oxford University Press, 1980.
La Mothe le Vayer. *De la vertu des payens*. Paris: F. Targa, 1642.
———. *Oeuvres de La Mothe le Vayer*. Dresden: M. Groell, 1758.
———. *Parallèles historiques*. Vol. 7. *Oeuvres de La Mothe le Vayer*. Dresden: M. Groell, 1758. 7, 287–97.

———. [Orasius Tubero, pseud.]. "Sur la divinité" ("De la Diversité des religions"). In *Deux Dialogues faits à l'imitation des anciens*. Edited by Ernest Tisserand. Paris: Editions Bossard, 1922.

La Peyrère, Isaac de. *Du Rappel des Juifs*. N.p.: n.p., 1643.

———. *Relation du Groenland*. Paris: A. Courbé, 1647.

———. *Praeadamitae*. N.p.: n.p., 1655.

———. *Systema theologicum ex prae Adamitarum hypothesi*. N.p.: n.p., 1655.

———. *A Theological Systeme upon that Presupposition that Men were before Adam*. London: n.p., 1655.

———. *Men before Adam, or a discourse upon the twelfth, thirteenth and fourteenth verses of the Epistle of the Apostle Paul to the Romans by which are proved that the first Men were created before Adam*. London: n.p., 1656.

———. *Lettre à Philotime, dans laquelle il expose les raisons qui l'ont obligé à abjurer la Secte de Calvin qu'il professait, et le Livre des Préadamites qu'il avait mis au jour: Traduit en Francais, du Latin imprimé à Rome, par l'Auteur même*. Paris: Courbé, 1658.

———. *Apologie de la Peyrère*. Paris: L. Billaine, 1663.

———. *Des Juifs, Elus, Rejetés, et Rapelés*. Cabinet des Manuscrits, Musée Condé, Chantilly. Ms. 191 (698).

Lachelier, Jules. "Notes sur le pari de Pascal." *Revue philosophique de la France et de l'étranger* 51 (1901): 625–39.

Lachèvre, Frédéric. *Le Prince des libertins du XVIIe siècle: Jacques Vallée des Barreaux, sa vie, ses poésies*. Paris: H. Leclerc, 1907.

———. *Voltaire mourant*. Paris: H. Champion, 1908.

———. *Le Procès de Théophile de Viau*. Paris: H. Champion, 1909. 2 vols.

———. *La Vie et les poésies libertines de Des Barreaux (1599–1673) et Saint-Pavin (1595–1670)*. Paris: Champion, 1911.

———. *Les Oeuvres libertines de Cyrano de Bergerac*. 2 vols. Paris: H. Champion, 1922.

Lacombe, Roger. "Le Pari de Pascal." *Revue philosophique* 137 (1947): 156–93.

———. *L'Apologétique de Pascal: Etude critique*. Paris: PUF, 1958.

Lafuma, Louis. *Recherches pascaliennes*. Paris: Delmas, 1949.

———. *Controverses pascaliennes*. Paris: Editions de Luxembourg, 1952.

———, ed. *Pascal: Oeuvres complètes*. L'Intégrale. Paris: Editions de Seuil, 1963.

Lagarde, François. "Le différement de Pascal." *Papers on French Seventeenth Century Literature* 20.38 (1993): 183–92.

Lanius, E.W. *Cyrano de Bergerac and the Universe of the Imagination*. Geneva: Droz, 1967.

Laporte, Jean. *La Doctrine de Port-Royal*. Paris: Vrin, 1951.

Le Brun, Jacques. *La Spiritualité de Bossuet*. Paris: Klincksieck, 1972.

Le Guern, Michel. *l'Image dans l'oeuvre de Pascal*. Paris: Armand Colin, 1969.

———, ed., *Blaise Pascal: Pensées*. 2 vols. Paris: Gallimard, 1977.

Le Guern, Michel and Marie-Rose. *Les Pensées de Pascal: De l'anthropologie à la théologie*. Paris: Larousse, 1972.

Lenoble, Robert. *Mersenne ou la naissance du mécanisme*. Paris: Vrin, 1971.

Lhermet, Jean. *Pascal et la Bible*. Paris: Vrin, 1930.

Lonning, Per. *Cet effrayant Pari*. Paris: Vrin, 1980.

Mackenzie, Louis. "To the Brink: The Dialectics of Anxiety in the *Pensées*." *Yale French Studies* 66 (1984): 57–66.

Marchand, Prosper. *Dictionnaire historique*. La Haye: P. de Hondt, 1758.

Marin, Louis. *La Critique du discours: Sur la "Logique de Port-Royal" et les "Pensées" de Pascal*. Paris: Minuit, 1975.

———. " 'Pascal': Text, Author, Discourse. . . ." *Yale French Studies* 52 (1975): 129–51.

Mariner, Frank. "The Order of Disorder: The Problem of the Fragment in Pascal's *Pensées*." *Papers on French Seventeenth Century Literature* 20.38 (1993): 171–82.

Martineau, Emmanuel. *Discours sur la religion et sur quelques autres sujets de Blaise Pascal, restitués et publiés par Emmanuel Martineau*. Paris: Fayard/Armand Colin, 1992.

Martini, Père Martin. *Histoire de la Chine, traduite du Latin du Père Martin Martini de la Compagnie de Jésus par l'abbé Le Peletier*. Paris: chez C. Barbin, 1692.

McKee, David Rice. "Isaac La Peyrère, a Precursor of the Eighteenth-Century Critical Deists." *PMLA* 59 (1944): 456–85.

McKenna, Antony. "L'Argument 'Infini-Rien.' " In *Méthodes chez Pascal: Actes du colloque tenu à Clermont-Ferrand 10–13 juin 1976*. Edited by Jean Mesnard. Paris, Presses universitaires de France, 1979. 497–508.

———. "Pascal et le corps humain." *XVIIe siècle* 177 (1992): 481–94.

———. "Une Question de cohérence: l'argument *ad hominem* dans les *Pensées* de Pascal." *Littératures Classiques* 20 (1994): 23–40.

Melzer, Sara E. "Pascal's *Pensées*: Economy and Interpretation of Fragments." *Stanford French Review* 6 (1982): 207–20.

———. *Discourses of the Fall: A Study of Pascal's Pensées*. Berkeley and Los Angeles: University of California Press, 1986.

Ménage, Gilles. *Ménagiana, ou Les Bons Mots et remarques critiques, historiques, morales et d'érudition de M. Ménage, recueillies par ses amis*. Vol. 4. Paris: F. Delaulne, 1715.

Mersenne, P. Marin. *L'Impiété des Déistes, Athées et Libertins de ce temps, combattue et renversée de point en point par raisons tirées de la Philosophie et de la Théologie*. 2 Vols. Paris: P. Bilaine, 1624.

Mesnard, Jean. *Blaise Pascal, Oeuvres complètes*. Paris: Desclée de Brouwer, Bibliothèque européenne, 1964–93. Vols. 1–5. *Pensées* will appear in Vol. 6.

———. *Pascal*. Paris: Desclée de Brouwer, coll. "Les Ecrivains devant Dieu," 1965.

———. "Aux origines de l'édition des *Pensées*: Les deux copies." In *Les "Pensées" de Pascal ont trois cents ans*. Clermont-Ferrand: G. de Bussac, 1971. 1–29.

———. *Les Pensées de Pascal*. Paris: S.E.D.E.S., 1976.

———. "Pourquoi les *Pensées* de Pascal se présentent-elles sous forme de fragments?" *Papers on French Seventeenth Century Literature* 10:19 (1983): 635–49.

———. "Le Thème des trois ordres dans l'organisation des *Pensées*." In *Pascal: Thématique des Pensées*. Edited by Lane M. Heller and Ian M. Richmond. Paris: Vrin, 1988.

———. *La Culture du XVIIe siècle*. Paris: P.U.F., 1991.

———. "Nombres et textes figurés chez Pascal." *XVIIe siècle* 177 (1992): 521–32.

———. "Structures binaires et structures ternaires dans les *Pensées* de Pascal." *Littératures Classiques* 20 (1994): 45–56.

Meurillon, Christian. "La Narration dans les *Pensées*." *XVIIe siècle* 177 (1992): 507–19.

Michon, Hélène. "*Deus absconditus*." *XVIIe siècle* 177 (1992): 495–506.

Mongrédien, Georges. *Cyrano de Bergerac*. Paris: Berger-Levrault, 1964.

Montaigne, Michel de. *Les Essais de Montaigne*. Edited by V.-L. Saulnier. Paris: P.U.F., 1965.

———. *The Complete Essays of Montaigne*. Translated by Donald M. Frame. Stanford, Calif.: Stanford University Press, 1965.

———. *Essais*. In *Oeuvres complètes*. Paris: Seuil, 1967.

Mungello, David E. *Curious Land: Jesuit Accommodation and the Origins of Sinology*. Stuttgart: Steiner, 1985.

Natoli, Charles. "Proof in Pascal's *Pensées*: Reason as Rhetoric." In *Meaning, Structure and History in the "Pensées" of Pascal*. Edited by D. Wetsel. Tübingen: Biblio 17, 1990. 19–32.

Naudé, Gabriel. *Instruction à la France sur la vérité de l'histoire des frères de la Rose-Croix*. Paris: F. Julliot, 1623.

———. *Apologie pour tous les grands personnages qui ont été faussement soupçonnés de magie*. Paris: F. Targa, 1625.

———. *Jugement de tout ce qui a été imprimé contre le cardinal Mazarin*. N.p.: n.p., 1649.

———. *Considérations politiques sur les coups d'estat, par Gabriel Naudé, parisien*. Paris: "Sur la copie de Rome," 1667.

———. *Political Considerations upon refined Politicks and the Master-Strokes of State as Practised by the Ancients and Moderns. Translated into English by Dr. King*. London: H. Clements, 1711.

Norman, Buford. *Portraits of Thoughts. Knowledge, Methods and Styles in Pascal*. Columbus: Ohio University Press, 1988.

Oddos, Jean-Paul. *Recherches sur la vie et l'oeuvre d'Isaac Lapeyère (1596?–1676)*. Unpublished "thèse de 3ème cycle," Université des Sciences Sociales, Grenoble II, 1971–74.

Orcibal, Jean. "Les Jansénistes face à Spinoza." *Revue de littérature comparée* October (1949): 441–68.

Orcibal, Jean. "Le Fragment Infini-Rien et ses sources." In *Blaise Pascal: L'homme et l'oeuvre*. Edited by M.-A. Bera. Paris: Editions de Minuit, 1956. 159–86.

Otto, Rudolf. *The Idea of the Holy: An Inquiry into the Nonrational Factor in the Idea of the Divine and Its Relation to the Rational*. Oxford: Oxford University Press, 1958.

Paganini, Gianni. "L'Anthropologie naturaliste d'un esprit fort: Thèmes et problèmes pomponaciens dans le *Theophrastus redivivus*." *XVIIe siècle* 149 (1985): 349–77.

Paine, Thomas. *The Age of Reason, Part the Second, Being an Investigation of True and Fabulous Theology*. London: n.p., 1795.

Pascal, Blaise. "Comparaison des chrétiens des premiers temps avec ceux d'aujourd'hui." *Pascal: Oeuvres complètes*. Edited by Lafuma. Paris: Seuil, 1963. 360–62.

———. "Lettre à Mlle de Roannez" (IV). *Pascal: Oeuvres complètes*. Edited by Lafuma. Paris: Seuil, 1963. 266–67.

———. "Préface sur le Traité du Vide." *Pascal: Oeuvres complètes*. Edited by Lafuma. Paris: Seuil, 1963. 230-32.

Pascal: Textes du tricentenaire. Paris: Fayard, 1963.

Les Pensées de Pascal ont trois cents ans. Clermont-Ferrand: G. de Bussac, 1971.

Périer, Gilberte. *La Vie de Monsieur Pascal. Pascal: Oeuvres complètes*. 17–33. Edited by Lafuma. Paris: Seuil, 1963.

Petau, Père Denis. *De Doctrina temporum*. 2 Vols. Paris: S. Cramoisy, 1627.

Pickthall, Mohammed Marmaduke, trans. *The Meaning of the Glorious Koran*. New York: Mentor, 1963.

Pinot, Virgile. *La Chine et la formation de l'esprit philosophique en France (1640–1740)*. Paris: Librairie Orientaliste, 1932.

Pintard, René. *Le Libertinage érudit dans la première moitié du XVIIe siècle*. Rev. ed. 1943; rpt. Geneva: Slatkine Reprints, 1983.

———. "Pascal et les libertins." In *Pascal présent*. Clermond Ferrand: G. de Bussac, 1962. 107–30.

———. "Les Problèmes de l'histoire du libertinage, notes et réflexions." *XVIIe siècle*. 127 (1980): 131–61.

Popkin, Richard H. "The Marrano Theology of Isaac La Peyrère." *Studi Internazionali di Filosofia* 5 (1973): 97–126.

———. "Menasseh ben Israel and Isaac La Peyrère." *Studia Rosenthaliana* 8 (1974): 59–63.

———. "La Peyrère, the Abbé Grégoire, and the Jewish Question in Eighteenth Century Culture." *Studies in Eighteenth Century Culture* 4 (1975): 209–22.

———. "The Pre-Adamite Theory in the Renaissance." In *Philosophy and Humanism: Renaissance Essays in Honor of Paul Oskar Kristeller*. Edited by Edward P. Mahoney. Leiden: Brill, 1976. 50–69.

———. "Menasseh ben Israel and La Peyrère II." *Studia Rosenthaliana* 18 (1984): 12–20.

———. *Isaac La Peyrère (1596–1676): His Life, Works and Influence*. New York: E. J. Brill, 1987.

Pugh, Anthony R. *The Composition of Pascal's Apologia*. Toronto: University of Toronto Press, 1984.

———. "La Disposition des matières." In *Pascal: Thématique des Pensées*. Edited by Lane M. Heller and Ian M. Richmond. Paris: Vrin, 1988. 9–28.

Quatrains du déiste [*Anti-Bigot ou le faux dévotieux*]. In F. Lachèvre's *Le Procès de Théophile*, 2, pp. 105–26, and *Voltaire Mourant* (Paris: H. Champion, 1908). Text also reproduced in Antoine Adam, *Les Libertins au XVIIe siècle*, pp. 90–109.

Raue, Christian [Ravius]. *Prima tredecim partium Alcorani arabico-latin . . . Opera et studio Christiani Ravii*. Amsterdam: n.p., 1646. Côte Bibliothèque Nationale: 40 O2g 122.

Rice, J. V. *Gabriel Naudé (1600–1653)*. Baltimore: Johns Hopkins University Press, 1939.

Robinson, Ira. "Isaac de la Peyrère and the Recall of the Jews." *Jewish Social Studies* 40 (1978): 117–30.

Rossi, Paolo. *The Dark Abyss of Time: The History of the Earth and the History of Nations from Hooke to Vico*. Chicago: University of Chicago Press, 1984.

Rouleau, F.A. "Chinese Rites Controversy." In *New Catholic Encyclopedia*. Vol. 3. 611–17.

Rousseau, J.-J. *Confessions*. Vol. 4. Paris: Pléiade, 1959.

———. *Les Confessions*. Paris: Pauvert, 1961.

Sacy, Louis-Isaac Le Maistre de. *La Genèse: traduite en françois avec l'explication du sens littéral et du sens spirituel*. Paris: Lambert Roulland, 1682.

———. *L'Exode et Le Lévitique: traduits en français avec l'explication du sens littéral et du sens spirituel*. Lyon: L. Plaignard, 1683.

———. *Les douzes petits prophètes: traduits en français . . . par Le Maistre de Sacy, Prêtre*. Brussels: chez Fricx, 1700.

———. *La Sainte Bible . . . traduite en françois . . . avec de courtes notes tirées des Saints Pères*. Liège: Chez Broncart, 1702.

Saint Evremond. *Oeuvres mêlées de Saint Evremond*. Paris: C. Barbin, 1680.

Sainte-Beuve. *Portraits littéraires*. Vol 3. Paris: Garnier frères, 1882.

Saint-Sorlin, Desmarests de. *Délices de l'esprit*. Paris: A. Courbé, 1658.

Sarrau, Claude. *Epistolae*. Orange: n.p. 1654.
Sellier, Philippe. *Pascal et la liturgie*. Paris: P.U.F.,1966.
———. *Pascal et Saint Augustin*. Paris: A. Colin, 1970.
———, ed. *Pensées: Nouvelle édition établie pour la première fois d'après la copie de référence de Gilberte Pascal par Philippe Sellier*. Paris: Mercure de France, 1976.
———. "Avant-Propos." In D. Wetsel. *L'Ecriture et le Reste: The Pensées of Pascal in the Exegetical Tradition of Port-Royal*. Columbus: Ohio State University Press, 1981. xi–xiii.
———. "La Bible de Pascal." In *La Bible au Grand Siècle*. Paris: Beauchesne, 1989.
———. "Seminar: Pascal's 'Trois Ordres.' " In *Meaning, Structure and History in the "Pensées" of Pascal*. Edited by D. Wetsel. Tübingen: Biblio 17, 1990. 75–83.
———. "Sur les fleuves de Babylone: The Fluidity of the World and the Search for Permanence in the *Pensées*." Translated by D. Wetsel. In *Meaning, Structure and History in the "Pensées of Pascal*. Edited by D. Wetsel. Tübingen: Biblio 17, 1990. 33–44.
———. "Dix ans d'études pascaliennes en occident: Positions et propositions." *Pascal, Port-Royal, Orient, Occident*. Paris: Klincksieck, 1991. 349–55.
———, ed. *Pensées, édition établie d'après la Copie de référence de Gilberte Pascal*. Paris: Bordas, 1991.
———. "L'Ouverture de l'apologie pascalienne." *XVIIe siècle* 177 (1992): 437–49.
———. "Une Préface 'retrouvée' de l'Apologie pascalienne." In *Travaux de littérature*. Paris: Klincksieck, 1993.
———. " 'Abondonné . . . dans une île déserte': fantasmatique et théologie dans les *Pensées*." *Littératures Classiques* 20 (1994): 67–74.
Sells, A. L. "Molière and La Mothe le Vayer." *Modern Language Review* 28 (1933): 352–67, 444–55.
Seltzer, Robert M. *Jewish People, Jewish Thought*. New York: Macmillan, 1980.
Semedo, Alvarez, S.J. *Histoire universelle du grand royaume de la Chine, traduite en notre langue par Louis Coulon*. Paris: chez S. Cramoisy, 1645.
Shiokawa, Tetsuya. *Pascal et les miracles*. Paris: Nizet, 1977.
Simon, Richard. *De l'inspiration des Livres sacrés*. Rotterdam: R. Leers, 1687.
———. *Lettres choisies de M. Simon*. Rotterdam: R. Leers, 1702.
———. *Lettres choisies*. Amsterdam: P. Mortier, 1730.
Spence, Jonathan. *The Memory Palace of Matteo Ricci*. New York: Viking, 1984.
Spink, J. S. *French Free-Thought from Gassendi to Voltaire*. London: Athlone Press, 1960.
Stanton, Domna. *The Aristocrat as Art: A Study of the Honnête Homme and the Dandy in Seventeenth- and Nineteenth-Century French Literature*. New York: Columbia University Press, 1980.
———. "Pascal's Fragmentary Thoughts: Dis-order and its Overdetermination." *Semiotica* 51.1–3 (1984): 211–35.
Steinmann, Père Jean. *Richard Simon et les origines de l'exégèse biblique*. Paris: Desclée de Brouwer, 1959.
Stillingfleet, E. *Origines Sacrae or rational account of the Grounds of Christian Faith as to the truth and divine authority of the Scriptures*. London: n.p., 1666.
Stolpe, Sven. *Christina of Sweden*. New York: Macmillan, 1966.
Théophile de Viau. *Oeuvres poétiques*. Edited by J. Strecher. Geneva: Droz, 1951.
Theophrastus redivivus. Bibliothéque Nationale, fonds latin 9324.
Thirouin, Laurent. "Raison des effets, essai d'explication d'un concept pascalien." *XVIIe siècle* 134 (1982): 31–50.

———. *Le Hasard et les règles: Le modèle du jeu dans la pensée de Pascal.* Paris: Vrin, 1991.

———. "Les Premières Liasses des *Pensées*: architecture et signification." *XVIIe siècle* 177 (1992): 451–68.

———. "Le défaut d'une droite méthode. *Littérature Classiques* 20 (1994): 7–17.

Topliss, Patricia. *The Rhetoric of Pascal: A Study of His Art and Persuasion in the Provinciales and the "Pensées."* Leicester: Leicester University Press, 1966.

Tourneur, Zacharie. *Pensées de Blaise Pascal: Édition paléographique des manuscrits originaux conservés à la Bibliothèque Nationale.* Paris: Vrin, 1942.

Valensin, Auguste. "Note sur le pari de Pascal." *Revue pratique d'apologétique* (October, 1919).

Valéry, P. *"Variation sur une pensée." Revue hebdomadaire.* Special issue (1932): 161–72.

Vanini, J. C. *De admirandis Naturae Reginae Deaeque mortalium Arcanis libri IV.* Lutetiae: Perier, 1616.

Voltaire. *Lettres philosophiques.* Oxford: Blackwell, 1965.

Vossius, G.-J. *De theologia Gentili et physiologia christiana sive de origine de progressu idolatriae.* Amsterdam: C. Blaen, 1642.

Wade, J. O. "The Manuscripts of J. Meslier's Testament." *Modern Philology* 30 (1932–33): 381–98.

Weber, H. Introduction, Cyrano de Bergerac. *L'Autre Monde.* Paris: Editions Sociales, 1960.

Wetsel, David. *L'Ecriture et le Reste: The "Pensées" of Pascal in the Exegetical Tradition of Port-Royal.* Columbus: Ohio State University Press, 1981.

———. "Biblicism and Historicity: The *Pensées* of Pascal and Christian Humanism." *South Central Review* 2.4 (1985): 9–16.

———. " 'Histoire de la Chine': Pascal and the Challenge to Biblical Time." *The Journal of Religion* 69.2 (1989): 199–219.

———. "Augustine's *Confessions*: A Problematic Model for Pascal's Conversion Itinerary in the *Pensées*." *Papers on French Seventeenth Century Literature* 17: 32 (1990): 123–43.

———. "Isaac de La Peyrère et la crise de la chronologie biblique." In *"Sur une note juste": Quarante-sept hommages à Jacques Body.* Tours: Publications de l'Université de Tours, 1990. 361–67.

———. "Pascal's *Pensées* and Recent Critical Theory: Illumination or Deformation of the Text?" *Papers on French Seventeenth Century Literature* 20.38 (1993): 117–22.

———. " 'La religion de Mahomet': Pascal and the Tradition of Anti-Islamic Polemics." *Papers on French Seventeenth Century Literature* 20.39 (1993): 467–88.

Wickelgren, Florence Louise. *La Mothe Le Vayer, sa vie et son oeuvre.* Paris: Impressions Pierre André, 1934.

Wilbur, E. M. *A History of Unitarianism.* Cambridge, Mass.: 1945–52.

Wilcox, Donald J. *The Measure of Times Past: Pre-Newtonian Chronologies and the Rhetoric of Relative Time.* Chicago: The University of Chicago Press, 1987.

Wood, Allen W. "Deism." In *Encyclopedia of Religions.* Edited by M. Eliade. New York: Macmillan, 1987. 262–64.

Yardeni, Miriam. "La Religion de La Peyrère et 'Le Rappel des Juifs.' " *Revue d'histoire et de philosophie religieuse* 51 (1971): 245–59.

Zuber, Roger. "Libertinage et humanisme: une rencontre difficile." *XVIIe siècle* 127 (1980): 163–79.

General Index

Index to "Pensées" Cited

Fragment numbers are those of the Lafuma *Oeuvres complètes* (Collection l'Intégrale, Editions du Seuil, 1963)